An Introduction to Programming Using Microsoft Visual Basic® 2010

Jan Marrelli

The data files used in this text can be downloaded from
www.emcschool.net/VisualBasic2010 (hardcover)
www.paradigmcollege.net/VisualBasic2010 (softcover)

Care has been taken to verify the accuracy of information presented in this book. However, the authors, editors, and publisher cannot accept responsibility for Web, e-mail, newsgroup, or chat room subject matter or content, or for consequences from application of the information in this book, and make no warranty, expressed or implied, with respect to its content.

Trademarks: Some of the product names and company names included in this book have been used for identification purposes only and may be trademarks or registered trade names of their respective manufacturers and sellers. The authors, editors, and publisher disclaim any affiliation, association, or connection with, or sponsorship or endorsement by, such owners.

We have made every effort to trace the ownership of all copyrighted material and to secure permission from copyright holders. In the event of any question arising as to the use of any material, we will be pleased to make the necessary corrections in future printings. Thanks are due to the aforementioned authors, publishers, and agents for permission to use the materials indicated.

ISBN 978-0-82196-202-2 (Hardcover)
ISBN 978-0-82196-206-0 (Softcover)

875 Montreal Way
St. Paul, MN 55102
E-mail: educate@emcp.com
Web site: www.emcp.com

Printed in the United States of America

20 19 18 17 16 15 14 13 12 11 1 2 3 4 5 6 7 8 9 10

Preface

We have strived to make this the most comprehensive and easy to understand Visual Basic 2010 text available. Our primary objective in this text is to present material in clear language with easy to follow examples. To meet this objective, we use our teaching experiences as well as the feedback, comments, and suggestions from other experienced teachers to determine how best to present programming concepts.

For the best classroom experience for both the student and the teacher, our comprehensive text book includes hands-on reviews, critical-thinking exercises, and projects of varying topics and difficulty levels. Additionally, our Instructor Resources CD correlates directly to the textbook and offers teaching strategies for explaining difficult concepts, additional lessons and exercises, and a comprehensive question bank for creating tests, quizzes, and reviews. The Instructor Resources CD also includes the applications, case studies, and vocabulary from the textbook, as well as answers to all the reviews and exercises.

It is our belief that learning to program offers the student an invaluable opportunity to develop problem-solving skills. The process of defining a problem, breaking it down into a series of smaller problems, and finally writing a computer program to solve it exercises a student's logical abilities. Additionally, the student is made aware of the capabilities and limitations of a computer and soon realizes that the programmer—the human element—is more important than the machine.

An Introduction to Programming Using Microsoft Visual Basic 2010 is written for a one-term or two-term course. No previous programming experience is required or assumed. It is our goal that this text provide students the best possible introduction to programming using Visual Basic 2010 and to prepare them for further study in the IT/programming/computer science field.

Topic Organization

Chapter 1 discusses computer technology, operating systems, and programming languages. Networks, Internet services, number systems, and the social, ethical, and environmental implications of computers are also discussed.

Chapter 2 introduces OOP and the Visual Basic 2010 IDE. The importance of good programming style is introduced in this chapter and emphasized throughout the text.

Chapter 3 introduces variables and constants. Automatic type conversion and scope are also discussed. The Visual Basic 2010 debugger is also introduced. The case study that ends the chapter produces a Calculator application.

The emphasis of Chapter 4 is on conditional control structures. Concepts presented include random numbers, pseudocode, and counters. Static variables and logic errors are also discussed. In the case study, a PizzaOrder application is created.

Chapter 5 covers loop structures. The `String` class and its members are presented, as well as the `Char` structure. Accumulators and string comparison considerations are also explained. In the case study, a WordGuess game is created.

Sub, function, and event procedures are discussed in Chapter 6. Adding graphics to an application is also explained. An advanced calculator application is created in the case study.

Chapter 7 covers the `Math` class and business functions. Windows application standards such as focus, access keys, and tab order are also discussed. The case study presents a LoanAnalyzer application.

Arrays, structures, and enumerated types are explained in Chapter 8. Two dimensional matrices are also discussed. A CafeOrders application is created in the case study.

In Chapter 9, color, graphics, sound, and animation are covered. The `Graphics` class, `SystemSounds` class, and the `My.Computer.Audio` object are discussed. In the case study, a ClickIt! game is created.

In Chapter 10 classes are created. Instantiation, encapsulation, inheritance, and polymorphism are explained. A TriangleCalculator application is created in the case study.

Files are discussed in Chapter 11. The `FileInfo`, `FileStream`, `StreamReader`, and `StreamWriter` classes are discussed. A WordGuessII application is created in the case study.

Chapter 12 introduces sorting and searching. Algorithms for bubble sort, selection sort, insertion sort, and binary search are introduced. The `DateTime` structure is used for creating timing code.

Chapter 13 discusses MDI applications that include dialog boxes. The case study for this chapter is a Bingo application.

Chapter 14 discusses databases and Web programming. Microsoft Visual Web Developer 2010 is introduced.

Design and Features

Programming Concepts This text emphasizes learning the fundamental concepts of programming so that this knowledge can be applied to other programming languages.

Problem Solving From the very beginning, students are taught to implement programming solutions with proper programming techniques.

Programming Style Throughout the text, proper programming style is emphasized so that students can make their applications easy to read, modify, and debug.

Demonstration Applications and Runs Many demonstration applications are included, complete with sample runs, so that students are shown both proper programming techniques and the output actually produced by an application.

Format Each Visual Basic 2010 statement is clearly defined, shown in sample code, and then used in an application.

Expectations An outline of the significant topics that will be covered in each chapter is presented in the chapter header.

Reviews Numerous reviews are presented throughout each chapter which provide immediate reinforcement to newly learned concepts. Reviews based on previous work are marked with a ⟳ symbol. Solutions to the reviews are provided on the Instructor Resources CD.

Case Studies Most chapters end by stating a problem and then developing the appropriate algorithm. The process of specification, design, coding, and debugging and testing is clearly outlined for producing the problem's solution.

Chapter Summaries Each chapter ends by summarizing the concepts, statements, and controls covered in the chapter.

Vocabulary Sections Each chapter contains a vocabulary section that defines new terms. A separate section lists Visual Basic 2010 controls, keywords, statements, and classes.

Critical Thinking Written response exercises that require critical thinking from the student are included at the end of each chapter.

Exercises Each chapter includes a large set of exercises of varying difficulty, making them appropriate for students with a range of abilities. Most exercises include a demonstration run to help make clear what output is expected from the student's application. Exercises based on previous work are marked with a ⟳ symbol. Advanced exercises are indicated as such, and require a carefully thought out algorithm as part of their solution, similar in form to that used in solving a case study. Answers to the exercises are included on the Instructor Resources CD.

Indexes A standard index is included at the end of the textbook.

Appendix Visual Basic for Applications (VBA) is introduced in the Appendix.

Online Resources Students can download all the files needed to complete the reviews and exercises from www.emcschool.net/VisualBasic2010 (hardcover) or www.paradigmcollege.net/VisualBasic2010 (softcover). At these sites, you will also find materials that complement and extend this text.

Software This text was written for the Express version of Visual Basic 2010. This software can be downloaded for free from: www.microsoft.com/express/Downloads. Microsoft Visual Web Developer 2010 Express, which is introduced in Chapter 14, can also be downloaded for free from the same site.

Instructor Resources

Our Instructor Resources correlate directly to the textbook and provide all the additional materials required to offer students an excellent programming course. The Instructor Resources CD features:

- **Lesson Plans** Lessons in PDF format keyed to the chapters in the text. Each lesson includes assignments and teaching notes.
- **Tutorials** Flash movie files that provide animations to illustrate searching and sorting concepts. Each movie is keyed to the text.
- **Visual Aids** Topics keyed to the text are in PowerPoint presentation files to support instruction.
- **Vocabulary** Word files of the vocabulary presented in the text.
- **Rubrics** Rubrics keyed to exercises in the text for assessment.
- **Worksheets** Programming assignments that supplement the exercises in the text provide additional reinforcement of concepts. Some worksheets introduce new topics.
- **Critical Thinking Answers** Answers for the critical thinking questions presented in the text.
- **Data Files** All the files the student needs to complete the reviews and exercises in the text, as well as the files needed to complete the worksheets and tests.
- **Application Files** All applications presented in the text and a cross reference guide.
- **Exam*View*® Assessment Suite** Question banks keyed to the text and the popular **Exam*View*®** software are included to create tests, quizzes, and additional assessment materials.
- **Answer files** Answers to the reviews, exercises, worksheets, and tests.

Using This Text

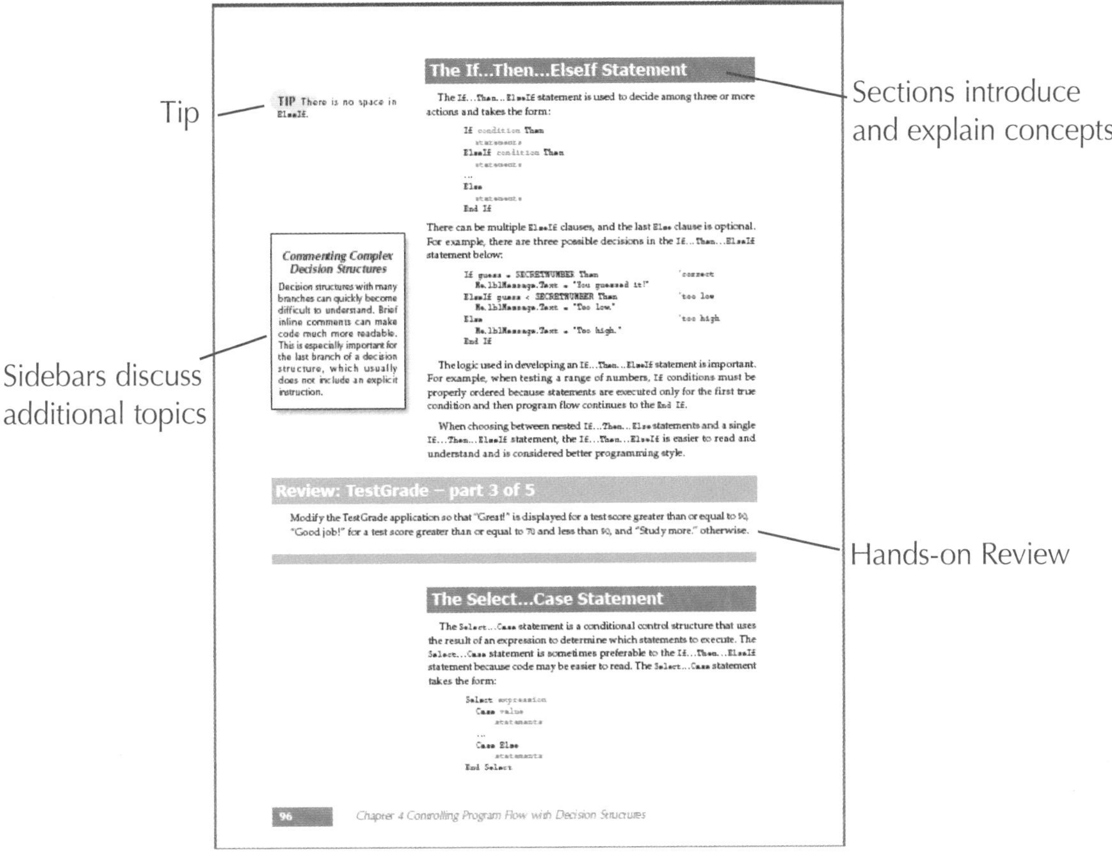

TIP There is no space in `ElseIf`.

The If...Then...ElseIf Statement

The `If...Then...ElseIf` statement is used to decide among three or more actions and takes the form:

```
If condition Then
   statements
ElseIf condition Then
   statements
...
Else
   statements
End If
```

There can be multiple `ElseIf` clauses, and the last `Else` clause is optional. For example, there are three possible decisions in the `If...Then...ElseIf` statement below:

```
If guess = SECRETNUMBER Then                       'correct
   Me.lblMessage.Text = "You guessed it!"
ElseIf guess < SECRETNUMBER Then                   'too low
   Me.lblMessage.Text = "Too low."
Else                                               'too high
   Me.lblMessage.Text = "Too high."
End If
```

Commenting Complex Decision Structures

Decision structures with many branches can quickly become difficult to understand. Brief inline comments can make code much more readable. This is especially important for the last branch of a decision structure, which usually does not include an explicit instruction.

The logic used in developing an `If...Then...ElseIf` statement is important. For example, when testing a range of numbers, `If` conditions must be properly ordered because statements are executed only for the first true condition and then program flow continues to the `End If`.

When choosing between nested `If...Then...Else` statements and a single `If...Then...ElseIf` statement, the `If...Then...ElseIf` is easier to read and understand and is considered better programming style.

Review: TestGrade – part 3 of 5

Modify the TestGrade application so that "Great!" is displayed for a test score greater than or equal to 90, "Good job!" for a test score greater than or equal to 70 and less than 90, and "Study more." otherwise.

The Select...Case Statement

The `Select...Case` statement is a conditional control structure that uses the result of an expression to determine which statements to execute. The `Select...Case` statement is sometimes preferable to the `If...Then...ElseIf` statement because code may be easier to read. The `Select...Case` statement takes the form:

```
Select expression
   Case value
      statements
   ...
   Case Else
      statements
End Select
```

96 *Chapter 4 Controlling Program Flow with Decision Structures*

Within each chapter, you will find:

Alternatives – Other ways to perform actions.

TIPs – Additional information that complements the text.

Sidebars – Additional topics that complement the text.

Text in the margin – Indicates new terminology and subtopics.

Reviews – Concepts are presented, discussed, and then followed by a "hands-on" review that allows you to try out newly learned programming skills and knowledge. Some reviews stand alone, while others build on work completed in previous reviews. Therefore, it is recommended that the reviews are completed in the order in which they are presented.

The end of each chapter contains:

Chapter Summaries – Concepts covered in the chapter are reviewed.

Critical Thinking Questions – Critical thinking questions that will let you review and deepen your understanding of the concepts covered in the chapter.

Vocabulary and Visual Basic Syntax Sections – A list of new terms and definitions and a list of the Visual Basic syntax covered in the chapter.

Table of Contents

Chapter 1
Computer Technology

Chapter 2
Introducing Visual Basic

Chapter 3
Variables and Constants

Chapter 4
Controlling Program Flow with Decision Structures

Chapter 5
Controlling Program Flow with Looping Structures

Chapter 6
Procedures

Chapter 7
Mathematical and Business Functions

Chapter 8
Arrays and Structures

Chapter 9
Color, Sound, and Graphics

Chapter 10
Creating Classes

Chapter 11
Using Files

Chapter 12
Sorting and Searching

Chapter 13
MDI Application

Chapter 14
Databases and Web Programming

Appendix A
Visual Basic for Applications (VBA)

Chapter 1
Computer Technology

Key Concepts

Desktop and mobile computing
Hardware components
Operating systems
Computer classifications and compatibility issues
Programming languages
Networks
Number systems
Files and folders
Storage devices
Internet services
Downloading files
Safe computing
Internet privacy issues
Social and ethical issues
Ergonomics
Environmental issues

Desktop and Mobile Computing

TIP PC (personal computer) is often used to refer to a desktop computer that is Windows compatible and to differentiate from Mac (Apple) computers.

Computers come in many sizes and with a variety of features. A *desktop computer* and its components are designed to fit on or under a desk:

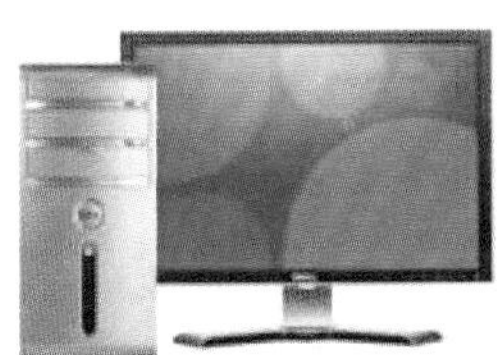

Desktop computers are single-user systems designed with microprocessor technology where an entire CPU (Central Processing Unit) is contained on a single computer chip.

Mobile computing devices, such as notebooks, tablet PCs, handhelds, and smartphones, contain long-lasting batteries and wireless technology that allow them to be portable:

Mobile computing devices also include *wearable computers*, which are used in many occupations. For example, auto mechanics can examine a car while wearing a head-mounted wearable computer which displays computer drawings of the car for comparison purposes. They are also used to monitor health problems, such as heart rate and respiration flow.

Mainframes and Supercomputers

A mainframe is a large computer system that supports multiuser applications and tasks that require the storage and processing of huge amounts of information. Large corporations, airlines, banks, government agencies, and universities use mainframes.

A supercomputer is the fastest and most powerful type of computer. Supercomputers focus on executing a few programs as fast as possible and are used for weather forecasting and nuclear energy research.

Computer Hardware

The physical components of the computer, such as the monitor and base unit, are referred to as *hardware*:

input devices

- *Input devices*, such as a keyboard, mouse, scanner, microphone, digital camera, and DVD drive are used to enter data and instructions into the computer.

Printers

A laser printer uses a laser and toner to generate characters and graphics on paper. An ink-jet printer uses an ink cartridge to place very small dots of ink onto paper to create characters and graphics.

- *Peripheral devices*, such as printers, webcams, and microphones, are added to make a computer more versatile. A peripheral device either has a wireless connection or is attached to a *port* on the computer. There are different types of ports, such as serial, parallel, FireWire, USB, and Bluetooth ports.
- Computers process data into meaningful, useful information. Processed data is conveyed using *output devices*. Monitors and printers display data, DVD+RWs, disk drives, and memory keys store data, and speakers communicate audio output.

The base unit also contains the *motherboard*, which is the main circuit board. The motherboard contains several components:

expansion boards

- *Expansion boards* are circuit boards that connect to the motherboard to add functionality to the computer. Examples include sound cards and video adapters.

TIP Intel and AMD are two processor manufacturers.

clock rate, megahertz gigahertz

- The *CPU (Central Processing Unit)* or processor processes data and controls the flow of data between the computer's other units. Within the CPU is the *ALU (Arithmetic Logic Unit)*, which can perform arithmetic and logic operations. It can also make comparisons, which is the basis of the computer's decision-making power. The ALU is so fast that the time needed to carry out a single addition is measured in nanoseconds (billionths of a second). The speed at which a CPU can execute instructions is determined by the computer's *clock rate*. The clock rate is measured in *megahertz* (*MHz*, million of cycles per second) or *gigahertz* (*GHz*, billion of cycles per second).
- A *bus* is a set of circuits that connect the CPU to other components. The data bus transfers data between the CPU, memory, and other hardware devices on the motherboard. The *address bus* carries memory addresses that indicate where the data is located and where the data should go. A *control bus* carries control signals. All data flows through the CPU:

Real-time Clock

A battery chip called a real-time clock keeps track of the date and time in a computer even when the computer is off.

Input → Memory → Output

Memory ↑↓ CPU

Integrated Circuits

Integrated circuits, also called chips, are created from silicon wafers which are etched with intricate circuits and coated with a metallic oxide that allows the circuits to conduct electricity. The silicon wafers are housed in special plastic cases that have metal pins. The pins allow the integrated circuits to be plugged into circuit boards.

- Memory in the form of *integrated circuits (ICs)* stores data electronically. *ROM* (*Read Only Memory)* contains the most basic operating instructions for the computer. The data in ROM is a permanent part of the computer and cannot be changed. *RAM (Random Access Memory)*, also called primary or main memory, is memory where data and instructions are stored temporarily. Data stored in RAM can be written to *secondary memory*, which includes any type of storage media, such as a hard disk, memory key, or DVD+RW. Secondary memory must be copied into primary memory before it is processed by the CPU. SRAM (Static Random Access Memory) is high-speed memory referred to as *cache* (pronounced "cash"). This memory is used to store frequently used data so that it can be quickly retrieved by an application.

Operating Systems and Environment

Computers also contain programs, or software. *Operating system* (OS) software is run automatically when the computer is turned on and is used to control processing and peripherals, run application software, and control input and output, among other tasks. Desktop operating system software includes Windows, Mac OS X, Unix, and Linux. Each of these operating systems have different features and functions. *Applications software* is written by programmers to perform a specific task, such as a word processor.

Environment refers to a computer's hardware and software configuration. For example, a Windows 7 environment means that the computer is running a version of the Windows 7 OS software and hardware includes a 1GHz processor or better, 1GB of RAM or more, and at least 16 GB of hard disk space available. The hardware requirements are based on what will be needed to allow the OS software to properly manage the computer's tasks. The term platform is sometimes synonymous with environment. Most environments run an OS with a graphical user interface (GUI). For example:

Windows 7 Operating System

utility program

device driver

memory-resident

OS functions are implemented through *utility programs* which have one clearly defined task. Utility programs manage input and output, read and write to memory, manage the processor, maintain system security, and manage files and disks. A *device driver* is one type of utility program. Device drivers are needed for printing, viewing graphics, using a CD/DVD drive, and using peripherals in general. Some utility programs load when the computer starts and are called *memory-resident* because they are always in memory. Features are added to an OS by incorporating utility programs to perform tasks that are in addition to the tasks required to run the computer. For example, an OS intended for a desktop or notebook environment will often include utilities for backing up the computer, restoring files, and other tools for improving performance:

TIP For information on operating systems, refer to www.emcschool.net/VisualBasic2010.

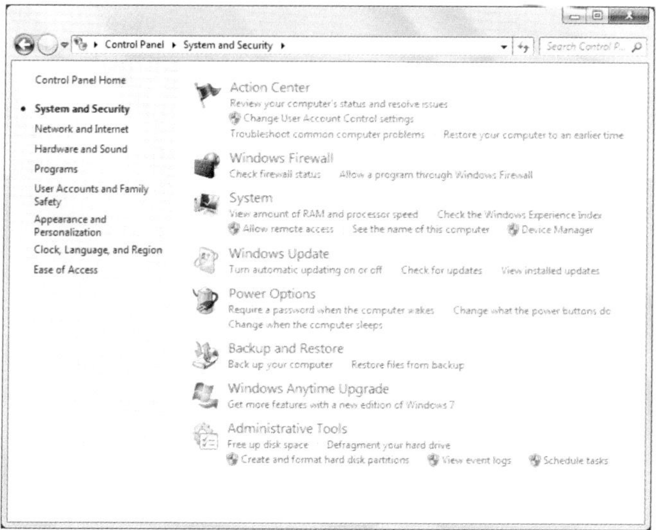

Windows 7 Utilities

> **Sync**
>
> Software utilities are available that allow a smartphone or handheld computer to sync with a desktop or notebook computer.

Cross-platform connectivity is the ability of one type of computer to link to and share data with a different type of computer. A conversion program may be required if the computers use a different OS and/or generate different file formats.

Programming Languages

A *programming language* is a set of words, codes, and symbols that allow a programmer to give instructions to the computer. Many programming languages exist, each with their own rules, or syntax, for writing these instructions.

low-level programming languages

Programming languages can be classified as low-level and high-level languages. *Low-level programming languages* include machine language and assembly language. Machine language, which is referred to as a first generation programming language, can be used to communicate directly with the computer. However, it is difficult to program in machine language because the language consists of 0s and 1s to represent the status of a switch (0 for off and 1 for on). Assembly language uses the same instructions and structure as machine language but the programmer is able to use meaningful names or abbreviations instead of numbers. Assembly language is referred to as a second generation programming language.

Fourth and Fifth Generation Languages

Fourth generation languages (4GL), such as SQL, have higher English-like instructions than most high-level languages and are typically used to access databases. Fifth generation languages are used for artificial intelligence.

High-level programming languages, which are often referred to as third generation programming languages (3GL), were first developed in the late 1950s. High-level programming languages have English-like instructions and are easier to use than machine language. High-level programming languages include Fortran, C, Basic, COBOL, and Pascal. In order for the computer to understand a program written in a high-level language, programmers convert the source code into machine language using a compiler or an interpreter. A *compiler* is a program that converts an entire program into machine code before the program is executed. An *interpreter* translates and executes an instruction before moving on to the next instruction in the program.

object-oriented programming

In the 1980s, *object-oriented programming* (OOP) evolved out of the need to better develop complex programs in a systematic, organized approach. The OOP approach allows programmers to create modules that can be used over and over again in a variety of programs. These modules contain code called classes, which group related data and actions. Properly designed classes encapsulate data to hide the implementation details, are versatile enough to be extended through inheritance, and give the programmer options through polymorphism. Object-oriented languages include Java, C++, Visual C#, Visual F#, and Visual Basic.

.NET Framework 4.0

The .NET Framework provides tools and processes developers can use to produce and run programs. Visual Studio 2010 provides the development environment for the developer to have access to the .NET Framework processes.

Networks

A *network* is a combination of hardware and software that allows computers to exchange data and share software and devices, such as printers. Networks are widely used by businesses, universities, and other organizations because a network:

- allows users to reliably share and exchange data.
- can reduce costs by sharing devices such as printers.
- offers security options including password protection to restrict access to certain files.
- simplifies file management through centralized software updates and file backups.
- provides communication tools such as e-mail for network users.

MAN and HAN

A MAN (Metropolitan Area Network) and a HAN (Home Area Network) are network technologies classified by the size of a network. A MAN is a high-speed network that typically connects LANs within a city or town. A HAN is used to connect personal devices within the home.

Networks are classified by their size, architecture, and topology. A common size classifications is *LAN (Local-Area Network)*, which is a network used to connect devices within a small area such as a building or a campus. A *WAN (Wide-Area Network)* is used to connect devices over large geographical distances. A WAN can be one widespread network or it can be a number of LANs linked together.

The computers and other devices in a LAN each contain an expansion card called a *network interface card*:

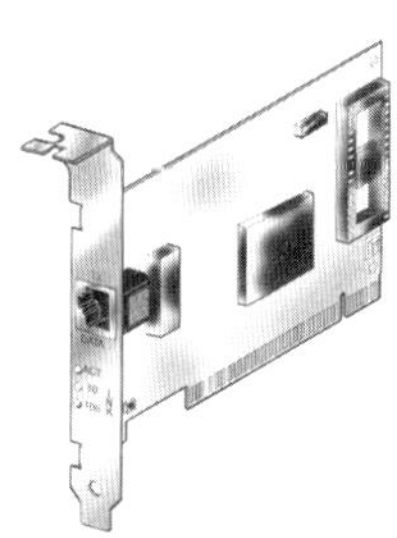

Network interface card

Transmission Media

Computers must be connected in order to transmit data between the nodes. Cable transmission media includes twisted-pair wiring, coaxial cable, and fiber optic cable.

Wireless transmission media includes infrared signals, broadcast radio, cellular radio, microwaves, and communications satellites.

The amount of data and the speed at which data can travel over a media is called bandwidth, which is measured in bits per second (bps). Each transmission media has a specific length or range restriction, data transmission rate, and cost.

A cable plugs into the adapter card to connect one device to another to form a LAN. Cables are not required for network cards that have wireless capabilities. Network interface cards are available for desktop and mobile computers and take various other forms including an adapter card, a PC card, or a Flash memory card.

Along with the physical, or hardware, aspects of setting up a network, there is also the software aspect. A *network operating system* is software that allow users and devices to communicate over the network. The operating system installed must be capable of supporting networking functions, such as security access features and support for multiple users. Operating systems capable of network functions are available for Linux, Windows, Unix, and Mac. The network architecture, discussed next, must also be considered when choosing a network OS.

Network architecture includes the type of computers on the network and determines how network resources are handled. Two common models are peer-to-peer and client/server. In a *peer-to-peer network*, each computer on the network is considered equal in terms of responsibilities and resource sharing. A *client/server network* consists of a group of computers, called *clients*, connected to a server. A *server* is a computer with more RAM, a larger hard disk, and sometimes multiple CPUs that is used to manage network functions.

topology
node

Physical *topology* refers to the arrangement of the nodes on a network. A *node* is a location on the network with a device capable of processing information, such as a computer or a printer. There are three common physical topologies:

bus topology

- The *bus topology* is a physical LAN topology that uses a single central cable, called the bus or backbone to attach each node directly:

Ethernet

The Ethernet LAN protocol was developed by Bob Metcalfe in 1976. Ethernet uses a bus or star topology with twisted-pair wiring, coaxial cable, or fiber optic cable transmission media. Newer protocols include 40 Gigabit Ethernet and 100 Gigabit Ethernet.

Baseband and Broadband Technology

Most LANs use baseband technology which means the transmission media carries one signal at a time. Broadband technology allows for data transmission of more than one signal at a time and is found in cable television transmission.

Bluetooth

Bluetooth is a wireless technology used to allow mobile computing devices to communicate.

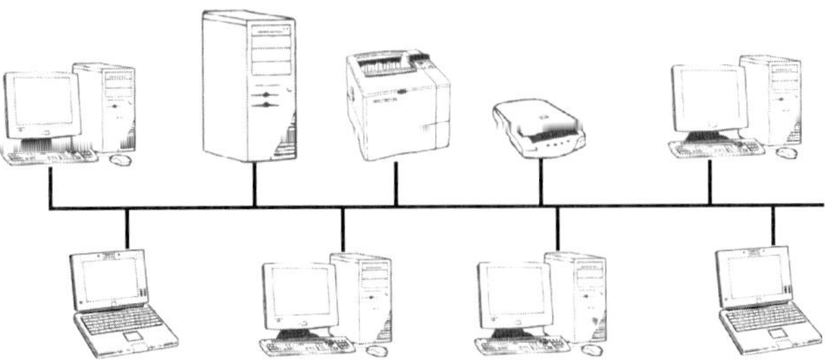

LAN using a bus topology

- In a *star topology*, each node is attached to a *hub*, which is a device that joins communication lines at a central location on the network:

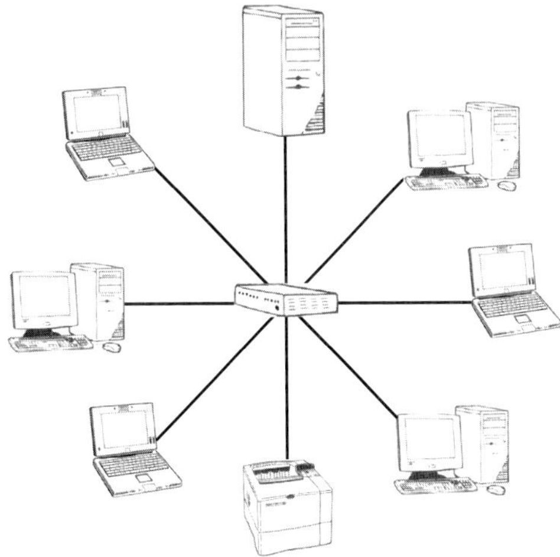

LAN using a star topology

- In a *ring topology*, each node is connected to form a closed loop. A LAN with a ring topology can usually cover a greater distance than a bus or star topology:

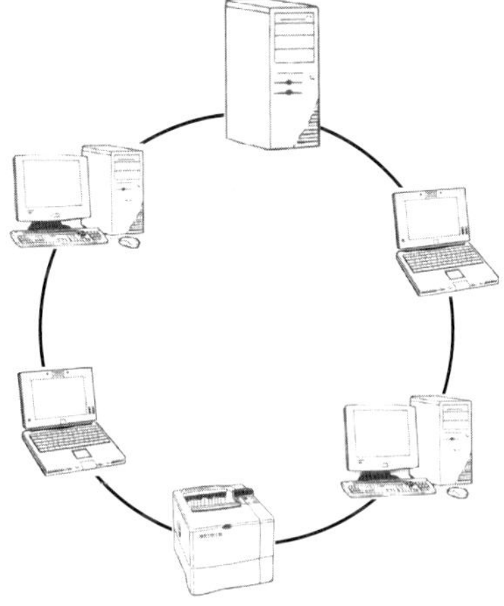

LAN using a ring topology

- *Wireless networks* use high frequency radio waves or infrared signals instead of cables to transmit data. A router/wireless access point device is used to allow nodes to transfer data wirelessly.

logical topology

Another type of topology is *logical topology*, which refers to the way data is passed between the nodes on a network. A LAN's logical topology is not always the same as its physical topology.

netiquette

Network users are given a user name and password to log on to a network through a computer connected to the network. Users are also assigned a level of access to maintain security. Network users should follow a certain etiquette referred to as *netiquette*:

- Do not attempt to access the account of another user without authorization.
- Do not share your password, and change it periodically.
- Use appropriate subject matter and language, and be considerate of other people's beliefs and opinions.

Number Systems

binary number system

bit

byte

The electrical circuits on an IC have one of two states, off or on. Therefore, the *binary number system* (base 2), which uses only two digits (0 and 1), was adopted for use in computers. To represent numbers and letters, a code was developed with eight binary digits grouped together to represent a single number or letter. Each 0 or 1 in the binary code is called a *bit* (BInary digiT) and an 8-bit unit is called a *byte*.

base 10

Our most familiar number system is the decimal, or *base 10*, system. It uses ten digits: 0 through 9. Each place represents a power of ten, with the first place to the left of the decimal point representing 10^0, the next place representing 10^1, the next 10^2, and so on (remember that any number raised to the zero power is 1). In the decimal number 485, the 4 represents 4×10^2, the 8 represents 8×10^1, and the 5 represents 5×10^0. The number 485 represents the sum $4\times100 + 8\times10 + 5\times1$ $(400 + 80 + 5)$:

Decimal	Base 10 Equivalent
485	$4\times10^2 + 8\times10^1 + 5\times10^0 = 400 + 80 + 5$

base 2

The binary, or *base 2*, system works identically except that each place represents a power of two instead of a power of ten. For example, the binary number 101 represents the sum $1\times2^2 + 0\times2^1 + 1\times2^0$ or 5 in base ten. Some decimal numbers and their binary equivalents are:

Decimal	Binary	Base 2 Equivalent		
0	0	$= 0\times2^1 + 0\times2^0$	$= 0\times2 + 0\times1$	$= 0 + 0$
1	1	$= 0\times2^1 + 1\times2^0$	$= 0\times2 + 1\times1$	$= 0 + 1$
2	10	$= 1\times2^1 + 0\times2^0$	$= 1\times2 + 0\times1$	$= 2 + 0$
3	11	$= 1\times2^1 + 1\times2^0$	$= 1\times2 + 1\times1$	$= 2 + 1$
4	100	$= 1\times2^2 + 0\times2^1 + 0\times2^0$	$= 1\times4 + 0\times2 + 0\times1$	$= 4 + 0 + 0$

base 16

The hexadecimal system is used to represent groups of four binary digits. The *hexadecimal*, or *base 16*, system is based on 16 digits: 0 through 9, and the letters A through F representing 10 through 15 respectively. Each place represents a power of sixteen. For example, the hexadecimal number 1F represents the sum $1\times16^1 + 15\times16^0$. Some decimal numbers and their hexadecimal equivalents are:

Decimal	Binary	Hexadecimal	Base 16 Equivalent		
0	0000 0000	0	$= 0\times16^0$	$= 0\times1$	$= 0$
10	0000 1010	A	$= 10\times16^0$	$= 10\times1$	$= 10$
25	0001 1001	19	$= 1\times16^1 + 9\times16^0$	$= 1\times16 + 9\times1$	$= 16 + 9$
30	0001 1110	1E	$= 1\times16^1 + 14\times16^0$	$= 1\times16 + 14\times1$	$= 16 + 14$

For clarity, a non-base 10 number should have the base subscripted after the number. For example, to show the difference between 100 in base 10 and 100 in base 2 (which represents 4), the base 2 number should be written as 100_2.

Unicode

Every letter of an alphabet (Latin, Japanese, Cherokee, and so on) and symbols of every culture (=, @, ½, and so on) have been given a representation in a digital code called Unicode. *Unicode* uses a set of sixteen 1s and 0s to form a 16-bit binary code for each symbol. For example, the uppercase letter V is Unicode 00000000 01010110, which can be thought of as the base 10 number 86 (86_{10}). Lowercase v has a separate code of 00000000 01110110, or 11810.

Storing Data in Memory

megabyte
gigabyte

Computer memory is measured in bytes. For example, a computer might have 1GB of RAM. In computers and electronics *MB* stands for *megabytes* where mega represents 2^{20} or 1,048,576 bytes and *GB* stands for *gigabytes,* which is 2^{30} or 1,073,741,820 bytes.

address

Data stored in memory is referred to by an address. An *address* is a unique binary representation of a location in memory. Therefore, data can be stored, accessed, and retrieved from memory by its address. For data to be addressable in memory, it must usually be at least one byte in length. For example, to store JIM in memory each character is converted to Unicode and stored in two bytes of memory with each memory location designated by its address:

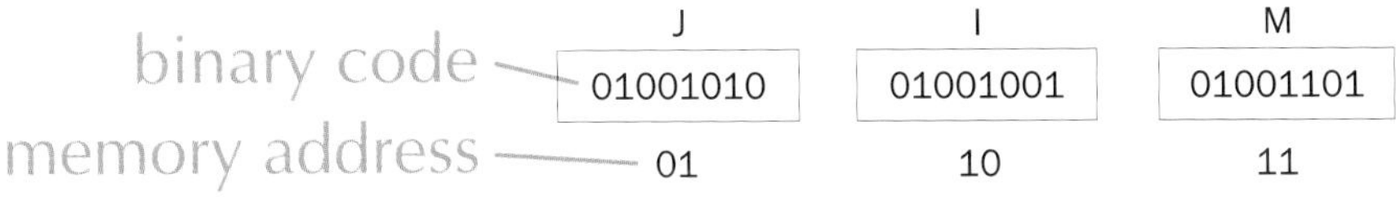

	J	I	M
binary code	01001010	01001001	01001101
memory address	01	10	11

Because JIM is a character string, it will probably be stored in adjacent memory addresses.

words

Bits grouped in units of 16 to 64 (2 to 8 bytes) are called *words.* Data stored in a word is also located by an address. The size of a word depends on the computer system.

overflow error

The binary representation of an integer number is usually stored in four bytes of memory. Because an integer is stored in four bytes, the range of integers that can be stored is –2,147,483,648 to 2,147,483,647. An *overflow error* occurs when the number of bits that are needed to represent the integer is greater than the size of four bytes.

real numbers

Real numbers, also called *floating point numbers,* are numbers that contain decimal points. The binary representation of a real number is usually 4 to 8 bytes of memory. The binary number 111.10 is equivalent to the real decimal number 7.5 and is stored in memory as the binary number 0.11110×2^3. In this form, the bits that represent the mantissa (fractional part) are stored in one section of a word and the exponent, in this example 3 (11_2), is stored in another section of the word:

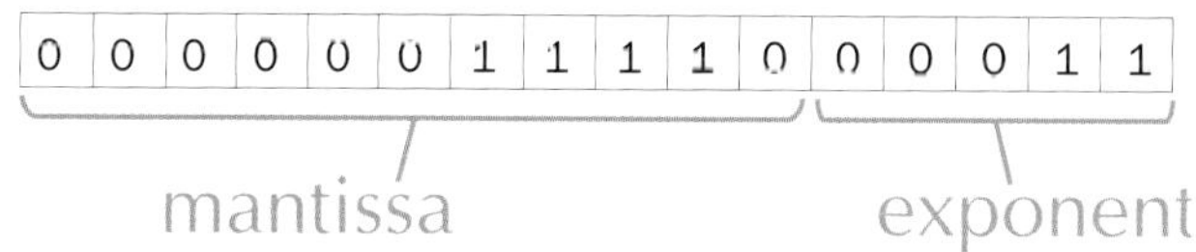

The overflow problem discussed for integers can also occur in real numbers if the part of the word storing the exponent is not large enough.

roundoff error

A *roundoff error* occurs when there are not enough bits to store the mantissa.

What is a File?

A *file* is related data stored on a persistent media. A file can be an application (program) or the product of an application. For example, a word processor application is used to create document files. A file is stored on a persistent media so that it is retained even after the computer or computerized device is turned off. A file can be used over and over again whenever the data it stores is needed.

A file is really just 1s and 0s because it is stored in binary code. Computers are programmed to translate bytes and words into symbols. Depending on the file type, these symbols are either human-readable or computer-readable after translation. Human-readable files are called *text files*, and computer-readable files are called *binary files*. Simple files, such as a text document, can be measured in *kilobytes*, for example 64K. The K comes from the word *kilo* and represents 2^{10} or 1,024. Therefore, a 64K file uses 65,536 bytes (64×2^{10}) of storage.

> **Extensions**
>
> Common extensions include:
>
> .vb - Visual Basic source file
> .zip - compressed file
> .gif - GIF image file
> .bmp - Bitmap graphic
> .xlsx - Excel file
> .odt - Open Document file

File types are distinguished by the *extension* that comes after the file name. An application adds a unique extension to the files it creates. For example, `MyResume.docx` is a document file type. A DOCX file is a file format created by Microsoft. A file named `TestData.txt` is a plain text file. A TXT file contains only letters, numbers, and common symbols readable by humans. An ODT file is an Open Document file format for saving documents such as text documents, spreadsheets, charts, and presentations. This standard was developed by the OASIS industry consortium and was based on the XML file format originally created by OpenOffice.org.

TIP The original form the file is saved in is referred to as the *native* format.

folders

Folders are used to organize commonly related files. A Visual Basic application consists of a series of files that are organized into a project folder.

Binary files are more complex than text files and often contain data for photos, formatted text, spreadsheets, sound, and so on. The disadvantage of binary files is that they require another application to interpret the contents. A binary file may have content similar to:

þ»ÿÿúªî¿þÿþûïûüÿ¾þïïÿ ÿÝþ_ÿÿ ÿwþuUuWýw÷÷ÿ{þÿß¿ß÷ÿuWwwu÷uu

A binary file is computer-readable

> **File Size Limitations**
>
> File size can be decreased or compressed using a compression program. This technique is often used to accommodate storage device and e-mail account limitations.

ODT files can be read any application that supports the Open Document file format, which reduces compatibility issues between applications.

Storage Devices

Storage devices use a persistent media to maintain files. These devices, which are also referred to as drives, mass storage, and auxiliary storage, can be categorized in three ways:

- internal, such as a hard disk, or external, such as a memory key
- removable or permanent media
- magnetic, optical, or solid state technology

Storage device technologies determine the media, size, and portability of a device. Magnetic technology uses a mechanical drive with tiny electromagnetic heads for reading and writing data to media. The media required with magnetic technology is a disk, usually made of aluminum or Mylar®, coated with iron oxide. The disk is either encased in hard plastic or several disks, called platters, are sealed in a case (hard disk). A data signal sent through the heads in the drive magnetize a bit of the media in one direction to store a 1 and in the other direction to store a 0.

Optical technology uses a drive with a laser and an optoelectronic sensor. The media required with optical technology is a compact or DVD disc made of polycarbonate plastic.

Solid state technology allows for the smallest, most portable storage devices because the technology requires no moving parts. The media is Flash memory, which consists of a grid with two tiny transistors at each cell. Each cell corresponds to a bit. Applying a charge to a cell stores a 0, while applying a stronger charge stores a 1. The grid of transistors is encased in hard plastic and is very small. Some devices can store 2MB or more within a package thinner and smaller than a quarter. Slightly larger media can store gigabytes of data. Encased media is often directly attached to a USB plug for use with a computer, or simply has conductive material imprinted so the media can slide into a digital camera slot.

Magnetic technology allows for storage devices that range in capacity up to many gigabytes (hard disk drives with many platters). Optical technology includes DVDs that can store at least 4GB of data. Solid-state devices store from 64KB of data to many gigabytes.

Storage media can be very sensitive. Care should be taken to avoid damaging files:

- Keep magnetic media away from magnets.
- Handle CD/DVDs by the center hole or by the edges.
- Store CD/DVDs in a jewel case or sleeve to prevent scratches.
- Keep media away from moisture and extreme temperatures.

Storage Media

The capacity of storage media varies. For example, a CD has a storage capacity of 650 MB, and a DVD has a storage capacity of over 4GB.

Blu-ray Disc

Blu-ray Disc is an optical disc storage media format that has the same dimensions as a CD or DVD. A dual layer Blu-ray Disc can store 50GB.

Tera, Peta, Exa

As more and more data is stored electronically, file sizes become very large and require storage devices with very large capacities. TB (terabyte) is 2^{40} bytes or 1 trillion bytes, petabyte (PB) is 2^{50} bytes or 1,024 terabytes, and EB (exabyte) is 2^{60} bytes or 1,024 petabytes. Devices with TB storage capacities are gradually coming into use, especially for database files.

Intranet, Extranet, Internet

An *intranet* is a network that is used by a single organization, such as a corporation or school, and is only accessible by authorized users. The purpose of an intranet is to share information. However, a firewall is also used to lock out unauthorized users. A *firewall* is a network security system that prevents unauthorized network access.

firewall

An *extranet* extends an intranet by providing various levels of accessibility to authorized members of the public. For example, a corporation may extend their intranet to provide access to specific information, such as their ordering system, to registered customers.

The largest and most widely accessed network is the *Internet*, a worldwide network of computers that is not controlled by any one organization. The Internet has had an undeniable impact on modern society because it allows users worldwide to communicate in a matter of seconds.

History of the Internet

The Internet evolved from ARPANET, a network created in the late 1960s by the Department of Defense's ARPA (Advanced Research Projects Agency), and the theory of open architecture networking.

The Internet is actually numerous networks all linked together through routers. A *router* is a device that connects different network technologies. Networks connected to routers use *TCP/IP* (Transmission Control Protocol/Internet Protocol) software to communicate.

Computers on the Internet are either servers or clients. The client is sent information from a server. The client/server structure of the Internet is called interactive because the information accessed is a result of selections made by the user. For example, a computer with just minimal software for accessing the Internet is a client. The client user selecting options from the Internet is receiving the information from a server, a computer with additional software and files that is also connected to the Internet.

Telecommunications

Telecommunications is the transmitting and receiving of data. Data can be in various forms including voice and video. Telecommunications requires a modem or adapter and a line or cable. The speed of data transmission (sending) and receipt (receiving) is measured in *Kbps* (thousands of bits per second) or *Mbps* (millions of bits per second). Numerous telecommunications options are available, which vary in speed and cost:

PLC

PLC (power line communications) uses existing power grid networks to send broadband data communications. Internet connections are established by plugging a computer device into a power outlet.

- A **conventional modem** uses standard telephone lines to convert analog signals to digital data. A conventional modem is a 56 Kbps modem, which transmits data at 28.8 Kbps and 36.6 Kbps, and receives data at 56 Kbps. Today, most home and business users select options other than conventional modems if they are available in their area, due to the slow access time associated with conventional modems.
- A **DSL** (Digital Subscriber Line) modem uses standard telephone lines with data transmission up to 640 Kbps. Data receipt is from 1.5 Mbps to 9 Mbps. A DSL (Asymmetric DSL) is the most common form used.
- A **cable modem** transmits data through a coaxial cable television network. Data transmission is from 2 Mbps to 10 Mbps and data receipt is from 10 Mbps to 36 Mbps.

- **Leased/Dedicated lines** are used by many businesses and schools for Internet access. They allow for a permanent connection to the Internet that is always active. The cost of a leased line is usually a fixed monthly fee. A T-1 carrier is a type of leased line that transmits data at 1.544 Mbps.
- **ISDN** (Integrated Services Digital Network) is a digital telephone network provided by a local phone company. ISDN is capable of transmitting and receiving data at up to 64 Kbps. ISDN requires the use of an ISDN terminal adapter instead of a modem.

Internet Services

> ***Blog***
>
> Blog is short for weblog and is a type of website where users can post entries in a journal format.

Internet services include the World Wide Web, e-mail, and mailing lists. The *World Wide Web* (WWW), also called the *Web* is the most widely used Internet service. The Web can be used to search and access information available on the Internet. A *web browser* application, such as Microsoft Internet Explorer, provides a graphical interface to present information in the form of a website:

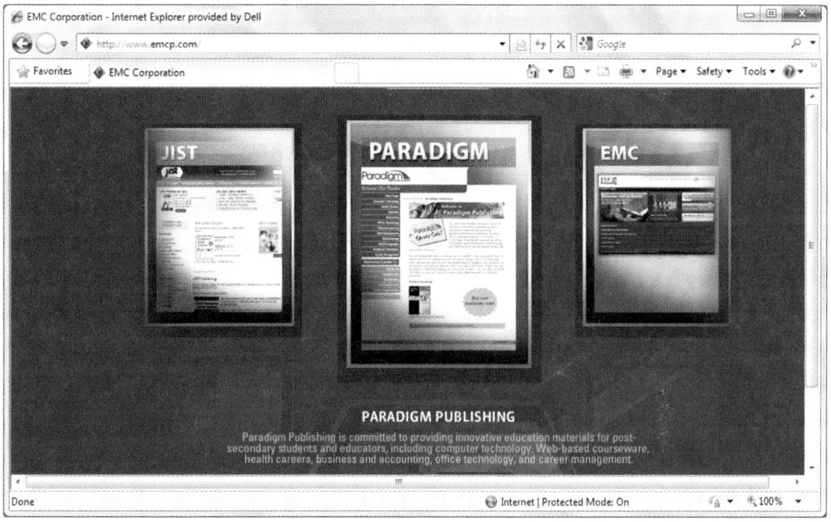

> ***Feeds***
>
> Feeds, also known as RSS feeds, XML feeds, syndicated content, or web feeds, contain frequently updated content published by a website. They are typically used for news and blog websites. Feeds can also be used to deliver audio content, typically in MP3 format. This is referred to as podcasting.

Another widely used Internet service is *e-mail* or *electronic mail*, which is the sending and receiving of messages and computer files over a communications network, such as a LAN (Local Area Network) or the Internet. E-mail can be received in a matter of seconds, even if the recipient is located half way around the world.

An e-mail address is required in order to send and receive e-mail messages. E-mail addresses are provided when you sign up with an ISP or an online service. A typical e-mail address is similar to:

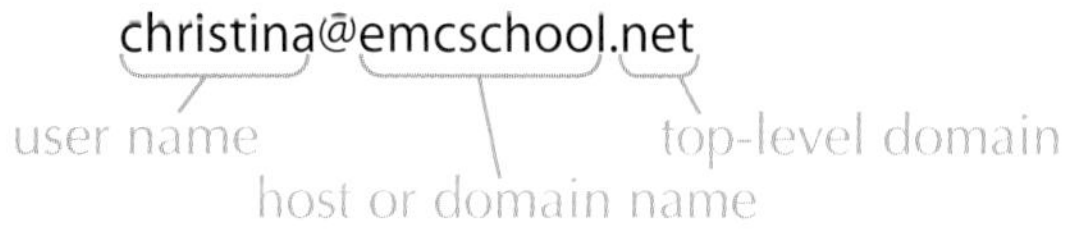

christina@emcschool.net

user name — host or domain name — top-level domain

> ***Digital Signature***
>
> A digital signature is a code that is attached to an electronic message to verify the authenticity of a website or e-mail message.

E-mail software is also required for sending and receiving e-mail messages. An example of e-mail software is Outlook. Browser-based e-mail only requires a web browser and is available through sites such as Yahoo!, Google, and Hotmail.

Certain rules should be followed when composing e-mail messages

- Use manners. Include "please" and "thank you" and also properly address people you do not know as Mr., Ms., Mrs., Dr., and so on.
- Be concise.
- Be professional, which includes using the proper spelling and grammar.
- Re-read a message before it is sent. Always fill in the To box last to avoid sending a message before it is complete.

E-mail messages are not private. An e-mail message goes through several mail servers before it reaches the recipient, making it easily accessible for others to read. Therefore, sending e-mail messages requires following a certain etiquette:

- Send messages through your account only.
- Use appropriate subject matter and language.
- Be considerate of other people's beliefs and opinions.

When sending e-mail at work or school, it is important to remember that employers and school administrators have the right to read any e-mail messages sent over the corporate or school network, as well as the right to track online activity.

A *mailing list server* is a server that manages mailing lists for groups of users. Two mailing list servers are Listserv and Majordomo. Often users subscribe to mailing lists for discussion purposes. When a subscriber posts a message to a mailing list server, every subscriber receives a copy of the message. Subscribers are identified by a single name or e-mail address.

E-mail Protocols

POP3 is an e-mail protocol that connects to an e-mail server to download messages to a local computer.

IMAP is an e-mail protocol that connects to an e-mail server to read message headers and then the user selects which e-mail messages to download to a local computer.

HTTP is used as an e-mail protocol when a web page is used to access an e-mail account.

Spam

Along with personal and business messages, most people also receive a lot of "junk e-mail" or spam. Most e-mail software includes features to filter and block messages from specific senders.

Finding Information on the Web and Downloading Files

A *search engine* is a program that searches a database of web pages for keywords and then lists hyperlinks to pages that contain those keywords. Commonly used search engines include:

Yahoo! (www.yahoo.com)
Google (www.google.com)
MSN (www.msn.com)

A search engine can be queried to display specific web pages. *Search criteria* can include single words or phrases that are then used by the engine to determine a match. A *match* is a web page that contains the search criteria. Surrounding phrases with quotation marks finds web pages that contain the entire phrase. The more specific the search criteria, the better the chance the information will be found.

Search Engines

A search engine usually works by sending out an agent, such as spider. A spider is an application that gathers a list of available web page documents and stores this list in a database that users can search by keywords.

When displaying information, search engines often show "Sponsored Sites Results" first. These are sites that contain the information being searched for but have paid the search engine to list their sites at the top of the list.

Most searches yield far too many matches to be useful. Limiting the number of matches to a reasonable number can usually be accomplished by using Boolean logic in the search criteria:

Boolean Logic

Boolean logic uses three logical operators:

AND locates pages that include both words

OR locates pages that include one word or the other or both

NOT locates pages that include the first word, but not the second word

A Boolean expression always evaluates to TRUE or FALSE with pages that match the search condition evaluating to TRUE.

- The **+** (plus sign) is used in search criteria to limit a search to only web pages that contain all of the specified words. For example, a search for florida +hotel or florida hotel returns only links to pages containing both words. **AND** can be used in place of + in most search engines.
- **OR** can be used in most search engines to find web pages that contain any one of the words in the criteria. For example, the criteria florida OR hotel returns links to pages containing either of the words.
- The – (minus sign) is used to exclude unwanted web pages. For example, the search for shakespeare –play returns hyperlinks to pages containing the word shakespeare, but eliminates pages that also contain the word play. **NOT** can be used in place of – in most search engines.

Some search engines provide a *subject tree*, or *web directory*, which is a list of sites separated into categories. The term subject tree is used because many of the categories "branch" off into subcategories. These subcategories allow the user to narrow down the subject and display a list of appropriate hyperlinks, which are at the lowest level of the tree.

TIP Just because a file is available on a website for download does not mean that it is legal to download the file. Downloading copyrighted files that have not been made freely available is a violation of copyright law.

Information on a website is sometimes in the form of a downloadable file. *Downloading* is the process of copying a file from a website to the user's computer. For example, virus definitions can be downloaded from an antivirus software company's website and software updates can be downloaded from the software company's website. When a file is downloaded, the user specifies where the file should be saved on the local computer. Files should only be downloaded from known, authentic websites since downloadable files are often associated with viruses.

MLA

If information from a website is to be referenced or quoted in a report, essay, or other document, a citation must be used to give credit to the original author and allow the reader to locate the cited information. A widely accepted form for citation is published by the Modern Language Association (MLA) in its publication *MLA Handbook for Writers of Research Papers, Seventh Edition.*

In general, a citation for material located at a Web site should look similar to:

Author's Last Name, First Name. "Article Title." Site Title. Publisher Name, Last-updated date. Web. Access date. <URL>.

TIP MLA no longer requires the use of URLs in MLA citations because Web sites are not static and typically documents can be located by searching the title in a search engine. If an instructor still requires the use of URLs, they are placed in angle brackets after the date of access.

If no publisher name is available, n.p. should be used and if no publication date is listed, n.d. is used. A citation of a page on a website:

Marrelli, J. "How to use Internet Explorer". *Lawrenceville Press - Download Data Files.* Lawrenceville Press, 23 Dec. 2010. Web. 15 May 2012.

Internet Privacy Issues

The growth of the Internet has caused additional concerns about personal privacy. Searching for information on the Internet is not as anonymous as it might seem.

Spyware

Spyware is software that uses the Internet to gather personal information from an unsuspecting user. Spyware is unknowingly downloaded and installed with another file, such as freeware or shareware programs.

The collection of data about consumers visiting a website is a marketing technique known as *online profiling*. When a commercial website is visited, information about the user may be collected using various methods such as cookies or web beacons.

A *cookie* is a text file created by the server computer when a user enters information into a website. The cookie file is then stored on the user's computer and accessed each time the user visits that website. Cookies are often created when online purchases are made. Although cookies can only store information that the user has selected or entered, their use has raised concerns over privacy issues.

IP Address

An IP address is an identifier for a computer or device on a TCP/IP network.

Web beacons, also called *web bugs* or *pixel tags*, are tiny, transparent graphics located on web pages or in e-mail messages that are used in combination with cookies to collect data about web page users or e-mail senders. Usually the monitoring is done by an outside advertising company. The information a web beacon collects includes the IP address of the computer, the URL being visited, the time the web page was viewed, the type of browser being used, and the cookie file.

TIP A website's privacy policy is typically found as a link at the bottom of the home page of a website.

Before providing a company with personal information through a website, check the site's privacy policy. A *privacy policy* is a legally binding document that explains how any personal information will be used.

The Internet has opened up access to many files that were previously inaccessible. To protect both the privacy of an individual and the accuracy of data stored about individuals, several laws have been passed:

- The **Electronic Communications Privacy Act of 1986 (ECPA)** makes it a crime to access electronic data without authorization. It also prohibits unauthorized release of such data.
- The **Electronic Freedom of Information Act of 1996 (E-FOIA)** requires federal government agencies to make certain agency information available for public inspection and is designed to improve public access to agency records by making more information available online.
- The **Children's Online Privacy Protection Act of 1998 (COPPA)** requires commercial websites that collect personal information from children under the age of 13 to obtain parental consent.
- The **Safety and Freedom through Encryption Act of 1999 (SAFE)** gives Americans the freedom to use any type of encryption to protect their confidential information.

NET Act

The NET (No Electronic Theft) Act of 1997 closed a loophole in the law which allowed copyrighted material to be given away on the Internet without any legal penalty.

Other laws have been passed that may invade the privacy of some to protect the safety of others. For example, the **Provide Appropriate Tools Required to Intercept and Obstruct Terrorism (PATRIOT) Act of 2001** gives law enforcement the ability to monitor individual's e-mail and web activity.

> ### *Encryption*
> Encryption is the process of translating data into a code that is not readable without the key to the code. Encryption prevents unauthorized access to the data. Data that is encrypted is referred to as cipher text.

Internet Acceptable Use Policy

Internet content, unproductive use, and copyright have prompted many schools and businesses to develop an Acceptable Use Policy or Internet Use Agreement. Acceptable Use Policies typically contain rules similar to:

- Use appropriate language.
- Do not reveal personal address or phone numbers.
- Do not access, upload, download, or distribute inappropriate materials.
- Do not access another user's account.
- Use of the network for private business is prohibited.
- Only administrator installed software may be used on the computers. Adding, deleting, or modifying installed software is not permitted.

> ### *Internet Filtering Software*
> Many schools and organizations install Internet filtering software to block offensive material.

The Social and Ethical Implications of Computer Use

information age

The society in which we live has been so profoundly affected by computers that historians refer to the present time as the *information age.* This is due to the our ability to store and manipulate large amounts of information (data) using computers. As an information society, we must consider both the social and ethical implications of our use of computers. By ethical questions we mean asking what are the morally right and wrong ways to use computers.

ergonomics

Ergonomics is the science that studies safe work environments. Many health-related issues, such as carpal tunnel syndrome and computer vision syndrome (CVS), are related to prolonged computer use.

Power and paper waste are environmental concerns associated with computer use. Suggestions for eliminating these concerns include recycling paper and printer toner cartridges and turning off monitors and printers when not in use.

Employee monitoring is an issue associated with computers in the workplace. It is legal for employers to install software programs that monitor employee computer use. As well, e-mail messages can be read without employee notification.

> ### *Identity Theft*
> Identity theft is a growing crime where personal information is stolen electronically in order to make fraudulent purchases or loans.

As discussed in a previous section in the chapter, the invasion of privacy is a serious problem associated with computers. Because computers can store vast amounts of data we must decide what information is proper to store, what is improper, and who should have access to the information. Every time you use a credit card, make a phone call, withdraw money, reserve a flight, or register at school, a computer records the transaction. These records can be used to learn a great deal about you—where you have been, when you were there, and how much money was spent. Should this information be available to everyone?

Computers are also used to store information about your credit rating, which determines your ability to borrow money. If you want to buy a car and finance it at a bank, the bank first checks your credit records on a computer to determine if you have a good credit rating. If you purchase the car and then apply for automobile insurance, another computer will check to determine if you have traffic violations. How do you know if the information being used is accurate? The laws listed below have been passed to help ensure that the right to privacy is not infringed by the improper use of data stored in computer files:

- The **Fair Credit Reporting Act of 1970** gives individuals the right to see information collected about them for use by credit, insurance, and employment agencies. If a person is denied credit they are allowed to see the files used to make the credit determination. If any of the information is incorrect, the person has the right to have it changed. The act also restricts who may access credit files to only those with a court order or the written permission of the individual whose credit is being checked.
- The **Privacy Act of 1974** restricts the way in which personal data can be used by federal agencies. Individuals must be permitted access to information stored about them and may correct any information that is incorrect. Agencies must insure both the security and confidentiality of any sensitive information. Although this law applies only to federal agencies, many states have adopted similar laws.
- The **Financial Privacy Act of 1978** requires that a government authority have a subpoena, summons, or search warrant to access an individual's financial records. When such records are released, the financial institution must notify the individual of who has had access to them.

Protecting Computer Software and Data

copyright

As society becomes more and more reliant on digital information, copyright and exposure to malicious code have become two important issues among computer users. *Copyright* is protection of digital information. Copyright infringement is the illegal use or reproduction of data (text, pictures, music, video, and so on). Laws, such as the NET Act (No Electronic Theft Act) of 1997, protect against copyright infringement. There have been several well-known cases of high penalties for individuals guilty of copyright infringement.

piracy

Copyright infringement includes duplication of computer software when copies are being used by individuals who have not paid for the software. This practice is called *piracy* when illegal copies are distributed. Developing, testing, marketing, and supporting software is an expensive process. If the software developer is then denied rightful compensation, the future development of all software is jeopardized. Therefore, it is important to use only legally acquired copies of software, and to not make illegal copies for others.

TIP It is usually legal to make one backup copy of a purchased software program.

Malicious code comes in many forms and is delivered in many ways. A virus, a Trojan horse, and an Internet worm are three forms of malicious code. They can appear on a system through executable programs, scripts, macros, e-mails, and some Internet connections. One devastating effect of malicious code is the destruction of data.

virus

A *virus* is a program or series of instructions that can replicate without the user's knowledge. Often a virus is triggered to run when given a certain signal. For example, a virus might check the computer's clock and then destroy data when a certain time is reached. A virus is easily duplicated when the file is copied, which spreads it to other computers.

Trojan horse

worm

A *Trojan horse* program appears as something else, usually a program that looks trustworthy. Running the program runs the malicious code and damages files on the computer. A *worm* is a program that is able to reproduce itself over a network. Worms are a threat because of the way they replicate and use system resources, sometimes causing the system to shut down.

antivirus programs

Malicious code has become so widespread that software called *antivirus programs* must be installed on computers and networks to detect and remove the code before it can replicate or damage data. Precautions can also be taken to prevent damage from malicious code:

- Update antivirus software. An antivirus program can only detect the viruses, Trojan horses, and worms it is aware of. Antivirus programs have a web link for updating the virus definitions on the computer containing the antivirus program.
- Do not open e-mail attachments without scanning for malicious code. One estimate states that 80% of virus infection is through e-mail.

crackers, hackers

Newspapers have carried numerous reports of *crackers*, or *hackers*, gaining access to large computer systems to perform acts of vandalism. This malicious act is illegal and can cause expensive damage. The Electronic Communications Privacy Act of 1986 specifically makes it a federal offense to access electronic data without authorization. Networks usually include a firewall, which is a combination of hardware and software, to help prevent unauthorized access.

The willful destruction of computer data is no different than any other vandalizing of property. Since the damage is done electronically the result is often not as obvious as destroying physical property, but the consequences are much the same. It is estimated that computer crimes cost billions of dollars each year.

phishing

Phishing is the act of sending an e-mail to a user falsely claiming to be a legitimate business in an attempt to trick the user into revealing personal information that could be used for crimes such as identity theft.

The Ethical Responsibilities of an IT Professional

An *IT* (information technology) professional has responsibilities that relate to system reliability. System reliability involves installing and updating appropriate software, keeping hardware working and up-to-date, and maintaining databases and other forms of data. Governments, schools, and employers rely on IT professionals to maintain their computer systems.

In addition to ensuring system reliability, an IT professional must take responsibility for the ethical aspects of the career choice. For example, IT professionals involved in creating software must ensure, as best he or she can, the reliability of the computer software. This means the ethical responsibility of the IT professional includes using the appropriate tools and methods to test and evaluate programs before distribution. A special cause for concern is the increased use of computers to control potentially dangerous devices such as aircraft, nuclear reactors, or sensitive medical equipment.

IT Careers

The growth of computers, the Internet, and the Web have created many new job opportunities in the IT field. IT careers include data-entry operator, systems analyst, programmer, computer engineer, and technical support technician.

IT professionals must also consider the impact they have on computer users. Web users for example often rely on data from websites providing real-time information. The information displayed is determined with a program written using a language that accesses a database. The IT professionals involved in such a project have the ethical responsibility to possibly millions of individuals for ensuring, as best they can, accurate data retrieval.

As capable as computers have proven to be, we must be cautious when allowing them to replace human beings in areas where judgement is crucial. As intelligent beings, we can often detect that something out of the ordinary has occurred which has not been previously anticipated and then take appropriate actions. Computers will only do what they have been programmed to do.

Chapter Summary

A desktop computer and its components are designed to fit on or under a desk. Mobile computers include notebooks, tablets, handhelds, smart phones, and wearables. A computer must run operating system (OS) software in order to control processing and peripherals, run application software, and control input and output, among other tasks.

A network is a combination of hardware and software that allows computers to exchange data and share software and devices, such as printers. Networks are classified by their size, architecture, topology, and protocol.

A programming language is a set of words, codes, and symbols that allows a programmer to communicate with the computer. Programming languages can be classified as low-level and high-level languages.

The electrical circuits on an IC have one of two states, off or on. Therefore, the binary number system (base 2), which uses only two digits (0 and 1), was adopted for use in computers. Our most familiar number system is the decimal or base 10 system. The binary number system is a base 2 system and the hexadecimal system is base 16. Every letter of an alphabet (Latin, Japanese, Cherokee, and so on) and symbols of every culture (=, @, ½, and so on) have been given a representation in a digital code called Unicode.

Computer memory, file sizes, and storage device capacities are measured in bytes. In computers and electronics MB stands for megabytes, GB stands for gigabytes, and K stands for kilobytes.

The binary representation of an integer number is usually stored in four bytes of memory. Real numbers are numbers that contain decimal points and the binary representation of a real number is usually 4 to 8 bytes of memory.

A file is related data stored on a persistent media. A file is really just 1s and 0s because it is stored in binary code. Computers are programmed to translate bytes and words into symbols. File types are distinguished by the extension that comes after the file name. Folders are used to organize commonly related files.

Storage devices use a persistent media to maintain files. These devices, which are also referred to as drives, mass storage, and auxiliary storage, can be categorized as internal or external.

An intranet is a network that is used by a single organization and is only accessible by authorized users. A firewall is a network security system that prevents unauthorized network access. An extranet extends an intranet by providing various levels of accessibility to authorized members of the public. The largest and most widely accessed network is the Internet.

Telecommunications is the transmitting and receiving of data. Telecommunication options include a conventional modem, a DSL modem, a cable modem, leased/dedicated lines, and ISDN.

A search engine is a program that searches a database of web pages for keywords and then lists hyperlinks to pages that contain those keywords. Limiting the number of matches to a reasonable number can be accomplished using Boolean logic.

Information found at a website should be evaluated for accuracy. There are guidelines for citing electronic material on the Internet. The primary purpose of a citation is to give credit to the original author and allow the reader to locate the cited information.

The growth of the Internet has caused concerns about personal privacy. Online profiling, cookies, and web bugs are all areas of concern. To protect an individual's privacy, several laws have been passed. Concerns about Internet content, unproductive use, and copyright have prompted many schools and businesses to develop an Internet Use Agreement.

Historians refer to our present time as the information age. The potential for the use of computers to invade our right to privacy has prompted legislation to protect individuals. Piracy is the illegal act of duplicating software without permission. A virus is a computer file that erases data and can cause considerable damage.

Working as an IT (information technology) professional includes taking responsibility for the ethical aspects of a career choice. IT professionals must also consider the impact they have on computer users.

Vocabulary

Address A unique binary representation of a location in memory.

Address bus Carries memory addresses that indicate data storage locations.

ALU (Arithmetic Logic Unit) The part of the CPU that handles arithmetic and logic operations.

Antivirus program Software installed on computers and networks to detect and remove viruses.

Applications software Program written to perform a specific task.

Base unit Housing that contains the motherboard, CD-RW/DVD drive, disk drive, and hard disk drive.

Binary files Computer-readable files.

Binary number system Number system used by computers that uses only digits 0 and 1. Also called base 2.

Bit (BInary digiT) A single 0 or 1 in binary code.

Bus A central network cable. Also a set of circuits that connect the CPU to other components.

Bus topology A physical LAN topology that uses a single central cable to attach each node directly.

Byte A group of 8 bits.

Cable modem A modem that transmits data through a coaxial cable television network.

Cache High-speed memory used to store frequently used data so that it can be quickly retrieved by an application.

Client A computer that is sent information from a server computer.

Client/server network A type of network that consists of a group of computers, called clients connected to a server computer.

Clock rate The speed at which a CPU can execute instructions, measured in megahertz or gigahertz.

Compiler A program that converts an entire program into machine code before the program is executed.

Control bus Carries control signals.

Conventional modem A modem that uses standard telephone lines to convert analog signals to digital data.

Cookie Text file created by the server computer when a user enters information into a website.

Copyright Protects a piece of work from reproduction without permission from the work's author.

CPU (Central Processing Unit) Processes data and controls the flow of data between the computer's other units. Also contains the ALU. Located on the motherboard.

Cracker Person who accesses a computer system without authorization.

Cross-platform connectivity The ability of one type of PC to link to and share data with a different type of PC.

Dedicated line *See* Leased line.

Desktop computer A computer designed to fit on or under a desk.

Device driver One type of utility program.

Downloading The process of copying a file from a website to the user's computer.

DSL (Digital Subscriber Line) modem A modem that uses standard telephone phone lines. ADSL is the most common form used.

E-mail (electronic mail) The sending and receiving of messages and electronic files over a communications network such as a LAN or the Internet.

Environment A computer's hardware and software configuration. Also referred to as platform. Environment types include desktop, multiuser, network, handheld, distributed, multiprocessing, and multitasking.

Ergonomics The science that studies safe work environments.

Expansion boards Circuit boards that connect to the motherboard to add functionality to the computer.

Extension Added after a file name to distinguish file types.

Extranet An extended intranet that provides various levels of access to authorized members of the public.

File A collection of related data stored on a lasting medium.

Firewall A network security system that prevents unauthorized network access.

Folder Used to organize commonly related files.

Gigabytes (GB) Approximately one billion bytes.

Gigahertz (GHz) Billion of cycles per second.

Hacker *See* Cracker.

Handheld computer A mobile computing device.

Hardware The physical components of the computer, such as the monitor and system unit.

Hexadecimal system Number system based on 16 digits. Also called base 16.

High-level programming languages Third generation programming languages that have English-like instructions.

Hub A communication device that joins communication lines at a central location on the network.

Information age Present time characterized by increasing dependence on the computer's ability to store and manipulate large amounts of information.

Input device Device used to enter data and instructions into the computer.

Integrated circuits (ICs) A silicon wafer with intricate circuits etched into its surface and then coated with a metallic oxide that fills in the etched circuit patterns. Also called a chip.

Interactive Information accessed as a result of selections made by the user.

Internet The largest and most widely accessed network.

Interpreter A program that translates and executes an instruction before moving on to the next instruction in the program.

Intranet A network that is used by a single organization and only accessible by authorized users.

ISDN (Integrated Services Digital Network) A digital telephone network provided by a local telephone company.

IT (Information Technology) A term that encompasses all aspects of computer-related technology.

Kbps Thousands of bits per second.

Kilobytes (K) Approximately a thousand bytes.

LAN (Local Area Network) A network used to connect devices within a small area.

Leased line A telecommunication option used for a permanent connection to the Internet that is always active.

Logical topology Refers to the way in which data is passed between the nodes on a network.

Low-level programming languages First and second generation programming languages including machine language and assembly language.

Mailing list server A server that manages mailing lists for groups of users.

Match A web page that contains the search criteria.

Mbps Millions of bits per second.

Megabytes (MB) Approximately one million bytes.

Megahertz (MHz) Million of cycles per second.

Memory-resident A program that is always in memory.

Minus sign (–) Used in search criteria to exclude unwanted web pages.

Modern Language Association (MLA) Organization that publishes standards used for citations.

Motherboard The main circuit board inside the base unit.

Netiquette The etiquette that should be followed when using a network.

Network A combination of software and hardware that allows computers to exchange data and to share software and devices, such as printers.

Network interface card A circuit board that goes into a computer or other device in a LAN.

Network operating system Software that allows users and devices to communicate over a network.

Node A location on the network capable of processing information, such as a computer or a printer.

Object-oriented programming (OOP) An approach to programming where modules are created that can be used over and over again.

Online profiling A marketing technique that collects online data about consumers.

Operating system Software that allows the user to communicate with the computer. Types include multiuser, multiprocessing, multitasking, multithreading, or real time.

Output device A device used to convey processed data.

Overflow error An error that occurs when the number of bits that are needed to represent the integer is greater than four bytes.

Peer-to-peer network A type of network that does not have a server.

Peripheral device A device attached to a PC.

Phishing The act of sending an e-mail to a user falsely claiming to be a legitimate business in an attempt to trick the user into revealing personal information that could be used for crimes such as identity theft.

Piracy Illegally copying or distributing software.

Plus sign (+) Used in search criteria to limit a search to only those web pages containing two or more specified words.

Port Used to attach a peripheral device to a computer.

Privacy policy A legally binding document that explains how any personal information will be used.

Programming languages A set of words, codes, and symbols that allows a programmer to communicate with the computer.

RAM (Random Access Memory) Memory that temporarily stores data and instructions. Also called primary or main memory.

Real numbers Numbers that contain decimal points. Also called floating point numbers.

Ring topology A physical LAN topology where each node is connected to form a closed loop.

ROM (Read Only Memory) Memory that stores data and is a permanent part of the computer.

Roundoff error An error that occurs when there are not enough bits to hold the mantissa.

Router A device that connects different network technologies.

Search criteria A single word or phrase that is used by the search engine to match web pages.

Search engine A program that searches a database of web pages for keywords and then lists hyperlinks to pages that contain those keywords.

Secondary memory Any type of storage media.

Server A computer used to manage network functions such as communication and data sharing.

Smartphone Cellular phone that is able to send and receive e-mail messages and access the Internet.

SRAM (Static Random Access Memory) High-speed memory referred to as cache.

Star topology A physical LAN topology where each node is attached to a hub.

Storage devices Devices that use persistent media to maintain files. Also referred to as drives, mass storage, and auxiliary storage.

Subject tree A list of sites separated into categories.

TCP/IP (Transmission Control Protocol/Internet Protocol) Software used by networks connected to routers to communicate.

Telecommunications The transmitting and receiving of data.

Text files Human-readable files.

Topology The physical or logical arrangement of the nodes on a network.

Transmission media The media that joins the nodes on a network to enable communication.

Trojan horse Malicious code in the form of a program that appears as something else, usually a program that looks trustworthy.

Ultra-portable devices Storage devices, such as keychains, that are small and easy-to-use.

Unicode A digital code that uses a set of sixteen 1s and 0s to form a 16-bit binary code for each symbol.

Utility program Program run by the operating system to manage input and output, read and write to memory, manage the processor, maintain system security, and manage files and disks.

Virus A program that is designed to reproduce itself by copying itself into other programs stored on a computer without the user's knowledge.

WAN (Wide Area Network) A network used to connect computers over large geographical distances.

Wearable computer A mobile computing device that is incorporated into clothing, eyewear, wristwear, and other wearables.

Web *See* World Wide Web.

Web beacon A tiny, transparent graphic located on a web page used to collect data about the web page user. Also called a web bug or pixel tag.

Web browser Interprets an HTML document to display a web page.

Web directory *See* Subject tree.

Wireless network A type of network that does not require the use of cables.

Word Bits grouped in units of 16 to 64.

World Wide Web The most widely used Internet service. Used to search and access information available on the Internet.

Worm Program that is able to reproduce itself over a network.

Review Questions

1. a) Describe a situation where a desktop computer might be preferred over a notebook computer.
   b) List three advantages of purchasing a notebook computer instead of desktop computer.
   c) Describe a situation or user that would prefer a tablet PC over a notebook computer.
   d) Describe two occupations where it would be useful to have a hand-held computer.
   e) Describe how wearable computers are used in the health care industry.

2. a) List and compare three input devices.
   b) List and compare three output devices.
   c) List and describe two peripheral devices.
   d) List three types of ports.

3. List and describe five components found on the motherboard.

4. Describe the flow of data between the components of a computer, starting with input.

5. What is cache memory used for?

6. a) Describe one difference between operating system software and applications software.
   b) List three different operating systems.
   c) What does environment refer to?
   d) What is another word for environment?

7. What is a utility program? Give an example.

8. Why is cross-platform connectivity important to many computer users?

9. a) What is the difference between low and high level programming languages?
   b) List three high-level programming languages.
   c) What is the difference between a compiler and an interpreter?
   d) List an advantage of using an object-oriented programming language.

10. List four benefits of using a network.

11. a) What are the two common size classifications for networks?
    b) What size classification is used to connect devices over large geographical distances?

12. a) What is a network operating system?
    b) What does a network environment refer to?

13. Describe two common network architecture models.

14. a) What does physical topology refer to?
    b) What is a node?
    c) Which topology uses a hub?
    d) Which topology connects each node to form a closed loop?
    e) What is the difference between physical and logical topology?

15. Which netiquette rules apply in your classroom?

16. Explain why the binary number system was adopted for use in computers.

17. a) What is the decimal equivalent of 1011_2?
    b) What is the decimal equivalent of $2A_{16}$?

18. What is Unicode?

19. a) How many bytes of data can 2 GB of RAM store?
    b) How many bytes of data can a 500 GB hard drive store?

20. a) When would an overflow error occur?
    b) What are real numbers?
    c) When would a roundoff error occur?

21. a) What is the difference between a text file and a binary file?
    b) Explain how an extension distinguishes file types.
    c) Describe how organizing your files into folders would help keep you organized.

22. List two ways storage devices can be classified and give an example of a storage device in each category.

23. List four rules that should be followed to avoid damaging files stored on disks or CD/DVDs.

24. a) What is the difference between an intranet and an extranet?
    b) Who controls the Internet?

25. a) What problem is associated with using a conventional modem?
    b) Describe the differences between a DSL modem and a cable modem.

26. a) What is the most widely used Internet service?
    b) List one benefit of e-mail over standard mail.
    c) Write your e-mail address and label the parts of the address.
    d) What are the two requirements for sending and receiving e-mail messages?
    e) List one example of a browser-based e-mail site.

27. a) Explain why sending an e-mail message should be thought of the same as sending a postcard.
    b) Discuss with a partner and then summarize issues that could occur if e-mail etiquette is not followed in the workplace.

28. a) List three commonly used search engines.
    b) Which search engine do you prefer to use, and why?
    c) Describe the importance of using effective search criteria.

29. Write search criteria to locate web pages that contain the following information:
    a) restaurants in Miami
    b) art museums in Montreal, Canada
    c) clothing stores in your city
    d) alligators, but not crocodiles
    e) the author James Patterson
    f) the phrase *garbage in garbage out*
    g) George Washington and John Adams, but not Thomas Jefferson
    h) travel to Florida, but not Orlando

30. Why should files only be downloaded from authentic sites?

31. a) List four questions to answer when evaluating a website source.
    b) Why is it necessary to cite sources?
    c) On August 2, 2012 you accessed a posting on the Clewiston Kite Surfing discussion list at http://www.emcschool.net/kitesurf/color.txt. The posting was made by Tara Perez on the topic of kite colors. Write a citation for a research paper that quotes Tara's posting.

32. a) What is online profiling?
    b) What is a cookie?
    c) What is a web beacon?
    d) Who usually monitors the information collected by web beacons?

33. Locate a website's privacy policy and document its contents.

34. Name and briefly describe one law that helps protect the privacy of an individual.

35. List three reasons why many schools have developed an Acceptable Use Policy.

36. What can you do if you are turned down for credit at a bank and believe that the data used to deny credit is inaccurate?

37. a) What is necessary for a federal government authority to access an individual's financial records?
    b) What must a financial institution do after releasing an individual's records?

38. a) What is copyright infringement?
    b) Why is computer piracy such a concern to software developers?
    c) What is a computer virus?
    d) Describe phishing.

39. What ethical responsibilities does an IT professional have?

True/False

40. Determine if each of the following are true or false. If false, explain why.
    a) Software refers to the physical components of the computer.
    b) Linux is an operating system.
    c) A utility program has one clearly defined task.
    d) Assembly language is a high-level programming language.
    e) A WAN connects devices over large geographical distances.
    f) A peer-to-peer network has a server.
    g) The binary number system uses only 1s and 0s.
    h) A conventional modem transmits data faster than a cable modem.
    i) An e-mail address is required to send e-mail messages.
    j) The present time is referred to as the industrial age.
    k) Ergonomics is the science that studies safe work environments.

Exercises

Exercise 1

In this exercise you will research the cost of purchasing a desktop computer.

a) Use computer websites, such as www.dell.com, www.apple.com or newspaper advertisements to research the costs of two comparable desktop computers.

b) Summarize the specifications and costs associated with each computer. Be sure to include the costs associated with any needed peripherals including auxiliary storage devices.

c) Decide which computer is a better choice. This may require additional research on company reliability and so forth. Be sure to assess the computer's warranty when making a decision.

d) Present your research and conclusion in a report.

Exercise 2

In this exercise you will research the capabilities and costs of mobile computers.

a) Assume you are a travelling salesman. You travel all over the country selling car parts. Keeping in mind the need to travel light, keep in contact with the main office, and have all price lists, inventory, and product information at your fingertips, research mobile computing devices and document what devices you think would be essential for this occupation. Include approximate costs in your documentation.

b) Assume you are a software engineer. You design software applications for the health services/medical industry. You work long hours both in the office and at home. You also need to travel frequently to provide on-site technical support to customers. Research and document what mobile computing devices you think would be essential for this occupation. Include approximate costs in your documentation.

Exercise 3

Processor manufacturers include Intel and AMD. Select one of these manufacturers and use the company's website (www.intel.com or www.amd.com) to research the features and specifications of one of their processors. Present your research in a report, citing the source of information.

Exercise 4

In this exercise you will analyze your classroom computer network by answering the following questions:

a) Is your computer network a LAN or a WAN?

b) List three advantages of having your classroom computers set up on a network.

c) Are there any disadvantages of having your classroom computers set up on a network?

d) List the input devices accessible on the classroom network. List advantages and disadvantages associated with each accessible input device.

e) List the output devices accessible on the classroom network. List advantages and disadvantages associated with each accessible output device.

f) What type of physical topology is used?

g) What type of transmission media is used?

h) What network protocol is used?

i) What operating system is used? Describe three computer maintenance tasks that can be performed using operating system utilities (i.e., emptying the Recycle Bin, defragmenting a hard drive)

j) Describe your workstation's environment.

k) What telecommunication option is used?

l) What advantages is there or would there be to having a wireless network in your classroom?

m) Does the school have an intranet?

n) List four rules on the school's Internet Use Agreement.

o) List five applications software programs available on your network. Describe tasks each application is designed to perform.

p) Use the Internet, magazines, and books to research tips additional for keeping your computer in good condition (i.e., dusting, using a surge protector). Describe at least three additional tips.

q) What storage devices are available to backup your files or to bring your files home? Comment on any cross platform connectivity issues you may encounter with using your classroom files on your home computer or on another computer in the school.

r) Does your computer network allow for resource sharing through a public drive or other means? If yes, explain the process.

s) Describe measures that are in place to protect the classroom network, such as a firewall and antivirus software.

Exercise 5

Repetitive stress injuries are caused by repeated movement of a particular part of the body and are often seen in workers whose physical routine is unvaried. The rise in computer usage is correlated to a substantial increase in the occurrences of repetitive stress injuries.

a) Conduct a search on the Internet using at least two search engines to find three web pages that have information about repetitive stress injuries.

b) Summarize your research in a report. Be sure to include information on preventative measures and possible treatments.

c) Write a citation for each source.

Exercise 6

Expand on the information presented in this chapter by researching one of the following topics:

- Network Protocols
- Operating Systems
- The History of the Internet
- Evolution of Programming Languages
- Identity Theft
- Number Systems
- Mobile Computing
- Wireless Networks
- Telecommunications
- Internet Services

a) Use the Internet, magazines, and books to find at least three sources of information.

b) Prepare a report or presentation that summarizes your research.

c) Write a citation for each source.

Exercise 7

In this exercise you will research and compare the advantages and cost of obtaining Internet access through three different telecommunication options.

a) Use the Internet and newspapers to find information about Internet service providers (ISPs).

b) Compare the costs and the advantages of at least three different telecommunication options.

c) Write a one paragraph conclusion that explains what telecommunication option would be the best choice.

d) Write a citation for each source.

Exercise 8

In this exercise you will further research emerging technologies and find real-life examples of how these technologies have impacted individuals and businesses.

a) Use the Internet, magazines, and books to learn more about at least three emerging technologies. Look specifically for information on how these emerging technologies impact individuals and businesses. For example, speech recognition technology greatly impacts those individuals who must rely on voice input rather than keyboard input for a PC.

b) Write a two-page report that summarizes the impact of and lists several functions of the emerging technologies you have researched.

c) Write a citation for each source.

Exercise 9

Many computer viruses have been associated with e-mail attachments.

a) Conduct a search on the Internet to find information about a virus associated with an e-mail attachments.

b) Write a one-paragraph description of the virus. Include details, such as the damage caused by the virus and steps necessary to remove the virus. Be sure to document prevention methods for similar viruses as well.

c) Write a citation for each source.

Exercise 10

You have decided to investigate computer-related careers.

a) Access the IT Careers PDF at www.emcschool.net/VisualBasic2010 to read about possible computer-related careers.

b) Conduct a search on the Internet using at least two search engines to find three appropriate degree programs.

c) List each program location (college name), the number of credits required to finish the degree, and the tuition cost per credit or per course.

d) If possible, interview a professional in your chosen field to learn more about the occupation.

Exercise 11

Environmental issues associated with computers include:

- significant energy use
- disposal of old computers
- health risks
- recycling

Select one of these topics to research further. Prepare a presentation that summarizes your research.

Exercise 12

In this exercise you will investigate mailing lists.

a) Join an appropriate computer-related mailing list.

b) Participate on the mailing list as a learner.

c) Contribute to the mailing list content.

Exercise 13

Ergonomics is the science that studies safe work environments. Using the correct type and configuration of mouse, keyboard, monitor, chair, and desk can help users work comfortably and efficiently while protecting their health.

a) Research tips for an ergonomically designed workstation (i.e, adjustable height chair with 5 legs for stability).

b) Analyze your school workstation. Comment on whether the workstation is ergonomically correct.

c) **Homework:** Analyze your home workstation. Comment on whether the workstation is ergonomically correct.

Exercise 14

Prepare a poster or document that outlines tips for safe computing. You may want to include tips on creating safe passwords, avoiding spyware, using anti-virus software effectively, backing up files, using screen saver passwords, wireless precautions, and so forth.

Chapter 2 Introducing Visual Basic

Key Concepts

Creating and running an application
Adding controls, objects, and menus
Object-oriented terminology
Event-driven applications
Writing assignment statements
Adding comments to program code
Finding help
Applying code conventions

Visual Basic Applications

GUI
interface

An *application* makes the computer a useful tool by enabling the user to perform a specific task, such as word processing. A Windows application has a graphical user interface, or *GUI* (sometimes pronounced "gooey"). The *interface* is what appears on the screen when the application is running. A Visual Basic GUI includes a form (window), labels, buttons, and other control objects. For example, the Visual Basic application interface below contains a form and a label:

BASIC

Visual Basic is derived from the BASIC (Beginner's All-Purpose Symbolic Instruction Code) computer language developed by John Kemeny and Thomas Kurtz at Dartmouth University in the 1960s.

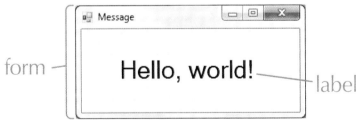

event-driven
event

A GUI is also event-driven. An *event-driven application* executes code in response to an event. An *event* can be an interaction from the user, such as a button click. For example, the Message application remains on the screen until the Close button in the upper-right corner of the form is clicked by the user. When clicked, the application responds to the event by closing the application.

Integrated Development Environment

Visual Basic applications are created in an *integrated development environment* or *IDE*. When the Visual Basic 2010 Express IDE is started, the Start Page is displayed:

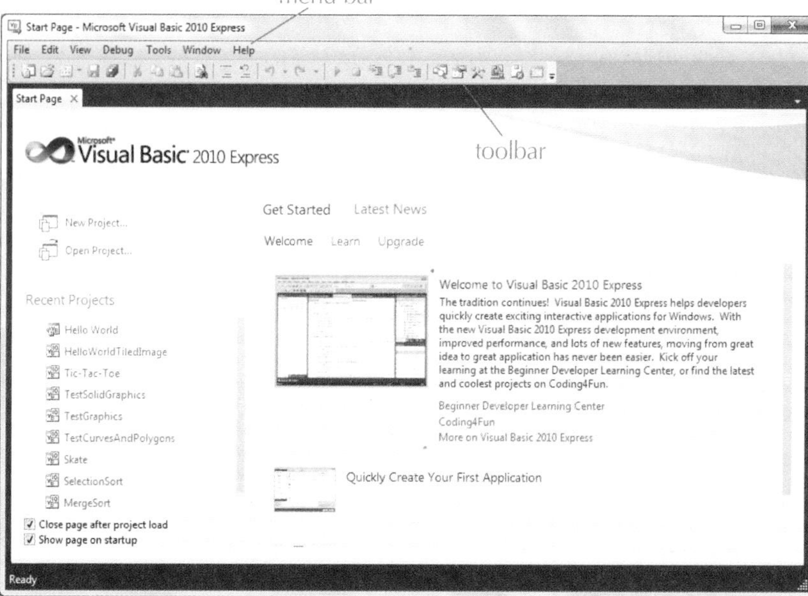

> ***Opening a Web Browser***
>
> A Web browser can be opened within the development environment by selecting View → Other Windows → Web Browser.

- The **menu bar** contains the names of drop-down menus that contain commands.
- The **toolbar** contain buttons that represent different actions.
- The **Start Page** is a help window for getting started with application development.

TIP Click View → Start Page to display the Start Page.

Creating a New Project

An application consists of several related files. In Visual Basic, these files are collectively maintained as a *project*. To create a new Windows project, click the New Project button on the toolbar or click the New Project link on the Start Page. The New Project dialog box is displayed:

Alternative New Project - Ctrl+N.

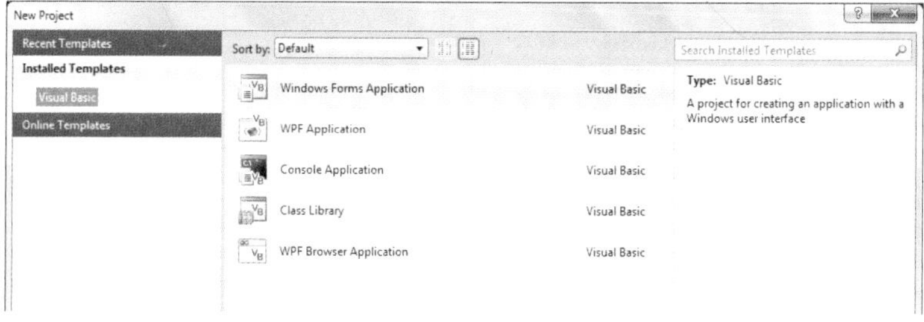

TIP The New Project dialog box may look slightly different depending on the installation options that were selected.

Select the Windows Forms Application template. In the Name box, replace the existing text with a descriptive application name. Application names can contain spaces, but developers typically use camel case. *Camel case* uses a capital letter at the beginning of each word and no spaces. Select OK. The new project is displayed in the Design window:

TIP A Visual Basic 2010 application includes a project file (.vbproj) and a solution file (.sln).

> **The Toolbox**
>
> Click the Toolbox tab or click the Toolbox button on the toolbar to display the Toolbox.
>
> The AutoHide button is used to dock and hide the Toolbox.

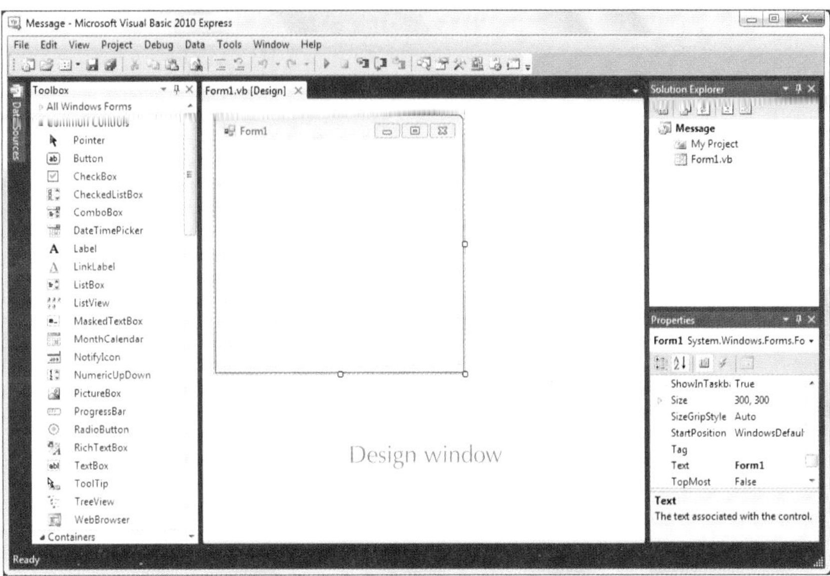

- The **Design window** displays the application interface.
- The **Toolbox** contains controls that are used to create objects on the interface. The controls are grouped for easy access.
- The **Solution Explorer** window is used to switch between the Design and Code windows.
- The **Properties window** lists the properties of a selected object.

TIP The View menu can be used to display and hide tools, such as the Properties window.

The IDE Navigator

The IDE Navigator is used to switch between open files and programming tools. Press Ctrl+Tab to open the IDE Navigator:

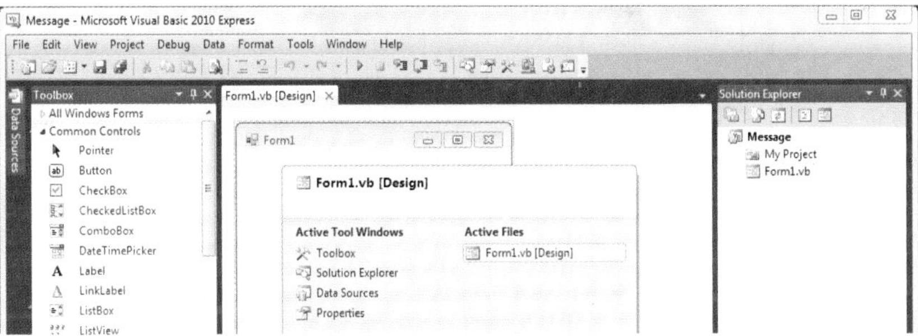

Hold the Ctrl key and then press the Tab key to scroll to a file or use the arrow keys to cycle through both the active files and the active tools. Release the Ctrl key to make the selected item active.

Customizing the IDE

The interface elements in the Visual Basic IDE can be moved, sized, docked, and hidden.

- To move one of the tool windows, click the title bar and drag the object to a new location. If the window is aligned along the edge of another window, it attaches to that window, or *docks* itself.

- Size a docked window by a dragging a window border.
- Close a window by clicking the Close button in the upper-right corner of the window. Use options in the View menu to redisplay the window.
- Click the Auto Hide button to reduce the window to a tab. To restore the window, click the tab and then click the Auto Hide button.

Review: Message – part 1 of 5

① START VISUAL BASIC

② CREATE A NEW PROJECT

a. On the toolbar, click the New Project button. The New Project dialog box is displayed.
   1. In the Templates list, select Windows Forms Application, if it is not already selected.
   2. In the Name box, replace the existing text with `Message`.
   3. Select OK. A project is created and the Design window is displayed.

b. Locate the Solution Explorer window and the Properties window.

c. Practice hiding and restoring the Toolbox.

d. Press Ctrl+ Tab. The IDE Navigator is displayed.

e. Use the IDE Navigator to make the Solution Explorer window active.

The Windows Form

form

A Windows application interface includes at least one form. A *form* is a graphical object that contains a title bar, a system menu, and Minimize, Maximize, and Close buttons.

selected object

A new Visual Basic Windows application automatically includes one Form object. To change the size of the Form object, click the form to select it. A *selected object* displays handles that appear as squares:

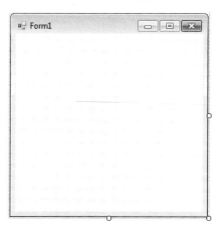

Drag a side handle to size the height or width. Drag a corner handle to size both height and width together.

properties
Text property

A Form object has *properties* that define its appearance, behavior, position, and other attributes. For example, the Text property of a form defines what is displayed in its title bar. Property values are displayed in the Properties window. Properties may be listed in alphabetical order or they may be grouped by category. The Alphabetical and Categorized buttons in the Properties window can be used to switch the list.

A property value is set by typing or selecting a new value. For example, selecting the form, clicking the Text property in the Properties window, and then typing `Message` displays the following:

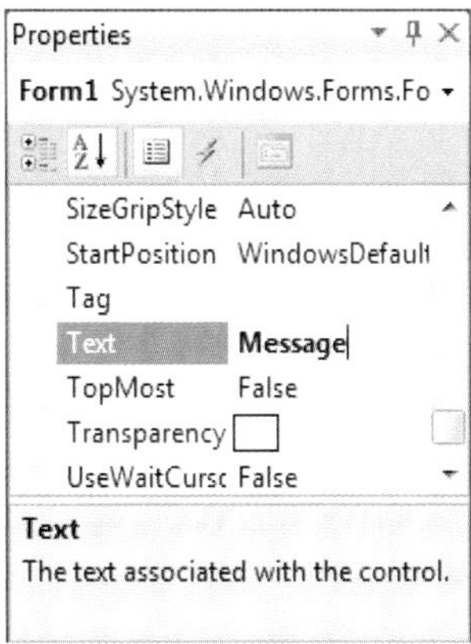

Pressing Enter or clicking outside the Properties window applies the new Text property value to the form:

TIP The Size property is used to size the height and width of a Windows form object.

The Label Control

The Toolbox in the Visual Basic IDE contains controls. A *control* is used to add objects to a form. *Control objects* display information or get user input. For example, a Label object displays text that cannot be changed by the user. An application interface typically contains many control objects on the Form object. The Message application has a simple interface with one label that displays Hello, world!:

Control Class Objects

An object is related data and the instructions for performing actions on that data as described by other code called a class. One class can be used to create multiple objects. Visual Basic provides many built-in classes. Controls are a type of class for creating graphical objects, such as a Label, that can be used in an application interface.

The Message Form object contains a Label control object

A Label

To add an object to a form, click a control in the Toolbox and then click the form. For example, clicking the Label control in the Toolbox and then pointing to the form displays:

The pointer shape displays an icon similar to the selected control. Clicking the form adds a new control object.

Marquee Selection

Multiple control objects can be selected together using a technique called marquee selection. Clicking the Pointer in the Toolbox and then dragging on the form displays a selection box called a marquee. Any objects within the boundaries of the marquee are selected.

Drag a control object to move it to a new location on the form. Multiple objects are moved together by selecting them as a group and then dragging one of the selected objects. This technique is useful when multiple objects need to be moved while maintaining their relative position. The arrow keys can also be used to move selected objects. Pressing the Ctrl key when clicking an object selects it in addition to already selected objects.

Label object properties are set in the Properties window. The Label control has the properties:

- **(Name)** identifies a control for the programmer. Label object names should begin with `lbl`.
- **Text** is the text displayed in the label.
- **Font** contains the … button that is clicked to display the Font dialog box where the font name, font style, and font size of label text is selected.
- **AutoSize** can be set to True or False. When True, the Label object is automatically sized to fit the text initially assigned in the Text property. When False, a Label object displays handles for sizing.
- **TextAlign** is the alignment of text in a label. Alignment can be set to TopLeft (the default), TopCenter, TopRight, MiddleLeft, MiddleCenter, MiddleRight, BottomLeft, BottomCenter, and BottomRight. TextAlign has no affect on Label text unless AutoSize is False.

TIP When AutoSize is True, a Label object displays just one handle, which is used for moving the label.

The properties of the label in the Message application below are `lblMessage` for (Name), `Hello, world!` for Text, and bold size 20 for Font:

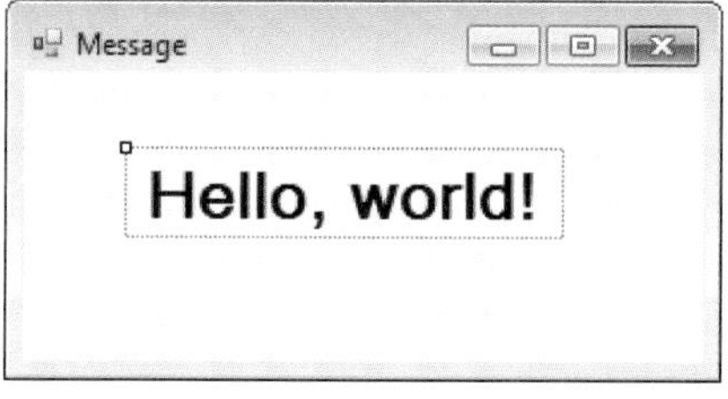

TIP To enter text on multiple lines in a Label object, click the Text property down-pointing arrow, type the text, and then press Ctrl+Enter.

For most objects, the (Name) property should always be set to a descriptive name. A proper object name begins with the appropriate prefix and then describes the purpose of the object. For example, the label in the Message application is named `lblMessage`. This name begins with the appropriate prefix, `lbl`, and is descriptive of the label's purpose.

Saving and Running an Application

An application should be saved frequently to avoid losing changes. To save a project, select File → Save All or click the Save All button on the toolbar.

To run an application from the IDE, click the Start Debugging button on the toolbar or select Debug → Start Debugging (F5). The IDE remains on the screen while the application runs. The application can be tested to see if events, such as clicking a button, produce the desired effect. An application can be run at any time during the development process to allow for testing at different stages.

To terminate a running application, click the Stop Debugging button on the toolbar or select Debug → Stop Debugging. The Close button in the upper-right corner of the window can also be clicked to close the application.

compile

Running an application means that a program is first converted to a language the computer understands in a process called *compiling*. During compilation, an output window is displayed with messages about the program. The Form StartPosition property is WindowsDefaultLocation by default, which means the operating system will determine the best location to display the form at run time. This property value can be set to **CenterScreen** to display the application form in the center of the screen at run time. The output window can be closed by clicking the Close button in the upper-right corner of the window after the program has run.

Review: Message – part 2 of 5

① SET THE FORM PROPERTIES

a. Click the Form to select it.

b. In the Properties window, the Text property is already selected.

c. Type `Message` and press Enter. The title bar now displays "Message."

② ADD A LABEL OBJECT TO THE FORM

a. In the Toolbox, click the Label control.

b. Click the form. A Label object is added to the form:

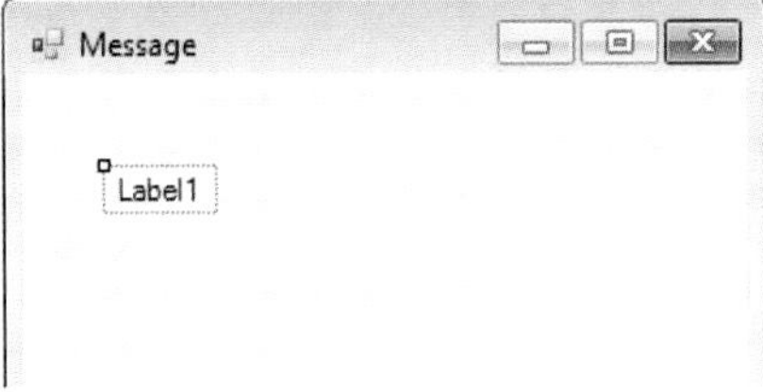

③ SET THE LABEL PROPERTIES

a. Click the Label object to select it, if it is not already selected.

b. Scroll the Properties window to display the (Name) property.

c. Click (Name) and enter `lblMessage`.

d. Scroll the Properties window to display the Text property.

e. Click Text and enter `Hello, world!` The Label object now displays "Hello, world!".

f. Scroll the Properties window to display the Font property.

g. Click Font and then click the [...] button. A dialog box is displayed.

   1. In the Font style list, select Bold.
   2. In the Size list, select 20.
   3. Select OK. The label text is displayed larger.

④ SIZE THE OBJECTS

a. Select the form. Size the form so that it is a smaller rectangular shape.

b. Drag the label so that it is in the center of the form.

Check – Your application interface should look similar to:

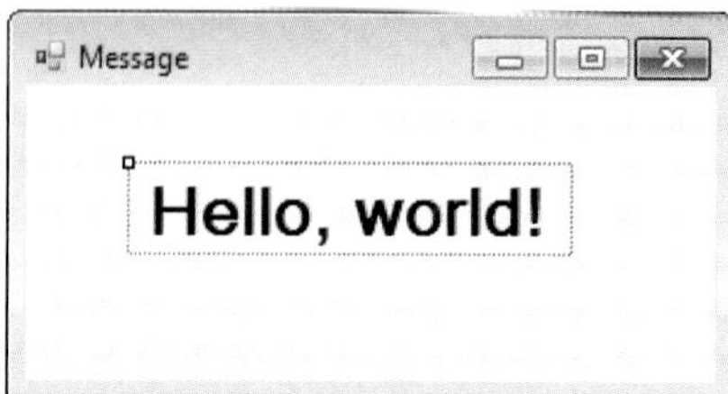

⑤ SAVE AND RUN MESSAGE

a. Select File → Save All. A dialog box is displayed.

   1. Use the Browse button to select the appropriate location for the project.
   2. Select Save.

b. On the toolbar, click the Start Debugging button ▶. The Message application is displayed.

c. Click the Close button [X] in the application window. The application is closed and the IDE is again active.

The MenuStrip Control

A Windows application typically includes menus that contain commands. For example, the Message application can be modified to include a Program menu with an Exit command:

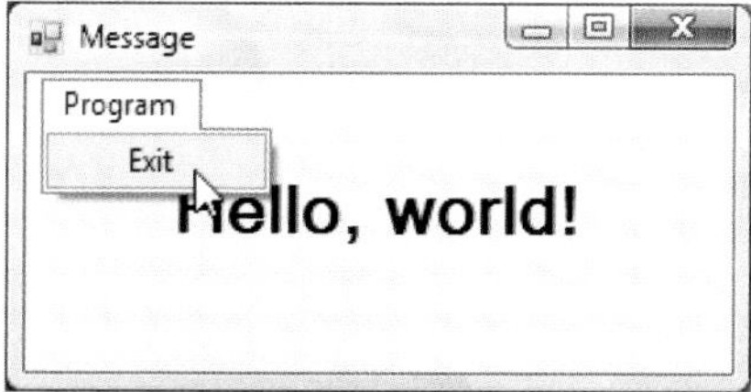

Message with a Program menu and an Exit command

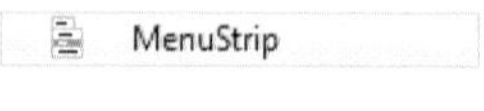

TIP The MenuStrip control is in the Menus & Toolbars section in the Toolbox.

To add a menu to an interface, click the MenuStrip control in the Toolbox and then click the form. A menu is automatically added to the upper-left corner of a form and the MenuStrip component is shown in the component tray at the bottom of the Design window. Typing a menu name displays boxes for typing a command and another menu:

The menu name Program has been typed

When a command or menu name is typed, another box is automatically added to allow for more commands and menus. If an added box is left blank, it will not be included in the menu. Each menu and command name typed is a MenuItem object with the properties:

- **(Name)** identifies an object for the programmer. Visual Basic assigns a descriptive name that begins with the menu or command name. For example, ProgramToolStripMenuItem.
- **Text** is the menu or command name and is set when text is typed into the MenuStrip box in the Design window.

TIP Exercise 12 at the end of the chapter introduces additional MenuItem properties.

A menu is modified in the Design window by clicking a MenuItem object and typing a new name. A MenuItem is deleted by right-clicking the item and selecting Delete from the menu. A new MenuItem is inserted above an existing one by right-clicking the existing item and selecting Insert → MenuItem from the menu.

Closing and Opening a Project and Quitting Visual Basic

When finished working with a project, it should be saved and closed. To close a project, select File → Close Project. A warning dialog box is displayed if the project has been modified since it was last saved. Closing a project removes it from the IDE. To quit Visual Basic, select File → Exit.

To open a project, select File → Open Project. The Open Project dialog box is displayed. Double-click a project folder to display its contents:

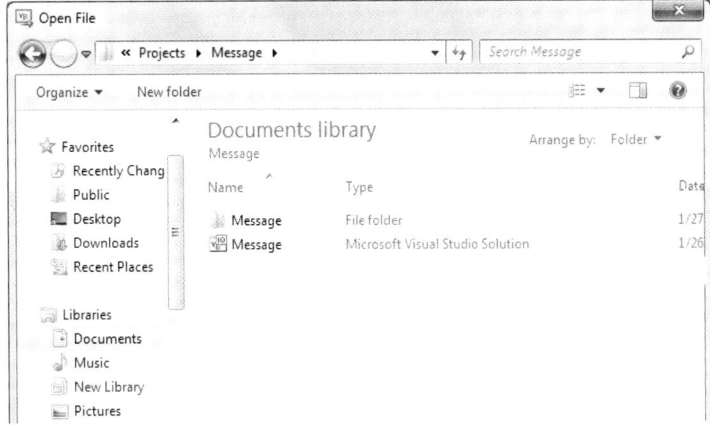

TIP In a file list, the solution file icons have a tiny number 10 because Visual Basic 2010 is the 10th version of the software.

Click the solution file and then select Open to open the project.

After opening a project, it may be necessary to double-click the form name in the Solution Explorer window to display the form in the Design window.

Review: Message – part 3 of 5

① ADD A MENU TO THE FORM

a. In the Toolbox, click the MenuStrip control.

b. Click the form. A menu is added to the upper-left corner of the form and a MenuStrip component is added to the component tray at the bottom of the Design window.

② ADD A MENU NAME AND A COMMAND

a. In the menu, click Type Here.

b. Type `Program` and then press Enter. Additional MenuItem boxes are displayed.

c. Click the MenuItem object below the Program menu and then type `Exit` and press Enter.

③ RUN MESSAGE

a. Save the modified Message application.

b. On the toolbar, click the Start Debugging button ▶. Note the Program menu.

c. Select Program → Exit. Nothing happens because code has not been written for this part of the interface.

d. Close the application.

Program Code

statement

program code

An application contains a set of instructions called *statements* that tells the computer how to perform tasks. Together, the statements for an application are called *program code*. Applications can contain tens to hundreds, even millions of lines of program code.

OOP
class
object

Visual Basic is an object-oriented programming (*OOP*) language. OOP code is organized into *classes*, each defining a set of data and actions. Classes are used to generate *objects*. Performing tasks with objects is the basis of an OOP application. Control classes have already been used to create Visual Basic interfaces. Additional code is needed for the interface to respond to events and perform other actions.

TIP Click the Solution Explorer button on the toolbar or select View → Other Windows → Solution Explorer to display the Solution Explorer window.

Program code for a Visual Basic application is typed into the Code window. The Code window is displayed by clicking the View Code button in the Solution Explorer window or selecting View → Code (F7). When displayed, the Code window automatically includes a class for the form:

The `Form1` class will need statements that instruct the computer how to respond to possible events. Tabs in the IDE can be clicked to switch between the Design window, as indicated by [Design], and the Code window. The IDE Navigator and buttons in the Solution Explorer window can also be used to switch between Design and Code windows.

The Event Procedure

procedure
event handler

A *procedure* is a block of code written to perform specific tasks. An *event procedure*, also called an *event handler*, is a type of procedure that performs tasks in response to user interaction with an object. Event procedures add functionality to an application. For example, when the user clicks a menu command, specific actions should occur. Procedures are written within a class.

Click event procedure

A *Click event procedure* executes in response to a mouse click. For example, clicking a command executes the Click event procedure for that MenuItem object. In the Message application, an Exit Click event procedure should quit the application. To add an event procedure to the Code window, select the object name in the Class Name list and then select the event from the Method Name list:

Method Name list

Class Name list

TIP The – icon in the Code window indicates a block of code is expanded to show all statements. The + icon indicates the statements are hidden.

An event procedure is added to the class. The new procedure does not contain any statements, but has a blank area indicating where the statements will go:

TIP The * at the end of a file name indicates that the file has been modified but not saved.

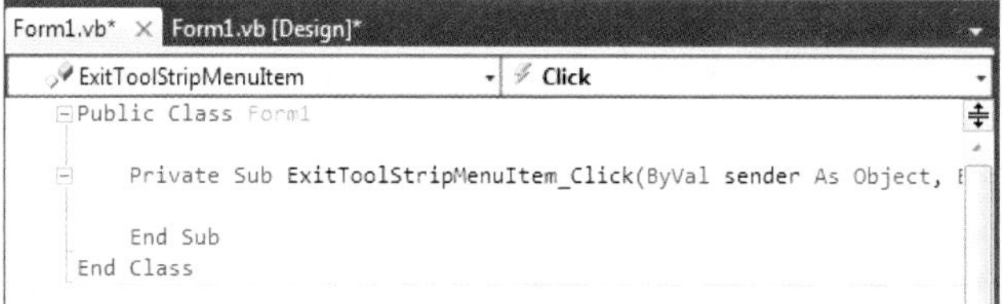

Form1.vb*
Form1.vb [Design]*
ExitToolStripMenuItem
Click
Public Class Form1
Private Sub ExitToolStripMenuItem_Click(ByVal sender As Object,
End Sub
End Class

The procedure heading that is automatically added by Visual Basic contains a set of parentheses with arguments after a descriptive procedure name. Arguments are values used by the procedure and will be discussed in Chapter 6. It is important not to modify the procedure heading, including deleting any of the arguments.

In an event procedure, `Private` indicates that the procedure cannot be accessed outside of the `Form1` class. `Sub` declares the procedure and `End Sub` is required to end the procedure. Between `Sub` and `End Sub` is the *body* with statements that execute when the event occurs.

body

The `Application.Exit()` statement stops program execution. `Application` is a Visual Basic class in the `Forms` class. The dot (.) followed by `Exit()` means that the Exit() method of the `Application` class should be executed. A *method* is a named set of statements that perform a single well-defined task. Visual Basic includes numerous built-in classes and methods for

method

use in applications. The ExitToolStripMenuItem Click event procedure is completed by adding the `Application.Exit()` statement:

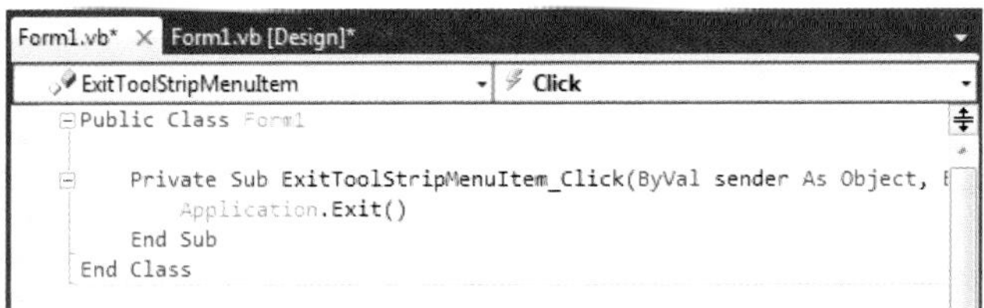

Form1.vb* × Form1.vb [Design]*
ExitToolStripMenuItem
Click
Public Class Form1
Private Sub ExitToolStripMenuItem_Click(ByVal sender As Object,
Application.Exit()
End Sub
End Class

The IDE automatically indents code for readability, but the Tab key can be used as well. Properly indenting code is good programming style.

The program code of an application is printed by selecting File → Print.

Using IntelliSense

TIP Press the Ctrl key and scroll the mouse wheel to zoom in on the program code.

The Visual Basic IDE IntelliSense feature makes coding easier and less error-prone. When a dot (.) is typed in a statement, a list of options is displayed:

TIP The arrow keys or mouse can be used to select an item in an IntelliSense list. Once the item is selected, pressing Tab or typing a space or period places the item in the statement.

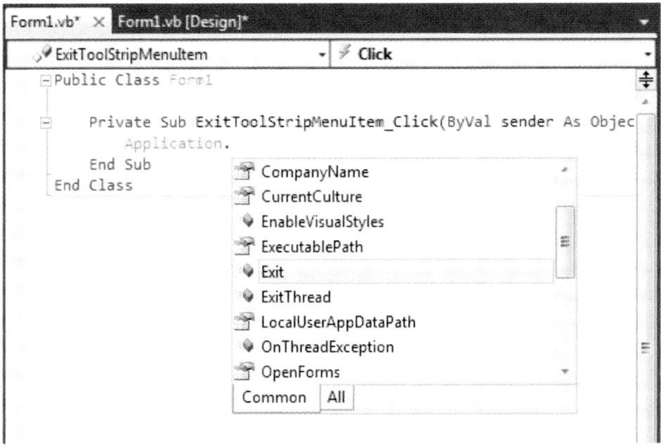

Form1.vb* × Form1.vb [Design]*
ExitToolStripMenuItem
Click
Public Class Form1
Private Sub ExitToolStripMenuItem_Click(ByVal sender As Objec
Application.
End Sub
End Class
CompanyName
CurrentCulture
EnableVisualStyles
ExecutablePath
Exit
ExitThread
LocalUserAppDataPath
OnThreadException
OpenForms
Common
All

IntelliSense displays properties and methods for an object

The options displayed in an IntelliSense list depend on what was typed just before the dot. For example, typing a class name and then a dot displays a list with the properties and methods of that class.

An IntelliSense list is also sometimes displayed when an equal sign (=) is typed. The list contains possible values for assignment to the object on the left.

Review: Message – part 4 of 5

① DISPLAY THE CODE WINDOW

a. In the Solution Explorer window, click the View Code button. The Message Code window is displayed.

b. In the Solution Explorer window, click the View Designer button. The Design window is once again displayed. Note the tabs in the IDE for switching between the windows.

c. In the IDE, click the Form1.vb tab. The Code window is again displayed.

② ADD A MENU ITEM CLICK EVENT PROCEDURE

a. From the Class Name list, select ExitToolStripMenuItem:

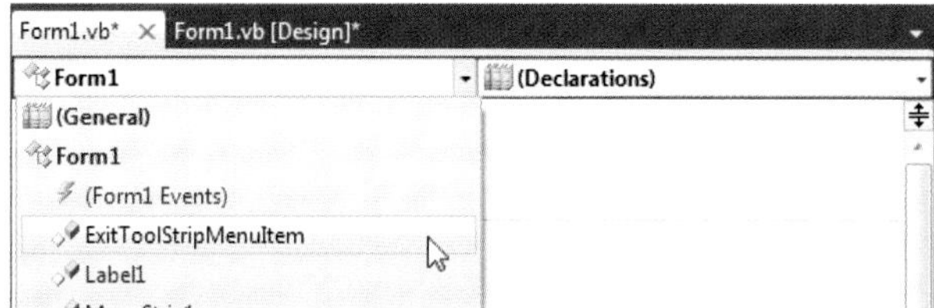

b. From the Method Name list, select Click:

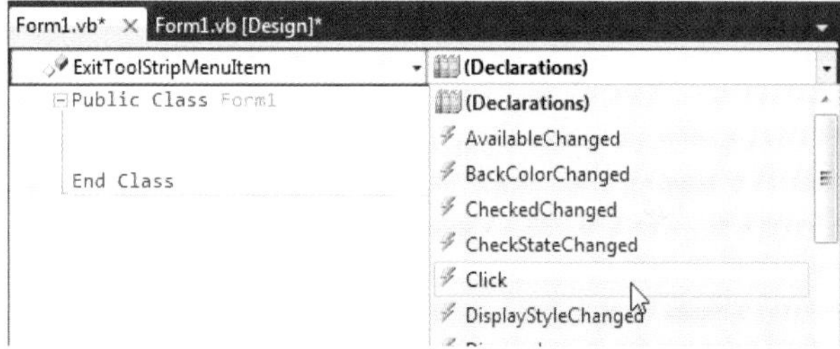

The ExitToolStripMenuItem_Click event procedure has been added to the program code:

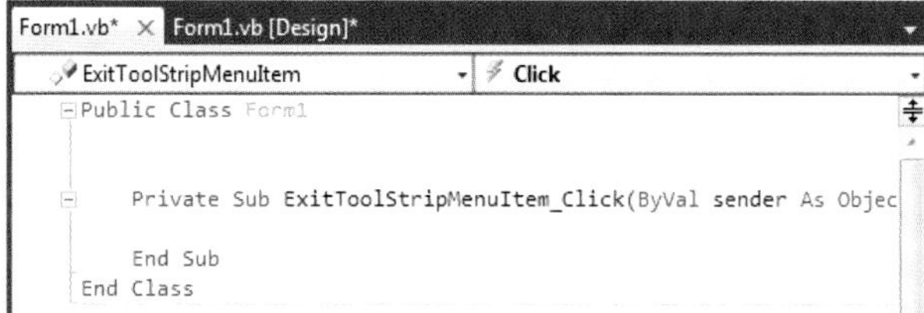

③ ADD A STATEMENT TO THE PROGRAM CODE

a. Click in the body of the ExitToolStripMenuItem_Click event procedure if the insertion point is not already there. Use the Tab key to indent the insertion point if it is not already properly indented.

b. Type `Application.` (Be sure to type the dot after the word Application.) An IntelliSense list is displayed.

c. From the IntelliSense list, select Exit if it is not already selected. Press Tab to insert the method name and then click the line below:

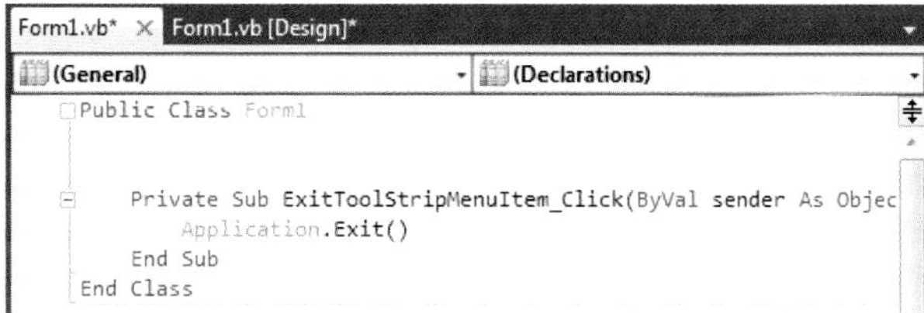

④ TEST THE EXIT COMMAND

a. Save the modified Message application.

b. Run the Message application.

c. On the Message menu bar, select Program → Exit. Message is quit.

⑤ PRINT THE CODE

a. Be sure the Code window is displayed and then select File → Print. A dialog box is displayed.

   1. Select OK. The program code is printed.

⑥ CLOSE THE PROJECT

Select File → Close Project. The project is removed from the IDE and the Start Page is displayed.

Review: MyName

Create a MyName application that displays your name centered, bold, and size 14. Include a Program menu with an Exit command that terminates the application when clicked. Use the Message application as a guide. The application interface should look similar to that shown on the right.

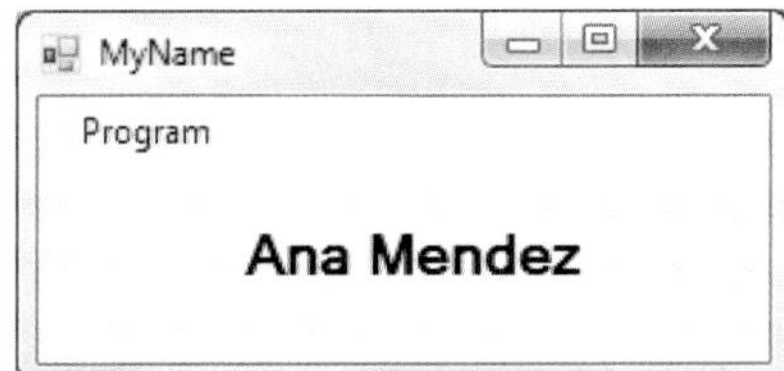

Assignment Statements

An *assignment statement* is used in a procedure to change a value at run time. One use of assignment is to set an object property at run time. In this case, an assignment statement takes the form:

```
Me.Object.Property = Value
```

where `Me` refers to the Form object, `Object` is the control object name, `Property` is the name of a property for that object, and `Value` is a valid property setting. A dot (.) is required between `Me` and `Object` to access the form's objects and again between `Object` and `Property` to access the object's properties. The *equal sign* (=) is an operator that indicates the property on the left is to receive the value on the right. For example, the statement

```
Me.lblMessage.Text = "Smile!"
```

sets the Text property of the lblMessage Label object to `Smile!` Note that text must be enclosed in quotation marks in an assignment statement.

Assignment statements allow a single label to display different text at run time. The Message application can be modified to demonstrate this. First, two menu commands are added to the interface:

Message with Hello World and Smile commands

Next, event procedures are added for the two new commands. Note that assignment statements are used to change the label text:

TIP To view the Code Editor and Design view windows side by side, drag the Code Editor window outside of the IDE.

```
Public Class Form1

    Private Sub ExitToolStripMenuItem_Click(ByVal sender As Object, ByVal e
        Application.Exit()
    End Sub

    Private Sub HelloWorldToolStripMenuItem_Click(ByVal sender As Object, ByV
        Me.lblMessage.Text = "Hello, world!"
    End Sub

    Private Sub SmileToolStripMenuItem_Click(ByVal sender As Object, ByVal e
        Me.lblMessage.Text = "Smile!"
    End Sub
End Class
```

As shown by the code, when Smile is clicked the label is assigned "Smile!" and when Hello World is clicked the label is assigned "Hello, World!" Both procedures use the same label to display a different message depending on the user's input.

An IntelliSense list will be displayed when typing the assignment statements. One list will display object names when the dot after `Me` is typed. A second list will display property names when the dot after the object is typed.

Review: Message – part 5 of 5

① OPEN MESSAGE

② ADD COMMANDS

a. In the upper-left corner of the Message form in the Design window, click the Program menu name. The Program menu is displayed.
b. Right-click Exit. A menu is displayed.
c. Select Insert → MenuItem. A MenuItem is inserted above Exit and selected.
d. Type `Hello World` and press Enter.
e. Right-click Exit and select Insert → MenuItem. A MenuItem is inserted above Exit.
f. Type `Smile` and press Enter.
g. Check the names of the two new menu items. Change their (Name) properties as appropriate to `HelloWorldToolStripMenuItem` and `SmileToolStripMenuItem`, if necessary.

③ ADD THE HELLO WORLD CLICK EVENT PROCEDURE

a. Display the Code window. The program contains one event procedure.
b. From the Class Name list, select HelloWorldToolStripMenuItem.
c. From the Method Name list, select Click. The HelloWorldToolStripMenuItem_Click event procedure is added to the program code.
d. Click in the body of the HelloWorldToolStripMenuItem_Click event procedure if the insertion point is not already there. Use the Tab key to indent the insertion point if it is not already properly indented.
e. Type `Me.` (Be sure to type the dot.) An IntelliSense list is displayed.
f. Type `l` (the letter L) to scroll to list items that begin with that letter.
g. Press the down-arrow key until lblMessage is selected.
h. Type a dot (period). lblMessage is added to the statement and a new IntelliSense list is displayed.

i. Type t (the letter T) to display list items that begin with that letter.
j. Press the down-arrow key until Text is selected.
k. Type = to add Text to the statement.
l. Type "Hello, world!" The event procedure should look similar to:

```
Private Sub HelloWorldToolStripMenuItem_Click(ByVal sender As Object, ByV
    Me.lblMessage.Text = "Hello, world!"
End Sub
```

④ ADD THE SMILE CLICK EVENT PROCEDURE

Use the techniques from step 3 above to create the SmileToolStripMenuItem_Click event procedure, which should look similar to:

```
    Private Sub SmileToolStripMenuItem_Click(ByVal sender As Object, ByVal e
        Me.lblMessage.Text = "Smile!"
    End Sub
End Class
```

⑤ SAVE THE PROJECT AND RUN THE APPLICATION

a. Save the modified Message project.
b. Run the application. Test the Smile and Hello World commands by selecting each one. Note how the assignment statements change the message displayed in the label. Also note that Smile is not centered in the label.
c. Close the application.

⑥ MODIFY THE LABEL OBJECT

a. Display the Design window.
b. Click the lblMessage label object to select it.
c. In the Properties window, change the AutoSize property to False. Handles are displayed around the entire label.
d. In the Properties window, click the TextAlign property and then click the arrow button. A list is displayed.
e. Click the middle center icon. The TextAlign property is set to MiddleCenter.

⑦ SAVE THE PROJECT AND RUN THE APPLICATION

a. Save the modified Message project and run the application.
b. Select Program → Smile. The Smile text is centered.

⑧ PRINT THE CODE AND THEN CLOSE THE PROJECT

a. Be sure the Code window is displayed and then print the code.
b. Close the project.

The RadioButton Control

A group of radio buttons is often used in an application to enable the user to choose from a set of options. Only one radio button in a set can be selected at a time. For example, the HelloWorldInternational application provides radio buttons so that the user can choose the language of the message:

Hello World International after clicking Spanish

RadioButton

TIP Be sure that control objects are appropriately named before adding event procedures to the Code window. Visual Basic does not automatically update procedure names if objects are later renamed.

The RadioButton control has the properties:

- **(Name)** identifies a control for the programmer. RadioButton object names should begin with `rad`.
- **Text** is the text displayed next to the button.
- **Checked** can be set to either True or False to display the radio button as selected or not selected, respectively. Only one radio button in a group can be checked at any given time. Therefore, changing the Checked value of one button to True automatically changes the other buttons in the group to False.

A Click event procedure is usually coded for each RadioButton object. The Click event procedure executes when the user clicks a button. For example, the Spanish Click event procedure includes an assignment statement that changes the Text property of the label to "Hola, mundo!".

GroupBox

A GroupBox object is used to group related radio buttons. In the application above, the language radio buttons were placed in the same group box. A GroupBox object must be added to a form before adding RadioButton objects. Radio buttons are then added to the group box by clicking the RadioButton control and then clicking the group box. Dragging a group box will move it along with the control objects within it.

Aligning Objects

Commands in the **Format** menu are useful for aligning objects on a form. Some commands require that multiple objects be selected first using marquee selection or holding the Shift key while objects are clicked.

Alternatively, objects can be aligned by clicking and holding an object to display gridlines for alignment.

The GroupBox control has the properties:

- **(Name)** identifies a control for the programmer. GroupBox object names should begin with `grp`.
- **Text** is the text displayed at the top of the group box.

Commenting Code

Comments are used to explain and clarify program code for other programmers. Comments have no effect on the way an application runs. In Visual Basic applications, a single quotation mark (') must begin a comment. Anything after the single quotation mark is considered a comment for that line of the program only. Comments placed on the same line as a statement are called *inline comments*. For example, the program line below includes an inline comment:

inline comments

```
Me.lblMessage.Text = "Hello, world!"   'change greeting
```

Multiline comments are created by placing a quotation mark at the beginning of each program line. Program statements do not appear in multiline comments. These comments are sometimes referred to as a *comment block*:

comment block

```
'HelloWorld application
'December 27, 2013
'This application displays a greeting
```

Comments should be used wherever code may be ambiguous, but not reiterate what is clear from the code. Comments are also used to include information such as the programmer's name and date of modifications.

Review: HelloWorldInternational

① CREATE A NEW PROJECT

a. Create a new Windows application naming it `HelloWorldInternational`.

b. Click the form to select it. Text is selected in the Properties window.

c. Enter `Hello World International` for the form text. The application's title bar now displays "Hello World International."

② COMPLETE THE INTERFACE

Add a label, a group box, and three radio buttons to the form. Be sure to add the group box before adding the radio buttons to the group box object. Size and move objects as necessary. Be sure to make the label large enough to display greetings of different lengths. Use the table on the next page for setting object properties:

Object	(Name)	Text	Font	AutoSize	TextAlign	Checked
Label1	`lblGreeting`	`Hello, world!`	Bold 20	False	MiddleCenter	
GroupBox1	`grpLanguage`	`Select a language`				
RadioButton1	`radEnglish`	`English`				True
RadioButton2	`radSpanish`	`Spanish`				False
RadioButton3	`radFrench`	`French`				False

③ WRITE THE APPLICATION CODE

a. Display the Code window.

b. Add comments that include your name, assignment, and today's date, similar to:

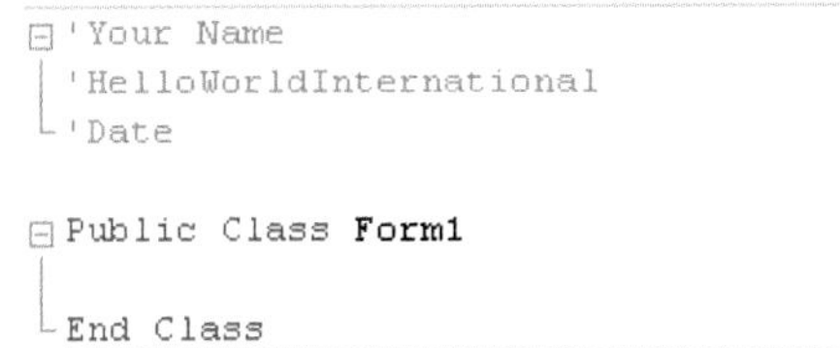

```
'Your Name
'HelloWorldInternational
'Date

Public Class Form1

End Class
```

c. From the Class Name list, select radEnglish.

d. From the Method Name list, select Click. A radEnglish_Click event procedure is added to the program code.

e. Add an assignment statement to the radEnglish_Click event procedure:

```
Me.lblGreeting.Text = "Hello, world!"
```

f. Create a radSpanish_Click event procedure and add an assignment statement to change the label text to `Hola, mundo!`

g. Create a radFrench_Click event procedure and add an assignment statement to change the label text to `Bonjour le monde!`

④ RUN AND TEST THE APPLICATION

Save the modified HelloWorldInternational project and then run the application. Select each radio button to test the application. Be sure the label changes and the text is displayed properly. If each of the greetings are not completely displayed, close the application and resize the label. Continue testing the application until it is working as expected.

⑤ PRINT THE CODE AND THEN CLOSE THE PROJECT

Arithmetic Operators and Numeric Expressions

Visual Basic includes a set of built-in arithmetic operators for exponentiation (^), multiplication (*), division (/), addition (+), and subtraction (–). Arithmetic operators are used to form a *numeric expression*. A numeric expression can be used anywhere a number is allowed. For example, the assignment statement below includes a numeric expression:

```
Me.lblAnswer.Text = 2 + 6 * 3
```

A numeric expression is not enclosed in quotation marks because quotation marks indicate text. When the above statement is executed at run time, the expression is evaluated by the computer and then the value assigned to the Text property of the Label object. Since a label displays text, the value is automatically converted to text.

Visual Basic evaluates a numeric expression using a specific order of operations, or operator precedence. Exponentiation is performed first, multiplication and division next, and then addition and subtraction. Two operators of the same precedence, for example + and –, are evaluated in order from left to right. For example, the numeric expression, `2 + 6 * 3`, evaluates to `20` because multiplication is performed first and then the addition.

Operator precedence can be changed by including parentheses in a numeric expression. The operations within parentheses are evaluated first. For example, the result of `(2 + 6) * 3` is `24` because `2` and `6` were added before multiplication was performed. It is also good programming style to include parentheses when there is any ambiguity or question about the numeric expression so a programmer reading the code will not have any doubts about what is intended.

The Button Control

A button is commonly used in Windows application interfaces. For example, the Calculations application below contains four Button objects and four Label objects. The labels initially display no text. When a button is clicked, the result of the numeric expression appears in the label next to the button. For example, 3+4 * 2 is clicked:

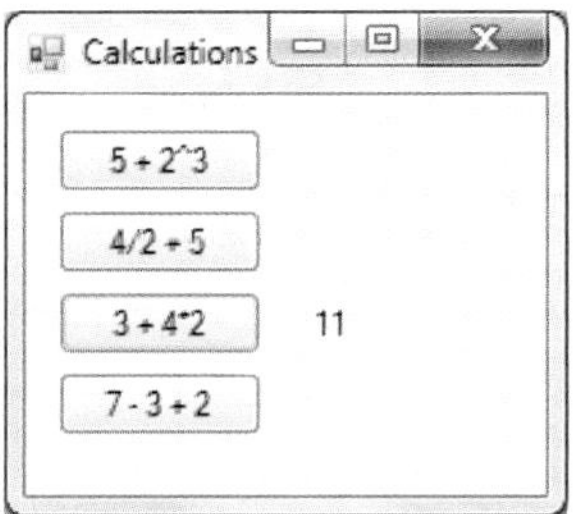

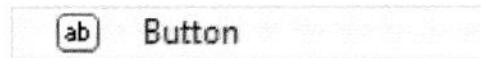

The Button control has the properties:

- **(Name)** identifies a control for the programmer. Button object names should begin with `btn`.
- **Text** is the text displayed on the button.

A Click event procedure is usually coded for a Button object and executes when the user clicks the button. For example, the Click event procedure coded for the 3+4 * 2 button is written as:

TIP The equal sign (=) is the operator used for assignment.

```
Private Sub btnExpression3_Click(ByVal sender As System.Object, ByVal
    Me.lblExpression3.Text = 3 + 4 * 2
End Sub
```

When the button is clicked, the statement in the Click event procedure evaluates the numeric expression and assigns the result to the label's Text property.

Review: Calculations

① CREATE A NEW PROJECT

a. Create a new Windows application naming it `Calculations`.

b. Set the Text property of the Form object to Calculations. The form title bar now displays "Calculations."

② COMPLETE THE INTERFACE

Add four buttons and four labels to the form. Size and move objects as necessary. Note the four empty labels are shown selected to help with placement. Use the table below for setting object properties.

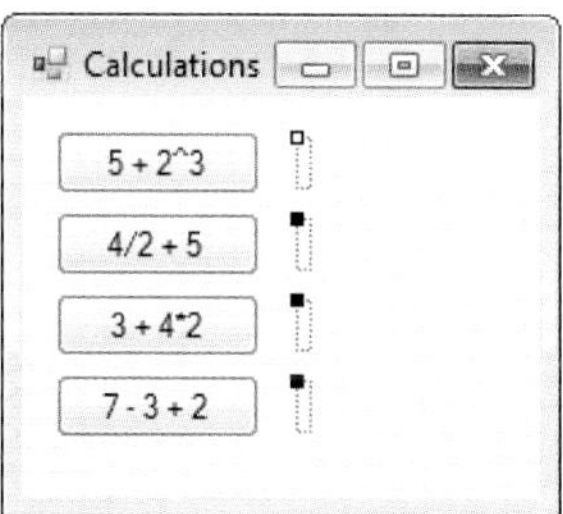

Control	(Name)	Text
Button1	btnExpression1	5 + 2^3
Label1	lblExpression1	*empty*
Button2	btnExpression2	4/2 + 5
Label2	lblExpression2	*empty*
Button3	btnExpression3	3 + 4*2
Label3	lblExpression3	*empty*
Button4	btnExpression4	7 - 3 + 2
Label4	lblExpression4	*empty*

③ WRITE THE APPLICATION CODE

a. Display the Code window.

b. Add comments that include your name and today's date.

c. From the Class Name list, select btnExpression1.

d. From the Method Name list, select Click. The btnExpression1_Click event procedure is added.

e. Add the following assignment statement to the btnExpression1_Click event procedure:

```
Me.lblExpression1.Text = 5 + 2 ^ 3
```

f. Add the remaining event procedures and statements so that the program code looks like:

```
Public Class Form1

    Private Sub btnExpression1_Click(ByVal sender As System.Object, ByVal e As Sys
        Me.lblExpression1.Text = 5 + 2 ^ 3
    End Sub

    Private Sub btnExpression2_Click(ByVal sender As System.Object, ByVal e As Sys
        Me.lblExpression2.Text = 4 / 2 + 5
    End Sub

    Private Sub btnExpression3_Click(ByVal sender As System.Object, ByVal e As Sys
        Me.lblExpression3.Text = 3 + 4 * 2
    End Sub

    Private Sub btnExpression4_Click(ByVal sender As System.Object, ByVal e As Sys
        Me.lblExpression4.Text = 7 - 3 + 2
    End Sub

End Class
```

④ RUN THE APPLICATION

Save the modified Calculations project and then run the application. Test each of the buttons and then close the application.

⑤ PRINT THE CODE AND THEN CLOSE THE PROJECT

⑥ QUIT VISUAL BASIC

Finding Help

Two types of Visual Basic help are available: local and online. Local help is installed with Visual Basic. If you have an Internet connection, it is better to use online help so that you will have access to the latest version of the help documentation.

The Help Library Manager is used to help manage your help settings. To open the Help Library Manager, select Help → Manage Help Settings. Select OK to accept the default location of the help files. The Help Library Manager dialog box is displayed:

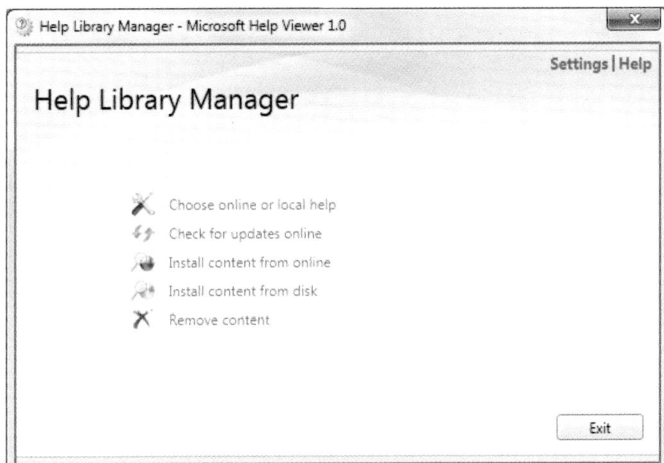

- Click Choose online or local help to select the type of help you want to use.
- Click Check for updates online to update local help documentation.

context-sensitive

Visual Basic displays *context-sensitive* help related to the keyword or task you are working on. Select a keyword or object and then press the F1 key. Help documentation opens in a browser window:

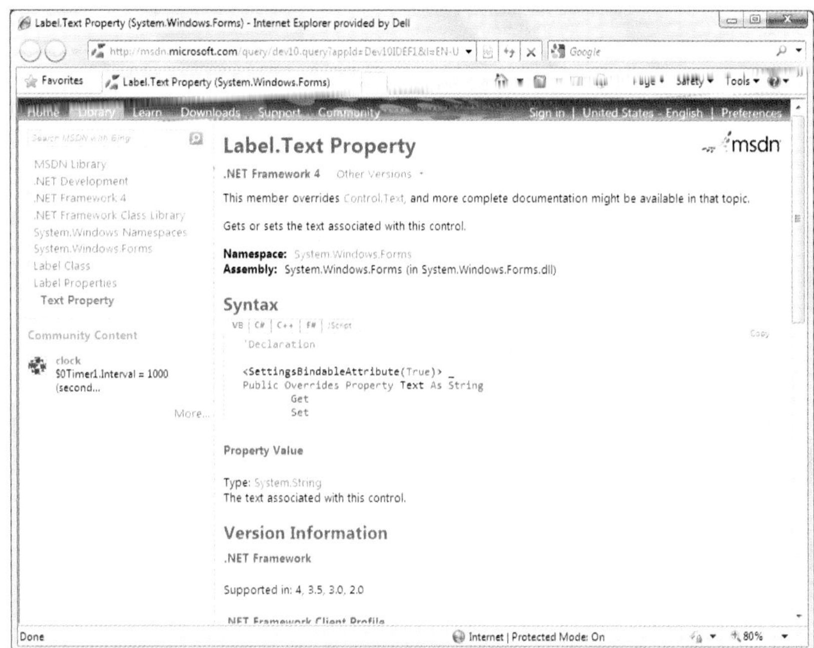

TIP The Search box can be used to search for additional help.

The Visual Studio product family shares a single site for Help documentation. Notice that the VB tab is selected in the browser window above.

Help can also be accessed by selecting Help → View Help or by opening http://msdn.microsoft.com/library/ in a browser.

Code Conventions

Code conventions are a set of guidelines for writing an application. These guidelines provide details about commenting, rules for naming methods, objects, and statement formatting. Just as comments inform a reader about a segment of code, a program that follows specific code conventions is easier to read and understand.

A company or organization that employs programmers will typically adhere to specific code conventions. A programmer familiar with the code conventions will more quickly become familiar with code written by another programmer in the company. Code conventions can make modifying and maintaining code faster, easier, and less expensive. Because of these benefits, organizations often not only encourage the use of code conventions, but require it.

The code conventions introduced in this chapter are:

- Control objects should be given a descriptive name that begins with an appropriate prefix.
- Begin object property assignment statements with `Me`.
- Use comments to include information such as the programmer's name and date.
- Comments should be used wherever code may be ambiguous, but not reiterate what is clear from the code.
- Statements in a procedure should be indented.

Chapter Summary

Visual Basic is an object-oriented programming language that is used to create event-driven applications for Microsoft Windows. Event-driven programs wait for an event to occur and then respond to it by executing a corresponding event handler.

The Visual Basic IDE (Integrated Development Environment) is used to create or modify an application. An application consists of several related files that are collectively maintained as a project. A project is created by clicking the New Project button on the toolbar.

An application interface is displayed in the Design window of the IDE. A form is a graphical object that contains a title bar, system menu, and Minimize, Maximize, and Close buttons. The Toolbox contains controls that are used to add objects to a form:

- A Label object displays text that cannot be modified by the user.
- A MenuStrip object displays a menu at run time.
- A set of RadioButton objects allow the user to choose from a set of options.
- Button objects are used to perform an action.

The Properties window lists the properties of a selected object. The Solution Explorer window is used to switch between the Design and Code windows.

An application consists of statements that are instructions for performing tasks. The statements for an application are called program code. Comments are used to explain and clarify program code for other programmers. A procedure is a block of code written to perform specific tasks. The event procedure executes to a corresponding event. An assignment statement is used in a procedure to change a value at run time.

The IDE displays an IntelliSense list of methods and properties when a dot (.) is typed. Using an IntelliSense list for selecting methods or properties can reduce typing errors.

An application is saved by selecting File → Save. An application is run by clicking the Start Debugging button on the toolbar.

Context sensitive help is accessed by selecting a keyword or object and then pressing the F1 key.

Code conventions are a set of guidelines for writing an application. The code conventions introduced in this chapter are:

- Control objects should be given a descriptive name that begins with an appropriate prefix.
- Begin object property assignment statements with `Me`.
- Use comments to include information such as the programmer's name and date.
- Comments should be used wherever code may be ambiguous, but not reiterate what is clear from the code.
- Statements in a procedure should be indented.

Vocabulary

Application A program which makes the computer a useful tool.

Assignment statement Uses the equal sign to give the object property on the left of the equal sign the value on the right of the equal sign.

Body The statements in a procedure.

Camel case Convention that uses a capital letter at the beginning of each word and no spaces.

Class A data type that can store data and includes methods.

Click event procedure A procedure that executes in response to a mouse Click event.

Code conventions A set of guidelines for writing an application.

Code window The part of the IDE that displays the Form1 class where event procedures and other code are entered.

Comment Text that explains and clarifies program code for other programmers. Comments are preceded by a single quotation mark.

Comment block A set of comments that are each on their own line.

Compiler Converts a program to a language that the computer understands.

Control Used to create a control class object that the user can interact with.

Design window Displays the application interface and allows control class objects to be added, deleted, and sized.

Equal sign An operator that indicates the property on the left is to receive the value on the right.

Event Occurs when the user interacts with an object.

Event-driven application Executes code in response to events.

Event handler *See* Event procedure.

Event procedure Block of code that executes in response to an event.

Form A control class object that is an application interface. Contains a title bar, system menu, and Minimize, Maximize, and Close buttons.

GUI Graphical User Interface.

IDE (Integrated Development Environment) Used to create or modify a Visual Basic application.

Inline comment A comment that appears on the same line as a statement.

Interface What appears on the screen when an application is running.

Menu bar The part of the IDE that contains the names of menus that contain commands. Can also be added to an application with a MenuStrip control.

Method A named set of statements that perform a well-defined task.

Numeric expression Formed with arithmetic operators.

Object A variable of a class.

OOP Object-Oriented Programming.

Operator precedence The order in which operators are evaluated in a numeric expression.

Procedure A block of code written to perform a specific task.

Program code The statements in an application.

Project The set of files that make up a Visual Basic application.

Project Explorer window The part of the IDE that lists the files in the current project.

Properties window The part of the IDE that lists the properties values of an object.

Property The part of a control object that defines its appearance, behavior, position, and other attributes.

Select Clicking an object, which displays a handle or handles.

Solution Explorer window Used to switch between the Design and Code windows.

Statement An instruction in an application.

Toolbox The part of the IDE that contains controls that are used to add objects to a form.

Visual Basic Object-oriented programming language used to create Windows applications.

^ Arithmetic operator for exponentiation.

* Arithmetic operator for multiplication.

/ Arithmetic operator for division.

+ Arithmetic operator for addition.

– Arithmetic operator for subtraction.

() Used to change operator precedence.

' Precedes a comment.

" Used to indicate a string in an assignment statement.

= Used in an assignment statement to give the property on the left of the equal sign the value on the right of the equal sign.

Alphabetical button Clicked to organize properties in alphabetical order. Found in the Properties window.

`Application.Exit()` Statement used to stop program execution.

Button **Button control** Used to add a Button control class object to a form. Properties include (Name) and Text. Events include Click.

Categorized button Clicked to organize properties by category. Found in the Properties window.

Close Project **command** Closes a project. Found in the File menu.

Delete **command** Deletes a menu item. Found in the menu displayed by right-clicking the menu item in the Form Design window.

`End Sub` Statement used to end a procedure.

Exit **command** Closes the Visual Basic IDE. Found in the File menu.

F1 key Displays help.

Form class Used to create a control class object that is an application interface. Properties include Text.

GroupBox **GroupBox control** Used to add a GroupBox control class object to a form. Properties include (Name) and Text.

Insert **command** Inserts a new menu item above an existing one. Found in the menu displayed by right-clicking the existing menu item in the Form Design window.

IntelliSense A Visual Basic feature for auto-completing statements.

A Label **Label control** Used to add a Label control class object to a form. Properties include (Name), Text, Font, AutoSize, and TextAlign.

`Me` Used in a statement to refer to the current Form object.

MenuItem objects The items added to a MenuStrip component. Properties include (Name) and Text. Events include Click.

MenuStrip **MenuStrip control** Used to add an application component that contains menu items.

New Project button Clicked to create a new project. Found on the toolbar. File → New Project can be used instead.

Open Project **command** Opens an existing project. Found in the File menu. The Open Project link on the Start Page can be used instead.

Print command Prints the program code of an application. Found in the File menu.

`Private` Used to indicate that a procedure cannot be accessed outside of the Form class.

RadioButton **RadioButton control** Used to add a RadioButton control class object to a form. Properties include (Name), Text, and Checked. Events include Click.

Save All **command** Saves the current project. Found in the File menu. The Save All button on the toolbar can be used instead of the command.

Start Debugging **command** Runs an application. Found in the Debug menu. The button on the toolbar can be used instead of the command.

Stop Debugging **command** Stops application execution. Found in the Debug menu. The button on the toolbar can be used instead of the command.

`Sub` Statement used to declare a procedure.

View Code button Displays the Code window. Found in the Solution Explorer window. View → Code can be used instead of the button.

View Designer button Clicked to view the Design window. Found in the Solution Explorer window. View → Designer can be used instead of the button.

Critical Thinking

1. Describe how the windows, components, and the features of the Visual Basic IDE are used to develop, run, and debug an application.

2. Indicate what would be displayed if each of these expressions were assigned to a label:

a) `10 + 3 - 6`	g) `2 + 4 / 2 + 1`
b) `2 ^ 3 + 5 * 4`	h) `5 - 3 ^ 2 + 1`
c) `4 + 3 * 2`	i) `15 / 3 + 2`
d) `2 + 9 ^ (1 / 2)`	j) `"6 + 3 - 2"`
e) `15 * 2 + 4`	k) `2 + 9 ^ 1 / 2`
f) `15 * (2 + 4)`	l) `5 - 3 ^ (2 + 1)`

3. Explain the term "event-driven."

4. List the controls presented in this chapter and explain if and how the user can interact with each one.

5. List at least one difference in the way a form looks between the Design window and at run time.

6. List two ways to terminate a running application.

7. Explain the difference between the (Name) and Text properties of a control.

8. Why is it better to type the statement `Me.lblMessage.Text = "Hello world!"` rather than just `lblMessage.Text = "Hello world!"`

9. Write the statements needed for the Click event procedures of `radSum` and `radDifference` based on the following application. Assume the first label is named `lblMessage` and the second is named `lblResult`:

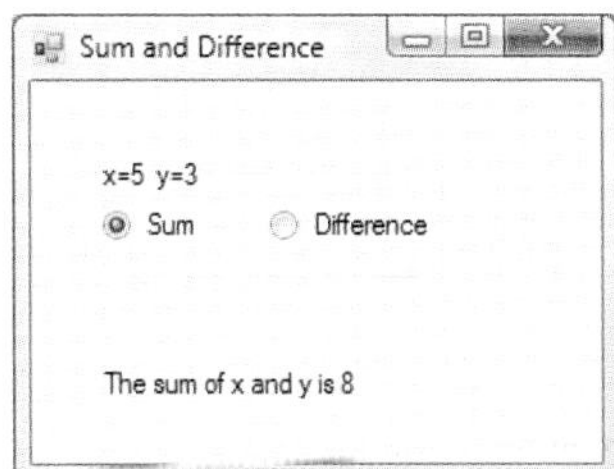

10. Explain the error(s) in the following comments:

```
'This is my first program
 9/9/12

'Display greeting  "Hi There!"
```

True/False

11. Determine if each of the following are true or false. If false, explain why.
    a) A Visual Basic application consists of a single file.
    b) A Windows application includes at least one form.
    c) The Text property of a form defines what is displayed in its title bar.
    d) The properties of an object can only be set in the Properties window.
    e) Text displayed in a label can be changed by the user.
    f) A MenuItem object can have a Click event procedure.
    g) A MenuStrip component can have only one MenuItem object.
    h) Each line of program code is called an object.
    i) Visual Basic is an object-oriented programming language.
    j) Program code is typed into the Design window.
    k) Buttons in the Toolbox are used to switch between the Code and Design window.
    l) Click is an example of an event.
    m) `Private` indicates that a procedure can be accessed outside of the Form1 class.
    n) Options displayed in an IntelliSense list vary depending on what is typed before the dot.
    o) An assignment statement is used to change a value at run time.
    p) More than one radio button in a set can be selected at a time.
    q) The only purpose of a GroupBox object is to display a title for a set of RadioButton objects.
    r) Comments affect the way an application runs.
    s) Multiline comments are created by placing a question mark (?) at the beginning of each line.
    t) Code conventions are a set of guidelines for writing an application.

Exercises

Exercise 1 — Address

Create an Address application that displays your name, city, and state in three separate labels. The interface should look similar to:

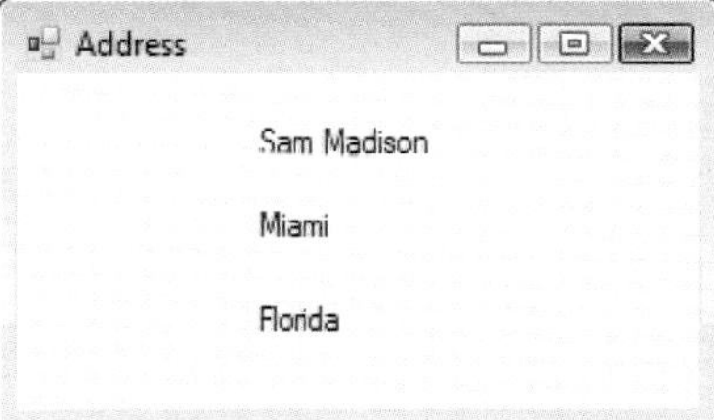

Exercise 2 — School

Create a School application that displays your school's name and mascot centered in two separate labels. Choose a different font, style, and size for the school name. Include a Program menu with an Exit command. The interface should look similar to:

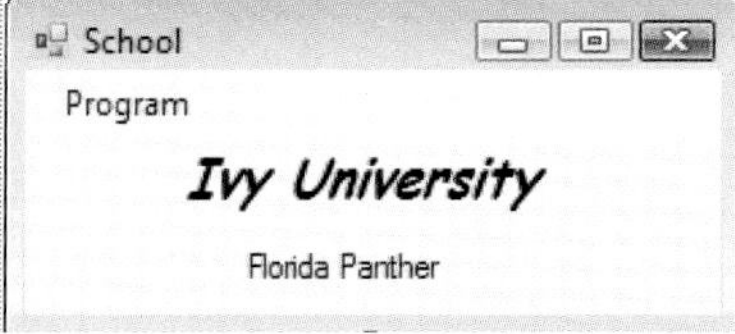

Exercise 3 — Band

Create a Band application that displays the members of a selected band. Include at least three of your favorite bands. The interface should look similar to:

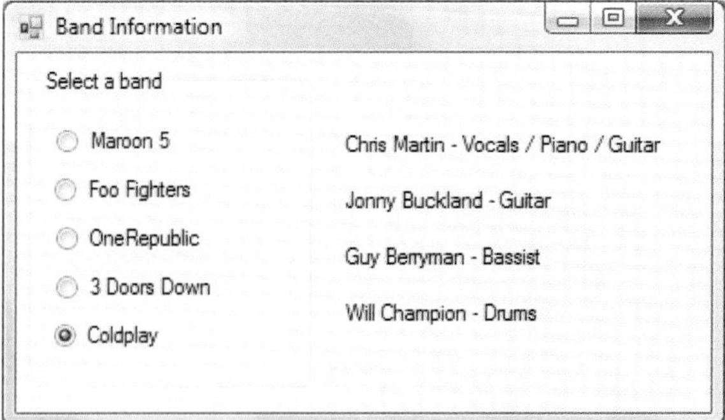

Exercise 4 — SchoolInformation

Create a SchoolInformation application that displays the city and state of a selected school. Include at least five of your favorite schools. The interface should look similar to:

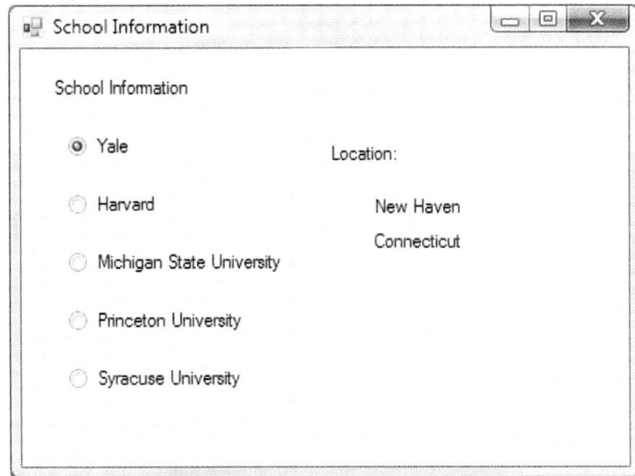

Exercise 5 — AdditionProperties

a) Create an AdditionProperties application that shows the associative property of addition, (a + b) + c = a + (b + c), in a label. The interface should look similar to:

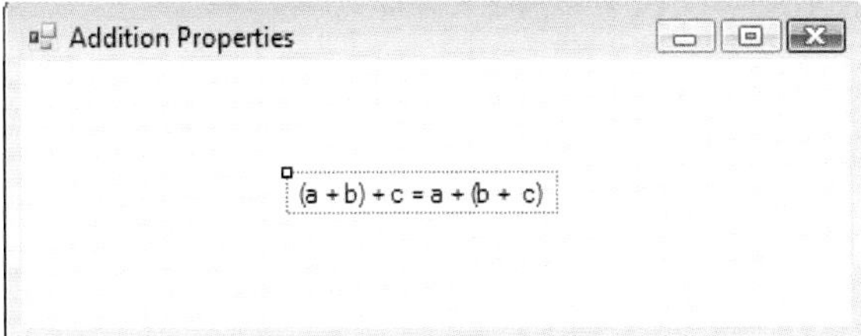

b) Modify the AdditionProperties application to display the associative property of addition when one button is clicked and the commutative property, a + b = b + a, when another button is clicked. The interface should look similar to the following after clicking **Commutative**:

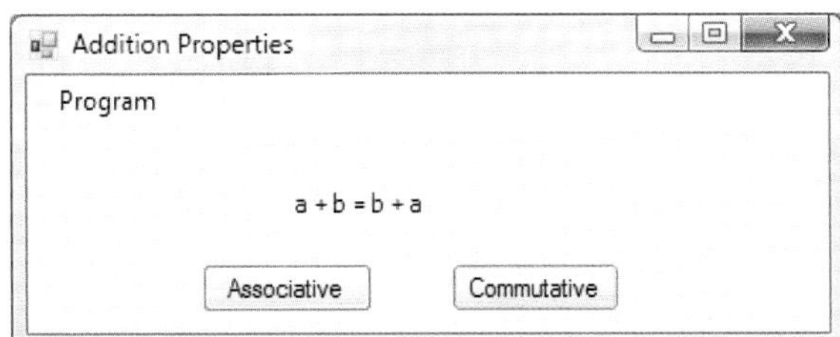

c) Modify the AdditionProperties application to include a **Program** menu with **Associative**, **Commutative**, and **Exit** commands.

Exercise 6 — HelloAndGood-bye

Create a HelloAndGood-bye application that displays a label centered, bold, and size 18 that reads Hello! or Good-bye! depending on the button clicked. Include a Program menu with Hello, Good-bye, and Exit commands. The interface should look similar to the following after clicking Hello:

Exercise 7 — CircleCircumference

Create a CircleCircumference application that displays in a label the circumference ($2\pi r$) of a circle with radius 15. Use the value 3.14 for π. Include a Program menu with an Exit command. The interface should look similar to the following after clicking Answer:

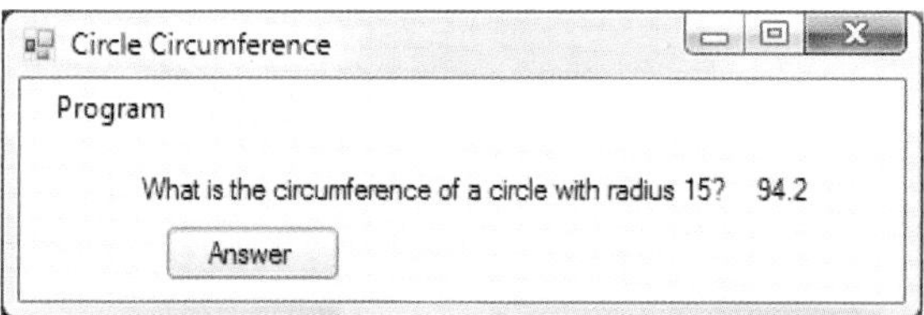

Exercise 8 — RectangleAreaAndPerimeter

Create a RectangleAreaAndPerimeter application that displays the area (length * width) and perimeter (2l + 2w) of a rectangle of length 5 and width 3. Include a Program menu with an Exit command. The interface should look similar to the following after clicking Answer:

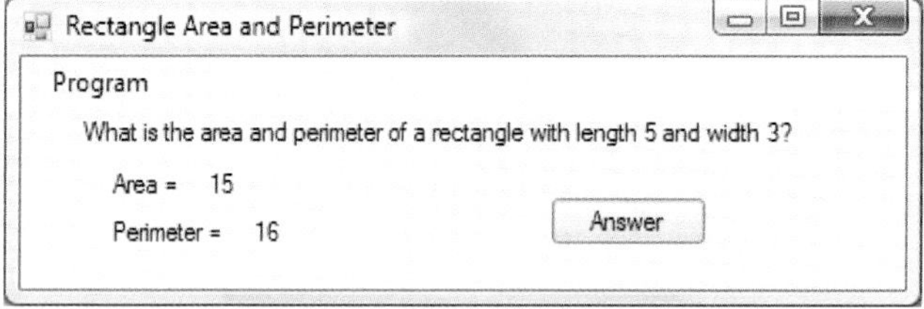

Exercise 9 — LongJumpAverage

Create a LongJumpAverage application that calculates and displays the average jump length of an athlete whose jumps were 3.3m, 3.5m, 4.0m, and 3.0m. Include a Program menu with an Exit command. The interface should look similar to the following after clicking Average:

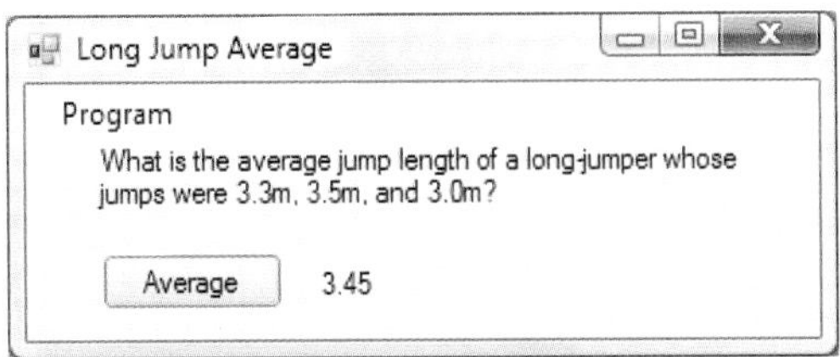

Exercise 10 — Position

Create a Position application that changes the position of text in a label according to the command selected by the user. The application should include a Program menu with an Exit command and a Position menu with TopLeft, TopCenter, TopRight, MiddleLeft, MiddleCenter, MiddleRight, BottomLeft, BottomCenter, and BottomRight commands. The interface should look similar to the following after selecting MiddleCenter from the Position menu:

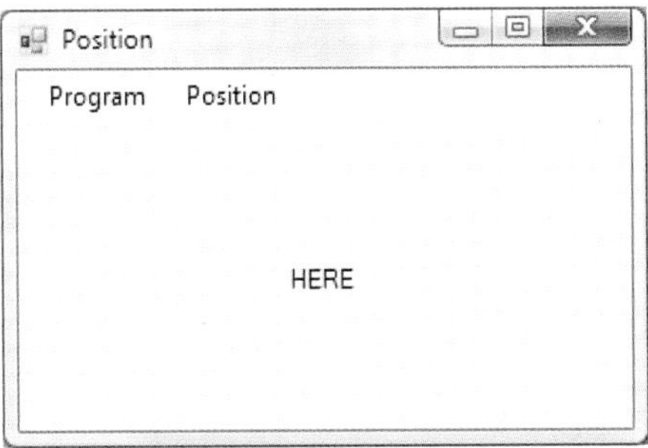

Hint: Be sure the label is large enough to show changes in text position. Also, use the IntelliSense list for selecting the assignment value for the TextAlign property.

Exercise 11 — WithStatement

The `With` statement can be used to change several properties of a designated object within a single statement. For example, the following statement changes the text, sizing, and alignment of a label:

```
With Me.lblCity
   .Text = "Dallas"
   .AutoSize = False
   .TextAlign = ContentAlignment.MiddleCenter
End With
```

Create a WithStatement application that uses the With statement to change the properties of a label when a Change button is clicked. Have a classmate test your application.

Exercise 12 — HiBye

Create a HiBye application that displays "Hi" when the user clicks a Hi button or selects the Hi command from the File menu. The application should also include a Bye button and a Bye command, which ends the application when selected. The Bye command should be disabled until the user clicks either the Hi command or the Hi button. An Exit command should be included to quit the application. Use the properties listed below to enhance your application.

MenuItem properties:

- **Enabled** can be set to either True or False. A MenuItem that is not enabled appears dimmed. A command should appear dimmed when it should not be selected at that time.
- **ShortcutKeys** can be set to a keyboard shortcut. The keyboard accelerator is selected from the list in the ShortcutKey property.
- **ShowShortcutKey** can be set to True or False. When True, the keyboard accelerator selected in the ShortcutKey property is displayed along with the MenuItem text at run time.

A menu can also be modified to include bars that separate groups of commands. Right-click an existing menu item in the Design window to display a menu and then select Insert → Separator. A bar is inserted above the menu item. Right-click a bar and select Delete from the displayed menu to remove the separator.

RadioButton and Button properties:

- **FlatStyle** can be set to Flat, Popup, Standard, or System. Flat gives the button a flat appearance, Popup gives the button a flat appearance until the mouse moves over the button at which time the button appears three-dimensional, Standard gives the button a three-dimensional appearance, and System gives the button the default appearance assigned by the user's operating system.

Exercise 13 — SystemClock

The system clock properties can be used display the current time and date. The TimeString property sets or returns the current time from the system clock and the DateString property returns the current date. The Now property returns a value that represents the current date and time. Design and create a SystemClock application that displays the current time and time in a label. Share your application design with a classmate. *Note that this exercise will be updated in Chapter 9 with a Timer, allowing the display of a running clock.*

Chapter 3
Variables and Constants

Key Concepts

Declaring and initializing variables and constants
Obtaining user input
Differentiating between data types
Understanding variable scope
Identifying Visual Basic keywords
Recognizing syntax and logic errors
Debugging an application
Creating an executable file
Application deployment
Problem-solving using a case study approach

Case Study

Calculator application

Declaring Variables

A *variable* is a name for a value stored in memory. Variables are used in programs so that values can be represented with meaningful names. For example, when a variable named `length` is used in a program, it is clear that its value is a distance. Variables should be used to represent values because they make code easier to read, understand, and modify.

declaration statement

A variable must be declared before it is used. A *declaration statement* takes the form:

```
Dim variableName As type
```

identifier
data type

A `Dim` statement must include the variable name, called the *identifier*, and the *data type*, which determines the type of data the variable will store. For example, the statement

```
Dim length As Integer
```

integer

declares a variable `length` to store data of type `Integer`. An *integer* is a numeric value that is a positive or negative whole number. When an `Integer` variable is declared it stores the value 0.

An identifier must begin with a letter and contain only letters, numbers, and some special characters. Typically variable identifiers begin with a lowercase letter. Any word after the first in a variable identifier should begin with an uppercase letter. For example, `rectangleLength`. This code convention allows variables to be easily recognized.

Multiple variables with the same data type can be declared in a single statement, similar to:

```
Dim length, width As Integer
```

Grouping variables together in a single statement is good programming style when the variables represent related items. Declarations should not be grouped together in the same statement just because the variables are all the same type.

Using Variables

TIP The Visual Basic IDE displays a green wavy underline below variables that have been declared, but not yet used in a statement.

Applications typically use many variables. The code segment below uses two variables:

```
Dim side As Integer = 5       'side of square
Dim area As Integer           'calculated area of square

area = side * side
```

The value of area after the last assignment statement is 25 (5 * 5).

Variable declarations should be grouped at the beginning of a procedure. A blank line after the declarations makes it easy to determine where the declarations end.

literal

As shown in the code segment above, the value of a variable is changed through assignment. A variable assignment statement is formed with the variable name on the left side of an equal sign and the value it is to receive on the right side of the equal sign. The equal sign (=) operator indicates that the variable on the left is to receive the value on the right. The value on the right can be a *literal,* which is any actual value. It could also be another variable or an expression. In the code segment above, area was assigned the value of an expression (side * side).

initialize

An assignment statement can be part of a variable declaration. In addition to being declared, the variable is *initialized.* For example, in the code segment above, variable side was assigned a value when declared.

TIP A common error is to reverse the variable name and the value it is being assigned. For example, 10 = side will generate an error.

It is important to realize that a variable can store only one value at any one time. For example, after the following statements execute:

```
Dim area As Integer
area = side * side
```

area: 0

area: 25

the value of area is 25 because this was the last value assigned to area.

Review: SquareArea – part 1 of 3

① START VISUAL BASIC

② CREATE A NEW PROJECT

Create a Windows application named SquareArea.

③ CREATE THE INTERFACE

Use the table on the next page for setting object properties.

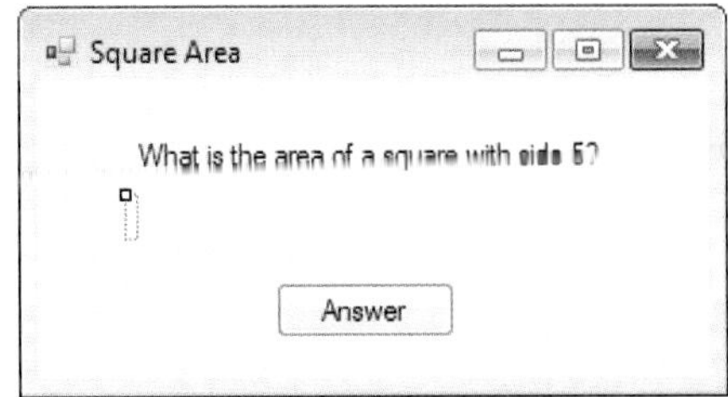

Object	(Name)	Text
Form1		Square Area
Label1	lblQuestion	What is the area of a square with side 5?
Label2	lblAnswer	*empty*
Button1	btnAnswer	Answer

④ WRITE THE APPLICATION CODE

a. Display the Code window.
b. Add comments that include your name, assignment, and today's date.
c. Create a btnAnswer_Click event procedure and then add the statements:

```
Dim side As Integer = 5     'side of square
Dim area As Integer

area = side * side
Me.lblAnswer.Text = area    'display answer
```

⑤ RUN AND TEST THE APPLICATION

a. Save the modified SquareArea project and then run the application. Click Answer to test the application.
b. Close the SquareArea application.

⑥ PRINT THE CODE

Obtaining a Value from the User

input

An application is more flexible when values can be entered, or *input*, at run time. A TextBox object is one way to allow users to enter values. For example, the SquareArea application could include a text box for the user to type a value for the length of the side:

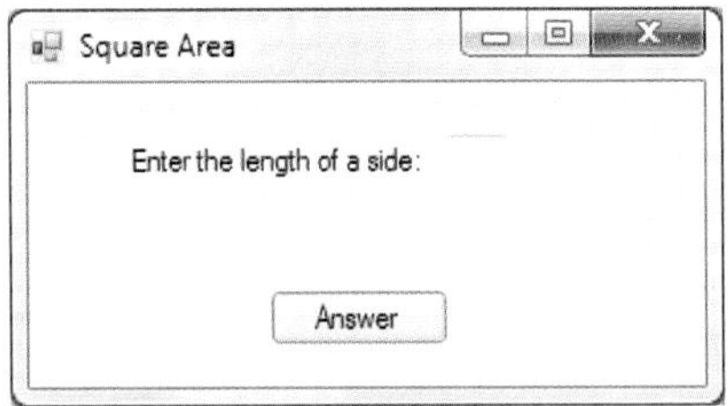

prompt

A label is often placed near a text box to tell the user what kind of input is expected. This label is called the *prompt*.

TextBox

The TextBox control has the properties:

- **(Name)** identifies a control for the programmer. TextBox object names should begin with `txt`.
- **MaxLength** can be set to a numeric value indicating the maximum number of characters allowed in the text box.
- **CharacterCasing** can be set to Normal, Upper, or Lower. Upper entries are converted to uppercase. Normal entries appear as typed and Lower entries are converted to lowercase.
- **Text** is what is displayed in the text box.
- **TextAlign** sets the alignment of text relative to the text box.

A TextChanged event procedure is sometimes coded for a TextBox object. This procedure executes when the user types in the text box.

At run time, the TextBox Text property stores whatever characters are currently in the text box. This property can be used in an assignment statement to retrieve the data typed by the user. The following statement assigns the data in a text box named txtRadius to the variable `side`:

```
side = Me.txtSide.Text     'retrieve data from text box
```

run-time error

function

If the text box does not contain data that matches the variable type, a *run-time error* occurs and the program is halted. To prevent this, the Val() function should be used to convert text box data to a numeric value. A *function* performs a single, well-defined task like a method or procedure, but then returns a value that is a result of the task performed. The Val() function requires a string value and then returns a number corresponding to the string. If the first character of the string is not a numeric character, Val() returns a 0. The statements below demonstrate Val():

TIP Functions often require data to perform their task. The data is included in parentheses after the function name.

```
Dim height As Integer
height = Val("62 inches")              'height is assigned 62
height = Val("Twenty inches")          'height is assigned 0
height = Val("Six feet 2 inches")      'height is assigned 0
```

To convert text box data to a numeric, the Val() function should be used in a statement similar to:

```
side = Val(Me.txtSide.Text)     'assign a numeric value to side
```

Review: SquareArea – part 2 of 3

① MODIFY THE INTERFACE

a. Change the lblQuestion Text property to `Enter the length of a side:`

b. Add a text box to the form:

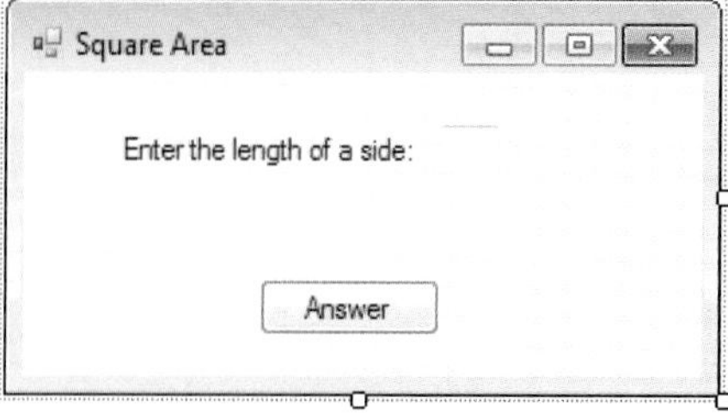

c. Name the TextBox object `txtSide` and set the Text property so that it is empty.

② MODIFY THE PROGRAM CODE

a. Display the Code window and then modify the btnAnswer_Click procedure as shown:

```
Dim side As Integer          'side of square
Dim area As Integer

side = Val(Me.txtSide.Text)
area = side * side
Me.lblAnswer.Text = area    'display answer
```

b. Run the application. Type `7` in the text box and then click Answer. The area 49 is displayed.

c. Replace text box contents by typing a `4` in the text box, but do not click Answer. Note the previous answer is still displayed.

d. Close the SquareArea application.

③ ADD A TEXTCHANGED EVENT PROCEDURE

a. Create a txtSide_TextChanged event procedure and then add the statement:

```
'Clear the current answer when the user begins to type a new value
Me.lblAnswer.Text = ""
```

b. Run the application. Type `2` in the text box and then click Answer. The area 4 is displayed.

c. Replace the text box contents by typing a `3` in the text box. The previous answer is cleared. Click Answer to display a new value.

d. Close the SquareArea application.

④ PRINT THE CODE AND THEN CLOSE THE PROJECT

Review: RectangleArea

Create a RectangleArea application that prompts the user for a length and width and then displays the area of a rectangle when Answer is clicked. Use appropriate variables and include TextChanged event procedures that clear the answer. The application interface should look similar to that shown on the right after typing `8` and `4` and clicking Answer.

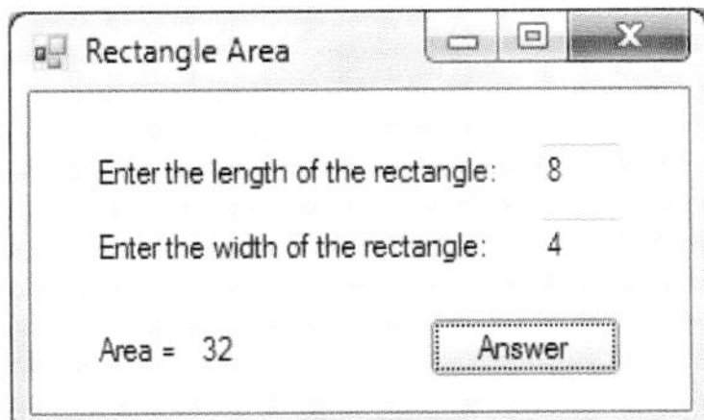

Built-In Data Types

The `Integer` data type is just one Visual Basic data type. Other built-in data types include:

Type	Data Range
`Integer`	integers from -2,147,483,648 to 2,147,483,647
`Double`	a positive or negative number that may contain a decimal portion in the range –1.8E+308 to 1.8E+308
`Decimal`	large numbers possibly containing a decimal.
`Date`	a date in m/d/yyyy format
`Char`	a single character

TIP Visual Basic also supports the `Short`, `UShort`, `UInteger`, `Long`, `ULong`, and `Single` data types.

TIP All but the `String` data types are primitive data types. A primitive data type stores a single piece of data.

`String`	a set of characters
`Boolean`	True or False

An `Integer` variable uses 4 bytes of memory to store its value and is used for representing whole numbers.

floating point

Values that are represented by the `Double` type are sometimes referred to as a *floating point*, meaning that the values contain numbers after the decimal point. Because of the many digits that are possible in a `Double`, a variable of this type uses 8 bytes of memory.

The `Decimal` data type is appropriate for storing values representing currency. `Decimal` variables use 16 bytes of memory.

A `Date` variable requires 8 bytes of memory. This type should be used to represent a date. Dates can be in the range 1/1/0001 through 12/31/9999. The value assigned to a `Date` variable must be enclosed with # signs, as in the statement below:

```
Dim birthDate As Date = #1/1/1998#
```

A `Char` variable requires 2 bytes of memory because Visual Basic uses the 16-bit Unicode character encoding. A character can include a letter of the alphabet, a digit, and in general any character that can be typed or displayed, such as $, %, and space. A `Char` assignment requires double-quotation marks ("):

```
Dim middleInitial As Char
middleInitial = "A"
```

The `String` type represents a set of characters, also called a *string*. A string can include the letters of the alphabet, digits, and in general any character that can be typed or displayed, such as $, %, and spaces. A `String` variable uses 2 bytes of memory for each character in the string. A `String` assignment requires double-quotation marks ("):

```
Dim lastName As String = "Lutz"
```

Variables that are type `Boolean` can have only one of two values—`True` or `False`. `Boolean` variables are particularly useful for representing on/off and yes/no values. `Boolean` assignment statements use the keywords `True` and `False`. A `Boolean` variable uses 2 bytes of memory.

Visual Basic automatically initializes variables to a default value when they are declared. Variables of numeric types, such as `Integer` and `Double` are initialized to 0. `Date` variables are initialized to 12:00:00 AM. `Boolean` variables are initialized to `False`. `Char` and `String` variables are initialized to nothing, which is equal to the keyword `Nothing`. This keyword can be used in place of an empty string ("") for clearing labels, and so forth.

When choosing a data type, it is important to choose the most appropriate type for the quantity being represented. If a value could possibly have a decimal portion, then `Double` is the best choice. If a variable will represent only whole numbers, then `Integer` is the best choice even though `Double` will work. Using the most appropriate data types for variables has two benefits. First, both the compiler and the reader will understand the possible values for a variable. Second, the compiler allocates the appropriate memory for the variable.

Automatic Type Conversion

> ***Type Casting***
>
> An *implicit conversion* takes place automatically when data of one type is assigned to a variable of a different type. An *explicit conversion* uses a type conversion keyword to convert data from one type to another and is also called *casting*.

In an assignment statement, Visual Basic automatically converts data to match the type of the variable it is being assigned to. For example, a value with a decimal portion is automatically rounded to a whole number when assigned to an `Integer` variable:

```
Dim x As Integer
x = 6.7          'x assigned 7
```

Visual Basic will try to convert from one data type to another as long as the data is valid for the receiving data type. For example, assigning `12.3` to an `Integer` variable is valid because the number can be converted to `12`. However, assigning `abc` to an `Integer` variable generates an error.

Review: TotalDistance

Create a TotalDistance application that prompts the user for the three segment lengths of a race and then calculates the total distance when **Distance** is clicked. The race segments can have lengths that contain a decimal portion. Use variables of the appropriate types and include a TextChanged event procedures that clears the distance. The application interface should look similar to that shown on the right after typing the data shown and clicking **Distance**.

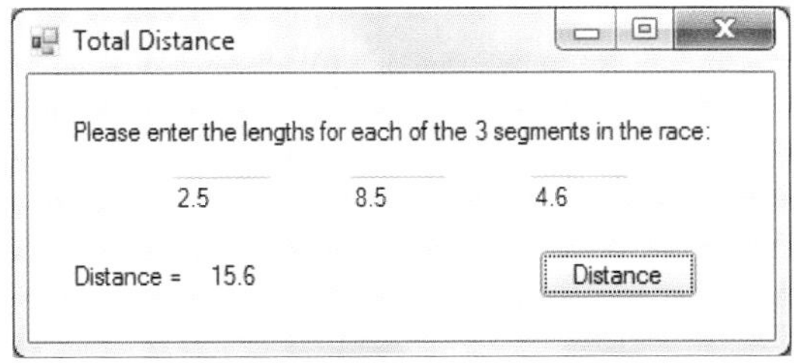

Variable Scope

The placement of a variable declaration is important because it determines the variable's scope. The *scope* of a variable is the set of statements that can access the variable. For example, a variable declared at the beginning of a procedure is accessible to any statement in that procedure. This means that any statement in the procedure can refer to the variable, change its value, and so on. This variable is said to be *local* to the procedure because its scope is limited to that procedure. Statements outside the procedure do not have access to the variable.

scope

local

When a variable needs to be accessed by several or all of the procedures in the Form class, the declaration should be placed in the Form class above any procedure declarations. This type of declaration is *module-level*. Module-level declarations are *global* to any code in the Form class, which means any statement in any procedure can refer to the variable or change its value. Global declarations should be used only when absolutely necessary. For example, the code on the next page includes both global and local variables:

module-level
global

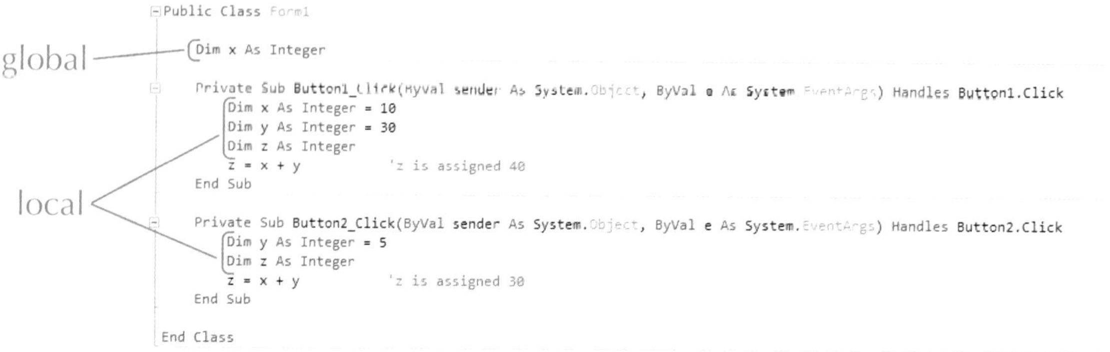

global
local
Public Class Form1
Dim x As Integer
Private Sub Button1_Click(ByVal sender As System.Object, ByVal e As System.EventArgs) Handles Button1.Click
Dim x As Integer = 10
Dim y As Integer = 30
Dim z As Integer
z = x + y 'z is assigned 40
End Sub
Private Sub Button2_Click(ByVal sender As System.Object, ByVal e As System.EventArgs) Handles Button2.Click
Dim y As Integer = 5
Dim z As Integer
z = x + y 'z is assigned 30
End Sub
End Class

One important programming practice is to declare variables so that their scope is limited to where they are needed. This is good programming style because it produces cleaner code and helps eliminate the possibility of errors.

Review: ScopeDemo

① CREATE A NEW PROJECT

Create a Windows application named `ScopeDemo`.

② COMPLETE THE INTERFACE

Use the table below for setting object properties.

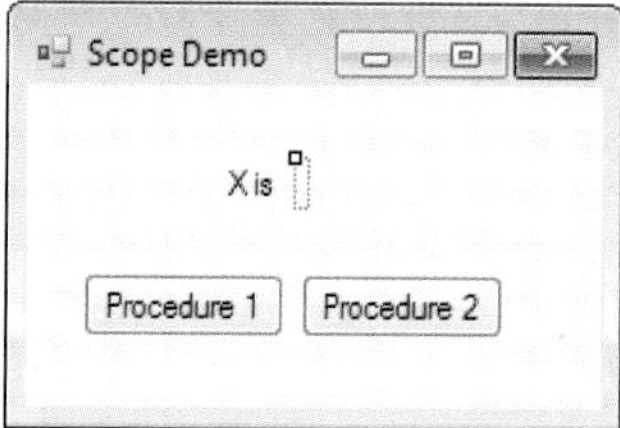

Object	**(Name)**	**Text**
Form1		`ScopeDemo`
Label1	`lblXis`	`X is`
Label2	`lblAnswer`	*empty*
Button1	`btnProc1`	`Procedure 1`
Button2	`btnProc2`	`Procedure 2`

③ WRITE THE APPLICATION CODE

a. Display the Code window.

b. Add comments that include your name, assignment, and today's date.

c. Create event procedures and add the global variable x as shown below:

```
Public Class Form1

    Dim x As Integer = 10

    Private Sub btnProc1_Click(ByVal sender As Object, ByVal e As System.EventArgs) Handles btnProc1.Click
        Dim x As Integer = 3
        Me.lblAnswer.Text = x
    End Sub

    Private Sub btnProc2_Click(ByVal sender As Object, ByVal e As System.EventArgs) Handles btnProc2.Click
        Me.lblAnswer.Text = x
    End Sub

End Class
```

④ RUN THE APPLICATION

a. Run the application. Click **Procedure 1**. 3 is displayed. Click **Procedure 2**. 10 is displayed. Note that the x variable in the btnProc1 procedure is local to that procedure. The x value displayed by the btnProc2 procedure uses the global variable. A procedure uses a local variable if available before looking for a global variable.

b. Close the ScopeDemo application.

Special Division Operators

In addition to the standard built-in operators (^, *, /, +, –), Visual Basic includes two additional division operators. The \ operator performs integer division, and the `Mod` operator performs modulus division.

integer division

Integer division truncates the decimal portion of the quotient, which results in an integer. For example, in the assignment statement

```
Dim x As Integer
x = 20 \ 7          'x is assigned 2
```

x is assigned 2 because the whole number portion of the quotient is 2:

```
   (2) r6  <--- 20\7
7)20
  14
   6
```

modulus division

Modulus division returns the remainder resulting from division. For example, in the assignment statement

```
Dim x As Integer
x = 20 Mod 7        'x is assigned 6
```

x is assigned 6 because the remainder of 20 divided by 7 is 6:

```
   2 (r6) <--- 20 Mod 7
7)20
  14
   6
```

Modulus division is used in applications where the separate digits of a number are needed, for finding the number of minutes left over after hours have been accounted for, and for other integer-related tasks.

Integer division is performed after multiplication and division. Modulus division is performed next, and then addition and subtraction. For example, the expression `5 * 2 Mod 3 \ 2` evaluates to 0 because `5 * 2` is performed first, then `3 \ 2`, and then `10 Mod 1`. Operator precedence can be changed by using parentheses.

Review: SkyhookInternational

Skyhook International sells skyhooks that ship 3 per box. Padded envelopes are used to ship individual skyhooks. Create a SkyhookInternational application that prompts the user for the number of skyhooks ordered, and then displays the number of boxes and envelopes required for the shipment when Ship is clicked. The application interface should look similar to that shown on the right after typing 47 and clicking Ship.

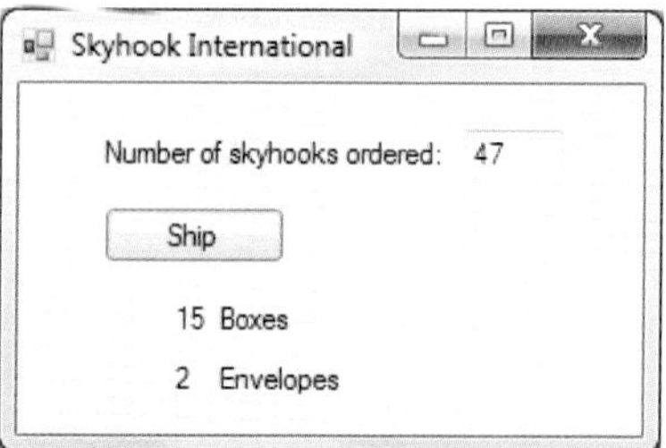

Using Named Constants

A *constant* is a name for a memory location that stores a value that cannot be changed from its initial assignment. Constants, like variables, are used in a program so that values can be represented with meaningful names. For example, the following statement declares a constant `PI` with the value `3.14`:

```
Const PI As Double = 3.14
```

TIP The area of a circle is calculated as πr^2.

A constant can be used wherever a value can be used. For example:

```
circleArea = PI * radius ^ 2
```

Constant identifiers are typically all uppercase and may include underscore (_) characters to separate words. For example, `MAX_PRICE`. The value of a constant is assigned only in the declaration. Trying to change the value of a constant after the initial assignment generates an error.

The placement of constant declarations determines their scope. Because the value of a constant does not change throughout a program run, it is usually safe to allow a broader scope. Therefore, constant declarations are often placed in the Form class, outside any procedures. Wherever constant declarations are placed, they should be grouped and declared before any variable declarations.

Identifiers and Keywords

TIP Right-click an identifier name and select **Rename** to display a dialog box where a new identifier name is typed. Visual Basic changes all occurrences of the identifier name to the new name.

Identifiers in Visual Basic must begin with a letter and may contain letters, numbers, and some special symbols. Periods and spaces are not allowed. Identifiers are not case sensitive, which means that an uppercase letter is the same as a letter in lowercase. For example, identifiers `Count` and `count` refer to the same variable. The IDE automatically changes the case of an identifier to match that of the first occurrence.

keywords

The Visual Basic language contains *keywords*, which have special meaning to the Visual Basic compiler and therefore cannot be used for a variable or constant identifier. Visual Basic keywords include:

`And`	`Dim`	`False`	`Long`	`Return`
`Boolean`	`Do`	`Finally`	`Me`	`Select`
`Byte`	`Double`	`For`	`Mod`	`Short`
`Call`	`Each`	`Friend`	`Module`	`Single`
`Case`	`Else`	`Function`	`New`	`Static`
`Catch`	`ElseIf`	`Get`	`Not`	`Stop`
`Const`	`End`	`Handles`	`Nothing`	`String`
`Date`	`Enum`	`If`	`Object`	`Structure`
`Decimal`	`Erase`	`In`	`Or`	`Sub`
`Declare`	`Error`	`Integer`	`Private`	`Then`
`Default`	`Event`	`Is`	`Protected`	`To`
`Delegate`	`Exit`	`Like`	`Public`	`True`

Review: CircleArea – part 1 of 2

Create a CircleArea application that prompts the user for the radius of a circle and then displays the circle area when **Area** is clicked. The application should include appropriate variables and a named constant `PI`. The application interface should look similar to that shown on the right after typing `4` and clicking **Area**.

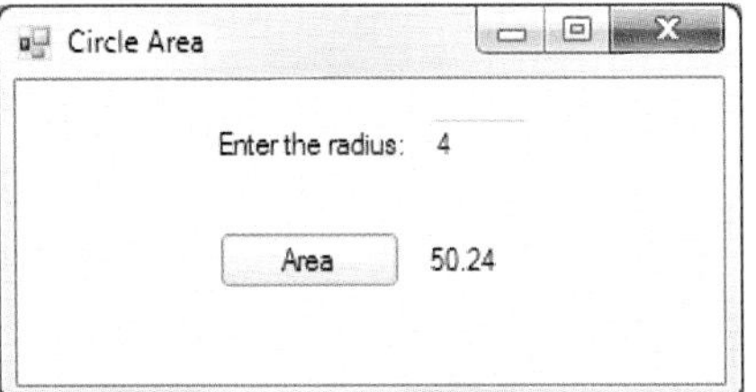

Programming Errors

Syntax errors, logic errors, and run-time errors are the three types of errors that can occur in a program. A statement that violates the rules of Visual Basic is a *syntax error*. For example, the second statement

syntax error

```
Const PI As Double = 3.14
PI = 3.141                          'Syntax error!
```

is not syntactically correct because constant assignment is illegal outside the declaration. Syntax errors display a blue wavy underline. Hovering with the mouse over the line displays help text:

TIP The Error List window displays a list of syntax errors.

```
Const PI As Double = 3.14
PI = 3.141
```

Constant cannot be the target of an assignment.

logic or semantic error

A *logic error*, also called a *semantic error*, is more difficult to detect. Logic errors are caused by statements that are syntactically correct, but produce undesired or unexpected results, as in the following example:

```
Dim length As Integer
Dim area As Double

length = 1.2                'l is actually assigned
area = length * length      'expected value is 1.44
```

The variable `length` was accidentally declared as an `Integer`. Therefore, 1.2 is converted to 1 in the statement `length = 1.2`.

Logic errors must be found by the programmer through testing of the application and by careful reading of the program code. Accurate and careful commenting, proper indentation, and descriptive identifiers can help in finding and preventing logic errors.

run-time error
exception

Errors that are not detected by the compiler may generate a *run-time error*. A run-time error, also called an *exception*, halts program execution at the statement that cannot be executed. The statement causing the error is highlighted and an exception helper box is displayed:

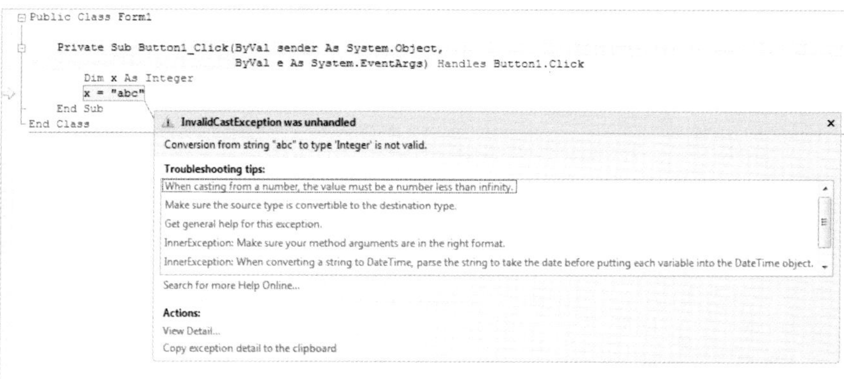

The box can be removed by clicking the Close button. The Stop Debugging button on the toolbar can then be clicked to stop program execution so that the program can be corrected.

Debugging an Application

The source of logic errors can be hard to determine without tools for debugging a program. *Debugging* is the process of getting an application to work correctly. One debugging technique uses breakpoints. A *breakpoint* is a statement that has been marked as a stopping point. The code below shows a breakpoint, which is highlighted in red:

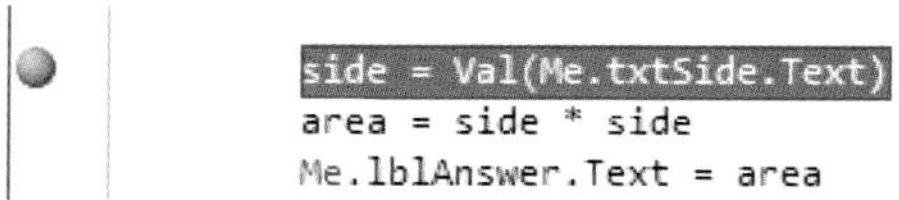

break mode

A breakpoint is created by clicking in the gray area to the left of a statement. When the application is run, program execution stops at the first breakpoint and the IDE goes into break mode. In *break mode*, the Watch window can be used to examine values. Right-clicking a variable, constant, or object name displays a menu with an `Add Watch` command. Selecting this command to add the variable, constant, or object name to the Watch window with its current value:

TIP Hovering over a variable with the mouse displays the variable's current value.

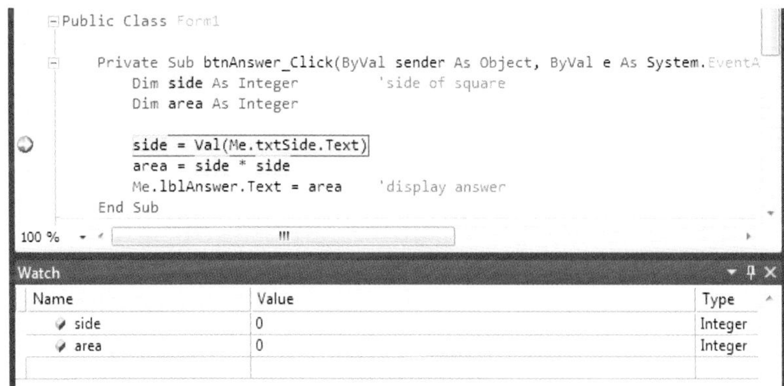

Program execution is continued from a breakpoint by clicking the Step Into button on the toolbar or pressing the F8 key, which executes one statement at a time. Debug → Step Into can also be used to step through a program. Values in the Watch window are automatically updated while stepping through a program.

Another debugging technique involves selecting lines of code and then clicking the "Comment out the selected lines" button. Commented statements will not be executed. The "Uncomment the selected lines." button on the toolbar removes the quotation mark (') from the beginning of the selected lines of code.

Review: SquareArea – part 3 of 3

① OPEN THE SQUAREAREA PROJECT

② ADD A BREAKPOINT TO THE CODE

a. Display the Code window.

b. Click the pointer in the gray area to the left of `side = Val(Me.txtSide.Text)`. A breakpoint is added, similar to:

```
Public Class Form1

    Private Sub btnAnswer_Click(ByVal sender As Object, ByVal e As System.EventArgs)
        Dim side As Integer         'side of square
        Dim area As Integer

        side = Val(Me.txtSide.Text)
        area = side * side
        Me.lblAnswer.Text = area    'display answer
    End Sub
```

③ RUN THE APPLICATION

a. Run the application. The SquareArea application is displayed.

b. Type `2` in the text box and then click Answer. The breakpoint is reached and the Code window is again displayed. Note the breakpoint statement is now selected in yellow.

c. Right-click `side` in the statement below the breakpoint. A menu is displayed.

d. Select Add Watch. `side` appears in the Watch window with its current value 0.

e. Add `area` to the Watch window. Note its value.

f. On the toolbar, click the Step Into button . The next statement is executed. In the Watch window, the value of `side` changes to 2.

g. Step into the next statement. `area` has been assigned 4, the result of the square area expression.

h. Continue stepping through the application until the SquareArea window is again displayed.

i. Close the application. The Watch window is closed and the Code window is again displayed.

④ CLEAR THE BREAKPOINT

Click the dot to the left of the breakpoint to remove the breakpoint.

Application Deployment

Chapter 2 introduced running an application within the Visual Basic IDE. To distribute a Visual Basic application to other computer systems, application deployment can be used. *Application deployment* packages an application using a process called ClickOnce publishing. This allows you to publish the application to a central location, such as a Web server, file share location, or removable media. The user then installs or runs the application from that location.

Alternative Publish Project - Project → Publish.

After an application has been tested and runs without error, right-click the project name in the Solution Explorer window and select Publish. The Publish Wizard is displayed.

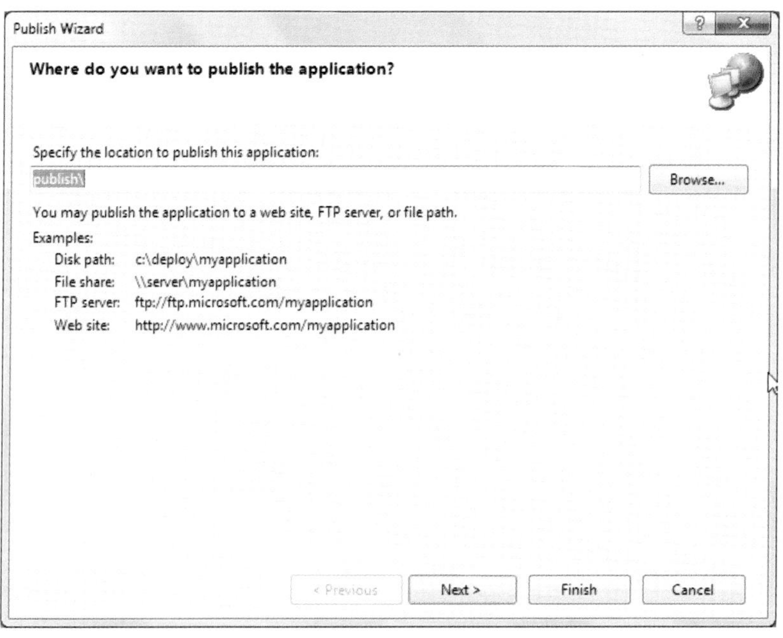

Enter a URL, FTP location, or click Browse to select a file path and then click Next. The second Publish Wizard dialog box is displayed:

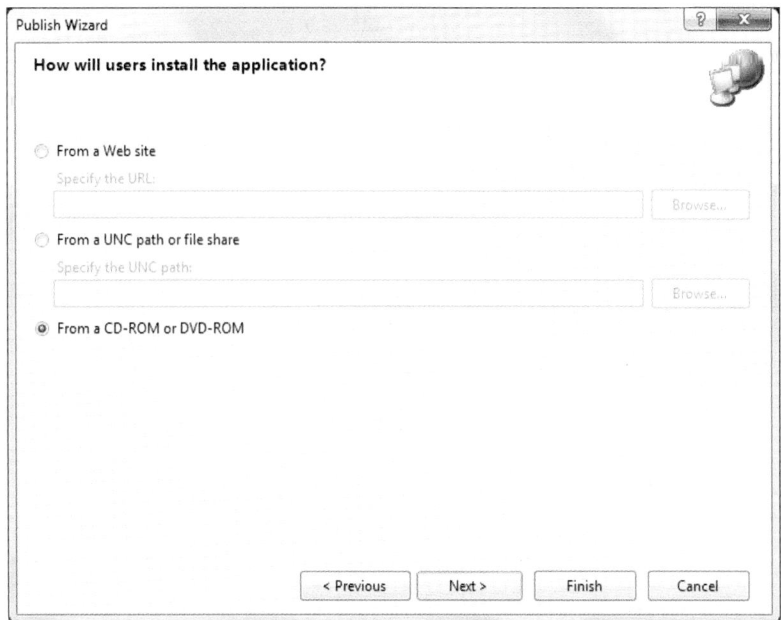

Select an option to indicate how users will install the application, such as CD-ROM or DVD-ROM and then click `Next`. The next Publish Wizard dialog box is displayed:

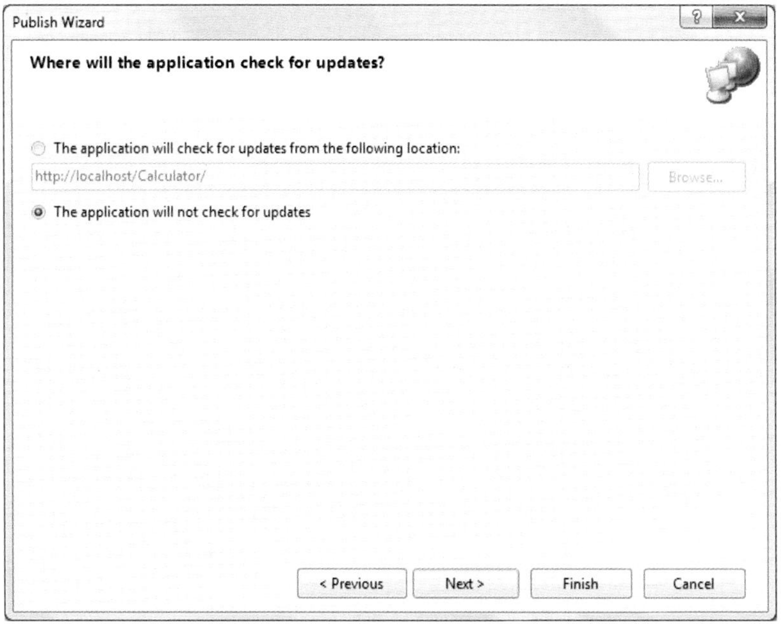

Options for checking for updates are displayed. Updates can be checked for if a website is available for doing so. Select `Next` to display the final Publish Wizard dialog box:

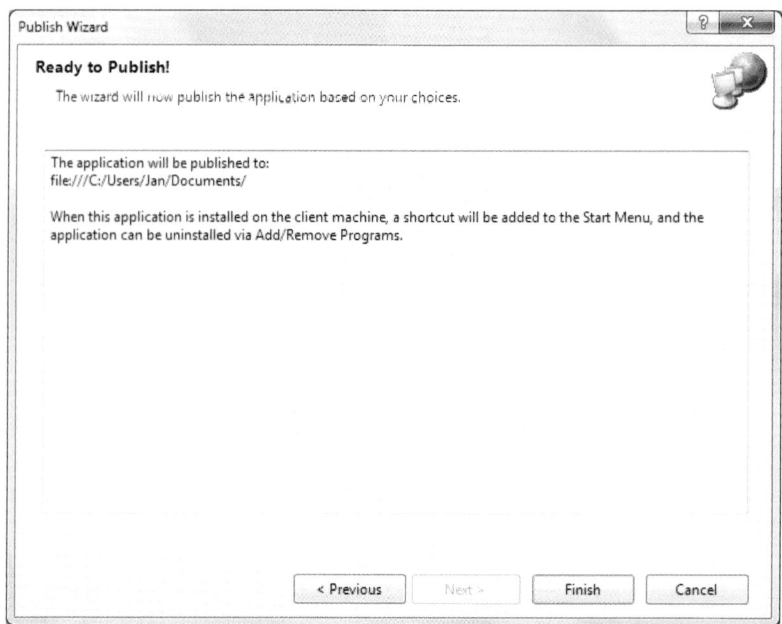

Select Finish to generate the files needed for installing the application on another computer.

Case Study

This and all subsequent chapters end with a case study. Case studies are used to learn problem-solving techniques. Each case study will include a description, program specification, code design, program implementation, and a discussion about testing and debugging.

In this case study, a Calculator application will be created. The Calculator application allows the user to enter two operands and select an operator and then the answer is displayed.

Calculator Specification

specification

The first step in creating an application is clearly defining what the application is to accomplish. This definition is called the *specification*, or *spec*, because it specifies what the application should do. In real-world situations, the specification is developed by talking with the end user and other computer professionals. In this text, the specification will be provided.

Calculator prompts the user for two numbers (operands) and allows the user to select an operator (^, *, /, \, `Mod`, +, –) from a set of radio buttons. When an operator is selected, the result of the expression formed by the operands and operator is displayed.

Calculator Design

application design

Application design includes how the interface looks and how the code is written to accomplish the specification. In this text, the interface and code designs will be presented.

The best way to design the interface is to sketch interface designs on paper. The Calculator interface design:

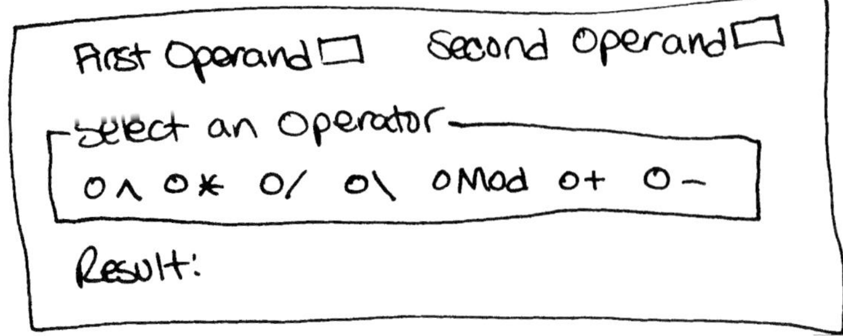

The code design describes how to accomplish the spec. Included in the code design are a description of the input, output, and the data generated. The code design for this Calculator is:

The input for Calculator is two numbers (operands) typed into text boxes and the selection of a radio button corresponding to the desired operator.

Click event procedures will respond to the user's selection of an operator for the expression. In each radio button Click event procedure, a `Double` variable `answer` will be used to store the result of the expression formed with the two operands and the selected operator.

The Output for Calculator is a label displaying the result for the expression formed with the operands and selected operator. This label will be set in the radio button Click event procedures.

TextChanged event procedures will be coded to clear the radio buttons and label.

Calculator Coding

coding *Coding* is creating the interface and writing the program code. The interface and code for this Case Study are:

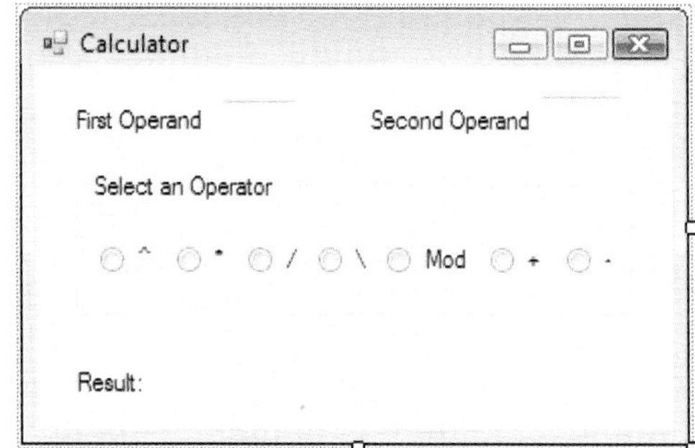

Object	**(Name)**	**Text**
Form1		`Calculator`
Label1	`lblOp1Prompt`	`First Operand:`
Label2	`lblOp2Prompt`	`Second Operand:`
TextBox1	`txtOperand1`	*empty*
TextBox2	`txtOperand2`	*empty*
GroupBox1	`grpOperators`	`Select an Operator`
RadioButton1	`radExponentiation`	`^`
RadioButton2	`radMultiplication`	`*`
RadioButton3	`radDivision`	`/`
RadioButton4	`radIntDivision`	`\`

RadioButton5	radModDivision	Mod
RadioButton6	radAddition	+
RadioButton7	radSubtraction	-
Label3	lblResult	Result:
Label4	lblExpressionValue	*empty*

```
Public Class Form1

    Private Sub txtOperand1_TextChanged(ByVal sender As Object,
    ByVal e As System.EventArgs) Handles txtOperand1.TextChanged
        Me.radAddition.Checked = False
        Me.radDivision.Checked = False
        Me.radExponentiation.Checked = False
        Me.radIntDivision.Checked = False
        Me.radModDivision.Checked = False
        Me.radMultiplication.Checked = False
        Me.radSubtraction.Checked = False
        Me.lblExpressionValue.Text = Nothing
    End Sub

    Private Sub txtOperand2_TextChanged(ByVal sender As Object,
    ByVal e As System.EventArgs) Handles txtOperand2.TextChanged
        Me.radAddition.Checked = False
        Me.radDivision.Checked = False
        Me.radExponentiation.Checked = False
        Me.radIntDivision.Checked = False
        Me.radModDivision.Checked = False
        Me.radMultiplication.Checked = False
        Me.radSubtraction.Checked = False
        Me.lblExpressionValue.Text = Nothing
    End Sub

    Private Sub radAddition_Click(ByVal sender As Object,
    ByVal e As System.EventArgs) Handles radAddition.Click
        Dim answer As Double
        answer = Val(Me.txtOperand1.Text) + Val(Me.txtOperand2.Text)
        Me.lblExpressionValue.Text = answer
    End Sub

    Private Sub radDivision_Click(ByVal sender As Object,
    ByVal e As System.EventArgs) Handles radDivision.Click
        Dim answer As Double
        answer = Val(Me.txtOperand1.Text) / Val(Me.txtOperand2.Text)
        Me.lblExpressionValue.Text = answer
    End Sub

    Private Sub radExponentiation_Click(ByVal sender As Object,
    ByVal e As System.EventArgs) Handles radExponentiation.Click
        Dim answer As Double
        answer = Val(Me.txtOperand1.Text) ^ Val(Me.txtOperand2.Text)
        Me.lblExpressionValue.Text = answer
    End Sub

    Private Sub radIntDivision_Click(ByVal sender As Object,
    ByVal e As System.EventArgs) Handles radIntDivision.Click
        Dim answer As Double
        answer = Val(Me.txtOperand1.Text) \ Val(Me.txtOperand2.Text)
        Me.lblExpressionValue.Text = answer
    End Sub

    Private Sub radModDivision_Click(ByVal sender As Object,
    ByVal e As System.EventArgs) Handles radModDivision.Click
        Dim answer As Double
```

```
        answer = Val(Me.txtOperand1.Text) Mod Val(Me.txtOperand2.Text)
        Me.lblExpressionValue.Text = answer
    End Sub

    Private Sub radMultiplication_Click(ByVal sender As Object,
    ByVal e As System.EventArgs) Handles radMultiplication.Click
        Dim answer As Double
        answer = Val(Me.txtOperand1.Text) * Val(Me.txtOperand2.Text)
        Me.lblExpressionValue.Text = answer
    End Sub

    Private Sub radSubtraction_Click(ByVal sender As Object,
    ByVal e As System.EventArgs) Handles radSubtraction.Click
        Dim answer As Double
        answer = Val(Me.txtOperand1.Text) - Val(Me.txtOperand2.Text)
        Me.lblExpressionValue.Text = answer
    End Sub
End Class
```

Calculator Testing and Debugging

testing
debugging

Testing is the process of running the application and entering data to test different possibilities to reveal any bugs. *Debugging* is the process of getting an application to work correctly.

Calculator should be tested by entering values that are positive, negative, and zero. What will happen when `0` is entered in the text box for the second operand? One way to prevent this error is discussed in the next chapter.

Running Calculator, entering two numbers, and then selecting the / operator displays the following:

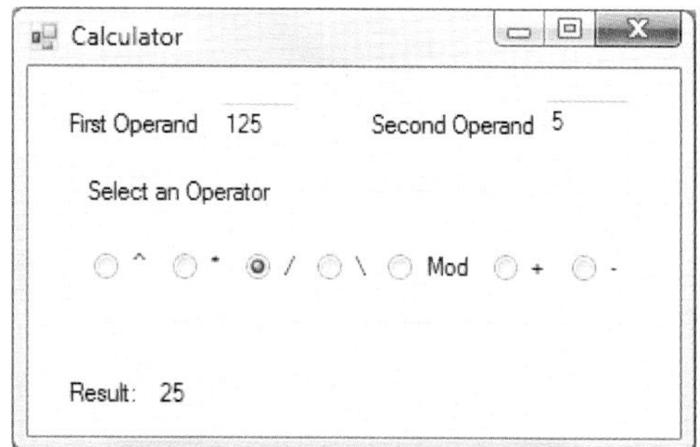

Chapter Summary

Variables and constants are used in a program so that values can be represented with meaningful names. A variable is declared with a `Dim` statement and a constant with a `Const` statement. Variable and constant identifiers must begin with a letter and contain only letters, digits, and the underscore character.

A TextBox is an object that allows the user to enter a value at run time. A label placed near a text box prompts the user for the type of data expected.

Visual Basic includes several built-in data types, including `Integer`, `Double`, `Decimal`, `Date`, `Char`, `String`, and `Boolean`. A variable or constant declaration should include the appropriate data type for the information to be stored.

The scope of a declaration is the set of statements that can access the declared variable or constant. A local declaration is declared at the beginning of a procedure is accessible to the statements in the procedure only. Global, or module-level, declarations are outside the procedures in a program and are accessible to all the procedures.

Visual Basic includes an integer division operator (\) that returns the whole portion of the quotient, and a modulus division operator (`Mod`) that returns the remainder of a division operation.

A statement that violates the rules of Visual Basic contains a syntax error. A logic error, also called a semantic error, is caused by syntactically correct statements that produce undesired or unexpected results.

Debugging is the process of getting an application to work correctly. One debugging technique uses breakpoints.

Application deployment packages an application using a process called ClickOnce publishing. This allows you to publish the application to a central location, such as a Web server, file share location, or removable media.

The sequence of steps and thinking that goes into the construction of an application are specification, design, coding, and testing and debugging.

The code conventions introduced in this chapter are:

- Variable identifiers should begin with a lowercase letter and any word after the first within the identifier should begin with an uppercase letter (camel case).
- Group variables together in the same declarations only when variables represent related items.
- Use a blank line after a group of declarations to make it clear where declarations end.
- Use a descriptive prompt next to a text box.
- Choose data types that are appropriate for the type of data being represented.
- Declare variables so that their scope is limited to where they are needed.
- Constant identifiers should be all uppercase with underscore characters separating words.
- Group constant declarations before variable declarations.

Vocabulary

Application deployment Packages an application so that it can be distributed to other computer systems.

Application design How an application's interface will look and how the program code will be written.

Break mode The point at which an application has stopped executing and the Visual Basic IDE is displayed with a Watch window.

Breakpoint A statement that has been marked as a stopping point.

Coding Creating the interface and writing the program code.

Constant A name for a memory location that stores a value that cannot be changed from its initial assignment.

Debugging The process of getting an application to work correctly.

Declaration statement A statement used to create a variable or constant.

Exception *See* Run-time error.

Floating point The `Double` data type that can represent values with numbers after the decimal point.

Function A procedure that performs a task and then returns a value.

Global declaration A declaration outside the procedures of a program. Also called module-level declaration.

Initialized Giving a variable a value in the declaration statement.

Integer division Division performed with the \ operator to return only the whole portion of the quotient.

Keyword Identifier reserved by Visual Basic.

Literal An actual value.

Local declaration A declaration at the beginning of a procedure.

Logic error An error caused by syntactically correct statements that produce unexpected results. Also called semantic error.

Module-level declaration *See* Global declaration.

Modulus division Division performed with the `Mod` operator to return only the remainder portion of the division operation.

Prompt A label placed near a text box describing the expected input from the user.

Run-time error A syntax or logic error that halts a program at run time. Also called an exception.

Scope The set of statements that can be accessed by a declared variable or constant.

Semantic error *See* Logic error.

Spec *See* Specification.

Specification Definition of what an application should do.

String A set of characters.

Syntax error An error caused by a statement that violates the rules of Visual Basic.

Testing The process of running an application and entering data to test different possibilities to reveal any bugs.

TextBox An object that allows the user to enter a value.

Variable A named memory location that stores a value.

Watch window The part of the IDE that can be used to examine values.

\ Arithmetic operator used to perform integer division.

`Boolean` A data type used to represent `True` or `False`.

`Char` A data type representing a single character.

Comment out the selected lines button Clicked to turn selected code into comment statements. Found on the toolbar.

`Const` Keyword used in a statement to declare a constant.

`Date` A data type representing dates and times.

`Decimal` A data type representing very large positive or negative real numbers. Best used for representing currency values.

`Dim` Keyword used in a statement to declare a variable.

`Double` A data type representing very large positive or negative real numbers.

`False` One of two possible `Boolean` values.

`Integer` A data type representing positive or negative whole numbers.

`Mod` Arithmetic operator used to perform modulus division.

`Nothing` Keyword that can be used in place of an empty string for clearing labels, and so forth.

Publish **command** Publishes an application to a website, FTP server, or file path. Found in the Project menu.

Step Into button Clicked to step through a program in break mode. Found on the toolbar.

`String` A data type representing a string.

TextBox **TextBox control** Used to add a TextBox control class object to a form. Properties include (Name), Text, and TextAlign. Events include TextChanged.

`True` One of two possible Boolean values.

Uncomment the selected lines button Clicked to remove the quotation mark (') from the beginning of the selected lines of code. Found on the toolbar.

Val() A function that takes a string and returns a number corresponding to the numeric characters.

Critical Thinking

1. a) List four legal identifier names.
   b) List four illegal identifier names and explain why each is illegal.

2. a) In two statements, declare a variable named `numCards` and assign it the value 5.
   b) In one statement, declare a variable named `numCards` and assign it the value 5.

3. a) What is the final value of `yourNumber` after the last statement executes?

```
Dim myNumber As Integer = 5
Dim yourNumber As Integer = 4
myNumber = yourNumber * 2
yourNumber = myNumber + 5
```

   b) What is the final value of `yourNumber` after the last statement executes?

```
Dim myNumber As Integer
Dim yourNumber As Integer = 4
myNumber = yourNumber + 7
yourNumber = myNumber
```

4. What is the primary purpose of a TextBox object?

5. Why is the Val() function used in a statement that assigns the data from a text box to a numeric variable?

6. a) What are labels near a text box called?
   b) Why should text boxes have labels near them?

7. Determine the appropriate data type for each of the following values:
   a) the number of basketballs in a department store.
   b) the price of a basketball.
   c) the number of players on a basketball team.
   d) the average age of the players on a basketball team.
   e) whether a basketball player has received a jersey or not.
   f) the first initial of a basketball player's first name.

8. The statement `Dim value As Integer = 3` appears in a Click event procedure for a button. The Click event procedure for a second button, contains the statements:

```
Dim value As Integer
Me.lblOutput.Text = value
```

   a) Is the scope of `value` local or global?
   b) What is shown in the label? Why?

9. What is the value of each of the following expressions?
   a) `10 / 5 * 4`
   b) `10 / 2 + 3`
   c) `6 Mod 3 + 4`
   d) `12 Mod 5 * 3`
   e) `12 Mod (5 * 3)`

10. What is the result of the following expression when x is 2005? When x is 1776? When x is 39?

```
(x\10)Mod10
```

11. Determine if each of the following are better represented by a variable or a constant and then write declarations using appropriate data types and descriptive identifiers:
    a) the number of votes received by an election candidate
    b) the percentage of votes won by a candidate
    c) the first, middle, and last initials of an election candidate
    d) the year of the election

12. For each of the following determine if the code contains a syntax error, logical error, or run-time error, and then correct the code.
    a) `Dim num = 6`
    b) `num = Value(Me.txtNum.Text)`
    c) `lblOutput = message`
    d)

```
Dim test1 As Integer
Dim test2 As Integer
Dim avg As Double
test1 = Val(Me.txtTest1.Text)
test2 = Val(Me.txtTest2.Text)
avg = test1 + test2 / 2
```

    e)

```
Dim numberTests As Integer
Dim test1 As Integer = 80
Dim test2 As Integer = 88
Dim avg As Double
avg = (test1 + test2) / numberTests
```

f)
```
Const MAX_CLASS_SIZE As Integer = 22
Dim currentSize As Integer
currentSize = Val(Me.txtSize.Text)
Me.lblEmptySeats.Text = MAX_CLASS_SIZE
```

13. What value is assigned to taxRate in the following statement if `seven percent` is typed in the txtTaxRate text box?

```
taxRate = Val(Me.txtTaxRate.Text)
```

14. Write each equation as a Visual Basic assignment statement, assuming π is a constant named PI:

a) $A=lw$ (geometry)

b) $P=\dfrac{R - C}{N}$ (business)

c) $A=\dfrac{h(b_1 + b_2)}{N}$ (geometry)

d) $V=\dfrac{4}{3}\pi r^3$ (geometry)

e) $A=\dfrac{F+S+T}{3}$ (algebra)

f) $P=\dfrac{5F}{4d^2}$ (physics)

g) $A=P+\mathrm{Pr}t$ (business)

h) $M=\dfrac{\mathrm{Pr}(1+r)^n}{(1+r)^n - 1}$ (algebra)

i) $x=\dfrac{-b\sqrt{b^2 - 4ac}}{2a}$ (algebra)

15. Rewrite the equations in parts (a) through (h) of question 14 to solve for the variable listed below and then write each equation as a Visual Basic assignment statement:
a) l
b) R
c) b1
d) r
e) T
f) F
g) P
h) P

True/False

16. Determine if each of the following statements is true or false. If false, explain why.
a) A variable must be declared before it is used.
b) Multiple variables with different data types can be declared in a single statement.
c) A runtime error results in the termination of program execution.
d) The Val() function converts text box data to a string value.
e) An `Integer` variable uses 4 bytes of memory to store its value.
f) `Boolean` variables are initialized to `True`.
g) In the variable assignment statement `x = 4.5`, where `x` is an `Integer` variable, `x` is assigned the value `4`.
h) Modulus division returns the remainder resulting from division.
i) In the variable assignment statement `x = 14 Mod 4 * 2`, where `x` is a `Double` variable, `x` is assigned the value `4`.
j) Constant declarations must be placed in the beginning of a program.
k) Visual Basic sees no difference between the variables `NEW` and `New`.
l) Keywords make good variable identifiers.
m) `Private` is a keyword.
n) The Visual Basic IDE informs the programmer of a syntax error.
o) Errors that violate the rules of Visual Basic are called semantic errors.
p) Run-time errors are always detected by the compiler.
q) A breakpoint temporarily stops the execution of a program, but pressing the right-arrow key continues execution.

Exercises

Exercise 1 — ObjectHeight

The height of an object at any given time dropped from a starting height of 100 meters is given by the equation `h=100-4.9*t²` where `t` is the time in seconds. Create an ObjectHeight application that prompts the user for a time less than 4.5 seconds and then displays the height of the object at that time when Height is clicked. The application interface should look similar to:

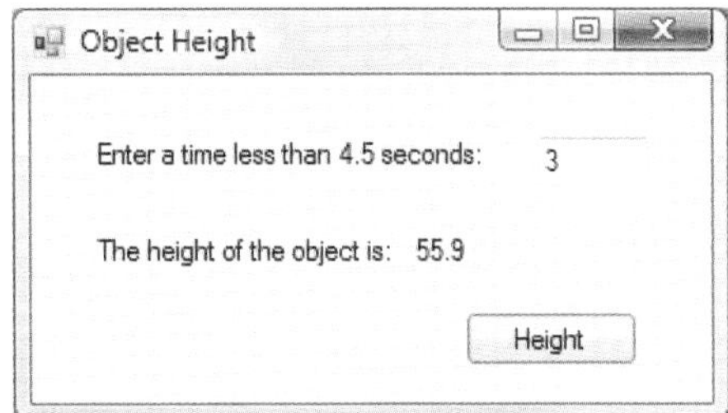

Exercise 2 — TemperatureConversion

a) Create a TemperatureConversion application that prompts the user for a temperature in degrees Fahrenheit and then displays the temperature in degrees Celsius when Celsius is clicked. Use the formula `C=5/9(F-32)` to make the conversion. Test the program with values `212`, `98.6`, `50`, `32`, and `-40`. The application interface should look similar to:

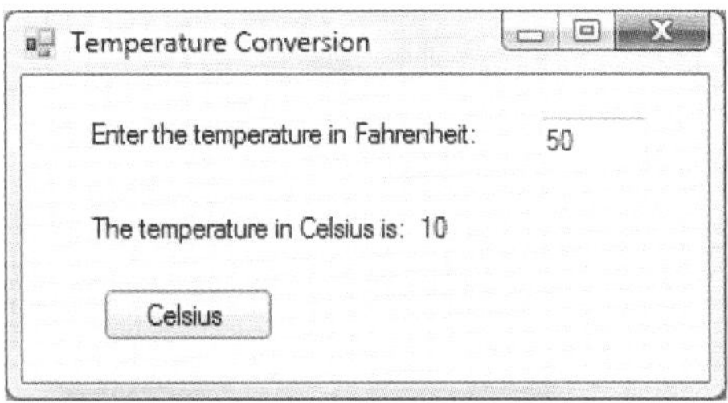

b) Modify the TemperatureConversion application to include a Program menu with Celsius, Fahrenheit, and Exit commands. Use the formula in part (a) above to determine the formula for converting from Celsius to Fahrenheit. Modify the prompt to display `Enter the temperature:` Modify the temperature label appropriately. Remove the Celsius button and corresponding code and size the form appropriately.

Exercise 3  ——— RectangleAreaAndPerimeter

Modify the RectangleAreaAndPerimeter application created in Chapter 2 Exercise 8 to prompt the user for the length and width of the rectangle and then display the area and perimeter of the rectangle when Answer is clicked. The application interface should look similar to:

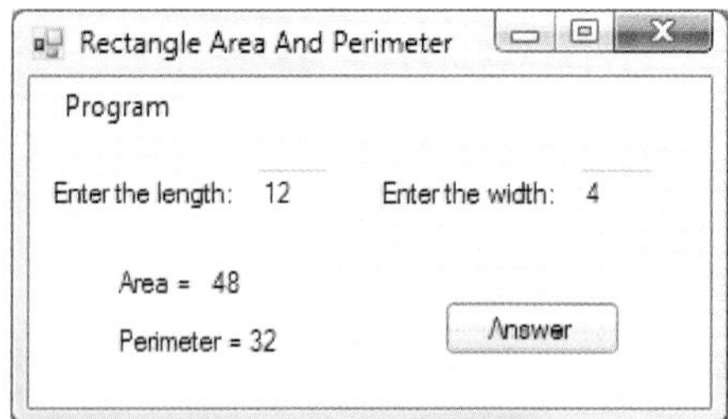

Exercise 4 ——— PizzaCost

The cost of making a pizza at a local shop is as follows:

- Labor cost is $0.75 per pizza, regardless of size
- Rent cost is $1.00 per pizza, regardless of size
- Materials is $0.05*diameter*diameter (diameter is measured in inches)

Create a PizzaCost application that prompts the user for the size of a pizza and then displays the cost of making the pizza when Cost is clicked. The application interface should look similar to:

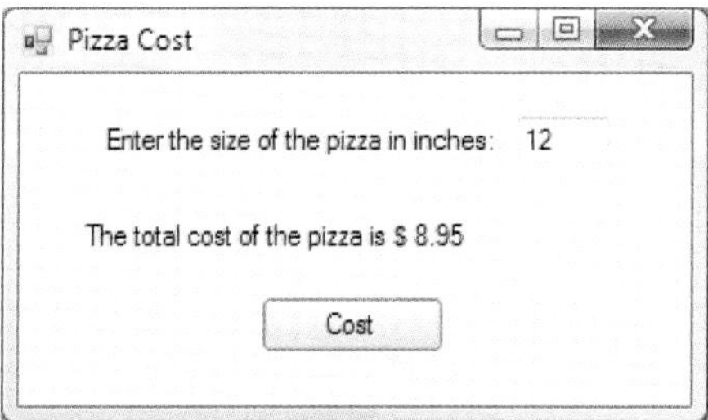

Exercise 5 ——— Energy

Einstein's famous formula, $e=mc^2$, gives the amount of energy released by the complete conversion of matter of mass m into energy e. If m represents the mass in kilograms and c represents the speed of light in meters per second ($3.0 * 10^8$ m/s), then the result is in the energy units Joules. It takes 360000 Joules to light a 100-watt light bulb for an hour. Create an Energy application that prompts the user for a mass in kilograms and then displays the energy and the number of light bulbs that could be powered when Energy is clicked. The application interface should look similar to:

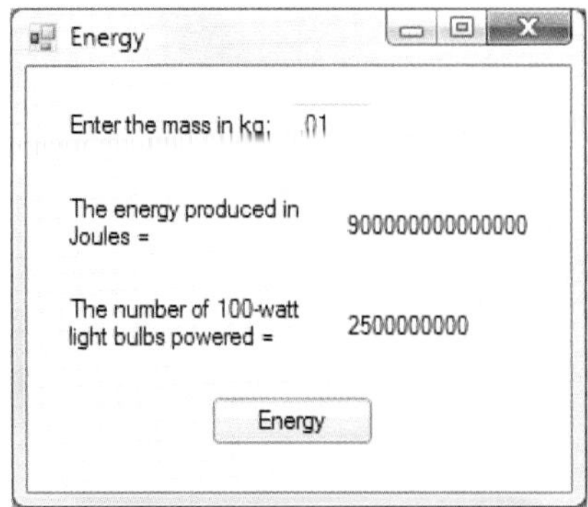

Exercise 6  LongJumpAverage

Modify the LongJumpAverage application created in Chapter 2 Exercise 9 to prompt the user for the lengths of four long jumps and then display the average jump length when Average is clicked. The application interface should look similar to:

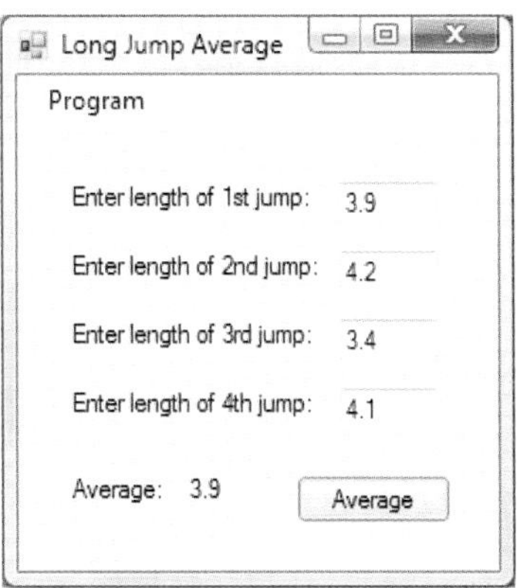

Exercise 7 Change

Create a Change application that prompts the user for an amount less than 100 and then displays the minimum number of coins necessary to make the change when Coins is clicked. The change can be made up of quarters, dimes, nickels, and pennies. The application interface should look similar to:

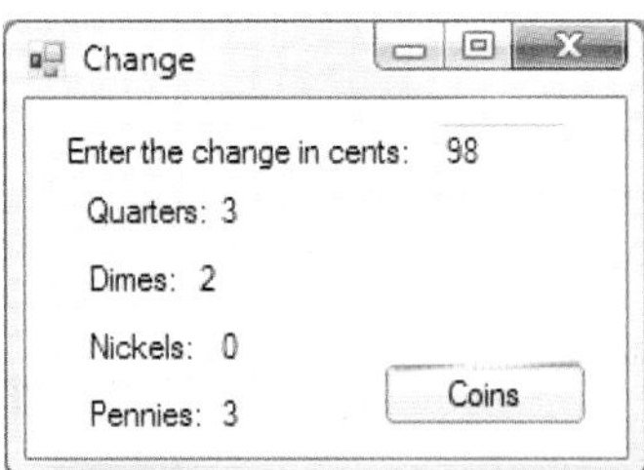

Exercise 8 — DigitsOfANumber

a) Create a DigitsOfANumber application that prompts the user for a two-digit number and then displays the digits separately when Digits is clicked. The application interface should look similar to:

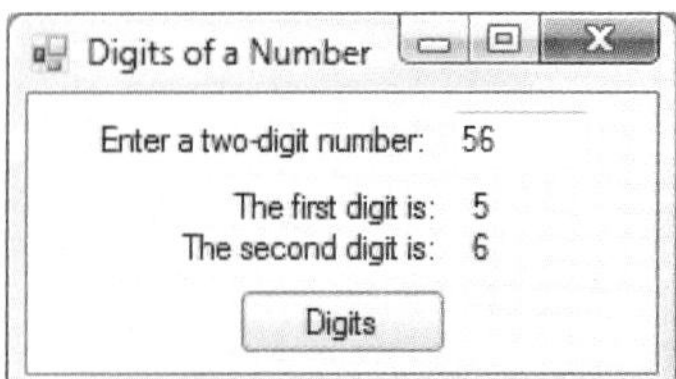

b) Modify the DigitsOfANumber application to include a Program menu with a Digits command.

Exercise 9 — TimeConversion

Create a TimeConversion application that prompts the user for a time in minutes and then displays the time in seconds or hour:minute format depending on the radio button clicked. Be sure to consider times where the number of minutes left over is less than 10. For example, 184 minutes in hour:minute format is 3:04 (*Hint*: use the modulus operator). The application interface should look similar to the following after clicking Minutes to hour:minute format:

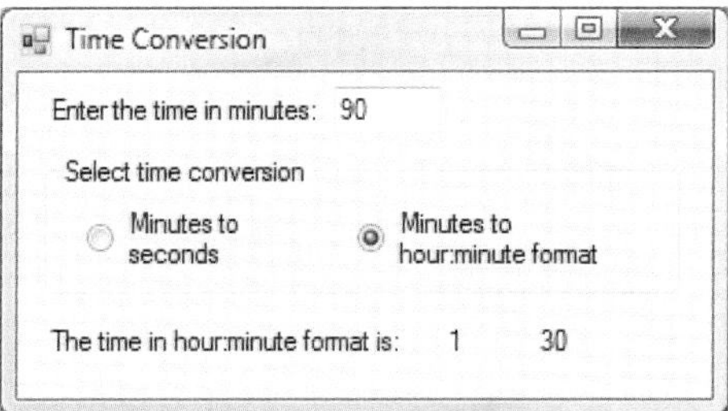

Exercise 10 — International

Create an International application that displays the phrase "My Name is" in English, Spanish, or French. Each radio button should display a tool tip. A *tool tip* displays information to the user about the purpose of an interface object and appears in a box when the mouse hovers on an object:

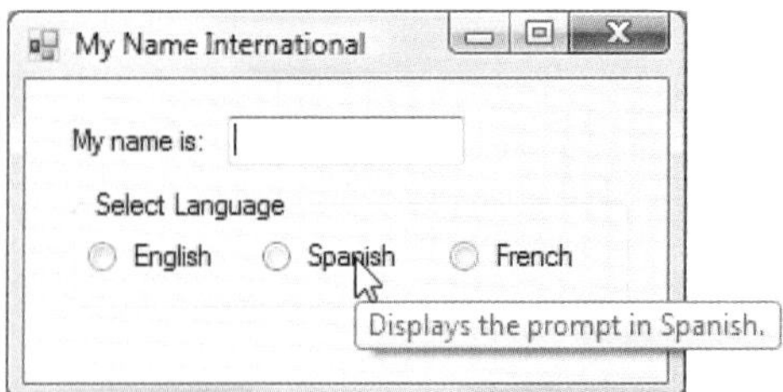

To add a ToolTip component, click the ToolTip control in the Toolbox and then click the form. The ToolTip component is shown in the component tray at the bottom of the Design window. The ToolTip property for each object should be set to the text that is to appear when the mouse hovers over that object.

Chapter 4
Controlling Program Flow with Decision Structures

Key Concepts

Controlling the flow of a program
Generating random numbers
Writing algorithms
Writing compound Boolean expressions
Using message boxes and counters
Selecting appropriate test data
Creating and modifying problem solutions

Case Study

Pizza Order application

The If...Then Statement

conditional control structure

The `If...Then` statement is a *conditional control structure*, also called a *decision structure*, which executes a set of statements when a condition is true. The `If...Then` statement takes the form:

```
If condition Then
  statements
End If
```

TIP The condition of an `If...Then` statement should never make an equality comparison between floating point numbers because of the possibility of roundoff error.

For example, in the following `If...Then` statement `guess = 7` is the `condition`, and there is one statement that will execute when this condition is true:

```
If guess = 7 Then
  Me.lblMessage.Text = "You guessed it!"
End If
```

In the condition, the equal sign (=) is used as a relational operator to determine if the value of `guess` is equal to `7`. If equal, then the Text property of lblMessage is changed. If not, program flow continues to the next statement after the `End If`.

Boolean expression
relational operators

The condition of an `If...Then` statement is a *Boolean expression*, which evaluates to either `True` or `False`. *Relational operators* can be used to form Boolean expressions. There are six relational operators:

TIP The equal sign (=) is used as a relational operator as well as an assignment operator.

Operator	Meaning
=	equal to
<	less than
<=	less than or equal to
>	greater than
>=	greater than or equal to
<>	not equal to

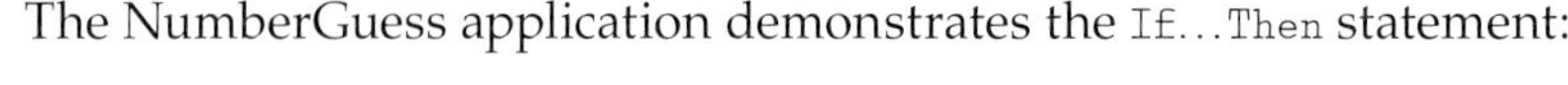

The NumberGuess application demonstrates the `If...Then` statement:

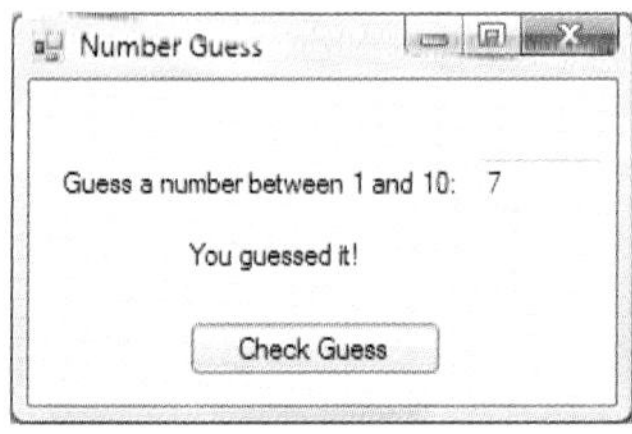


```
Public Class Form1

    Private Sub btnCheckGuess_Click(ByVal sender As System.Object, ByVal e As System.EventArgs)
        Const SECRET_NUMBER As Integer = 7
        Dim guess As Integer
        guess = Val(Me.txtUserGuess.Text)
        If guess = SECRET_NUMBER Then
            Me.lblMessage.Text = "You guessed it!"
        End If
    End Sub
End Class
```

Running the application, typing 5 in the text box, and then clicking **Check Guess** displays no message. Typing 7 and clicking **Check Guess** displays the message "You guessed it!"

A `Boolean` variable may also be used as the condition of an `If...Then` statement because its value is either `True` or `False`. For example, the `If...Then` statement below uses a `Boolean` variable as its condition:

```
Dim gameOver As Boolean = True
If gameOver Then
  Application.Exit()
End If
```

Review: TestGrade – part 1 of 5

Create a TestGrade application that prompts the user for a test score and then displays "Good job!" for a test score greater than or equal to 70 when **Check Grade** is clicked. The application interface should look similar to that shown on the right after typing 75 and clicking **Check Grade**. Be sure to include a TextChanged event procedure for the text box.

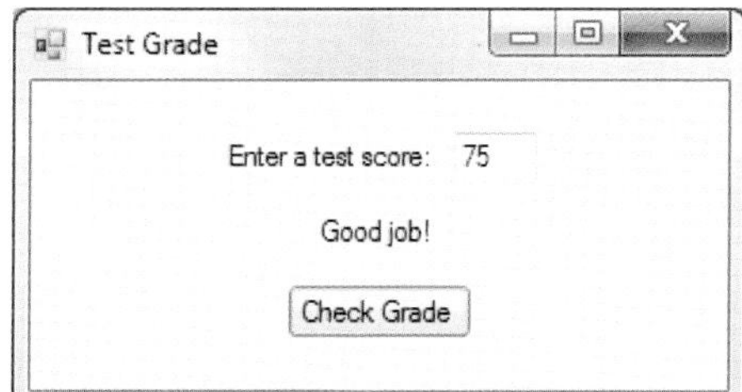

The If...Then...Else Statement

The `If...Then` statement can include an optional `Else` clause that is executed when the `If` condition evaluates to `False`. The `If...Then...Else` statement takes the following form:

```
If condition Then
  statements
Else
  statements
End If
```

The NumberGuess application could be modified to include an `If...Then...Else` statement:

```
If guess = SECRETNUMBER Then
    Me.lblMessage.Text = "You guessed it!"
Else
    Me.lblMessage.Text = "Try again."
End If
```

Running the application, typing a number other than 7, and then clicking **Check Guess** displays the message "Try again." Typing 7 and then clicking **Check Guess** displays the message "You guessed it!"

The indentation used in the `If...Then...Else` statement is a code convention that makes the statement easier to read. It has no effect on the execution of the statement. The indentation also makes it easier for a programmer reading the code to follow the logic of the statement.

Review: TestGrade – part 2 of 5

Modify the TestGrade application so that "Good job!" is displayed for a score greater than or equal to 70 and "Study more." is displayed for a score less than 70.

Review: CircleArea – part 2 of 2

Modify the CircleArea application created in Chapter 3 to display the message "Negative radii are illegal.". when a negative radius value is entered, otherwise the area of the circle should be displayed.

Nested If...Then...Else Statements

nested

An `If...Then...Else` statement can contain another `If...Then...Else` or `If...Then` statement, which is said to be *nested*. For example, the NumberGuess application could be modified to give the user a hint:

```
If guess = SECRETNUMBER Then          'correct
  Me.lblMessage.Text = "You guessed it!"
Else
  If guess < SECRETNUMBER Then        'too low
      Me.lblMessage.Text = "Too low."
  Else                                'too high
      Me.lblMessage.Text = "Too high."
  End If
End If
```

TIP When you click a keyword in a control structure, all of the keywords in the structure are highlighted.

Nested statements should be indented as good programming style.

The If...Then...ElseIf Statement

TIP There is no space in ElseIf.

The If...Then...ElseIf statement is used to decide among three or more actions and takes the form:

```
If condition Then
  statements
ElseIf condition Then
  statements
...
Else
  statements
End If
```

There can be multiple ElseIf clauses, and the last Else clause is optional. For example, there are three possible decisions in the If...Then...ElseIf statement below:

```
If guess = SECRETNUMBER Then                    'correct
  Me.lblMessage.Text = "You guessed it!"
ElseIf guess < SECRETNUMBER Then                'too low
  Me.lblMessage.Text = "Too low."
Else                                            'too high
  Me.lblMessage.Text = "Too high."
End If
```

The logic used in developing an If...Then...ElseIf statement is important. For example, when testing a range of numbers, If conditions must be properly ordered because statements are executed only for the first true condition and then program flow continues to the End If.

When choosing between nested If...Then...Else statements and a single If...Then...ElseIf statement, the If...Then...ElseIf is easier to read and understand and is considered better programming style.

Commenting Complex Decision Structures

Decision structures with many branches can quickly become difficult to understand. Brief inline comments can make code much more readable. This is especially important for the last branch of a decision structure, which usually does not include an explicit instruction.

Review: TestGrade – part 3 of 5

Modify the TestGrade application so that "Great!" is displayed for a test score greater than or equal to 90, "Good job!" for a test score greater than or equal to 70 and less than 90, and "Study more." otherwise.

The Select...Case Statement

The Select...Case statement is a conditional control structure that uses the result of an expression to determine which statements to execute. The Select...Case statement is sometimes preferable to the If...Then...ElseIf statement because code may be easier to read. The Select...Case statement takes the form:

```
Select expression
  Case value
     statements
  ...
  Case Else
     statements
End Select
```

The `expression` must evaluate to a built-in data type. There can be multiple `Case` clauses, and the `Case Else` clause is optional. The `value` type should match the `expression` type and can be a single value, a list separated by commas, or a range separated by the keyword `To`. `End Select` is required to complete the `Select...Case` statement.

The `Select...Case` statement below uses the value of a score to determine the message to display:

```
Select Case score
   Case 0, 10                    'score is 0 or 10
      Me.lblMessage.Text = "Nice try."
   Case 20 To 23                 'score is 20, 21, 22, or 23
      Me.lblMessage.Text = "Great!"
   Case Else                     'score not 0, 10, 20, 21, 22, 23
      Me.lblMessage.Text = "Invalid score."
End Select
```

Review: Hurricane

The Saffir-Simpson Hurricane Scale provides a rating (a category) depending on the current intensity of a hurricane. Create a Hurricane application that prompts the user for a wind speed and then displays the hurricane category. Display the speed in miles per hour (mph), knots (kts), and kilometers per hour (km/hr). Refer to the Saffir-Simpson Hurricane Scale below for wind speeds. The application interface should be similar to that shown on the right after typing 100 and clicking **Category**.

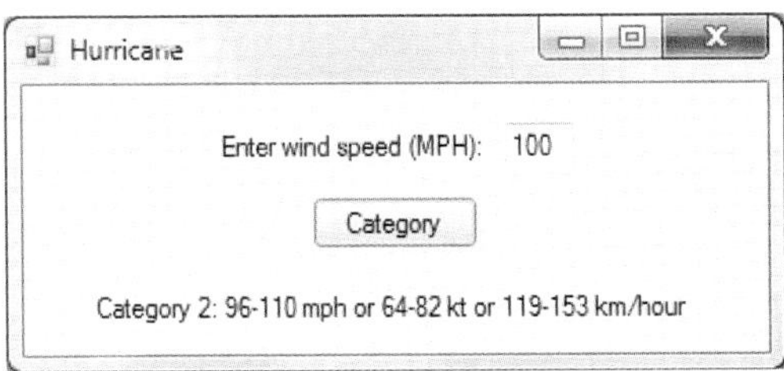

Category 1: 74-95 mph or 64-82 kt or 119-153 km/hr

Category 2: 96-110 mph or 83-95 kt or 154-177 km/hr

Category 3: 111-130 mph or 96-113 kt or 178-209 km/hr

Category 4: 131-155 mph or 114-135 kt or 210-249 km/hr

Category 5: greater than 155 mph or 135 kt or 249 km/hr

The Select...Case Is Statement

The `Select...Case Is` statement compares the result of an expression to a range of values when a relational operator is part of the value. For example, the following statement uses ranges to determine the message to display:

```
Select Case score
   Case Is < 10                  'less than 10
      Me.lblMessage.Text = "Nice try."
   Case Is < 25                  'less than 25
      Me.lblMessage.Text = "Good."
   Case Is >= 25              'greater than or equal to 25
      Me.lblMessage.Text = "Great!"
End Select
```

Review: TestGrade – part 4 of 5

Modify the TestGrade application to use a Select...Case Is and ranges of values to determine which grade to display. An A is for scores greater than 90, a B is for scores greater than or equal to 80 and less than 90, a C for scores greater than or equal to 70 and less than 80, a D for scores greater than or equal to 60 and less than 70, and a F for scores less than 60.

Generating Random Numbers

Games, simulators, screen savers, and many other types of applications require random numbers. For generating random numbers, Visual Basic includes the built-in Rnd() function. This function uses a formula to generate a sequence of numbers and then returns one number from the sequence. Although the numbers in the sequence vary and for most applications can be considered random, the sequence will at some point repeat. Therefore, random numbers in a computer application are referred to as *pseudorandom* (like random).

pseudorandom

The Rnd() function returns a number that is greater than or equal to 0 and less than 1. For example, the RandomNumbers application generates and displays six random numbers when Random Numbers is clicked:

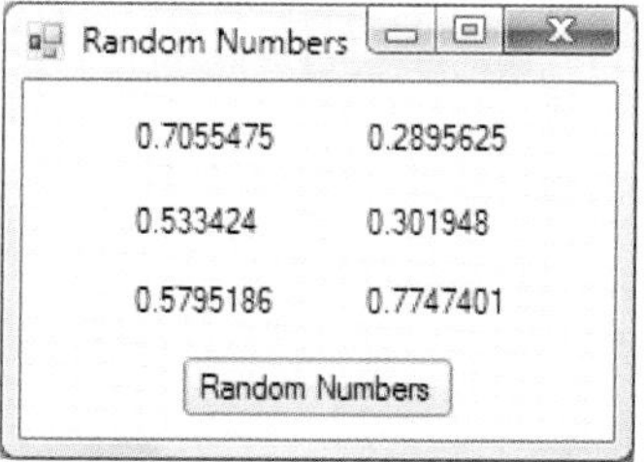

The RandomNumbers application code includes a statement similar to:

```
Me.lblRandNum1.Text = Rnd()
```

Using Rnd() alone generates random numbers greater than or equal to 0 and less than 1. To generate random numbers in a greater range, Rnd() is multiplied by the upper limit of the range. This produces numbers from 0 to one less than the upper limit. For example, to generate random numbers greater than or equal to 0 and less than 10, the following expression is used:

```
Rnd() * 10
```

A random number in a specific range is generated by using the following expression:

```
(highNumber - lowNumber + 1) * Rnd() + lowNumber
```

> ***The Fix() Function***
>
> Fix() is a built-in Visual Basic function similar to Int(). Int() and Fix() work the same for positive numbers. However, for negative numbers Int() returns the first negative integer less than or equal to its argument, while Fix() returns the first negative integer that is greater than or equal to its argument. For example, Fix(-5.4) returns -5 and Int(-5.4) returns -6.

`highNumber` is the maximum value desired and `lowNumber` is the minimum value. For example, the following statement generates a number greater than or equal to 10 and less than 31 ((30 – 10 + 1) * Rnd() + 10) and then assigns it to a label:

```
Me.lblRandNum1.Text = 21 * Rnd() + 10
```

Using this type of expression, the RandomNumbers application can be modified to display six floating point numbers in the range 10 to 30:

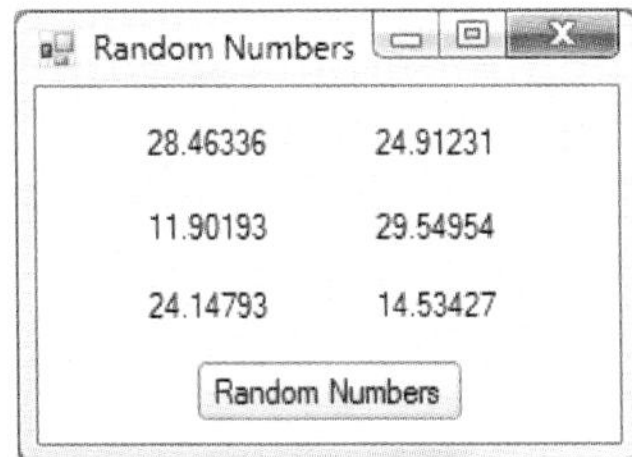

Numbers generated by Rnd() are floating point numbers with a decimal portion. To produce random integers (whole numbers), the Int() function can be used. Int() requires a numeric value and then returns the integer portion of that number without rounding. For example, in the following statement an integer is assigned to a label:

```
Me.lblRandNum1.Text = Int(21 * Rnd() + 10)
```

The RandomNumbers application modified to display six integers in the range 10 to 30 looks similar to:

> ***How Random Numbers are Generated***
>
> The Randomize() statement uses a value based on the computer's clock as a seed for the random number generator. The seed is a starting value for calculating the sequence of pseudorandom numbers.

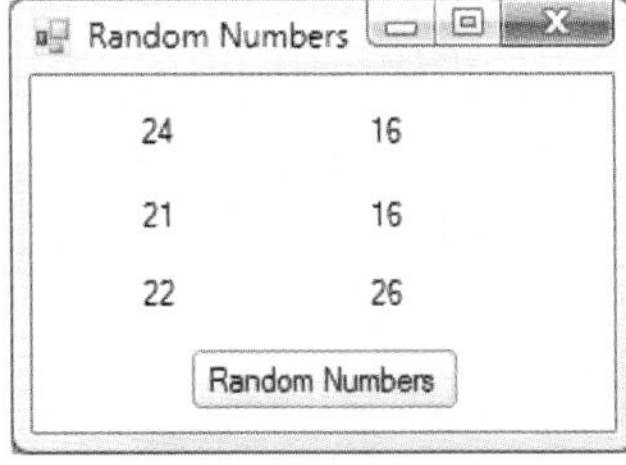

Programs using Rnd() should also include one Randomize() statement in the beginning of the event procedure before the Rnd() function is used. Randomize() initializes the random number generator so that different random numbers are generated from run to run.

Review: RandomNumbers

① CREATE A NEW PROJECT

Create a Windows application named RandomNumbers.

② CREATE THE INTERFACE

Use the table below for setting object properties.

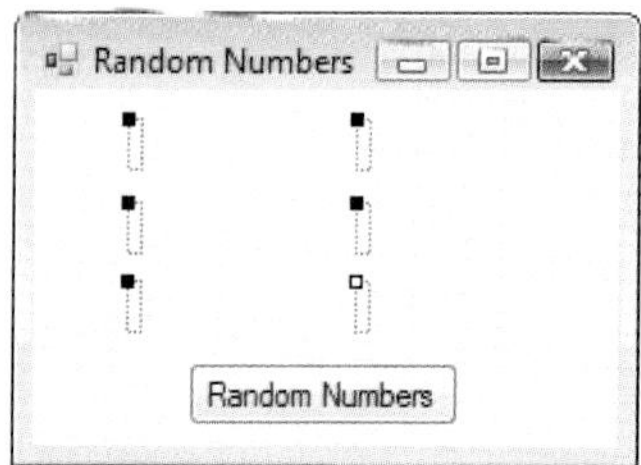

Object	(Name)	Text
Form1		Random Numbers
Label1	lblRandNum1	*empty*
Label2	lblRandNum2	*empty*
Label3	lblRandNum3	*empty*
Label4	lblRandNum4	*empty*
Label5	lblRandNum5	*empty*
Label6	lblRandNum6	*empty*
Button1	btnRandomNumbers	Random Numbers

③ WRITE THE APPLICATION CODE

a. Display the Code window.

b. Add comments that include your name, assignment, and today's date.

c. Create a btnRandomNumbers_Click event procedure and then add the statements:

```
Me.lblRandNum1.Text = Rnd()
Me.lblRandNum2.Text = Rnd()
Me.lblRandNum3.Text = Rnd()
Me.lblRandNum4.Text = Rnd()
Me.lblRandNum5.Text = Rnd()
Me.lblRandNum6.Text = Rnd()
```

④ RUN THE APPLICATION

a. Save the modified RandomNumbers project.

b. Run the application. Click Random Numbers. Write down on a piece of paper the six numbers generated.

c. Click Random Numbers again. Note that the numbers are the same as before.

d. Close the RandomNumbers application.

⑤ ADD THE RANDOMIZE() STATEMENT

a. In the btnRandomNumbers_Click event procedure, add a Randomize() statement:

```
Randomize()
Me.lblRandNum1.Text = Rnd()
Me.lblRandNum2.Text = Rnd()
Me.lblRandNum3.Text = Rnd()
Me.lblRandNum4.Text = Rnd()
Me.lblRandNum5.Text = Rnd()
Me.lblRandNum6.Text = Rnd()
```

b. Save the modified RandomNumbers project and then run the application. Click Random Numbers a few times. Note that the numbers now vary.

⑥ GENERATE INTEGERS IN A RANGE

Modify the btnRandomNumbers_Click event procedure to generate random integers between 10 and less than 31, similar to:

```
Randomize()
Me.lblRandNum1.Text = Int(21 * Rnd() + 10)
Me.lblRandNum2.Text = Int(21 * Rnd() + 10)
Me.lblRandNum3.Text = Int(21 * Rnd() + 10)
Me.lblRandNum4.Text = Int(21 * Rnd() + 10)
Me.lblRandNum5.Text = Int(21 * Rnd() + 10)
Me.lblRandNum6.Text = Int(21 * Rnd() + 10)
```

⑦ RUN THE APPLICATION

Save the modified RandomNumbers project and then run the application. Click Random Numbers a few times.

⑧ PRINT THE CODE AND THEN CLOSE THE PROJECT

Algorithms

Programs are created to solve problems. However, problems of any complexity require outlining, or designing, a solution before typing source code. One method of designing a solution is to create an algorithm. An *algorithm* is a set of steps that outline how to solve a problem. There are various methods for implementing an algorithm. For example, an algorithm written in plain English for the NumberGuess application:

algorithm

1. Determine a secret number.
2. Get a number from the player.
3. Compare the player's number with the secret number.
4. If the player's number is the same as the secret number go to step 5, otherwise tell the player if the number entered was too low or too high and then go back to step 2.
5. Display a message telling the player the secret number was guessed.

pseudocode

Another way to implement an algorithm is to write it in *pseudocode,* which is a mix of English and program code. For example, the NumberGuess algorithm in pseudocode:

```
Sub btnCheckGuess_Click()
    secretNumber = 7
    Get guess from text box
    If guess = secretNumber Then
        Display "You guessed it!"
    ElseIf guess < secretNumber Then
        Display "Too low."
    Else
        Display "Too high."
    End If
End Sub
```

Creating an algorithm allows a programmer to think through a program before actually typing code. This helps a programmer focus on the overall structure of a program and may reduce errors in logic.

Static Variables

As discussed in Chapter 3, the scope of a variable is the set of statements that can access the variable. In addition to scope, variables have a lifetime in which they exist in memory. The *lifetime* of a local variable is the duration of the procedure in which it was declared. A global variable's lifetime is the duration of the program.

lifetime

The lifetime of a local variable can be extended by using a `Static` declaration statement, which takes the form:

```
Static variableName As type = initialValue
```

static variable

A *static variable* is declared using the keyword `Static` instead of `Dim`. It should also be explicitly initialized in the declaration. A static variable's scope is local to the procedure in which it is declared, but its lifetime is the duration of the program. When either a static or global variable can be used, the static variable is a better choice because it is good programming style to keep the scope of a variable as narrow as possible.

Static variables are necessary in event procedures with variables that should be retained in memory throughout program execution. A variable declared in a Click event procedure is redeclared and reinitialized each time the Click event occurs unless the variable is declared as static. For example, the following declaration assigns a random number to a static variable. Unless the variable is assigned a new value, this value is retained throughout program execution:

```
Static secretNumber As Integer = Int(50*Rnd()+1)
```

Review: GuessingGame – part 1 of 4

GuessingGame is a game that it can be played again and again by the same user because a new random number between 1 and 50 is generated for the secret number each time the application is started. The algorithm for Guessing Game is:

1. Generate a random secret number between 1 and 50.
2. Get a number from the player.
3. Compare the player's number with the secret number.
4. If the player's number equals the secret number go to step 5, otherwise tell the player if the number entered was too low or too high and then go back to step 2.
5. Display a message telling the player the secret number was guessed.

The GuessingGame algorithm in pseudocode:

```
Sub btnCheckGuess_Click()
    Generate a random number between 1 and 50 once when program starts
    Get guess from text box
    If guess = secret number Then
        Display "You guessed it!"
    ElseIf guess < secret number Then
```

```
            Display "Too low."
        Else
            Display "Too high."
        End If
End Sub
```

① CREATE A NEW PROJECT

Create a Windows application named `GuessingGame`.

② CREATE THE INTERFACE

Use the table below for setting properties.

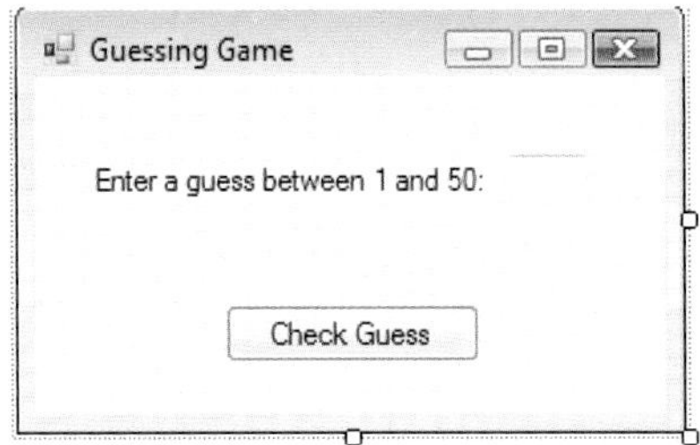

Object	Name	Text
Form1		`Guessing Game`
Label1	`lblPrompt`	`Enter a guess between 1 and 50:`
TextBox1	`txtPlayerGuess`	*empty*
Label2	`lblMessage`	*empty*
Button1	`btnCheckGuess`	`Check Guess`

③ WRITE THE APPLICATION CODE

a. Display the Code window.

b. Add comments that include your name, assignment, and today's date.

c. Create two global variables and then create a btnCheckGuess_Click event procedure with the statements:

```
Public Class Form1

    Const MIN As Integer = 1
    Const MAX As Integer = 50

    Private Sub btnCheckGuess_Click(ByVal sender As Object, ByVal e As System.EventArgs) Handles btnCheckGuess.Click
        Randomize()
        Static secretNumber As Integer = Int((MAX - MIN + 1) * Rnd() + MIN)
        Dim guess As Integer

        guess = Val(Me.txtPlayerGuess.Text)
        If guess = secretNumber Then                'correct
            Me.lblMessage.Text = "You guessed it!"
        ElseIf guess < secretNumber Then            'low num
            Me.lblMessage.Text = "Too low."
        ElseIf guess > secretNumber Then            'high num
            Me.lblMessage.Text = "Too high."
        End If
    End Sub
End Class
```

d. Create a txtPlayerGuess_TextChanged event procedure that assigns `Nothing` to the lblMessage label.

④ RUN THE APPLICATION

Save the modified GuessingGame application and then play the game a few times to test it.

⑤ PRINT THE CODE AND THEN CLOSE THE PROJECT

Compound Boolean Expressions

logical operators

Conditions with complex criteria are formed using the *logical operators* And and Or. And is used to form an expression that evaluates to True only when both operands are true. An expression formed with Or evaluates to True when either operand is true. For example, the If condition is an expression formed with Or:

```
If guess < 1 Or guess > 50 Then                'invalid guess
  Me.lblMessage.Text = "Invalid guess."
ElseIf guess = secretNumber Then               'correct guess
  Me.lblMessage.Text = "You guessed it!"
...
```

compound Boolean expression

When guess is either less than 1 *or* greater than 50, "Invalid guess." is displayed. The condition in the If...Then...ElseIf statement is called a *compound Boolean expression* because more than one Boolean expression determines whether the condition is true or false.

truth table

How a compound Boolean expression evaluates with And and Or operators can be shown in a truth tables. A *truth table* shows the possible outcomes of compound Boolean expressions:

And

Exp1	Exp2	Result
True	True	True
True	False	False
False	True	False
False	False	False

Or

Exp1	Exp2	Result
True	True	True
True	False	True
False	True	True
False	False	False

As another example, consider an application that computes a discount depending on the quantity and type of purchase:

```
If itemNum = 220 And quantity > 50 Then
  discount = 1                                 '$1.00 discount
End If
```

This If...Then statement executes the discount = 1 statement if both itemNum is 220 and quantity is greater than 50.

A third logical operator is Not. An expression including Not is evaluated according to the following truth table:

Not

Exp	Result
True	False
False	True

For example, the following statements change the label because `itemNum` is not 220:

```
If Not itemNum = 220 Then
  Me.lblMessage.Text = "No discount given."
End If
```

In the order of operations, `Not` is evaluated before `And`. `Or` is evaluated last. For example, the expression `Not 5 < 6 Or 2 > 4 And 3 < 6` evaluates to `False` because `Not 5 < 6` is performed first, then `2 > 4 And 3 < 6`, and then `False Or False`. Operator precedence can be changed by using parentheses.

Review: RockPaperScissors – part 1 of 4

Rock Paper Scissors is a popular game used for decision making between two individuals. The rules of the game are Rock dulls Scissors, Scissors cut Paper, and Paper covers Rock. In this computer-game version, the user plays against the computer. The RockPaperScissors algorithm is:

1. The player selects either Rock, Paper, or Scissors.
2. A random number between 1 and 3 is generated to represent the computer's choice. A 1 corresponds to Rock, a 2 to Paper, and a 3 to Scissors.
3. Compare the player's choice to the computer's choice.
4. Display an appropriate message.

The RockPaperScissors algorithm in pseudocode:

```
Sub btnPlay_Click()
    Get user's choice from radio buttons
    Generate a random number between 1 and 3
    If user = radRock and comp = Rock Then
        draw
    ElseIf user = radRock and comp = Paper Then
        computer wins
    ElseIf user = radRock and comp = Scissors Then
        user wins
    End If
    If user = radPaper and comp = Rock Then
        user wins
    ElseIf user = radPaper and comp = Paper Then
        draw
    ElseIf user = radPaper and comp = Scissors Then
        computer wins
    End If
    If user = radScissors and comp = Rock Then
        computer wins
    ElseIf user = radScissors and comp = Paper Then
        user wins
    ElseIf user = radScissors and comp = Scissors Then
        draw
    End If
End Sub
```

① CREATE A NEW PROJECT

Create a Windows application named RockPaperScissors.

② CREATE THE INTERFACE

Use the table below for setting properties.

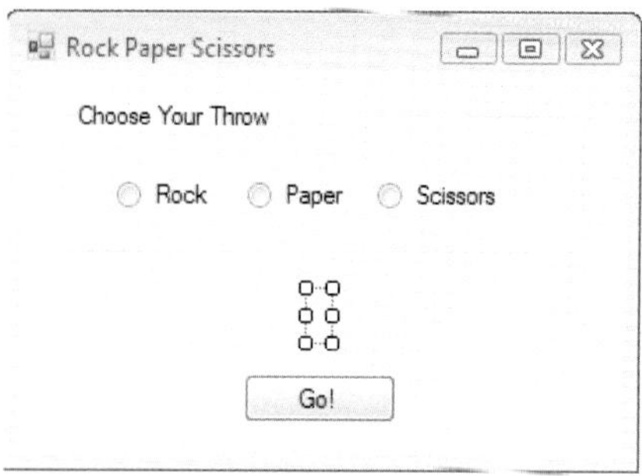

Object	(Name)	Text	Checked
Form1		Rock Paper Scissors	
GroupBox1	grpThrows	Choose Your Throw	
RadioButton1	radRock	Rock	False
RadioButton2	radPaper	Paper	False
RadioButton3	radScissors	Scissors	False
Label1	lblWinner	*empty*	
Button1	btnGo	Go!	

③ WRITE THE APPLICATION CODE

a. Display the Code window.

b. Add comments that include your name, assignment, and today's date.

c. Create a btnGo_Click event procedure and then add the statements:

```
Const ROCK As Integer = 1
Const PAPER As Integer = 2
Const SCISSORS As Integer = 3
Dim computerThrow As Integer

'Generate computer throw
Randomize()
computerThrow = Int(3 * Rnd() + 1)

If Me.radRock.Checked And computerThrow = ROCK Then
    Me.lblWinner.Text = "Computer throws Rock. It's a Draw!"     'Rock Rock
ElseIf Me.radRock.Checked And computerThrow = PAPER Then
    Me.lblWinner.Text = "Computer throws Paper. Computer wins!"     'Rock Paper
ElseIf Me.radRock.Checked And computerThrow = SCISSORS Then
    Me.lblWinner.Text = "Computer throws Scissors. You win!"        'Rock Scissors
End If

If Me.radPaper.Checked And computerThrow = ROCK Then
    Me.lblWinner.Text = "Computer throws Rock. You win!"            'Paper Rock
ElseIf Me.radPaper.Checked And computerThrow = PAPER Then
    Me.lblWinner.Text = "Computer throws Paper. It's a Draw!"       'Paper Paper
ElseIf Me.radPaper.Checked And computerThrow = SCISSORS Then
    Me.lblWinner.Text = "Computer throws Scissors. Computer wins!"  'Paper Scissors
End If

If Me.radScissors.Checked And computerThrow = ROCK Then
    Me.lblWinner.Text = "Computer throws Rock. Computer wins!"      'Scissors Rock
ElseIf Me.radScissors.Checked And computerThrow = PAPER Then
    Me.lblWinner.Text = "Computer throws Paper. You win!"           'Scissors Paper
ElseIf Me.radScissors.Checked And computerThrow = SCISSORS Then
    Me.lblWinner.Text = "Computer throws Scissors. It's a Draw!" 'Scissors Scissors
End If
```

④ RUN THE APPLICATION

Save the modified RockPaperScissors application and then play the game a few times to test it. Close the application.

⑤ PRINT THE CODE

Review: RockPaperScissors – part 2 of 4

Modify the RockPaperScissors application to use nested `If...Then...ElseIf` statements to determine the outcome of game.

Review: RockPaperScissors – part 3 of 4

Modify the RockPaperScissors application to use a `Select...Case` statement and `If...Then...ElseIf` statements to determine the outcome of game. *Hint*: Use the `computerThrow` value as the expression in the `Select...Case` statement.

Displaying a Message Box

A *message box* is a predefined dialog box that displays a message for the user. A message can be displayed to alert the user to invalid data or as a reminder of options required for an application to continue. For example, the GuessingGame application could be modified to alert the user to a guess that is out of range:

Message Box Parameters

A message box can display text in the title bar by including a string as the second parameter. For example, the statement `MessageBox.Show("Good guess!", "Game")` displays a message box with "Game" in the title bar.

The `MessageBox` class includes a Show() method for displaying a message box and is used in a statement that takes the form:

```
MessageBox.Show(message)
```

`message` is a variable, constant, or a string literal. For example, the `If...Then...ElseIf` statement alerts the user to a number outside the allowed range:

```
If guess < MIN Or guess > MAX Then                'invalid guess
  MessageBox.Show("Guess out of range.")
ElseIf guess = secretNumber Then                  'correct
  Me.lblMessage.Text = "You guessed it!"
ElseIf guess < secretNumber Then                  'too low
  Me.lblMessage.Text = "Too low."
Else                                              'too high
  Me.lblMessage.Text = "Too high."
End If
```

TIP A string literal is the actual string enclosed in quotation marks.

Review: GuessingGame – part 2 of 4

Modify the GuessingGame application to display a message box with an appropriate message if the user's guess is less than the minimum allowed number or greater than maximum.

Review: TestGrade – part 5 of 5

Modify the TestGrade application so that "Invalid grade." is displayed in a message box if the grade entered is less than `0` or greater than `100`.

Counter Variables

Many algorithms involve counting. Information such as the number of times a user enters a guess require counting each guess. Calculations such as averaging a set of numbers require counting because the sum of the numbers must be divided by the count of the numbers. Applications written for algorithms that involve counting use a *counter variable* for storing a number that is incremented by a constant value.

Counters are useful for keeping track of the number of times a user clicks a button, enters a guess, or types a password. The statement for incrementing a counter, often called updating a counter, takes the form:

```
counter = counter + constant
```

`counter` is the numeric variable that is updated. `constant` is the number that is added to the current value of `counter`. In an assignment statement the expression on the right side of the equal sign is evaluated first and then that value given to the variable on the left. This makes it possible to use the current value of `counter` in the expression itself. For example, the following statement updates the counter `numTries` by 1:

```
numTries = numTries + 1
```

Each time the statement is executed, `1` is added to the current value of `numTries` and then this new value is assigned to `numTries`.

Counters are used often in programming. Therefore, Visual Basic has additional assignment operators just for updating counters. These operators perform an operation before making an assignment. For example, the `+=` allows the statement above to be written as:

```
numTries += 1
```

Counters sometimes count backward. For these counters, the `-=` operator can be used.

A counter should be initialized when it is declared and then updated by an unchanging amount. A counter in an event procedure should be declared as a `Static` variable so that it is initialized only once.

Review: RockPaperScissors – part 4 of 4

Modify the RockPaperScissors application to include three counters that maintain the number of wins by the player, the number of wins by the computer, and the number of draws. The scores should be updated and displayed in labels at the end of each game.

The CheckBox Control

Check boxes allow the user to select options. Unlike radio buttons, more than one check box can be selected at a time. For example, in the MorningToDo application, CheckBox objects give the user options:

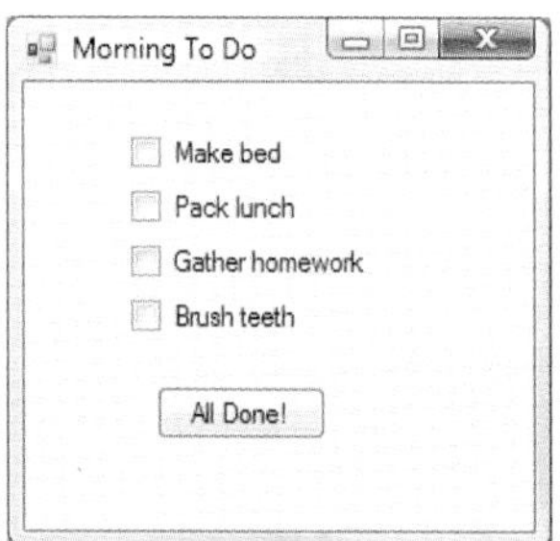

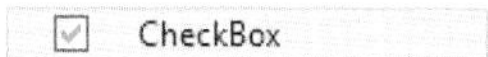

The CheckBox control has the properties:

- **(Name)** identifies a control for the programmer. CheckBox object names should begin with `chk`.
- **Text** is the text displayed next to the box.
- **Checked** can be set to either True or False to display the check box with or without a check, respectively.

Related check boxes are sometimes placed together in a GroupBox object. As with radio buttons, a group box should be added to the form before adding check boxes.

An `If...Then` statement can be used in a program to determine if a check box is selected or cleared. For example, the following statement displays a message that depends on the state of the check box:

```
If Me.chkLunch.Checked Then          'check box selected
  MessageBox.Show("Don't forget your bottled water!")
Else                                 'check box cleared
  MessageBox.Show("Take lunch money!")
End If
```

A Click event procedure is sometimes coded for a check box. This procedure executes when a check box is clicked and usually includes code to determine the state of the check box and then perform actions depending on whether the check box was selected or cleared.

Implicit Line Continuation

TIP A line of code can be more than 65,000 characters in length. However, it is easier to work with lines of 80 characters or less.

A statement typically fits on one line, but can be continued onto the next line using a line-continuation sequence, which consists of a space followed by an underscore character (_), followed by a carriage return. For example, a condition placed onto two lines looks similar to:

```
If Not (Me.chkBed.Checked And Me.chkLunch.Checked _
And Me.chkHomework.Checked And Me.chkTeeth.Checked) Then
...
```

In many cases, you can continue a statement on the next consecutive line without using the underscore character (_). Syntax elements that implicitly continue the statement on the next line of code include:

- after a comma (,)
- after an open parenthesis (() or before a closing parenthesis ())
- after an open curly brace ({) or before a closing curly brace (})
- after assignment operators (=, &=, :=, +=, -=, *=, /=, \=, ^=)
- after binary operators (+, -, /, *, Mod, <>, <, >, <=, >=, And, Or)

Review: MorningToDo

① CREATE A NEW PROJECT

Create a Windows application named MorningToDo.

② CREATE THE INTERFACE

Use the table below for setting properties.

Object	(Name)	Text	Checked
Form1		Morning To Do	
CheckBox1	chkBed	Make bed	False
CheckBox2	chkLunch	Pack lunch	False
CheckBox3	chkHomework	Gather homework	False
CheckBox4	chkTeeth	Brush teeth	False
Button1	btnAllDone	All Done!	

③ WRITE THE APPLICATION CODE

a. Display the Code window.

b. Add comments that include your name, assignment, and today's date.

c. Create a chkLunch_Click event procedure and then add the statements:

```
If Me.chkLunch.Checked Then
    MessageBox.Show("Don't forget bottled water!")
End If
```

d. Create a btnAllDone_Click event procedure and then add the statements:

```
If Not (Me.chkBed.Checked And Me.chkLunch.Checked And
    Me.chkHomework.Checked And Me.chkTeeth.Checked) Then
    MessageBox.Show("Did you forget something?")
Else
    Application.Exit()
End If
```

④ RUN THE APPLICATION

a. Save the modified MorningToDo application and then run it. Select the Pack Lunch check box and note the message box.

b. Select all the check boxes and then select All Done! The application ends.

c. Run the application again. Select only two or three of the check boxes and then select All Done! A message box is displayed. Select the remaining check boxes and then select All Done!

⑤ PRINT THE CODE AND THEN CLOSE THE PROJECT

Case Study

In this case study a PizzaOrder application will be created.

PizzaOrder Specification

PizzaOrder allows a user to select a pizza size and toppings. Topping choices include pepperoni, mushrooms, onions, and hot peppers. Once the order is placed, an order number and the pizza price are displayed. A new order clears the current order information and allows the next order to be generated. The order number should automatically increment with each new order. The following prices and toppings prices should be used:

Regular:	$6.00
Large:	$10.00
one topping:	$1.00 additional
two toppings:	$1.75 additional
three toppings:	$2.50 additional
four toppings:	$3.25 additional

PizzaOrder Design

For each pizza order there can be only one size, but many toppings. Therefore, radio buttons should be used to select the size and check boxes should be used to select the toppings:

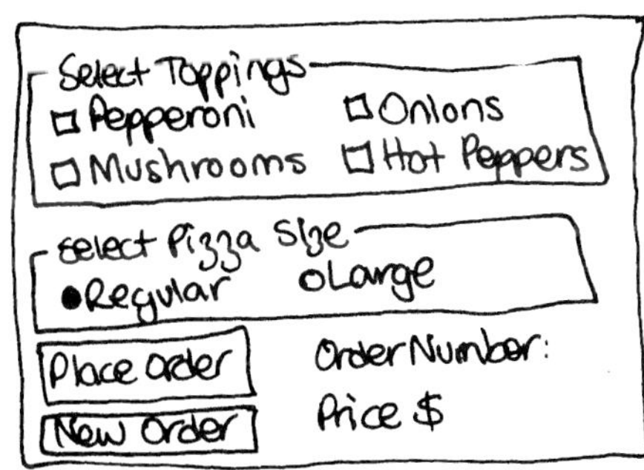

The code design should start with an algorithm:

1. Increment order number.
2. Determine toppings price based on the selected number of toppings.
3. Determine pizza price based on the selected size and then add toppings price.
4. Display pizza price and order number.
5. When a new order is started, select the Regular radio button and clear the check boxes and labels.

The algorithm is implemented with the following pseudocode:

```
Sub btnPlaceOrder_Click()
    Const REGULAR As Decimal = 6
    Const LARGE As Decimal = 10
    Const ONE_TOPPING As Decimal = 1
    Const TWO_TOPPINGS As Decimal = 1.75
    Const THREE_TOPPINGS As Decimal = 2.5
    Const FOUR_TOPPINGS As Decimal = 3.25
    Static orderNumber As Integer = 0
    Dim numToppings As Integer
    Dim toppingsPrice As Decimal
    Dim pizzaPrice As Decimal

    Increment orderNumber

    For each topping check box selected, increment numToppings

    Use numToppings to select ONE_TOPPING, TWO_TOPPINGS,
    THREE_TOPPINGS, or FOUR_TOPPINGS

    If radLarge.Checked Then
        pizzaPrice = LARGE + toppingsPrice
    Else
        pizzaPrice = REGULAR +  toppingsPrice
    End If

    lblOrder = "Order Number:"
    lblOrderNumber.Text = OrderNumber
    lblPrice = "Price: $"
    lblPizzaPrice.Text = PizzaPrice
End Sub

Sub btnNewOrder_Click()
    Clear check boxes
    Select the Regular radio button
    Clear labels
End Sub
```

PizzaOrder Coding

The interface and code for this Case Study are:

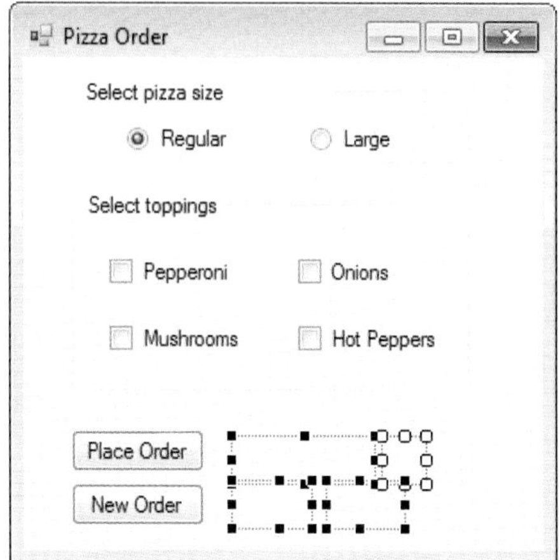

Object	**(Name)**	**Text**
Form1		Pizza Order
GroupBox1	grpPizzaSize	Select pizza size
RadioButton1	radRegular	Regular
RadioButton2	radLarge	Large
GroupBox2	grpToppings	Select toppings
CheckBox1	chkPepperoni	Pepperoni
CheckBox2	chkMushrooms	Mushrooms
CheckBox3	chkOnions	Onions
CheckBox4	chkHotPeppers	Hot Peppers
Button1	btnPlaceOrder	Place Order
Button2	btnNewOrder	New Order
Label1	lblOrder	*empty*
Label2	lblOrderNumber	*empty*
Label3	lblPrice	*empty*
Label4	lblPizzaPrice	*empty*

The Checked property of the radRegular radio button must be set to True.

```
Public Class Form1

  Private Sub btnPlaceOrder_Click(ByVal sender As Object,
  ByVal e As System.EventArgs) Handles btnPlaceOrder.Click
      Const REGULAR As Decimal = 6            '$6
      Const LARGE As Decimal = 10             '$10
      Const ONE_TOPPING As Decimal = 1        '$1
      Const TWO_TOPPINGS As Decimal = 1.75    '$1.75
      Const THREE_TOPPINGS As Decimal = 2.5  '$2.50
      Const FOUR_TOPPINGS As Decimal = 3.25  '$3.25
      Static orderNumber As Integer = 0
      Dim numToppings As Integer = 0
      Dim toppingsPrice As Decimal = 0
      Dim pizzaPrice As Decimal = 0

      'Increment order number
      orderNumber += 1

      'Count selected toppings
```

```
        If Me.chkHotPeppers.Checked = True Then
            numToppings += 1
        End If
        If Me.chkMushrooms.Checked = True Then
            numToppings += 1
        End If
        If Me.chkOnions.Checked = True Then
            numToppings += 1
        End If
        If Me.chkPepperoni.Checked = True Then
            numToppings += 1
        End If

        'Determine toppings price
        Select Case numToppings
            Case 1
                toppingsPrice = ONE_TOPPING
            Case 2
                toppingsPrice = TWO_TOPPINGS
            Case 3
                toppingsPrice = THREE_TOPPINGS
            Case 4
                toppingsPrice = FOUR_TOPPINGS
        End Select

        "Determine pizza price
        If Me.radLarge.Checked Then             'large pizza
            pizzaPrice = LARGE + toppingsPrice
        Else                                    'regular pizza
            pizzaPrice = REGULAR + toppingsPrice
        End If

        'Display order number and pizza price
        Me.lblOrder.Text = "Order Number:"
        Me.lblOrderNumber.Text = orderNumber
        Me.lblPrice.Text = "Price: $"
        Me.lblPizzaPrice.Text = pizzaPrice
    End Sub

    Private Sub btnNewOrder_Click(ByVal sender As Object,
    ByVal e As System.EventArgs) Handles btnNewOrder.Click
        Me.radLarge.Checked = False
        Me.radRegular.Checked = True
        Me.chkHotPeppers.Checked = False
        Me.chkMushrooms.Checked = False
        Me.chkOnions.Checked = False
        Me.chkPepperoni.Checked = False
        Me.lblOrder.Text = Nothing
        Me.lblOrderNumber.Text = Nothing
        Me.lblPrice.Text = Nothing
        Me.lblPizzaPrice.Text = Nothing
    End Sub
End Class
```

Running PizzaOrder, selecting options, and then clicking Place Order displays:

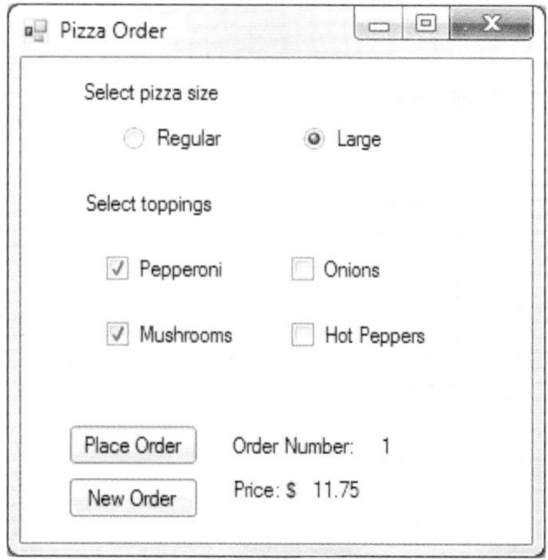

TIP Formatting numeric output is discussed in Chapter 7.

This case study should be tested by generating several different pizza orders and checking the price displayed by hand.

Review: PizzaOrder

Modify the PizzaOrder case study to include Pickup and Delivery radio buttons in a new group box. If Delivery is selected, $1.50 should be added to the total price of the pizza. Pickup should add nothing to the total price of the pizza and should be selected when the program starts and when a new order is started.

Chapter Summary

Conditional control structures, also called decision structures, include the `If...Then`, `If...Then...Else`, `If...Then...ElseIf`, `Select...Case`, and `Select...Case Is` statements. Each of these structures evaluates a condition to determine program flow. The condition in the `If...Then` statements is a Boolean expression that evaluates to true or false. The `If...Then...ElseIf` statement is used to decide among three, four, or more actions. The `Select...Case` statements are also used to decide among many actions.

A Boolean expression may be a Boolean variable or an expression formed using relational operators (=, <, <=, >, >=, <>). A compound Boolean expression uses logical operators (`And`, `Or`, `Not`).

The Rnd() function generates a random number greater than or equal to 0 and less than 1. The Int() function is used to return the integer portion of a number. The Randomize() statement is used to initialize the Rnd() function so that different random numbers are generated from program run to program run.

An algorithm is a set of steps that tell how to solve a problem. An algorithm refined using both English and program code is called pseudocode. Creating an algorithm before using the computer helps reduce logic errors.

Static variables have a local scope but a lifetime the duration of the program. Static variables are necessary in event procedures with variables that should be retained in memory throughout a program run.

A message box is used to provide information to the user, such as when invalid data has been entered. The MessageBox class includes a Show() method that displays a predefined dialog box.

A counter is a variable storing a number that is incremented by a constant value. A counter in an event procedure should be declared as a `Static` variable so that it is initialized only once.

A check box is an object that allows the user to select one or more options from a set of options. A Click event is sometimes coded for a check box. The procedure should include an `If...Then` statement to determine if the check box has been selected or cleared. Related check boxes are sometimes placed together in a group box.

The line-continuation character (_) is used to divide a statement over two or more lines. However, in many cases, such as after a comma or after an assignment operator, you can continue a statement on the next consecutive line without using the underscore character (_).

The code conventions introduced in this chapter are:

- The statements of an `If...Then` statement should be indented.
- The statements of an `If...Then...Else` statement should be indented.
- The statements of an `If...Then...ElseIf` statement should be indented.
- Nested statements should be indented.
- The `Case` statements of a `Select...Case` statement should be indented.
- Choose a static variable over a global variable when possible because the scope of the static variable can be kept more narrow.
- Use implicit line continuation syntax to divide long statements into two or more lines.

Vocabulary

Algorithm A set of steps that outline how to solve a problem.

Compound Boolean expression More than one Boolean expression determines whether the condition is `True` or `False`.

Conditional control structure *See* Decision structure.

Counter A variable used to store a value that is updated by a constant value.

Decision structure A statement that uses a condition to determine which set of statements to execute.

Lifetime The duration in which a declared variable exists in memory.

Logical operators Operators (`And`, `Or`, and `Not`) that may be used to form a Boolean expression.

Message box A predefined dialog box that displays a message for the user.

Nested statements One or more statements within a statement.

Pseudocode An algorithm written in both English and program code.

Pseudorandom Not truly random, but like random.

Relational operators Operators (=, <, <=, >, >=, and <>) that can be used to form a Boolean expression.

Static variable A variable with a local scope but a lifetime the duration of the program.

Truth table Shows the possible outcomes of compound Boolean expressions.

Update To increment a counter variable.

_ (underscore) The line-continuation character.

`+=` Assignment operator that adds the value on the right of the statement to the current value of the variable on the left and then updates the variable to store the new value.

`-=` Assignment operator that subtracts the value on the right of the statement from the current value of the variable on the left and then updates the variable to store the new value.

`=` (equal to) Relational operator used to determine if one value is equal to another.

`<` (less than) Relational operator used to determine if one value is less than another.

`<=` (less than or equal to) Relational operator used to determine if one value is less than or equal to another.

`>` (greater than) Relational operator used to determine if one value is greater than another.

`>=` (greater than or equal to) Relational operator used to determine if one value is greater than or equal to another.

`<>` (not equal to) Relational operator used to determine if one value is not equal to another.

`And` Logical operator used to form a Boolean expression. An expression formed using `And` is `True` only when the expressions it joins are all `True`.

CheckBox **CheckBox control** Used to add a CheckBox control class object to a form. Properties include (Name), Text, and Checked. Events include Click.

`If...Then` Statement that executes code when a condition is `True`.

`If...Then...Else` Statement that executes code in the `Else` clause when a condition is `False`.

`If...Then...ElseIf` Statement that is used to decide among three or more actions.

Int() A function that returns the integer portion of a number without rounding.

`MessageBox` **class** Used to display a predefined dialog box that displays a message and an OK button. Methods include Show().

`Not` Logical operator used to form a Boolean expression. An expression formed using `Not` is `True` only when the expression it is used with is `False`.

`Or` Logical operator used to form a Boolean expression. An expression formed using `Or` is `True` when any of the expressions it joins are `True`.

Randomize() Statement used to initialize the Rnd() function so that different random numbers are generated from run to run.

Rnd() A function used to generate a random number greater than or equal to 0 and less than 1.

`Select...Case` Statement that executes code depending on the result of an expression.

`Select...Case Is` Statement that executes code depending on a comparison of a range of values to the result of an expression.

`Static` Statement used to declare a static variable.

Critical Thinking

1. Assuming the comment is correct, determine the logic error in the following statement:

```
If grade > 90 Then
    'Display A for grade greater than or
    'equal to 90
    Me.lblGrade.Text = "You have an A"
End If
```

2. What is displayed in the label after the following statement executes? Does the label assignment reflect what was intended? If not, how should the statement be rewritten to produce the intended result?

```
Dim score As Integer = 25
If score >= 100 Then
    Me.lblMessage.Text = "You won!"
ElseIf score < 100 Then
    Me.lblMessage.Text = "Good try."
ElseIf score < 50 Then
    Me.lblMessage.Text = "Practice more."
End If
```

3. Check boxes, radio buttons, and text boxes all accept user input.
   a) List the differences in the way the three accept input.
   b) Give an example of how each should be used in an application.

4. Given the statements

```
Dim quantity As Integer = 20
Dim price As Double = 5
```

   determine the value, true or false, for each of the following expressions:

   a) `quantity > 10 And price > 5`
   b) `quantity = 15 Or price = 5`
   c) `quantity >= 20 And price >=2 And quantity * price >= 40`
   d) `Not price = 5`
   e) `quantity < 100 Or price > 4 And Not quantity = 20`

5. Write an appropriate decision statement for each of the following:
   a) Display "Great Job" in a label named lblMessage if grade is 90 or above.
   b) Display "High Scorer" in a label named lblHigh for `totalPoints` between 100 and 200, inclusive.
   c) Display "Number must be less than 100." in a message box if the value in txtGrade is greater than 100.

6. a) Which is the appropriate word for the first blank below, odd or even? Which is the appropriate word for the second blank?

```
If number Mod 2 = 0 Then
    MessageBox.Show ("Your number is ______")
Else
    MessageBox.Show ("Your number is ______")
End If
```

   b) Rewrite the `If...Then...Else` statement from part (a) as a `Select...Case` statement.

7. List the errors in the statement below and then rewrite the statement so that it will execute as expected:

```
If 50 <= numTickets <= 100 And _
Me.radStu.Checked
    MessageBox.Show = ("Both discounts.)
ElseIf 50 <= numTickets <= 100
    MessageBox.Show = ("Volume discount.)
ElseIf Me.radStu.Checked
    MessageBox.Show = ("Student discount.)
    Case Else
        MessageBox.Show = ("No discount.)
    End If
End If
```

8. Rewrite the following statement so that it does not include a nested `If...Then` statement:

```
If Me.chkValue1.Checked Then
    If Me.chkValue2.Checked Then
        MessageBox.Show("Both applied.")
    End If
End If
```

9. Assume txtTest1, txtTest2, and txtTest3 contain numeric values. Write an `If...Then...Else` statement that displays in a label the average of the three numbers only if all of the numbers are between 0 and 100, otherwise a message box with an appropriate message should be displayed and the text boxes cleared.

10. Assume txtNum1 and txtNum2 contain numeric values. Write an `If...Then...ElseIf` statement that displays a message box with one of the following messages as appropriate:

```
First number is larger
Second number is larger
Both numbers are equal
```

11. Write a statement that generates a random whole number between 5 and 50, inclusive.

12. a) List the errors in the statement below and then rewrite the statement so that it will execute as expected:

```
Select Case num
    Case 2 Or 3, num > 10
        MessageBox.Show("1st Case")
    Case 20 <= num < 30
        MessageBox.Show("2nd Case")
End Case
```

b) Rewrite the `Select...Case` statement in part (a) using an `If...Then...ElseIf` statement.

13. Assume txtMonth contains all uppercase text that is a month of the year, for example, SEPTEMBER. Another text box, txtYear, contains the year. Write a `Select...Case` statement that displays in a message box the number of days in the month entered. Hint: An efficient statement does not require 12 case values. The days in February can be determined by using the following pseudocode:

```
If year Mod 4 <> 0 Then
    use 28 days for February
ElseIf year Mod 400 = 0 Then
    use 29 days for February
ElseIf year Mod 100 = 0 Then
    use 28 days for February
Else
    use 29 for days in February
End If
```

14. Write a btnPurchase_Click event procedure that calculates the cost of tickets and gives free tickets on every 100th purchase. The txtNumTickets text box contains the number of tickets for a purchase and each ticket price is $8.00. A counter variable should be updated by one each time Purchase is clicked. On the 100th purchase, a message box should display "Congratulations, the tickets are free!" The counter should then be reset to zero. If the purchase is not the 100th, a message box should display the cost of the tickets. Use appropriate constants and variables.

15. Write a btnMessage_Click event procedure that displays one of the messages below in a message box:

`You win $100`	2% of the time
`You win $10`	10% of the time
`You win $1`	50% of the time
`Thanks for trying.`	The rest of the time.

Hint: Use a random number between 1 and 100 and a `Select..Case` to determine the message to display.

True/False

16. Determine if each of the following statements is true or false. If false, explain why.
    a) The condition of an `If...Then` statement is a `Boolean` expression
    b) A decision structure must have an `Else` clause.
    c) It is good programming style to line up the `If`, the `Else`, and the `End If` in a decision structure, and to indent the lines in between.
    d) The `Select...Case` statement must have the `Case Else` clause.
    e) The `Select...Case` statement can only be used if you have more than two cases.
    f) Using Rnd() without including Randomize() will produce a run-time error.
    g) Numbers generated by the statement Rnd() are integers.
    h) Algorithms are designed after the source code is typed.
    i) The value of local variables are always retained in memory for the duration of a program execution.
    j) A compound Boolean expression uses more than one Boolean expression to determine whether a condition is true or false.
    k) In a logical `And` expression, both operands must be true for the expression to evaluate to true.
    l) In a logical expression, `Or` is evaluated before `Not`.
    m) Message boxes can only be used in decision statements.
    n) Counter variables are useful for keeping track of the number of times a specific event occurs.
    o) `sum`, assigned as `sum = 1 + 2 + 3`, is a counter variable.
    p) Only one check box can be selected at a time.
    q) A Visual Basic statement must be typed in its entirety on a single line.

Exercises

Exercise 1 — NumberOfDigits

Create a NumberOfDigits application that prompts the user for a number less than 100 and then when Check Number is clicked displays whether the number is one digit or two digits:

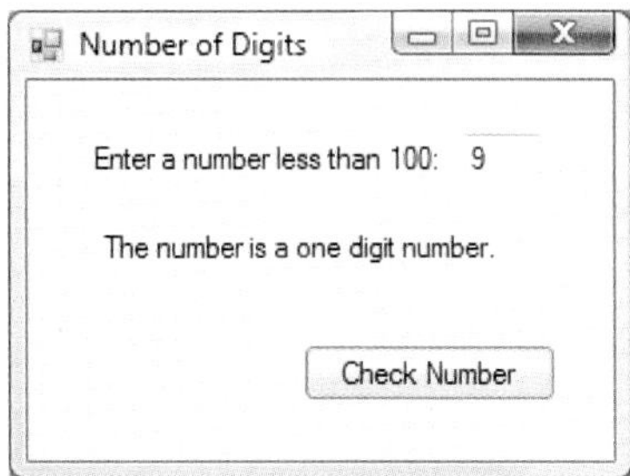

Exercise 2 — Payroll

An employee should receive pay equal to time and a half for every hour worked over 40 hours.

a) Create a Payroll application that prompts the user for the number of hours worked and the hourly rate of pay and then calculates the gross weekly wages (before taxes) when Pay is clicked:

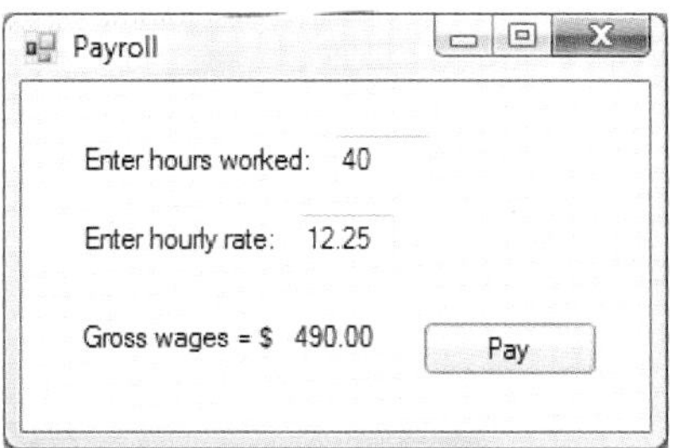

b) Modify the Payroll application so that there is an 18% deduction from gross pay, unless the employee is exempt. If an employee is exempt, "NO TAXES DEDUCTED" should be displayed in a message box and then the wages displayed. The application interface should look similar to the following for an employee that is not exempt:

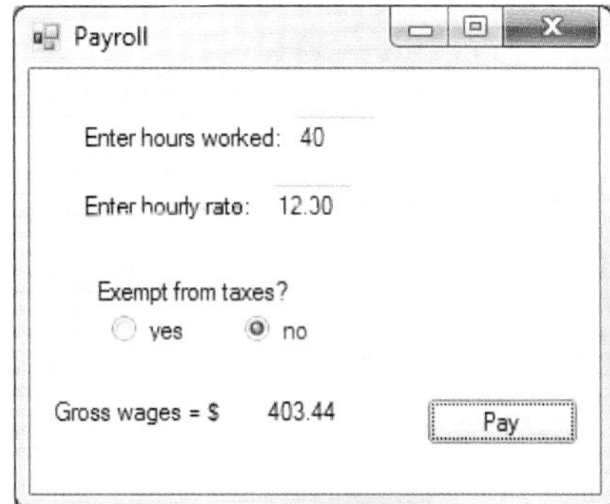

Exercise 3 — PrintingPrices

Printing prices are typically based on the number of copies to be printed. For example:

0 - 499 copies	$0.30 per copy
500 - 749 copies	$0.28 per copy
750 - 999 copies	$0.27 per copy
1000 copies or more	$0.25 per copy

Create a PrintingPrices application that prompts the user for the number of copies to print and then when Price is clicked displays the price per copy and the total price:

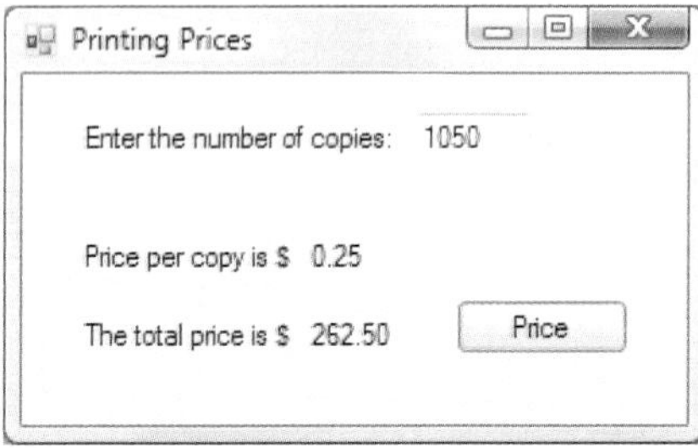

Exercise 4 — PackageCheck

A delivery service does not accept packages heavier than 27 kilograms or larger than 0.1 cubic meters (100,000 cubic centimeters). Create a PackageCheck application that prompts the user for the weight of a package and its dimensions, and when `Check Package` is clicked displays an appropriate message if the package does not meet the requirements (e.g., too large, too heavy, or both):

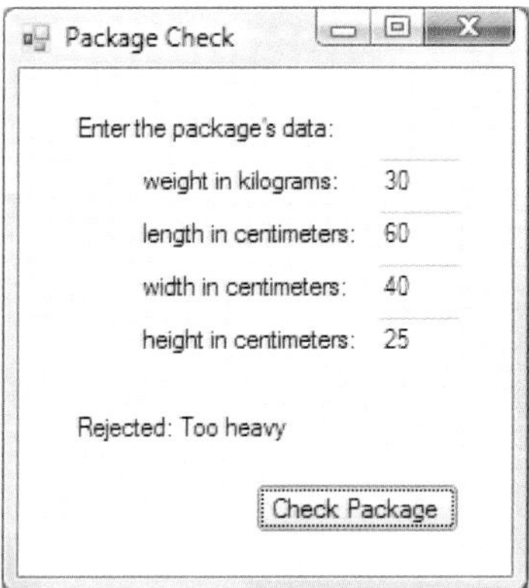

Exercise 5 — ComputerTroubleshooting

Create a ComputerTroubleshooting application that asks the user if the ailing computer beeps on startup and if the hard drive spins. If it beeps and the drive spins, have the application display "Contact tech support." If it beeps and the drive doesn't spin, have the application display "Check drive contacts." If it doesn't beep and the hard drive doesn't spin, have the application display "Bring computer to repair center." Finally, if it doesn't beep and the hard drive spins, have the application display "Check the speaker connections." The application interface should look similar to:

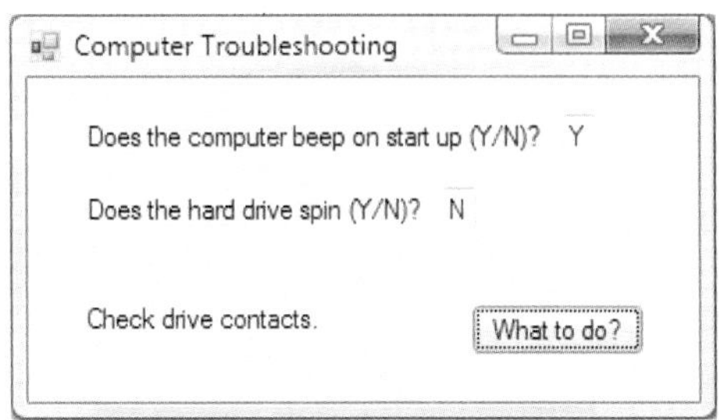

Exercise 6 — CarModels

An auto company produced some models of cars that may be difficult to drive because the car wheels are not exactly round. Cars with model numbers 119, 179, 189 through 195, 221, and 780 have been found to have this defect. Create a CarModels application that prompts a customer for the model number of their car to find out if it is defective. When Evaluate is clicked, the message "Your car is not defective." should be displayed if the user typed a model number without a defect. Otherwise, the message "Your car is defective. Please have it fixed." should be displayed:

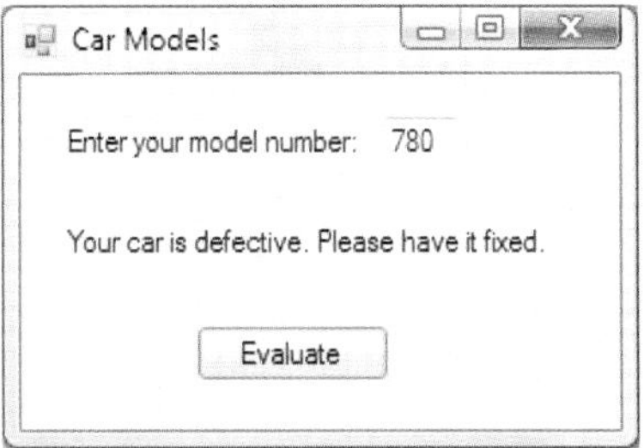

Exercise 7 — Grades

Create a Grades application that allows the user to enter one letter grade (uppercase or lowercase) after another and continuously displays the number of students who passed (D or better) and the number who failed. The application interface should look similar to the following after entering 15 grades and clicking Enter Grade:

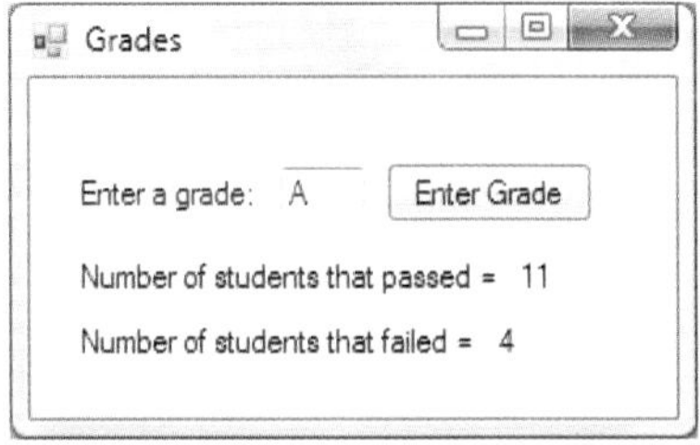

Exercise 8 — PhoneBill

Create a PhoneBill application that determines a phone bill by prompting the user for calling options (call waiting, call forwarding, and caller ID). The monthly basic service charge is $25.00 and each additional calling option is $3.50. The application interface should look similar to the following after selecting options and clicking Calculate:

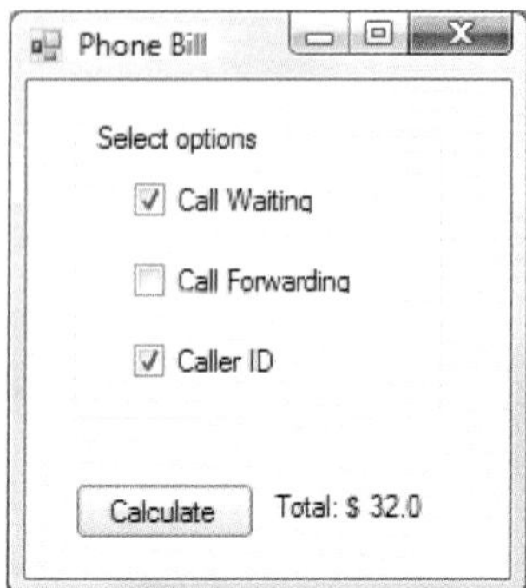

Exercise 9 — Welcome

Many programs are password protected and require the user to enter a user ID and password to get access to the application. A welcome dialog box usually looks similar to:

The password is kept secret by showing a special character, often an asterisk (*), in place of each letter typed in the text box. This can be specified from the Design window by typing * in the PasswordChar property of the text box object.

a) Create a Welcome application that prompts the user for an ID and a password. If the ID and password are correct, display a message box stating so and then end the application. If the ID is not correct display an "Incorrect ID." message box and then clear the ID text box and allow the user to enter another ID. If the password is not correct display an "Incorrect password." message box and then clear the Password text box and allow the user to enter another password. If the ID and password are both not correct display an "Incorrect ID and password." message box and then clear both text boxes and allow the user to enter another ID and password. If the user has made three incorrect attempts then display a "Sorry, access denied." message box and then end the application.

b) Modify the application to check for three different user IDs and their corresponding passwords.

Exercise 10 — MathTutor

Create a MathTutor application that displays math problems by randomly generating two numbers, 1 through 10, and an operator (*, +, –, /) and prompts the user for an answer. The application should check the answer and display a message, display the correct answer, and generate a new problem. The application interface should look similar to the following after typing a correct answer and clicking Check Answer:

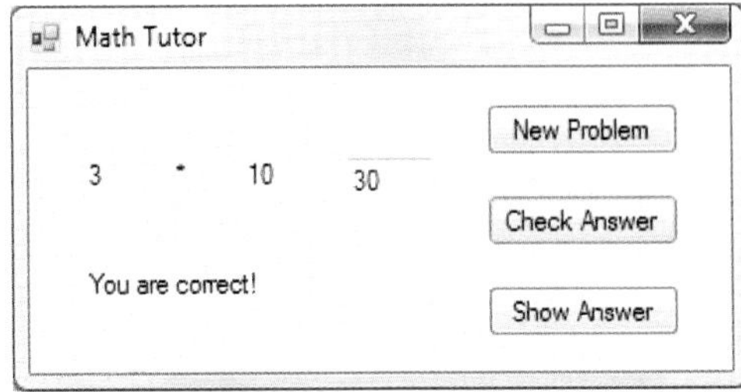

Exercise 11 — SandwichOrder

Create a SandwichOrder application that creates a sandwich order by prompting the user for the size of the sandwich (small or large) and the fixings (lettuce, tomato, onion, mustard, mayonnaise, cheese). A small sandwich is $2.50 and a large sandwich is $4.00. Mustard and mayonnaise are free, lettuce and onion are $0.10 each, tomato is $0.25, and cheese is $0.50. The defaults should be a small sandwich with no fixings. The application interface should look similar to the following after selecting options and clicking Place Order:

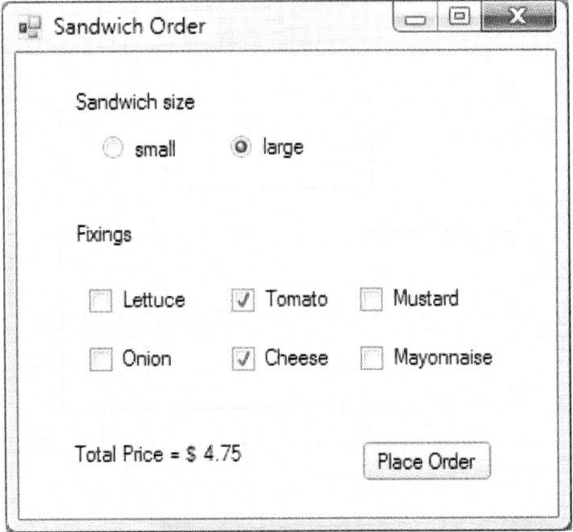

Exercise 12  GuessingGame

The GuessingGame application created in this chapter would be better if the number of guesses the user took were displayed at the end of the game.

a) Modify the GuessingGame code to include a counter that keeps track of the number of guesses made by the user. Have the application display the total number of guesses in a message box after the user correctly guesses the secret number.

b) A *binary search* is a divide-and-conquer technique for efficiently searching a list of numbers that are sorted from lowest to highest. A strategy that incorporates the binary search technique can be used by the GuessingGame player when making guesses about the secret number:

1. Guess the number halfway between the lowest and highest numbers.
2. If the number guessed matches the secret number, then the player wins.
3. If the number guessed is too high, then take the number guessed minus one and make this the highest number and go back to Step 1.
4. If the number guessed is too low, then take the number guessed plus one and make this the lowest number and go back to Step 1.

For example, assuming 15 is the random number generated in the GuessingGame application, the game would play out as follows when the player uses a divide-and-conquer technique:

Current Low	Current High	Player Types	Message Displayed
1	50	26 (i.e., (1+50)/2=25.5)	Too high.
1	25	13 (i.e., (1+25)/2=13)	Too low.
14	25	20 (i.e., (14+25)/2=19.5)	Too high.
14	19	16 (i.e., (14+19)/2=16.5)	Too high.
14	15	14 (i.e., (14+15)/2=14.5)	Too low.
15	15	15 (i.e., (15+15)/2=15)	You guessed it!

In another program run, assuming the random number generated is 20, the game would play out as follows using the same divide-and-conquer technique:

Current Low	Current High	Player Types	Message Displayed
1	50	26 (i.e., (1+50)/2=25.5)	Too high.
1	25	13 (i.e., (1+25)/2=13)	Too low.
14	25	20 (i.e., (14+25)/2=19.5)	You guessed it!

When this approach is taken, it has been proven that a player will not be required to make more than $\text{Log}_2 n$ guesses, in this case $\text{Log}_2 50$, or at most 6 guesses. Try this technique yourself. Explain in your own words why this works. Would this strategy be possible if hints were not given after each guess?

Exercise 13 — GuessTheBlocks

Create a GuessTheBlocks application to simulate a modified version of the game Mastermind. In this game, three different colored blocks are lined up and hidden from the player. The player then tries to guess the colors and the order of the blocks. There are four colored blocks (red, green, blue, yellow) to choose from. After guessing the color of the three hidden blocks the program displays how many of the colors are correct and how many of the colors are in the right position. Based on this information the player makes another guess and so on until the player has determined the correct order and color of the hidden blocks. Use R for Red, G for Green, B for Blue, and Y for Yellow. The application interface should look similar to the following after making a guess and clicking Check Guess:

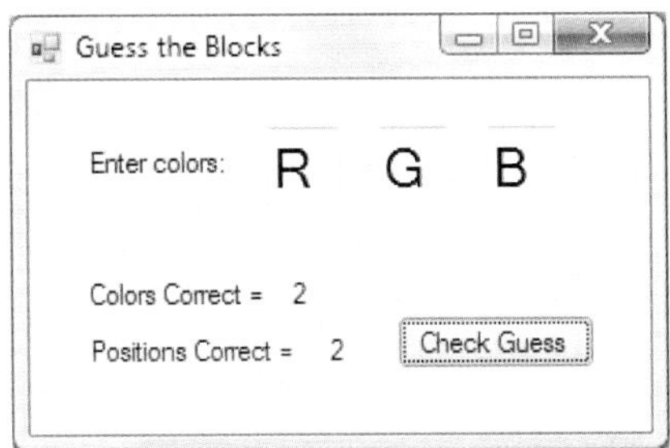

Exercise 14  — RockPaperScissors

Modify the RockPaperScissors application created in the reviews to include a Program menu with New Game and Exit commands. The New Game command should clear the labels and set all the radio buttons to False.

Exercise 15 (advanced) — GameOf21

Create a GameOf21 application to simulate a simplified version of the game "21" against the computer. A deck with cards numbered 1 through 10 is used and any number can be repeated. The program starts by dealing the user two randomly picked cards and itself three randomly picked cards that are not revealed until Check Scores is clicked. The user may then draw one card. If the user and computer scores are both over 21, or if both are equal but under 21, the game is declared a draw. Otherwise, the winner is the one with the highest score less than or equal to 21. If one score is over 21 and the other is 21 or less, the player with 21 or less is declared the winner. The result should be displayed in a message box. The application interface should include a Program menu with Play Game and Exit commands. The application should look similar to the following after cards have been dealt and drawn and Check Scores clicked:

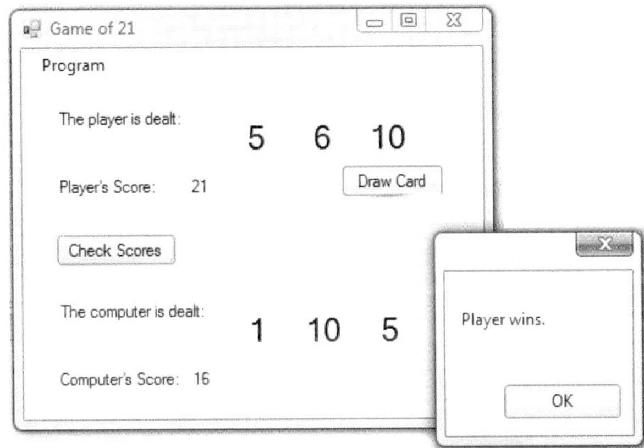

Exercise 16 — BasicMultiplication

Create a BasicMultiplication application that allows the user to multiply two numbers that are each in the range 0 through 10. The application should allow the user to select the first operand and the second operand. The NumberUpDown object is a good choice for getting input within a range. The NumberUpDown control looks similar to a text box, but includes arrows for scrolling through a list of numbers:

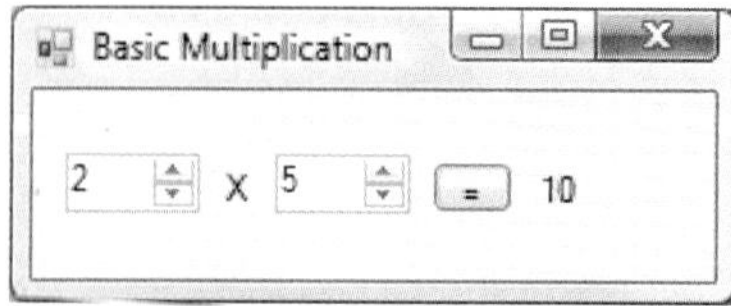

The NumberUpDown control has the properties:

- **(Name)** identifies a control for the programmer. NumberUpDown object names should begin with `num`.
- **Minimum** can be set to a value that will be the least value the user can select.
- **Maximum** can be set to a value that will be the greatest value the user can select.
- **Value** is the number selected by the user.

Exercise 17

The Show() method of the MessageBox class has several optional parameters. A MessageBox.Show() statement can take any of the following forms:

```
MessageBox.Show(message, title)
MessageBox.Show(message, title, buttons)
MessageBox.Show(message, title, buttons, icon)
```

The message and title parameters must be strings. Arguments for the buttons and icon parameters should be selected from the IntelliSense list that is displayed when a comma is typed after the second and third parameters. The IntelliSense list will include arguments for the following sets of buttons:

- `Abort, Retry, and Ignore`
- `OK`
- `OK and Cancel`
- `Retry and Cancel`
- `Yes and No`
- `Yes, No, and Cancel`

A second IntelliSense list will include arguments for the following icons:

- `asterisk`
- `error`
- `exclamation`
- `hand`
- `information`
- `question`
- `stop`
- `warning`

Experiment with the Show() method of the MessageBox class by modifying an existing exercise to include a message box.

Chapter 5
Controlling Program Flow with Looping Structures

Key Concepts

Using repetition control structures
Debugging infinite loops
Using input boxes, counters, and accumulators
Manipulating and comparing strings
Using the Char structure and its methods
Understanding Unicode
Applying problem solving strategies

Case Study

Word Guess application

The Do...Loop Statement

loop structure

iteration

The Do...Loop statement is a *loop structure* that executes a set of statements over and over again based on a condition. Repeating a set of statements is called *looping*, or *iteration*. Loop structures are used to perform tasks such as summing a set of numbers as they are entered by the user or repeatedly prompting the user for a value until valid data is entered. The first type of Do...Loop structure takes the form:

```
Do
   statements
Loop While condition
```

statements is executed at least once. condition is a Boolean expression used to determine if the loop is to be repeated. If condition is True, statements is executed again and then the condition reevaluated. The loop is repeated until condition evaluates to False. For example, in the statements

```
Dim number As Integer = 0
Do
   number = number + 2      'increment by 2
Loop While number < 10
```

the Do...Loop structure executes the loop five times. On the fifth iteration, number is 10 making the loop condition (number < 10) False.

Another form of Do...Loop evaluates a condition before executing the loop and takes the form:

```
Do While condition
   statements
Loop
```

In this case, if condition is True, statements is executed and then condition reevaluated. The loop is repeated until condition evaluates to False.

The first form of Do...Loop executes the loop at least once. The second form of Do...Loop may execute zero or more times. This is because, if condition is initially False, the loop never executes.

Infinite Loops

The condition of a loop is used to determine when the loop should stop executing. A Do...Loop continues until its condition is False. What happens, though, if the condition never becomes false? The result is an *infinite loop*—one which continues forever.

A logic error can lead to an infinite loop. For example, the following statements create an infinite loop. Can you see why?

```
Dim number As Integer = -1
Do While number < 0
   number = number - 1
Loop
```

Because number is initialized to -1 and never incremented to a positive number in the loop, the condition of the loop structure is always True. However, in this case, number is eventually assigned a number that results in an overflow and a run-time error is generated:

TIP Click the Stop Debugging button to end an infinite loop.

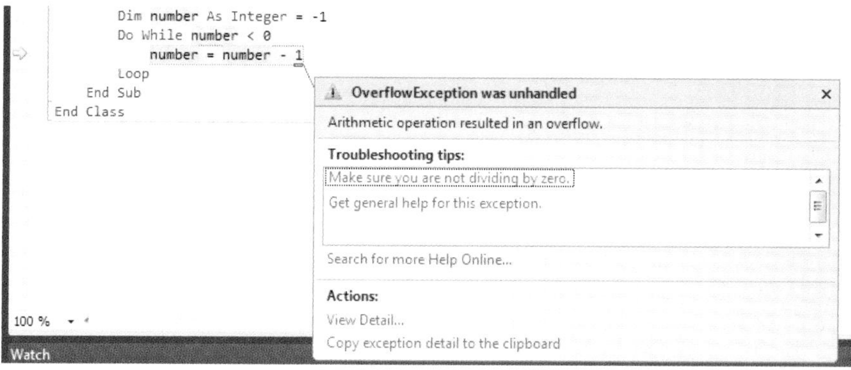

An assignment statement similar to the following will not generate an overflow error:

```
Dim number As Integer = -1
Do While number < 0
   number = -1
Loop
```

Instead, the program will simply stop responding to user events such as mouse clicks. When this happens, right-click the program icon on the Windows Taskbar and select Close window from the menu to display the following dialog box:

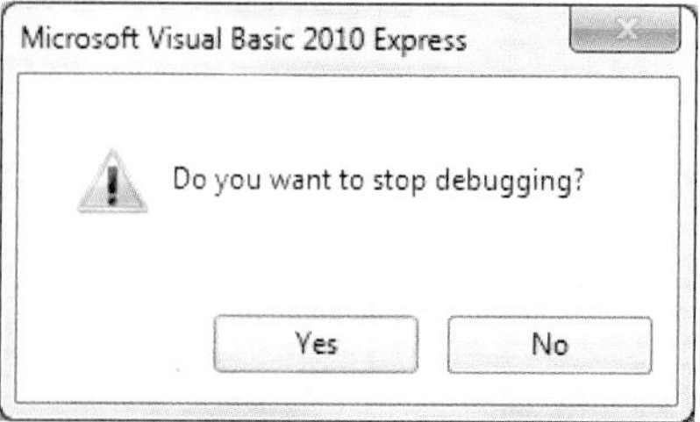

Select Yes to end the application.

Review: PrimeNumber

A prime number is an integer greater than 1 that is evenly divisible by only 1 and itself. For example, 2, 3, and 7 are prime numbers, but 4, 6, and 9 are not. Mod can be used to determine if one number evenly divides into another, and a loop can be used to generate divisors between 1 and the number entered. The pseudocode for determining a prime number is:

```
Get testNum from user
divisor = 1
If testNum <= 1 Then
    Display message that testNum is not prime
Else
    Do
        Increment divisor by 1
    Loop While testNum Mod Divisor <> 0
    If divisor = testNum Then
        Display message that testNum is prime
    Else
        Display message that testNum is not prime
    End If
End If
```

① CREATE A NEW PROJECT

Create a Windows application named PrimeNumber.

② CREATE THE INTERFACE

Use the table below for setting object properties.

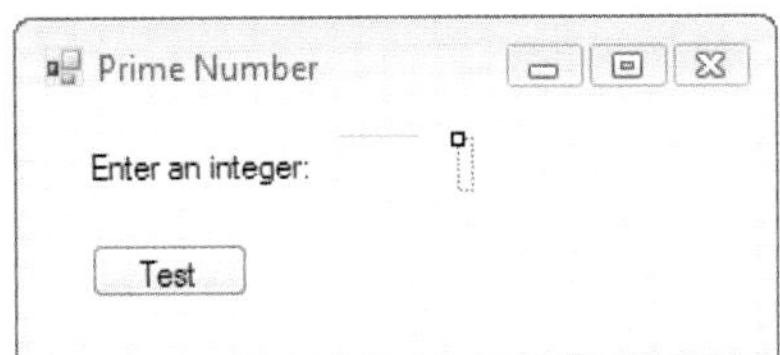

Object	(Name)	Text
Form1		Prime Number
Label1	lblIntegerPrompt	Enter an integer:
TextBox1	txtInteger	*empty*
Label2	lblPrimeResult	*empty*
Button1	btnTest	Test

③ WRITE THE APPLICATION CODE

a. Display the Code window.

b. Add comments that include your name, assignment, and today's date.

c. Create a btnTest_Click event procedure and then add the statements:

```
'Get number from user
Dim testNum As Integer = Val(Me.txtInteger.Text)

'Test number
Dim divisor As Integer = 1
If testNum <= 1 Then                    '1 and negatives are not prime numbers
    Me.lblPrimeResult.Text = "Not a prime number."
Else
```

```
        Do
            divisor += 1
        Loop While testNum Mod divisor <> 0
        If divisor = testNum Then
            Me.lblPrimeResult.Text = "Prime number."
        Else
            Me.lblPrimeResult.Text = "Not a prime number."
        End If
    End If
```

d. Create a txtInteger_TextChanged event procedure and then add the statements:

```
'Clear the previous test result
Me.lblPrimeResult.Text = Nothing
```

④ RUN THE APPLICATION

a. Save the modified PrimeNumber project.
b. Run the application. Type 7 and then click Test. The number is prime.
c. Try other prime and nonprime numbers to test the application.
d. Close the PrimeNumber application.

⑤ PRINT THE CODE AND THEN CLOSE THE PROJECT

Using an Input Box

An input box is a predefined dialog box that has a prompt, a text box, and OK and Cancel buttons. It is used to get information from the user and looks similar to:

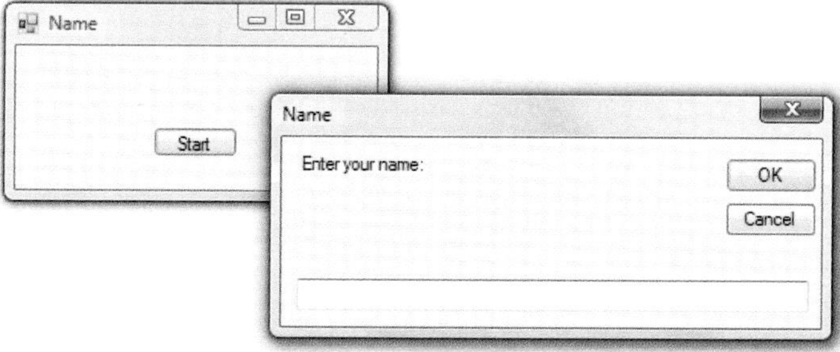

The InputBox() function displays an input box and is used in a statement that takes the form:

```
stringVar = InputBox(prompt, title)
```

`prompt` is a `String` variable or a string enclosed in quotation marks that is displayed as a prompt in the input box. `title` is an optional `String` variable or a string enclosed in quotation marks that is displayed in the title bar of the input box. When OK is selected, the data in the text box is assigned to `stringVar`, a `String` variable. For example, the following statement prompts the user for a name and then assigns the text entered to a label:

```
Me.lblUserName.Text = InputBox("Enter your name", "Name")
```

TIP Use `Me.Text` for the title in the InputBox() function call to display the text from the form's title bar.

If the user selects Cancel or leaves the text box blank, `Nothing` is returned by the InputBox() function. Testing for `Nothing` is good programming style and can be done using code similar to:

```
Dim textEntered As String
textEntered = InputBox("Enter your name", "Name")

'Test data entered
If textEntered = Nothing Then          'Cancel or empty textbox
  Me.lblUserName.Text = "Canceled."
Else                                   'text entered
  Me.lblUserName.Text = textEntered
End If
```

If the user is expected to enter a numeric value in an input box, the Val() function should be used to convert the entry to a number after checking for `Nothing`. For example, the following statements assign a numeric value to an `Integer` variable:

```
Dim stock As Integer
Dim numEntered As String
numEntered = InputBox("Enter the amount in stock", "Stock")

If numEntered <> Nothing Then
  stock = Val(numEntered)
End If
```

Accumulator Variables

An *accumulator* is a variable storing a number that is incremented by a changing amount. The statement for updating an accumulator takes the form:

```
accumulator = accumulator + value
```

`accumulator` is the numeric variable that is updated. `value` is the number that is added to the current value of `accumulator`. Unlike a counter which is updated by a set amount, the value that is used to update an accumulator can vary. An accumulator is often within a loop structure and is useful for keeping a *running total* or sum, as in the statement:

running total

```
totalScore += newScore
```

In this statement, `totalScore` is the name of the accumulator variable. Each time the statement is executed, the value of `newScore` is added to the current value of `totalScore` and then this new value assigned to `totalScore`.

In addition to `+=` and `-=`, Visual Basic includes the `*=`, `\=`, `/=`, and `^=` operators for updating accumulators.

An accumulator should be initialized when it is declared. An accumulator in an event procedure should be declared as a `Static` variable so that it is initialized only once.

Using Flags

sentinel

A *flag*, also called a *sentinel*, is a condition used to signify that a loop should stop executing. This approach provides a clear and easy-to-change method for ending a loop. For example, in the loop below the value -1 "flags" the loop to stop executing:

```
Const FLAG As Integer = -1
Dim newNumber As Integer
Dim total As Integer = 0
Dim tempNumber As String

tempNumber = InputBox("Enter a positive number (-1 to stop)")
Do While tempNumber <> Nothing And Val(tempNumber) <> FLAG
    newNumber = Val(tempNumber)
    total += newNumber
    tempNumber = InputBox("Enter a positive number (-1 to stop)")
Loop
```

The code above defines the sentinel as a constant. Another approach is to use a variable and prompt the user for the sentinel value.

Review: AverageScore

The average of a set of scores is calculated by dividing the sum of the scores by the number of scores. The pseudocode for computing an average score is:

```
Prompt user for a score
Do While score is not equal to Nothing and score is not equal to flag
    Increment count by 1
    score = Val(userEntry)
    Add score to sum of scores
    Prompt user for next score
Loop
Average Score = (sum of scores)/(count of scores)
```

① CREATE A NEW PROJECT

Create a Windows application named `AverageScore`.

② CREATE THE INTERFACE

Use the table on the next page for setting object properties.

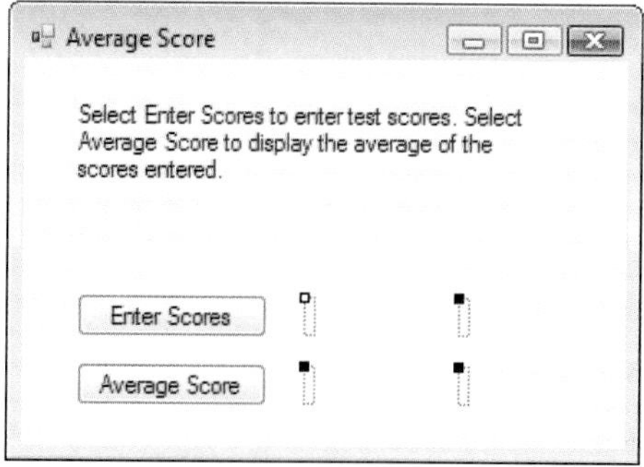

Object	(Name)	Text
Form1		Average Score
Label1	lblInstructions	*See interface*
Button1	btnEnterScores	Enter Scores
Button2	btnAverageScore	Average Score
Label2	lblScoresMessage	*empty*
Label3	lblNumberofScores	*empty*
Label4	lblAverageMessage	*empty*
Label5	lblAverage	*empty*

③ WRITE THE APPLICATION CODE

a. Display the Code window.

b. Add comments that include your name, assignment, and today's date.

c. Add two global variable declarations:

```
Dim numberOfScores As Integer = 0
Dim sumOfScores As Integer = 0
```

d. Create a btnEnterScores_Click event procedure and then add the statements:

```
Const TITLE As String = "Scores"
Const PROMPT As String = "Enter a score (-1 to stop):"
Const FLAG As Integer = -1                'loop flag
Dim tempScore As String
Dim newScore As Integer
numberOfScores = 0                        'reinitialize global counter
sumOfScores = 0                           'reinitialize global accumulator

'Clear labels
Me.lblAverageMessage.Text = Nothing
Me.lblAverage.Text = Nothing
Me.lblScoresMessage.Text = Nothing
Me.lblNumberofScores.Text = Nothing

'Get scores
tempScore = InputBox(PROMPT, TITLE)
Do While tempScore <> Nothing And Val(tempScore) <> FLAG
    newScore = Val(tempScore)
    numberOfScores += 1                   'update scores count
    sumOfScores += newScore               'update scores sum
    tempScore = InputBox(PROMPT, TITLE)   'get next score
Loop

Me.lblScoresMessage.Text = "Scores entered:"
Me.lblNumberofScores.Text = numberOfScores
```

e. Create a btnAverageScore_Click event procedure and then add the statements:

```
Dim average As Double
Me.lblAverageMessage.Text = "Average score:"
If numberOfScores > 0 Then
    average = sumOfScores / numberOfScores     'compute average
    Me.lblAverage.Text = average
Else
    Me.lblAverage.Text = 0
End If
```

④ RUN THE APPLICATION

a. Save the modified AverageScore project.

b. Run the application. Test AverageScore with several sets of scores and then close the application.

⑤ PRINT THE CODE AND THEN CLOSE THE PROJECT

Review: UniqueRandomNumbers

Create a UniqueRandomNumbers application that prompts the user for a number greater than 3 and then generates three unique random numbers between 1 and the number entered. Use a loop to repeatedly generate three random numbers until all three numbers are different. Include a counter in the loop to count the number of loop iterations required. The application interface should look similar to that shown on the right after clicking Generate Numbers and entering 5.

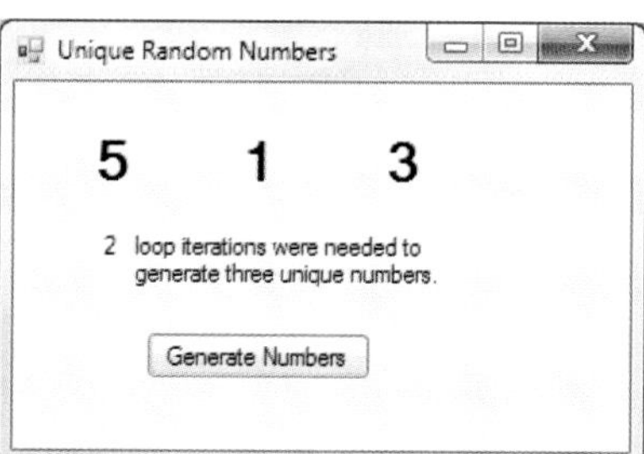

The For...Next Statement

The `For...Next` statement is a loop structure that executes a set of statements a fixed number of times. Unlike a `Do...Loop` that executes while a condition is true, `For...Next` executes until a counter reaches an ending value. The `For...Next` statement takes the form:

```
For counter As Integer = start To end
  statements
Next counter
```

`counter`, `start`, and `end` are `Integer` variables, values, or expressions. `counter` is initialized to `start` (`counter = start`) only once when the loop executes, and compared to `end` before each loop iteration. `counter` is automatically incremented by 1 each time the `Next` clause is reached.

Note that the counter variable is declared in the `For...Next` statement (`counter As Integer`). When a declaration is in this location, the scope of the variable is from the initialization to the `Next` statement. The variable will not be recognized outside of the `For...Next` statement. This code convention produces cleaner code and helps eliminate the possibility of errors.

With each iteration of the following `For...Next`, a message box is displayed. In this case, 10 message boxes in all will be displayed with numbers counting from 1 to 10:

```
For number As Integer = 1 To 10
  MessageBox.Show(number)
Next number
```

While it is possible to modify the value of the counter or to terminate the loop prematurely, this is considered poor programming style.

A `For...Next` statement can include the keyword `Step` to change the way `counter` is incremented. For example, the following `For...Next` loop increments the counter by 2 with each iteration to sum all the even numbers between 2 and 8:

```
Dim start As Integer = 2
Dim end As Integer = 8
Dim stepAmt As Integer = 2
Dim sum As Integer = 0

For count As Integer = start To end Step stepAmt
   sum += count                    'update sum
Next count
Me.lblEvenSum.Text = sum          '2+4+6+8
```

`Step` may also be used to decrement a counter. For example, the statements below count down from 10 to 1 with each number being displayed in a message box:

```
For number As Integer = 10 To 1 Step -1
   MessageBox.Show(number)
Next number
```

Review: Factorial

The factorial of a number is the product of all the positive integers from 1 to the number. For example, 3 factorial, written as 3!, is 3 * 2 * 1, or 6. The pseudocode for computing the factorial of a number is:

```
Get a number from the user
factorial = 1
For count = 1 To number
    factorial *= count
Next count
```

① CREATE A NEW PROJECT

Create a Windows application named `Factorial`.

② CREATE THE INTERFACE

Use the table below for setting object properties.

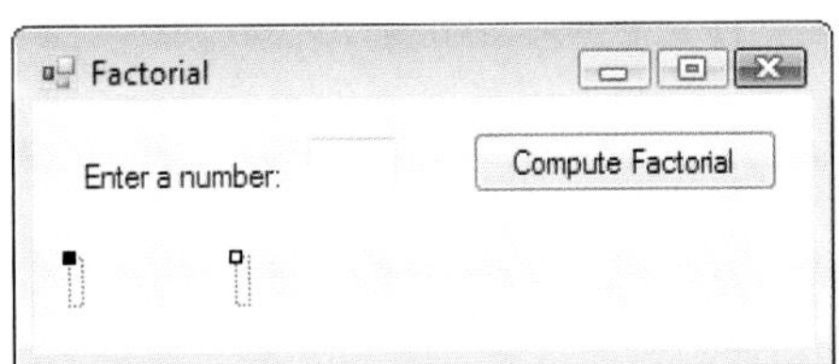

Object	(Name)	Text
Form1		`Factorial`
Label1	`lblNumberPrompt`	`Enter a number:`
TextBox1	`txtNumber`	*empty*
Button1	`btnComputeFactorial`	`Compute Factorial`
Label2	`lblFactorialMessage`	*empty*
Label3	`lblFactorial`	*empty*

③ WRITE THE APPLICATION CODE

a. Display the Code window.

b. Add comments that include your name, assignment, and today's date.

c. Create a btnComputeFactorial_Click event procedure and then add the statements:

```
Dim factorial As Double = 1
Dim number As Integer

number = Val(Me.txtNumber.Text)     'get number from user
For count As Integer = 1 To number
    factorial *= count
Next count

Me.lblFactorialMessage.Text = "Factorial is:"
Me.lblFactorial.Text = factorial
```

d. Create a txtNumber_TextChanged event procedure and then add the statements:

```
Me.lblFactorialMessage.Text = Nothing
Me.lblFactorial.Text = Nothing
```

④ RUN THE APPLICATION

a. Save the modified Factorial project and then run the application. Test the application with several different numbers, including 0 and 1.

b. Close the Factorial application.

⑤ PRINT THE CODE AND THEN CLOSE THE PROJECT

Review: OddNumbersSum

Create an OddNumbersSum application that displays the sum of the odd numbers from 1 to a maximum value entered by the user.

The String Class

members
object

The `String` data type is a class. A class includes properties and methods called *members*. When a class is used to create a variable, the variable is called an *object*. An object accesses a member of its class with a dot (.) between the object name and the member name. Property members of the `String` class are:

TIP A class is an abstract data type.

- **Chars(*index*)** returns the character at the specified position `index` in a `String` object, with the first character of a string at index 0.
- **Length** returns the number of characters in a String object.

The code below demonstrates the `String` class properties:

```
Dim season As String = "Summer"
Dim letter As Char
Dim numChars As Integer

letter = season.Chars(4)       'e
numChars = season.Length       '6
```

method

A *method* is a procedure in a class. The `String` class contains several method members for manipulating strings:

StrConv() Function

The built-in StrConv() function can be used to change each word in a string to mixed case, with the first letter of each word in uppercase and the remaining letters in lowercase.

- **ToUpper** converts a `String` object to all uppercase characters.
- **ToLower** converts a `String` object to all lowercase characters.
- **Trim** removes all spaces from the beginning and end of a `String` object.
- **TrimEnd** removes all spaces from the end of a `String` object.
- **TrimStart** removes all spaces from the beginning of a `String` object.
- **PadLeft(*len*, *char*)** adds a specified character to the beginning of a `String` object until the string is a specified length. `len` is the padded length of the string and `char` is a character in quotation marks or a `Char` variable.
- **PadRight(*len*, *char*)** adds a specified character to the end of a `String` object until the string is a specified length. `len` is the padded length of the string and `char` is a character in quotation marks or a `Char` variable.

The code below demonstrates the `String` methods:

```
Dim season As String = "SummerTime"
Dim newString As String

newString = season.ToUpper             'SUMMERTIME
newString = season.ToLower             'summertime

season = "     SummerTime     "
newString = season.Trim                'SummerTime
newString = season.TrimEnd             '     SummerTime
newString = season.TrimStart           'SummerTime

season = "SummerTime"
newString = season.PadLeft(15, "x")    'xxxxxSummerTime
newString = season.PadLeft(9, "x")     'SummerTime
newString = season.PadRight(13, "x")   'SummerTimexxx
```

substring

The `String` class also contains methods that return a portion of a string called a *substring*. Other methods modify or insert substrings. These methods include:

- **Substring(*startPos*, *numOfChars*)** returns a substring of the `String` object. `startPos` indicates the position of the character that starts the substring, with the first character of a string at position 0. `numOfChars` indicates the length of the substring.
- **Remove(*startPos*, *numOfChars*)** deletes a substring from the `String` object. `startPos` indicates the position of the character to start deleting, with the first character of a string at position 0. `numOfChars` indicates the number of characters to delete.

- **Replace(*oldString, newString*)** exchanges every occurrence of a substring in the `String` object with a new string. `oldString` is an existing substring. `newString` is the string to replace *oldString*.
- **Insert(*startPos, substring*)** inserts a substring in the `String` object. *startPos* indicates the position to place `substring`, with the first character of a string at position 0.
- **IndexOf(*substring*)** returns the position of the first occurrence of `substring` in the `String` object, with the first character of a string at position 0. `-1` is returned if the `substring` is not found.

When using the Substring() and Remove() methods, it may be necessary to first use the Length property to determine how many characters are in a string. Otherwise, if `numOfChars` exceeds the number of characters in the string, a run-time error will occur. An application is considered *robust* if it can perform even under unexpected circumstances, such as when a string isn't the expected length.

robust

The following code demonstrates the `String` methods:

```
Dim season As String = "SummerTime"
Dim newStr As String
Dim pos As Integer

newStr = season.Substring(6, 4)              'Time
newStr = season.Remove(0, 6)         'Time
newStr = season.Replace("Time", " is fun!")  'Summer is fun!
newStr = season.Insert(6, " is a fun ")      'Summer is a fun Time
pos = season.IndexOf("mer")                  '3
```

Review: LetterCount

Create a LetterCount application that displays the number of times a specific letter occurs in a word or phrase. Uppercase and lowercase characters should be counted. The application interface should look similar to that on the right after typing `Is it summer vacation yet?`, the letter `i`, and clicking Count Letter.

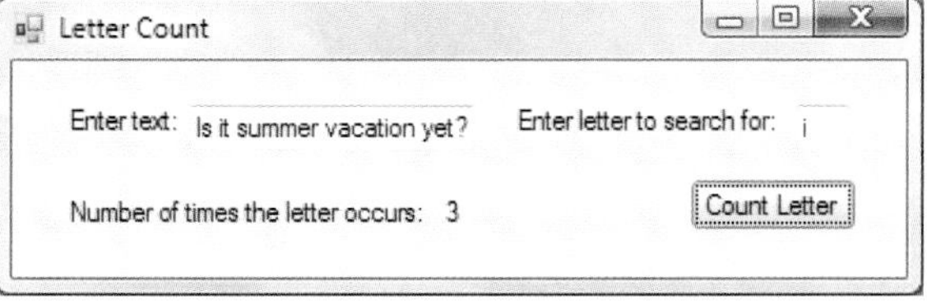

Review: StringTest

Create a StringTest application that displays the first letter, last letter, and middle letter of a word or phrase. The application interface should look similar to that shown on the right after typing `directory` and clicking Display Data.

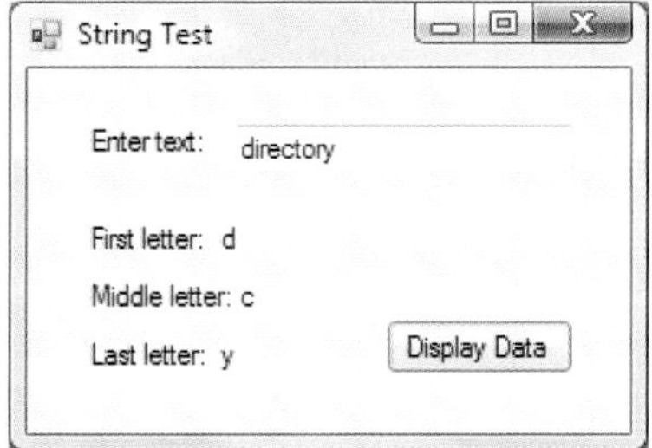

Review: FindString

Create a FindString application that displays the first position of a word or phrase in another word or phrase. Use text boxes to prompt the user for a string and a search substring. The application interface should look similar to that shown on the right after typing the strings and clicking **Find String**.

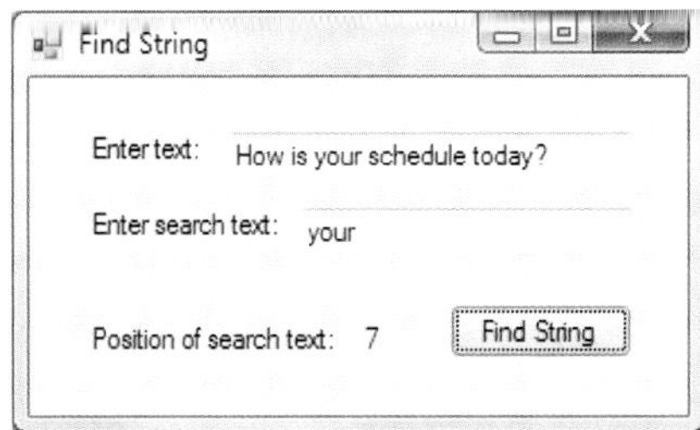

String Concatenation

Two or more strings can be joined together in a process called concatenation. Strings that have been joined are said to be *concatenated*. The String class method for concatenation is:

- **Concat(*string1*, *string2*, ...)** concats two or more strings into one string. `string1`, `string2`, and so on can be strings in quotation marks or `String` variables.

shared method

The Concat() method is a *shared method* which means that it must be used with the `String` class, not with a particular object. The code below demonstrates the Concat() method:

```
Dim season As String = "Summertime"
Dim message As String = " is a fun time!"
Dim newString As String

'Summertime is a fun time!
newString = String.Concat(season, message)
```

The `&=` assignment operator can be used in place of the Concat() method. For example,

```
Dim season as String = "Summertime"
season &= " is a fun time!"    'Summertime is a fun time!
```

The `&` operator can also be used to concatenate strings. The `&` operator is used in an expression similar to the following:

```
newString = string1 & string2
```

`newString` is a `String` variable that will store the result of the expression. `string1` and `string2` are `String` variables or strings enclosed in quotation marks. The following code demonstrates `&`:

```
Dim firstName As String, lastName As String
Dim fullName As String

firstName = "Carlos"
lastName = "Celino"
fullName = firstName & " " & lastName        'Carlos Celino
```

The Space() function is a built-in function that returns a string of spaces. The Space() function takes the form:

```
Space(numOfSpaces)
```

`numOfSpaces` is an `Integer` variable or a value indicating the number of spaces for the returned string. The following code demonstrates Space():

```
Dim blanks As String
blanks = "10" & Space(10) & "spaces"   '10          spaces
```

Visual Basic contains two built-in constants that are useful for formatting strings. The `vbTab` constant can be used to place a string into the next field of eight characters. The `vbCrLf` constant represents a carriage return-linefeed combination and is used to move text to a new line. The following statements demonstrate `vbTab` and `vbCrLf`:

```
Dim message As String
message = "Hello" & vbTab & "and" & vbCrLf & "Good-bye"
MessageBox.Show(message)
```

Review: FullName

Create a FullName application that prompts the user for a first name and last name in two separate input boxes when Start is clicked and then displays in a label the first name and last name concatenated with a space between. The application interface should look similar to that shown on the right after clicking Start and entering two names.

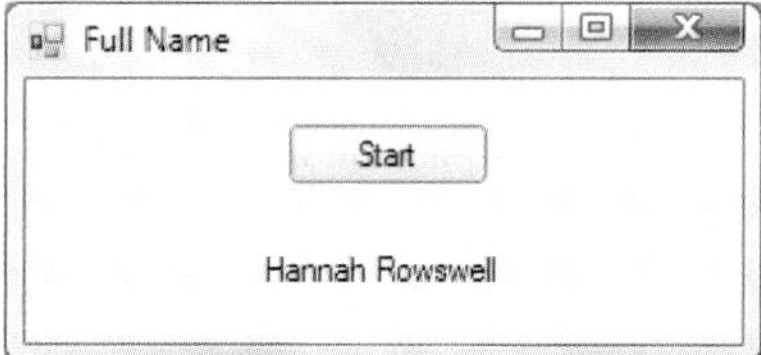

The Char Structure

structure

The `Char` data type is a structure. A *structure* is a simple form of a class. Like a class, a structure has properties and methods. The differences between structures and classes are discussed later in the text.

The ToUpper() and ToLower() Char methods are similar to the `String` class methods ToUpper() and ToLower(). However, the `Char` methods are shared methods that must be used with the `Char` structure. The code below demonstrates the methods:

```
Dim letter1 As Char = "b"
Dim letter2 As Char = "E"
Dim newLetter As Char

newLetter = Char.ToUpper(letter1)      'B
newLetter = Char.ToLower(letter2)      'e
```

Unicode

> ### *The Unicode Set*
>
> Unicode uses 2 bytes to represent a character. When 2 bytes are used, there are 2^{16} or 65,536 possible codes.

Every letter of an alphabet (Latin, Japanese, Cherokee, and so on) and symbols of every culture (=, @, ½, and so on) have been given a representation in a digital code called Unicode. *Unicode* uses a set of sixteen 1s and 0s to form a 16-bit binary code for each symbol. For example, the uppercase letter V is Unicode 00000000 01010110, which can be thought of as the base 10 number 86 (86_{10}). Lowercase v has a separate code of 00000000 01110110, or 118_{10}. Below is a table of some Unicode symbols and their corresponding decimal and binary equivalents.

Visual Basic includes two built-in functions for converting between characters and Unicode:

- **AscW(*char*)** returns the integer Unicode value of `char`. `char` is a character in quotation marks or a `Char` variable.
- **ChrW(*integer*)** returns the character corresponding to `integer`.

The following code demonstrates the conversion functions:

```
Dim testChar As Char
Dim charCode As Integer

testChar = ChrW(65)        'A
testChar = ChrW(37)        '%
charCode = AscW("A")       '65
charCode = AscW("%")       '37
```

Decimal	Binary	Unicode Symbol
32	00000000 00100000	*space*
33	00000000 00100001	!
34	00000000 00100010	"
35	00000000 00100011	#
36	00000000 00100100	$
37	00000000 00100101	%
38	00000000 00100110	&
39	00000000 00100111	'
40	00000000 00101000	(
41	00000000 00101001	)
42	00000000 00101010	*
43	00000000 00101011	+
44	00000000 00101100	,
45	00000000 00101101	-
46	00000000 00101110	.
47	00000000 00101111	/
48	00000000 00110000	0
49	00000000 00110001	1
50	00000000 00110010	2
51	00000000 00110011	3
52	00000000 00110100	4
53	00000000 00110101	5
54	00000000 00110110	6
55	00000000 00110111	7
56	00000000 00111000	8
57	00000000 00111001	9
58	00000000 00111010	:
59	00000000 00111011	;
60	00000000 00111100	<
61	00000000 00111101	=
62	00000000 00111110	>
63	00000000 00111111	?

Decimal	Binary	Unicode Symbol
64	00000000 01000000	@
65	00000000 01000001	A
66	00000000 01000010	B
67	00000000 01000011	C
68	00000000 01000100	D
69	00000000 01000101	E
70	00000000 01000110	F
71	00000000 01000111	G
72	00000000 01001000	H
73	00000000 01001001	I
74	00000000 01001010	J
75	00000000 01001011	K
76	00000000 01001100	L
77	00000000 01001101	M
78	00000000 01001110	N
79	00000000 01001111	O
80	00000000 01010000	P
81	00000000 01010001	Q
82	00000000 01010010	R
83	00000000 01010011	S
84	00000000 01010100	T
85	00000000 01010101	U
86	00000000 01010110	V
87	00000000 01010111	W
88	00000000 01011000	X
89	00000000 01011001	Y
90	00000000 01011010	Z
91	00000000 01011011	[
92	00000000 01011100	\
93	00000000 01011101	]
94	00000000 01011110	^
95	00000000 01011111	_

Decimal	Binary	Unicode Symbol
96	00000000 01100000	`
97	00000000 01100001	a
98	00000000 01100010	b
99	00000000 01100011	c
100	00000000 01100100	d
101	00000000 01100101	e
102	00000000 01100110	f
103	00000000 01100111	g
104	00000000 01101000	h
105	00000000 01101001	i
106	00000000 01101010	j
107	00000000 01101011	k
108	00000000 01101100	l
109	00000000 01101101	m
110	00000000 01101110	n
111	00000000 01101111	o
112	00000000 01110000	p
113	00000000 01110001	q
114	00000000 01110010	r
115	00000000 01110011	s
116	00000000 01110100	t
117	00000000 01110101	u
118	00000000 01110110	v
119	00000000 01110111	w
120	00000000 01111000	x
121	00000000 01111001	y
122	00000000 01111010	z
123	00000000 01111011	{
124	00000000 01111100	|
125	00000000 01111101	}
126	00000000 01111110	~

Review: SecretMessageDecoder

Create a SecretMessageDecoder application that uses a loop to prompt the user for six uppercase letters in six input boxes when Start is clicked. After the user enters the letters, a coded message is displayed in a label. The code is the set of base 10 numbers corresponding to the lowercase of the letters entered. The application interface should look similar to that shown on the right clicking Start and entering H, O, M, B, R, E.

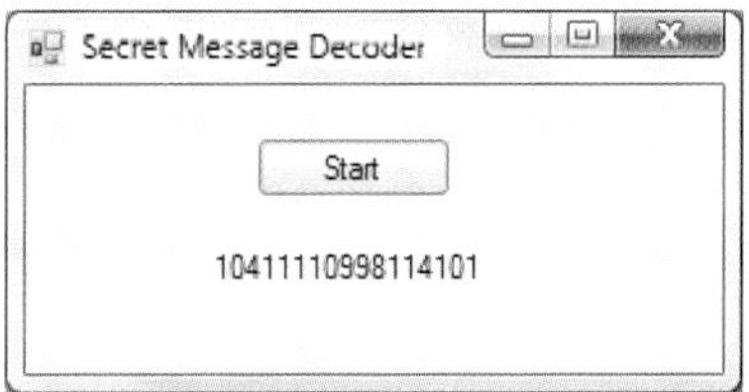

Comparing Strings

> ***The String Equals() Method***
>
> **Equals(*string1, string2*)** returns `True` if *string1* and *string2* are the same, including case. Otherwise `False` is returned.

A program will often need to alphabetically compare strings. For example, a list of names may need to be displayed in alphabetical order or a user's name may need to be compared to a list of permitted users. Relational operators (=, >, <, >=, <=, <>) can be used to compare strings. However, they use the Unicode values of the strings to determine the relationship between the strings. This can give unexpected results because uppercase and lowercase letters have different values. For example, "j" and "J" are two different Unicode values.

The Compare() method in the `String` class should be used to alphabetically compare strings:

- **Compare(*string1, string2, Case-insensitive*)** returns `0` if `string1` and `string2` are the same. A positive number is returned if `string1` is greater than `string2` and a negative number if `string1` is less than `string2`. Case-insensitive should be `True` if the case of the strings should not be considered. A `False` will compare the case of the strings as well.

The following code demonstrates the String Compare() method:

```
Dim name As String = "Chris"
Dim newName As String

newName = "chris"
Select String.Compare(name, newName, True)
  Case 0
      Me.lblMessage.Text = "The same."
  Case Is < 0
      Me.lblMessage.Text = "Alphabetically before."
  Case Is > 0
      Me.lblMessage.Text = "Alphabetically after."
End Select
```

Review: CompareWords

Create a CompareWords application that prompts the user for two words and then textually compares the words to determine if they are equal or if the first word comes alphabetically before or after the second word. The application interface should look similar to that shown on the right after entering `minimum` and `maximum` and clicking Compare Words.

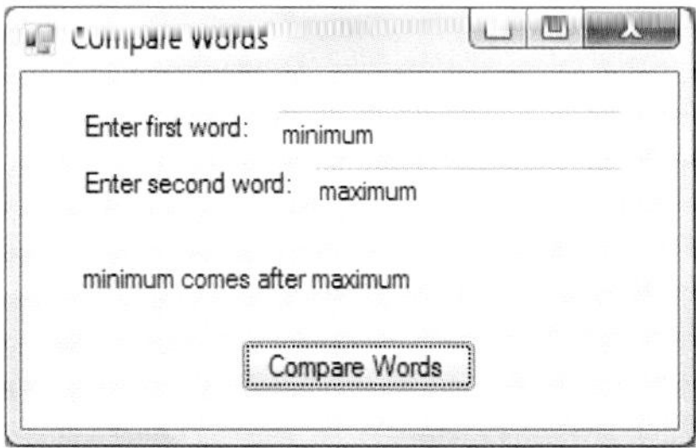

The Like Operator

pattern matching

The `Like` operator is also used to perform a textual comparison between two strings. However, `Like` can be used to perform pattern matching. *Pattern matching* allows wildcard characters, character lists, and character ranges to match strings. The `Like` operator is used in a statement and takes the form:

```
result = string Like pattern
```

`result` is a `Boolean` variable that is assigned `True` if `string` matches `pattern` and `False` otherwise. `string` is a `String` variable or a string enclosed in quotation marks. pattern can be in many forms:

- ? used in place of any single character
- * used in place of many characters
- # used in place of any single number
- [] used to enclose a list of characters
- – used to indicate a range of characters in a character list
- , used to separate characters in a character list

The following code demonstrates `Like`:

```
Dim word As String
Dim pattern As String
word = "Run"
pattern = "?un"
Me.lblMessage.Text = word Like pattern        'displays True

word = "Run"
pattern = "?um"
Me.lblMessage.Text = word Like pattern        'displays False

word = "Letter to Suzy"
pattern = "Letter to *"
Me.lblMessage.Text = word Like pattern        'displays True

word = "Case 9876"
pattern = "Case 987#"
Me.lblMessage.Text = word Like pattern        'displays True

word = "Case 9876"
pattern = "Case ##6#"
Me.lblMessage.Text = word Like pattern        'displays False
```

```
word = "C"
pattern = "[A,B,C,D,E,F]"
Me.lblMessage.Text = word Like pattern        'displays True

word = "B"
pattern = "[A-F]"
Me.lblMessage.Text = word Like pattern        'displays True
```

Case Study

In this case study a WordGuess application will be created. The WordGuess application allows the player to guess the letters of a secret word. At the start of the game, the player is shown only how many letters the word contains through a set of dashes. When a letter matching one in the word is guessed, it replaces the appropriate dash. Play continues until the entire word is guessed letter-by-letter or when the player chooses to guess the entire word.

WordGuess Specification

WordGuess is played between the computer and a single player. The secret word is VELOCITY. At the start of the game, eight dashes are displayed (--------), one for each letter of the word. The player is repeatedly prompted for a letter guess. When a letter matching one in the word is guessed, the letter replaces the corresponding dash. Letters may be entered as uppercase or lowercase. However, only uppercase letters should be displayed. If the player enters an exclamation point (!), the player is prompted to guess the word. At that point the player either wins (a correct guess) or loses (an incorrect guess). Alternatively, the player can continue to guess letters until the entire word is revealed. The games ends by showing the player the total number of guesses.

WordGuess Design

The interface design should have a label with a font sized large enough to show the secret word prominently on the form. Since the user is to be prompted automatically, an input box will be used, so there is no need for a text box. A button allows the user to start the game:

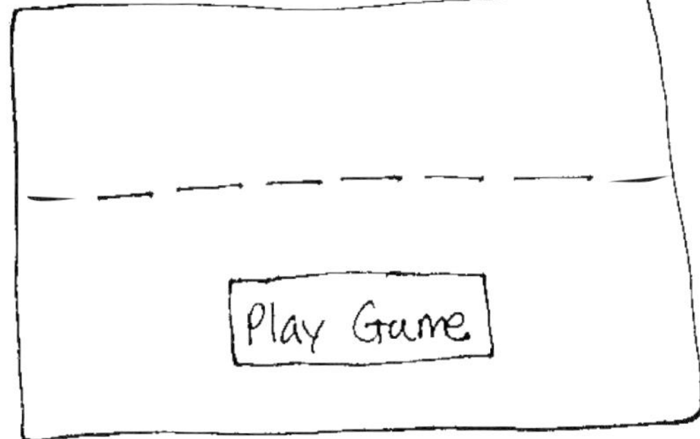

The code design should start with an algorithm and also pseudocode:

1. Display the same number of dashes as in the secret word.
2. Prompt the user for a letter, but also allow the user to enter a flag if ready to guess the entire word.

3. Increment a guess counter.
4. If a letter was entered determine if the letter is in the secret word and then display the letter entered in the proper position on the form.
5. If the flag was entered, prompt the user for the entire word.
6. Repeat step 1 until the word has been guessed or the user gives up by clicking Cancel in the input box or leaves the input box empty.

The algorithm is implemented with the following pseudocode:

```
Sub btnPlayGame_Click()
    Const SECRET_WORD As String = "VELOCITY"
    Const FLAG As Char = "!"
    Static numGuesses As Integer = 0
    Dim letterGuess As Char
    Dim wordGuess As String
    Dim letterPos As Integer
    Dim tempWord As String
    Dim endGame As Boolean

    Dim wordGuessedSoFar = ""
    Dim length = SECRET_WORD.Length
    wordGuessedSoFar = wordGuessedSoFar.PadLeft(Length, "-")
    Show wordGuessedSoFar in a label

    Get letterGuess from user, ending game if Cancel is clicked
    Do While letterGuess <> FLAG And _
    wordGuessedSoFar <> SECRET_WORD And Not endGame
        Increment number of guesses
        Compare each letter of secretWord to letterGuess
        If letterGuess matches a letter in secretWord Then
            Replace dash in wordGuessedSoFar with letterGuess
        If wordGuessedSoFar <> secretWord Then
            Get letterGuess from user, ending game if Cancel clicked
    Loop

    If wordGuessedSoFar = secretWord Then
        Display message with number of guesses
    Else If letterGuess = FLAG Then
        Show input box prompting for wordGuess
        If wordGuess = secretWord Then
            Display message with number of guesses
        Else
            Display "you lose" message
    Else
        Display "game over" message
End Sub
```

Note that the string of dashes is created by padding an empty string with the same number of dashes as characters in the secret word. This allows more flexibility in the program because creating a new secret word means just changing one variable assignment.

WordGuess Coding

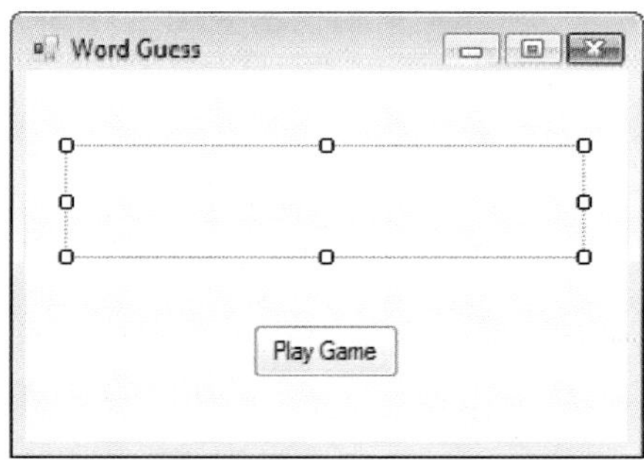

Object	(Name)	Text	AutoSize	TextAlign	Font
Form1		Word Guess			
Label1	lblSecretWord	*empty*	False	MiddleCenter	Size 36
Button1	btnPlayGame	Play Game			

```
Public Class Form1

    Private Sub btnPlayGame_Click(ByVal sender As Object,
    ByVal e As System.EventArgs) Handles btnPlayGame.Click
        Const SECRET_WORD As String = "VELOCITY"
        Const FLAG As Char = "!"
        Const GUESS_PROMPT As String = "Enter a letter or " & FLAG & " to guess word:"
        Dim numGuesses As Integer = 0
        Dim letterGuess As Char
        Dim wordGuess As String
        Dim tempWord As String
        Dim endGame As Boolean

        'Set number of dashes as letters in SECRET_WORD
        Dim wordGuessedSoFar As String = ""
        Dim length As Integer = SECRET_WORD.Length
        wordGuessedSoFar = wordGuessedSoFar.PadLeft(length, "-")
        Me.lblSecretWord.Text = wordGuessedSoFar           'initialize game

        'Get first guess
        Dim tempLetterGuess = InputBox(GUESS_PROMPT, Me.Text)
        'Test data entered
        If tempLetterGuess = Nothing Then
            endGame = True
        Else
            letterGuess = tempLetterGuess
        End If

        Do While letterGuess <> FLAG And wordGuessedSoFar <> SECRET_WORD And Not endGame
            numGuesses += 1
            For letterPos As Integer = 0 To SECRET_WORD.Length - 1
                If SECRET_WORD.Chars(letterPos) = Char.ToUpper(letterGuess) Then
                    'Remove dash at position of letter guessed
                    tempWord = wordGuessedSoFar.Remove(letterPos, 1)
                    'Insert guessed letter
                    wordGuessedSoFar = tempWord.Insert(letterPos, Char.ToUpper(letterGuess))
                    'Update interface
                    Me.lblSecretWord.Text = wordGuessedSoFar
                End If
            Next letterPos
```

```
                'Get next letter if word hasn't been guessed
                If wordGuessedSoFar <> SECRET_WORD Then
                    'Get user guess
                    tempLetterGuess = InputBox(GUESS_PROMPT, Me.Text)
                    'Test data entered
                    If tempLetterGuess = Nothing Then
                        endGame = True
                    Else
                        letterGuess = tempLetterGuess
                    End If
                End If
            Loop

            If wordGuessedSoFar = SECRET_WORD Then
                MessageBox.Show("You guessed it in " & numGuesses & " guesses!")
            ElseIf letterGuess = FLAG Then
                wordGuess = InputBox("Enter a word: ", Me.Text)
                If wordGuess.ToUpper = SECRET_WORD Then
                    MessageBox.Show("You guessed it in " & numGuesses & " guesses!")
                    Me.lblSecretWord.Text = SECRET_WORD
                Else
                    MessageBox.Show("Sorry you lose.")
                End If
            Else
                MessageBox.Show("Game over.")
            End If
        End Sub
    End Class
```

WordGuess Testing and Debugging

Running WordGuess and guessing two correct letters displays:

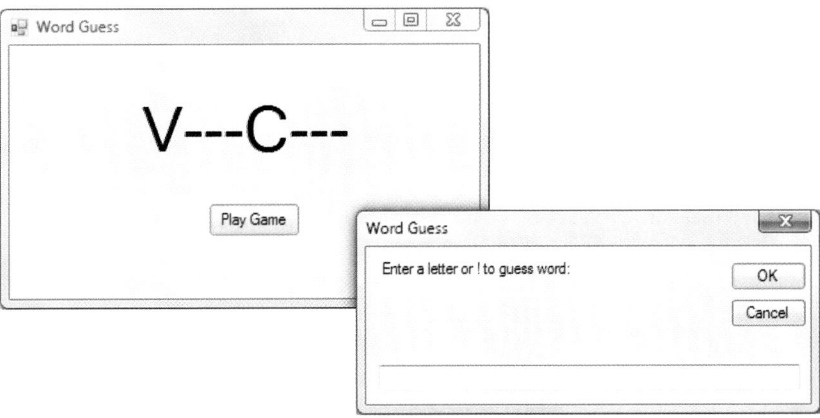

This application should be tested by entering correct and incorrect characters and correct and incorrect word guesses.

Review: WordGuess

Modify WordGuess to display the player's score on the form. The player should start with a score of 100, and lose 10 points for each incorrect guess. The score should be updated and displayed as the game is played.

Chapter Summary

Loop structures are used to control program flow and allow for iteration. In this chapter the `Do...Loop` and `For...Next` statements were used to control program flow. The `Do...Loop` executes a set of statements as long as a condition is true. The `For...Next` executes a set of statements a fixed number of times. Another form of `Do...Loop` evaluates a condition before executing the loop.

An infinite loop is a loop which continues forever. An infinite loop may result in a run-time error. If a program stops responding, edit and recompile the program or select Close window from the menu displayed by right-clicking the program icon on the Windows Task bar.

An input box is used to get information from the user. The InputBox() function returns the text entered by the user or an empty string if Cancel is clicked.

An accumulator is a variable that stores a value that accumulates, or gets added to by a varying amount during run time. A sentinel is a constant that holds a special value that "flags" a loop to stop executing. A sentinel provides a clear and easy-to-change method for ending a loop.

The `String` class includes several properties and methods for converting and manipulating strings. Some methods return, modify, or insert substrings. Two or more strings can be joined together in a process called concatenation. The Concat() method is a shared method and is used with the String type itself. The `&` operator can also be used to concatenate two or more strings.

The `Char` type is a structure that includes the ToUpper() and ToLower() shared methods for converting a character to uppercase or lowercase, respectively.

The Space() function returns a string of spaces. The `vbTab` and `vbCrLf` built-in constants are used to format a string.

Unicode uses a 16-bit binary code to represent letters and symbols from every language and culture. The AscW() and ChrW() functions can be used to convert between Unicode and characters. Strings can be alphabetically compared with the Compare() String method. The `Like` operator uses pattern matching and wildcards to compare strings.

Code conventions introduced in this chapter are :

- The statements of an `Do...Loop` statement should be indented.
- The statements of a `For...Next` statement should be indented.
- The counter variable of a `For...Next` statement should be declared in the statement to limit its scope.
- A counter variable should not be modified within a `For...Next` loop, and the loop should end only when the condition is false.

Vocabulary

Accumulator A variable used to store a number that is incremented by a changing amount.

Concatenated Strings that have been joined.

Concatenation The process of joining two or more strings into one string.

Flag A condition used to signify that a loop should stop executing.

Infinite loop A loop that continues forever.

Input box A predefined dialog box that accepts input from the user.

Iteration *See* looping.

Loop A set of statements that repeatedly perform a task based on a condition.

Loop structure A statement that executes a loop as long as a condition is true.

Looping Repeating one or more statements.

Members Properties and methods of a class.

Method A procedure in a class.

Object A variable that is declared with a data type that is a class.

Pattern matching Allows wildcard characters (?, *, #), character lists, and character ranges ([A–M, Z]) to match strings using the `Like` operator.

Robust Describes an application that performs even under unexpected circumstances.

Sentinel *See* Flag.

Shared method A method that is used with a class, not with a particular object of that class.

Structure A simple form of a class.

Substring A portion of a string.

Textual comparison Comparing characters without distinguishing case.

Unicode A digital code that represents every letter of an alphabet and symbols of every culture. Each code uses 16 bits or 2 bytes.

`*=` Assignment operator that multiplies the value on the right of the statement and the current value of the variable on the left and then updates the variable to store the new value.

`/=` Assignment operator that uses the value on the right of the statement to divide the current value of the variable on the left and then updates the variable to store the new value.

`\=` Assignment operator that uses the value on the right of the statement to divide the current value of the variable on the left and then updates the variable to store the integer portion of the new value.

`^=` Assignment operator that raises the current value of the variable on the left to the power of the value on the right of the assignment statement and then updates the variable to store the new value.

`&=` Assignment operator that concatenates the string on the right of the statement and the current string of the variable on the left and then updates the variable to store the new string.

`&` Used to concatenate two or more strings.

AscW() Function that returns the integer Unicode value that corresponds to a character argument.

`Char` **structure** Used to manipulate characters. Methods include ToLower() and ToUpper().

ChrW() Function that returns the character corresponding to an integer representing a Unicode value.

`Do...Loop` Statement that repeatedly executes a loop as long as a condition is True.

`For...Next` Statement that executes a loop a fixed number of times.

InputBox() Function used to generate a predefined dialog box that has a prompt, a text box, and OK and Cancel buttons.

`Like` Operator used to perform textual comparison on strings and pattern matching using characters such as ?, *, #, [].

Space() Function used to generate a string of spaces.

`Step` Keyword used in a `For...Next` statement to increment or decrement the counter by a set amount.

`String` **class** Used to manipulate strings. Properties include Chars and Length. Methods include Concat(), Compare(), IndexOf(), Insert(), PadLeft(), PadRight(), Remove(), Replace(), Substring(), Trim(), ToUpper(), ToLower(), TrimEnd(), and TrimStart().

`vbCrLf` Built-in constant that represents a carriage return-linefeed combination.

`vbTab` Built-in constant that places a string in the next field of eight characters.

Critical Thinking

1. What is the primary purpose of a loop?

2. Explain the difference between the `Do...Loop` and the `Do While...Loop`.

3. a) What is an infinite loop?
   b) What causes an infinite loop?

4. a) What are the two predefined dialog boxes discussed so far?
   b) How are they similar?
   c) How do they differ?

5. An *input validation* loop is a loop that checks user input for the valid data. If valid data is not entered, the loop reiterates until valid data is entered. Write code that checks the data in txtNumStudents for a value between 1 and 30 inclusive and displays an appropriate prompt in an InputBox if valid data is not typed. This check loop should continue until a valid value is typed. Be sure to consider what happens if Cancel is selected in the Input box.

6. Compare and contrast counters and accumulators. List two uses for each.

7. Explain the difference between the `Do...Loop` and the `For...Next` statements.

8. Write code to average the sum of every third integer from 2 through 99 (i.e. 2 + 5 + ...) using
   a) a `Do...Loop`.
   b) a `For...Next`.

9. How is the `String` data type different from the `Integer` and `Double` data types?

10. What are variables created with the `String` data type called?

11. Complete the code below that sums the digits in a number. For example, 1234 in txtNumber displays "The sum of the digits in 1234 is 10" in a message box.

```
number = Me.txtNumber.Text
For i As Integer = ___ To number. ________ - 1
    sum = ___ + ___(number.Substring(__,__))
Next i
MessageBox.Show("The sum of the digits in " &
number & " is " & ___)
```

12. What are the two ways strings can be combined to create a new string?

13. Write code that prompts the user for a starting value and an ending value, and then displays a table of each number in the range and its square in a label. Be sure to account for the fact that the user may not necessarily type a smaller number first.

14. Write code that prompts the user for words in an input box and concatenates them together with a space between until a period is entered. The concatenated words should then be displayed in a label.

15. Consider the statement: `str1 = "TesT Now"` What value is assigned to the variables in the statements?
    a) `new1 = str1.ToLower`
    b) `new2 = str1.Substring(0, 4)`
    c) `new3 = (str1.ToUpper).Substring(3, 4)`
    d) `pos1 = str1.IndexOf("T")`
    e) `pos2 = str1.IndexOf("NOW")`

16. Correct the errors in the code:

```
Dim first As Char = "f"
Dim middle As Char = "m"
Dim last As Char = "l"
'Create monogram
Me.lblMonogram.Text = first.ToUpper &
middle.ToUpper & last.ToUpper
```

17. Write code that prompts the user for a date in the form mm/dd/yy and then displays the date in form month, day, year. For example, 12/25/13 displays December 25, 2013.

18 What is displayed by the message box?

```
nums = "0123456789012345678901234567890"
MessageBox.Show(nums & vbCrLf & vBTab &
"This" & vbTab & "Is" & vbCrLf &
"So Wonderful" & "and Marvelous")
```

19. What is displayed in the label?

```
original = "Visual Basic is so much fun!"
length = original.Length
For i As Integer = 0 To length - 1
    char = original.Substring(i, 1)
    If i Mod 2 = 0 Then
        output = output & char.ToUpper
    Else
        output = output & char.ToLower
    End If
Next i
Me.lblOutput.Text = output
```

20. a) Write an algorithm to count the number of words in a sentence.
    b) Write an algorithm to count the number of letters in a sentence.

True/False

21. Determine if each of the following is true or false. If false, explain why.
    a) Each execution of a loop is called an iteration.
    b) A `Do...Loop` that evaluates the condition before executing a loop may never execute.
    c) An infinite loop continues forever.
    d) Accumulator variables can only be Integer variables.
    e) An accumulator signifies that a loop is to stop iterating.
    f) Sentinel values must always be the value –1.
    g) The statement `sum += 1` uses `sum` as an accumulator variable.
    h) The counter in a `For...Next` statement is always incremented or decremented by 1.
    i) The `String` data type is a primitive data type.
    j) A string can be changed by methods of the `String` class.
    k) `String.Compare("Test", "TEST", False)` returns a negative value.
    l) `vbTab` is a variable that allows the programmer to control the spaces in a string.
    m) The Unicode value for an uppercase letter is the same for the corresponding lowercase letter.
    n) The Compare() method returns a `Boolean` variable.
    o) A wildcard character is a ?, *, or #, which matches an unknown character or group of characters.

Exercises

Exercise 1 — GroomingServices

Create an GroomingServices application that allows the user to select pet grooming services. A shampoo is $15, a flea dip is $5, a trim is $15, and a full shave is $20. The displayed price should reflect the total of the services currently selected. If a service is cleared, the price should change immediately to reflect the correct price. *Hint*: Use Click event procedures for each check box to update an accumulator. The application interface should look similar to the following after selecting the Shampoo and Trim check boxes:

Exercise 2 — CDCalculator

A certificate of deposit (CD) is a type of investment that matures at a specified interest rate for a specified period. Create a CDCalculator application that prompts the user for the initial investment amount, the annual interest rate, and the desired ending value and then displays the number of years required for the CD to be worth the specified ending value when interest is compounded annually. The CD value at the end of each year can be calculated by the formula CD Value = CD Value + (CD Value * Interest Rate). To determine the number of years it will take for the CD to reach the desired ending value, repeatedly execute the formula until the CD Value is greater than or equal to the desired ending value. The application interface should look similar to:

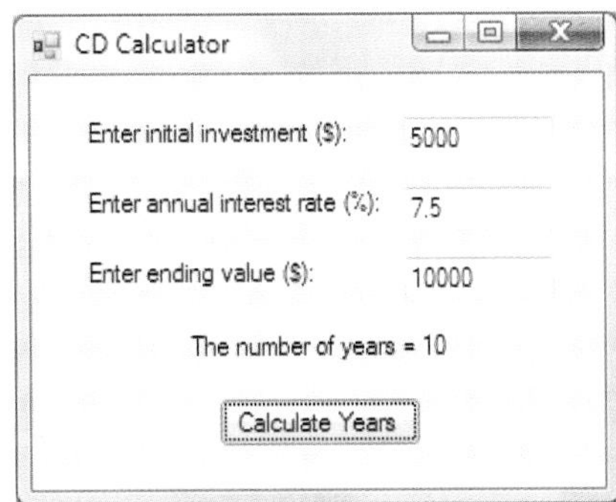

Exercise 3 — BowlingScores

a) Create a BowlingScores application that prompts the user to enter as many bowling scores as desired and then displays the high score and the low score. The application interface should look similar to the following after clicking Enter Scores, entering a set of scores, and then clicking Statistics:

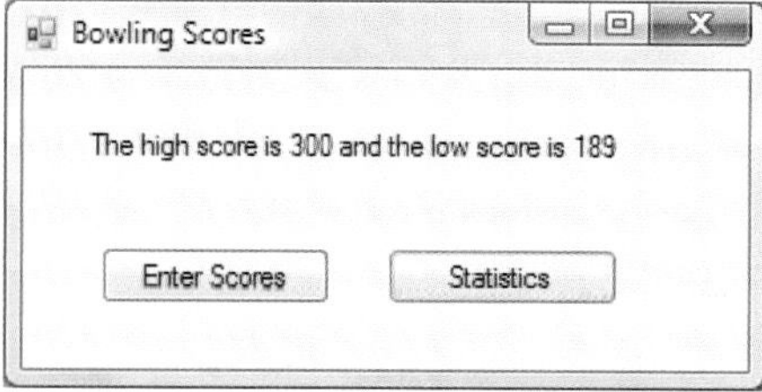

b) Modify the application to display the average bowling score in a label.

Exercise 4 — Initials

Create an Initials application that prompts the user to enter his or her first and last names and then displays the initials of the name in uppercase. The application interface should look similar to:

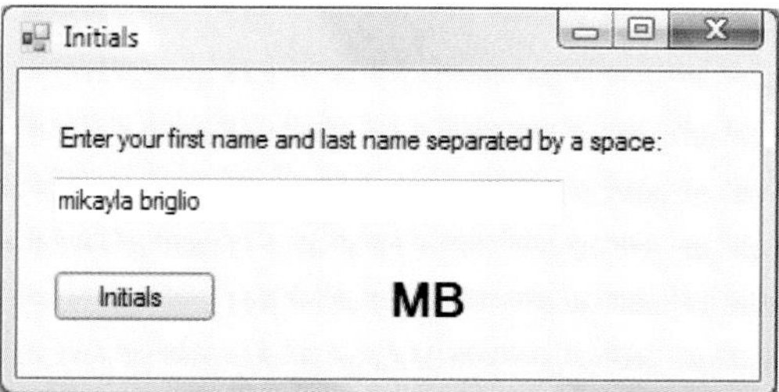

Exercise 5 — Monogram

Create a Monogram application that prompts the user to enter his or her first, middle, and last names and then displays a monogram with the first and middle initials in lowercase and the last initial in uppercase. The application interface should look similar to:

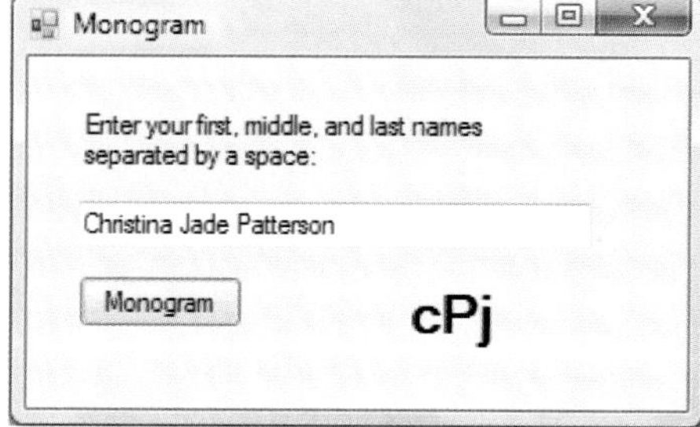

Exercise 6 — Average

Create an Average application that calculates the average of a set of numbers from 1 to a number entered by the user. For example, if the user enters 5, the average of 1, 2, 3, 4, and 5 would be calculated. The application interface should looks similar to:

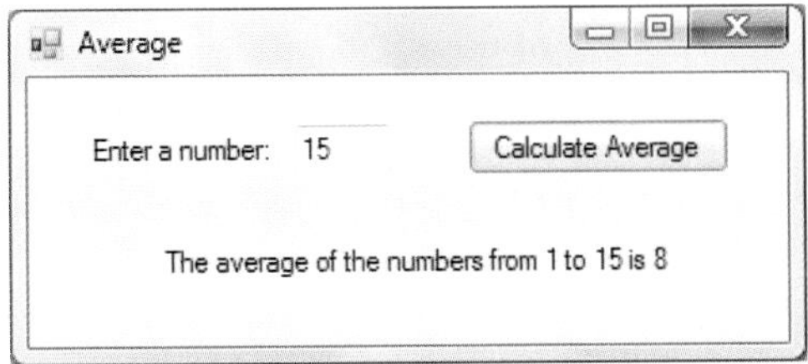

Exercise 7 — ReplaceString

Create a ReplaceString application that displays a new string in a label. The new string should take a sentence entered by the user and replace every occurrence of a substring with a new string supplied by the user. The application interface should look similar to:

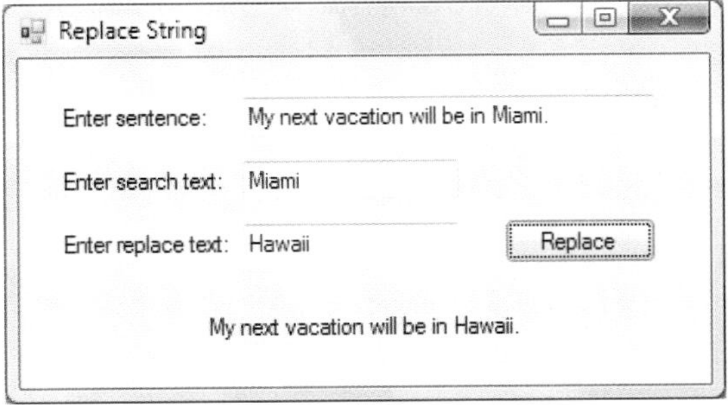

Exercise 8 — RemoveString

Create a RemoveString application that displays a new string in a label. The new string should take a sentence entered by the user and remove every occurrence of a substring supplied by the user. The application interface should look similar to:

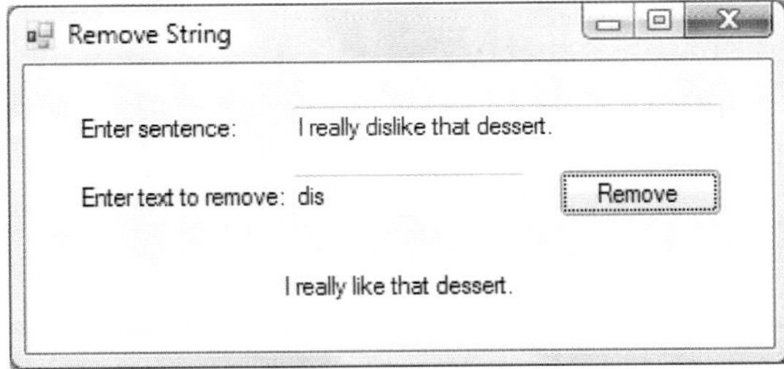

Exercise 9 — SumNumbers

Create a SumNumbers application that calculates the sum of a range of numbers entered by the user and displays in a label an expression with the numbers in the range. The application interface should look similar to:

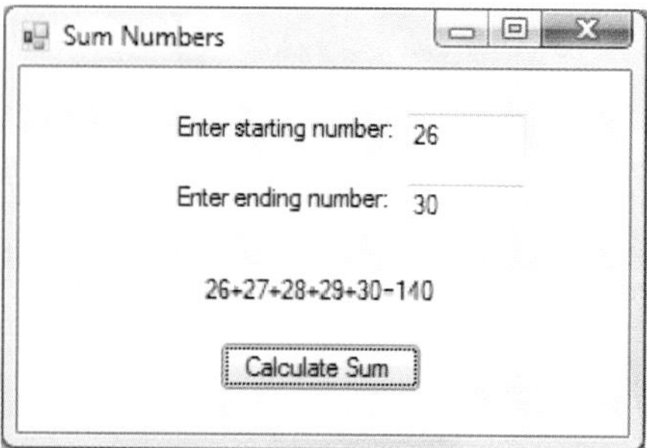

Exercise 10 — Acronym

An acronym is a word formed from the first letters of a few words, such as GUI for graphical user interface. Create an Acronym application that displays an acronym for the words entered by the user. The application should first display an input box asking the user how many words will make up the acronym, then display separate input boxes to get each word, and finally display the acronym in all uppercase. The application interface should look similar to the following after clicking **Create Acronym**, entering 6, and then entering `brackets exponents division multiplication addition subtraction` as the words:

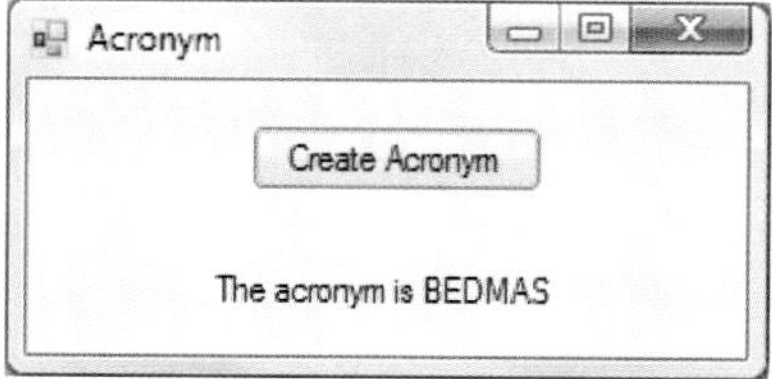

Exercise 11 — NameBackwards

As a young boy Franklin Roosevelt signed his letters to his mother backwards: tlevesoor nilknarf. Create a NameBackwards application that prompts the user to enter his or her name and then displays the name backwards in all lowercase in a label. The application interface should look similar to:

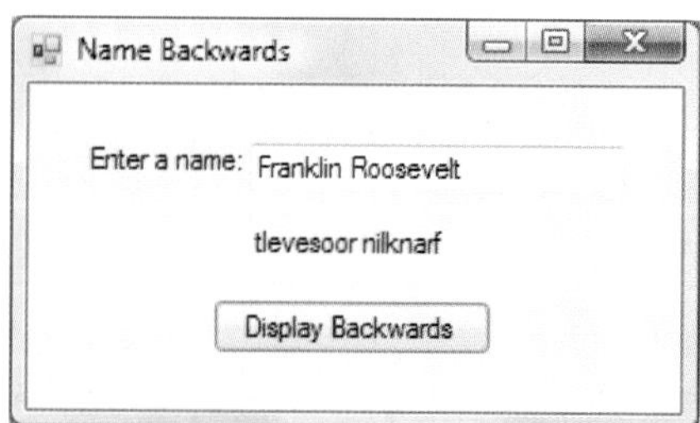

Exercise 12 ——— CountVowels

Create a CountVowels application that counts the number of vowels in a word or phrase. The application interface should look similar to:

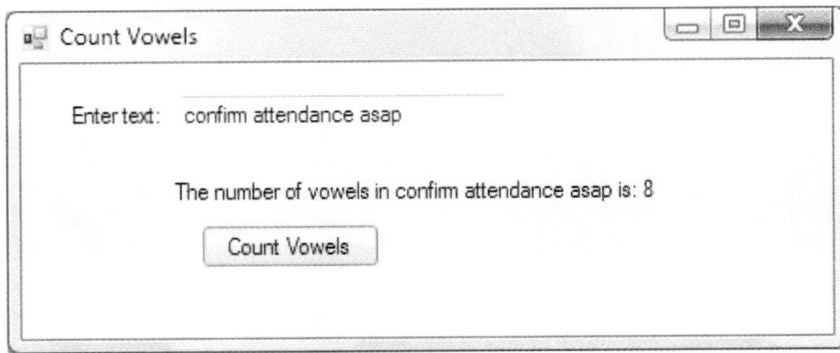

Exercise 13 ——— Unicode

Create a Unicode application that prompts the user for a word and then displays the Unicode base 10 number for each letter in the word. The application interface should look similar to:

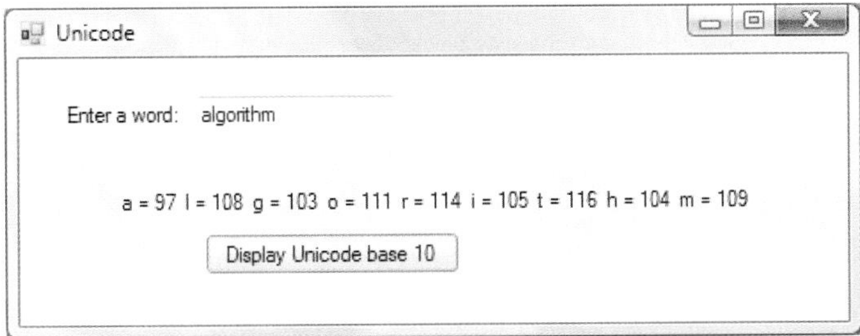

Exercise 14 ——— Coder

a) Create a Coder application that encodes or decodes a message using Unicode. The application interface should look similar to the following after clicking Enter Message, entering `Meet me for lunch` in an input box, and then selecting Encode:

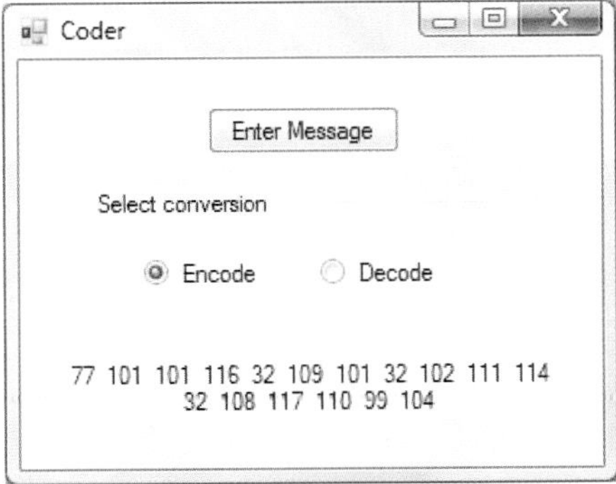

b) Modify Coder to produce the code by converting each letter in the original message to its corresponding Unicode number, add 2 to each number, and then convert these numbers back to characters to display a coded message. Keep all spaces between the words in their original places and realize that the letters "Y" and "Z" are to be converted to A and B.

Exercise 15 — Palindrome

A palindrome is a word or phrase that is spelled the same backwards and forwards, such as madam, dad, or race car. Create a Palindrome application that uses a loop to determine if the word or phrase entered by the user is a palindrome. The application interface should look similar to:

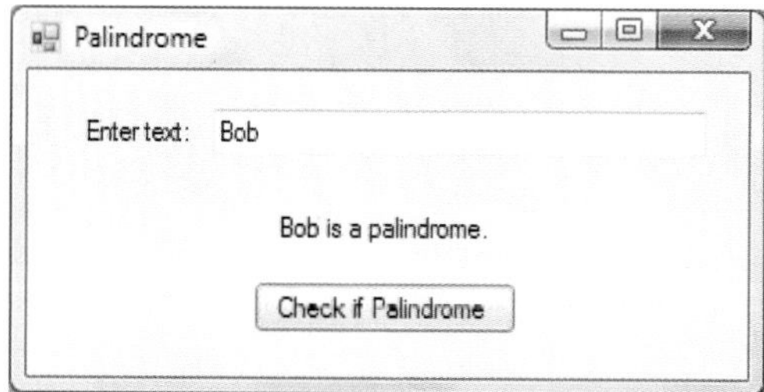

Exercise 16 — StudentGroup

Create a StudentGroup application that prompts the user to enter a student name and then displays what group a student is assigned to depending on the first letter in the student's last name. Last names beginning with A through I are in Group 1, J through S are in Group 2, T through Z are in Group 3. The application interface should look similar to the following after entering text and clicking Determine Group:

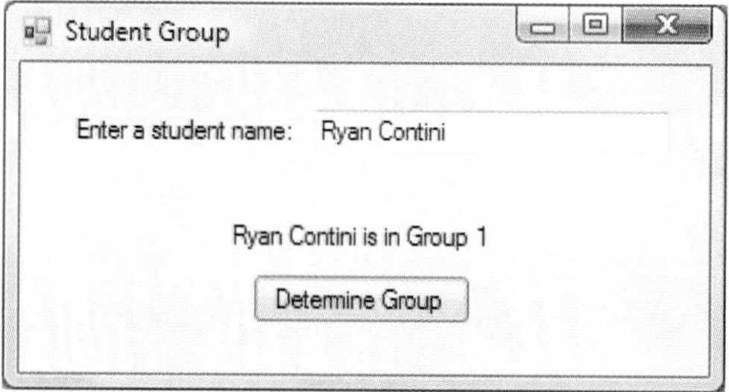

Exercise 17 — SlotMachineGame

Create a SlotMachineGame application that acts as a simple slot machine. The user starts with 100 tokens. With each "pull" of the handle, the user loses 1 token and the computer "spins" three wheels, each consisting of the numbers 1, 2, and 3. If all three numbers are 1, the user gets 4 tokens; if all are 2, the user gets 8 tokens; if all are 3, the user gets 12 tokens. The number of tokens that the user has should be displayed on the form and the result of the spin should be displayed in a message box. The application interface should look similar to the following after Pull has been clicked several times:

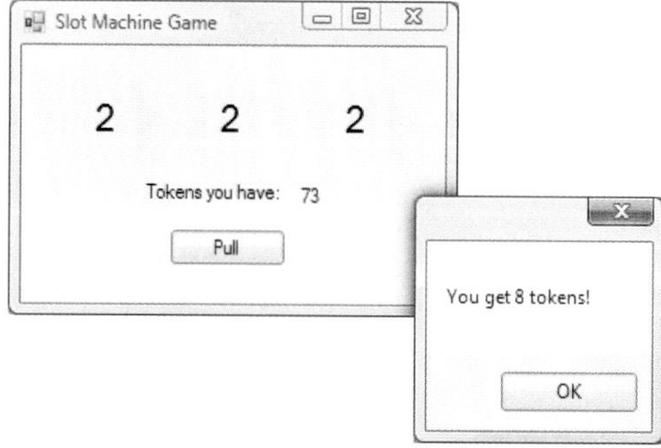

Exercise 18

Create a Fibonacci application that gets two seeds from the user and then generates a Fibonacci Sequence of 50 values:

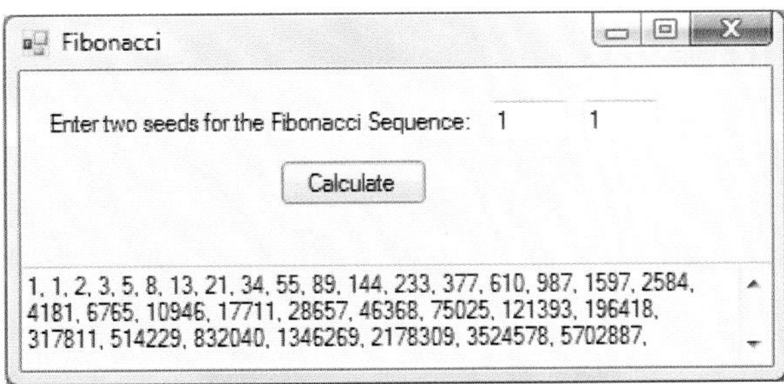

A *Fibonacci Sequence* is a sequence of numbers that is generated from two starting values called seeds. The two seeds are the first two numbers in the sequence. The seeds are then added together to generate the third number in the sequence. Each additional number in the sequence is created by adding the previous two numbers. For example, if the seeds are 1 and 1, the sequence is 1, 1, 2, 3, 5, 8, ... As another example, the seeds 3 and 6 generate the sequence 3, 6, 9, 15, 24, 39, ...

A long series of numbers will need to be displayed. A label is not a good choice for such a long list of numbers. TextBox objects have additional properties from those listed in Chapter 3. The properties listed below can be set to make a text box appropriate for displaying lines of text, such as a sequence of numbers. Use the TextBox properties listed below to enhance your application:

- **Dock** is the location of docking for the text box. Setting Dock to Bottom automatically sizes the text box so that the bottom, right, and left borders are anchored to the form. Dock can also be set to Top, Left, Right, or Fill.
- **ReadOnly** is set to True when the text box should be used for display only. When ReadOnly is True, text can be displayed in the text box, but the user will not be able to type in the text box.
- **Multiline** is set to True to allow the text box to display multiple lines of text. The box can then be sized vertically.
- **WordWrap** is set to True to wrap lines of text at the right border of the text box. WordWrap can be set to False, but it is not recommended because only one line of text will be displayed and it may extend beyond the right border of the text box.
- **ScrollBars** is set to Vertical to add a vertical scroll bar to the text box. A vertical scroll bar appears only when the WordWrap and Multiline properties are also set to True. ScrollBars can also be set to None, Horizontal, or Both.

Exercise 19 — BirthDate

Create a BirthDate application that uses the DateTimePicker control to prompt the user for their date of birth and then displays that information in a message box when the user clicks a button. The DateTimePicker control allows users to select a date using a graphical calendar:

Hint - Try using the following code:

```
MsgBox("You were born on: " & DateTimePicker1.Text)
MsgBox("Day of the week: " & DateTimePicker1.Value.DayOfWeek.ToString)
```

Experiment further with the DateTimePicker control sharing your results with a classmate. Note that the DateTimePicker control can display times instead of dates by setting the object's Format property to Time.

Chapter 6
Procedures

Key Concepts

Writing Sub procedures for specific tasks
Adding images
Passing data to a procedure
Writing documentation
Using reference parameters
Creating event handlers for multiple events
Writing function procedures
Applying code conventions to procedures

Case Study

Calculator II

Review Data Files

cat.jpg, dog.jpg, fish.jpg
shell.gif, pearl.gif

Exercise Data Files

die1.gif - die6.gif
cardback.gif
card1.gif - card10.gif

Sub Procedures

In Visual Basic there are several types of procedures. One type is called the *Sub procedure*, which is a set of statements that performs a specific task. An event procedure is a Sub procedure written for a specific object event. A Sub procedure can also perform tasks not specifically related to an event, and takes the form:

```
Sub ProcedureName()
   statements
End Sub
```

`ProcedureName` is a name describing the task performed by the procedure. Procedure names should indicate an action. A procedure name should also begin with an uppercase letter and then an uppercase letter should begin each word within the name. Procedure names may not contain spaces. `statements` is one or more statements that perform the task. `Sub` declares the procedure and `End Sub` ends the procedure.

Sub procedures divide a program into smaller, more manageable blocks of code. There is less code redundancy because the statements for a specific task appear just once in the Sub procedure. A program with Sub procedures is more flexible because changes to the statements for a task need only be made in the Sub procedure. For example, the following Sub procedure displays a message to the user:

```
Sub PromptUser()
   MessageBox.Show("Please complete all text boxes.")
End Sub
```

The PromptUser() procedure can be used whenever a message of this type needs to be displayed. If a different message is needed, only the statement in the Sub procedure is changed.

A Sub procedure must be called from another procedure in order to execute. The `Call` statement takes the form:

```
Call ProcedureName()
```

`ProcedureName()` is the Sub procedure name followed by parentheses. The parentheses indicate a procedure.

From the Code window, add a procedure by typing `Sub` followed by the procedure name and then pressing Enter. When this is done, the IDE automatically adds an `End Sub` statement and places the insertion point in the body of the procedure where statements can then be typed.

The PictureBox Control

Images can make an application more interesting or improve usability. For example, the Online Shopping application includes three images:

TIP The form's background color is changed using the BackColor property.

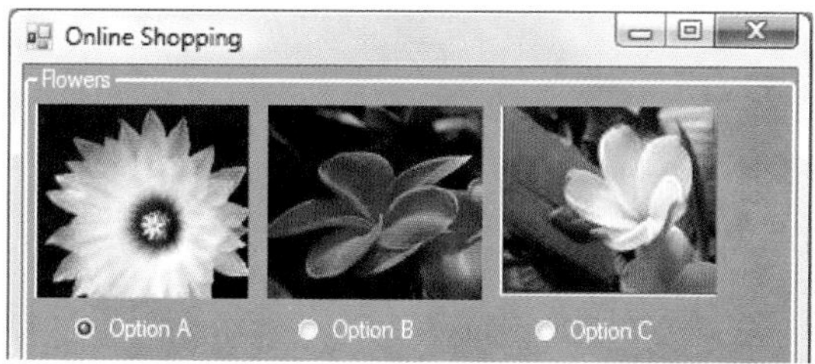

An image is added to an application by placing it in a picture box. The PictureBox control has the properties:

- **(Name)** identifies a control for the programmer. PictureBox object names should begin with `pic`.
- **Image** contains the ... button that is clicked to display the Select Resource dialog box. In this dialog box, images can be added to the Resources folder of a project and an image selected for a picture box. Once an image is added to the Resource folder, it is available for any picture box on the form. Image files can be BMP, JPG, GIF, PNG, and WMF formats. Right-clicking Image and then selecting Reset removes the picture from the picture box.
- **SizeMode** can be set to either Normal, StretchImage, AutoSize, CenterImage, or Zoom. AutoSize is often the best choice because the picture box is automatically sized to fit the image. Normal places an image in the upper-left corner of the picture box. If the image is too big, it is clipped. If the image is too small, blank area is displayed. StretchImage sizes an image to fit the picture box, which may distort some images.
- **Visible** can be set to either True or False. Visible is often used at run time to display or hide an image.
- **Size** is the picture box size in pixels. The size of a pixel depends on the screen resolution. Size changes automatically when SizeMode is AutoSize.

A Click event procedure can be coded for a picture box. The Click event procedure is executed when the user clicks the displayed image.

My.Resources Object

The My.Resources object provides access to a project's resources. Besides adding resources through the Select Resource dialog box, the My Project icon in the Solution Explorer window can be double-clicked to display the My Project window with many application options including a Resources tab with options for adding and deleting resources.

The image in a picture box can be changed at run time by retrieving the resource from the Resources folder. The `My.Resources` object is used to access a resource in a statement similar to:

TIP Image files must already be in the Resources folder in order to access them at run time.

```
Me.pictureBox.Image = My.Resources.imageName
```

`pictureBox` is the name of the PictureBox object and `imageName` is the name of the resource in the Resources folder. When a dot is typed after `Resources`, Visual Basic displays an IntelliSense list with available resources.

The LinkLabel Control

A LinkLabel

A Visual Basic Windows application can include a link to a website by adding a LinkLabel object. The LinkLabel control has the properties:

- **(Name)** identifies a control for the programmer. LinkLabel object names should begin with `lnk`.
- **ActiveLinkColor** sets the color of the link when clicked.
- **LinkColor** sets the color of the link.
- **Text** sets the text for the destination website.
- **VisitedLinkColor** sets the color of a link that has been previously visited.

Review: PetStore

① CREATE A NEW PROJECT

Create a Windows application named `PetStore`.

② CREATE THE INTERFACE

a. Set the Form1 BackColor property to White.

b. Use the table below for setting object properties.

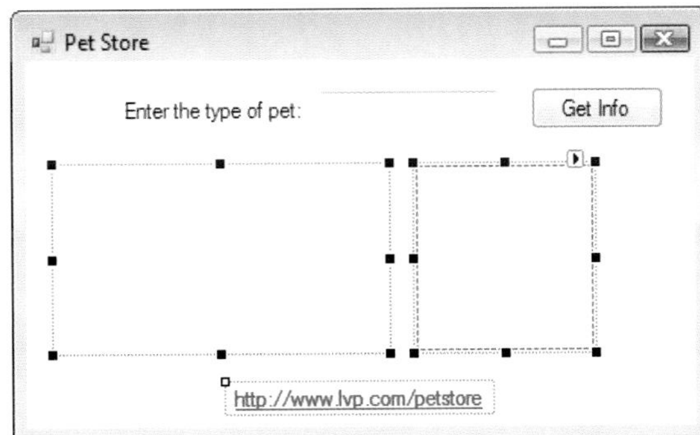

Object	(Name)	Text	AutoSize	SizeMode	Size
Form1		Pets			
Label1	lblPrompt	*see interface*	True		
TextBox1	txtPetName	*empty*			
Label2	lblPetInfo	*empty*	False		
PictureBox1	picPetPhoto			AutoSize	100, 100
Button1	btnGetInfo	Get Info			

c. Add a LinkLabel control and set the Text property to: `http://www.lvp.com/petstore`

③ IMPORT IMAGE RESOURCES AND ADD TO INTERFACE

a. Select the picPetPhoto picture box.

b. In the Properties window, select the Image property. The [...] button is displayed.

c. Click the [...] button. The Select Resource dialog box is displayed.

   1. Select Project resource file if it is not already selected.
   2. Select Import. The Open dialog box is displayed.
   3. Navigate to the location of the `cat.jpg` file, a data file for this text.
   4. Select `cat.jpg` and then select Open. The file is added to the project.
   5. Select Import again and add the `dog.jpg` data file to the project.
   6. Select Import a third time and add the `fish.jpg` data file to the project.
   7. In the files list, select (none) because there should be no image displayed initially and then select OK.

④ WRITE THE APPLICATION CODE

a. Display the Code window.

b. Add comments that include your name, assignment, and today's date.

c. Create a btnGetInfo_Click event procedure and then add the following statements. Note that a blue wavy underline will appear below the procedure names because they do not yet exist:

```
Dim PetName As String

PetName = Me.txtPetName.Text

'Show pet info
Select Case PetName.ToUpper
    Case "CAT"
        Call CATInfo()
    Case "DOG"
        Call DOGInfo()
    Case "FISH"
        Call FISHInfo()
    Case Else
        MessageBox.Show("Sorry, no information available.")
End Select
```

d. After the `End Sub` statement of the btnGetInfo_Click event procedure, press Enter twice, type `Sub CATInfo`, and then press Enter again. An `End Sub` statement is added and the insertion point is placed in the body of the new procedure. Add the following statements to the procedure:

```
Sub CATInfo()
    Me.picPetPhoto.Image = My.Resources.cat
    Me.lblCatInfo.Text = "This kitten is 4 months old and loves playing with children."
End Sub
```

e. After the `End Sub` statement of CATInfo(), press Enter twice, type `Sub DOGInfo`, and press Enter again. Add statements to the DOGInfo() procedure:

```
Sub DOGInfo()
    Me.picPetPhoto.Image = My.Resources.dog
    Me.lblPetInfo.Text = "This puppy is just 3 months old and needs a good home."
End Sub
```

f. Create a FISHInfo() procedure:

```
Sub FISHInfo()
    Me.picPetPhoto.Image = My.Resources.fish
    Me.lblPetInfo.Text = "We have a variety of goldfish."
End Sub
```

⑤ RUN THE APPLICATION

a. Save the modified PetStore project and then run the application. Type `Cat` and then click Get Info. A picture and information are displayed:

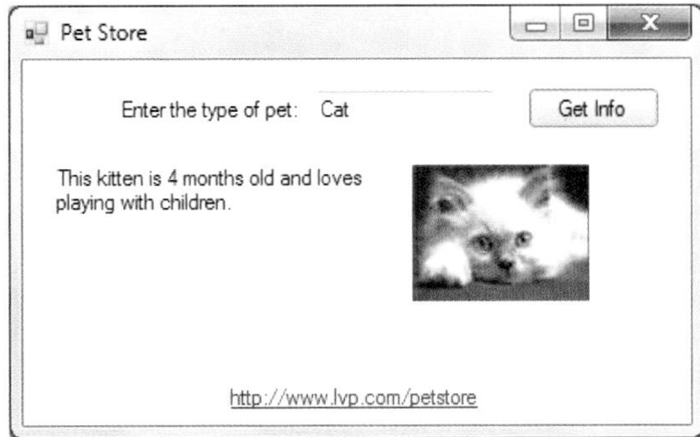

b. Display information for Dog, Fish, and then an animal that does not have a procedure.

c. Close the PetStore application.

⑥ PRINT THE CODE AND THEN CLOSE THE PROJECT

Value Parameters

pass

A procedure often needs data in order to complete its task. Data is given, or *passed*, to a procedure by enclosing it in parentheses in the procedure call. For example, the statement below calls a procedure named GiveHint() and passes it two values, `secretNumber` and `guess`:

```
Call GiveHint(secretNumber, guess)
```

argument

A variable or value passed to a procedure is called an *argument*. In the statement, `secretNumber` and `guess` are the arguments to be used by the procedure.

A procedure that requires arguments is declared with *parameters* and takes the following form:

```
Sub ProcedureName(ByVal parameter1 As type, ...)
  statements
End Sub
```

parameters

`ProcedureName` is the name describing the procedure. `ByVal` indicates that the parameter is a value parameter, `parameter1` is the name of the parameter, and `type` is the data type of the expected value. A *value parameter* is only used as a local variable by the called procedure. This means that after the procedure has executed, the value of the argument in the procedure call has not changed. There can be many parameters separated by commas. `statements` is the body of the procedure.

The GiveHint() procedure has two parameters. When GiveHint() is called, the first argument is assigned to `firstNum` and the second argument is assigned to `secondNum`:

```
Sub GiveHint(ByVal firstNum As Integer,
ByVal secondNum As Integer)
   If firstNumber > secondNumber Then
      MessageBox.Show("Too low.")
   Else
      MessageBox.Show("Too high.")
   End If
End Sub
```

GiveHint() does not rely on any other information except what it is passed, and its parameters have names meaningful to GiveHint() but not necessarily to the calling procedure. Generic procedures such as this one can be easily reused in other programs, making coding more efficient.

The following points are important to keep in mind when working with procedures that have value parameters:

- The order of the arguments passed corresponds to the order of the parameters. For example, the first argument in a procedure call corresponds to the first parameter in a procedure declaration.
- The number of arguments in a procedure call must match the number of parameters in the procedure declaration.
- Arguments passed by value can be in the form of constants, variables, values, or expressions. For example, the GiveHint() procedure call may take any of the following forms:

```
Call GiveHint(secretNumber, guess)
Call GiveHint(2*5, 10*2)
Call GiveHint(10, guess)
Call GiveHint(10, 20)
```

- Variable arguments passed by value are not changed by the procedure. For example, consider the following code. Assume the Demo() procedure executes first:

```
Sub Demo()
   Dim counter As Integer = 1
   Call ShowCount(counter)
   Me.lblNumber.Text = counter          'displays 1
End Sub

Sub ShowCount(ByVal counter As Integer)
   counter = counter + 1
   MessageBox.Show(counter)             'displays 2
End Sub
```

When the `Call ShowCount(counter)` statement executes, the value of the counter variable in demo, `1`, is passed to the `counter` parameter in ShowCount(). A `ByVal` parameter is used like a local variable for the duration of the procedure. When the procedure finishes executing, the `ByVal` parameter is no longer maintained in memory. The code above demonstrates that `counter` in ShowCount() has no relation to `counter` in Demo().

Procedure Documentation

Just as comments are used to clarify statements, comments should also be used to describe, or *document*, procedures. Procedure documentation should include a brief description of what the procedure does followed by any preconditions and postconditions. The assumptions, or initial requirements, of a procedure are called its *preconditions*. The *postcondition* is a statement of what must be true at the end of the execution of a procedure if the procedure has worked properly. A procedure may not have a precondition, but every procedure must have a postcondition.

A precondition is indicated by `pre:`, and a postcondition is indicated by `post:`. The GiveHint() procedure at the top of the next page includes proper documentation. Note that there is no precondition:

```
'Determines if firstNum is larger than secondNum and
'then displays an appropriate message.
'
'post: A message has been displayed in a message box.
'
Sub GiveHint(ByVal firstNum As Integer,
ByVal secondNum As Integer)
  If firstNum > secondNum Then
     MessageBox.Show("Too low.")
  Else
     MessageBox.Show("Too high.")
  End If
End Sub
```

Review: GuessingGame – part 3 of 4

① OPEN THE GUESSING GAME PROJECT

Open the GuessingGame project, which was last modified in Chapter 4.

② MODIFY THE PROGRAM CODE

a. Display the Code window.

b. Add the GiveHint() procedure after the existing procedures:

```
'Determines if firstNum is larger than secondNum and then displays an
'appropriate message.
'
'post: A message has been displayed in a message box.
'
Sub GiveHint(ByVal firstNum As Integer, ByVal secondNum As Integer)
    If firstNum > secondNum Then
        MessageBox.Show("Too low.")
    Else
        MessageBox.Show("Too high.")
    End If
End Sub
```

c. Change the `If...Then...ElseIf` statement in the btnCheckGuess_Click() procedure to include a procedure call:

```
...
If guess < MIN Or guess > MAX Then          'invalid guess
    MessageBox.Show("Guess out of range.")
ElseIf guess = secretNumber Then            'correct
    Me.lblMessage.Text = "You guessed it!"
    MessageBox.Show(count)
Else                                        'too low or too high
    Call GiveHint(secretNumber, guess)
End If
```

③ RUN THE APPLICATION

Save the modified GuessingGame project and then run the application. Test the application.

④ PRINT THE CODE AND THEN CLOSE THE PROJECT

Reference Parameters

TIP Reference parameters are sometimes called called *actual parameters* because they can change the actual value of the variable argument used in the procedure call.

A procedure can use *reference parameters* to send values back to the calling procedure. Reference parameters can alter the value of the actual variables used in the procedure call. A procedure with reference parameters takes the following form:

```
Sub ProcedureName(ByRef parameter1 As type, ...)
  statements
End Sub
```

`ProcedureName` is the name describing the procedure. `ByRef` indicates that the parameter is by reference, `parameter1` is the name of the parameter, and `type` is the data type of the parameter. There can be many parameters separated by commas. A procedure can have both reference (`ByRef`) and value (`ByVal`) parameters. `statements` is the body of the procedure.

The TwoDigits() procedure assigns the first and second digits of a two-digit number to the variables passed by reference:

```
'The digits of a two-digit number are returned in
'separate parameters.
'
'pre: num is a number less than 100 and greater than -100.
'post: firstDigit stores a number between 0 and 9 inclusive.
'secondDigit stores a number between 0 and 9 inclusive.
'
Sub TwoDigits(ByVal num As Integer,
ByRef firstDigit As Integer, ByRef secondDigit As Integer)
  firstDigit = num \ 10
  secondDigit = num Mod 10
End Sub
```

address

When TwoDigits() is called, the value of the first argument is assigned to a new memory location also called `num`. The next two arguments give their address to `firstDigit` and `secondDigit`. The *address* of a variable is the location in memory where its value is stored. A `ByRef` parameter uses the same memory location as the argument:

27
0
0
num
tensDigit
onesDigit
27
0
0
27
num (copy)
firstDigit/ tensDigit
secondDigit/ onesDigit
num (original)
27
2
0
27
num (copy)
firstDigit/ tensDigit
secondDigit/ onesDigit
num (original)
27
2
7
27
num (copy)
firstDigit/ tensDigit
secondDigit/ onesDigit
num (original)
Private Sub btnDisplayDigits_Click(ByVal sender As Object,
ByVal e As System.EventArgs) Handles btnDisplayDigits.Click
Dim num As Integer = 27
Dim tensDigit As Integer
Dim onesDigit As Integer
Call TwoDigits(num, tensDigit, onesDigit)
Me.lblTensDigit.Text = tensDigit '2
Me.lblOnesDigit.Text = onesDigit '7
End Sub
'The digits of a two-digit number are returned in separate
'parameters
'
'pre: num is a number less than 100 and greater than -100
'post: firstDigit stores a number between 0 and 9 inclusive.
'secondDigit stores a number between 0 and 9 inclusive.
'
Sub TwoDigits(ByVal num As Integer,
ByRef firstDigit As Integer, ByRef secondDigit As Integer)
firstDigit = num \ 10
secondDigit = num Mod 10
End Sub

As another example, the LowestToHighest() procedure below also uses reference parameters:

```
'Determines if lowest is the lesser of two values and
'then swaps lowest and highest if necessary.
'
'post: lowest has the lesser of the two arguments passed.
'highest has the greater of the two arguments passed.
'
Sub LowestToHighest(ByRef lowest As Integer,
ByRef highest As Integer)
  Dim temp As Integer
  If lowest > highest Then            'swap values
    temp = lowest
    lowest = highest
    highest = temp
  End If
End Sub
```

When LowestToHighest() is called, the values of the passed arguments are switched if the first argument's value is greater than the second. For example, when the following statements are executed

```
num1 = 30
num2 = 12
Call LowestToHighest(num1, num2)
Me.lblOrderedNumbers.Text = num1 & "  " & num2        '12 30
```

LowestToHighest() is passed the addresses of `num1` and `num2`. Since `lowest` has a greater value than `highest`, `temp` is assigned 30, then `lowest` is assigned 12, and finally `highest` is assigned 30, the value of `temp`.

The following points are important to keep in mind when working with procedures with reference parameters:

- The order of the arguments corresponds to the order of the parameters.
- `ByRef` parameters accept only variable arguments. For example, a run-time error is generated when LowestToHighest() is called with constants, as in the statement:

```
Call LowestToHighest(5, 1)    'Bad Call Statement
```

- Variable arguments passed by reference may be changed by the procedure.

Review: NumberBreakdown

① CREATE A NEW PROJECT

Create a Windows application named `NumberBreakdown`.

② CREATE THE INTERFACE

Use the table below for setting object properties.

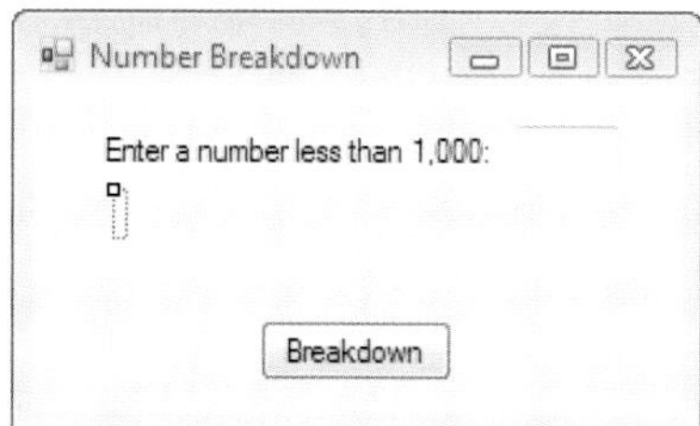

Object	(Name)	Text
Form1		`Number Breakdown`
Label1	`lblPrompt`	`Enter a number less than 1,000:`
TextBox1	`txtNumber`	*empty*
Label2	`lblDigits`	*empty*
Button1	`btnBreakdown`	`Breakdown`

③ WRITE THE APPLICATION CODE

a. Display the Code window.

b. Add comments that include your name, application, and today's date.

c. Create a btnBreakdown_Click event procedure and then add the statements:

```
Dim numberEntered As Integer
Dim onesDigit As Integer
Dim tensDigit As Integer
Dim hundredsDigit As Integer

numberEntered = Val(Me.txtNumber.Text)
If numberEntered < 10 Then
    Me.lblDigits.Text = "The first digit is: " & numberEntered
ElseIf numberEntered < 100 Then
    Call TwoDigits(numberEntered, tensDigit, onesDigit)
    Me.lblDigits.Text = "The first digit is: " & tensDigit &
        vbCrLf & "The second digit is: " & onesDigit
ElseIf numberEntered < 1000 Then
    Call ThreeDigits(numberEntered, hundredsDigit, tensDigit, onesDigit)
    Me.lblDigits.Text = "The first digit is: " & hundredsDigit &
        vbCrLf & "The second digit is: " & tensDigit &
        vbCrLf & "The third digit is: " & onesDigit
Else
    Me.lblDigits.Text = "Invalid entry."
End If
```

d. Add the TwoDigits procedure:

```
'The digits of a two-digit number are returned in separate parameters.
'
'pre: num is a number less than 100 and greater than -100.
'post: firstDigit stores a number between 0 and 9 inclusive.
'secondDigit stores a number between 0 and 9 inclusive.
'
Sub TwoDigits(ByVal num As Integer, ByRef firstDigit As Integer,
ByRef secondDigit As Integer)
    firstDigit = num \ 10
    secondDigit = num Mod 10
End Sub
```

e. The ThreeDigits procedure uses integer division to determine the third digit (the hundreds digit) of the number and then calls TwoDigits to get the first two digits of a number. Add the ThreeDigits procedure after the TwoDigits procedure:

```
'The digits of a three-digit number are returned in separate parameters.
'
'pre: num is a number less than 1000 and greater than -1000.
'post: firstDigit stores a number between 0 and 9 inclusive.
'SecondDigit stores a number between 0 and 9 inclusive.
'thirdDigit stores a number between 0 and 9 inclusive.
'
Sub ThreeDigits(ByVal num As Integer, ByRef firstDigit As Integer,
ByRef SecondDigit As Integer, ByRef thirdDigit As Integer)
    firstDigit = num \ 100
    num = num Mod 100
    Call TwoDigits(num, SecondDigit, thirdDigit)
End Sub
```

f. Add a TextChanged event procedure for the text box.

④ RUN THE APPLICATION

Save the modified NumberBreakdown project and then run the application. Test the application using single, double, and triple-digit numbers, and invalid data, such as four-digit numbers.

⑤ PRINT THE CODE AND THEN CLOSE THE PROJECT

Review: SortNumbers

Create a SortNumbers application that prompts the user for two numbers and then displays the numbers sorted from lowest to highest when **Sort** is clicked. The program should use the LowestToHighest procedure from the previous section. The application interface should look similar to that shown on the right after entering 5 and 2 and then clicking **Sort**.

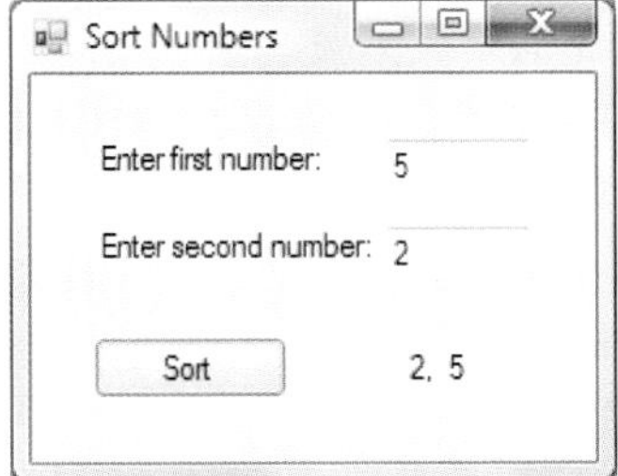

Control Object Parameters

control class

Control objects, such as labels, are a data type called a *control class*. A control class has a visual element that is displayed on the form and properties for storing data. Control classes include CheckBox, Label, RadioButton, Button, TextBox, and PictureBox. A control object can be passed as an argument to a procedure. For example, a call that passes a reference to an actual label on the form looks similar to:

```
Call GiveHint(Me.lblMessage, secretNumber, guess)
```

Control object parameters should be declared `ByRef` in a procedure using the appropriate control class name. For example, GiveHint() has a Label parameter:

```
'Determines if firstNum is larger than secondNum and then
'displays an appropriate message.
'
'post: A message has been displayed in a label.
'
Sub GiveHint(ByRef lblHint As Label,
ByVal firstNum As Integer, ByVal secondNum As Integer)
   If firstNum > secondNum Then
       lblHint.Text = "Too low."
   Else
       lblHint.Text = "Too high."
   End If
End Sub
```

Note that the keyword `Me` is *not* used in the assignment statements because the label being referred to is the one passed to the parameter. This allows a procedure to be written without actually knowing the names of the objects on the form. A procedure written this way can be used again and again in other programs without being modified. Development time for larger and more complex programs can be reduced by using generic procedures like this one after thorough testing and debugging.

Review: GuessingGame – part 4 of 4

Modify the GuessingGame application to include a control object parameter in the GiveHint() procedure so that a hint is displayed to the user in a label on the form rather than in a message box. Use the procedure in the previous section. The application interface should look similar to that shown on the right after guessing a number that is too low and clicking **Check Guess**.

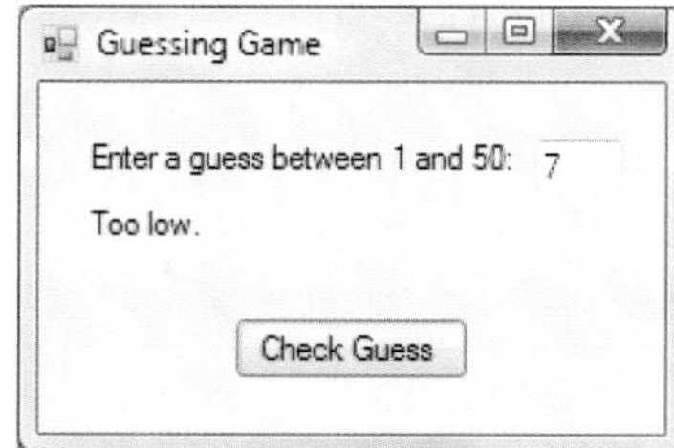

The Event Handler Procedure

Event procedures are used in every program. They are also called event handler procedures because they execute in response to events. For example, the following event procedure executes when a check box named chkRelish is clicked:

procedure name

```
Private Sub chkRelish_Click(ByVal sender As Object, ByVal e As System.EventArgs) Handles chkRelish.Click
    If chkRelish.Checked Then
        price += 0.25 'Relish selected
    Else
        price -= 0.25 'Relish cleared
    End If
End Sub
```

event

Event procedure declarations include the `Handles` keyword followed by the events to be "handled." This keyword, not the procedure name, determines when an event procedure executes. Therefore, changing an event procedure name has no effect on procedure execution.

Event procedures always include two parameters, as shown in the chkRelish_Click heading. `sender` is the object that raised the event, and `e` is information about the event and will be explained later in the text. sender is type `Object`, a data type that can be used to represent any value.

An event procedure handles multiple events when event names, separated by commas, are added after the `Handles` keyword. For example, the HotDog application uses a single Click event procedure to handle click events for three different check boxes. Note that an assignment statement uses the `sender` parameter to access the properties of the object that caused the event:

```
Public Class Form1

    'Updates the price of a hot dog.
    '
    'post: The hot dog price has been updated in the label.
    '
    Private Sub Topping_Click(ByVal sender As Object, ByVal e As System.EventArgs) Handles chkRelish.Click,
        chkKraut.Click, chkCheese.Click
        Const TOPPING_PRICE As Double = 0.25
        Static price As Double = 2                      'hot dog base price
        Dim chkSelectedTopping As CheckBox = sender     'object that raised event

        If chkSelectedTopping.Checked Then
            price += TOPPING_PRICE
        Else
            price -= TOPPING_PRICE
        End If

        Me.lblCurrentPrice.Text = "Price: $" & price    'display updated price
    End Sub
End Class
```

- The procedure name was changed to a more generic name. This was done by modifying the name of the chkRelish_Click event procedure after it was added to the Code window.
- Additional events to be handled by the procedure were typed after the `Handles` keyword. An IntelliSense list is displayed when a comma is typed after the `Handles` keyword in the procedure heading.
- `sender` was assigned to a CheckBox variable so that its properties can be accessed.

The Tag Property

Every control has a Tag property. The Tag property of an object can be set in the Properties window to any string expression and is useful for identifying, or "tagging," objects for the programmer. When an event procedure is handling more than one object, the string in the Tag property can be used to determine which object raised the event. This is important when different actions should be taken for different objects. For example, the HotDogII application prices a hot dog by an amount that varies depending on the selected check box:

```
Public Class Form1
    'Updates the price of a hot dog.
    'pre: sender has a valid Tag expression.
    'post: The hot dog price has been updated in the label.
    '
    Private Sub Topping_Click(ByVal sender As Object, ByVal e As System.EventArgs) Handles chkRelish.Click,
        chkKraut.Click, chkCheese.Click
        Const RELISH As Double = 0.15
        Const KRAUT As Double = 0.25
        Const CHEESE As Double = 0.5
        Static price As Double = 2                          'hot dog base price
        Dim chkSelectedTopping As CheckBox = sender         'object that raised event

        If chkSelectedTopping.Checked Then                  'topping selected
            Select Case chkSelectedTopping.Tag
                Case "Relish"
                    price += RELISH
                Case "Kraut"
                    price += KRAUT
                Case "Cheese"
                    price += CHEESE
            End Select
        Else                                                'topping cleared
            Select Case chkSelectedTopping.Tag
                Case "Relish"
                    price -= RELISH
                Case "Kraut"
                    price -= KRAUT
                Case "Cheese"
                    price -= CHEESE
            End Select
        End If
        Me.lblCurrentPrice.Text = "Price: $" & price        'display updated price
    End Sub
End Class
```

The Tag property for each of the check boxes was set to a descriptive string. This property value is then used to determine which action to take.

Review: ShellGame

The Shell Game displays pictures of three shells. Under one shell is a "hidden" pearl. The user guesses which shell is hiding the pearl by clicking a shell. The hidden pearl is then displayed along with a message telling the player if a correct guess was made. The pearl is hidden again after each try so that the game can be played again and again. An algorithm for implementing this kind of guessing game is:

1. Generate a random number between 1 and 3. Use this number to determine which shell is "hiding" the pearl.
2. Show a pearl picture below the shell that corresponds to the random number.
3. Using one procedure that handles click events for all three shells, determine if the user clicked the shell that corresponds to the random number.
4. Display a message to the player. The player won if the shell clicked corresponds to the generated random number.
5. Make the pearl picture no longer visible so that the game can be played again without quitting and running the application again.

The algorithm can then be refined into the following pseudocode:

```
Sub picShell_Click(sender, e) Handles Shell1.Click, Shell2.Click, Shell3.Click
    Generate a random number between 1 and 3 inclusive
    Show the pearl that corresponds to the random number
    If picShellClicked.Tag = randomNumber then
        Display "You won!"
    Else
        Display "Sorry, you lose."
    End If
    Hide the displayed pearl
End Sub
```

① CREATE A NEW PROJECT

Create a Windows application named `ShellGame`.

② CREATE THE INTERFACE

Use the table below for setting object properties:

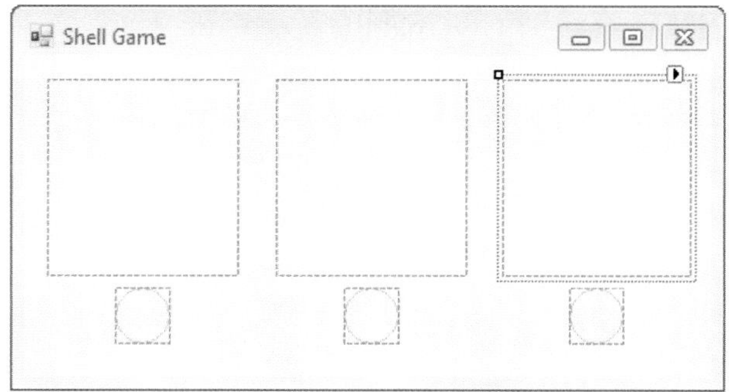

Object	(Name)	Text	SizeMode	Visible	Tag	Size
Form1		`Shell Game`				
PictureBox1	`picShell1`		AutoSize	True	1	110, 110
PictureBox2	`picPearl1`		AutoSize	False	1	32, 32
PictureBox3	`picShell2`		AutoSize	True	2	110, 110
PictureBox4	`picPearl2`		AutoSize	False	2	32, 32
PictureBox5	`picShell3`		AutoSize	True	3	110, 110
PictureBox6	`picPearl3`		AutoSize	False	3	32, 32

③ IMPORT IMAGE RESOURCES AND ADD TO INTERFACE

a. Select the picShell1 picture box.

b. In the Properties window, select the Image property. The [...] button is displayed.

c. Click the [...] button. The Select Resource dialog box is displayed.

   1. Select Project resource file and then select Import. The Open dialog box is displayed.
   2. Navigate to the location of the `shell.gif` file, a data file for this text.
   3. Select `shell.gif` and then select Open. The file is added to the project.
   4. Import the `pearl.gif` file, a data file for this text.
   5. In the files list, select Shell to display the shell image in the picture box.
   6. Select OK. The dialog box is removed.

d. Display the shell image in the picShell2 and picShell3 picture boxes.

e. Display the pearl image in the picPearl1, picPearl2, and picPearl3 picture boxes.

Check – The application interface should look similar to:

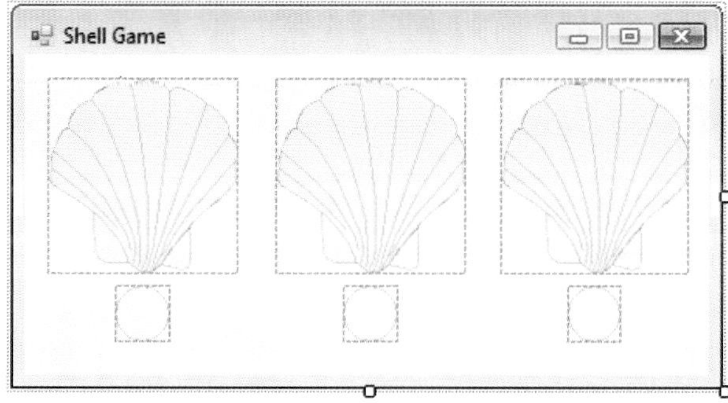

④ WRITE THE APPLICATION CODE

a. Display the Code window.

b. Add comments that include your name, assignment, and today's date.

c. Create a picShell1_Click event procedure.

d. Modify the procedure name, document the procedure, add events after the `Handles` keyword, and add statements so that the procedure is like:

```
'Determines which shell was clicked and displays a message if shell clicked is the
'same as a randomly chosen shell.
'
'pre: Shell picture objects have valid Tag properties.
'post: The hidden pearl has been shown and a message box has been displayed.
'
Private Sub picShell_Click(ByVal sender As Object, ByVal e As System.EventArgs)
Handles picShell1.Click, picShell2.Click, picShell3.Click

    'Determine which shell was clicked by user
    Dim picShellClicked As PictureBox = sender
    Dim shellClicked As Integer = Val(picShellClicked.Tag)

    'Pick the shell that hides the pearl
    Randomize()
    Dim shellWithPearl As Integer = Int(3 * Rnd()) + 1

    'Show the pearl
    Select Case shellWithPearl
        Case 1
            Me.picPearl1.Visible = True
        Case 2
            Me.picPearl2.Visible = True
        Case 3
            Me.picPearl3.Visible = True
    End Select

    'Display message to player
    If shellClicked = shellWithPearl Then
        MessageBox.Show("You won!")
    Else
        MessageBox.Show("Sorry, you lose.")
    End If

    'Hide pearl again
    Select Case shellWithPearl
        Case 1
            Me.picPearl1.Visible = False
        Case 2
            Me.picPearl2.Visible = False
        Case 3
            Me.picPearl3.Visible = False
    End Select

End Sub
```

⑤ RUN THE APPLICATION

a. Save the modified ShellGame project.

b. Run the application. Click a shell. Select OK in the message box and play a few more times.

c. Close the ShellGame application.

⑥ PRINT THE CODE AND THEN CLOSE THE PROJECT

Function Procedures

A *function procedure*, often just called a *function*, performs a specific task and then returns a value. Several built-in functions have been discussed in previous chapters, including Int() and Rnd(). A function procedure takes the following form:

```
Function ProcedureName(ByVal parameter1 As type, ...)
As Returntype
   statements
   Return value
End Function
```

ProcedureName describes the task performed by the function. ByVal indicates that the parameter is by value, parameter1 is the name of the parameter, and type is the data type of the parameter. There can be many parameters separated by commas. Returntype indicates the data type of the value returned by the function. statements is one or more statements needed to perform the task. The Return statement returns a value to the calling statement. There can be more than one Return, but the function ends after the first Return statement executes. Function declares the function procedure and End Function ends the function procedure.

A function often has at least one parameter for data that is required to perform its task. However, parameters are ByVal because a function performs a task and returns a single value. It should not alter the arguments it has been passed.

Functions are called from within a statement that will make use of the return value, as in the assignment statement below:

```
Me.lblStudentGrade.Text = LetterGrade(average)
```

The lblStudentGrade label displays the character returned by the LetterGrade() function:

```
'Returns a letter grade corresponding to score.
'
'post: A letter grade has been returned.
'
Function LetterGrade (ByVal score As Double) As Char
   If score >= 90 Then
      Return "A"
   ElseIf score >= 80 Then
      Return "B"
   ElseIf score >= 70 Then
      Return "C"
   ElseIf score >= 60 Then
      Return "D"
   Else
      Return "F"
   End If
End Function
```

Functions are useful for validating user input. For example, an application that prompts the user for a value between 1 and 10 could use the following Boolean function to determine if user input is valid:

```
'Returns True if lowerLimit <= userNum <= upperLimit.
'
'post: True has been returned if
'lowerLimit <= userNum <= upperLimit.
'False returned otherwise.
'
Function ValidEntry (ByVal userNum As Integer,
ByVal upperLimit As Integer, ByVal lowerLimit As Integer)
As Boolean
  If userNum > upperLimit Or userNum < lowerLimit Then
      Return False
  Else
      Return True
  End If
End Function
```

The following code uses ValidEntry() to check user input:

```
...
guess = Val(Me.txPlayerGuess.Text)
If Not ValidEntry(guess, MAX, MIN) Then
  MessageBox.Show("Invalid guess. Please try again.")
...
```

Note how the `Boolean` value returned by the function is used as the condition of the `If...Then` statement.

A function is a better choice over a Sub procedure when a well-defined task that results in a single value is to be performed. The following points are important to keep in mind when working with functions:

- The order of the arguments corresponds to the order of the parameters.
- Only `ByVal` parameters should be declared in a function because a function should not alter the arguments it has been passed.
- A function returns a single value and therefore must be used in a statement such as an assignment statement that makes use of the returned value.

Review: LetterGrade

① CREATE A NEW PROJECT

Create a Windows application named `LetterGrade`.

② CREATE THE INTERFACE

Use the table below the form for setting object properties.

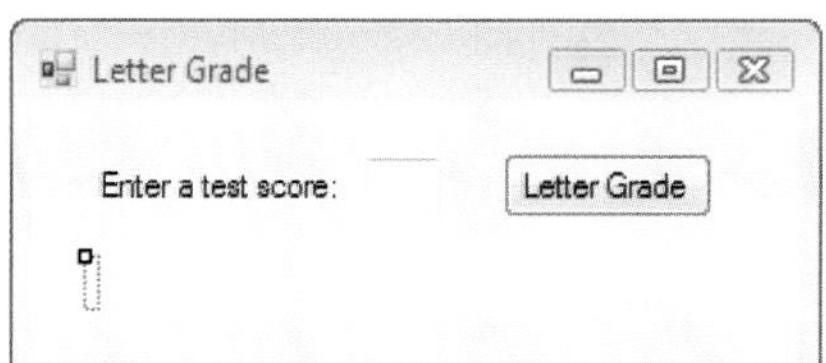

Object	(Name)	Text
Form1		`Letter Grade`
Label1	`lblPrompt`	`Enter a test score:`

TextBox1	`txtScore`	*empty*
Button1	`btnLetterGrade`	Letter Grade
Label2	`lblLetterGrade`	*empty*

③ WRITE THE APPLICATION CODE

a. Display the Code window.

b. Add comments that include your name, assignment, and today's date.

c. Create a btnLetterGrade_Click event procedure and then add the statements:

```
Const LOWEST_SCORE As Double = 0
Const HIGHEST_SCORE As Double = 100
Dim scoreEntered As Double

scoreEntered = Val(Me.txtScore.Text)

If Not ValidEntry(scoreEntered, HIGHEST_SCORE, LOWEST_SCORE) Then
    MessageBox.Show("Enter a score between " & LOWEST_SCORE & " and " &
    HIGHEST_SCORE)
    Me.txtScore.Text = Nothing
    Me.lblLetterGrade.Text = Nothing
Else
    Me.lblLetterGrade.Text = "Your grade is " & LetterGrade(scoreEntered)
End If
```

d. Add the ValidEntry function:

```
'Returns True if lowerLimit <= userNum <= upperLimit.
'
'post: True has been returned if lowerLimit <= userNum <= upperLimit.
'False has been returned otherwise.
'
Function ValidEntry (ByVal userNum As Integer, ByVal upperLimit As Integer,
ByVal lowerLimit As Integer) As Boolean
    If userNum > upperLimit Or userNum < lowerLimit Then
        Return False
    Else
        Return True
    End If
End Function
```

e. Add the LetterGrade function:

```
'Returns a letter grade corresponding to score.
'
'post: A letter grade (A, B, C, D, or F) has been returned.
'
Function LetterGrade (ByVal score As Double) As Char
    If score >= 90 Then
        Return "A"
    ElseIf score >= 80 Then
        Return "B"
    ElseIf score >= 70 Then
        Return "C"
    ElseIf score >= 60 Then
        Return "D"
    Else
        Return "F"
    End If
End Function
```

f. Add an appropriate TextChanged event procedure.

④ RUN THE APPLICATION

a. Save the modified LetterGrade project.

b. Run the application. Test the application by entering several valid and invalid scores.

c. Close the LetterGrade application.

⑤ PRINT THE CODE AND THEN CLOSE THE PROJECT

Case Study

The Chapter 4 case study was a simple calculator. In this case study a CalculatorII application will be created. This calculator will provide an interface similar to standard calculators and will be able to perform calculations involving many operands.

CalculatorII Specification

The CalculatorII application is an onscreen calculator with buttons for digits 0 through 9, the decimal point (.), and operators +, –, *, /, and = . The = button displays the result of a calculation. The user should be able to enter a series of numbers and operators which are evaluated as they are entered. For example, clicking 2, +, 3, and * displays 5. Continuing on and clicking 4 and then = displays 20. A Clear button should change the display to 0. After clearing, the number entered is considered the first operand. An Off button should close the application.

CalculatorII Design

The interface design for this CalculatorII is based on the appearance of a standard calculator:

The code design starts with an algorithm:

1. When the user clicks the decimal point button or a digit other than 0, replace the 0 on the display with the digit or decimal point clicked.

2. As the user clicks buttons, concatenate the digits and the decimal point to the display until an operator button is clicked.

3. When an operator button is clicked, convert the calculator display to a number and store this number as the first operand. Store the operator clicked for use in a calculation after the second operand is entered.
4. When a digit or decimal point button is clicked, display this value to replace the current display.
5. As the user clicks buttons, concatenate the digits and the decimal point to the display until an operator or equal sign button is clicked.
6. When an operator or equal sign button is clicked, convert the calculator display to a number and store this number as the second operand. Perform a calculation using the stored operator and the two operands. Display the result on the calculator display and also store the result as the first operand for use in another operation, if necessary.
7. If another operator button is clicked, store the operator and then start again with step 4.
8. If Clear is clicked, assign the operands 0, assign the operator nothing, show a 0 on the display, and then start again with step 1.
9. If Off is clicked, end the application.

From the algorithm, event procedures, variables, and functions can be identified by carefully reading the description. For example, "clicks," "clicking," and "clicked" indicates a Click event procedure. The words "store" and "stored" indicate a variable. An action to be performed could mean the need for a function. In this case, "perform a calculation" indicates the need for a function that takes two operands and an operator and returns the result of a calculation.

Analyzing the algorithm further reveals some aspects of the code:

- The same or similar actions are needed for the digit buttons and the decimal point button so a single event procedure should handle a Click event for the ., 0, 1, 2, 3, 4, 5, 6, 7, 8, and 9 buttons.
- The same or similar actions are needed for the operator buttons so a single event procedure should handle a Click event for the =, +, −, x, and / buttons.
- Variables representing the first operand, the second operand, and the last operator clicked need to be global because both the digit and operator Click event procedures require access to the variables.
- The Click event procedure that handles digit clicks needs a flag to determine if the digit or decimal point clicked should be concatenated to the current display or if the current display should be replaced by the clicked value.

Based on the algorithm and analysis of the algorithm, the pseudocode for this application appears like:

Dim operand1 As Double = 0
Dim operand2 As Double = 0
Dim op As String = Nothing
Dim newOperand As Boolean = True

```
Sub btnNumber_Click(sender, e) Handles buttons for 0 through 9
and the decimal point
    Dim btnNumberClicked As Button = sender
    If newOperand Then
        Change calculator display to digit clicked
        newOperand = False
    Else
        Concatenate digit clicked to current display
    End If
End Sub

Sub btnClear_Click(sender, e)
    Change calculator display to 0
    operand1 = 0
    operand2 = 0
    op = Nothing
    newOperand = True
End Sub

Sub btnOff(sender, e)
    Application.Exit()
End Sub

Sub btnOperator_Click(sender, e) Handles operator buttons
    Dim btnOperatorClicked As Button = sender
    If (operand1 = 0 And operator = Nothing) Or operator = "=" Then
        operand1 = value displayed
    Else
        operand2 = value displayed
        operand1 = Calculate(operand1, operand2, operator)
        Change calculator display to operand1
    End If
    operator = operator clicked
    newOperand = True
End Sub

Function Calculate(ByVal firstOperand As Double_
ByVal secondOperand As Double, ByVal operator As String) As Double
    Select Case operator
        Case "+"
            Return(firstOperand + secondOperand)
        Case "–"
            Return(firstOperand – secondOperand)
        Case "x"
            Return(firstOperand * secondOperand)
        Case "/"
            Return(firstOperand / secondOperand)
    End Select
End Function
```

Complex applications often require many Sub procedures and functions to perform tasks that together meet the overall program specification. Each new Sub procedure and function should be developed with the specification, design, coding, and testing and debugging steps used in creating a larger application. Solidly written and tested Sub procedures and functions can then be used in an application without introducing bugs and side effects.

In this case study, a function is needed to perform a calculation with two operands. Its pseudocode appears above. Next, the function needs to be coded and then tested and debugged. This can be done in an application created just for testing the function, as shown below:

```
Public Class Form1

    Private Sub btnResult_Click(ByVal sender As Object,
    ByVal e As System.EventArgs) Handles btnResult.Click
        Dim op1 As Double = Val(Me.txtFirstOperand.Text)
        Dim op2 As Double = Val(Me.txtSecondOperand.Text)
        Dim op As String = Me.txtOperator.Text
        Me.lblResult.Text = Calculate(op1, op2, op)
    End Sub

    'Performs a calculation using two operands and an operator
    '
    'post: The result of a calculation has been returned
    '
    Function Calculate(ByVal firstOperand As Double,
    ByVal secondOperand As Double, ByVal op As String) As Double
        Select Case op
            Case "+"
                Return (firstOperand + secondOperand)
            Case "-"
                Return (firstOperand - secondOperand)
            Case "x"
                Return (firstOperand * secondOperand)
            Case "/"
                Return (firstOperand / secondOperand)
        End Select
    End Function
End Class
```

CalculatorII Coding

The interface for CalculatorII is:

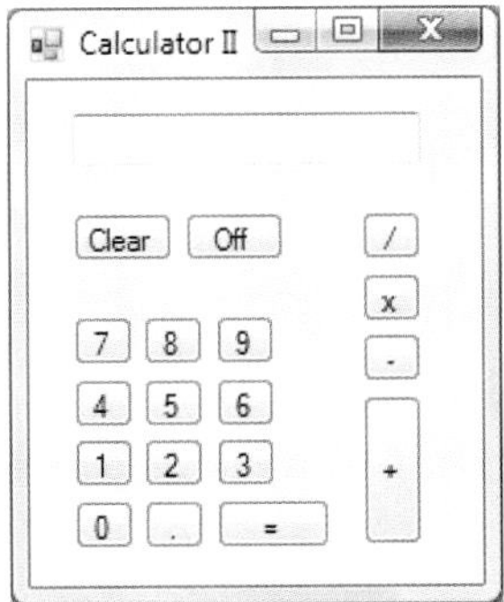

Object	(Name)	Text	Tag
Form1		Calculator II	
TextBox1	txtDisplay	0	
Button1	btn0	0	0
Button2	btnDot	.	.
Button3	btn1	1	1
Button4	btn2	2	2
Button5	btn3	3	3
Button6	btn4	4	4

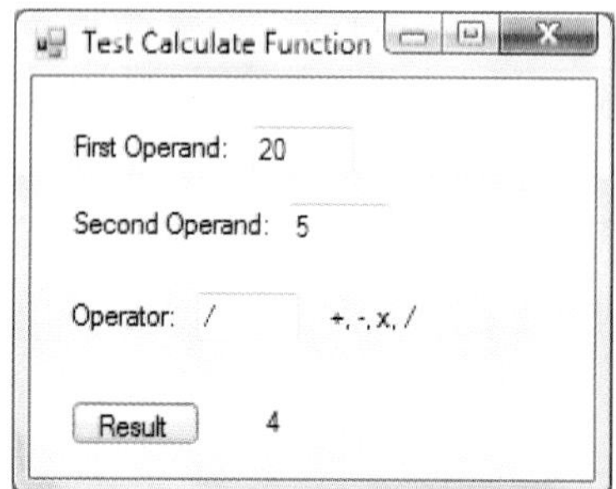

Button7	btn5	5	5
Button8	btn6	6	6
Button9	btn7	7	7
Button10	btn8	8	8
Button11	btn9	9	9
Button12	btnEqual	=	=
Button13	btnPlus	+	+
Button14	btnMinus	-	-
Button15	btnTimes	X	X
Button16	btnDivide	/	/
Button17	btnClear	Clear	
Button18	btnOff	Off	

The final coding for CalculatorII is shown below. The Calculate() function was copied from the function tested previously:

```
Public Class Form1

    Dim operand1 As Double = 0
    Dim operand2 As Double = 0
    Dim op As String = Nothing
    Dim newOperand As Boolean = True


    'Updates the calculator display.
    '
    'pre: Global variable newOperand is True when the current display should be changed
    'to a new number and False when the current display should be updated with a
    'new digit.The Tag property of the button clicked contains the number
    'corresponding to the number on the button.
    '
    'post: The calculator display has been updated to show a new number or an
    'additional digit.
    '
    Private Sub Number_Click(ByVal sender As Object, ByVal e As System.EventArgs)
    Handles btnDot.Click, btn0.Click, btn1.Click, btn2.Click, btn3.Click, btn4.Click, btn5.Click,
    btn6.Click, btn7.Click, btn8.Click, btn9.Click
        Dim btnNumberClicked As Button = sender
        If newOperand Then
            Me.txtDisplay.Text = btnNumberClicked.Tag
            newOperand = False
        Else
            Me.txtDisplay.Text &= btnNumberClicked.Tag
        End If
    End Sub


    'Clears the calculator display.
    '
    'post: The calculator display has been changed to 0 and the global variables
    'have been reinitialized.
    '
    Private Sub btnClear_Click(ByVal sender As Object, ByVal e As System.EventArgs)
    Handles btnClear.Click
        Me.txtDisplay.Text = "0"
        operand1 = 0
        operand2 = 0
        newOperand = True
        op = Nothing
    End Sub
```

```
    'Ends the applications.
    '
    'post: The application has been ended.
    '
    Private Sub btnOff _ Click(ByVal sender As Object, ByVal e As System.EventArgs)
    Handles btnOff.Click
        Application.Exit()
    End Sub


    'Updates the value of the operands and updates the calculator display to show the result
    'of a calculation if two operands have been entered.
    '
    'post: The calculator display has been changed to show the result of a calculation if a
    'second operator had been clicked, otherwise the display has not been changed.
    '
    Private Sub btnOperator _ Click(ByVal sender As Object, ByVal e As System.EventArgs)
    Handles btnPlus.Click, btnMinus.Click, btnTimes.Click, btnDivide.Click, btnEqual.Click
        Dim operatorSelected As Button = sender

        'No operator previously clicked or a calculation just performed
        If (operand1 = 0 And op = Nothing) Or op = "=" Then
            operand1 = Val(Me.txtDisplay.Text)
        Else    'second operand entered and a second operator clicked
            operand2 = Val(Me.txtDisplay.Text)
            operand1 = Calculate(operand1, operand2, op)
            Me.txtDisplay.Text = operand1
        End If

        'Store operator for use when the next operator is clicked
        op = operatorSelected.Tag
        newOperand = True
    End Sub


    'Performs a calculation using two operands and an operator.
    '
    'post: The result of a calculation has been returned.
    '
    Function Calculate(ByVal firstOperand As Double, ByVal secondOperand As Double,
    ByVal op As String) As Double
        Select Case op
            Case "+"
                Return (firstOperand + secondOperand)
            Case "-"
                Return (firstOperand - secondOperand)
            Case "x"
                Return (firstOperand * secondOperand)
            Case "/"
                Return (firstOperand / secondOperand)
        End Select
    End Function
End Class
```

CalculatorII Testing and Debugging

Running CalculatorII displays the following:

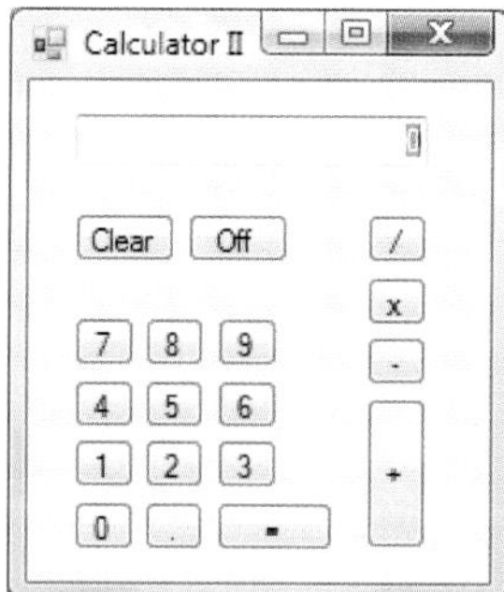

The CalculatorII application should be tested by trying several calculations and verifying by hand that the result is correct.

Review: CalculatorII – part 1 of 2

Modify the CalculatorII case study to include a button for integer division (\).

Review: CalculatorII – part 2 of 2

Modify the CalculatorII case study to display "ERROR" if a division by 0 is attempted. "ERROR" should also be displayed if more than one decimal point is entered for a single number.

Review: TestRndIntFunction

Write a RndInt() function that has lowNum and highNum parameters and returns a random integer in the range lowNum to highNum. Test and debug the function in a project named TestRndIntFunction. Properly document the function.

Chapter Summary

A Sub procedure is a set of statements that performs a specific task. Sub procedures simplify a program by dividing it into smaller, more manageable blocks of code. There is also less code redundancy and more program flexibility. A `Call` statement is used to execute a procedure.

A PictureBox object displays an image. A Click event is sometimes coded for a picture box. An image can be loaded at run time by using the `My.Resources` object.

A procedure can be passed data for use in completing its task. The data passed is called the arguments and a procedure that requires arguments is declared with parameters. `ByVal` parameters create a local copy of the argument passed and cannot alter the actual value of the variable. `ByRef` parameters use the actual variable passed and can alter the value of the variable. Objects can also be passed as arguments to procedures. Control object parameters should be declared using the appropriate control class names.

Comments are used to properly document a procedure. Documentation should include a brief description of what the procedure does followed by any preconditions and postconditions.

An event handler procedure always has two parameters. The `sender` parameter can be assigned to a variable of the appropriate control object type so that the properties of the object can be accessed. The `Handles` keyword in the procedure declaration indicates the events to be handled by the procedure. Adding additional control object events allows one procedure to handle several related objects. Every control has a Tag property. The Tag property can be set to any string expression and is useful for identifying objects in an event procedure.

A function is a procedure that returns a value. Functions often have at least one parameter for data that is required to perform its task. However, parameters are `ByVal` because a function performs a task and returns a value. It should not alter the arguments it has been passed. Functions are called from within a statement that make use of the return value. A Return statement within a function is terminates the function and returns a value to the calling statement.

Code conventions introduced in this chapter are:

- Procedure names should indicate an action and begin with an uppercase letter and then an uppercase letter should begin each word within the name.
- Procedure documentation should include a brief description of the task the procedure performs, a precondition when needed, and a postcondition.

Vocabulary

Address A variable's location in memory where its value is stored.

Argument A variable or value passed to a procedure.

Control class The data type used to create a control object.

Documentation Comments that describe a procedure and any preconditions or postconditions of the procedure.

Function procedure A procedure that performs a specific task and then returns a value. Also referred to as "function."

Parameter A variable declared in a procedure to accept the value or address of an argument.

Pass Giving data to a procedure.

Postcondition A statement of what must be true at the end of the execution of a procedure if the procedure has worked properly. Also referred to as "post."

Precondition The initial requirements of a procedure. Also referred to as "pre."

Reference parameter A variable declared in a procedure to accept the address of an argument. Reference parameters can alter the value of the variable arguments used in the procedure call.

Sub procedure A set of statements that perform specific tasks. Event procedures and general procedures are Sub procedures.

Value parameter A variable declared in a procedure to accept a copy of an argument. Value parameters cannot alter the value of the actual arguments used in the procedure call.

`ByRef` Keyword used to declare a reference parameter in a procedure.

`ByVal` Keyword used to declare a value parameter in a procedure or function.

`Call` Statement used to execute a procedure.

`End Function` Statement used to end the `Function` statement.

`End Sub` Statement used to end the `Sub` statement.

`Function` Statement used to declare a function procedure.

`Handles` Keyword that determines which events cause an event procedure to execute.

LinkLabel **LinkLabel control** Used to create a link to a website. Properties include (Name), ActiveLinkColor, LinkColor, Text, and VisitedLinkColor.

`My.Resources` Object used to retrieve a resource at run time.

`Object` A data type that can be used to represent any value.

PictureBox **PictureBox control** Used to create a control class object that can display an image. Properties include (Name), Image, SizeMode, Visible, and Size.

`Return` Statement used in a function procedure to send a value back to the calling statement.

`sender` Parameter in an event procedure that is the object that raised the corresponding event.

`Sub` Statement used to declare a procedure.

Tag Control class property that can be set to a string expression for identifying objects.

Critical Thinking

1. What has the SizeMode property (Normal, StretchImage, AutoSize, or CenterImage) of a PictureBox object been set to for each of the following situations to occur?
   a) Size of image is as designed, but outer edges have been clipped.
   b) Size of image is as designed, but blank area is displayed to the right and below the picture.
   c) Size of image is as designed, but blank area surrounds the picture.
   d) Size of image is shrunk to fit picture box and image is distorted.
   e) Size of image is as designed, but bottom and right edges are not visible.
   f) Image is as designed, but size of PictureBox is automatically changed to display entire image.

2. Explain the similarities and differences between:
   a) parameters and arguments
   b) Sub procedures and function procedures
   c) the keywords `ByVal` and `ByRef`

3. Determine if a Sub procedure or a function procedure should be used for each of the following tasks. State any parameters needed and if they are `ByVal` or `ByRef`. If a function procedure should be used, indicate the data type of the value returned by the function.
   a) Encode a string.
   b) Find the largest and the smallest of four whole numbers.
   c) Display an appropriate message in a message box for a numerical average.
   d) Display the rules to a game application.

4. Write code that:
   a) calls a procedure named LookFor() that has two value parameters named first and second and a reference parameter named foundIt.
   b) contains the Sub procedure heading for the Call statement in part (a).
   c) calls a procedure named ShowMe(), which has no arguments.
   d) contains the Sub procedure heading for the Call statement in part (c).
   e) calls a function named FindAverage() that has parameters test1, test2 and test3 and assigns the return value to a variable named average.
   f) contains the function procedure heading for the function used in part (e).
   g) contains an event procedure heading for btnChoose_Click that handles the click events for btnDelivered, btnPickUp, and btnSpeedy.

5. Given the function:

```
Function Testing(ByVal num As Integer)
    If num > 100 Then
        Return (num * 4)
    Else
        Return (num - 20)
    End If
    Return 500
End Function
```

   What do each of the Call statements display?
   a) `Me.lblAnswer.Text = Testing(60)`
   b) `Me.lblAnswer.Text = Testing(100)`
   c) `Me.lblAnswer.Text = Testing(200)`

6. What is displayed by the following application code when Display is clicked?

```
Private Sub btnDisplay _ Click(ByVal sender As
System.Object, ByVal e As System.EventArgs) Handles
btnDisplay.Click
    Dim a As Integer = 0
    Dim b As Integer = 0
    Dim c As Integer = 0

    Call Sub1(a, c, Me.lblOutput)
    Me.lblOutput.Text &= a & " " & b & " " &
    c & vbCrLf
    Call Sub2(a, c, b, Me.lblOutput)
    Me.lblOutput.Text &= a & " " & b & " " &
    c & vbCrLf
    Call Sub3(a, b, c, Me.lblOutput)
    Me.lblOutput.Text &= a & " " & b & " " &
    c & vbCrLf
End Sub

Sub Sub1(ByRef x As Integer, ByRef y As Integer,
ByRef lblOutput As Label)
    x = 2
    y = x
    lblOutput.Text &= x & " " & y & vbCrLf
End Sub
```

```
Sub Sub2(ByVal x As Integer, ByRef y As Integer,
ByRef z As Integer, ByRef lblOutput As Label)
    x = x - 1
    y = z
    lblOutput.Text &= x & " " & y & " " & z &
    vbCrLf
End Sub

Sub Sub3(ByVal x As Integer, ByRef y As Integer,
ByVal z As Integer, ByRef lblOutput As Label)
    x = 5
    y = 5
    z = 5
    lblOutput.Text &= x & " " & y & " " & z &
    vbCrLf
End Sub
```

True/False

7. Determine if each of the following is true or false. If false, explain why.
   a) A Sub procedure must always be declared with parameters.
   b) A procedure can call another procedure.
   c) Once an image is assigned to a picture box it cannot be changed.
   d) A PictureBox object can respond to a Click event.
   e) Arguments passed by value must be in the form of a constant.
   f) Every procedure must have documentation before it can be compiled.
   g) A `ByRef` parameter only exists for the duration of a procedure.
   h) A `ByRef` parameter uses the same memory location as the argument it is passed.
   i) A control object can be passed to a procedure as an argument.
   j) The parameters sender and e are optional in an event handler procedure.
   k) A Click event procedure can be coded to handle multiple events for more than one control object.
   l) Only the Button control has a Tag property.
   m) A function can only have one `Return` statement.
   n) A `Call` statement must be used in order to execute any type of procedure.
   o) Every type of procedure ends with `End Sub`.

Exercises

Exercise 1 — CD-DVDTips

Create a CD-DVDTips application that displays one of the following messages when Tip is clicked:

Handle CD/DVDs by the center hole or by the edges.
Keep CD/DVDs away from extreme temperatures and moisture.
Store discs in a jewel case or sleeve to prevent scratches.

The program code should include a DisplayTip() procedure that uses RndInt() function from the TestRndIntFunction review in this chapter to randomly display one of the tips in a label. The application interface should look similar to the following after clicking Tip:

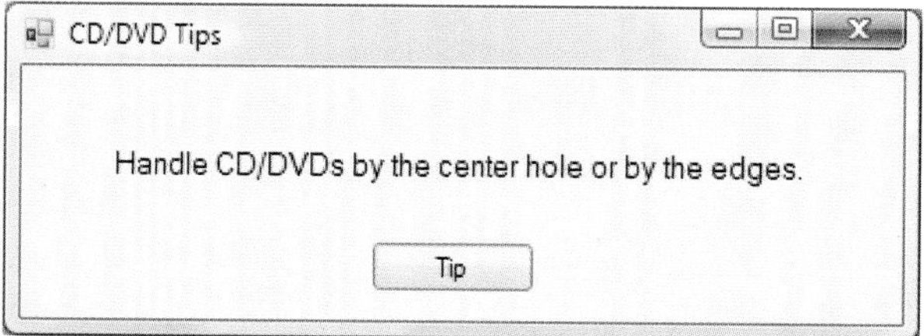

Exercise 2 — AddCoins

Create an AddCoins application that prompts the user for the number of quarters, dimes, nickels, and pennies and then displays the total dollar amount. The program code should include a TotalDollars() function with quarters, dimes, nickels, and pennies parameters. The application interface should look similar to:

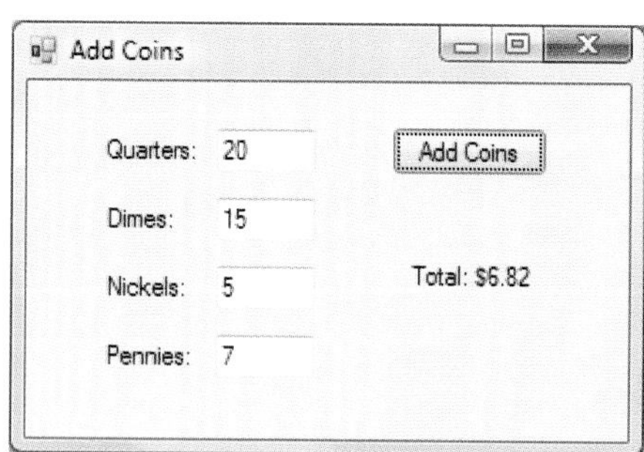

Exercise 3 — ReduceFraction

Create a ReduceFraction application that takes the integer numerator and denominator of a fraction and then displays the fraction reduced or a message stating the fraction cannot be reduced. A fraction may be reduced by finding the largest common factor and dividing both the numerator and denominator by this factor. The program code should include a Reduce() procedure with num and denom parameters that are changed, if possible, to the reduced values. The application interface should look similar to:

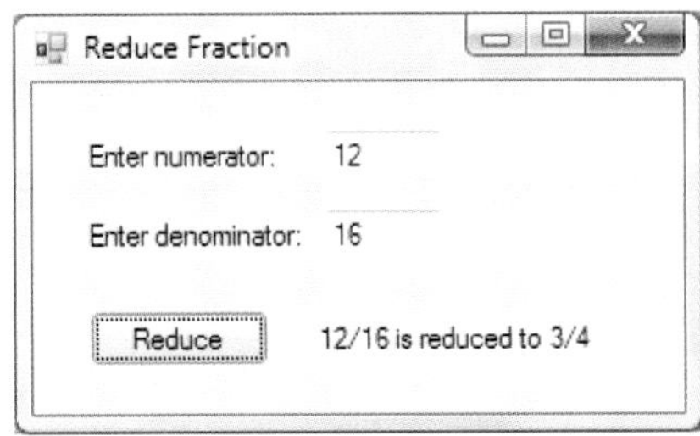

Exercise 4 — TestBuild

Create a TestBuild application that breaks up and then rebuilds numbers 100 through 125 and displays them in a label. The application interface should look similar to the following after clicking Break Up and Rebuild:

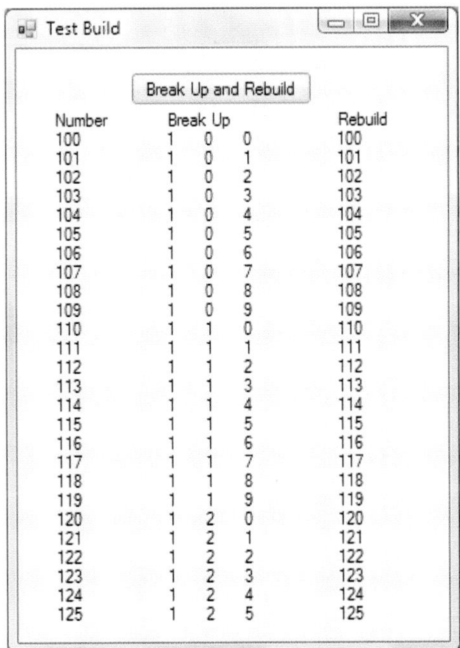

The program code should include:

- the ThreeDigits() and TwoDigits() procedures from the NumberBreakdown review.
- a Build() procedure that has firstDigit, SecondDigit, and thirdDigit parameters and returns, in a builtNumber parameter, a value that consists of the number represented by the three digits.

Exercise 5 ——— AlarmSystem

An office building uses an alarm system that is turned off by entering a master code and then pressing Enter. The master code is 62498. Create an AlarmSystem application that displays a message box with an appropriate message after a code is typed and then Enter is clicked. The application interface should look similar to the following after clicking five number buttons:

Exercise 6 ——— MetricConversion

The following formulas can be used to convert English units of measurement to metric units:

inches * 2.54 = centimeters
feet * 30 = centimeters
yards * 0.91 = meters
miles * 1.6 = kilometers

Create a MetricConversion application that prompts the user for a number and then converts it from inches to centimeters, feet to centimeters, yards to meters, and miles to kilometers and vice versa when a button is clicked. The program code should include separate functions to perform the conversions. The application interface should look similar to:

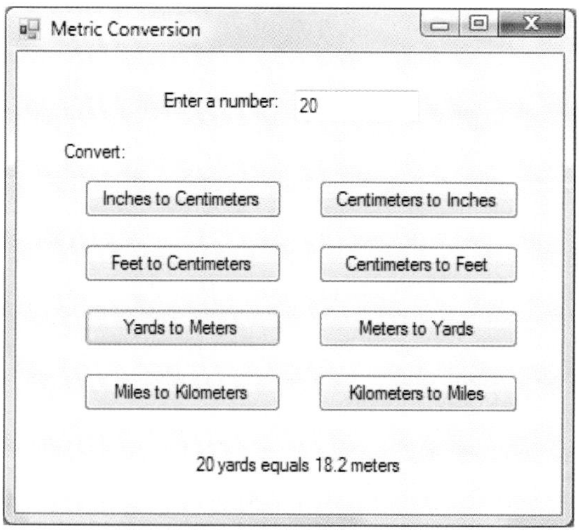

Exercise 7 — TestEntries

Validating user input is often required in programs. Create a TestEntries application that prompts the user for an integer, decimal number, and letter and then determines if the values are valid. The application interface should look similar to:

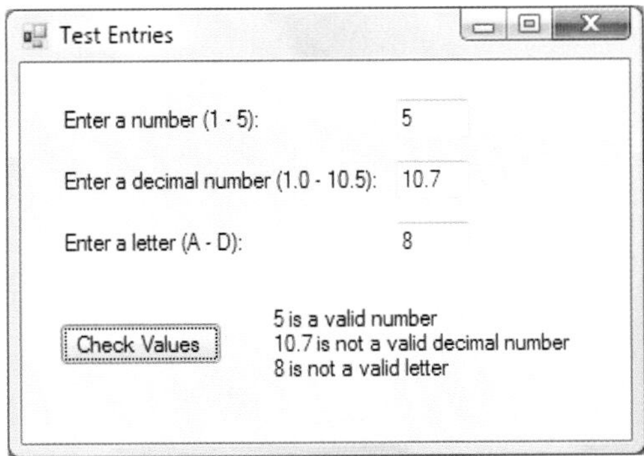

The program code should include:

- a ValidInt() function that has highNum, lowNum, and number parameters and returns True if number is in the range lowNum to highNum, and False otherwise.
- a ValidDouble() function that has highNum, lowNum, and number parameters and returns True if number is in the range lowNum to highNum, and False otherwise.
- a ValidChar() function that has highChar, lowChar, character parameters and returns True if character is in the range lowChar to highChar, and False otherwise.

Exercise 8 — LumberyardHelper

The basic unit of lumber measurement is the board foot. One board foot is the cubic content of a piece of wood 12 inches by 12 inches by 1 inch thick. For example, a board that is 1 inch thick by 8 feet long by 12 inches wide is 8 board feet:

((1 * (8 * 12) * 12) / (12 * 12 * 1)) = 8

Milled wood is cut to standardized sizes called board, lumber, and timber. A board is one-inch thick or less, timber is more than four inches thick, and lumber is anything between one and four inches thick. Create a LumberyardHelper application that prompts the user for the thickness, length, and width of a piece of wood and then displays the board feet and the classification of the cut. The application interface should look similar to:

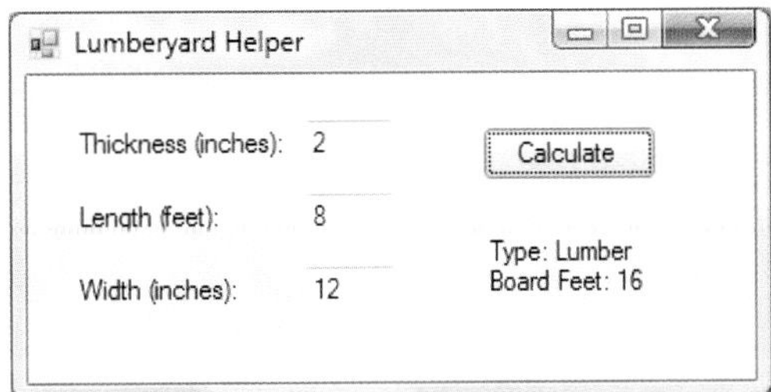

The program code should include a BoardFeet() function that has `thickness`, `length`, and `width` parameters and returns the number of board feet and a CutClassification() function that has a `thickness` parameter and returns the classification of the cut.

Exercise 9 — Hi-LoGame

In the Hi-LoGame, the player begins with a score of 1000. The player enters the number of points to risk and chooses High or Low. The player's choice of high or low is compared to a random number between 1 and 13, inclusive. If the number is between 1 and 6 inclusive, it is considered "low." If it is between 8 and 13 inclusive, it is considered "high." The number 7 is neither high nor low, and the player loses the points at risk. If the player guesses correctly, he or she receives double the points at risk. If the player guesses incorrectly, he or she loses the points at risk. Create a Hi-LoGame application that prompts the user for the number of points. The player then clicks either High or Low to play. The program code should include RndInt() from the TestRndIntFunction review to generate the random number between 1 and 13 inclusive. The application interface should look similar to:

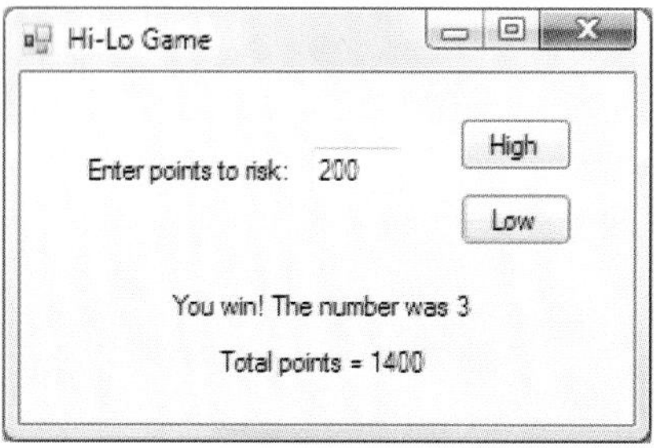

Exercise 10 — DiceGame

Create a DiceGame application. The player begins with a score of 1000. After entering the number of points to risk, the player clicks Roll Dice. The points on each die is displayed. If the total is even, the player loses the points at risk. If the total is odd, the player receives double the points at risk. The program code should include a RollDice() procedure with picDie1, picDie2, and total parameters that generates a two random numbers in the range 1 to 6 to determine the die faces to display in the picture boxes. RollDie() then updates the total parameter. The `die1.gif`, `die2.gif`, `die3.gif`, `die4.gif`, `die5.gif`, and `die6.gif` data files for this text are required to complete this exercise. The program code should also include RndInt() from the TestRndIntFunction review. The DiceGame application should look similar to:

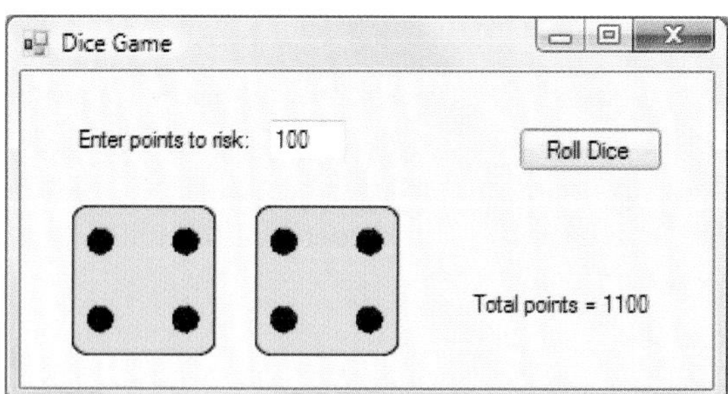

Exercise 11 — ShellGame

The ShellGame application from the reviews in this chapter gives the user just one chance at choosing the shell with the pearl. Modify the ShellGame application to give the user a better chance of finding the pearl:

1. After the user selects a shell but before the hidden pearl is displayed, remove (hide) one of the other two shells that does not contain the pearl.
2. Use an input box to ask the user if he or she wants to keep the original guess or choose the remaining shell as the new guess.
3. Display the result in a message box.

Improve the ShellGame application by appropriately separating tasks into procedures and functions, including using the RndInt() function from the TestRndIntFunction review to generate a random number from 1 to 3 for the shell that hides the pearl. The application interface should look similar to the following after playing one game:

Exercise 12 — Nim

The game of Nim starts with a random number of stones between 15 and 30. Two players alternate turns and on each turn may take either 1, 2, or 3 stones from the pile. The player forced to take the last stone loses. Create a Nim application that allows the user to play against the computer. In this version of the game, the application generates the number of stones to begin with, the number of stones the computer takes, and the user goes first. The application interface should look similar to:

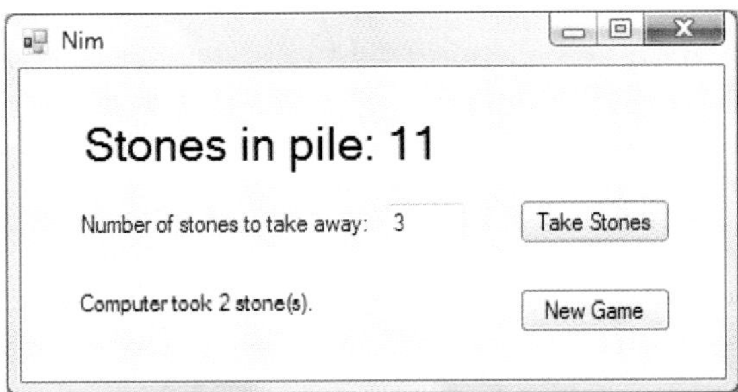

The program code should:

- prevent the user and the computer from taking an illegal number of stones. For example, neither should be allowed to take three stones when there are only 1 or 2 left.

- include the ValidEntry() function presented in this chapter to check user input.
- include RndInt() from the TestRndIntFunction review to generate a random number from 1 to 3 for the computer's turn to remove stones from the pile.
- include separate procedures for the user's turn and the computer's turn.

Exercise 13 — Mastermind

The game of Mastermind is played as follows: one player (the codemaker) chooses a secret arrangement of colored pegs and the other player (the codebreaker) tries to guess it. After each guess, the codemaker reports two numbers:

1. The number of pegs that are the correct color in the correct position.
2. The number of pegs that are the correct color regardless of whether they are in the correct position.

Create a Mastermind application where the computer is the codemaker and the player is the codebreaker. For simplicity, do not allow the secret arrangement of colored pegs to have duplicate colors and do not allow the codebreaker to guess duplicate peg colors. The application interface should look similar to the following after making several guesses:

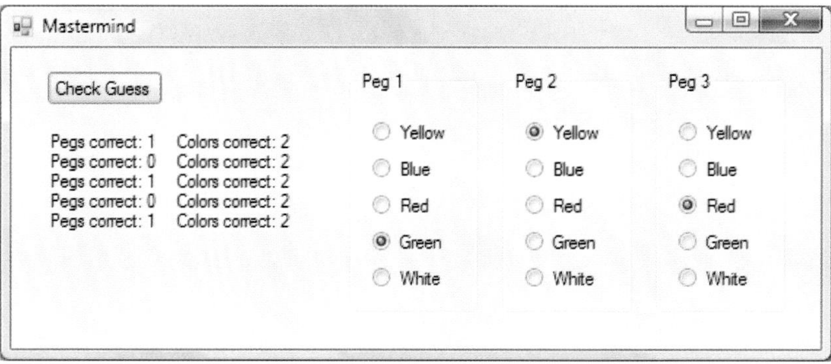

The program code should:

- include a ChooseColors() procedure that has `peg1Color`, `peg2Color`, and `peg3Color` parameters to generate unique colors for the secret arrangement of the colored pegs. Use numbers 1 through 5 to represent colors and use RndInt() from the TestRndIntFunction review to generate a random number.
- generate the secret arrangement of the colored pegs in the btnCheckGuess_Click() procedure. `peg1Color`, `peg2Color`, and `peg3Color` should be static variables that get assigned a color the first time the player makes a guess. Code similar to the following can be used to make peg color assignments:

```
If peg1Color = 0 Then         'first time variable used
   Call ChooseColors(peg1Color, peg2Color, peg3Color)
End If
```

- use separate functions to determine the number of correct colors and the number of correct pegs each time the player makes a guess.

Exercise 14 — FunnySentences

Create a FunnySentences application that prompts the user for a noun, verb, and adjective and then displays a sentence using these words. The program code should include a MakeSentence() procedure that has noun, verb, adjective, and lblLabel parameters and displays the sentence in the label. Use numbers 1 through 5 to represent five different sentences of your choosing and use RndInt() from the TestRndIntFunction review to generate a random number. The application interface should look similar to:

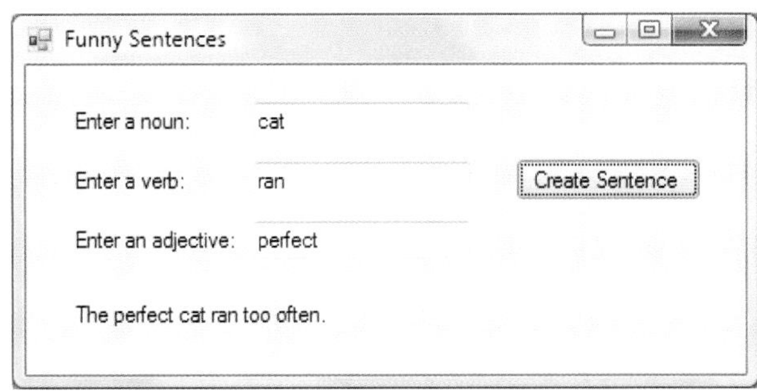

Exercise 15 (advanced) — ArithmeticDrill

Computers are used to test a student's ability to solve arithmetic problems. Create an ArithmeticDrill application that tests a student on addition, subtraction, or multiplication using random integers between 1 and 100. The student begins by choosing the type of problem and is then asked 10 problems with 3 chances to answer each correctly. If after 3 chances the answer is still incorrect, the correct answer is displayed. A score is calculated by awarding 10 points for a correct answer on the first try, 5 points on the second try, 2 points on the third try, and 0 points if all three attempts are wrong. Your program code should contain procedures, functions, and static variables. RndInt() from the TestRndIntFunction review should be used as well.

Exercise 16 (advanced) — PetAdoption

A new pet adoption agency has opened up in your neighborhood and needs an application to keep track of pets in need of a home. The agency currently has 15 puppies, 10 kittens, 3 canaries, and 2 iguanas. Create a PetAdoption application that keeps a running total of how many pets are available by subtracting animals that have been adopted and adding new animals in need of a home to the total.

Exercise 17 (advanced) — CardGame

The CardGame application that deals three cards to the user (player) and three cards to the computer. The cards dealt are randomly selected and are in the range 1 to 10, inclusive. The winner is the one with the highest score. After each game, a message should be displayed (You won!, Computer won!, or It's a draw!) and a score updated and displayed (1 point for each win). The user can repeatedly play the game. The scores are maintained until the user quits the application. The application interface should look similar to the following after playing the game five times:

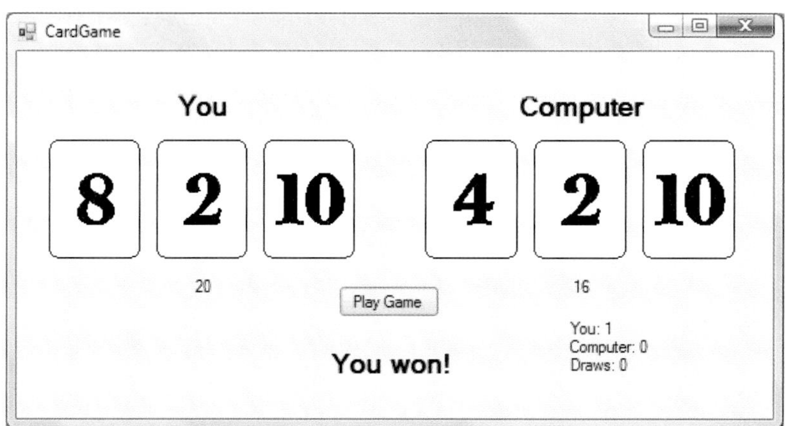

Use the pseudocode below when designing the application:

```
Sub btnPlayGame_Click()
    Deal 3 cards to player
    Deal 3 cards to computer

    If winner = player Then
        UpdateScore(playerScore)
        ShowScore
    ElseIf winner = computer Then
        UpdateScore(compScore)
        ShowScore
    Else
        UpdateScore(drawScore)
        ShowScore
    End If
End Sub
```

The interface should display six picture boxes that show the cards dealt. These picture box images should display cardback.gif when the application starts. The `cardback.gif`, `card1.gif`, `card2.gif`, `card3.gif`, `card4.gif`, `card5.gif`, `card6.gif`, `card7.gif`, `card8.gif`, `card9.gif`, and `card10.gif` data files for this text are required to complete this exercise.

The program code should include:

- a DealCard() procedure with picCard and intTotal parameters that generates a random number in the range 1 to 10 to determine the card to display in a picture box. DealCard() then updates the total and returns this value in a parameter.
- RndInt() from the TestRndIntFunction review.
- a Winner() function that compares the totals of the two hands and returns the winner. An UpdateScore() procedure adds 1 to the winner's score, and the ShowScore() procedure displays the current scores in a label.

Exercise 18 — CatchTheSquare

Create a CatchTheSquare application, which includes a label instructing the user to try to click the square and a square picture box object that moves when the user points to it. Objects have additional properties and can respond to events in addition to those discussed in the text. Use the properties and event listed below for this application.

Form properties also include:

- **Size** has properties Height and Width that correspond to the height and width of the Form object. Note: The Height and Width refer to the entire form. When positioning objects on the form, consider that the title bar has an approximate height of 32 and the borders have an approximate width of 6.

PictureBox properties also include:

- **BackColor** is the background color of an object. Clicking the arrow in this property displays a list of colors to choose from. (Change the background color of the PictureBox so that it visible against the form.)
- **Location** has properties X and Y, which can be changed by assigning Location a new Point structure that corresponds to the form location for the upper-left corner of the PictureBox object.
- **Size** has properties Height and Width that correspond to the height and width of the PictureBox object.

For example, the following statement changes the location of a PictureBox object:

```
Me.picSquare.Location = New Point(100, 100) 'upperleft of PictureBox at 100,100
```

A MouseEnter event can be coded for a picture box. A MouseEnter event occurs when the mouse pointer is over the PictureBox object. (This event can be used to move the square before the user has a chance to click.)

Chapter 7
Mathematical and Business Functions

Key Concepts

Using the Math class and its methods
Formatting numeric output
Using the IsNumeric() function
Understanding the Pmt(), PV(), and FV() business functions
Processing business data
Applying Windows application standards
Using trigonometric, logarithmic, and exponential methods in applications

Case Study

Loan Analyzer

Exercise Data Files

cart.gif

The Math Class

Computers and Math

Most of the earliest uses for computers were for performing mathematical calculations. Although still valued for their efficiency with mathematical calculations, computers are used in just about every field.

The Visual Basic `Math` class includes method members that perform common math functions. Three of these methods are:

- **Abs(*num*)** returns the absolute value of a number. `num` is a numeric variable or value.
- **Sqrt(*num*)** returns a `Double` value that is the square root of a number. `num` is a positive numeric variable or value. A negative number generates a run-time error.
- **Sign(*num*)** returns the `Integer` value `1`, `-1`, or `0` when a number is positive, negative, or 0 respectively. `num` is a numeric variable or value.

The following code demonstrates the `Math` methods discussed above:

```
Dim number As Integer

number = -5
Me.lblResult.Text = Math.Abs(number)          '5

number = 16
Me.lblResult.Text = Math.Sqrt(number)         '4

number = 8
Me.lblResult.Text = Math.Sign(number)         '1
```

The IsNumeric() Function

The IsNumeric() function is a Visual Basic built-in function that returns `True` if its argument can be evaluated as a number and `False` if it cannot. The IsNumeric() function takes the form:

```
IsNumeric(argument)
```

`argument` is a numeric or string expression or variable. The code below demonstrates IsNumeric():

```
Dim text As String
text = "123"
Me.lblAnswer.Text = IsNumeric(text)          'True

text = "abc"
Me.lblAnswer.Text = IsNumeric(text)          'False

Me.lblAnswer.Text = IsNumeric("2+4")         'False
Me.lblAnswer.Text = IsNumeric(2 + 4)         'True
```

Note that "123" evaluates to a number because the string contains only numbers. However, "2+4" is False because the string contains characters other than numbers. In this case, since the + character is not a number, the expression evaluates to a string.

Review: MathematicalFunctions

Create a MathematicalFunctions application that prompts the user for a number and then depending on which button is clicked, displays the absolute value, square root, or whether the number is positive, negative, or zero. Use the IsNumeric() function to verify user input is numeric. Display an appropriate message if the user enters nonnumeric data. The application interface should look similar to that shown on the right after typing 25 and clicking Square Root.

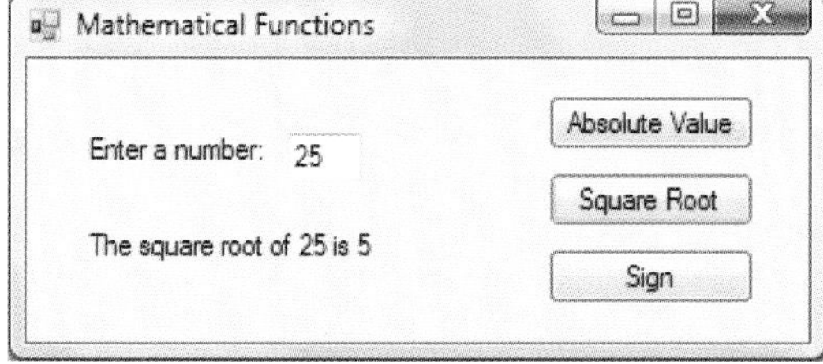

The Round() Method

The `Math` class contains the Round() method for rounding numeric data to a specified number of decimal places:

- **Round(*num*, *places*)** returns a `Double` representing a value rounded to a specified number of decimal places. `num` is a numeric variable or value. `places` is a numeric variable or value.

The following code demonstrates Round():

```
Dim number As Double = 3.4567
Me.lblRoundedValue.Text = Math.Round(number, 2)        '3.46
```

> ***Rules of Rounding***
>
> A number with a decimal portion greater than or equal to 0.5 is rounded up and a number with a decimal portion less than 0.5 is rounded down. When the decimal portion is exactly 0.5, an odd number is rounded up and an even number remains the same.

Review: RoundTheNumber

Create a RoundTheNumber application that prompts the user for a number and number of decimal places and then displays that number rounded to the specified decimal place when Round is clicked. The application interface should look similar to that shown on the right after typing 0.679999 and 2 and clicking Round.

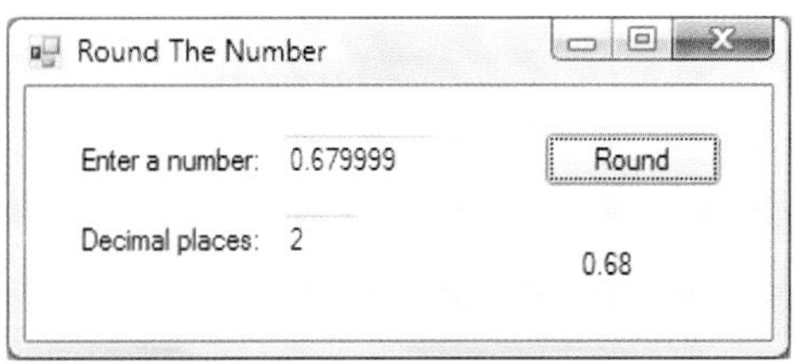

Formatting Numeric Output

Applications that display numeric data are more user-friendly when the numbers are formatted for the values they represent. For example, a value that represents a percentage should display a percent sign (%). The Visual Basic built-in Format() function converts a number to a formatted string. This string can be displayed on the interface. However, the actual value used in a calculation is just a number with no formatting.

The Format() function takes the form:

```
Format(number, "format type")
```

number is a numeric variable or value and format type is a predefined Visual Basic format. The following code demonstrates Format() and some format types:

```
Me.lblAnswer.Text = Format(8789, "General Number") '8789
Me.lblAnswer.Text = Format(8789, "Currency")       '$8,789.00
Me.lblAnswer.Text = Format(8789, "Fixed")          '8789.00
Me.lblAnswer.Text = Format(8789, "Standard")       '8,789.00
Me.lblAnswer.Text = Format(89, "Percent")          '8900.00%
Me.lblAnswer.Text = Format(8789, "Scientific")     '8.79E+3
Me.lblAnswer.Text = Format(8, "Yes/No")            'Yes
Me.lblAnswer.Text = Format(0, "True/False")        'False
Me.lblAnswer.Text = Format(1, "On/Off")            'On
```

The Yes/No, True/False, and On/Off formats display No, False, or Off when number is 0 and Yes, True, and On otherwise.

Business Functions

annuity

An *annuity* is a set of payments made on a regular basis for a specified period. When an annuity is a loan it is sometimes called an installment loan. An annuity can also refer to an investment, such as a retirement plan. Visual Basic includes built-in business functions that return information about an annuity. These functions include a payment function called Pmt(), a present value function called PV(), and a future value function called FV().

The Pmt() function takes the form:

```
Pmt(rate, term, principal)
```

rate is the monthly interest rate, term is the total number of monthly payments to be made, and principal is the amount borrowed. For example, the Pmt() function would be used to determine the monthly payment on a mortgage loan. The statements below calculate the monthly payments for a 30-year, $100,000 loan with an interest rate of 6%:

```
Dim payments As Decimal
payments = Pmt(0.06/12, 360, -100000)   'calculate payment
Me.lblPayment.Text = Format(payments, "Currency")      '$599.55
```

rate and term must be in the same units. Since the payments are monthly, the interest rate is calculated as monthly by dividing 6% by 12. The number of payments is 360, 30 years * 12 months. The principal is negative because it is the amount borrowed or owed.

PV() returns the present value of an annuity. The PV() function takes the form:

```
PV(rate, term, amount)
```

rate is the monthly interest rate, term is the total number of monthly payments, and amount is the dollars paid per payment. For example, PV() would be used to determine the cost of financing a car. The statements below calculate the cost of financing when $250 per month over a 4-year period is applied to a loan with an interest rate of 8%:

Amortization

Amortization is a method of computing equal periodic payments for an installment loan. Each installment, or payment, is the same and consists of two parts: a portion to pay interest due on the principal and the remainder which reduces the principal.

```
Dim amountSpent As Decimal
Dim financing As Decimal
Dim presentValue As Decimal
amountSpent = 250 * 12 * 4                       '12,000
presentValue = PV(0.08/12, 48, -250)             '10,240.48
financing = amountSpent - presentValue           '1,759.52
Me.lblPV.Text = Format(financing, "Currency")  '$1,759.52
```

This means that when you apply $250 a month for 4 years to an 8% loan, $1,759.52 is spent on financing, and $10,240.48 is applied to the purchase price of the car.

As another example of PV(), the following statements determine the maximum amount that should be borrowed for a 15-year mortgage at 10% when the desired monthly payment should not go over $650:

```
Dim borrowAmt As Decimal
borrowAmt = PV(0.10/12, 180, -650)
Me.lblAmount.Text = Format(borrowAmt, "Currency")   '$60,487.34
```

FV() returns the future value of an annuity. The FV() function takes the form:

```
FV(rate, term, amount)
```

rate is the monthly interest rate, term is the total number of monthly payments to be made, and amount is the dollars invested per month. For example, assume $500 per month is invested in a retirement plan that earns 8% interest per year. The statements below determine how much the retirement plan will be worth after 20 years:

```
Dim fund As Decimal
fund = FV(0.08/12, 240, -500)           'calculate future value
Me.lblRetirement.Text = Format(fund, "Currency")   '$294,510.21
```

Processing Business Data

Business applications that prompt the user for currency values and percentage rates should be written to accept a variety of formats. For example, a user may type $45,000.00 or 45000 for an amount. Each of these inputs reflect a currency amount, but a run-time error will occur if code is not written to handle the dollar sign and comma. The same is true for data that could include the percent sign (%).

The IsNumeric() function returns True when a string begins with $. For example, IsNumeric($45) returns True. However, the Val() function returns 0 for Val("$45") because $ is not recognized. When the user is expected to enter a currency value, the Replace() String method can be used to find and replace the dollar sign and commas with empty strings before converting the entry to a numeric value. The following procedure processes data in a text box and returns a number. The isValid variable is True only when a valid number greater than 0 is in the text box:

```
'Processes data in a text box to read a dollar amount,
'if any
'
'post: dollars has been assigned a number if numeric data
'with or without a $ and commas is stored in the text box.
'isValid has been set to True if a numeric value is stored
'in the text box.
'
Sub GetDollarAmount(ByVal txtUserData As TextBox,
ByRef dollars As Decimal, ByRef isValid As Boolean)
  Dim testAmount As String

  isValid = False                    'assume nonnumeric data
  If txtUserData.Text <> Nothing Then
      testAmount = txtUserData.Text            'data typed
      testAmount = testAmount.Replace("$", "") 'delete $
      testAmount = testAmount.Replace(",", "") 'delete commas
      If IsNumeric(testAmount) Then            'numeric data
          dollars = Val(testAmount)
          isValid = True
      End If
  End If
End Sub
```

The way in which a percentage value is entered must also be considered. For example, a decimal value such as 0.10 may be typed or just 10. Percentage values are sometimes entered with %, which must be removed from an entry. The TrimEnd() String method can be used to remove a percent sign from a string. The TrimEnd() method removes spaces when no other character is specified. However, it will also remove a specified character as shown in the procedure on the next page:

```
'Processes data in a text box to read a percentage amount,
'if any
'
'post: percent has been assigned a decimal number if numeric
'data with or without a % is stored in the text box.
'isValid has been set to True if a numeric value is stored
'in the text box.
'
Sub GetPercentAmount(ByVal txtUserData As TextBox,
ByRef percent As Double, ByRef isValid As Boolean)
  Dim testAmount As String

  isValid = False          'assume nonnumeric data
  If txtUserData.Text <> Nothing Then
      testAmount = txtUserData.Text
      testAmount = testAmount.TrimEnd("%")     'delete %
      If IsNumeric(testAmount) Then            'numeric data
          If Val(testAmount) >= 1 Then         'convert data
              percent = Val(testAmount) / 100
          Else
              percent = Val(testAmount)
          End If
          isValid = True
      End If
  End If
End Sub
```

Review: LoanPayment – part 1 of 3

① CREATE A NEW PROJECT

Create a Windows application named `LoanPayment`.

② CREATE THE INTERFACE

Use the table below for setting object properties.

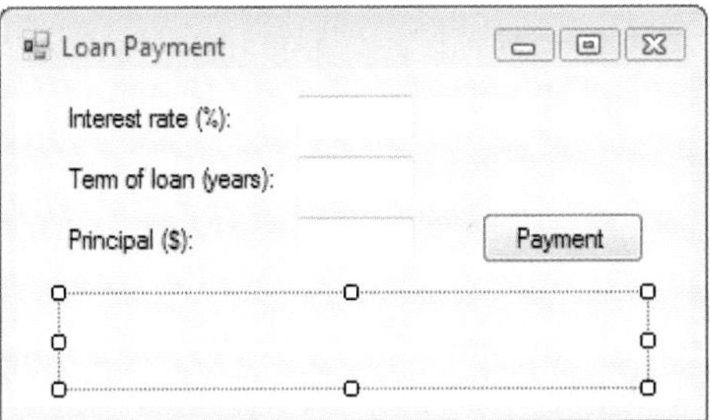

Object	(Name)	Text	AutoSize
Form1		`Loan Payment`	
Label1	`lblRatePrompt`	*see interface*	True
TextBox1	`txtRate`	*empty*	
Label2	`lblTermPrompt`	*see interface*	True
TextBox2	`txtTerm`	*empty*	
Label3	`lblPrincipalPrompt`	*see interface*	True
TextBox3	`txtPrincipal`	*empty*	
Label4	`lblMonthlyPayment`	*empty*	False
Button1	`btnPayment`	`Payment`	

③ WRITE THE APPLICATION CODE

a. Display the Code window.

b. Add comments that include your name, application, and today's date.

c. Create a btnPayment_Click event procedure and then add the statements:

```
Dim rate As Double
Dim principal As Decimal
Dim term As Integer
Dim payment As Decimal
Dim validData As Boolean

'Get interest rate
GetPercentAmount(Me.txtRate, rate, validData)

'Get term if interest rate is valid
If validData Then
    term = Val(Me.txtTerm.Text)
    If term <= 0 Then
        validData = False
    End If
End If

'Get principal if interest rate and term are valid
If validData Then
    GetDollarAmount(Me.txtPrincipal, principal, validData)
End If

'Calculate payment if all data entered by user is valid
If validData Then
    payment = Pmt(rate / 12, term * 12, -principal)
    Me.lblMonthlyPayment.Text = "The monthly payment for a loan of  " &
    Format(principal, "Currency") & " at " & Format(rate, "Percent") &
    " for " & term & " years is " & Format(payment, "Currency")
Else
    Me.lblMonthlyPayment.Text = "Enter valid data."
End If
```

d. Add the GetPercentAmount() and GetDollarAmount() procedures shown in the previous section of this chapter.

e. Create an event procedure that handles TextChanged events for all three text boxes. Change the procedure name to NewDataEntered and add the statement:

```
Me.lblMonthlyPayment.Text = Nothing
```

④ RUN THE APPLICATION

a. Save the modified LoanPayment project and then run and test the application.

b. Close the LoanPayment application.

⑤ PRINT THE CODE AND THEN CLOSE THE PROJECT

Review: CreditCardLoan – part 1 of 2

Create a CreditCardLoan application that prompts the user for the interest rate of the card, the total amount charged, and the minimum payment desired. Clicking Number of Payments displays the number of payments required to pay off the credit card loan, the total amount that will be paid, and the amount that will be paid to interest. The application interface should look similar to that shown on the right.

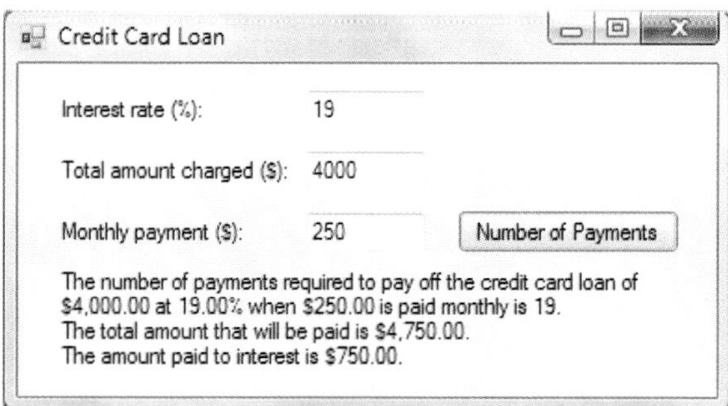

Review: WatchYourMoneyGrow

Create a WatchYourMoneyGrow application that prompts the user for the interest rate, term, and the amount invested each month and then displays the value of the investment (future value) when Future Value is clicked. The application interface should look similar to that shown on the right.

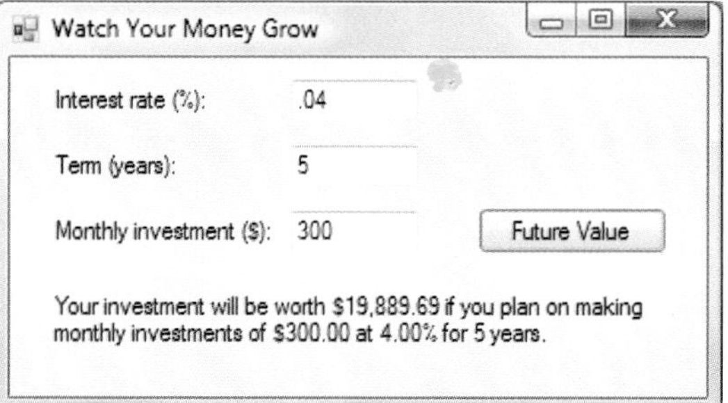

The ListBox Control

A list box is used to display a list of items. A scroll bar automatically appears in the list box if the number of list items exceeds the height of the list box. For example, in the TuitionCalculator application, a list box contains course level names:

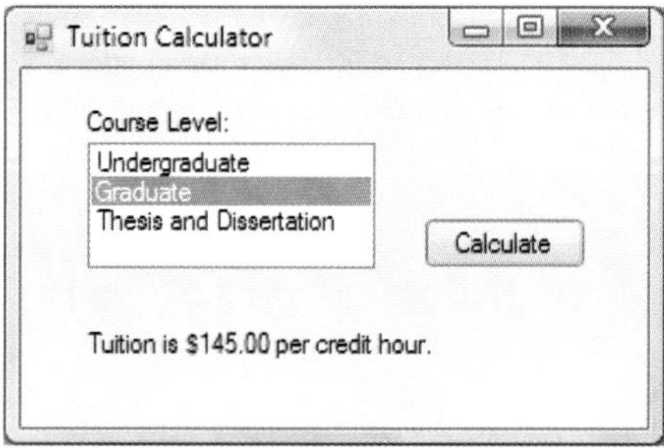

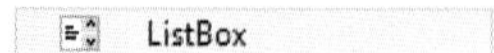

A ListBox control has the properties:

- **(Name)** identifies a control for the programmer. ListBox object names should begin with `lst`.
- **Items** contains the button that is clicked to display the String Collection Editor dialog box where a set of strings is typed.
- **Sorted** is set to True to display the list items in alphabetical order.

- **SelectedItem** is the selected list item. This property is available only at run time.
- **SelectedIndex** is the index of the selected list item. This property is available only at run time.

The items in a list box have an index value, with 0 being the index of the first item, 1 the index of the next, and so on. An index value of –1 means that none of the list items are selected.

A SelectedIndexChanged event procedure is sometimes coded for a list box. This procedure executes when a list item is clicked. The specific item clicked is determined with the SelectedItem or the SelectedIndex properties. The `Select...Case` statement below uses the SelectedItem property to determine the selected item:

```
Select Case Me.lstCourseLevels.SelectedItem
  Case "Undergraduate"
      creditHour = 75
  Case "Graduate"
      creditHour = 145
  Case "Thesis and Dissertation"
      creditHour = 160
End Select
```

The ListBox control class contains methods that can be used to display output at run time. Up to this point, labels have primarily been used to display output. However, a list box is a good choice for output that should be displayed as one item after another. The height of the list box is of little concern because a scroll bar is automatically displayed when the list gets longer than the box.

The Items.Add() method is used to add an item to a list at run time and takes the form:

```
lstControl.Items.Add(item)
```

`lstControl` is the name of the list box object and `item` is a value or string. The item is added to the end of the list, or in the proper position if the list is sorted. The following code demonstrates Items.Add():

```
For num As Integer = 2 To 20 Step 2
  Me.lstByTwos.Items.Add(num & " x 5 = " & num * 5)
Next num
```

Note that the `&` was used for concatenation. The `vbTab` constant can also be used to form strings with consistent spacing.

The Items.Remove() method is used to delete a specified item from the list and takes the form:

```
lstControl.Items.Remove(item)
```

`lstControl` is the name of the list box object and `item` is a value or string.

The Items.Clear() method is used to delete the contents of the list box and takes the form:

```
lstControl.Items.Clear()
```

`lstControl` is the name of the list box object.

Review: TuitionCalculator – part 1 of 3

① CREATE A NEW PROJECT

Create a Windows application named `TuitionCalculator`.

② CREATE THE INTERFACE

a. Use the table below for setting object properties.

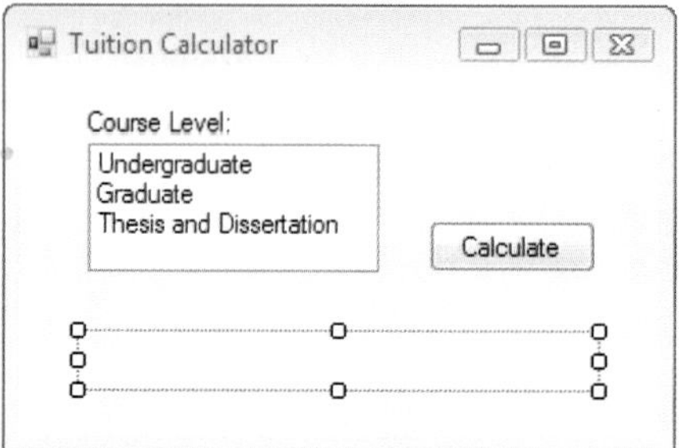

Object	(Name)	Text	AutoSize
Form1		`Tuition Calculator`	
Label1	`lblCourseLevelList`	`Course Level:`	True
ListBox1	`lstCourseLevels`		
Label2	`lblTuition`	*empty*	False
Button1	`btnCalculate`	`Calculate`	

b. Click the list box to select it and then click the Items property in the Properties window. Click the [...] button to display a dialog box. Type the following items, pressing Enter after each except the last:

```
Undergraduate
Graduate
Thesis and Dissertation
```

③ WRITE THE APPLICATION CODE

a. Display the Code window.

b. Add comments that include your name, application, and today's date.

c. Create a btnCalculate_Click event procedure and then add the statements:

```
Const UNDERGRADUATE_PER_HOUR As Decimal = 75
Const GRADUATE_PER_HOUR As Decimal = 145
Const THESIS_PER_HOUR As Decimal = 160
Dim tuition As Decimal

Select Case Me.lstCourseLevels.SelectedItem
    Case "Undergraduate"
        tuition = UNDERGRADUATE_PER_HOUR
    Case "Graduate"
        tuition = GRADUATE_PER_HOUR
    Case "Thesis and Dissertation"
        tuition = THESIS_PER_HOUR
End Select

Me.lblTuition.Text = "Tuition is  " & Format(tuition, "Currency") &
"  per credit hour."
```

d. Create a lstCourseLevels_SelectedIndexChanged event procedure and then add the following statement to clear the label when a different list item is clicked:

```
Me.lblTuition.Text = Nothing
```

④ RUN THE APPLICATION

a. Save the modified TuitionCalculator project and then run the application. Test the application by clicking each of the list items and then Calculate.
b. Close the TuitionCalculator application.
c. Print the application code.

The ComboBox Control

A combo box displays a text box for typing an entry and an arrow that can be clicked to choose an item from a list. A scroll bar automatically appears in the list when necessary. For example, the Tuition Calculator application can be modified to include a combo box for the user to enter or select the number of credit hours:

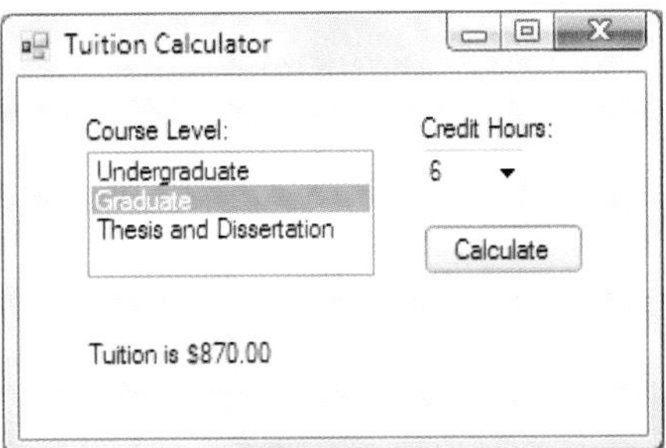

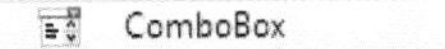

A ComboBox control has the properties:

- **(Name)** identifies a control for the programmer. ComboBox object names should begin with `cbo`.
- **Items** contains the [...] button that is clicked to display the String Collection Editor dialog box where a set of strings is typed for the list box of the combo box.
- **Text** is the text displayed in the text box of the combo box.
- **Sorted** is set to True to display the list items in alphabetical order.
- **SelectedItem** is the currently selected list item. This property is available only at run time.
- **SelectedIndex** is the index of the selected list item. This property is available only at run time.

The items in the list box of a combo box have an index value, with 0 being the index of the first item, 1 the index of the next, and so on. An index value of –1 means that none of the list items are selected. The Text property contains the item typed by the user in the text box.

The entry in a combo box changes when the user either types a value or selects a value from the list. Typing a value raises a TextChanged event, and selecting a value raises a SelectedIndexChanged event. Two different event procedures can be written for these events or a single event procedure can be written to handle both events. An `If...Then...Else` statement can be used to determine if a value was entered or an item selected, as in the statement below:

```
If Me.cboCreditHours.SelectedIndex >= 0 Then
   'Show item selected
   MessageBox.Show(Me.cboCreditHours.SelectedItem)
Else
   'Show value typed
   MessageBox.Show(Me.cboCreditHours.Text)
End If
```

The ComboBox control class also contains methods for adding and clearing list items at run time. The Items.Add() method is used to add an item to a list at run time and takes the form:

```
cboControl.Items.Add(item)
```

`cboControl` is the name of the combo box object and `item` is a value or a string. The item is added to the end of the list, or in the proper position if the list is sorted. The following statement demonstrates Items.Add():

```
Me.cboCreditHours.Items.Add("18")
```

The Items.Remove() method is used to delete a specified item from the list and takes the form:

```
cboControl.Items.Remove(item)
```

`cboControl` is the name of the combo box object and `item` is a value or a string.

The Items.Clear() method is used to delete the contents of the list in the combo box takes the form:

```
cboControl.Items.Clear()
```

`cboControl` is the name of the combo box object.

Review: TuitionCalculator – part 2 of 3

① OPEN THE TUITIONCALCULATOR PROJECT

Display the TuitionCalculator Design window if it is not already displayed.

② MODIFY THE INTERFACE

a. Use the table on the next page for setting object properties.

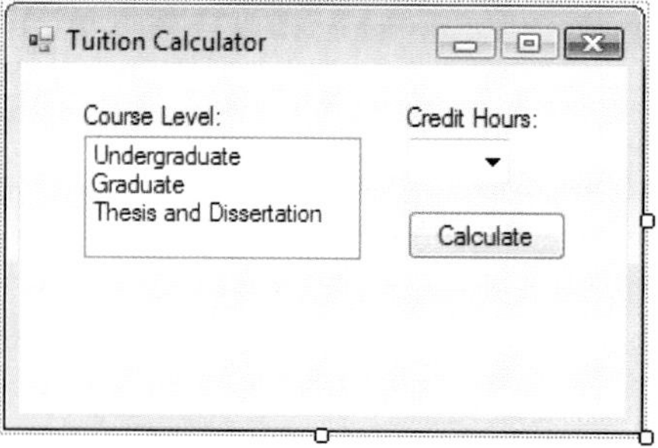

Object	(Name)	Text
Label1	lblCreditHours	Credit Hours:
ComboBox1	cboCreditHours	*empty*

b. Use the ComboBox Items property to add the list items 3, 6, 9, 12, and 15 to the combo box.

③ MODIFY THE APPLICATION CODE

a. Display the Code window.

b. Modify the btnCalculate_Click event procedure:

```
Const UNDERGRADUATE_PER_HOUR As Decimal = 75
Const GRADUATE_PER_HOUR As Decimal = 145
Const THESIS_PER_HOUR As Decimal = 160
Dim creditHours As Integer
Dim tuition As Decimal

If Me.cboCreditHours.SelectedIndex >= 0 Then    'list item selected
    creditHours = Val(Me.cboCreditHours.SelectedItem)
Else
    creditHours = Val(Me.cboCreditHours.Text)    'value typed
End If

Select Case Me.lstCourseLevels.SelectedItem
    Case "Undergraduate"
        tuition = UNDERGRADUATE_PER_HOUR * creditHours
    Case "Graduate"
        tuition = GRADUATE_PER_HOUR * creditHours
    Case "Thesis and Dissertation"
        tuition = THESIS_PER_HOUR * creditHours
End Select

Me.lblTuition.Text = "Tuition is:  " & Format(tuition, "Currency")
```

c. Modify lstCourseLevels_SelectedIndexChanged() to handle SelectedIndexChanged events for lstCourseLevels and cboCreditHours and the TextChanged event for cboCreditHours. Change the procedure name to DataChanged.

④ RUN THE APPLICATION

Save the modified TuitionCalculator project and then run the application. Test the application by selecting different combinations of course levels and credit hours.

⑤ PRINT THE CODE AND THEN CLOSE THE PROJECT

Review: LoanPayment – part 2 of 3

Modify the LoanPayment application so that combo boxes prompt the user for the interest rate and term. The interest rate combo box should contain 6%, 6.5%, 7%, 7.5%, 8%, 8.5%, and 9%. Modify GetPercentAmount() accordingly. The term combo box should contain 3, 5, 10, 15, 20, and 30. Modify the NewDataEntered() procedure to handle the five possible TextChanged and SelectedIndexChanged events. The application interface should look similar to that shown on the right after entering the loan information and clicking Payment.

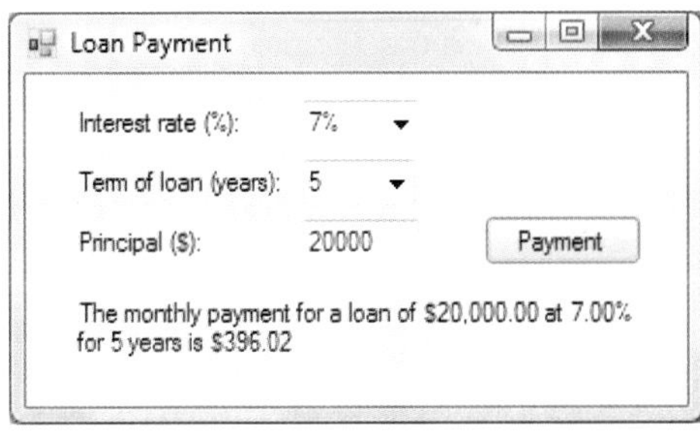

Windows Application Standards

Windows applications have a standard look and feel about them. An application that has features similar to other Windows applications is easier for the user to learn and understand. For example, the application below has several features found in a Windows application:

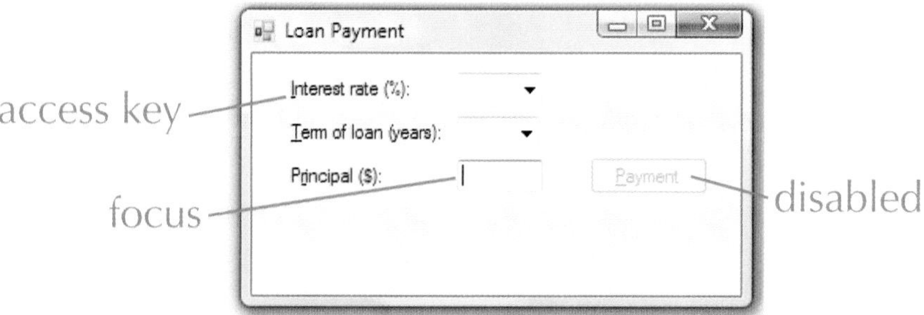

focus
access key
disabled object

The Principal text box contains the insertion point. This indicates it has the focus. An object with *focus* will receive the user input from the keyboard. The underlined r in the Principal ($) label is an access key. An *access key* is the key pressed while holding down the Alt key to select an object. For example, Alt+T moves the insertion point to the Term of loan (years) combo box. The tab order has been set so that the focus will move from one object to the next in a logical order when the Tab key is pressed. Payment appears dimmed because it is disabled. A *disabled object* cannot be selected by the user. In this case, Payment is not appropriate to select at this time because all the loan information has not be entered.

A button that has the focus appears with a dashed line around it. A text box that has the focus contains an insertion point and any text typed will be displayed in that text box. When a list box or combo box has the focus, the arrow keys can be used to select a list item. Labels cannot receive focus.

An ampersand (&) is used in the Text property for an object to define an access key. For example, typing `&Payment` for a button's Text property displays Payment on the button and allows the user to press Alt+P at run time to select the button. Access keys are not displayed until the user presses the Alt key.

TIP Select Tools → Settings → Expert Settings and then select View → Tab Order to display the TabIndex setting for each object on the interface. Click the tab number on the interface to change the value.

A logical tab order allows for easier and faster data entry. For example, when the LoanPayment application is started, the interest rate combo box should have the focus. Pressing the Tab key should logically move the focus to the term combo box, and then the principal text box, and finally the payment button. The tab order is determined by the order in which objects are added to a form. However, this order can be changed by setting the TabIndex property of the objects, with the first object to be selected given TabIndex 0.

Although labels cannot receive focus, their tab order is important. When the access key of a label is selected, the object that comes after the label in tab order receives the focus. For example, in the LoanPayment application, the Interest rate (%) label has tab order 0 and the cboRate combo box has tab order 1. When Alt+I is pressed, the label cannot receive focus, so the combo box gets the focus, which is exactly what the user expects.

The Enabled property for an object can be set to False to make the object appear dimmed. Disabled objects cannot be selected. For example, in the LoanPayment application, the rate, term, and principal are required to calculate a payment. Therefore, the button is disabled until valid data is entered.

The Visible property for an object can be used to hide an object. An object with False for the Visible property does not appear on the form at run time. This is useful when an object is not relevant at the current time. Setting the Visible property of a group box to False hides the group box and every object within the group box.

Review: LoanPayment – part 3 of 3

① OPEN THE LOANPAYMENT PROJECT

a. Open the Loan Payment project.

b. Display the Design window.

② DISABLE A BUTTON

a. Set the Enabled property of btnPayment to False.

b. Run the application. Note that the Payment button is dimmed and nothing happens when it is clicked.

c. Close the application and display the Design window.

③ ADD ACCESS KEYS

a. Set the Text property of lblRatePrompt to &Interest rate (%):

b. Use the table below to set other Text properties:

Object	Text
lblTermPrompt	`&Term of loan (years):`
lblPrincipalPrompt	`P&rincipal ($):`
btnPayment	`&Payment`

④ RUN THE APPLICATION AND TEST THE TAB ORDER AND ACCESS KEYS

a. Run the application. Press the Tab key a few times. Notice how the focus does not go from one object to another in a logical order.

b. Press Alt+I. Note how the interest rate combo box does not receive the focus like expected.

c. Close the application and display the Design window.

⑤ SET THE TAB ORDER

a. Set the TabIndex property of lblRatePrompt to 0 if it is not already 0.

b. Use the table shown below to set other TabIndex properties:

Object	TabIndex
cboRate	1
lblTermPrompt	2
cboTerm	3
lblPrincipalPrompt	4
txtPrincipal	5
lblMonthlyPayment	6
btnPayment	7

⑥ MODIFY THE APPLICATION CODE

a. Display the Code window.

b. Modify the NewDataEntered() procedure to enable the Payment button when appropriate:

```
Private Sub NewDataEntered(ByVal sender As System.Object,
ByVal e As System.EventArgs) Handles txtPrincipal.TextChanged,
cboRate.SelectedIndexChanged, cboTerm.SelectedIndexChanged,
cboRate.TextChanged, cboTerm.TextChanged

    Me.lblMonthlyPayment.Text = Nothing
    Me.btnPayment.Enabled = False

    If Me.cboRate.Text <> Nothing And Me.cboTerm.Text <> Nothing And _
    Me.txtPrincipal.Text <> Nothing Then
        Me.btnPayment.Enabled = True
    End If
End Sub
```

⑦ RUN THE APPLICATION

a. Save the modified LoanPayment project and then run the application. Press the Alt key to display access keys. Press the Tab key several times. The focus moves in a logical order.

b. Enter all the necessary loan information. Note how Payment is enabled. Use the appropriate access key to select Payment.

⑧ PRINT THE CODE AND THEN CLOSE THE PROJECT

Review: CreditCardLoan – part 2 of 2

Modify the CreditCardLoan application so that the focus is in the first text box when the application is started and the focus moves to the next object in the application in a logical order when the Tab key is pressed. Set appropriate access keys. Modify the interface so that the Number of Payments button is disabled at startup and add code to enable the button when valid data has been entered.

Review: TuitionCalculator – part 3 of 3

Modify the TuitionCalculator application so that the focus is in the list box when the application is started and the focus moves to the next object in the application in a logical order when the Tab key is pressed. Set appropriate access keys. Modify the interface so that the Calculate button is disabled at startup and add code to enable the button when valid data has been entered.

In this case study a Loan Analyzer application will be created. A loan analyzer should calculate payments and/or loan sizes for auto and home loans.

LoanAnalyzer Specification

The LoanAnalyzer application provides the user with a loan payment and a loan amount for car and house loans. Terms available are 2, 3, 5, and 7 years for an auto loan and 10, 15, and 30 years for a mortgage (house loan). The user should be required to enter only the information necessary for a particular loan. LoanAnalyzer should then display either a loan payment amount or a total loan amount.

LoanAnalyzer Design

The LoanAnalyzer interface will vary depending on what type of loan the user is inquiring about. A car loan will have a different set of term options from a home loan. If the user wants to know payment information, a loan size will be required. However, for loan size information, the payment amount will be required.

To get the user started, images that respond to clicks will provide an intuitive way to choose either a car or home loan. After selecting the loan type, the user must choose to calculate the loan size or the payment amount. Since the user must choose one or the other, radio buttons should be used. Because the term options are limited, a list box is the best choice for getting this input. A combo box is the best choice the interest rate because rates can vary, but there are some typical values. A New Loan button clears all options except the icons. A Calculate button displays the result of a calculation based on the information entered. The interface sketch shows all the require elements, but at run time only some of the elements will be displayed:

The code design starts with an algorithm:

1. When LoanAnalyzer starts, only an auto icon and a home icon are displayed. All other objects should not be visible.
2. Clicking an image displays the What do you want to know? options. Term options can be added to the Select Term list, but the list should not be displayed until the user selects the type of information wanted. A New Loan button should also appear to allow the user to clear the form and start over.
3. Selecting the type of information wanted displays the loan options. A Calculate button should also appear, but should not be enabled until all the required data has been entered or selected. If How much can I borrow? is selected, a text box should prompt for a payment amount. If What will be the size of my payments? is selected, the text box should prompt for a loan amount.
4. After required data has been entered, clicking Calculate uses either the Pmt() or PV() function to determine the information wanted by the user. This information should then be displayed in a label.
5. If New Loan is clicked, all options except the images are hidden.

Analyzing the algorithm further reveals some aspects of the code:

- The Visible property should be used in the Design window to hide many of the options. At run time, the Visible option can be set to True to display options as they are required.
- The Enabled property should be used to disable Calculate until all the required data is entered or selected.
- The same or similar actions are needed for the radio buttons so a single event procedure should handle a Click event for How much can I borrow? and What will be the size of my payments?
- When either the term, amount, or interest rate data is entered, selected, or changed, the other options need to be checked for required data to determine if Calculate should be displayed. This should all be done in a single event procedure that handles selected index changes and text changes.

Based on the algorithm and analysis of the algorithm, the pseudocode for this application appears like:

```
Sub Image_Click(sender, e) Handles picAuto.Click, picHome.Click
    ImageClicked = sender

    Show the group box of radio button options
    Show the New Loan button
    Show the disabled Calculate button

    Select Case ImageClicked.Tag
        Case auto
            lstTerm.Items.Add("2 years")
            lstTerm.Items.Add("3 years")
            lstTerm.Items.Add("5 years")
            lstTerm.Items.Add("7 years")
```

```
        Case home
            lstTerm.Items.Add("10 years")
            lstTerm.Items.Add("15 years")
            lstTerm.Items.Add("30 years")
    End Select
End Sub

Sub btnNewLoan_Click(sender, e)
    Hide all objects except picture boxes
    Clear result label
End Sub

Sub WhatDoYouWantToKnow_Click(sender, e) Handles radHowMuch.Click,
radPaymentSize.Click
    Show term prompt and term list
    Show textbox for principal or payment with appropriate prompt
    Show interest rate prompt and combo box
End Sub

Sub InfoEntered(sender, e) Handles lstTerm.SelectedIndexChanged,
txtPrincipalOrPayment.TextChanged, cboInterestRate.SelectedIndexChanged,
cboInterestRate.TextChanged
    Clear result label
    Disable Calculate button
    If txtPrincipalOrPayment.Text <> Nothing And
    cboInterestRate.Text <> Nothing Then
        Enable Calculate button
    End If
End Sub

Sub btnCalculate
    Term = Val(lstTerm.SelectedItem)
    Get Principal or payment
    If Principal or payment is valid Then
        Get Interest rate
    End If
    If Interest rate is valid Then
        If radHowMuch.Checked
            Use PV() function to calculate loan amount. Show message.
        Else
            Use Pmt() function to calculate payment amount. Show message.
        End If
    Else
        Display message that data is invalid
    End If
End Sub
```

LoanAnalyzer Coding

The interface and code for this Case Study are:

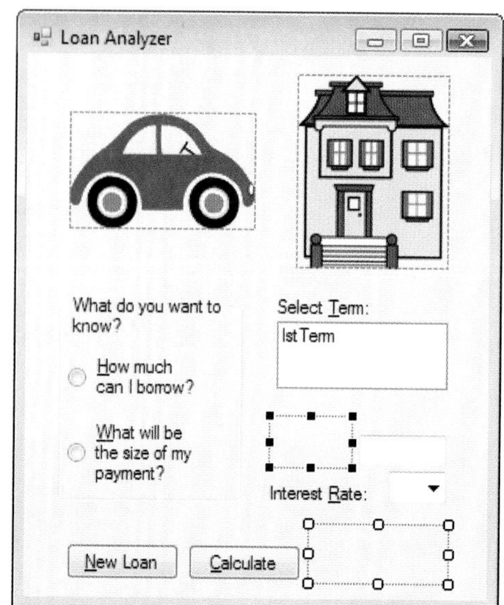

Object	(Name)	Text	Tag	TabIndex
Form1		Loan Analyzer		
PictureBox1	picAuto		auto	
PictureBox2	picHome		home	
GroupBox1	grpWhatToKnow			0
RadioButton1	radHowMuch	*see interface*	how much	1
RadioButton2	radPaymentSize	*see interface*	payment size	2
Button1	bntNewLoan	&New Loan		3
Label1	lblTermPrompt	Select &Term:		4
ListBox1	lstTerm			5
Label2	lblPrincipalOrPaymentPrompt	*empty*		6
TextBox1	txtPrincipalOrPayment	*empty*		7
Label3	lblRatePrompt	Interest &Rate:		8
ComboBox1	cboRate	*empty*		9
Button2	btnCalculate	&Calculate		10
Label4	lblResult	*empty*		11

- The `auto.gif` and `home.gif` files need to be added to the Resources folder of the project and then used for the PictureBox images.
- The picture boxes should also be set to AutoSize for the SizeMode.
- The radio buttons, lblPrincipalOrPaymentPrompt, and lblRatePrompt must have AutoSize set to False so that text can properly wrap.
- The values `5, 5.5, 6, 6.5, 7, 7.5, 8, 8.5, 9, 9.5, 10, 10.5, 11, 11.5, 12` need to be added to the combo box.
- The Visible property should be set to False for every object except the picture boxes, radio buttons, lblResult, and the form.
- The Calculate button should also be disabled.

```
Public Class Form1

    'Displays options for choosing loan information and adds
    'appropriate choices to list box
    '
    'post: Options have been displayed.
    '
    Private Sub ImageClicked(ByVal sender As Object,
    ByVal e As System.EventArgs) Handles picAuto.Click, picHome.Click
        Dim picImageClicked As PictureBox = sender

        'Display options for choosing loan information
        Me.grpWhatToKnow.Visible = True
        Me.btnNewLoan.Visible = True
        Me.btnCalculate.Visible = True
        'Calculate button should be displayed but disabled
        Me.btnCalculate.Enabled = False

        'Clear any existing list items
        Me.lstTerm.Items.Clear()

        'Add appropriate terms to list box depending on image clicked
        Select Case picImageClicked.Tag
            Case "auto"
                Me.lstTerm.Items.Add("2 years")
                Me.lstTerm.Items.Add("3 years")
                Me.lstTerm.Items.Add("5 years")
                Me.lstTerm.Items.Add("7 years")
            Case "home"
                Me.lstTerm.Items.Add("10 years")
                Me.lstTerm.Items.Add("15 years")
                Me.lstTerm.Items.Add("30 years")
        End Select
    End Sub

    'Hides loan information options. Clears label text.
    '
    'post: Loan options have been hidden and text in label
    'text set to an empty string.
    '
    Private Sub btnNewLoan_Click(ByVal sender As Object,
    ByVal e As System.EventArgs) Handles btnNewLoan.Click
        Me.grpWhatToKnow.Visible = False
        Me.radHowMuch.Checked = False
        Me.radPaymentSize.Checked = False
        Me.lblTermPrompt.Visible = False
        Me.lstTerm.Visible = False
        Me.lblPrincipalOrPaymentPrompt.Visible = False
        Me.txtPrincipalOrPayment.Visible = False
        Me.lblRatePrompt.Visible = False
        Me.cboInterestRate.Visible = False
        Me.btnNewLoan.Visible = False
        Me.btnCalculate.Visible = False
        Me.lblResult.Text = Nothing
    End Sub
```

```
'Displays options for entering loan information
'
'post: Options have been displayed.
'
Private Sub WhatDoYouWantToKnow_Click(ByVal sender As Object,
ByVal e As System.EventArgs) Handles radHowMuch.Click, radPaymentSize.Click
    Dim radOptionClicked As RadioButton = sender

    'Display term options
    Me.lblTermPrompt.Visible = True
    Me.lstTerm.Visible = True

    'Display either principal or payment options
    Select Case radOptionClicked.Tag
        Case "how much"
            Me.lblPrincipalOrPaymentPrompt.Text = "Desired Payment:"
        Case "payment size"
            Me.lblPrincipalOrPaymentPrompt.Text = "Loan Amount:"
    End Select
    Me.lblPrincipalOrPaymentPrompt.Visible = True
    Me.txtPrincipalOrPayment.Visible = True
    Me.txtPrincipalOrPayment.Text = Nothing

    'Display interest rate options
    Me.lblRatePrompt.Visible = True
    Me.cboInterestRate.Visible = True
    Me.cboInterestRate.Text = Nothing
End Sub


'Clears the last loan results. Checks for numeric loan information and
'enables the Calcualte button if required data has been entered or
'selected.
'
'post: The Results label has been cleared. The Calculate button has been
'enabled if data has been entered or selected.
'
Private Sub InfoEntered(ByVal sender As Object, _
ByVal e As System.EventArgs) Handles lstTerm.SelectedIndexChanged,
txtPrincipalOrPayment.TextChanged, cboInterestRate.SelectedIndexChanged,
cboInterestRate.TextChanged
    Me.lblResult.Text = Nothing
    Me.btnCalculate.Enabled = False

    If Me.txtPrincipalOrPayment.Text <> Nothing And
    Me.cboInterestRate.Text <> Nothing Then
        Me.btnCalculate.Enabled = True
    End If
End Sub


'Displays either the monthly payment for a loan or a loan amount that can
'be borrowed.
'
'post: The calculation result for the selected term, principal or
'payment, and interest rate have been displayed.
'
Private Sub btnCalculate_Click(ByVal sender As Object,
ByVal e As System.EventArgs) Handles btnCalculate.Click
    Dim term As Integer
    Dim principalOrPayment As Decimal
    Dim rate As Double
    Dim result As Decimal
    Dim validData As Boolean
```

```
    'Get term
    term = Val(Me.lstTerm.SelectedItem)

    'Get principal or payment
    GetDollarAmount(Me.txtPrincipalOrPayment, principalOrPayment, validData)

    'Get interest rate if principal or payment is valid
    If validData Then
        GetPercentAmount(Me.cboInterestRate, rate, validData)
    End If

    'Calculate result if principal or payment and interest are valid
    If validData Then
        If Me.radHowMuch.Checked Then
            result = PV(rate / 12, term * 12, -principalOrPayment)
            Me.lblResult.Text = "Loan amount: " & Format(result, "Currency")
        Else
            result = Pmt(rate / 12, term * 12, -principalOrPayment)
            Me.lblResult.Text = "Payment amount: " & Format(result, "Currency")
        End If
    Else
        Me.lblResult.Text = "Data not valid."
    End If
End Sub


'Processes data in a text box to read a dollar amount,
'if any
'
'post: dollars has been assigned a number if numeric data
'with or without a $ and commas is stored in the text box.
'isValid has been set to True if a numeric value is stored
'in the text box.
'
Sub GetDollarAmount(ByVal txtUserData As TextBox, ByRef dollars As Decimal,
ByRef isValid As Boolean)
    Dim testAmount As String

    isValid = False      'assume nonnumeric data
    If txtUserData.Text <> Nothing Then
        testAmount = txtUserData.Text                'data typed
        testAmount = testAmount.Replace("$", "") 'delete $
        testAmount = testAmount.Replace(",", "")     'delete commas
        If IsNumeric(testAmount) Then                'numeric data
            dollars = Val(testAmount)
            isValid = True
        End If
    End If
End Sub
```

```
    'Processes data in a combo box to read a percentage amount,
    'is any
    '
    'post: percent has been assigned a decimal number if numeric data
    'with or without a % is stored in the combo box. isValid has been
    'set to True if a numeric value is stored in the combo box.
    '
    Sub GetPercentAmount(ByVal cboUserData As ComboBox, ByRef percent As Double,
    ByRef isValid As Boolean)
        Dim testAmount As String

        isValid = False          'assume nonnumeric data
        If cboUserData.Text <> Nothing Then
            testAmount = cboUserData.Text
            testAmount = testAmount.TrimEnd("%")        'delete %
            If IsNumeric(testAmount) Then               'numeric data
                If Val(testAmount) >= 1 Then            'convert data
                    percent = Val(testAmount) / 100
                Else
                    percent = Val(testAmount)
                End If
                isValid = True
            End If
        End If
    End Sub
End Class
```

LoanAnalyzer Testing and Debugging

Running LoanAnalyzer, clicking the auto picture, and entering data displays the following:

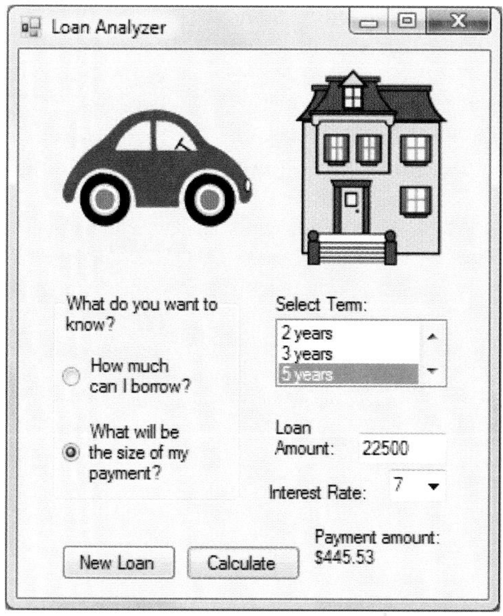

LoanAnalyzer should be tested by selecting different items to calculate and different rates, terms, and payments or loan amounts. Entering invalid rates, terms, and loan amounts (text instead of numbers) will test the error handling in the code.

Trigonometric Methods

The Visual Basic `Math` class also includes trigonometric method members. These methods include Sin(), Cos(), and Tan():

- **Sin(*angle*)** returns the sine of an angle. `angle` is a numeric variable or value, and is in radians.
- **Cos(*angle*)** returns the cosine of an angle. `angle` is a numeric variable or value, and is in radians.
- **Tan(*angle*)** returns the tangent of an angle. `angle` is a numeric variable or value, and is in radians.

The following code demonstrates the Trigonometric Math methods discussed above:

```
Dim radians As Double

radians = 0.79                              '45 Degrees
Me.lblSine.Text = Math.Sin(radians)         '0.710353

radians = 0.79                              '45 Degrees
Me.lblCosine.Text = Math.Cos(radians)       '0.703845

radians = 0.79                              '45 Degrees
Me.lblTangent.Text = Math.Tan(radians)      '1.009246
```

The Sin(), Cos(), and Tan() functions require an argument in radians. An angle in degrees can be converted to radians using a formula that requires π. The `Math` class includes a member constant `PI` with the value 3.14159265358979323846, which can be used in the conversion formula:

```
radians = (Math.PI / 180) * degrees
```

This formula works because 180 degrees equals π radians. To convert from radians to degrees, the following formula is used:

```
degrees = radians * (180 / Math.PI)
```

Review: TestDegreesToRadiansFunction

Write a DegreesToRadians() function that has a `degrees` parameter and returns the angle in radians. Test and debug the function in a project named TestDegreesToRadiansFunction. Properly document the function, including the following:

```
'Returns a value in radians that corresponds to degrees, a value
'in degrees.
'
'pre: 0 <= degrees <= 360
'post: The radians equivalent of degrees has been returned.
'
```

Review: TestRadiansToDegreesFunction

Write a RadiansToDegrees() function that has a `radians` parameter and returns the angle in degrees. Test and debug the function in a project named TestRadiansToDegreesFunction. Properly document the function, including the following:

```
'Returns a value in degrees that corresponds to radians, a value
'in radians.
'
'pre: 0 <= radians <= 2PI
'post: The degrees equivalent of radians has been returned.
'
```

Review: TrigonometricFunctions

Create a TrigonometricFunctions application that prompts the user for an angle in degrees and then displays the sine, cosine, or tangent of the angle rounded to 2 decimal places depending on the function selected from a list box. Include the DegreesToRadians() function created in a previous review. The application interface should look similar to that shown on the right after typing `50` and selecting Tangent in the list box.

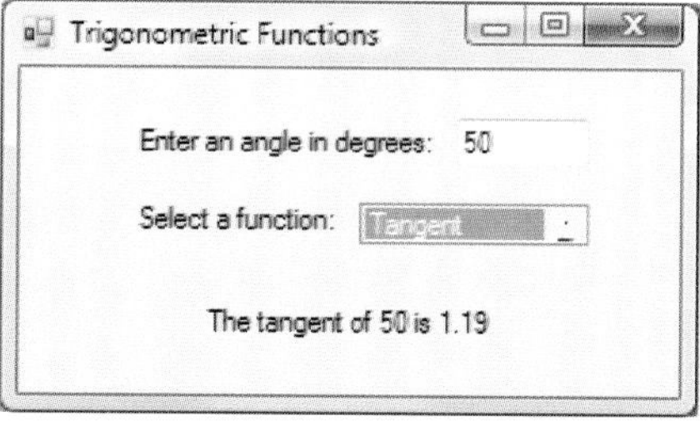

Review: SineCosineTable

① CREATE A NEW PROJECT

Create a Windows application named `SineCosineTable`.

② CREATE THE INTERFACE

Use the table below for setting object properties.

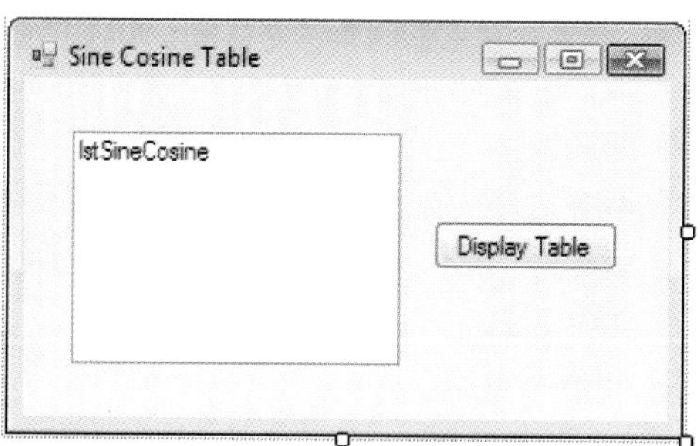

Object	(Name)	Text	Items
Form1		`Sine Cosine Table`	
ListBox1	`lstSineCosine`		*empty*
Button1	`btnDisplayTable`	`Display Table`	

③ WRITE THE APPLICATION CODE

a. Display the Code window.

b. Add comments that include your name, assignment, and today's date.

c. Create a btnDisplayTable_Click event procedure and then add the following statements:

```
Me.lstSineCosine.Items.Add("Angle" & vbTab & "Sin" & vbTab & "Cos")

Dim angleRadians As Double
Dim sin As Double
Dim cos As Double

For angle As Integer = 0 To 360 Step 15
    angleRadians = DegreesToRadians(angle)
    sin = Math.Round(Math.Sin(angleRadians), 2)
    cos = Math.Round(Math.Cos(angleRadians), 2)
    Me.lstSineCosine.Items.Add(angle & vbTab & sin & vbTab & cos)
Next angle
```

d. Add the DegreesToRadians() function from a previous review in this chapter.

④ RUN THE APPLICATION

a. Save the modified SineCosineTable project and then run the application.

b. Close the SineCosineTable application.

⑤ PRINT THE CODE AND THEN CLOSE THE PROJECT

Inverse Trigonometric Methods

arcsine, arccosine, arctangent

Mathematical work often requires finding the angle that corresponds to a trigonometric value. This is called the inverse trigonometric function. The inverse of sine is called *arcsine*, the inverse of cosine is called *arccosine*, and the inverse of tangent is called *arctangent*. The Visual Basic `Math` class includes these inverse trigonometric method members:

- **Asin(*num*)** returns the radian angle that corresponds to a sine. `num` is a numeric variable or value.
- **Acos(*num*)** returns the radian angle that corresponds to a cosine. `num` is a numeric variable or value.
- **Atan(*num*)** returns the radian angle that corresponds to a tangent. `num` is a numeric variable or value.

The following code demonstrates the inverse trigonometric `Math` methods discussed above:

```
Dim number As Double

number = 0.710353
Me.ArcSine.Text = Math.Asin(number)             '0.79 Radians

number = 0.703845
Me.ArcCosine.Text = Math.Acos(number)           '0.79 Radians

number = 1.009246
Me.lblArcTangent.Text = Math.Atan(number)       '0.79 Radians
```

Review: InverseTrigonometricFunctions

Create an InverseTrigonometricFunctions application that prompts the user for a value and then displays the arcsine, arccosine, or arctangent in degrees rounded to 2 decimal places depending on the button clicked. Include the RadiansToDegrees() function from a previous review in this chapter. The application interface should look similar to that shown on the right after typing `0.703845` and clicking **Arccosine**.

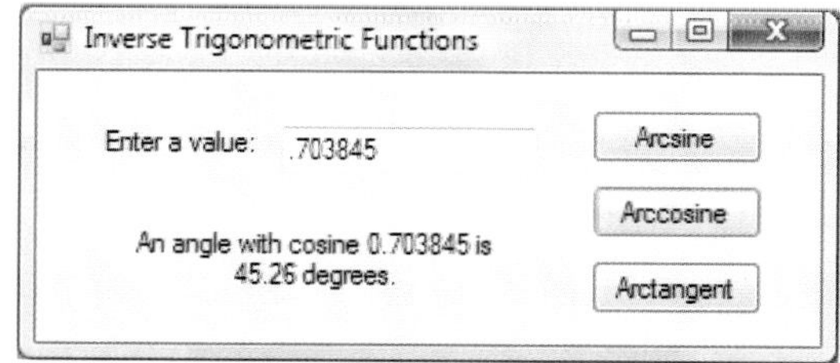

Logarithmic and Exponential Methods

The Visual Basic `Math` class also includes methods for logarithmic and exponential operations. These methods include:

- **Log(*num*)** returns the natural logarithm (base e) of a number. `num` is a variable or value that is greater than 0.
- **Log(*num, base*)** returns the logarithm of a number in a specified base. `num` is a numeric variable or value that is greater than 0. `base` is a numeric variable or value that is greater than 0.
- **Log10(*num*)** returns the base 10 logarithm of a number. `num` is a numeric variable or value that is greater than 0.
- **Exp(*power*)** returns *e* raised to a power (e^x). `power` is a numeric variable or value. Exp() is the inverse function of Log().
- **Pow(*num, power*)** returns a number raised to a power. `num` and `power` are numeric variables or values.

Note that the Log() function can have either one or two arguments. When only one argument is used, the natural logarithm is returned. When two numbers are used, the logarithm is returned in the specified base. A function that performs a different action depending on the number of arguments it receives is called an *overloaded function*.

overloaded function

The `Math` class also includes a member constant `E` with the value 2.7182818284590452354, which represents the base of natural logarithms.

The following code demonstrates the `Math` methods logarithmic and exponential functions:

```
Dim num1 As Double = 10
Dim num2 As Double = 8
Me.lblLogE.Text = Math.Log(num1)            'base e, 2.3025
Me.lblLogX.Text = Math.Log(num1, num2)      'base 8, 1.1073
Me.lblLog10.Text = Math.Log10(num1)         'base 10, 1
num1 = 2
num2 = 4
Me.lblExp.Text = Math.Exp(num1)             'e2, 7.389
Me.lblPow.Text = Math.Pow(num1, num2)  '24, 16
```

Review: LogAndExpFunctions

Create a LogAndExpFunctions application that prompts the user for a number and then displays the natural logarithm of the number or *e* raised to that number depending on the button clicked. The application interface should look similar to that shown on the right after typing `1` and clicking **Natural Logarithm**.

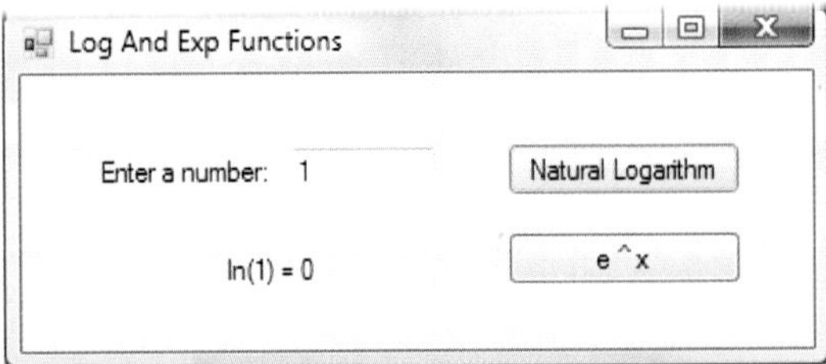

Chapter Summary

This chapter introduced the Visual Basic `Math` class and built-in mathematical and business functions.

The `Math` class members include the Abs(), Sqrt(), Sign(), Round(), Sin(), Cos(), Tan(), Asin(), Acos(), Atan(), Log(), Log10(), Exp(), and Pow() methods. The `Math` class also includes constants `PI` and `E`.

Built-in functions include IsNumeric() and Format(). The IsNumeric() and Val() functions can be used with `String` methods to allow the user to enter data that includes a dollar sign.

The Pmt(), PV(), and FV() built-in functions are used for payment, present value, and future value business calculations.

A ListBox object can contain several items for the user to choose from. The items in a list box have an index value beginning with 0 and a SelectedIndexChanged event procedure is sometimes coded for a list box.

A list box is a good choice for displaying items that should appear one after the other. The ListBox control class contains the Items.Add(), Items.Remove(), and Items.Clear() methods for controlling the contents of a list box at run time.

A ComboBox object combines a text box and a list box. The items in the list box of the combo box have an index value beginning with 0. Because a user can type or select a value in a combo box, both TextChanged and SelectedIndexChanged events need to be considered. The ComboBox control class also contains Items.Add(), Items.Remove(), and Items.Clear() methods for controlling the contents of the list box part of the combo box at run time.

An object that has focus receives the user input. An ampersand (&) may be used in an object's Text property to define an access key. The tab order for the objects in an application can be set with the TabIndex property. The Enabled property can be set to False so that the user cannot select an object. The Visible property can be used to hide an object.

Vocabulary

Access key The underlined character in an application that indicates which key can be pressed while holding down the Alt key to select an object.

Annuity A set of payments made on a regular basis for a specified period.

Arccosine The inverse of cosine.

Arcsine The inverse of sine.

Arctangent The inverse of tangent.

Disabled An object that cannot be selected by the user.

Focus Describes an object that will receive user input from the keyboard.

Overloaded function A function that performs a different action depending on the number and type of the arguments it receives.

Visual Basic

`&` Used in the Text property of an object to define an access key. Also used to concatenate items to form a single item to be added to a list box or combo box.

ComboBox **ComboBox control** Used to create a ComboBox control class object. Properties include Name, Items, Text, Sorted, SelectedItem, and SelectedIndex. Methods include Items.Add(), Items.Clear(), and Items.Remove(). Events include TextChanged and SelectedIndexChanged.

`E` `Math` class constant for the base of natural logarithms (2.7182818284590452354).

Enabled Control object property used to disable an object so that it cannot be selected.

Format() Function used to convert a number to a formatted string.

FV() Function that returns the future value of an annuity.

IsNumeric() Function that returns True if its argument can be evaluated as a number and False if it is not.

ListBox **ListBox control** Used to create a ListBox control class object. Properties include Name, Items, Sorted, SelectedItem, and SelectedIndex. Methods include Items.Add(), Items.Remove(), and Items.Clear(). Events include SelectedIndexChanged.

`Math` **class** Used to perform common math functions. Methods include Abs(), Acos(), Asin(), Atan(), Cos(), Exp(), Log(), Log100(), Pow(), Round(), Sign(), Sin(), Sqrt(), and Tan(). Other members include `PI` and `E`.

`PI` `Math` class constant (3.14159265358979323846).

Pmt() Function that returns the payment for an annuity.

PV() Function that returns the present value of an annuity.

TabIndex Control class property used to set the tab order for an application interface.

Visible Control class property used to hide or display an object.

Critical Thinking

1. List the similarities and differences between radio buttons and list boxes.

2. Why might a programmer decide to use a combo box over a list box?

3. What are the two ways a user can enter data into a combo box?

4. a) Why might a programmer decide to set an object's Enabled property to False instead of setting Visible to False?
   b) Why might a programmer decide to set an object's Visible property to False instead of setting Enabled to False?

5. A button displays Exit.
   a) What functionality does the underlined x indicate?
   b) How was this functionality added to the button?
   c) What must the user do to display the underlining at run time?

6. How do you know when a:
   a) text box has the focus?
   b) button is disabled?
   c) button has the focus?
   d) list box has the focus?

7. List three ways the user can change which object has the focus in a running application.

8. Explain how access keys can be used to give the focus to a combo box.

9. a) Why should a programmer consider the tab order of objects on an interface?
   b) Without any programmer intervention, how is the tab order of objects determined?
   c) How is tab order changed?

10. List three ways to determine the square root of the value stored in a variable `num`.

11. a) What does it mean to say a function is overloaded?
    b) Name the overloaded function covered in this chapter and give an example of how both versions can be used.

12. State the numeric expression needed to evaluate the following:
    a) The money you will have in 10 years if you invest $100 monthly at 6%.
    b) The monthly payment for a $15,000 4-year car loan at 8%.
    c) The lump sum equivalent to receiving $1,000 a month for 10 years invested at 10%.
    d) The total amount paid on a 30-year mortgage with monthly payments of $800.
    e) The total interest amount paid on a 30-year mortgage with monthly payments of $800 at 7.25%.

13. Write a statement that includes the appropriate function(s) to:
    a) store a number in `value` that indicates the absolute value of `guess`.
    b) assign the square root of (b2 – 4ac) to `deter`.
    c) replace the current value of `value` with its value rounded to 2 decimal places.
    d) determine if the data in txtNum1 and txtNum2 are numbers. If the data is numeric, btnCalculate should be enabled, otherwise, "Enter valid data." should be displayed in a message box. What must be done in the Design window for the code to work as expected?
    e) determine the logarithm of `num` in base `base` as long as both `num` and `base` are positive.

14. Use the following interface to answer parts (a), (b), and (c):

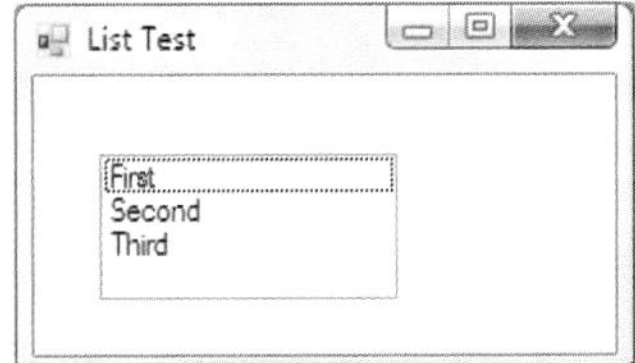

    a) If Second was selected, its _______________ would have a value of 1.
    b) If the list was not sorted, where would the statement Me.lstTest.Items.Add("Fourth") place the new item?
    c) If the list was sorted, where would the statement Me.lstTest.Item.Add("Fourth") place the new item?

15. Write an event procedure that executes when the user selects an item in `lstStudentName`. The code should determine if the radio button `radRemove` is selected. If it is, the selected list item should be removed from the list box.

16. Write code that adds the value typed in a combo box to the combo box list and then clears the text box of the combo box. Include code that checks the Text property for a valid entry before trying to add the item to the list.

17. An application contains a txtNumSand object, which prompts the user for the number of sandwiches, and a lstSize object, which contains Small, Medium, and Large list items. Write code that executes when a list item is clicked. Include a statement that displays the total cost of the sandwiches in lblCost or the message "Invalid number." The cost of a sandwich is stored in constants named `COST_SMALL`, `COST_MEDIUM`, and `COST_LARGE`.

18. Write a btnCalculate_Click event procedure that adds to lstResult the numbers 1 through 10 and next to each number either their square root rounded to 1 decimal place or their square, depending on the selected radSquareRoots or radSquares radio button. Make the first list item an appropriate title.

19. Use the following interface to answer parts (a) and (b):

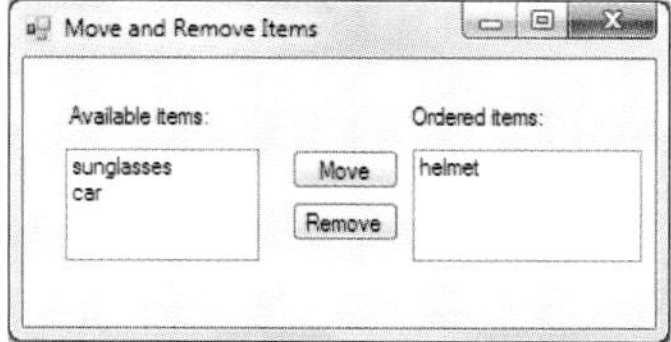

   a) Write event handlers for each button. The Move button should move a selected item from the Available Items list to the Ordered Items list. The Remove button should move a selected item from the Ordered Items list back to the Available Items list. The buttons should be enabled only when items are available for moving in their respective lists.
   b) When the application starts, should there be items in `lstAvailable`, `lstOrdered`, or both? Explain.

True/False

20. Determine if each of the following are true or false. If false, explain why.
   a) The Sqrt() function returns the square root of any number.
   b) `IsNumeric(3 - 7)` evaluates to True.
   c) `Format(0.079, "Percent")` would display 79%.
   d) `Val("$100")` returns 100.
   e) The Items.Add() method always adds the new item to the bottom of a list box or combo box.
   f) A SelectedIndex value of 0 means no item has been selected in a list box or combo box.
   g) The Sorted property of a list box or combo box cannot be set at run time.
   h) A Click event is raised when the user selects an item in either a combo box or list box.
   i) The Text property of a combo box contains the value of the selected list item.
   j) If a list box or combo box cannot display all the items added to the list, a vertical scroll bar is automatically displayed.
   k) It is possible to have both Calculate and Choose buttons on the same form.
   l) TabIndex values should start at 0.
   m) An object with Enabled set to False is not displayed on the form at run time.
   n) The trigonometric methods use degree as the angle of measurement.
   o) It is possible for certain functions to accept a varying number of arguments.

Exercises

Exercise 1 — PerfectSquare

A perfect square is an integer whose square root is a whole number. For example, 4, 9, and 16 are perfect squares. Create a PerfectSquare application that determines if the number entered by the user is a perfect square. The program code should include a PerfectSquare() `Boolean` function that has an `number` parameter. *Hint*: Use the Int() function in determining if a square root is a whole number. The application interface should look similar to:

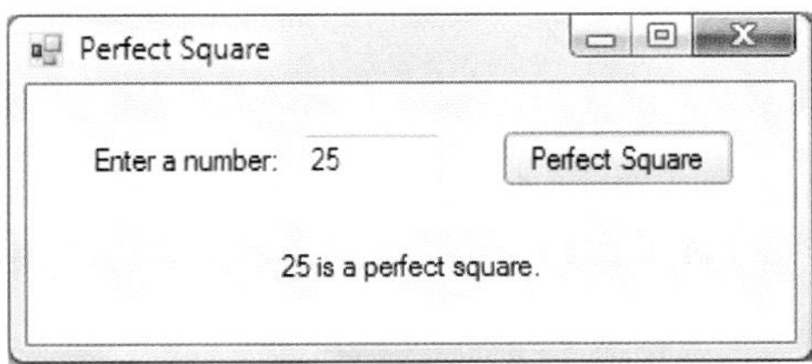

Exercise 2 — PaymentCalculator

Create a PaymentCalculator application the prompts the user for a loan amount, interest rate, loan term in years, and payments term (daily, monthly, or yearly). Keep in mind the payments must be converted so that the number used in the calculation is in the appropriate units. For this conversion, assume that there are 30 days in each month and there are 360 days in a year. The application should display the payments, total amount paid over the length of the loan, and the total amount of interest paid. The application interface should look similar to:

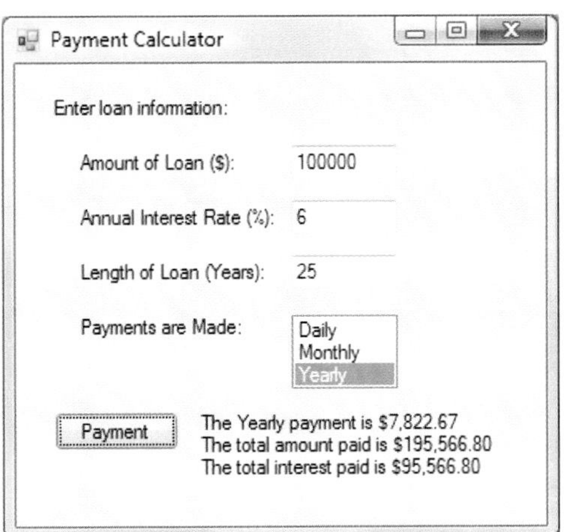

Exercis 3 — LoanCalculator

Create a LoanCalculator application the prompts the user for the monthly payment, interest rate, and term of a loan in years. The application should display the loan amount, total amount paid, and the total amount of interest paid. The application interface should look similar to:

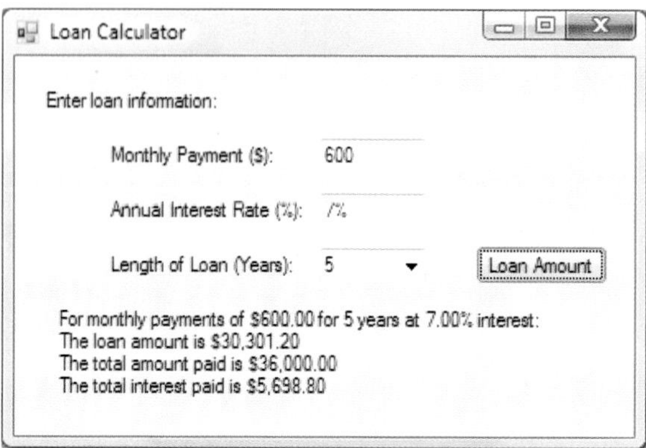

Exercise 4 — InvestmentCalculator

Create an InvestmentCalculator application that prompts the user for the amount invested monthly, interest rate, and term of the investment in years. The application should display the value of the investment at 5 year intervals in a list box and look similar to:

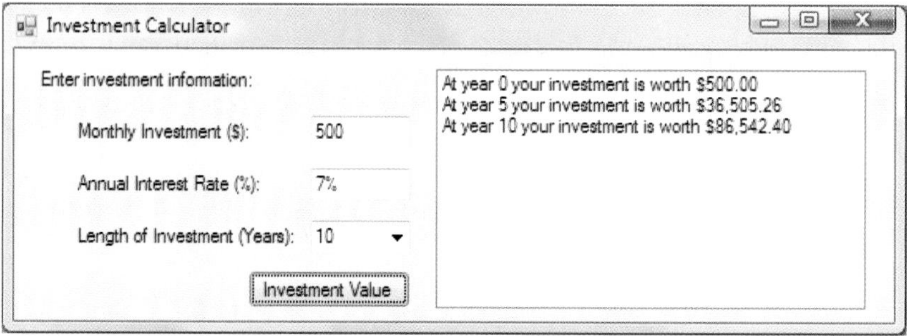

Exercise 5 PythagoreanTriples

A Pythagorean triple is a set of three integers that solves the equation $a^2 + b^2 = c^2$. Create a PythagoreanTriples application that displays all Pythagorean triples with values of A and B less than 100. The program code should include a PerfectSquare() function like the one created in Exercise 1. The application interface should look similar to the following after clicking **Compute**:

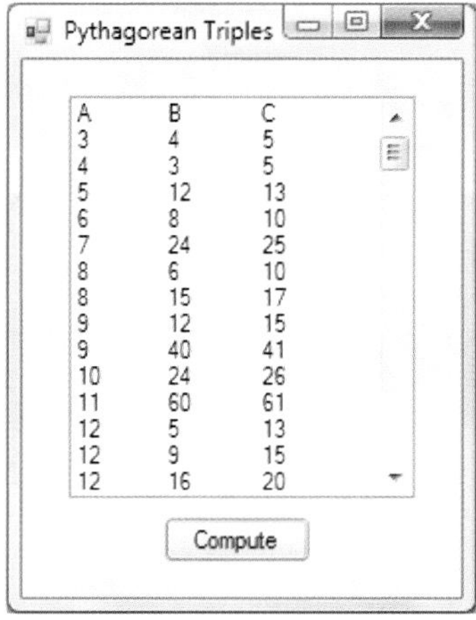

Exercise 6 SquareRootRoundoffError

Create a SquareRootRoundoff Error application that compares the square of the square root of a number with the number itself for all integers from 1 to 100. This difference in values is due to the computer's rounding error. The application interface should look similar to the following after clicking **Compute**:

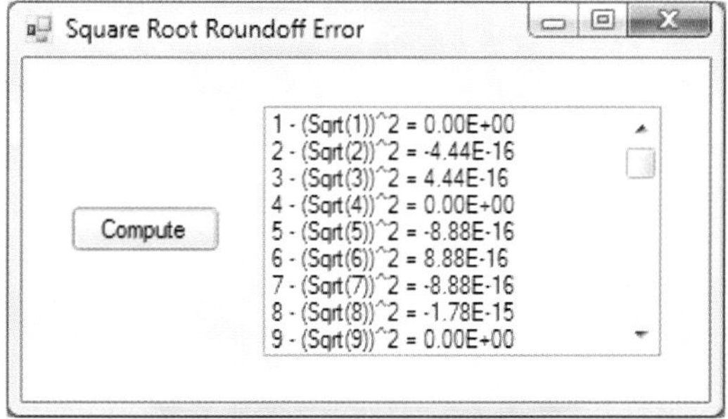

Exercise 7 ——— BookstoreOrderForm

Create a BookstoreOrderForm application the prompts the user to select different items and quantities to purchase and then displays the order information in a list box that is on top of a `cart.gif` graphic, a data file for this text. The application interface should look similar to:

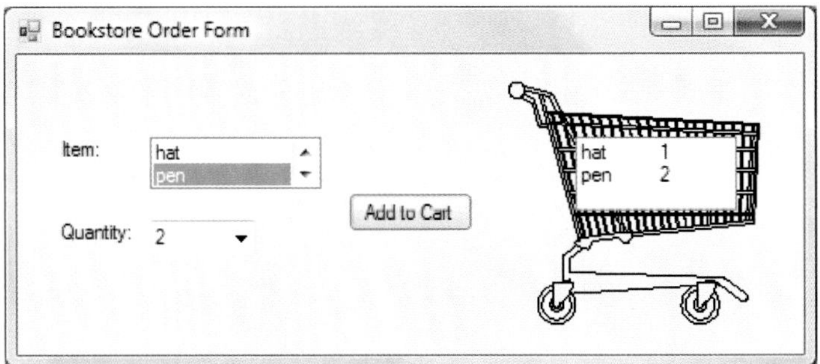

Exercise 8 ——— PythagoreanTheorem

The Pythagorean Theorem is $a^2 + b^2 = c^2$ where a and b are the lengths of two sides of a right triangle and c is the length of the side opposite the right angle (the hypotenuse). Create a PythagoreanTheorem application that prompts the user for the lengths of sides `a` and `b` and then displays the length of the hypotenuse when **Hypotenuse** is clicked. The application interface should look similar to:

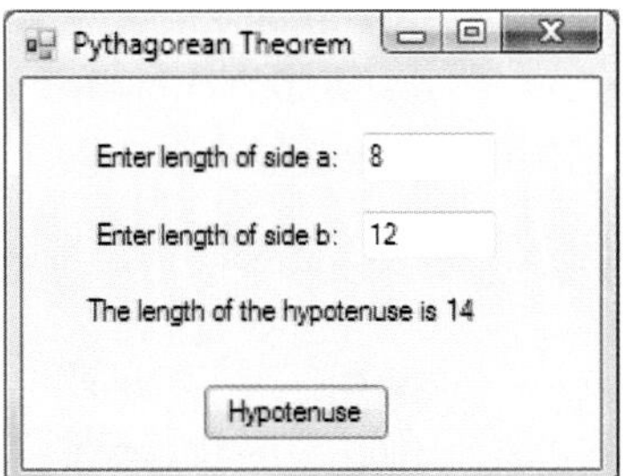

Exercise 9 (trigonometry required) ——— AngleConversion

Create an AngleConversion application that converts an angle in degrees to radians and vice versa. The application should include the options 30, 0.52, 45, 0.79, 60, and 1.05 in a combo box. Refer to the functions created in the reviews for this chapter. The application interface should look similar to:

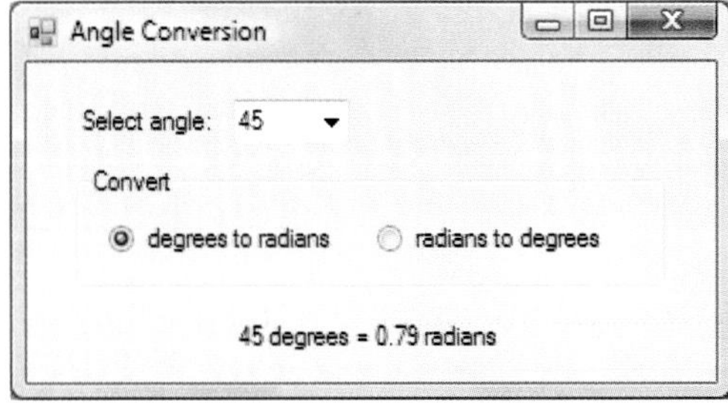

Exercise 10 (trigonometry required) ——— MyRandomNumbers

Create a MyRandomNumbers application that produces a sequence of random numbers without using the Rnd() function. To do this, let `X` vary from 1 to 100 in steps of 1. Obtain Sin(`X`) and multiply this by `1000`, which results in a value `Y`. Then take the absolute value of `Y` and divide `Int(Y)` by `16`, and let the remainder serve as the random number. The application interface should look similar to the following after clicking **Random Numbers**:

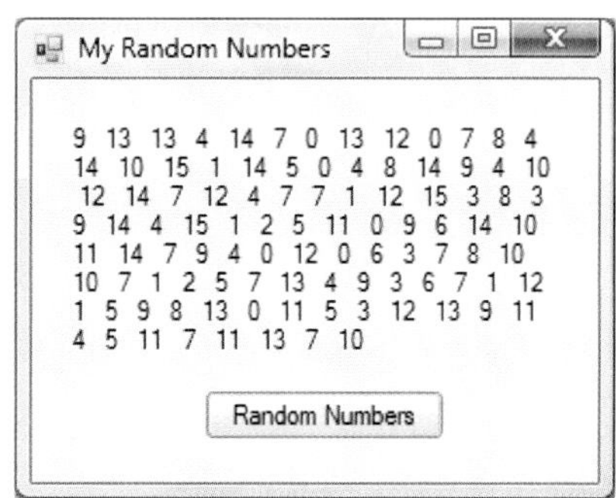

Exercise 11 ——— TriangleArea

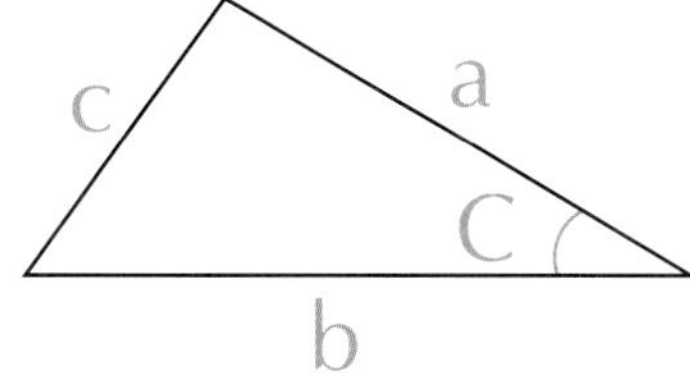

a) The formula Area = $\sqrt{s(s-a)(s-b)(s-c)}$ computes the area of a triangle where `a`, `b`, and `c` are the lengths of the sides and `s` is the semiperimeter (half the perimeter). Create a TriangleArea application that prompts the user with text boxes for lengths of sides `a`, `b`, and `c` and then displays the area of the triangle in a label.

b) *Trigonometry required.* The trigonometric formula Area = ½ * a * b * Sin C computes the area of a triangle where `C` is the angle formed by sides `a` and `b`, in degrees. Modify TriangleArea to use this formula. The application interface should look similar to:

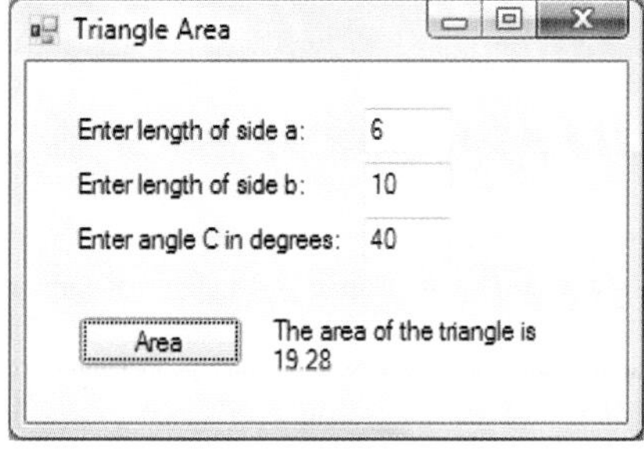

Exercise 12 (trigonometry required) ——— SOH–CAH–TOA

SOH-CAH-TOA is a mnemonic for the trigonometric formulas that can be used to find the sine, cosine, and tangent of an angle in a right triangle:

Sine = Opposite/Hypotenuse   Cosine = Adjacent/Hypotenuse   Tangent = Opposite/Adjacent

For example, the sine of angle A is calculated by dividing the opposite side a by the hypotenuse c. Likewise, the cosine of angle A is b/c, and the tangent of angle A is a/b:

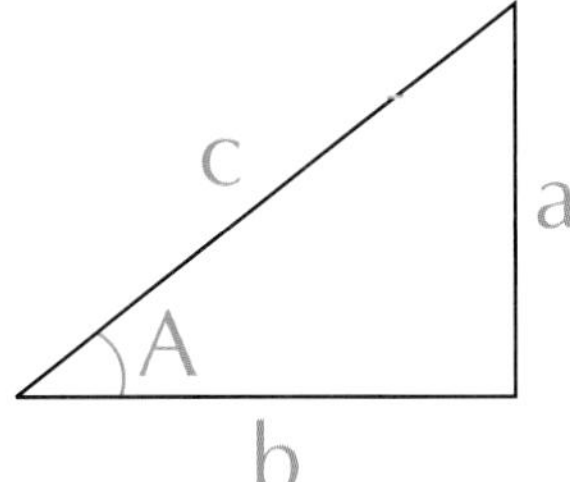

Create a SOH-CAH-TOA application that prompts the user for the lengths of the three sides of a triangle and then calculates the sine, cosine, and tangent of angle A depending on which button is clicked. The application should use the RadiansToDegrees() function from the reviews in this chapter to determine angle A in degrees. The code should also include a CheckSides() `Boolean` function that checks that the sides entered form a right triangle (Hint: Refer to Exercise 8) and if not, displays a message box and clears the text boxes to allow for new entries. The application interface should look similar to:

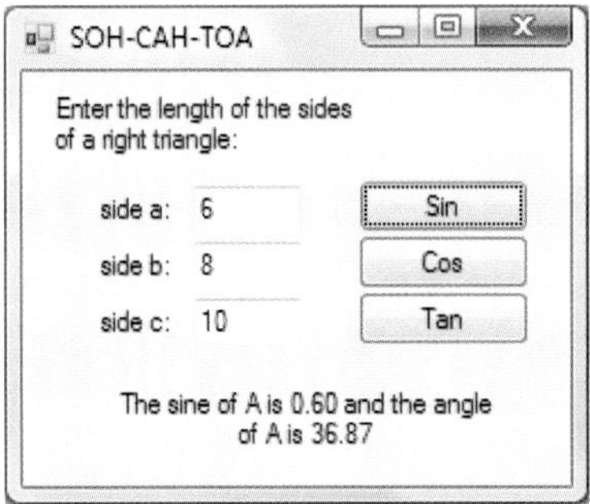

Exercise 13 — BacteriaGrowth

The formula $y = ne^{kt}$ can be used for estimating growth where:

`y` is the final amount
`n` is the initial amount
`k` is a constant
`t` is the time

For example, this formula could be used for estimating population growth in a region or for estimating cell growth in a lab experiment. Create a BacteriaGrowth application that calculates how many bacteria will be present based on this formula. The application interface should look similar to:

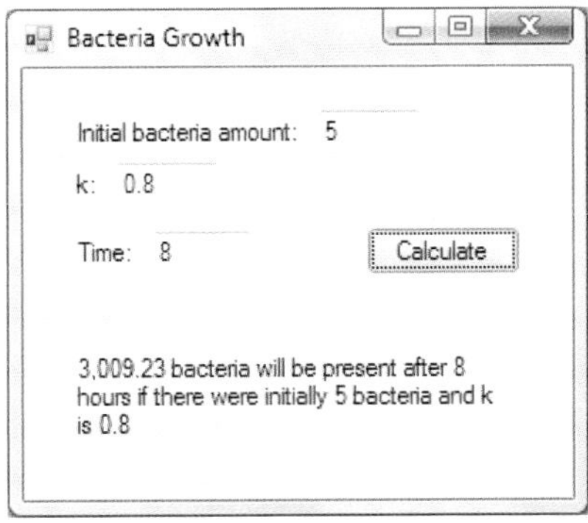

Exercise 14 — Depreciation

The formula $V_n = P (1 + r)^n$ is can be used to estimate depreciation or appreciation where:

V_n is the value at the end of n years
`P` is the initial value of the equipment
`r` is the rate of appreciation (positive) or depreciation (negative)
`n` is the time in years

For example, this formula could be used to determine the current value of a mainframe that a company has owned for 10 years. From this formula you can also determine how long it will take a piece of equipment to depreciate to a specific value using the formula: $n = \log (V_n / P) / \log (1 + r)$. Create a Depreciation application that calculates how long it will take a piece of equipment to depreciate using this formula. The application interface should look similar to:

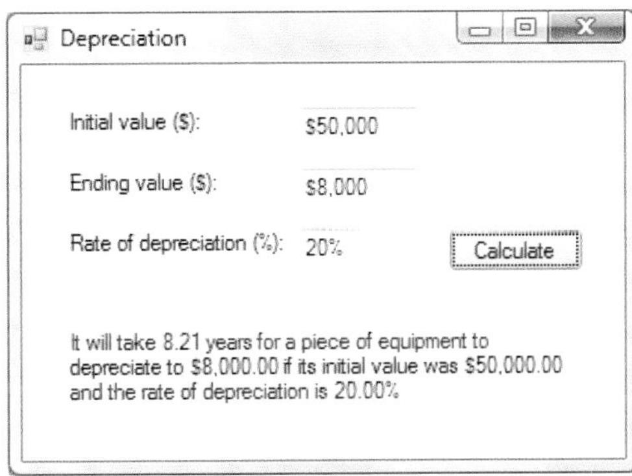

Exercise 15 (trigonometry required) (advanced) — Triangle

Create an application that solves a triangle (compute the unknown sides and angles) for the following situations:

- given two sides and the included angle
- given two angles and any side
- given three sides

The application should prompt the user to select one of the three choices, and based on the selected option prompts the user to enter the appropriate known information. Angles should be entered in degrees and displayed in degrees.

Exercise 16 (advanced) — Decay

The formula used in Exercise 13 for growth problems can also be used in decay problems. In decay problems, `k` is negative. Create an application that allows the user to select from the following options:

- calculate the final amount `y`: ne^{-kt}
- calculate the initial amount `n`: $y \ / \ e^{-kt}$
- calculate the constant `k` (called the half-life): `(log (y/n)) / t`

The application should prompt the user to select one of the three choices and based on the selected option prompts the user to enter the appropriate known information. For example, a radioactive mass of 200 grams will reduce to 100 grams in 10 years. Based on this information, the half-life is calculated to be –0.06931.

Chapter 8
Arrays and Structures

Key Concepts

Creating one and two dimensional arrays
Using array parameters
Passing array arguments
Applying search algorithms
Understanding dynamic arrays
Using structures and structure arrays
Declaring an enumerated type
Using control objects as array elements

Case Study

Cafe Order

Arrays

Up to this point, only variables that hold a single value at a time have been used in applications. With this approach, many separate variables are required to represent a collection of related values such as names of students in a class or game scores for a team's season. A better way to represent related values is with an *array*, which stores many of the same kind of data together at once. For example, an array containing five `String` elements could be visualized as:

index

The elements of an array have an *index* value, with 0 being the index of the first item, 1 the index of the second, and so on. In the example above, `Rose` is the fourth element of the array and has index 3.

composite data type

Arrays are an important programming concept because they allow a collection of related values to be stored together with a single descriptive name. Because an array is made up of a collection of elements, it is called a *composite data type*.

An array is declared with a `Dim` statement that includes the array name followed by the index of the last element in parentheses and then the data type of the elements. For example, the statement

```
Dim stuNames(4) As String     '5 elements
```

TIP Array identifiers are often plural to indicate that several values are being stored by the variable.

declares a `stuNames` array that has five `String` elements with indexes 0, 1, 2, 3, and 4. Note that the size of the array is indicated with the index of the last element. The elements are automatically initialized to the default value of the element data type. In this case, each element is initialized to `Nothing`.

An array declaration may also include initial values for each element by using an array literal. An *array literal* consists of a list of comma separated values that are enclosed in braces:

```
Dim stuNames() As String = {"Mia", "Eli", "Eva", "Rose", "Wu"}
```

The index is not included in the parentheses because the number of values in the braces indicate the size. Strings must be enclosed in quotation marks, but numeric and Boolean values are not. Note that when an array literal is used, type inference can be used to determine the array type. Therefore, the array declaration above could also be written as:

```
Dim stuNames() = {"Mia", "Eli", "Eva", "Rose", "Wu"}
```

The compiler determines the type by examining each element in the array and calculating the dominant type.

Using Arrays

An array element is accessed by including its index in parentheses after the array name. For example, the following statement displays the element at index 4 in a label:

TIP Index is sometimes referred to as subscript.

```
Me.lblStudentName.Text = stuNames(4)   'Wu
```

Assignment to an array element works similarly. For example, the following statement assigns `Tori` to the element at index 3:

```
stuNames(3) = "Tori"
```

A run-time error occurs when an invalid index is used. For example, the assignment statement causes the exception IndexOutOfRangeException:

```
Dim strNames(9) As String
strNames(10) = "Constance"     'invalid index
```

The message produced for this exception is "Index was outside the bounds of the array."

Arrays are objects of the `Array` class that includes many properties and methods. One property is Length, which returns the number of elements in an array, as in the statement:

```
Me.lblNumElements.Text = stuNames.Length      '5
```

A `For...Next` loop is often used to access the elements of an array because the loop counter can be used as the array index. Accessing each element of an array is called *traversing* the array. For example, in the following statements, a `For...Next` loop and an input box are used to assign values to the elements of an array:

traversing an array

```
For name As Integer = 0 To stuNames.Length - 1
   stuNames(name) = InputBox("Enter first name:", "Students")
Next name
```

Note that the loop iterates from 0 to one less than the length of the array because Length is a count of the number of elements, not the greatest index value.

Review: StudentNames

① CREATE A NEW PROJECT

Create a Windows application named `StudentNames`.

② CREATE THE INTERFACE

Use the table below for setting object properties.

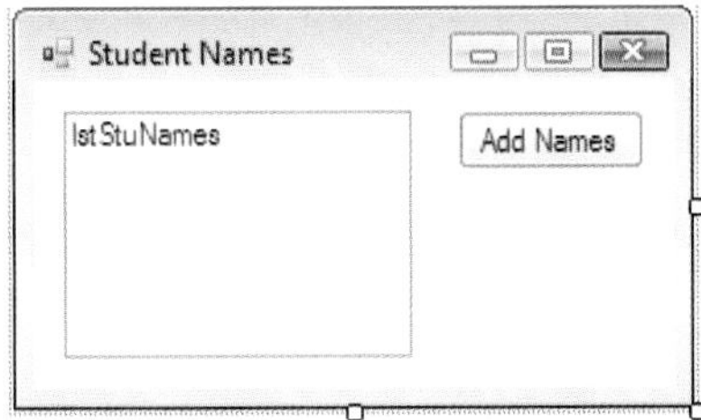

Object	(Name)	Text
Form1		Student Names
ListBox1	lstStuNames	
Button1	btnAddNames	Add Names

③ WRITE THE APPLICATION CODE

a. Display the Code window.

b. Add comments that include your name, assignment, and today's date.

c. Create a btnAddNames_Click event procedure and then add the statements:

```
Const NUM_NAMES As Integer = 5
Dim stuNames(NUM_NAMES - 1) As String

'Get student names from user
For nameCount As Integer = 0 To stuNames.Length - 1
    stuNames(nameCount) = InputBox("Enter student's first name:", "Students")
Next nameCount

'Add names to list box
For nameCount As Integer = 0 To stuNames.Length - 1
    Me.lstStuNames.Items.Add(stuNames(nameCount))
Next nameCount
```

④ RUN THE APPLICATION

a. Save the modified StudentsNames project.

b. Run the application. Click Add Names and then type one name in each input box. Note how the names are added to the list after all of the names have been entered.

c. Close the StudentNames application.

⑤ PRINT THE CODE AND THEN CLOSE THE PROJECT

Array Parameters

A procedure can include array parameters. The array passed to a procedure can be either an entire array or an element of the array. Arrays can get very large so it is usually more efficient if the parameter is `ByRef` because this parameter type refers to the actual array and does not make a copy of the array for use in the procedure. The SumOfValues() function on the next page has a `ByRef` array parameter and returns the sum of the array elements:

TIP The array parameter is declared as the array name followed by empty parentheses.

```
'Returns the sum of the values in numArray.
'
'post: Sum of the values in numArray has been returned.
'0 has been returned if array has no elements.
'
Function SumOfValues (ByRef numArray() As Integer) As Integer
   Dim sum As Integer = 0

   For index As Integer = 0 To numArray.Length - 1
      sum += numArray(index)
   Next index
   Return sum
End Function
```

A procedure call uses just the array name when an array argument is passed. For example, the statement below passes `dataArray` to the SumOfValues() function:

```
total = SumOfValues(dataArray)
```

A single array element may also be used as an argument. Passing a single element to a procedure means that only that element can be included in the procedure call. For example, the following code segment passes the fourth element of `dataArray` to DisplayElement():

TIP The procedure declares a non-array parameter with a data type that matches the element data type.

```
Call DisplayElement(dataArray(3), Me.lblOutput)
...

'Sets the Text property of lblLabel to number.
'
'post: number has been displayed in a label.
'
Sub DisplayElement (ByVal number As Integer,
ByRef lblLabel As Label)
   lblLabel.Text = number
End Sub
```

Arrays with Meaningful Indexes

Many algorithms make use of the index value of an array element for simplifying the storage and retrieval of data. For example, a `testScores` array with 101 elements indexed from 0 to 100 could store a count of all the scores of 90 in the element with index 90, the scores of 82 in element 82, and so on. The DiceRolls and LetterOccurrences applications described in this section implement similar algorithms.

The DiceRolls application counts the frequency of dice roll outcomes. A roll is simulated by generating two random numbers between 1 and 6 inclusive. The outcome of each roll is used to update a counter in an array of counters at the index corresponding to the outcome. For example, if 3 is rolled, then `counts(3)` is incremented:

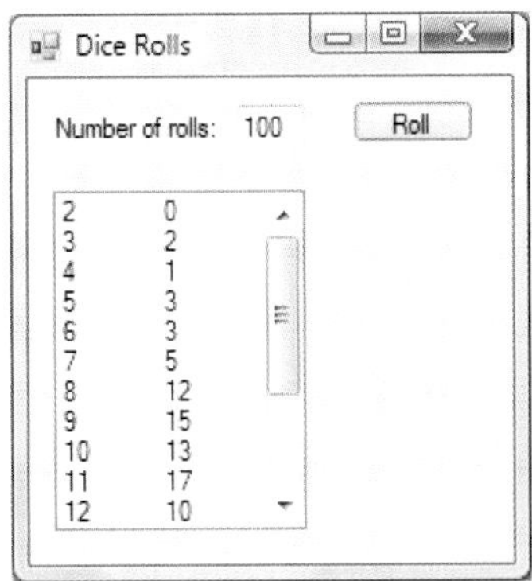


```
Private Sub btnRollDice _ Click(ByVal sender As Object,
ByVal e As System.EventArgs) Handles btnRollDice.Click
   Dim counts(12) As Integer
   Dim numRolls As Integer = Val(Me.txtRolls.Text)

   Call CountTrials(numRolls, counts)
   Call DisplayRollsCounts(counts, Me.lstRollsOutcomes)
End Sub


'Simulates numRolls rolls of two dice and keeps a count
'of the outcomes.
'
'pre: counts has elements with at least index values
'2 through 12.
'post: numRolls dice rolls have been simulated.
'Counts of numRolls simulated dice rolls has been
'stored in counts.
'
Sub CountTrials(ByVal numRolls As Integer,
ByRef counts() As Integer)
   Dim rollOutcome As Integer

   Randomize()
   For roll As Integer = 1 To numRolls
       rollOutcome = (Int(6 * Rnd() + 1)) + (Int(6 * Rnd() + 1))
       counts(rollOutcome) += 1
   Next roll
End Sub


'Displays the contents of counts in a list box.
'
'pre: counts has elements with at least index values
'2 through 12.
'post: Elements of counts have been displayed in a
'list box.
'
Sub DisplayRollsCounts(ByRef counts() As Integer,
ByRef lstList As ListBox)

   For rollOutcome As Integer = 2 To 12
       lstList.Items.Add(rollOutcome & vbTab &
       counts(rollOutcome))
   Next rollOutcome
End Sub
```

```
Private Sub txtRolls_TextChanged(ByVal sender As Object,
ByVal e As System.EventArgs) Handles txtRolls.TextChanged
    Me.lstRollsOutcomes.Items.Clear()
End Sub
```

The LetterOccurrences application counts the occurrences of letters in a string. The storage of the letter counts is simplified by using an array with index values that correspond to the Unicode values of letters A (Unicode 65) through Z (Unicode 90). A run of the LetterOccurrences application and its code are:

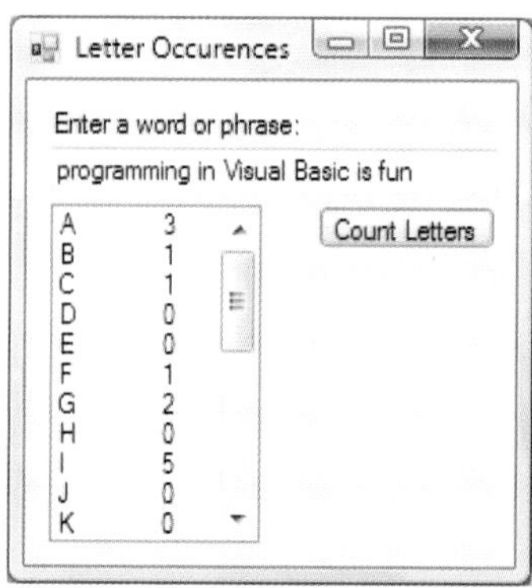


```
Private Sub btnCountLetters_Click(ByVal sender As Object,
ByVal e As System.EventArgs) Handles btnCountLetters.Click
  Const UNICODE_Z As Integer = AscW("Z")
  Dim letterCounts(UNICODE_Z) As Integer

  Dim phrase As String = Me.txtPhrase.Text
  Call CountLetters(phrase, letterCounts)
  Call DisplayLetterCounts(letterCounts,
  Me.lstLetterCounts)
End Sub

'Counts the occurrences of letters a through z in a string,
'regardless of case.
'
'pre: letterCounts has elements with at least index
'values 65 through 90 corresponding to the Unicode value
'for A through the Unicode value for Z.
'post: Counts of letters in a phrase have been stored in
'letterCounts.
'
Sub CountLetters(ByVal phrase As String,
ByRef letterCounts() As Integer)
  Dim letterIndex As Integer
  Dim uppercaseLetter As Char

  For character As Integer = 0 To phrase.Length - 1
      uppercaseLetter = Char.ToUpper(phrase.
      Chars(character))
      If uppercaseLetter >= "A" And
      uppercaseLetter <= "Z" Then
          letterIndex = AscW(uppercaseLetter)
          letterCounts(letterIndex) += 1
      End If
  Next character
End Sub
```

```
'Displays the contents of letterCounts in a list box.
'
'post: Elements of letterCounts have been displayed
'in a list box.
'
Sub DisplayLetterCounts(ByRef letterCounts() As Integer,
ByRef lstList As ListBox)

  For letter As Integer = AscW("A") To AscW("Z")
      lstList.Items.Add(ChrW(letter) & vbTab &
      letterCounts(letter))
  Next letter
End Sub

Private Sub txtPhrase_TextChanged(ByVal sender As Object,
ByVal e As System.EventArgs) Handles txtPhrase.TextChanged
  Me.lstLetterCounts.Items.Clear()
End Sub
```

Offset Array Indexes

In some cases, it is not efficient to use array indexes that directly correspond to outcomes. For example, a range of years from 1900 to 2000 would require an array of 2001 elements with only the last 100 elements in use. In this situation, offset array indexes should be used. For example, for an outcome of 1900, the counter at index 0 should be incremented. For an outcome of 1901, the counter at index 1 would be updated, and so forth.

The CountLetters() procedure converts each letter of the phrase to uppercase to simplify counting. In DisplayLetterCounts(), the loop control variable, `letter`, is converted to a character to act as a label in the list.

Review: DiceRolls

The DiceRolls application displays statistics for rolling two dice. Modify DiceRolls to display statistics on rolling three dice. The application interface should look similar to that shown on the right after typing `1000` and clicking **Roll Dice**.

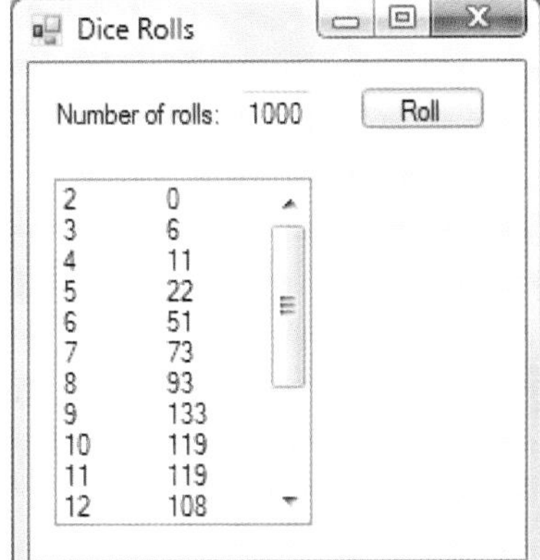

Review: NumberOccurences

Create a NumberOccurrences application that displays the counts of the occurrences of each digit in a number entered by the user. *Hint*: treat the number entered as a string. The application interface should look similar to that shown on the right after typing the number `12664590` and clicking **Count Numerals**.

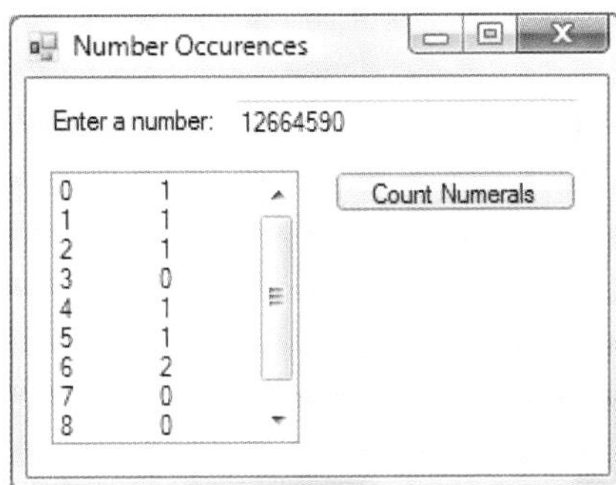

Searching an Array

linear search

There are many ways to search an array for a specific value. The simplest searching algorithm is called *linear search* and works by proceeding from one array element to the next until the specified value is found or until the entire array has been searched. The function FindItemIndex() implements the linear search algorithm:

```
'Returns the index of the first occurrence of searchItem in
'dataArray or -1 if searchItem not found.
'
'post: Index of the first occurrence of searchItem has
'been returned, or -1 has been returned if searchItem
'not found.
'
Function FindItemIndex(ByRef dataArray() As Integer,
ByVal searchItem As Integer) As Integer
   'Empty array
   If dataArray.Length = 0 Then
      Return -1                    'item not found
   End If

   'Find search item
   Dim index As Integer = 0
   Do While (dataArray(index) <> searchItem) And
   (index < dataArray.Length - 1)
      index += 1
   Loop
   If dataArray(index) = searchItem Then
      Return index                 'item found
   Else
      Return -1                    'item not found
   End If
End Function
```

The loop used in FindItemIndex does not explicitly check the last item in `dataArray`. However, if `searchItem` has not yet been found the `If...Then` compares it to the last array item.

Dynamic Arrays

A *dynamic array* varies in size during run time and is used in situations where the size of an array may need to grow or shrink or when the array size is unknown at the start of a program. The size of an existing array is changed at run time with a `ReDim` statement. The code below demonstrates `ReDim`:

```
Dim dataArray(-1) As Integer  'array contains 0 elements
ReDim dataArray(4)            'array now contains 5 elements
```

An array with size –1 contains zero elements. The `ReDim` statement sizes the array to contain five elements.

`ReDim` can be executed again and again to change the size of an array throughout program execution. However, each time a `ReDim` statement is executed, all the values in the array are lost. To keep the existing values in an array when sizing it, a `ReDim Preserve` statement must be used. For example, the following statements demonstrate `Preserve`:

```
Dim dataArray() As Integer = {25, 50} 'array with 2 elements
ReDim dataArray(3)                    'array with 4 elements
x = dataArray(1)                      '0 because value not preserved
dataArray(1) = 300
ReDim Preserve dataArray(4)                   'array with 5 elements
x = dataArray(1)                      '300 because value preserved
```

The DynamicArrayDemo application demonstrates dynamic arrays:

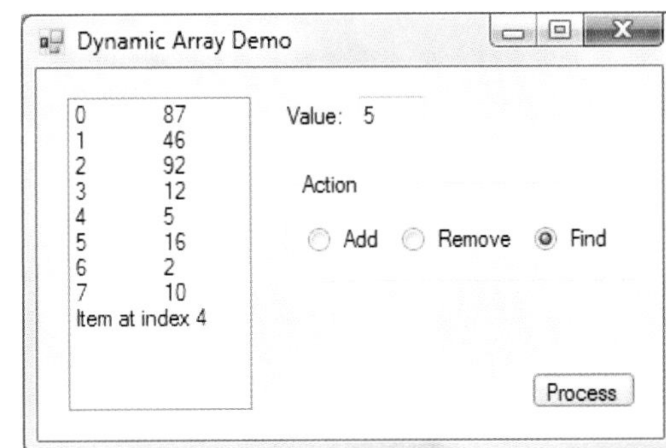

The DynamicArrayDemo application after adding values and then finding a value

```
Private Sub btnProcess _ Click(ByVal sender As Object,
ByVal e As System.EventArgs) Handles btnProcess.Click
  Static dataArray(-1) As Integer   'array with zero elements
  Dim index As Integer
  Dim numEntered As Integer = Val(Me.txtValue.Text)

  If Me.radAdd.Checked Then
      Call AddItem(dataArray, numEntered)
      Call DisplayData(dataArray, Me.lstOutput)
  ElseIf Me.radRemove.Checked Then
      Call RemoveItem(dataArray, numEntered)
      Call DisplayData(dataArray, Me.lstOutput)
  ElseIf Me.radFind.Checked Then
      index = FindItemIndex(dataArray, numEntered)
      Me.lstOutput.Items.Add("Item at index " & index)
  End If
End Sub


'Adds new element numToAdd as the last element of dataArray.
'
'pre: dataArray contains zero or more elements.
'post: dataArray has a new element numToAdd as the
'last element of the array.
'
Sub AddItem(ByRef dataArray() As Integer,
ByVal numToAdd As Integer)
  'Use Length to size array because that value is one
  'greater than the current highest index value
  ReDim Preserve dataArray(dataArray.Length)
  dataArray(dataArray.Length - 1) = numToAdd
End Sub
```

```
'Removes the first occurrence of numToRemove from dataArray
'and sizes the array with one less element.
'
'post: If numToRemove found, dataArray now has one less
'element and numToRemove has been deleted from array.
'
Sub RemoveItem(ByRef dataArray() As Integer,
ByVal numToRemove As Integer)
   Dim itemIndex As Integer

   itemIndex = FindItemIndex(dataArray, numToRemove)
   'move remaining elements up one position in array
   If itemIndex > -1 Then
       For index As Integer = itemIndex To
       dataArray.Length - 2
           dataArray(index) = dataArray(index + 1)
       Next index
       ReDim Preserve dataArray(dataArray.Length - 2)
   End If
End Sub


'Returns the index of the first occurrence of searchItem in
'dataArray or -1 if searchItem not found.
'
'post: Index of the first occurrence of searchItem has been
'returned, or -1 has been returned if searchItem not found.
'
Function FindItemIndex(ByRef dataArray() As Integer,
ByVal searchItem As Integer) As Integer
   'Empty array
   If dataArray.Length = 0 Then
       Return -1                'item not found
   End If

   'Find search item
   Dim index As Integer = 0
   Do While (dataArray(index) <> searchItem) And
   (index < dataArray.Length - 1)
       index += 1
   Loop
   If dataArray(index) = searchItem Then
       Return index             'item found
   Else
       Return -1                'item not found
   End If
End Function


'Clears a list box and then displays dataArray elements
'in the list box.
'
'pre: dataArray.Length > 0
'post: List box has been cleared of any previous items.
'dataArray elements are now displayed in the list box.
'
Sub DisplayData(ByRef dataArray() As Integer,
ByRef lstList As ListBox)
   lstList.Items.Clear()

   For index As Integer = 0 To dataArray.Length - 1
       lstList.Items.Add(index & vbTab & dataArray(index))
   Next index
End Sub
```

Note that in the btnProcess_Click event procedure, `dataArray` is declared as a static array so it would not be reinitialized each time Process is clicked. The RemoveItem() procedure finds the first location of the element to be removed and then overwrites it by moving the elements ahead of it up by one index. Finally, the "extra" element is removed from the array by sizing the array down by one.

Review: DynamicArrayDemo

Modify the DynamicArrayDemo application so that "Item not found" is displayed in the list box rather than "Item at index –1" when a search item is not found.

Review: FindName

Create a FindName application that allows the user to add, delete, and find names. The application interface should look similar to the DynamicArrayDemo interface.

Two-Dimensional Arrays

An array with two dimensions can be used to represent data that corresponds to a grid. For example, a checkerboard, the streets in a city, and seats in a theater can all be represented with a grid. A tic-tac-toe board represented in a two-dimensional array can be visualized as:

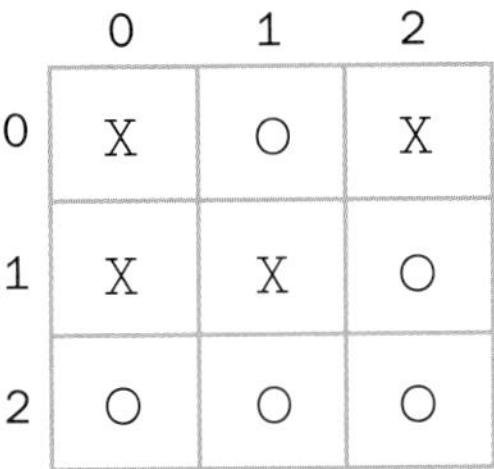

TTTBoard

A two-dimensional array is declared with a `Dim` statement that includes the array name followed by the index of the last element of each dimension separated by commas in parentheses and then the data type of the elements. For example, the statement

```
Dim TTTBoard(2, 2) As Char            '9 elements
```

declares a 3 x 3 TTTBoard with rows 0 through 2 and columns 0 through 2 for a total of nine `Char` elements. An element is accessed by including the appropriate row and column indexes in parentheses after the array name. For example, the following statement assigns the letter `X` to the first row (0) in the third column (2):

```
TTTBoard(0, 2) = "X"
```

The Length property returns the total number of elements in all the dimensions of an array. For example, 9 is the length of the `TTTBoard` array. The Array class contains other properties and methods useful when working with arrays with more than one dimension:

- **Rank** returns the number of dimensions in the array.
- **GetLength(*dimension*)** returns the number of elements in a dimension of an array. `dimension` is the dimension of the array, with 0 being the first dimension, 1 being the second, and so on.

Nested `For...Next` loops are often used to traverse the elements of a two-dimensional array because one loop counter indicates the row of the array and the other counter indicates the column. For example, in the following statements, nested `For...Next` loops are used to display the contents of a two-dimensional array in a list box:

```
Dim TTTBoard(2, 2) As Char
For row As Integer = 0 To TTTBoard.GetLength(0) - 1
      For col As Integer = 0 To TTTBoard.GetLength(1) - 1
          Me.lstElements.Items.Add(TTTBoard(intRow, col))
      Next col
Next row
```

A `ReDim` statement can be used to change the size of individual dimensions, but the number of dimensions in an array cannot be changed once declared.

Two-dimensional array parameters should be declared `ByRef` with the array name followed by an empty set of parentheses that includes a comma indicating two dimensions. For example, `ByRef numArray(,) As Integer` could be the parameter for a procedure.

The Tic-Tac-Toe application allows two players to play a computerized game of tic-tac-toe. The application keeps track of whether X or O is the next player and with each move checks to see if there is a winner or if the game is a draw. The application uses a two-dimensional array to keep track of the board. A run of the Tic-Tac-Toe application and its code are:

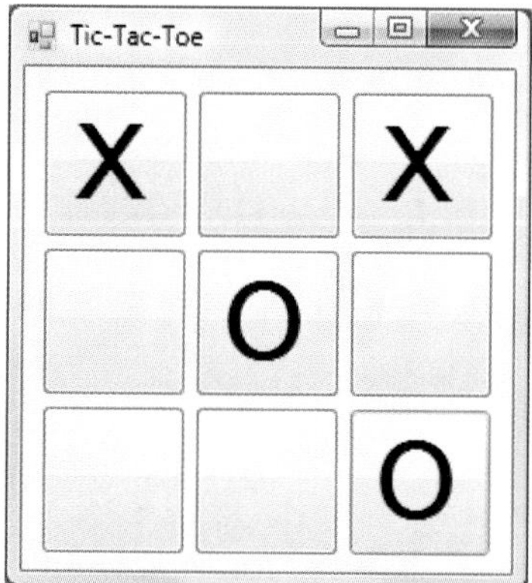

Tic-Tac-Toe after four moves

```
'Two player game of Tic-Tac-Toe.
'
'pre: Buttons representing the board have Tags that
'correspond to:
'             0,0  0,1  0,2
'             1,0  1,1  1,2
'             2,0  2,1  2,2
'post: Tic-Tac-Toe has been played until a winner or a draw is
'declared.
'
Private Sub btnMoveMade_Click(ByVal sender As Object,
ByVal e As System.EventArgs) Handles btn00.Click,
btn01.Click, btn02.Click, btn10.Click, btn11.Click,
btn12.Click, btn20.Click, btn21.Click, btn22.Click
   Dim btnSquareClicked As Button = sender
   Static chrTTT(2, 2) As Char          'store player moves
   Static player As Char = "X"          'X goes first

   'Check for existing X or O
   If btnSquareClicked.Text <> Nothing Then
       MessageBox.Show("Invalid move.")
   Else
       'Show move
       btnSquareClicked.Text = player

       'Store move in chrTTT
       Dim index As String
       index = btnSquareClicked.Tag
       Dim x As Integer = Val(index.Chars(0))
       Dim y As Integer = Val(index.Chars(2))
       Call StoreMove(x, y, player, chrTTT)

       'Check for winner
       If IsWinner(chrTTT) Then
           MessageBox.Show("Game over!")
       Else                                 'next player's turn
           If player = "X" Then
               player = "O"
           Else
               player = "X"
           End If
       End If
   End If
End Sub


'Store Tic-Tac-Toe move in chrTTT.
'
'pre: x and y is a valid index. chrTTT is a 3 x 3 array.
'post: Tic-Tac-Toe move has been stored in chrTTT.
'
Sub StoreMove(ByVal x As Integer, ByVal y As Integer,
ByVal player As Char, ByRef TTT(,) As Char)
   TTT(x, y) = player
End Sub
```

```
'Determines if there is a winner.
'
'pre: chrTTT is a 3 x 3 array.
'post: True has been returned if a winner is found
'or if all squares are filled.
'
Function IsWinner(ByRef TTT(,) As Char) As Boolean
   'Check all rows
   For row As Integer = 0 To 2
       If TTT(row, 0) = TTT(row, 1) And
       TTT(row, 1) = TTT(row, 2) And
       (TTT(row, 0) = "X" Or TTT(row, 0) = "O") Then
           Return True      'winner
       End If
   Next row

   'Check all columns
   For col As Integer = 0 To 2
       If TTT(0, col) = TTT(1, col) And
       TTT(1, col) = TTT(2, col) And
       (TTT(0, col) = "X" Or TTT(0, col) = "O") Then
           Return True      'winner
       End If
   Next col

   'Check one diagonal
   If TTT(0, 0) = TTT(1, 1) And TTT(1, 1) = TTT(2, 2)
   And (TTT(0, 0) = "X" Or TTT(0, 0) = "O") Then
       Return True          'winner
   End If

   'Check other diagonal
   If TTT(0, 2) = TTT(1, 1) And TTT(1, 1) = TTT(2, 0)
   And (TTT(0, 2) = "X" Or TTT(0, 2) = "O") Then
       Return True          'winner
   End If

   'Check for empty squares
   Dim movesLeft As Boolean = False
   For row As Integer = 0 To 2
       For col As Integer = 0 To 2
           If TTT(row, col) = Nothing Then
               movesLeft = True
           End If
       Next col
   Next row
   If Not movesLeft Then
       Return True          'all squares filled
   End If

   Return False             'no winner found
End Function
```

Structures

> **Structure Members**
>
> A structure is a simple form of a class and can have members that include methods, properties, constants, and events.

A *structure* is a composite data type that groups related variables. Unlike arrays that have elements of the same data type, structures have members that can be different data types. For example, the following is a declaration for a structure named `Student`:

```
Structure Student
  Dim firstName As String
  Dim lastName As String
  Dim middleInitial As Char
  Dim gpa As Single
  Dim credits As Integer
End Structure
```

A structure name typically begins with an uppercase letter, similar to other data type names and members follow variable naming code conventions. The names used for structures should be descriptive without exposing specific types.

In general, a structure takes the form:

```
Structure StructureName
  member declarations
End Structure
```

`StructureName` is a name describing the data grouped by the structure. `member declarations` is one or more statements that declare variables of any data type to store information. `Structure` declares the structure and `End Structure` ends the structure. A structure must be declared outside of any procedures and is usually placed at the beginning of a program with other global declarations.

A structure variable declaration can appear anywhere in a program. A structure variable accesses members of its structure with a dot (.) between the variable name and the member name. For example, the following statements declare a variable of type `Student` and then assigns a value to its `gpa` member:

```
Dim newStudent As Student
newStudent.gpa = 3.4
```

A procedure can include a structure parameter that is either `ByRef` or `ByVal`. A structure argument is passed to a procedure by including the variable name. A single member of a structure is passed to a procedure by using the structure name followed by a dot and then the member name. For example, both of the following statements are valid procedure calls:

```
Call ShowStudentData(newStudent)
Call ShowName(newStudent.FirstName, newStudent.LastName)
```

The procedure heading must declare a variable using the data type for the single member.

Structure Arrays

An array of structures can be used to store related information for a group of elements. For example, information for the students in a school could be stored in an array with elements of type `Student`:

```
Structure Student
   Dim firstName As String
   Dim lastName As String
   Dim middleInitial As Char
   Dim gpa As Single
   Dim credits As Integer
End Structure

...

Dim students(99) As Student          '100 students
```

> ***UDTs***
>
> Structures and arrays are sometimes referred to as user-defined types (UDTs) because the programmer decides the characteristics of the type.

Note that an array of structures can be declared anywhere in the program and does not need to be global like the `Structure` declaration itself.

The members of each element are accessed by using the index of the element and then a dot with a member name:

```
students(3).firstName = "Faith"          'Faith is fourth student
```

Review: Customers

Create a Customers application that prompts the user with input boxes for the first name, last name, and account balance of 5 customers and then displays the customer with the highest account balance and the average account balance. Store the customer data in an array of structures. The application interface should look similar to that shown on the right after clicking Enter Customer Information and entering data for five customers.

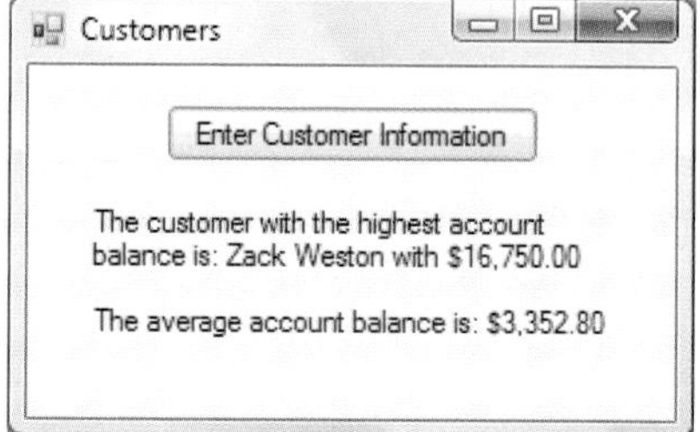

Enumerated Types

An *enumerated type* is a data type that defines a related set of named constants. An enumeration is useful when a variable that should be limited to a set of values. For example, student level is either freshman, sophomore, junior, or senior, based on the years in school. A `String` variable can be used to store a student level, but this type of variable can hold any string, not just the four possible levels, which could lead to hard-to-find bugs. Instead `Enum` can be used to declare an enumeration:

```
Enum Level
   Freshman
   Sophomore
   Junior
   Senior
End Enum
```

Enumerated type names should begin with an uppercase letter, similar to other data type names. The constants defined by the enumerated type, called *fields*, should also begin with an uppercase letter.

field

A variable declared with an enumerated type is limited to storing the values defined in the enumeration. Visual Basic enforces this in the IDE with an IntelliSense list. For example, in a `Level` variable assignment statement a list is displayed when the equal sign is typed:

Dim year As Level
year =
Level.Freshman
Level.Junior
Level.Senior
Level.Sophomore

The values allowed for assignment to this variable are displayed in alphabetical order in the IntelliSense list.

An enumerated type must be declared outside of any procedures and is usually placed at the beginning of a program with other global declarations. Variables declared as an enumerated type can appear anywhere in the program.

The fields of an enumerated type correspond to a set of integer constants, starting with 0 if no other values are assigned in the `Enum` statement. The `Level` members correspond to `Freshman` = 0, `Sophomore` = 1, `Junior` = 2, and `Senior` = 3. Therefore, the following statements display `1` in the label:

```
Year = Level.Sophomore
Me.lblShowLevel.Text = Year            '1 is displayed!
```

A `Select...Case` statement is often used to determine what action to take based on the value of an enumerated type variable. In the Code window, an IntelliSense list is displayed after `Case` is typed:

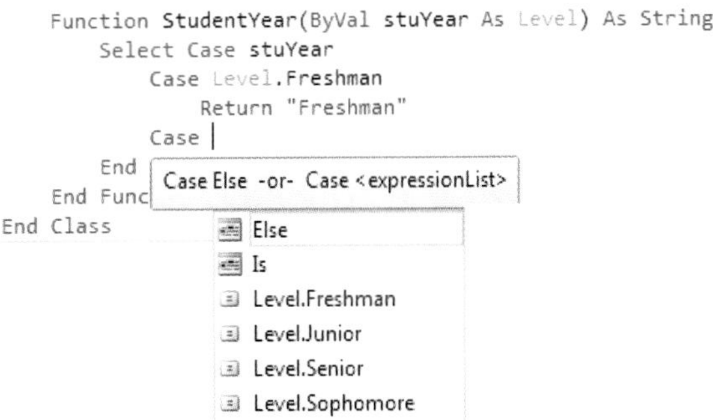
Function StudentYear(ByVal stuYear As Level) As String
Select Case stuYear
Case Level.Freshman
Return "Freshman"
Case
End
End Func
End Class
Case Else -or- Case <expressionList>
Else
Is
Level.Freshman
Level.Junior
Level.Senior
Level.Sophomore

In this example, the `Select...Case` statement is part of a function that returns the string equivalent of an enumerated type member.

Enumerated type members can be explicitly assigned values, as in the statement:

```
Enum Summer
  June = 6
  July = 7
  August = 8
End Enum
```

Review: Students

Create a Students application that maintains an array of student information using an appropriate data type for the array members. The application should prompt the user with text boxes for the first name, middle initial, last name, GPA, and credits for a student. A list box should prompt the user for the student's year. Add Student adds the student to the array. Show Student displays an input box prompting the user for a last name and then displays student information in a message box. The application should use a modified FindItemIndex() function from this chapter. The interface should look similar to that shown on the right after adding students and then displaying information about a student.

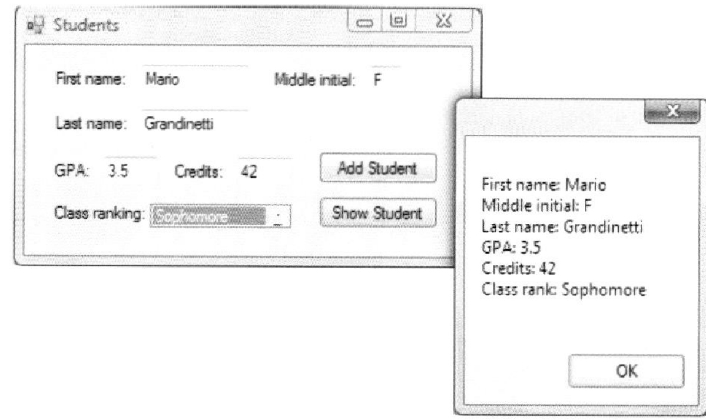

Case Study

In this case study an application for generating orders for Lucy's Cuban Cafe will be created.

CafeOrders Specification

Lucy's Cuban Cafe is a small restaurant that offers nine menu items: Arroz con Pollo for $9.95, Ropa Vieja for $9.95, Masitas for $8.95, Cuban Sandwich for $6.95, Moros for $2.75, Yuca for $2.75, Cafe con Leche for $1.75, Flan for $2.50, and Pudin de Pan for $2.95. The CafeOrders application should maintain a list of the items ordered and a running total price for the order. The user should be able to create a new order, which clears the list and the total, and select items to order by clicking buttons.

CafeOrders Design

The interface for CafeOrders should provide a button for each menu item. A list box displays any number of items ordered and a label displays the total price of an order. A New Order button clears the list box and total price.

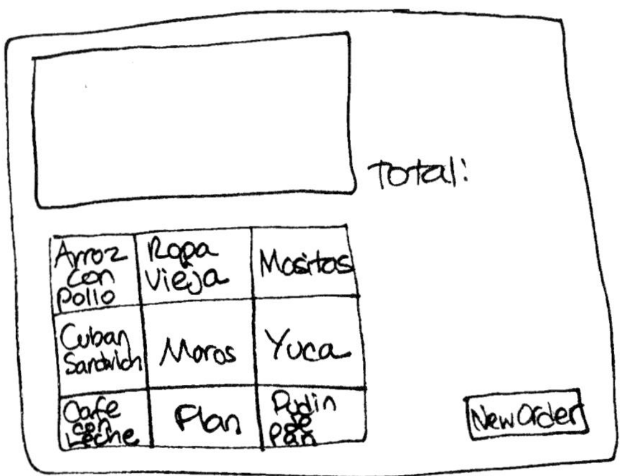

The code design starts with an algorithm:

1. Start the application to show only a `New Order` button. All other objects are not visible.
2. Click `New Order` to load the menu items into an array and display buttons with item names.
3. Clicking a menu item button adds that item and its price to the list and updates the current total price label.
4. Clicking `New Order` removes any items from the list box and removes the price from the total price label.

Analyzing the algorithm further reveals some aspects of the code:

- The Visible property should be used in the Design window to hide options.
- The same or similar actions are performed by the `New Order` and menu item buttons.
- The data for the menu items could be stored as structure elements in an array, with the structure containing the item name and price.

Based on the algorithm and analysis of the algorithm, the pseudocode for this application appears like:

```
Structure MenuItem
    itemName
    price
End Structure

MAX_FOOD_ITEMS = 9

Sub ProcessOrder (sender, e) Handles btnNewOrder.Click, btnItem0.Click, btnItem1.Click,
btnItem2.Click, btnItem3.Click, btnItem4.Click, btnItem5.Click, btnItem6.Click, btnItem7.Click,
btnItem8.Click
    Static lucyMenu(MAX_FOOD_ITEMS) As MenuItem
    Static totalPrice As Decimal
    Dim menuItem As Integer

    Dim ButtonClicked As Button = sender
    Select Case ButtonClicked.Tag
        Case "NewOrder"
            LoadMenu(lucyMenu)
            LoadButtons(lucyMenu)
            totalPrice = 0
            Clear list box items and label
            Show list box
        Case Else
            menuItem = ButtonClicked.Tag
            AddToList(lucyMenu(intMenuItem), list box)
            totalPrice += lucyMenu(menuItem).Price
            ShowTotal
    End Select
End Sub
```

```
Sub LoadMenu(ByRef menu() As MenuItem)
    menu(0).ItemName = "Arroz con Pollo"
    menu(0).Price = 9.95

    … Repeat block for remaining eight menu items …
End Sub

Sub LoadButtons(ByRef menu() As MenuItem)
    btnItem0.Text = menu(0).ItemName
    Show button

    … Repeat block for remaining eight menu items …
End Sub

Sub AddToList(ByVal item As MenuItem, ByRef lstOrderList As ListBox)
    lstOrderList.Items.Add(Item.ItemName & vbTab & _
    Format(item.Price, "Currency")
End Sub

Sub ShowTotal(ByVal amount As Decimal, ByRef lblAmount As Label)
    lblAmount.Text = "Total:" & Format(amount, "Currency")
End Sub
```

CafeOrders Coding

The interface for CafeOrders is:

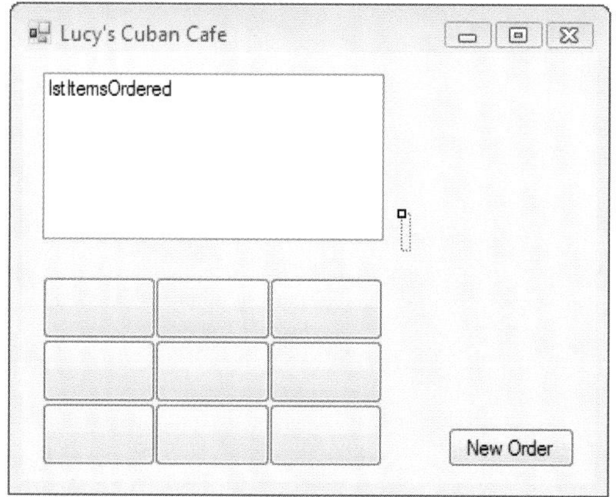

Object	**(Name)**	**Text**	**Tag**
Form1		Lucy's Cuban Cafe	
ListBox1	lstItemsOrdered		
Label1	lblTotal	*empty*	
Button1	btnItem0	*empty*	0
Button2	btnItem1	*empty*	1
Button3	btnItem2	*empty*	2
Button4	btnItem3	*empty*	3
Button5	btnItem4	*empty*	4
Button6	btnItem5	*empty*	5
Button7	btnItem6	*empty*	6
Button8	btnItem7	*empty*	7
Button9	btnItem8	*empty*	8
Button10	btnNewOrder	New Order	NewOrder

The Visible property is set to False for every object except the New Order button and the lblTotal label. The label should also be bold, size 10.

The final coding for CafeOrders is shown below:

```
Public Class Form1

    Structure MenuItem
        Dim itemName As String
        Dim price As Decimal
    End Structure

    Const MAX_FOOD_ITEMS As Integer = 9   'number of items on interface

    'Processes orders by showing selected items in a list and maintaining a
    'current total
    '
    'post: A total price has been displayed and selected items have been displayed
    'in a list if menu items were selected. The list has been cleared and the
    'price has been cleared if the New Order button was clicked.
    '
    Private Sub ProcessOrder(ByVal sender As Object, ByVal e As System.EventArgs)
    Handles btnNewOrder.Click, btnItem0.Click, btnItem1.Click, btnItem2.Click,
    btnItem3.Click, btnItem4.Click, btnItem5.Click, btnItem6.Click,
    btnItem7.Click, btnItem8.Click
        Static lucyMenu(MAX_FOOD_ITEMS) As MenuItem
        Static totalPrice As Decimal
        Dim menuItem As Integer
        Dim btnButtonClicked As Button = sender

        Select Case btnButtonClicked.Tag
            Case "NewOrder"
                'Load menu items and display on buttons
                Call LoadMenu(lucyMenu)
                Call LoadButtons(lucyMenu)
                'Initialize price and clear total from interface
                totalPrice = 0
                Me.lblTotal.Text = Nothing
                'Clear list of existing items and show list
                Me.lstItemsOrdered.Items.Clear()
                Me.lstItemsOrdered.Visible = True
            Case Else
                menuItem = Val(btnButtonClicked.Tag)
                Call AddToList(lucyMenu(menuItem), Me.lstItemsOrdered)
                totalPrice += lucyMenu(menuItem).price
                Call ShowTotal(totalPrice, Me.lblTotal)
        End Select
    End Sub


    'Stores item names and prices in Menu array.
    '
    'post: Menu item names and prices have been stored in an array.
    '
    Sub LoadMenu(ByRef menu() As MenuItem)
        menu(0).itemName = "Arroz con Pollo"
        menu(0).price = 9.95

        menu(1).itemName = "Ropa Vieja"
        menu(1).price = 9.95

        menu(2).itemName = "Masitas"
        menu(2).price = 8.95

        menu(3).itemName = "Cuban Sandwich"
        menu(3).price = 6.95
```

```
        menu(4).itemName = "Moros"
        menu(4).price = 2.75

        menu(5).itemName = "Yuca"
        menu(5).price = 2.75

        menu(6).itemName = "Cafe con Leche"
        menu(6).price = 1.75

        menu(7).itemName = "Flan"
        menu(7).price = 2.5

        menu(8).itemName = "Pudin de Pan"
        menu(8).price = 2.95
    End Sub


    'Displays menu item names on interface
    '
    'post: Menu item names have been displayed on buttons.
    '
    Sub LoadButtons(ByRef menu() As MenuItem)
        Me.btnItem0.Text = menu(0).itemName
        Me.btnItem0.Visible = True

        Me.btnItem1.Text = menu(1).itemName
        Me.btnItem1.Visible = True

        Me.btnItem2.Text = menu(2).itemName
        Me.btnItem2.Visible = True

        Me.btnItem3.Text = menu(3).itemName
        Me.btnItem3.Visible = True

        Me.btnItem4.Text = menu(4).itemName
        Me.btnItem4.Visible = True

        Me.btnItem5.Text = menu(5).itemName
        Me.btnItem5.Visible = True

        Me.btnItem6.Text = menu(6).itemName
        Me.btnItem6.Visible = True

        Me.btnItem7.Text = menu(7).itemName
        Me.btnItem7.Visible = True

        Me.btnItem8.Text = menu(8).itemName
        Me.btnItem8.Visible = True
    End Sub

    'Adds selected menu item to a list
    '
    'post: Selected menu item and price have been added to list
    '
    Sub AddToList(ByVal item As MenuItem, ByRef lstOrderList As ListBox)
        lstOrderList.Items.Add(item.itemName & vbTab & Format(item.price, "Currency"))
    End Sub

    'Displays a total price for the current order in a label
    '
    'post: A price has been displayed in a label.
    '
    Sub ShowTotal(ByVal amount As Decimal, ByRef lblAmount As Label)
        lblAmount.Text = "Total:" & Format(amount, "Currency")
    End Sub
End Class
```

Running CafeOrders, clicking New Order, and selecting a few menu items displays the following:

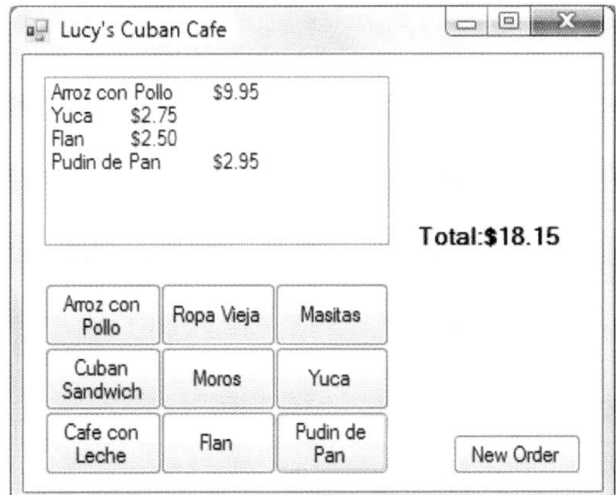

Lucy's Cuban Cafe

Lucy serves only authentic Cuban food at her restaurant. The menu items are in Spanish and translate to English as Chicken and Yellow Rice (Arroz con Pollo), Shredded Beef (Ropa Vieja), Pork and Plantains (Masitas), Cuban Bread with Meat and Cheese (Cuban Sandwich), Black Beans and Rice (Moros), Cassava (Yuca), Coffee with Milk (Cafe con Leche), Baked Custard (Flan), and Bread Pudding (Pudin de Pan).

CafeOrders should be tested by selecting each of the menu items at least once and verifying that the items appear correctly in the list and that the total is updated correctly. The New Order button should also be clicked to verify that it performs as expected.

Arrays of Objects

An array can store a reference to a set of control class objects, such as a set of buttons on a form. For example, the following statement declares an array of the menu buttons in the CafeOrders application:

```
Dim itemButtons() As Button = {Me.btnItem0, Me.btnItem1,
Me.btnItem2, Me.btnItem3, Me.btnItem4, Me.btnItem5,
Me.btnItem6, Me.btnItem7, Me.btnItem8}
```

An array of objects must be declared with the appropriate control class data type. In addition to the `Button` data type used in the declaration, there are `CheckBox`, `Label`, `TextBox`, `RadioButton`, and `PictureBox` classes.

An array of control class objects can simplify code that sets the same property for multiple objects of the same type. For example, the CafeOrders LoadButtons() procedure could be rewritten to include a `Button` array parameter:

```
Sub LoadButtons(ByRef menu() As MenuItem,
ByRef itemButtons() As Button)

  'Set each button to an item name
  For item As Integer = 0 To menu.Length - 1
      itemButtons(item).Text = Menu(item).itemName
      itemButtons(item).Visible = True
  Next item
End Sub
```

Review: CafeOrders

Modify the CafeOrders application to include an English button when the application is started. Clicking this button displays the menu items in English and the language button then displays Spanish to allow the user to switch the application display back to Spanish menu items. Refer to the sidebar on the previous page to determine the English names of the menu items. The application changes will require modifying the MenuItem structure to contain appropriate members for storing English and Spanish names, using arrays of objects to simplify code, modifying ProcessOrder(), LoadMenu(), LoadButtons(), and AddToList() procedures, and sizing the list box and buttons appropriately.

Chapter Summary

An array is a composite data type that stores many of the same type of data together. A data item stored by an array is called an element. The elements of an array have an index value, with the first element being index 0, the second being index 1, and so on. Arrays are objects of the `Array` class, which has member Length that returns the number of elements.

An array is declared using a `Dim` statement that includes the array name followed by the index of the last element in parentheses and then the data type of the elements. Array elements can include built-in types, such as `Double` and `String`, structures, or control class objects, such as `Button`. An array can be initialized to a specific set of values when it is declared by including in braces the values of the elements separated by commas.

An array element is accessed by including the index in parentheses after the array name. A `For...Next` loop is used to traverse an array. An exception occurs if an invalid index is used.

An array parameter can be declared `ByVal` or `ByRef` and uses the array name followed by an empty set of parentheses. An array argument uses just the array name. A single array element may also be used for parameters and arguments. A single element is passed by including the array name followed by the index of the element in parentheses.

Many algorithms make use of the index value of an array element for simplifying the storage and retrieval of data.

The linear search algorithm proceeds from one array element to the next until a specified value is found or until the entire array has been searched.

A dynamic array varies in size during run time and is used in situations where the size of an array may need to grow or shrink or when the array size is unknown at the start of a program. An array declared with a size of –1 contains 0 elements. A `ReDim` statement changes the size of an existing array. A `ReDim Preserve` statement changes the size of an array and leaves existing values.

A two-dimensional array is often used to represent data that relates to a grid and is declared using a `Dim` statement that includes the array name followed by the size of each dimension separated by commas in parentheses and then the data type of the elements. Nested `For...Next` loops are used to traverse a two-dimensional array. Elements of a two-dimensional array are accessed using both the row and column indexes. The Rank and GetLength members of the `Array` class are often used with two-dimensional arrays.

A structure is a composite data type grouping related variables that can be of different types. Structures must be declared outside of any procedures and are usually placed at the beginning of a program with other global declarations. Structure members are accessed using a dot between the structure variable name and the member name. An array of structures can be used to store related information for a group of elements.

An enumerated type is a data type that defines a related set of named constants. Enumerations are used to declare variables that should store a value from a limited set of values. Enumerated types must be declared outside of any procedures and are usually placed at the beginning of a program with other global declarations. The fields of an enumerated type can be assigned specific values.

Code conventions introduced in this chapter are:

- Structure names should begin with a uppercase letter and members should follow variable naming conventions.
- Enumerated type names should begin with an uppercase letter. Field names should also begin with an uppercase letter.

Vocabulary

Array A composite data type consisting of a set of elements that are all the same data type.

Composite data type A data type that is made up of a collection of elements.

Dynamic array An array that varies in size during run time.

Enumerated type A data type that defines a related set of named constants.

Field One of the constants of an enumerated type.

Index The number used to identify an array element.

Linear search A simple algorithm for searching an array for a specific value.

Structure A composite data type that groups related variables that can be of different data types.

Traversing Iterating through each element of an array.

Visual Basic

`()` Parentheses are used to enclose an index that refers to an array element.

`{}` **Braces** are used to enclose initial array element values.

`Array` **class** Used to manipulate array elements. Properties include GetLength, Length, and Rank.

`End Enum` Statement used to end an enumerated type declaration.

`End Structure` Statement used to end a structure data type.

`Enum` Statement used to declare an enumerated data type.

`Preserve` Keyword used in a `ReDim` statement to keep the existing values of an array when it is sized.

`ReDim` Statement used to change the size of an array at run time.

`Structure` Statement used to declare a structure data type.

Critical Thinking

1. Write declarations for an array storing 15 test grades (integer values), an array storing 100 prices (decimal values), and an array storing 50 true/false test answers (Boolean values).

2. What are the similarities and differences between `Structure` declarations and enumerated type declarations?

3. Show the contents of the `grid` array after the following statements execute:

```
Dim grid(3, 2) As Integer
Dim value As Integer
For i As Integer = 0 To 3
    For j As Integer = 0 To 2
        value = i + j
        grid(i, j) = value
    Next j
Next i
```

4. Write an event handler procedure for the following interface:

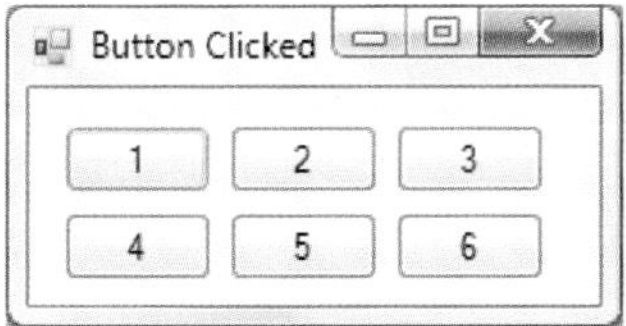

The Tag properties of the buttons are assigned the same values as the Text properties of the buttons. The procedure responds to the clicking of the buttons and uses array `timesSelected` to keep track of the number of times each button has been clicked. Use meaningful array indexes. For example, if the **3** button has been clicked 5 times then the value of `timesSelected(3)` will be 5.

5. a) Why is it not possible to create a two-dimensional array that stores movie titles in its first dimension and gross money earned in its second dimension?
   b) Write a declaration for a structure named `MovieInfo` that stores a movie title and a gross money earned amount.
   c) Where must the structure in part (b) be declared in a program?
   d) Using the structure declared in part (b), write a declaration for an array named `TopActionMovies` that stores information for 50 movies.
   e) Write an assignment statement for the first element of the `TopActionMovies` array declared in part (d) so that Star Wars, which grossed $460,395,655, is stored.

6. Write an array declaration for:
   a) `prices` which initially stores `1.50`, `2.25`, `3.15`, `4.30`.
   b) `names` which initially contains zero elements.
   c) `scores` which has 30 rows and 5 columns.

7. a) Write a function RowSum() that returns the sum of the values in the elements of a specific row for a two-dimensional array. The header is:

```
Function RowSum(ByRef ints(,) As Integer,
ByVal row As Integer) As Integer
```

   b) Write a function ColSum() that returns the sum of the values in the elements of a specific column for a two-dimensional array. The header is:

```
Function ColSum(ByRef ints(,) As Integer,
ByVal col As Integer) As Integer
```

   c) Write a decision structure that calls RowSum() in part (a) only if the value of the row number is valid. If the row number is not valid, a message box with an appropriate message is displayed.

8. The array `values` can be visualized as:

4	6	2	0
10	9	1	12

   a) What will `values.Length` return?
   b) What will `values.Rank` return?
   c) What will `values.GetLength(0)` return?
   d) What will `values.GetLength(1)` return?
   e) What is stored at `values(2, 2)`?
   f) What is stored at `values(1, 2)`?
   g) What will lstOutput display after the following code segment executes:

```
For i As Integer = 0 To 3
  For j As Integer = 0 To 1
    Me.lstOutput.Items.Add(values(j, i))
  Next j
Next i
```

9. For each of the following, determine the error(s):

a)
```
'procedure header which accepts an array
'declared as (2, 3) for an argument
Sub GetName(ByRef names(2, 3) As String)
```

b)
```
Dim cost(7) As Decimal  'array of 7 items
```

c)
```
'The winner is the last element in an
'array that holds 20 names
Me.lblOutput.Text = "Winner is " &
name(20)
```

d)
```
Sub Test()
    Enum Card
        Ace = 1
        Deuce = 2
        King = "Highest Value"
    End Enum
    Card.Ace = 14
    Dim card1 As Card
    card1 = Card.Ace
    ...
```

10. a) What is the purpose of using a `ReDim` statement?

b) What happens if the keyword `Preserve` does not follow `ReDim`?

11. a) Show the contents of lstOutput after the following statements execute:

```
Dim values() As Integer = {2, 4, 6, 8}
ReDim Preserve values(6)
For i As Integer = 5 To 0 Step -1
    Me.lstOutput.Items.Add(values(i))
Next i
```

b) Is `values` in part (a) an example of a dynamic array or a non-dynamic array?

12. Use the following code to answer the questions below:

```
Enum AnimalType
    Bird
    Cat
    Dog
    Fish
End Enum

Structure PetType
    Dim name As String
    Dim animal As AnimalType
End Structure

Dim pets(9) As PetType
```

a) What is the result of:

```
Pets(2).Animal = AnimalType.Dog
```

b) What integer value does Fish correlate to?

c) What will the following code display:

```
For pet As AnimalType = AnimalType.Bird _
    To AnimalType.Fish
        MessageBox.Show(pet)
Next pet
```

13. Assume an interface has seven Label objects. Write statements that create an array of the Label objects and then sets each to a random number between 1 and 7.

True/False

14. Determine if each of the following is true or false. If false, explain why.

a) The length of a one-dimensional array is one more than the index of the last element.

b) An array declaration must have a number in the parentheses.

c) "Index was outside the bounds of the array" is a syntax error message that is displayed when an invalid index is used.

d) An array being passed in a `Call` statement must have its size indicated in parentheses.

e) An array used as a parameter must have its size in parentheses.

f) Arrays must be passed into procedures by reference.

g) A dynamic array is an array that has been assigned values in its declaration statement.

h) `ReDim` reinitializes all the elements in an array to `Nothing`.

i) In a `Dim` statement, the size of an array must be a positive number.

j) All columns in a two-dimensional array must be of the same type.

k) Structures can have members of different types.

l) To pass a structure requires that each individual member be listed.

m) A linear search looks at one element after another until the desired element is found or the entire array has been searched.

n) A structure can be declared in the procedure that uses it.

o) The `Preserve` keyword is used when the programmer wants to make sure the array size is not changed.

p) An enumerated type cannot be defined in the procedure that uses it.

q) The first member declared in an enumerated type has a default value of 0 (zero).

r) An array can contain elements from the application interface that are all the same control class type.

Exercises

Exercise 1 — StudentNames

Modify the StudentNames application created in the first review of this chapter so that the names are displayed in the list box in the reverse order in which they were entered.

Exercise 2 — MaxAndMinNumbers

Create a MaxAndMinNumbers application that generates an array of 10 random numbers between 1 and 99 and then displays the array elements in a list box when Numbers is clicked. The application should display the highest number in the array when Max is clicked and the lowest number in the array when Min is clicked. The application interface should look similar to:

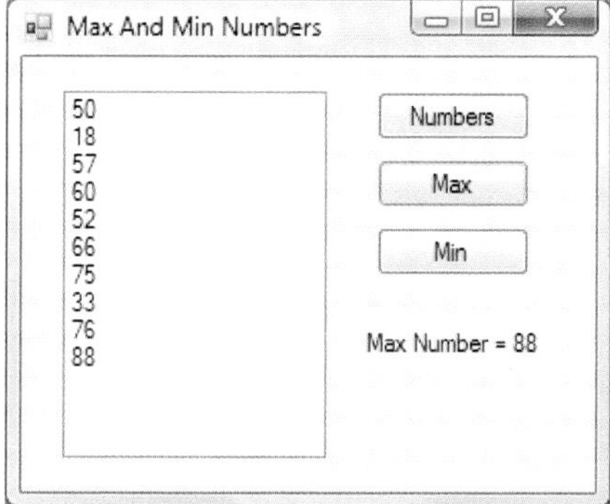

Exercise 3 — GeneratedNumbers

Create a GeneratedNumbers application that stores in an array with indexes 1 through 100 numbers generated by the index values when Generate is clicked. Generate the number to be stored at each index by summing the index and its individual digits. For example, 25 should be stored at index 17 because 17 + 1 + 7 = 25 and 4 should be stored at index 2 because 2 + 0 + 2. The application interface should look similar to:

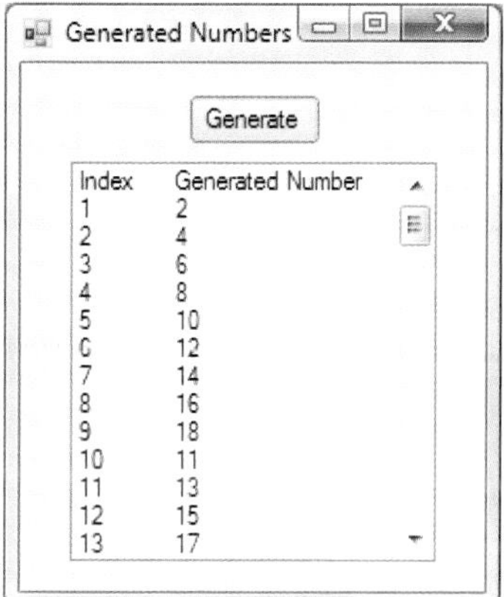

Your program code should use a FillArray() procedure to generate the numbers and a DisplayArray() procedure that displays each index and its element in the list box.

Exercise 4 — WordGuess

Modify the WordGuess case study from Chapter 5 to keep track of the letters guessed in an array with meaningful indexes. Include in the modifications code that displays a message box if the user enters the same guess twice.

Exercise 5 — DynamicNumbers

a) Create a DynamicNumbers application that prompts the user for an array size and then loads the array with random numbers between 1 and 99 and displays the index and contents of each array element in a list box when **Create Array** is clicked. The application interface should look similar to:

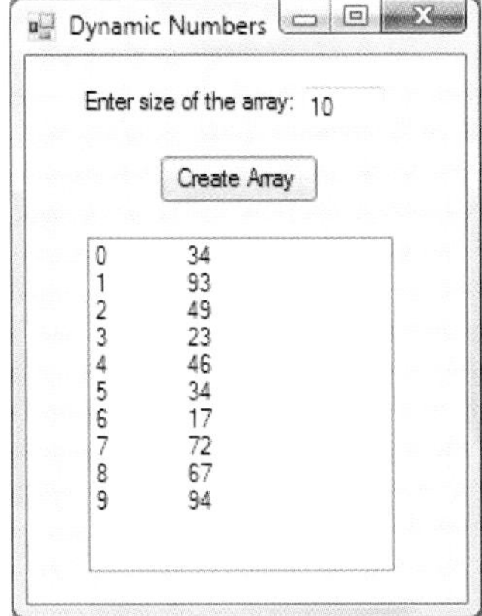

b) *Advanced.* An array is said to be sorted if its elements are in either increasing or decreasing order. One way the selection sort algorithm works is by repeatedly taking the lowest item from an array and adding it to a new array, so that all the elements in the new array are sorted from low to high. Modify the DynamicNumbers application so that it also displays the array sorted from low to high in the list box. Your program code should use a:

- FindLowest() function that returns the index of the lowest value in the array.
- Sort() procedure that repeatedly finds the lowest value in an array A, removes it, and adds it to array T. When all the values of A have been moved, the elements of T are copied to A with an assignment statement and a loop. Use the FindLowest() function and refer to the AddItem() and RemoveItem() procedures from the text.

Exercise 6 — MatchingIndexAndElement

Create a MatchingIndexAndElement application that prompts the user with an input box for an array size and then randomly fills each element of the array with a number that is in the range of 0 to one less the length of the array and displays the array elements in a list box. Have the application count the indexes of the array that match its corresponding element value. For example, if the random number generated is 2 and stored in index 2, then update the count. The application interface should look similar to the following, after clicking Generate/Match and entering 10 in the input box:

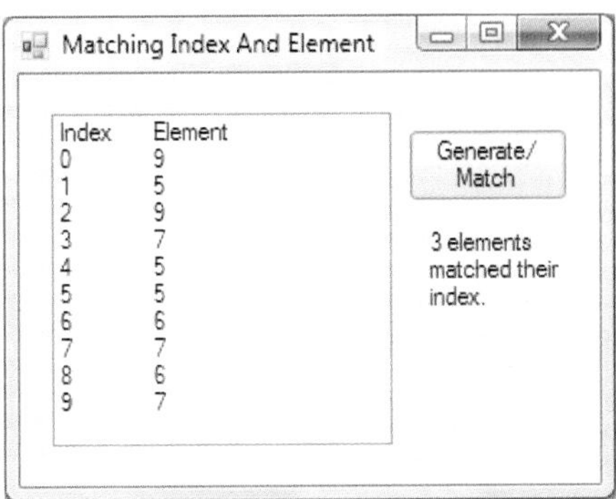

Exercise 7 — EvenAndOddNumbers

Create an EvenAndOddNumbers application that generates an array of 10 random numbers between 1 and 99 and displays in a list box the index and array value of each element, the even number array values, and the odd number array values when Generate is clicked. The application interface should look similar to:

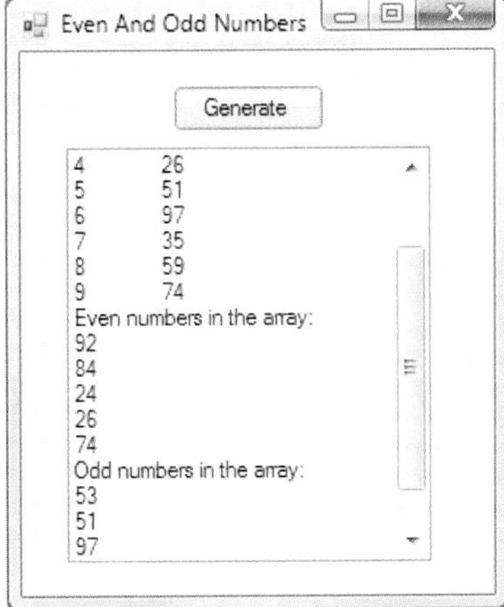

Your program code should use a:

- FillArray() procedure to generate and store the random numbers in the array.
- DisplayArray() procedure that displays the index and its element in the list box.
- EvenNumbers() procedure that adds the even numbers to the list box.
- OddNumbers() procedure that adds the odd numbers to the list box.

Exercise 8 ——— DuplicateValues

Create a DuplicateValues application that prompts the user with input boxes for numbers between 1 and 99 until a duplicate value is entered. When a duplicate value is entered, the numbers entered before the duplicate value are displayed in a list box and a message in a label displays how many numbers where entered. The application interface should look similar to the following after the user has clicked Input Numbers and entered 67, 87, 90, and 67 in input boxes:

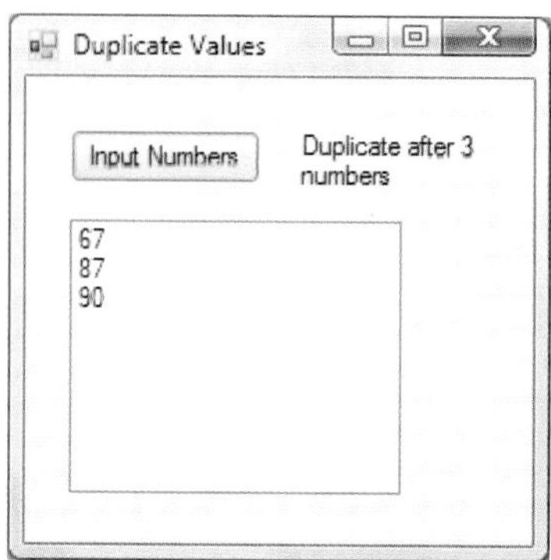

Exercise 9  ——— Mastermind

Modify the Mastermind application from Chapter 6 Exercise 13 to use arrays with the following features:

- The number of pegs (from 1 to 10) can be specified at the start of the application.
- The number of colors (from 1 to 9) can be specified at the start of the program.
- Both the guess and the secret code can contain duplicates. This will require extra care when counting the number of pegs of the correct color. For example, if the secret code is 1, 2, 3, 4, 5 and the guess is 2, 1, 1, 2, 2 then the program should only report two correct colors (a single 1 and a single 2).

Exercise 10 ——— Lockers

Create a Lockers application that simulates a progressive cycle of closing and opening every nth locker in a hall of 100 lockers, with n starting at the 2nd locker and continuing through to the 100th locker. The application should represent the locker status (opened or closed) as a `Boolean` array with `True` representing opened. When the application first starts, all of the lockers should be open and their status displayed in a list box when Initialize is clicked. When the user clicks Simulate, the status of every 2nd locker should be switched (if it is open then close it and if it is closed, open it). Then, the status of every 3rd locker should be switched. Continue this process for every 4th through the 100th locker. Display the concluding locker statuses in a list box. The application interface should look similar to that shown on the next page after clicking Initialize and then Simulate:

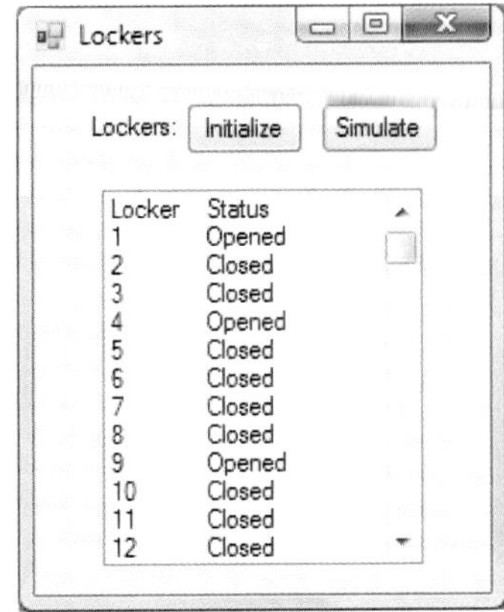

Can you identify what pattern the open lockers represent in the concluding array?

Exercise 11 — GameBoard

a) Create a GameBoard application that represents a game board with 16 spots. Use buttons to represent the 16 spots. The application should simulate 100 dice rolls when the user clicks `100 Dice Rolls` and store in an array with meaningful indexes the total number of times each spot was landed on based on the dice roll (moving around the board clockwise from the Start location). The total count should be displayed on each button. The application interface should look similar to the following after clicking `100 Dice Rolls`:

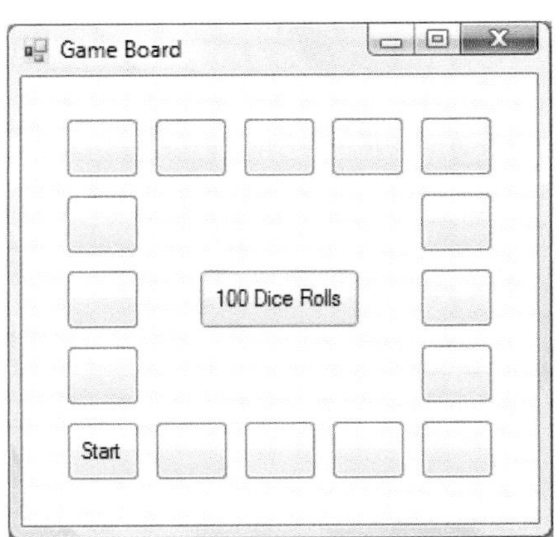

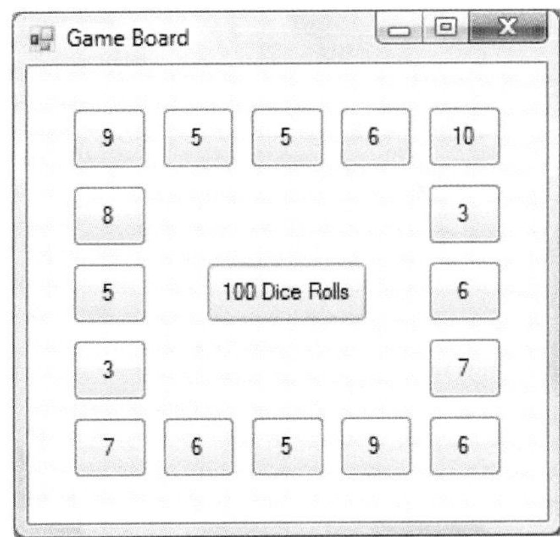

b) *Advanced*. Modify the application so that spot 13 is a "Go Back" location. If spot 13 is landed on, count it as being landed on but go back to spot 5, count it as being landed on and continue from spot 5. Also, if doubles are consecutively rolled then go back to spot 5.

Exercise 12 — GolfGame

a) Create a GolfGame application that uses a two-dimensional array representing 4 golfers playing 9 holes of golf (4 x 9 array) to store 36 randomly generated golf scores (integer values 1 through 9) and displays the contents of the array in a list box when Play Golf! is clicked. The golfer with the lowest number of strokes on a hole wins that hole. Display how many holes each player won overall. The application interface should look similar to:

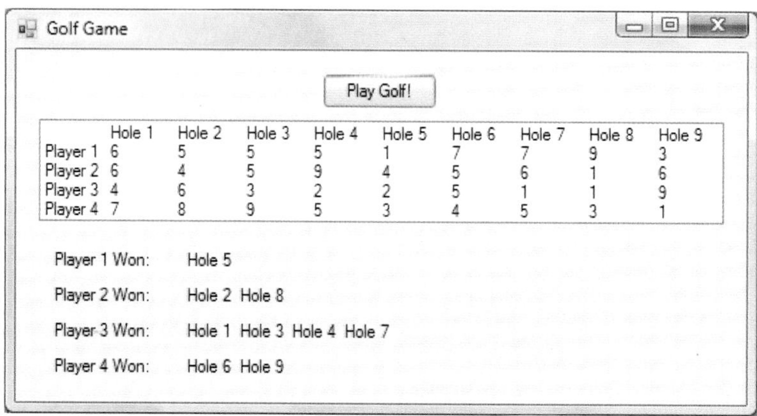

b) *Advanced*. Modify the GolfGame application to include an option that prompts the user for the golf scores.

Exercise 13 — HiddenPrizes

Create a HiddenPrizes application that uses buttons to represent a 5 x 5 board. The user is allowed five guesses to find the two randomly selected buttons that contain the text `Comp` and `uter` that are "hidden" when Hide the Prizes! is clicked. If the user finds both of the hidden words "You're a winner!" is displayed in a message box, otherwise "You lose." is displayed and the text `Comp` and `uter` are shown. The application interface should look similar to:

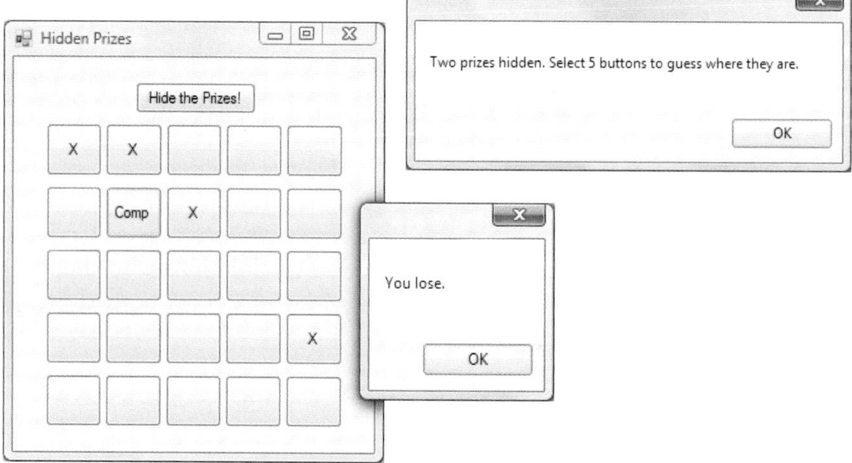

Exercise 14 (advanced)

The game of Life was devised by a mathematician as a model of a very simple world. The Life world is a grid of cells, a 10 x 10 grid in this case. Each cell may be empty or contain a single creature. Each day, creatures are born or die in each cell according to the number of neighboring creatures on the previous day. A neighbor is a cell that adjoins the cell either horizontally, vertically, or diagonally. The rules are:

- If the cell is alive on the previous day then

  if the number of neighbors was 2 or 3 the cell remains alive
  else the cell dies (of either loneliness or overcrowding)

- If the cell is not alive on the previous day then

  if the number of neighbors was exactly 3 the cell becomes alive
  else it remains dead

Start Game initializes the world by randomly generating 20 cells and displaying them on a grid:

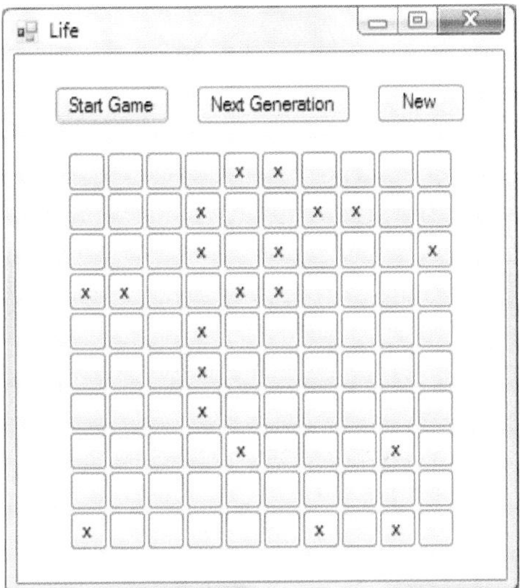

Next Generation displays a new generation each time it is clicked:

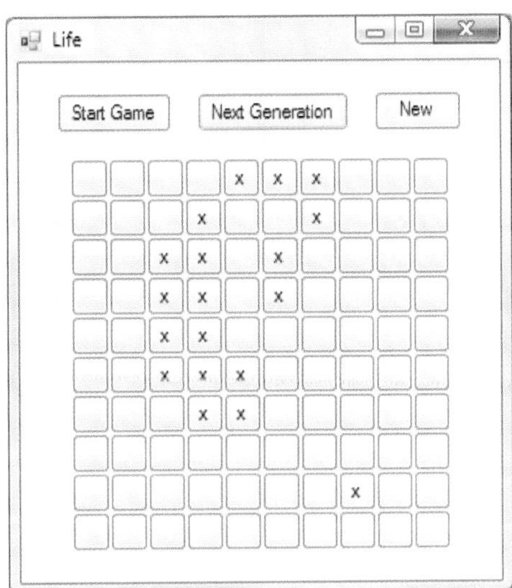

Next Generation can be clicked until there are no more live cells. Clicking New Life displays a new Life world.

Exercise 15 (advanced) —— PennyPitch

The penny pitch game is popular in amusement parks. Pennies are tossed onto a board that has certain areas marked with different prizes. Create a PennyPitch application that simulates the penny pitch game. For example, clicking New Game randomly marks a 5 x 5 board of 25 buttons with prizes of puzzle, game, ball, poster, and doll:

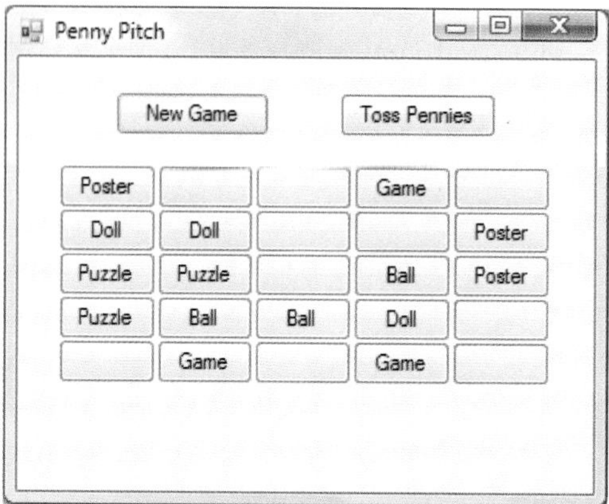

Each prize appears on 3 randomly chosen squares so that 15 squares contain prizes. Clicking Toss Pennies simulates ten pennies being randomly pitched onto the board. Each penny is represented by an "x" character on a square. If all of the squares that say Ball in them are covered by a penny, the player wins a ball. This is also true for the other prizes. Clicking Toss Pennies shows where the ten pennies landed and displays a list of the prizes won or "No prizes.":

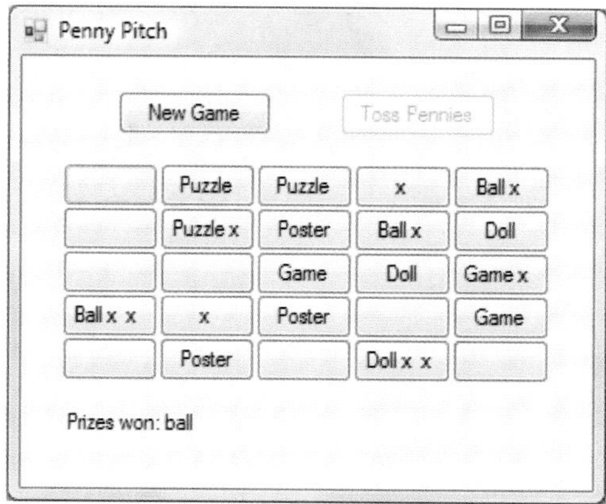

Chapter 9
Color, Sound, and Graphics

Key Concepts

Applying color to an interface
Including a Color dialog box
Using images in an application
Adding sound
Using a Timer control to create animation
Using the Graphics class and its methods
Responding to mouse events
Modifying existing code

Case Study

Click It

Review Data Files

orange.jpg, pink.jpg, green.jpg, red.jpg
roostercrow.wav, ball0.bmp - ball3.bmp

Exercise Data Files

arrow.jpg, anemone.jpg, grayangel.jpg
sponges.jpg, starfish.jpg, scorpionfish.jpg
bubbles.wav, word-dog.wav, word-cat.wav
word-fluffy.wav, word-I.wav, word-is.wav
word-see.wav, word-the.wav, word-walk.wav
bird1.gif-bird3.gif, gull.wav
turtle1.bmp-turtle3.bmp

Using Color

> **Inheritance**
>
> A child control *inherits* properties and other features from a parent control. Inheritance is an important object-oriented concept that means a new class can be created from an existing class and then the new class can be extended or customized. Inheritance allows for code reusability.

Color can be used to enhance an application's interface. For example, buttons can be Lime (a green color) and a form can be Plum (a purple color). Visual Basic provides more than 100 defined colors to choose from, as well as a palette of system colors. When setting colors in the Design window, a tabbed list is provided. The Web colors provide the most choices:

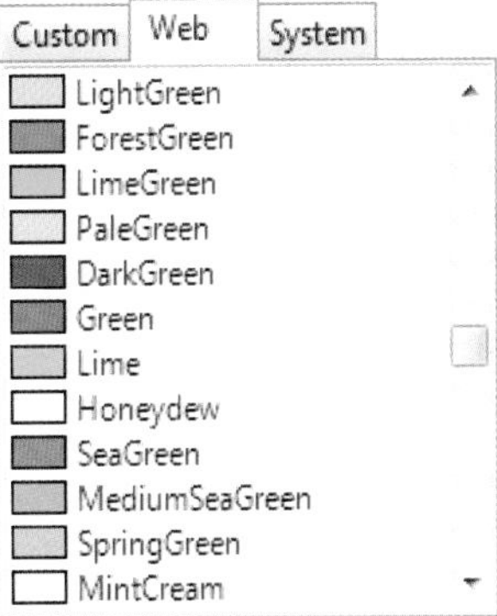

Control objects have BackColor and ForeColor properties that can be set from the Properties window.

- **BackColor** is the background color of an object, which refers to the object area not including any text. Clicking the arrow in the property displays a list of colors to choose from.
- **ForeColor** is the color of the text displayed on an object. Clicking the arrow in the property displays a list of colors to choose from.

Web colors include Transparent. Objects on a form can be set to this "color" so that the form BackColor shows through the object.

parent control
child control

Controls, including Button, CheckBox, and Label, are derived from the Form control. Form is said to be the *parent control* and the other controls are said to be *child controls*. When a parent control property value is changed, the corresponding child property value is also changed unless the child property is explicitly set. For example, changing the BackColor of a form means that the background color of objects on the form will also be changed to that color. New objects will inherit the form BackColor. To have objects with a background color different from the form's, the BackColor property must be individually set for each child control.

BackColor and ForeColor can be changed at run time in assignment statements. An `Imports System.Drawing` statement must be included at the top of a program so that the members of the `Drawing` class are accessible. The `Drawing` class includes the Visual Basic color constants:

TIP The color constants are displayed in an IntelliSense list when `Color.` is typed.

```
Imports System.Drawing

other code ...

Me.btnDisplay.BackColor = Color.Honeydew        'button color
Me.BackColor = Color.Lime                       'form color
```

Review: ChangeFormColor – part 1 of 2

Create a ChangeFormColor application that changes the background color of the form only to the color indicated on the clicked button. The form should initially be white. The buttons should be a blue with white text. The application interface should look similar to that shown on the right.

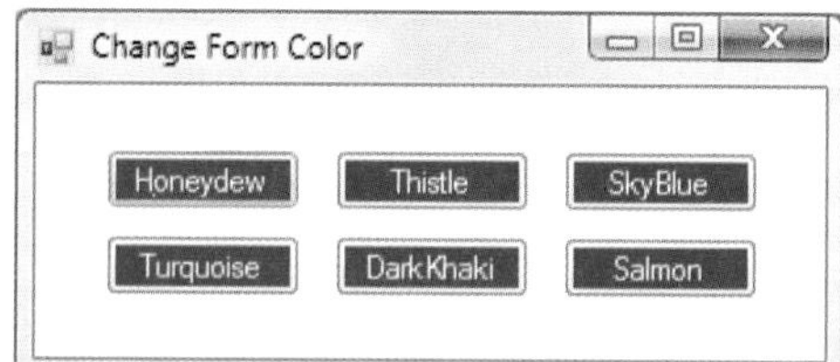

The ColorDialog Control

The Color dialog box is a predefined dialog box that has many colors for the user to choose from:

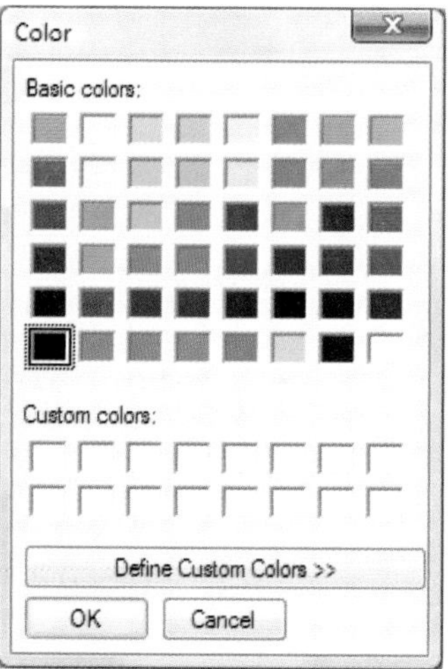

This dialog box can be displayed at run time to allow a user to choose which color to assign to the BackColor or ForeColor of an object.

To add a Color dialog box to an application, click the ColorDialog control in the Toolbox, and then click the form. A component is displayed in the component tray at the bottom of the Design window. The ColorDialog control is a component that has no graphical element.

ColorDialog

The ColorDialog control has the properties:

- **Color** is the color selected in the dialog box.
- **AllowFullOpen** is set to True to allow the user to create a custom color or False to allow the user to select only from the displayed colors.

The Color dialog box is displayed with a statement similar to:

```
Me.ColorDialog1.ShowDialog()
```

`ColorDialog1` is the name of the component added to the interface. ShowDialog() is the method of the `ColorDialog` class that displays the dialog box.

The Color property of a ColorDialog component contains the color selected by the user. For example, the first statement below displays a Color dialog box. The application waits until the user makes a selection before continuing to the next statement. The second statement sets the form background color to that selected by the user:

```
Me.ColorDialog1.ShowDialog()           'show dialog box
Me.BackColor = Me.ColorDialog1.Color   'set form color
```

If the user selects Cancel in the Color dialog box, the default color in the Color dialog box is returned. The first time a Color dialog box is displayed in an application, the default color is black. The Color dialog box defaults to the last selected color after it is first displayed.

Review: ChangeFormColor – part 2 of 2

Modify the ChangeFormColor application to include a Choose Color button that displays a Color dialog box and then changes the background color to that selected in the dialog box. The interface should look similar to that shown on the right.

Using Images

There are different ways to include images in an application. A picture box, as discussed in Chapter 6, can be used to display an image in a box on the form. Objects can also include a background image. For example:

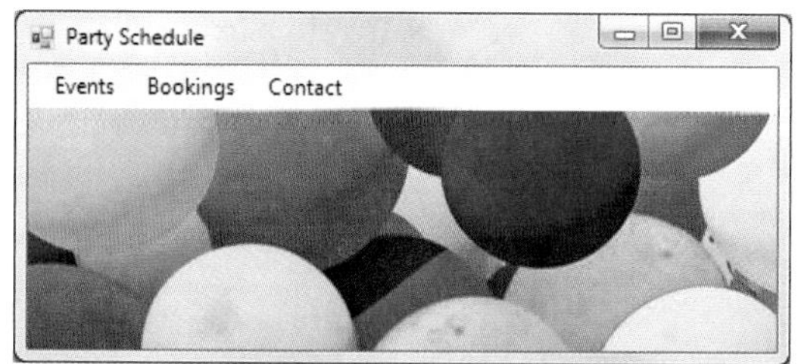

tiled An image is *tiled* on a form, which means that it is repeated to fill the form. Objects on the form can be set to a BackColor of Transparent to better show the tiled form image.

Most control objects have a BackgroundImage property that can be set in the Properties window:

- **BackgroundImage** contains the [...] button that is clicked to display the Select Resource dialog box. In this dialog box, images can be added to the Resources folder of a project and an image selected for the background. Image files can be BMP, JPG, GIF, PNG, JPEG, and WMF formats. Right-clicking BackgroundImage and then selecting Reset removes the image.

TIP Once an image is added to the Resources folder, it is available for any object in the application.

The Image property is available with the Button and Label controls. Setting this property places a single image that is not tiled as the background of a button or label:

- **Image** contains the [...] button that is clicked to display the Select Resource dialog box. Images can then be added to the Resources folder and an image selected for the background. Image files can be BMP, JPG, GIF, PNG, ICO,

and WMF formats. Right-clicking Image and then selecting Reset clears the picture box.

The image on an object can be changed at run time by retrieving the resource from the Resources folder. The `My.Resources` object is used to access a resource in statements similar to:

```
Me.btnEvents.Image = My.Resources.Flower         'button image
Me.BackgroundImage = My.Resources.Balloons       'form image
```

When changing images at run time, the image files must already be in the Resources folder of the project before running the application.

Review: ChangeImage

Create a ChangeImage application that changes the background of a form to the image shown on the clicked button. The form should initially be the default color with no image. Use the `red.jpg`, `green.jpg`, `orange.jpg`, and `pink.jpg` files, which are data files for this text. The application interface should look similar to that shown on the right after the clicking the pink button.

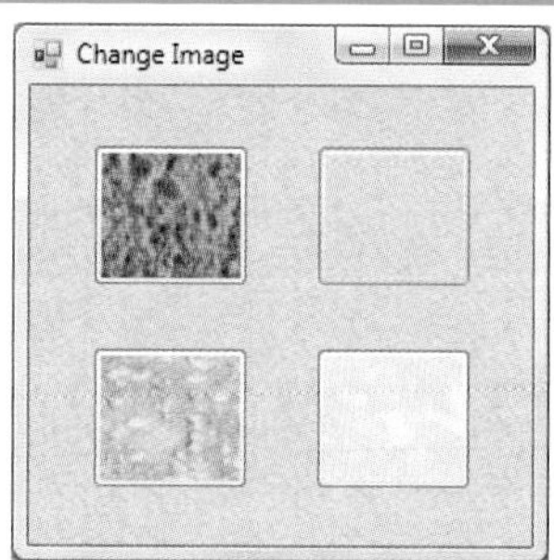

Making Sounds

TIP The Windows operating system sounds are in the Hardware and Sound category in the Control Panel.

Applications often make use of simple sounds, such as a beep, to provide feedback to the user. For example, when the wrong type of data is entered into a text box, the application could clear the text box and then beep. The beep notifies the user to check the input.

The Visual Basic `SystemSounds` class includes five properties for making Windows operating system sounds. The properties, which are `Asterisk`, `Beep`, `Exclamation`, `Hand`, and `Question`, return an object that makes a sound when the Play() method is called. For example, the following statement plays the sound of the operating system beep:

```
SystemSounds.Beep.Play()
```

An `Imports System.Media` statement must be included at the top of a program that uses the `SystemSounds` class.

The Beep() Function

Visual Basic also provides the Beep() function for playing a continuous tone through the computer's speaker. The statement `Beep()` is all that is required to play the tone.

Review: TestSounds

Create a TestSounds application that plays the sound of the button that is clicked. The application should include Asterisk, Beep, Exclamation, Hand, and Question buttons on an interface that looks similar to that shown on the right.

Playing Sound Files

Audio can be in the form of instrumental music, voice recording, and sound effects to name a few. Visual Basic applications can include any audio file that is in the Windows WAV format. The `My.Computer.Audio` object provides methods for working with audio:

- **Play(*resource, playmode*)** Plays a sound file. `resource` is the sound file in the Resources folder of the project. `playmode` is one of the AudioPlaymode constants `Background`, `BackgroundLoop`, and `WaitToComplete`. `Background` and `BackgroundLoop` starts a sound file while still allowing user interaction with the application interface. `BackgroundLoop` also plays the sound file repeatedly until the Stop() method is called. `WaitToComplete` prevents any user interaction until after the sound file has loaded and completely played.
- **Stop()** Stops the current sound file from playing.

When adding `My.Computer.Audio` statements to the Code window, Visual Basic IntelliSense displays lists for choosing object and constant names.

The Music Demo application plays a sound file once when Listen is clicked:

The My.Computer Object

The `My.Computer` object provides access to many of a computer's components, such as the keyboard, the clock, and the file system.

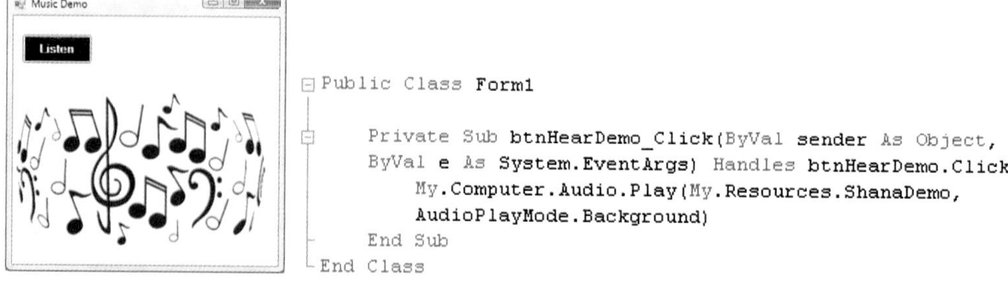

Music Demo
Listen
Public Class Form1
Private Sub btnHearDemo_Click(ByVal sender As Object,
ByVal e As System.EventArgs) Handles btnHearDemo.Click
My.Computer.Audio.Play(My.Resources.ShanaDemo,
AudioPlayMode.Background)
End Sub
End Class

To access an audio file, it must first be added to the project Resources folder. To add an audio file to the Resources folder, double-click the My Project icon in the Solution Explorer window to display the My Project window. Click the Resources tab to display those options. Click the Add Resource arrow and then select Add Existing File. A dialog box is displayed. In the Files of type list, select Audio. Navigate to the WAV file, select it, and then select Open to add the audio resource to the project.

Review: WakeUp

① CREATE A NEW PROJECT

Create a Windows application named `WakeUp`.

② CREATE THE INTERFACE

a. Use the table on the next page and the steps below it for setting object properties.

Object	(Name)	Text	SizeMode	BackColor
Form1		`Wake Up!`		Gold
PictureBox1	`picRooster`		AutoSize	

b. Select the picRooster picture box.

c. Use the Image property to add the `rooster.gif` file to the Resources folder and display the rooster image in the picture box.

d. In the Solutions Explorer window, double-click the My Project icon. The WakeUp project window is displayed.

e. On the left of the window, click the Resources tab. The project resources, including the rooster image, are displayed. If the rooster image is not displayed, select Images from the first button of the Resources tab:

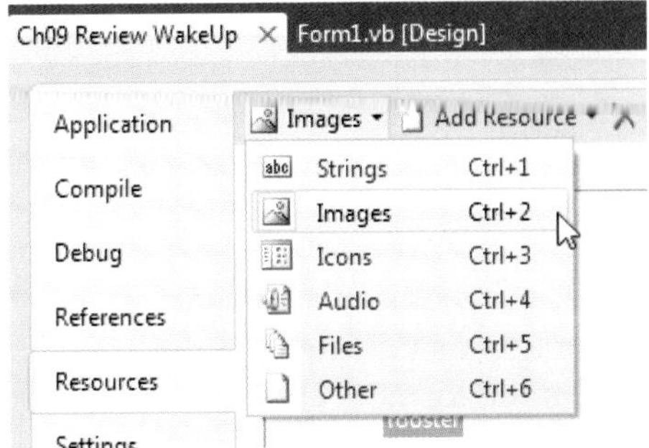

f. On the Add Resource button, click the arrow and then select **Add Existing File**:

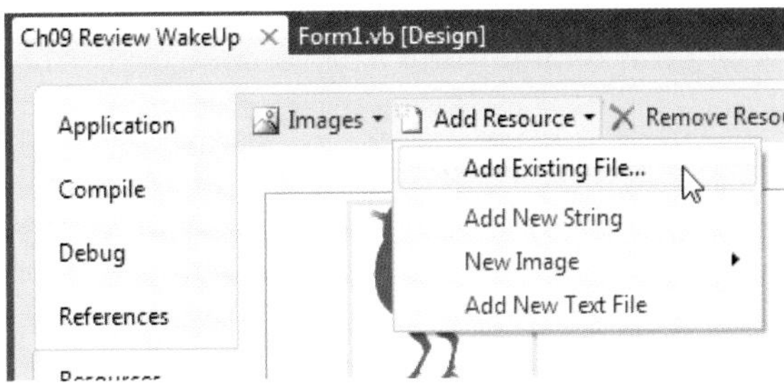

The Add existing file to resources dialog box is displayed.

1. In the **Files of type** list, select Audio.
2. Navigate to the location of the `rooster_crow.wav` file, a data file for this text.
3. Select `rooster_crow.wav` and then select **Open**. The file added to the project.
4. Save the project and close the WakeUp Project window.

③ WRITE THE APPLICATION CODE

a. Display the Code window.

b. Add comments that include your name, assignment, and today's date.

c. Create a picRooster_Click event procedure and then add the statements:

```
Static crow As Boolean = False

crow = Not crow
If crow Then
    My.Computer.Audio.Play(My.Resources.rooster_crow, AudioPlayMode.BackgroundLoop)
Else
    My.Computer.Audio.Stop()
End If
```

④ RUN THE APPLICATION

a. Save the modified WakeUp project and then run the application.

b. Click the rooster. There is crowing. Notice that the crowing repeats. Click the rooster again to stop the audio loop.

c. Close the WakeUp application.

⑤ PRINT THE CODE AND THEN CLOSE THE PROJECT

The Timer Control

Applications often perform actions at regular intervals. For example, a game application might display a "Time's up!" message if the user hasn't answered a question in 10 seconds.

A timer object is used to execute code at specified intervals. To add a timer to an application, click the Timer control in the Toolbox, and then click the form. A component is displayed in the component tray at the bottom of the Design window. The Timer control is a component that has no graphical element.

Timer

The Timer control has the properties:

- **(Name)** identifies a control for the programmer. Timer object names should begin with `tmr`.
- **Interval** is the amount of time that passes before the Tick event procedure is executed. Interval is specified in milliseconds between 0 and 64,767 where 1,000 milliseconds equals 1 second.
- **Enabled** is set to True to allow a Tick event to occur at the end of each interval. Setting Enabled to False stops Tick events from occurring. Note that Enabled is set to False by default.

A Tick event procedure is coded for each timer object added to an application. A Tick event occurs after the time specified in the Interval property elapses. For example, if a timer is enabled and its Interval property is set to 1000, then a Tick event occurs every second (1000 milliseconds). After the Tick event procedure executes, timing automatically starts over again.

The following Tick event procedure switches the ForeColor of a button back and forth from HotPink to Chocolate every second when Enabled is True and Interval of tmrColorChange is set to 1000:

```
Private Sub tmrColorChange_Tick(ByVal sender As Object,
ByVal e As System.EventArgs) Handles tmrColorChange.Tick
   Static colorChange As Boolean = True
   If colorChange Then
       Me.btnCheck.ForeColor = Color.HotPink
       colorChange = False
   Else
       Me.btnCheck.ForeColor = Color.Chocolate
       colorChange = True
   End If
End Sub
```

The Timer control also has two methods available:

- **Start()** starts a timer. This method can be used instead of the Enabled property and is used in a statement that takes the form Timer.Start().
- **Stop()** stops a timer. This method is used in a statement that takes the form Timer.Stop().

These methods can be used from any procedure in the application.

Review: Blinky

Create a Blinky application that cycles through three background form colors that change every 2 seconds. The Go button should switch between two green colors every 1 second and the Stop button should switch between two red colors every 1 second. Clicking Go starts the timer and Stop stops the timer. The application interface should look similar to that shown on the right.

Animation

> ***Video vs. Animation***
>
> Video breaks continuous motion up into separate images, while animation uses separate images to simulate continuous motion.

Animation can be added to an application with a timer and a set of images. Similar images displayed quickly one after the other in a picture box gives the impression of continuous motion, or *animation*. For example, the Skate! application changes the image of a picture box every 180 milliseconds using a set of six similar images. The images appear so quickly that a skater appears to skate down a hill. The Skate! images are:

The Skate! interface has a PictureBox control and a Timer control. A Tick event procedure is used to animate the images:

```
Private Sub tmrChangeImage_Tick(ByVal sender As Object,
ByVal e As System.EventArgs) Handles tmrChangeImage.Tick
  Const MAX_IMAGES As Integer = 6
  Static imageNum As Integer = 0

  'display an image from array
  Select Case imageNum
      Case 0
          Me.picImage.Image = My.Resources.skateboard0
      Case 1
          Me.picImage.Image = My.Resources.skateboard1
      Case 2
          Me.picImage.Image = My.Resources.skateboard2
      Case 3
          Me.picImage.Image = My.Resources.skateboard3
      Case 4
          Me.picImage.Image = My.Resources.skateboard4
      Case 5
          Me.picImage.Image = My.Resources.skateboard5
  End Select

  'determine next image number
  imageNum = (imageNum + 1) Mod MAX_IMAGES
End Sub
```

Review: BouncingBall

The BouncingBall application shows a ball that repeatedly falls from the top of the form to the bottom and then bounces back to the top. The algorithm for BouncingBall is:

1. Show ball images, one at a time, that progress from the top of the form to the bottom.
2. Show ball images, one at a time, that progress from the bottom of the form to the top.
3. Repeat Step 1.
4. Repeat Step 2.

The same set of images can be used for the balls falling to the bottom of the form as for the balls bouncing up to the top of the form. A variable can be used to determine which ball position to show. The position will increment by 1 for balls falling down and decrement by 1 for balls bouncing up. With this in mind, the BouncingBall algorithm can be refined into the following pseudocode:

```
Sub tmrAnimateBall_Tick()
    Const MAX_IMAGES As Integer = 4
    Static newPosition As Integer
    Static direction As Integer

    ballImage=Me.Resources.ball image

    Determine direction (1 or –1) based on newPosition
    newPosition += direction

    Use newPosition number (0, 1, 2, or 3) to determine which ball image (ball0, ball1, ball2, or
    ball3) to display.
End Sub
```

① CREATE A NEW PROJECT

Create a Windows application named `BouncingBall`.

② CREATE THE INTERFACE

a. Use the table below for setting object properties.

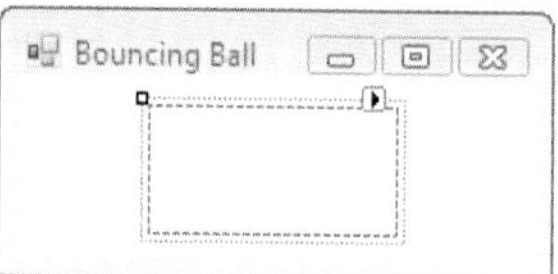

Object	(Name)	Text	SizeMode	BackColor
Form1		`Bouncing Ball`		White
PictureBox1	`picBall`		AutoSize	
Timer1	`tmrAnimateBall`			

b. Set the tmrAnimateBall Enabled property to True and the Interval property to `150`.

③ ADD IMAGE FILES TO THE PROJECT RESOURCES

a. In the Solutions Explorer window, double-click the My Project icon. The BouncingBall project window is displayed.

b. Click the Resources tab and then select Images from the first button, if Images is not already shown on the button.

c. On the Add Resource button, click the arrow and then select Add Existing File. A dialog box is displayed

   1. In the Files of type list, select Bitmaps, if Bitmaps is not already showing.
   2. Navigate to the location of the `ball0.bmp` file, a data file for this text.
   3. Select `ball0.bmp` and then select Open. The file is added to the project.
   4. Add the `ball1.bmp`, `ball2.bmp`, and `ball3.bmp` files to the project.

d. Save the modified BouncingBall project and then close the BouncingBall project window.

④ WRITE THE APPLICATION CODE

a. Display the Code window.

b. Add comments that include your name, assignment, and today's date.

c. Create a tmrAnimateBall_Tick event procedure and then add the statements:

```
Const MAX_IMAGES As Integer = 4
Static newPosition As Integer = 0
Static direction As Integer

'Display an image from array
Me.picBall.Image = My.Resources.ball0

'Determine next image
If newPosition = 0 Then                     'change to upward direction
    direction = 1
ElseIf newPosition = MAX_IMAGES - 1 Then    'change to downward direction
    direction = -1
End If
newPosition += direction

'display next image
Select Case newPosition
    Case 0
        Me.picBall.Image = My.Resources.ball0
    Case 1
        Me.picBall.Image = My.Resources.ball1
    Case 2
        Me.picBall.Image = My.Resources.ball2
    Case 3
        Me.picBall.Image = My.Resources.ball3
End Select
```

⑤ RUN THE APPLICATION

Save the modified BouncingBall project and then run the application. You may need to adjust the form size so that the ball appears to be bouncing from the top to the bottom of the form.

Check – Your application should look similar to:

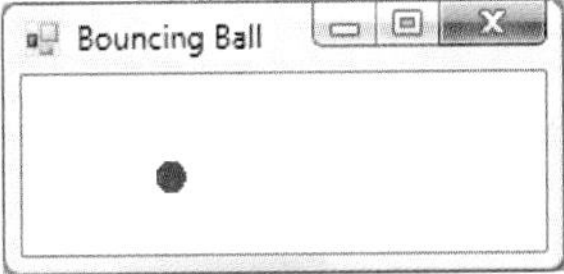

⑥ PRINT THE CODE AND THEN CLOSE THE PROJECT

The Graphics Class

drawing surface

Visual Basic includes the `Graphics` class with methods for creating circles, lines, rectangles, and other shapes on a drawing surface. A *drawing surface* can be the surface of a form, the surface of a button, or the surface of almost any other object. The drawing surface is defined by assigning an object's surface to a `Graphics` object. The following statement creates a `Graphics` object from the surface of the form:

```
'Form surface
Dim formSurface As Graphics = Me.CreateGraphics
```

The CreateGraphics method is a control class method that encases a specific object's surface area. This method is available with most control objects.

Drawing on a surface requires a `Pen` object. The pen, pen color, and line thickness are all declared in the same statement, similar to:

```
Dim thinAquaPen As New Pen(Color.Aqua, 2)
```

TIP The color constants are displayed in an IntelliSense list when `Color.` is typed.

The keyword `New` declares a new object. A Visual Basic color constant is used to define the pen color. The color is followed by a comma and then a line thickness.

pixel

After defining a surface and a pen, `Graphics` class methods are used to draw onto the surface. A drawing surface can be thought of a grid consisting of a set of points with x values and y values. Each point is a *pixel* (picture element) and the number of pixels in a surface depends on the screen resolution. The point with coordinates (0, 0) is the pixel in the very upper-left corner of the drawing surface. The Coordinates application below has a form that is 300 by 300, but the actual drawing surface is about 292 by 265:

```
Private Sub btnShowGrid_Click(ByVal sender As Object, ByVal e As System.EventArgs) Handles btnShowGrid.Click
    Dim formSurface As Graphics = Me.CreateGraphics
    Dim maxX As Integer = Me.Size.Width
    Dim maxY As Integer = Me.Size.Height
    Dim magentaPen As New Pen(Color.Magenta, 1)
    Dim greenPen As New Pen(Color.Green, 1)

    'Draw a grid that is 10 pixels by 10 pixels
    For xCoord As Integer = 0 To maxX Step 10
        For yCoord As Integer = 0 To maxY Step 10
            If xCoord Mod 50 = 0 Or yCoord Mod 50 = 0 Then
                'makes every 50th pixel a green square
                formSurface.DrawRectangle(greenPen, xCoord, yCoord, 10, 10)
            Else
                formSurface.DrawRectangle(magentaPen, xCoord, yCoord, 10, 10)
            End If
        Next yCoord
    Next xCoord

    Me.lblCoords.Text = "Max x is " & maxX & ", " & "Max y is " & maxY
End Sub
```

Each square on the grid is 10 pixels by 10 pixels. For easier measuring, every fifth grid square is green. Count the grid squares and notice that the actual drawing space is less than 300 by 300 because of the form's title bar and borders.

The Size property of an object stores both a height and width. For many objects, such as a label, the height and width correspond to the point in the lower-right of the object. For a form object, as demonstrated in the Coordinates application above, the Size property returns the size of the form, not the coordinates in the lower-right corner:

```
Dim formMaxX As Integer = Me.Size.Width      '300
Dim formMaxY As Integer = Me.Size.Height     '300
```

The Graphics class methods require a pen along with the shape position and size. Graphics methods include:

- **DrawLine(*pen, x1, y1, x2, y2*)** draws a line that extends from coordinates (x1, y1) on a Graphics object to coordinates (x2, y2).
- **DrawRectangle(*pen, x1, y1, width, height*)** draws a rectangle with the upper-left corner at coordinates (x1, y1) on a Graphics object and is width wide and height high.
- **DrawEllipse(*pen, x1, y1, width, height*)** draws an ellipse within a rectangular area that has its upper-left corner at coordinates (x1, y1) on a Graphics object and is width wide and height high.
- **DrawArc(*pen, x1, y1, width, height, startAngle, sweepAngle*)** draws an arc that starts at angle startAngle and continues clockwise sweepAngle degrees. The arc is within a rectangular area that has its upper-left corner at coordinates (x1, y1) on a Graphics object and is width wide and height high.
- **Clear(*color*)** clears the drawing surface with color, which can be a System.Drawing color constant or the current object color. For example, Me.BackColor uses the form color.

Drawing an Arc

An arc is part of an ellipse. A circle is an ellipse with the same width and height. The start angle and sweep angle of an arc can be determined with the diagram:

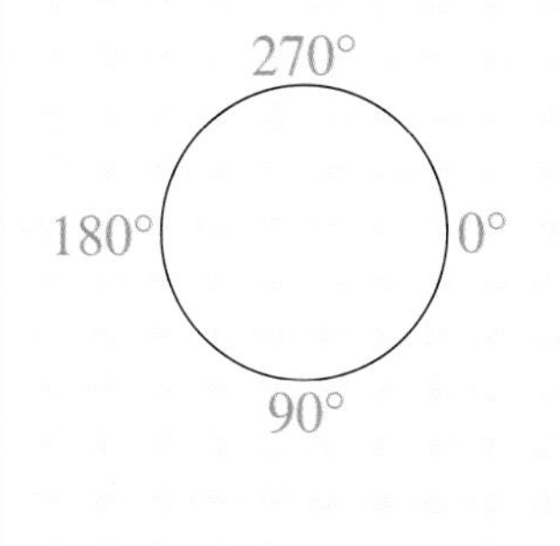

A Click event procedure in the TestGraphics application demonstrates these methods:

```
Private Sub btnDrawNow _ Click(ByVal sender As Object,
ByVal e As System.EventArgs) Handles btnDrawNow.Click
   'Create drawing surface
   Dim formSurface As Graphics = Me.CreateGraphics
   'Define pen
   Dim indigoPen As New Pen(Color.Indigo, 5)
   Dim salmonPen As New Pen(Color.Salmon, 3)
   Dim tealPen As New Pen(Color.Teal, 2)

   'Draw on form
   formSurface.DrawRectangle(indigoPen, 0, 0, 200, 200)
   formSurface.DrawEllipse(salmonPen, 0, 0, 200, 200)
   formSurface.DrawArc(tealPen, 0, 0, 100, 100, 0, 120)
End Sub
```

Clicking Draw Here in the TestGraphics application produces shapes similar to:

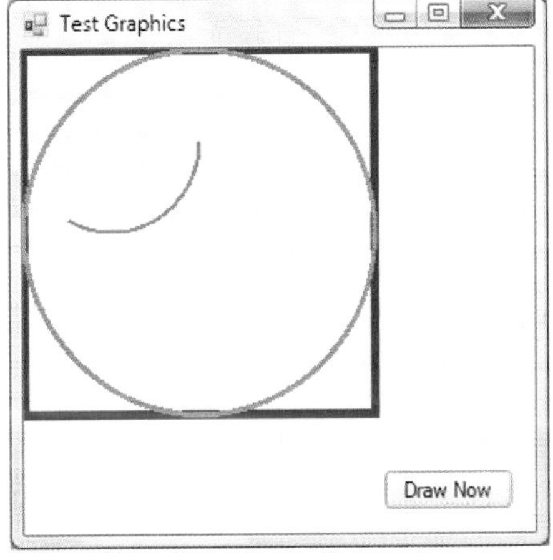

absolute and relative coordinates

The shapes in the TestGraphics application have been drawn using *absolute coordinates*, meaning that actual values, such as `0` and `200` were used to specify the shape sizes. A better approach is to use *relative coordinates*, which are based on the size of the form. When relative coordinates are used, the shapes maintain their relative size and position should the form be resized by the user at run time. The DrawShapes review on the next page practices using relative coordinates.

Pen Styles

The `Pen` class contains the DashStyle property for defining a pen style. Dashed lines, dotted lines, and dash-dot lines are a few examples of pen styles. An IntelliSense list with Visual Basic pen-style constants is displayed when setting the property:

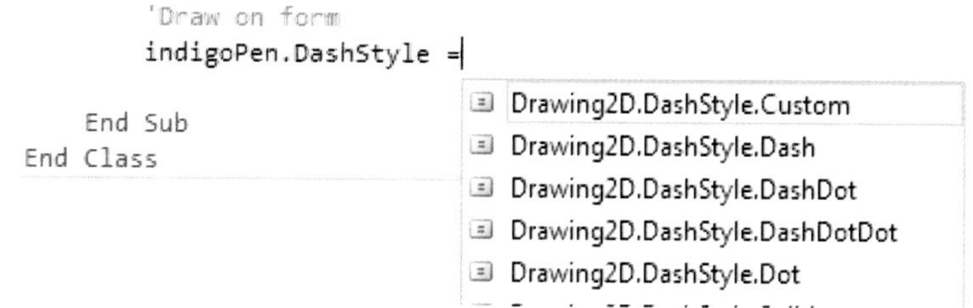

The TestGraphics application uses the indigoPen `Pen` object with the DashStyle property set to DashDot:

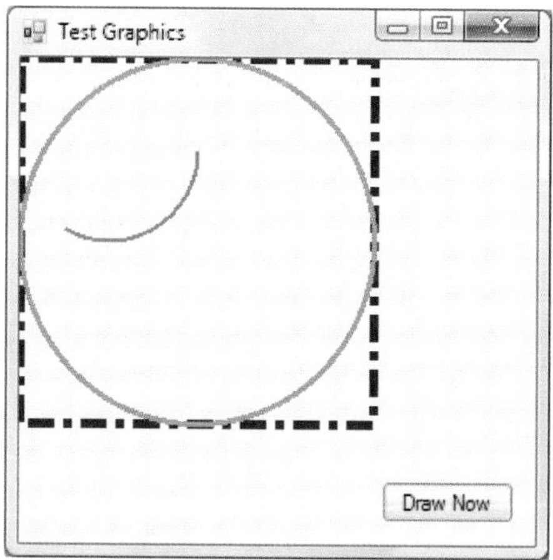

Review: DrawShapes

① CREATE A NEW PROJECT

Create a Windows application named `DrawShapes`.

② CREATE THE INTERFACE

Use the table below for setting object properties.

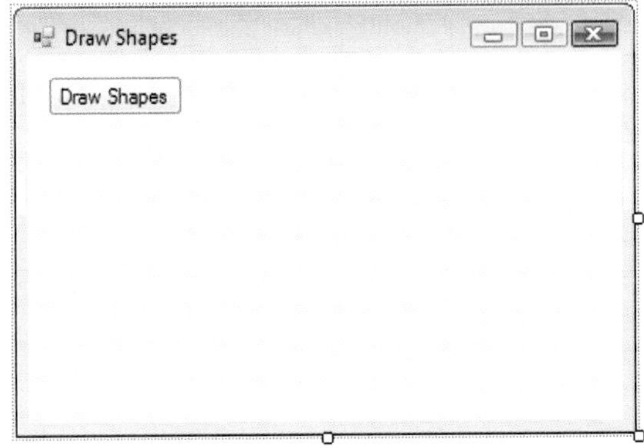

Object	(Name)	Text	Size
Form1		Draw Shapes	360, 245
Button1	btnDrawShapes	Draw Shapes	

③ WRITE THE APPLICATION CODE

a. Display the Code window.

b. Add comments that include your name, application, and today's date.

c. Create a btnDrawShapes_Click event procedure and then add the statements:

```
'Create a drawing surface
Dim formSurface As Graphics = Me.CreateGraphics
formSurface.Clear(Me.BackColor)
'Determine max X and max Y values
Dim maxX As Integer = Me.Size.Width
Dim maxY As Integer = Me.Size.Height

'Define all the pens
Dim lightSeaGreenPen As New Pen(Color.LightSeaGreen, 2)
Dim thickerDeepPinkPen As New Pen(Color.DeepPink, 10)
Dim thickDodgerBluePen As New Pen(Color.DodgerBlue, 5)
Dim thinRedPen As New Pen(Color.Red, 3)

'Draw thin LightSeaGreen horizontal line
formSurface.DrawLine(lightSeaGreenPen, 30, maxY \ 3, maxX - 30, maxY \ 3)

'Draw thicker DeepPink circle (ellipse)
formSurface.DrawEllipse(thickerdeepPinkPen, maxX \ 2, maxY \ 2, 40, 40)

'Draw thick DashDotDot DodgerBlue rectangle
thickDodgerBluePen.DashStyle = Drawing.Drawing2D.DashStyle.DashDotDot
formSurface.DrawRectangle(thickDodgerBluePen, 80, maxY \ 4, maxX \ 3, 70)

'Draw thin Red arc
formSurface.DrawArc(thinRedPen, 30, 0, maxX - 60, maxY - 60, 0, 180)
```

④ RUN THE APPLICATION

a. Run the application. Click Draw Shapes. The application interface looks similar to:

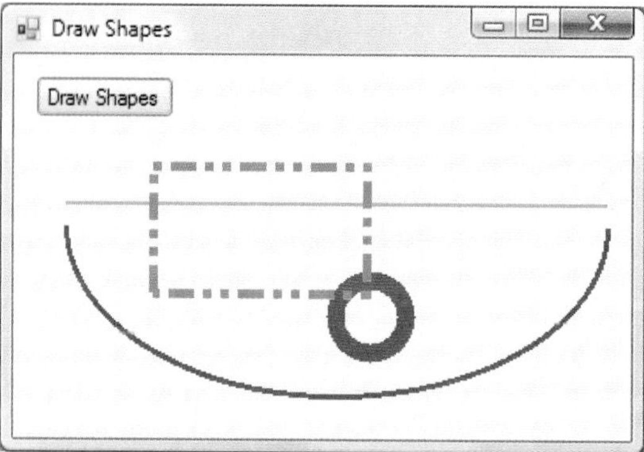

b. Drag the lower-right corner of the form. Make the application interface smaller and then click Draw Shapes. The application interface looks similar to:

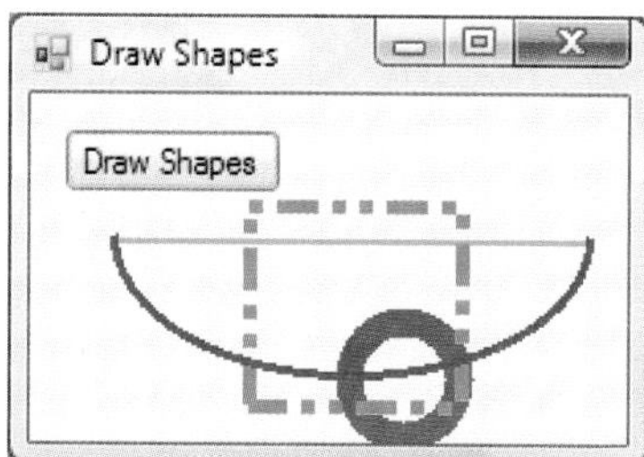

The shapes are proportional to the drawing surface because the code statements use shape coordinates that are relative to the maximum X and Y coordinates of the drawing surface.

⑤ PRINT THE CODE AND THEN CLOSE THE PROJECT

Drawing Solid Shapes

The `Graphics` class also includes methods for creating solid shapes such as filled circles and solid rectangles. A `SolidBrush` object is needed to fill shapes. The following statement declares a `SolidBrush` object that draws in a purple color. Note that the line thickness is not indicated since the brush fills the shape:

```
Dim purpleBrush As New SolidBrush(Color.BlueViolet)
```

The `Graphics` class methods that fill shapes require a brush along with the shape position and size. Some of these methods are:

- **FillRectangle(*brush*, *x1*, *y1*, *width*, *height*)** draws a solid rectangle with the upper-left corner at coordinates (`x1`, `y1`) on a `Graphics` object and is `width` wide and `height` high.
- **FillEllipse(*brush*, *x1*, *y1*, *width*, *height*)** draws a solid ellipse within a rectangular area that has its upper-left corner at coordinates (`x1`, `y1`) on a `Graphics` object and is `width` wide and `height` high.

- **FillPie(*brush, x1, y1, width, height, startAngle, sweepAngle*)** draws a filled pie shape that starts at angle `startAngle` and continues clockwise `sweepAngle` degrees. The pie shape is within a rectangular area that has its upper-left corner at coordinates (`x1`, `y1`) on a `Graphics` object and is `width` wide and `height` high.

A click event procedure in the TestSolidGraphics application demonstrates these methods:

```
Private Sub btnDrawNow _ Click(ByVal sender As Object,
ByVal e As System.EventArgs) Handles btnDrawNow.Click
   'Create drawing surface
   Dim formSurface As Graphics = Me.CreateGraphics
   'Define pen
   Dim indigoBrush As New SolidBrush(Color.Indigo)
   Dim limeGreenBrush As New SolidBrush(Color.LimeGreen)
   Dim goldBrush As New SolidBrush(Color.Gold)

   'Draw on form
   formSurface.FillPie(indigoBrush, 0, 210, 50, 50, 0, 180)
   formSurface.FillRectangle(limeGreenBrush, 0, 0, 200, 200)
   formSurface.FillEllipse(goldBrush, 0, 0, 200, 200)
End Sub
```

Running TestSolidGraphics shows solid shapes similar to:

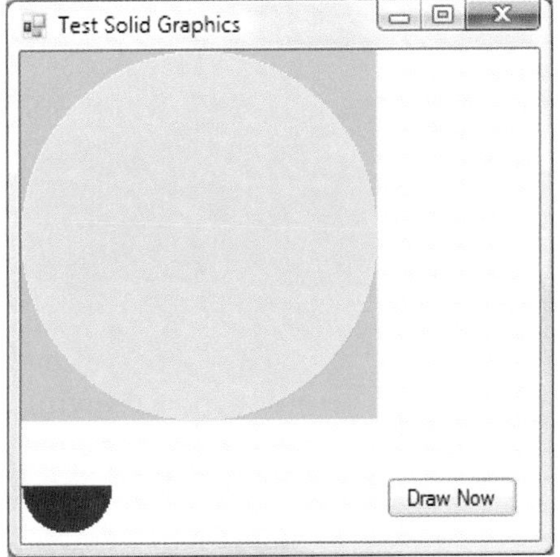

Review: Face

Create a Face application that displays a happy face when Happy is clicked and a sad face when Sad is clicked. Use a picture box and the FillRectangle, FillEllipse, and FillPie methods with different brush colors. The application interface should look similar to that shown on the right after clicking Sad.

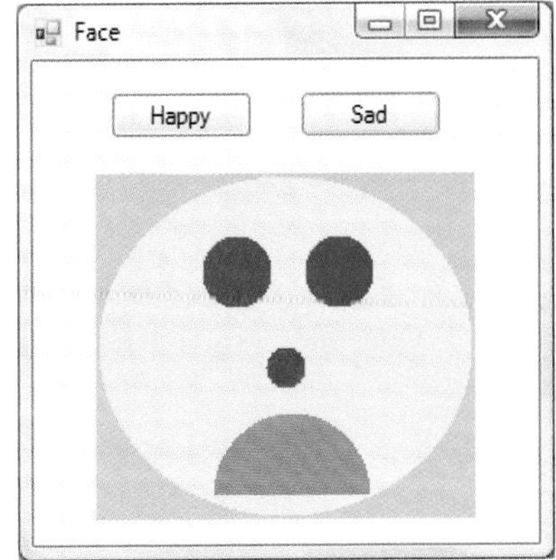

The Point Structure

point

A *point* has an x-coordinate and a y-coordinate that together indicate a specific location. The `Point` structure has members X and Y. For example, the following three statements declare a point and set the X and Y values to 0:

```
Dim minPoint As Point
minPoint.X = 0
minPoint.Y = 0
```

The X and Y values of a point can be included in the declaration when the keyword `New` is used, as in the statement:

```
Dim minPoint As New Point(0, 0)
```

The DrawLine Graphics method is overloaded to accept `Point` variables in place of coordinates, as in the statements below:

```
Dim labelSurface As Graphics = Me.lblDrawLine.CreateGraphics
Dim orangePen As New Pen(Color.Orange, 5)

Dim minPoint As New Point(0, 0)
Dim maxPoint As New Point(Me.lblDrawLine.Size.Width,
Me.lblDrawLine.Size.Height)

labelSurface.DrawLine(OrangePen, minPoint, maxPoint)
```

The segment of code above draws a line from the upper-left corner of the label to the lower-right corner of the label.

Drawing Curves and Polygons

The `Graphics` class also includes methods for creating polygons and curves on a drawing surface. The number of points that define a curve or polygon vary depending on the specific shape. Therefore, a set of points in an array is required by these methods:

- **DrawCurve(*pen, points*)** creates a curve on a `Graphics` object using the points in the `points` array.
- **DrawClosedCurve(*pen, points*)** creates a closed curve on a `Graphics` object using the points in the `points` array. The curve is automatically continued from the last point to the first point to close the curve.
- **FillClosedCurve(*brush, points*)** creates a filled, closed curve on a `Graphics` object using the points in the `points` array. The curve is automatically continued from the last point to the first to close the curve.
- **DrawPolygon(*pen, points*)** creates a closed polygon on a `Graphics` object using the points in the `points` array. A line is automatically created from the last point to the first to close the polygon.
- **FillPolygon(*brush, points*)** creates a filled, closed polygon on a `Graphics` object using the points in the `points` array. A line is automatically created from the last point to the first to close the polygon.

A click event procedure in the TestCurvesAndPolygons application on the next page demonstrates these methods. One set of points can be used because each shape is drawn on a separate surface. Note that the array elements are initialized with a set of point declarations:

```
Private Sub btnDraw _ Click(ByVal sender As Object,
ByVal e As System.EventArgs) Handles btnDraw.Click
    'Create Drawing surfaces
    Dim labelDrawCurve As Graphics = Me.lblDrawCurve.CreateGraphics
    Dim labelDrawClosedCurve As Graphics = Me.lblDrawClosedCurve.CreateGraphics
    Dim labelFillClosedCurve As Graphics = Me.lblFillClosedCurve.CreateGraphics
    Dim labelDrawPolygon As Graphics = Me.lblDrawPolygon.CreateGraphics
    Dim labelFillPolygon As Graphics = Me.lblFillPolygon.CreateGraphics

    'Define pen and brush
    Dim tomatoPen As New Pen(Color.Tomato, 1)
    Dim tomatoBrush As New SolidBrush(Color.Tomato)

    'Define points
    Dim curvePoints() As Point = {New Point(10, 30), New Point(35, 35),
    New Point(75, 80), New Point(120, 20)}

    'Draw shapes
    labelDrawCurve.DrawCurve(tomatoPen, curvePoints)
    labelDrawClosedCurve.DrawClosedCurve(tomatoPen, curvePoints)
    labelFillClosedCurve.FillClosedCurve(tomatoBrush, curvePoints)
    labelDrawPolygon.DrawPolygon(tomatoPen, curvePoints)
    labelFillPolygon.FillPolygon(tomatoBrush, curvePoints)
End Sub
```

Running TestCurvesAndPolygons and clicking Draw shows curves and polygons produced with the `Graphics` class:

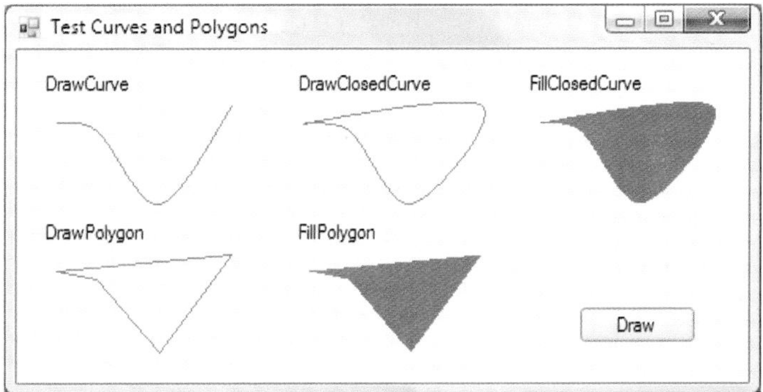

Review: Sailboat

Create a Sailboat application. Clicking Draw displays a coral-colored sailboat with a black mast and white sails in medium blue waves on a light sky blue background. Use the DrawLine, FillRectangle, FillClosedCurve, DrawCurve, and FillPolygon methods. The application interface should look similar to that shown on the right after clicking Draw.

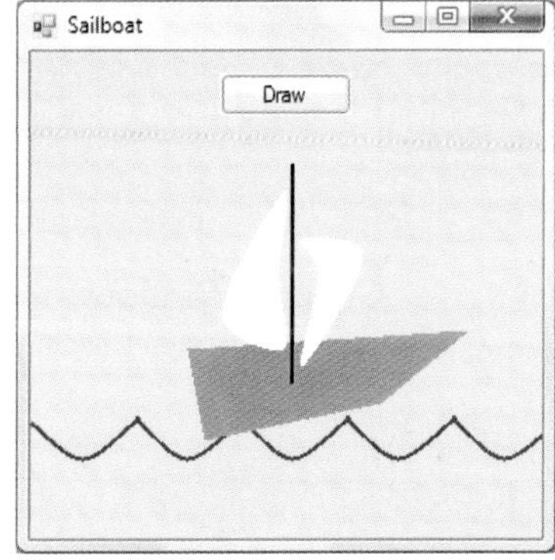

Handling Mouse Events

Event procedures can be coded for mouse events, similar to event procedures for objects on a form. Mouse events include MouseDown, which occurs when the user clicks the mouse on an application interface. By coding a MouseDown event, actions can be taken every time the user clicks an object.

To add a MouseDown event procedure to the Code window, click the object name in the Class Name list and then in the Method Name list, select MouseDown. To add a MouseDown event that occurs when the user clicks the form, select Form1 Events in the Class Name list and then in the Method Name list, select MouseDown:

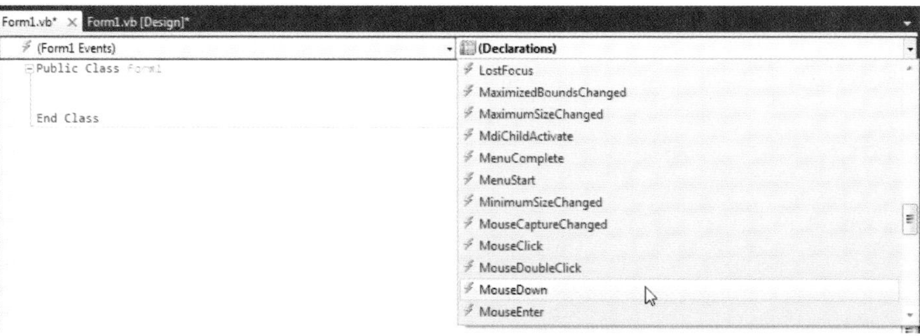

The MouseDown event procedure is added to the Code window with room for statements that will execute each time the user clicks the mouse on the form:

```
Private Sub Form1_MouseDown(ByVal sender As Object,
ByVal e As System.Windows.Forms.MouseEventArgs)
Handles Me.MouseDown

End Sub
```

In the procedure heading, the `e` parameter contains properties specific to the mouse click that raised the event. These properties store the values the x and y coordinates of the mouse click, and are accessed by typing `e` followed by a dot and then the property name (`X` or `Y`). The procedure below displays a message box with the mouse click coordinates:

```
Private Sub Form1_MouseDown(ByVal sender As Object,
ByVal e As System.Windows.Forms.MouseEventArgs)
Handles Me.MouseDown
  MessageBox.Show("X:" & e.X & "  Y:" & e.Y)
End Sub
```

Review: Tracker

① CREATE A NEW PROJECT

Create a Windows application named `Tracker`.

② CREATE THE INTERFACE

The interface contains only a form. Set the Text property to `Tracker`.

③ WRITE THE APPLICATION CODE

a. Add comments that include your name, application, and today's date.
b. Create a Form1_MouseDown event procedure and then add the statements:

```
Static previousPoint As Point       'remember the previous mouse click
Dim formSurface As Graphics = Me.CreateGraphics
Dim orangeRedPen As New Pen(Color.OrangeRed, 3)
Dim mouseClick As Point

'Get point of mouse click
mouseClick.X = e.X
mouseClick.Y = e.Y

'Draw line from previous point to point clicked
formSurface.DrawLine(orangeRedPen, previousPoint, mouseClick)

'Make point clicked the next starting point
previousPoint = mouseClick
```

④ RUN THE APPLICATION

a. Save the modified Tracker project and then run the application. Click the form. A line is created from the upper-left corner to where the mouse was clicked. Continue clicking. Lines are created from the previous click to the next.
b. Close the Tracker application.

⑤ PRINT THE CODE AND THEN CLOSE THE PROJECT

Case Study

In this case study a game application will be created.

ClickIt Specification

The Click It! game randomly displays a blue triangle, a red diamond, or a pink circle in one of six different locations of the application window. The user must click the blue triangle to score 5 points or the pink circle to score 10 points. Clicking the red diamond is a deduction of 3 points.

Each image is displayed for 1 second at a time. The game ends after one minute (60 seconds). The user's score is displayed in a message box after the game ends.

ClickIt Design

The interface for ClickIt is a form with six picture boxes and a Go! button. The Go! button should not be visible after it is clicked:

The code design starts with an algorithm:

1. Every second, generate a random number between 0 and 2 and use this number to determine which shape to display. Generate a random number between 0 and 5 and use this number to determine which picture box to display the shape.
2. When the user clicks a picture box, determine if a shape was clicked and then update the player's score.
3. After 60 seconds display a message box with the player's score.

Analyzing the algorithm further reveals some aspects of the code:

- Timer controls are needed for timing the shape display time and the game time.

Based on the algorithm and analysis of the algorithm, the pseudocode for this application appears like:

```
Const NUM_SHAPES As Integer = 3
Dim score As Integer = 0
Dim boxNum As Integer
Dim shapeNum As Integer

Sub btnGo_Click (sender, e) Handles btnGo.Click
    Hide Go button
    Start timers
End Sub

Sub tmrShowShape_Tick(sender, e) Handles tmrShowShape.Tick
    picBoxes() As PictureBox = {6 picture boxes  on interface}
    Randomize()
    ClearBoxes(picBoxes)
    boxNum = random number between 0 and picBoxes.Length
    shapeNum = random number between 0 and NUM_SHAPES
    DisplayShape(picBoxes, boxNum, shapeNum)
End Sub
```

```
Sub ClearBoxes(picBoxes))
    Show default image in all picture boxes
End Sub

Sub DisplayShape(boxes(), box, shape)
    Select Case shape
        Case 0
            display triangle in boxes(box)
        Case 1
            display diamond in boxes(box)
        Case 2
            display circle in boxes(box)
    End Select
End Sub

Sub ShapeClicked(sender, e) Handles picShape0.MouseDown,
picShape1.MouseDown, picShape2.MouseDown,
picShape3.MouseDown, picShape4.MouseDown,
picShape5.MouseDown
    Dim picClicked As PictureBox = sender
    If picClicked.Tag = boxNum Then
        Select Case shapeNum
            Case 0
                score += 5
            Case 1
                score -= 3
            Case 2
                score += 10
        End Select
    End If
End Sub

Sub tmrGameLength_Tick(sender, e) Handles tmrGameLength.Tick
    tmrGameLength.Stop()
    tmrShowShape.Stop()
    MessageBox.Show("Score: " & score)
End Sub
```

ClickIt Coding

The interface for ClickIt is:

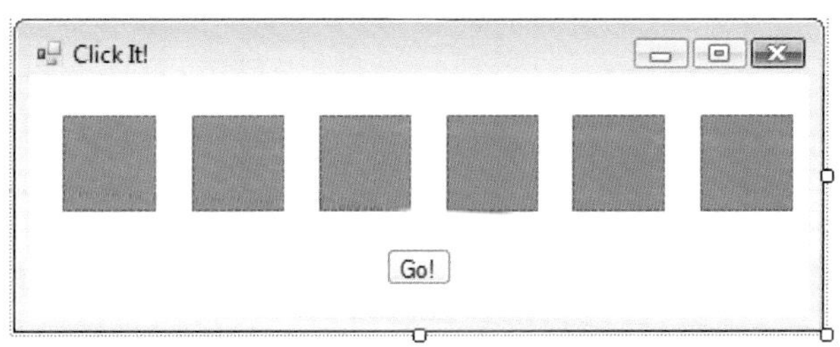

Object	(Name)	Text	Tag
Form1		Click It!	
Button1	btnGo	Go!	
PictureBox1	picShape0		0

PictureBox2	picShape1	1
PictureBox3	picShape2	2
PictureBox4	picShape3	3
PictureBox5	picShape4	4
PictureBox6	picShape5	5
Timer1	tmrShowShape	
Timer2	tmrGameLength	

The PictureBox objects should each display the `greensquare` image. The Interval property of the tmrShowShape timer control should be set to 1000, so that a new shape is displayed approximately every second. The Interval property of the tmrGameLength timer control should be set to 60000, so that the game lasts for approximately 1 minute.

The final coding for ClickIt is:

```
Public Class Form1

    Const NUM _ SHAPES As Integer = 3    'number of shapes
    Dim score As Integer = 0             'player's score
    Dim boxNum As Integer                'box displaying the shape
    Dim shapeNum As Integer              '0 blue triangle, 1 red diamond, 2 pink circle

    'Starts the game.
    '
    'post: The game has displayed various shapes for one minute for the
    'player to click.
    '
    Private Sub btnGo _ Click(ByVal sender As Object,
    ByVal e As System.EventArgs) Handles btnGo.Click
        Me.btnGo.Visible = False
        Me.tmrShowShape.Start()
        Me.tmrGameLength.Start()
    End Sub

    'Displays a shape in one of a set of picture boxes
    '
    'pre: There are six picture boxes on the interface named
    'picShape0, picShape1, picShape2, picShape3, picShape4, and
    'picShape5
    'post: A shape has been displayed in one of the picture boxes.
    'The remaining picture boxes display the default shape.
    '
    Private Sub tmrShowShape _ Tick(ByVal sender As Object,
    ByVal e As System.EventArgs) Handles tmrShowShape.Tick
        Dim picBoxes() As PictureBox = {Me.picShape0, Me.picShape1, Me.picShape2,
        Me.picShape3, Me.picShape4, Me.picShape5}
        Randomize()

        'Clear the previous shape by showing default shape in all boxes
        Call ClearBoxes(picBoxes)
        'Assign global variable box number for shape
        boxNum = Int(picBoxes.Length * Rnd())
        'Assign global variable shape number for box
        shapeNum = Int(NUM _ SHAPES * Rnd())

        Call DisplayShape(picBoxes, boxNum, shapeNum)
    End Sub
```

```
    'Places a default image in all the picture boxes of the PictureBox array
    '
    'post: The picture boxes have been set to display the default image
    '
    Sub ClearBoxes(ByRef boxes() As PictureBox)

        For box As Integer = 0 To boxes.Length - 1
            boxes(box).Image = My.Resources.greensquare  'green square is default image
        Next box
    End Sub

    'A shape is displayed in one of the boxes of the PictureBox
    'array
    '
    'pre: The Resources folder contains the bluetriangle,
    'reddiamond, and pinkcircle image files. 0 <= box <= PictureBox.Length.
    'shape is 0, 1, or 2.
    'post: A shape has been displayed in a picture box
    '
    Sub DisplayShape(ByRef boxes() As PictureBox, ByVal box As Integer,
    ByVal shape As Integer)
        Select Case shape
            Case 0
                boxes(box).Image = My.Resources.bluetriangle
            Case 1
                boxes(box).Image = My.Resources.reddiamond
            Case 2
                boxes(box).Image = My.Resources.pinkcircle
        End Select
    End Sub

    'Determines if clicked picture box is the one with the shape
    '
    'pre: The picture boxes have appropriate Tag values. shapeNum is 0, 1, or 2.
    'post: Player's score has been updated if shape was clicked
    '
    Private Sub ShapeClicked(ByVal sender As Object,
    ByVal e As System.Windows.Forms.MouseEventArgs) Handles picShape0.MouseDown,
    picShape1.MouseDown, picShape2.MouseDown, picShape3.MouseDown,
    picShape4.MouseDown, picShape5.MouseDown
        Dim picClicked As PictureBox = sender

        If picClicked.Tag = boxNum Then
            Select Case shapeNum
                Case 0    'blue triangle
                    score += 5
                Case 1    'red diamond
                    score -= 3
                Case 2    'pink circle
                    score += 10
            End Select
        End If
    End Sub

    'Ends the game and displays the player's score
    '
    'post: Timers have been stopped and the player's score displayed
    '
    Private Sub tmrGameLength_Tick(ByVal sender As Object,
    ByVal e As System.EventArgs) Handles tmrGameLength.Tick
        Me.tmrGameLength.Stop()
        Me.tmrShowShape.Stop()
        MessageBox.Show("Score: " & score)
    End Sub
End Class
```

ClickIt Testing and Debugging

Playing the entire Click It! game displays the interface and a message box similar to:

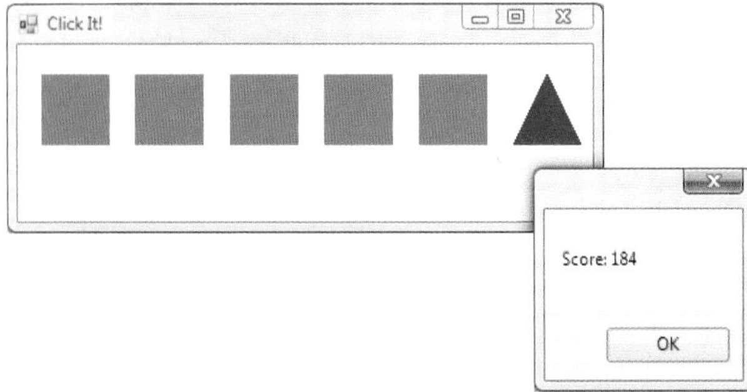

Click It! should be tested by comparing the score against actual mouse clicks.

Review: ClickIt

Modify the ClickIt! tmrGameLength_Tick event procedure to include a call to NewGame(). The NewGame() procedure should execute after the player clicks OK in the message box and prepare the application for a new game. A new game requires the score reset to 0, the picture boxes cleared, and the Go! button displayed.

Chapter Summary

Color can be used to enhance an application interface. Visual Basic provides more than 100 predefined colors to choose from. Control objects have BackColor and ForeColor properties that can be set to a color. The Transparent color is used to allow color behind an object to show through. BackColor and ForeColor can be set at run time in assignment statements.

A ColorDialog control is an component that displays a Color dialog box at run time, but has no graphical element. The ShowDialog() method is used to display the dialog box at run time and the Color property is used to determine what color the user clicked.

Images can also be used to enhance an application interface. Images can be added to almost any control by setting the BackgroundImage property. This property tiles an image on the object. The Label control does not have a BackgroundImage property. However, the Label control has an Image property that displays a single image on a label. The Button control also has this property. An image can be loaded at run time by using the `My.Resources` object.

Sounds and audio files can also be used to make an application more interesting and informative. The `SystemSounds` class includes five objects that play Windows operating system sounds. The Play() method is used to play a sound from this class. Audio files in the WAV format can also be used in an application. The `My.Computer.Audio` object provides methods for working with audio files.

A Timer control is an component that raises a Tick event after a specified amount of time has elapsed. A Timer control has no graphical element. A Tick event procedure is coded for a timer object. The Interval is specified in milliseconds with 1000 ms in 1 second. Animation uses a Timer object and several similar images.

Visual Basic includes the `Graphics` class with methods for creating circles, lines, rectangles, and other shapes on a drawing surface. A drawing surface is defined by assigning an object's surface to a `Graphics` object and calling the CreateGraphics() method for the object. After creating a drawing surface, the Pen and SolidBrush classes can be used to create a pen or brush object for drawing. Next, methods are called with a pen or brush and a set of coordinates to create a shape on the drawing surface. Methods include DrawLine(), DrawRectangle(), DrawEllipse(), DrawArc(), Clear(), FillRectangle(), FillEllipse(), FillPie(), DrawCurve(), DrawClosedCurve(), FillClosedCurve(), DrawPolygon(), FillPolygon().

The `Point` structure includes X and Y members. A `Point` variable can be used in place of a set of coordinates in the `Graphics` class methods.

Form events can include the MouseDown event, which is raised when the user clicks an interface object. A MouseDown event procedure includes a parameter named `e` that contains properties specific to the mouse click. The `e` parameter has properties X and Y, which are the coordinates of the mouse click.

Vocabulary

Actual coordinates Actual x and y values on a drawing surface.

Animation Similar images displayed quickly one after the other to give the impression of continuous motion.

Child control The objects on a form as they relate to the form.

Drawing surface The surface of a form, button, or almost any other object used for creating shapes.

Parent control A form as it relates to its objects.

Pixel Each point on a surface. The number of pixels in a surface depends on the screen resolution.

Point An x-coordinate and y-coordinate that together indicate a specific location.

Relative coordinates x and y coordinates which are specified relative to a form.

Tiled An image that is repeated to fill an object.

Visual Basic

ColorDialog **ColorDialog control** Used to add an application component that displays the Color dialog box. Properties include Color and AllowFullOpen. Methods include ShowDialog().

CreateGraphics() Method used for making the surface area of a specific control object a graphics drawing surface. Available with most control class objects.

`Drawing` **class** Contains the Visual Basic color constants that can be used to change background and foreground colors of objects. Also used with `Pen` and `SolidBrush` objects.

`Graphics` **class** Used to create graphic objects. Methods include Clear(), DrawCurve(), DrawArc(), DrawClosedCurve(), DrawEllipse(), DrawLine(), DrawPolygon(), DrawRectangle(), FillClosedCurve(), FillPie(), FillEllipse(), FillPolygon(), and FillRectangle().

`Imports` Statement used to make the members of a class accessible in an application.

`New` Statement used to declare a new object.

`Pen` **class** Used to create an object for drawing on a graphics surface. Properties include DashStyle.

`Point` Structure that has members X and Y for defining a point.

`SolidBrush` **class** Used to create an object for filling shapes on a surface.

`SystemSounds` **class** Includes five properties that return Windows operating system sounds which can be played with the Play() method.

Timer **Timer control** Used to add an application component that executes code at specific intervals. Properties include (Name), Interval, and Enabled. Methods include Start() and Stop(). Events include Tick.

Critical Thinking

1. a) Explain the parent/child relationship as it relates to the BackColor property of a form and the objects on the form.
   b) What is meant by inherits?

2. Give an example of when a label should be Transparent.

3. a) What is meant by a predefined dialog box?
   b) List the three predefined dialog boxes discussed in the text so far.

4. What is the difference between the BackgroundImage and Image properties?

5. What happens when the BackgroundImage property of a form is right-clicked and then Reset selected?

6. a) List the five properties in the `SystemSounds` class that play Windows operating system sounds.
   b) For each property listed for part (a) give an example of how the sound could be used to enhance an application.
   c) Which method is used to make the sound associated with the object returned by the `SystemSounds` properties?
   d) Which statement must be included at the top of a program that uses the `SystemSounds` class?

7. Which file format must audio be in to be used in a Visual Basic application?

8. Which object provides methods for working with audio?

9. a) What does it mean when a component has no graphical element?
   b) Why does the Timer control have no graphical element?

10. a) What happens when the following code executes in a Tick event procedure for an enabled timer with Interval 7000?

```
Static keepTrack As Integer = 0
If keepTrack Mod 2 = 0 Then
    Me.Text = "Who's on First?"
Else
    Me.Text = "What's on Second?"
End If
keepTrack += 1
```

   b) What would happen if the keyword `Static` was changed to `Dim`?

11. An application uses a Timer object to automatically display a message box with a message every 2 minutes.
   a) If the Interval property of a timer can be no higher than 64,767 milliseconds, how can the application use a timer to display a message every 2 minutes?
   b) Write the Tick event procedure for the application. Have the message box display "2 minutes."

12. Explain how animation works.

13. Write statements that display a filled quarter circle in the upper-left quadrant of a label that is size 100 by 100.

14. a) Write statements that draw a solid blue circle with radius `r` on a form starting at (50, 70).
   b) Modify the statements in part (a) to use the FillPie() method to create a solid circle.

15. a) What does the following code produce?

```
Dim x1 As Integer = 0
Dim y1 As Integer = _
Int(Me.lblShow.Height / 2)
Dim x2 As Integer = Me.lblShow.Width
Dim y2 As Integer = _
Int(Me.lblShow.Height / 2)
labelSurface.DrawLine(AquaPen,x1,y1,x2,y2)
```

   b) Modify the statements in part (a) to use the `Point` structure.

16. a) Explain what happens when the following code executes in a form's MouseDown event procedure.

```
Dim hey As Integer = Me.Size.Width / 2
Dim you As Integer = Me.Size.Height / 2
If e.X < hey + 10 And e.X > hey - 10 _
And e.Y < you + 10 _
And e.Y > you - 10 Then
    MessageBox.Show("Bull's Eye!")
End If
```

   b) Why are < and >, rather than =, being used in the `If` condition above?

True/False

17. Determine if each of the following is true or false. If false, explain why.
    a) A child control will always inherit property values from the parent control.
    b) The ForeColor of an object is the color of its text.
    c) The color of a form can be changed at run-time.
    d) Visual Basic applications support audio files in WAV format.
    e) A program can only have one Timer object.
    f) A Click event executes at every timer interval.
    g) If a timer should process an action every 10 seconds, then its Interval property should be set to 10.
    h) The coordinate (0, 0) is the coordinate of the center of the object.
    i) A line thickness must be indicated when declaring a `SolidBrush` object.
    j) DrawCurve() would be the method to draw a pentagon.
    k) A form Click event occurs when a form is clicked.
    l) A Timer object can be turned on and off at run time by setting its Visible property.

Exercises

Exercise 1 — PhotoAlbum

a) Create a PhotoAlbum application that allows the user to scroll through photographs and their corresponding captions by clicking a button that displays an image of an arrow. The `arrow.jpg`, `anemone.jpg`, `grayangel.jpg`, `sponges.jpg`, `starfish.jpg`, and `scorpionfish.jpg` images are data files for this text. The application interface should look similar to the following:

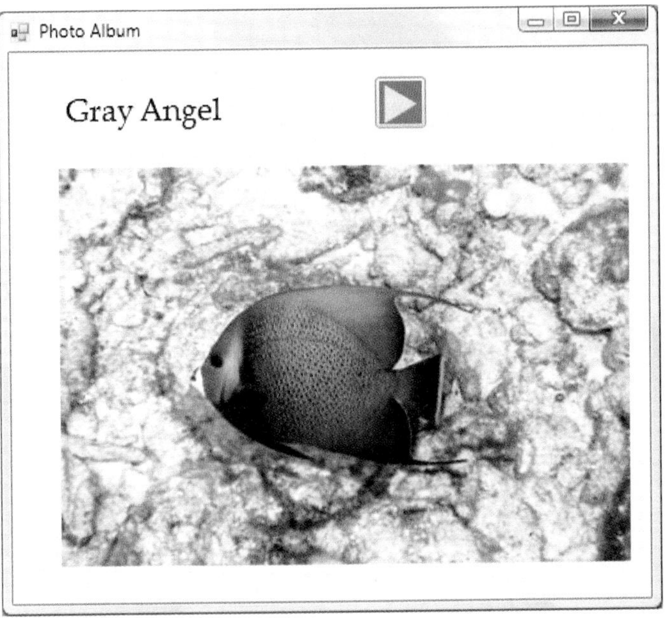

b) Modify the PhotoAlbum application to play a bubble background sound while the application is running. Use the `bubbles.wav` file, which is a data file for this text.

Exercise 2 — Speak

Create a Speak application that allows the build a string by clicking buttons on the interface. When the string is complete, the user can then click **Speak** to hear the string as a spoken phrase. The `word-dog.wav`, `word-cat.wav`, `word-fluffy.wav`, `word-I.wav`, `word-is.wav`, `word-see.wav`, `word-the.wav`, and `word-walk.wav` sound files are data files for this text. The application interface should look similar to:

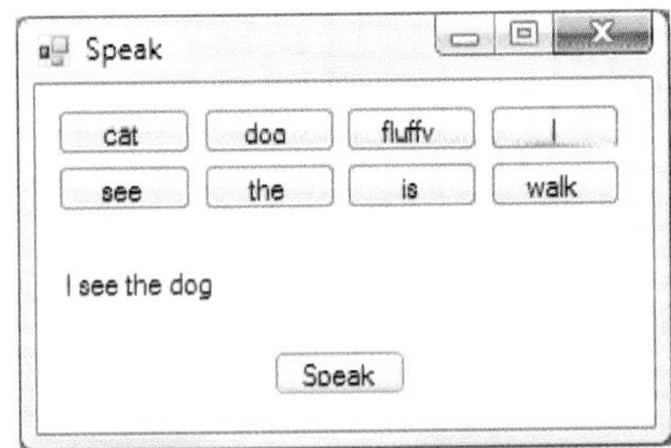

Exercise 3 — DrawHouse

Create a DrawHouse application that allows the user to select the color of the sky, sun, roof, house, and door to draw in a label by clicking radio buttons. The application interface should look similar to:

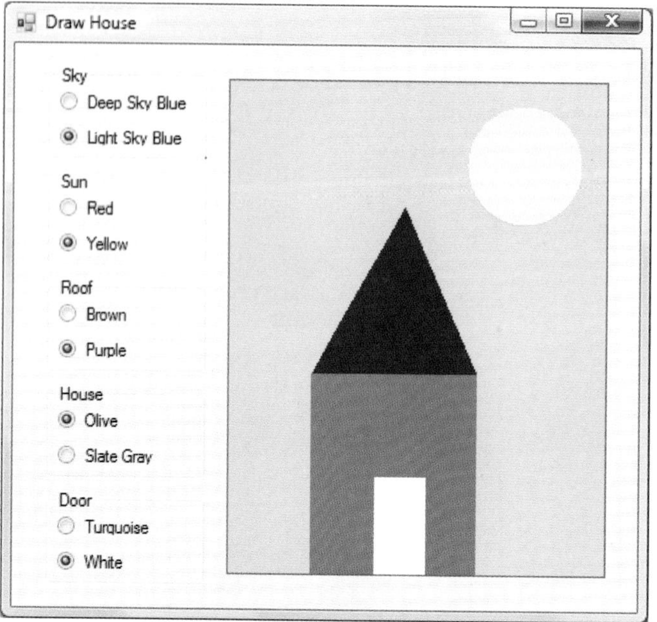

Exercise 4 — MoveLine

a) Create a MoveLine application that displays a blue line that randomly changes position every 3 seconds after clicking **Start**. Clicking **Stop** should stop the animation. Hint: Use the size of the form and the Rnd() function to define starting and ending coordinates and the DrawLine() method to draw the lines. The form will need to be cleared before a new line is drawn. The application interface should look similar to the following after clicking **Start**:

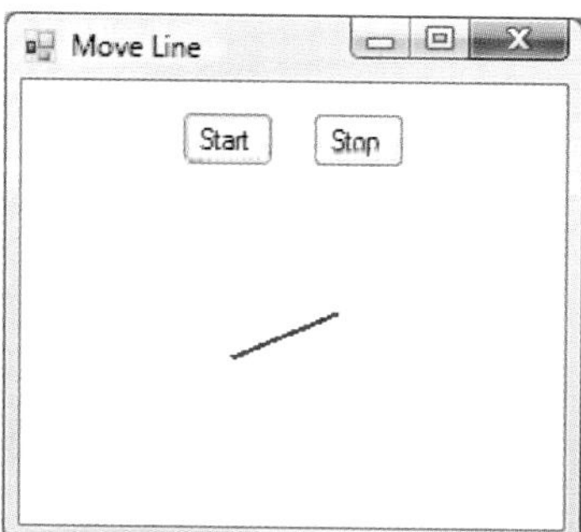

b) Modify the MoveLine application to randomly display the moving line in either blue, green, or red when **Start** is clicked.

c) Modify the MoveLine application to beep each time the line is displayed.

Exercise 5 — MoveFilledEllipse

a) Create a MoveFilledEllipse application that displays a filled ellipse that randomly changes position every 3 seconds after clicking **Start**. Clicking **Stop** should stop the animation. Hint: Use the size of the form and the Rnd() function to define coordinates and the FillEllipse() method to draw the ellipses. The form will need to be cleared before a new ellipse is drawn. The application interface should look similar to the following after clicking **Start**:

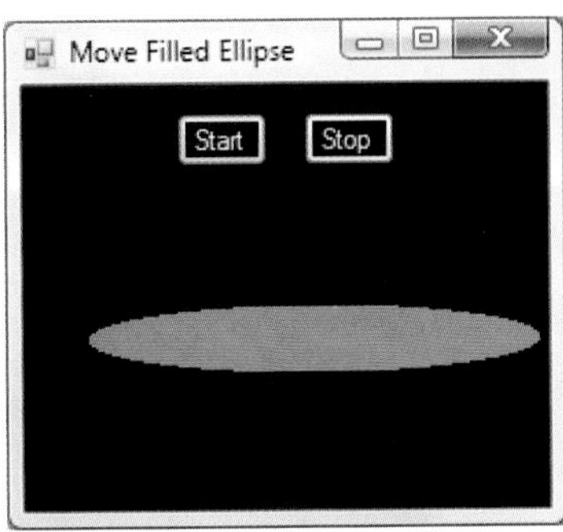

b) Modify the MoveFilledEllipse application to randomly display the moving filled ellipse in either blue, green, or red when Start is clicked.

Exercise 6 — BirdFlying

a) Create a BirdFlying application that simulates a bird flying. Use the `bird1.gif`, `bird2.gif`, and `bird3.gif` images that are data files for this text. The three different animations should look similar to:

b) Modify the BirdFlying application to include the sound of a flying seagull. Use the `gull.wav` sound file that is a data file for this text.

Exercise 7 — DigitalClock

In Chapter 2, Exercise 13, a SystemClock application was created that displayed the current time. Use a timer to create a similar application that displays the time as a running digital clock. *Hint*: Set the time interval to 1000 and create a Timer1_Tick event procedure that uses the system clock TimeString property.

Exercise 8 — TurtleRun

Create a TurtleRun application that allows the user to control the speed of the animation by clicking a button. Use the `turtle1.bmp`, `turtle2.bmp`, and `turtle3.bmp` images that are data files for this text. The background color of the form should be white and the background color of the buttons should be MediumSeaGreen. The application interface should look similar to:

Exercise 9  — BouncingBall

Modify the BouncingBall application created in a review in this chapter to include a MouseDown event procedure that reverses the direction of the ball when the form is clicked. For example, if the ball is falling down from the top of the form, clicking the form makes the ball move from the bottom to the top.

Exercise 10 — Shapes

Create a Shapes application that allows the user to enter the information needed to draw a line, ellipse, or rectangle in a MistyRose background colored label. The Select Color button should display a Color dialog box for the user to choose from. Hint: Make the color assignment to a global variable. The application interface should look similar to:

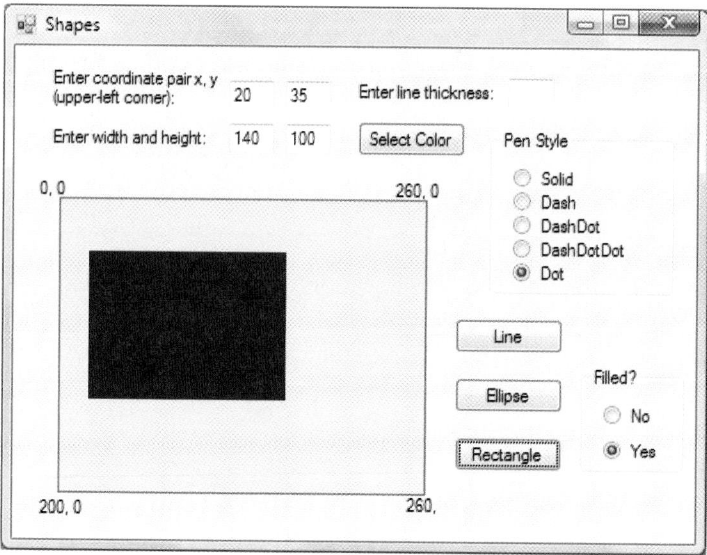

Exercise 11 — DrawArcs

Create a DrawArcs application that allows the user to enter the information needed to draw an arc in a MistyRose background colored label. The application interface should look similar to:

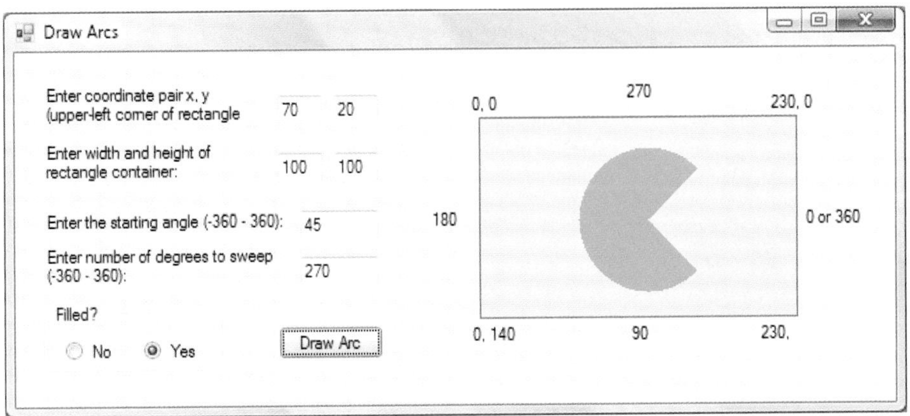

Exercise 12 — EllipseDimensions

Create an EllipseDimensions application that draws a solid purple ellipse from boundary coordinates (0, 0) in the width and height determined by where the user clicks the form. Indicate in a message box the width and height dimensions of the ellipse. Every time the form is clicked, it should be cleared before drawing the new ellipse and displaying a message box. The application interface should look similar to:

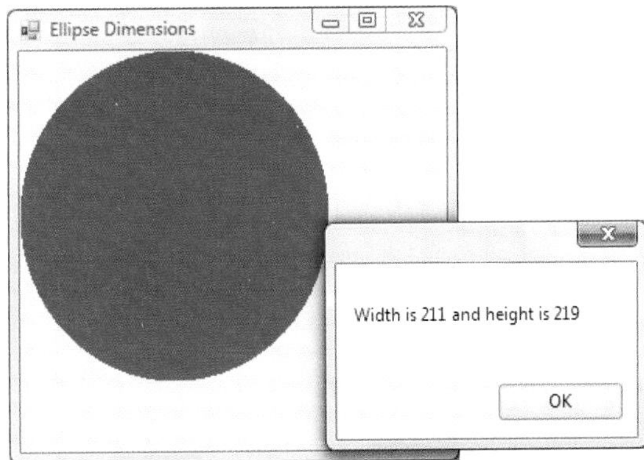

Exercise 13 — CurvesAndPolygons

Create a CurvesAndPolygons application that allows the user to draw in a label by clicking the mouse to define the points of the curve or polygon before clicking the button indicating the shape to draw. If the user clicks less than three times, display a message box with an appropriate message. The Select Color button should display a Color dialog box for the user to choose from. Hint: Make the color assignment to a global variable. The Clear button should clear the label. The application interface should look similar to the following after drawing many shapes and curves:

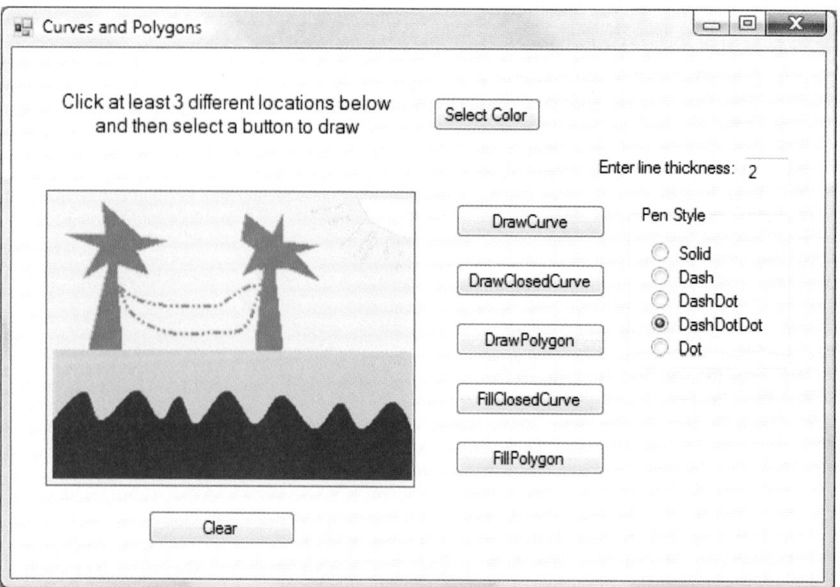

Exercise 14 —————— Face

Modify the Face application created in a review in this chapter to include a Wink button that, when clicked, winks an eye every second. The Wink button should be disabled until the Happy or Sad button is clicked. Clicking Wink starts the timer and Happy and Sad stops the timer. Your application interface should look similar to the following after clicking Happy and then Wink:

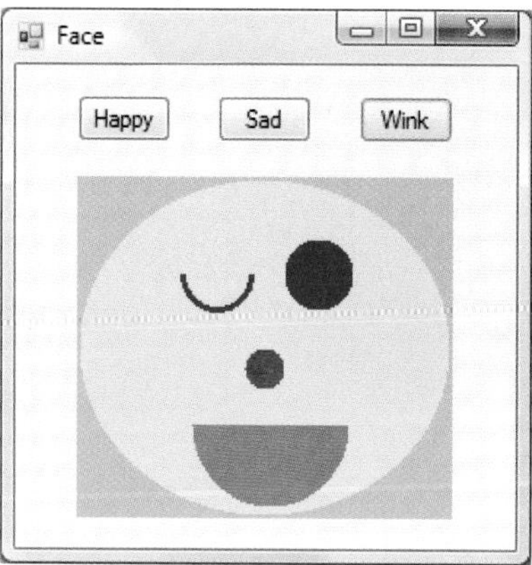

Exercise 15 (advanced) —————— PieChart

Create a PieChart application that allows the user to enter four values to represent relative pie slices in a pie chart. The percentage of the total that each value represents and a pie chart drawing with different color pie slices should be displayed when the Chart button is clicked. *Hint*: Use the percentage of the total values to determine the degree each pie slice will sweep out of the 360 degrees available.

Chapter 10 Creating Classes

Key Concepts

Instantiating objects
Designing and creating a class
Applying encapsulation
Writing constructors
Overloading methods
Extending a class using inheritance
Polymorphism
Reusing existing code

Case Study

Triangle Calculator

Classes

TIP Classes are similar to structures.

Classes have been used in all the applications presented in this text. For example, each control in the Toolbox represents a different class. A Button control is a class with a Text property. Another example is the `String` class which has methods such as ToUpper() for converting the string to all uppercase characters. These classes are precompiled code that are part of Visual Basic.

object

A Visual Basic application can also include classes created by the programmer. A *class* is an abstract data type. When a class is used to declare a variable, the variable is called an *object*. For example, the class `Account` could be used to create an `acct1` object:

```
Dim acct1 As New Account()
```

instantiation

A statement that creates an object is *instantiating* the object. In general, instantiation takes the form:

```
Dim ClassObjectName As New ClassName(parameters)
```

`ClassObjectName` is a name describing the object. The keyword `New` creates the `ClassName` object. `parameters` are sometimes required in the creation of an object.

An object may also be declared and then later instantiated:

```
Dim acct1 As Account
...statements...
acct1 = New Account()
```

Using two statements to create an object can be helpful when an object requires parameters for instantiation. By instantiating in a separate statement, values for parameters can be obtained from the user and then used for instantiation.

Classes have members. A member can be a field member, data member, property, or method. An object accesses members of its class with a dot (.) between the object name and member name. For example, the statement

```
Me.lblAcctBal.Text = acct1.Balance    'display balance
```

uses the Balance property of the `Account` class to get the current balance of the `acct1` object. This value is assigned to the Text property of the lblAcctBal object that is on the form.

Classes with a Graphical Element

A control class, such as Button, is a class with a graphical element.

The concepts covered in this chapter are the basis of object-oriented programming. Although the terminology may seem a bit overwhelming, keep in mind that a class is simply a data type and objects are variables of a class. Classes are used to create objects. The process of creating a new object is called instantiation. Class members are accessed with a dot between the object name and member name.

Designing a Class

A class groups related variables and procedures. Therefore, a class should be created for a program that requires a related set of data and actions. For example, many banks use a computer application to maintain customer accounts. In the application, these accounts are better implemented as objects of a class because each object (account) requires similar data and actions to be performed.

field
data member
property
method

A class is designed based on a description, or specification. By carefully analyzing the class specification, field and data members, properties, and methods can be determined. A *field* is piece of data that will not change. A *data member* is a variable used by the class, but not accessible to objects of the class. A *property* is an attribute of an object that can be viewed and optionally set. A *method* is a procedure that performs an action on an object. The following list of members was created from the specification for a class in a program that manages bank accounts:

- An `activity` array data member stores the transactions on the account.
- An AcctNum property retrieves or sets the account number for an existing account.
- FirstName and LastName properties retrieve or set a customer's first and last names.
- A read-only Balance property for retrieving the current balance.
- A MakeDeposit() method for depositing money.
- A MakeWithdrawal() method for withdrawing money.
- A ShowTransactions() method for listing transactions.

TIP The case study at the end of this chapter shows the steps for designing as well as creating a class.

Throughout the chapter, this list of members will be used to create a class named `Account`.

The Class Module

A new class is coded in a separate file called a *Class module*. Adding a Class module to a project allows objects of that class to be instantiated in the Form1 module. To add a Class module to an open project, select **Project → Add Class**. The Add New Item dialog box is displayed with the Class template selected:

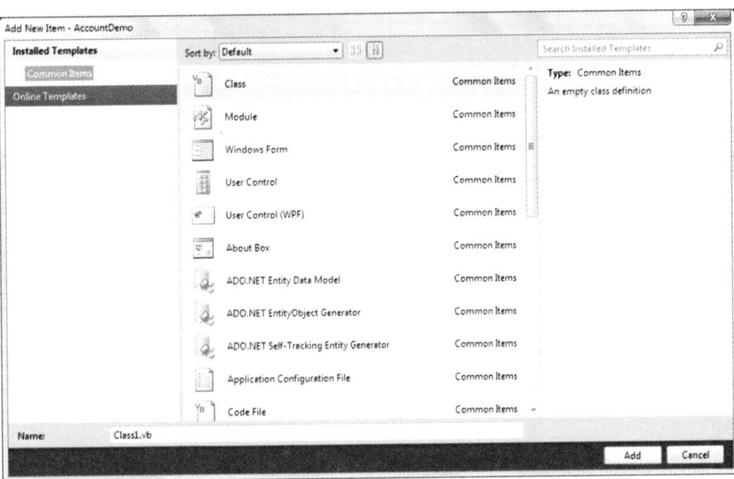

Type the class name in the **Name** box (be sure to keep the `.vb` extension) and then select **Add**. Class names should be a noun and begin with an uppercase letter. Class names may not contain spaces. The class file is displayed in its own Code window in the IDE. The Class module below was named `Account`, which is the name automatically used for the class declaration:

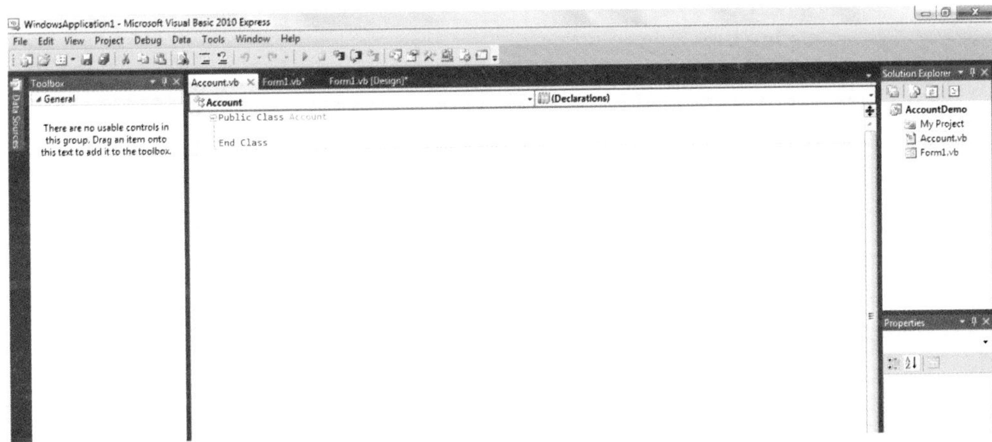

A new Class module contains a class declaration that takes the form:

```
Public Class ClassName

End Class
```

ClassName is automatically replaced with the name of the class typed in the Add New Item dialog box.

Review: AccountDemo – part 1 of 5

① **CREATE A NEW PROJECT**

Create a Windows application named `AccountDemo`.

② **CREATE THE INTERFACE**

Use the table below the form on the next page for setting object properties.

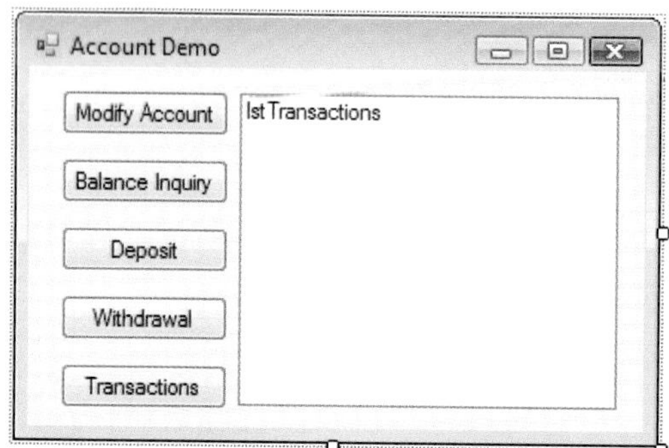

Object	(Name)	Text
Form1		`Account Demo`
Button1	`btnModifyAccount`	`Modify Account`
Button2	`btnBalanceInquiry`	`Balance Inquiry`
Button3	`btnDeposit`	`Deposit`
Button4	`btnWithdrawal`	`Withdrawal`
Button5	`btnTransactions`	`Transactions`
ListBox1	`lstTransactions`	

③ **ADD A CLASS MODULE**

a. Display the Code window.

b. Add comments that include your name, assignment, and today's date.

c. Select Project → Add Class. A dialog box is displayed.

1. In the Templates list, click Class, if it is not already selected.
2. In the Name box, type `Account.vb`.
3. Select Add. The Account.vb Code window is displayed.

d. Save the project.

Encapsulation

TIP *Client code* refers to the code module that uses a class. Client code can access the Public methods of a class, but cannot directly change the data stored in a class.

One important aspect of classes is that the methods of a class are the only way an object of the class can change data values. For example, the `Account` class includes MakeDeposit() and MakeWithdrawal() methods that update the balance, similar to a real bank that would not allow a customer to directly change an account balance without properly making a deposit or a withdrawal. The balance data is not directly accessible to an `Account` object and is said to be "encapsulated" by the class. Limiting access to data is called *data hiding*, and is the basis for *encapsulation*.

data hiding

access modifier

Encapsulation is accomplished by using an *access modifier* in declarations. Access modifiers are keywords that control access to members:

- `Private` declares a member as accessible to the methods of the class only.
- `Protected` declares a member that can be used from within the class only.
- `Public` explicitly declares a member available to an object of the class. In a Form1 module, public members appear in an IntelliSense list after typing an object name followed by a dot.

Field, Data, and Property Members

field

A class usually requires variables and constants for its private use. A constant of a class is called a *field*. Fields declared as `Private Const` are constants that are accessible to the methods of the class only. Variables of a class are called data members. They are declared as `Private` to make them accessible to the methods of the class only.

class constant

A second type of field, called a class constant, is usually accessed from the class itself. A *class constant* is declared `Public Const` and is accessible to objects and methods of a class, as well as from the class itself. For example, the following statements define class constants:

```
Public Class Account

  Public Const MIN_REQUIRED_BALANCE As Decimal = 100  '$100
  Public Const LOW_BALANCE_FEE As Decimal = 1         '$1
...
```

Next, a decision structure in the Form module could compare the current balance to the minimum required:

```
If acct1.Balance < Account.MIN_REQUIRED_BALANCE Then
  ...
```

Note the class constant was accessed from the class itself.

property member

A *property member* is used to return or change information about an object. For example, the `Account` class is designed to include an AcctNum property for getting and setting an account number. The first statement below gets an account number and assigns it to the label's text. The second statement sets an account number to a new value:

```
Me.lblInfo.Text = martinAccount.AcctNum     'show acct number
martinAccount.AcctNum = "1234"              'change acct number
```

Previous versions of Visual Basic required a property declaration to be written in an expanded syntax:

```
Private DataMember As DataType

Property PropertyName() As ReturnType
      Get
          Return DataMember value
      End Get
      Set(ByVal Value As DataType)
          DataMember = value
      End Set
  End Property
```

DataMember stores the property data. PropertyName is the name describing the information available from the property and ReturnType is the data type of the value returned to the calling object. Get() and Set() are property procedures. Get() returns the current DataMember value to the calling object, and Set() assigns Value to DataMember. Property declares the property and End Property ends the property.

In Visual Basic 2010, *auto-implemented* properties allow the Visual Basic compiler to automatically create a private field to store the property variable in addition to creating the associated Get and Set procedures. The code on the previous page can now be simply written as:

```
Property PropertyName() As DataType
```

However, some property definitions still require use of the standard or expanded property syntax. This includes creating properties that are `WriteOnly` or `ReadOnly`. It also includes situations where you want to validate incoming values in the Set procedure. For example, in the code below, you are validating the password:

```
Public Class Account
...
   Property AcctNum As String
        Get
             Return acctNumber
        End Get
        Set(ByVal value As String)
             Const PASSWORD As String = "money"
             Dim passwordEntered As String = _
             InputBox("Enter password:")
             If passwordEntered = PASSWORD Then
                 acctNumber = value
             End If
        End Set
   End Property
...
```

A property declared as `ReadOnly` can return its data member value, but an object cannot change, or set, the property value. The `Account` class includes the read-only Balance property, which contains only a Get() method:

```
Public Class Account
...
   'private data member
   Private acctBalance As Decimal
...
   ReadOnly Property Balance() As Decimal
        Get
             Return acctBalance
        End Get
   End Property
...
```

A property is added to the Class module by typing `Property` followed by the property name. Typing `ReadOnly Property` adds `Get` and `End Get` statements and an `End Property` statement. Statements can then be typed for each method.

Review: AccountDemo – part 2 of 5

① ADD DATA MEMBERS

a. In the Solution Explorer window, double-click the Account.vb module icon to open it, if necessary.

b. In the Account class Code window, add a comment and then the data members. Note that the structures used to declare two of the data members should be declared just below the data members:

```
Public Class Account

    'Private data members

    Private acctNumber As String
    Private acctBalance As Decimal
    Private activity(-1) As Transaction
    Private customer As PersonalInfo

    Private Structure Transaction
        Dim transType As String
        Dim transCode As Boolean        'false if no errors
        Dim endingBalance As Decimal
    End Structure

    Private Structure PersonalInfo
        Dim firstName As String
        Dim lastName As String
    End Structure
```

Note the structures are `Private`, which makes them available to the class only.

② ADD PROPERTIES

a. Below the structures, add the following code to validate the incoming value in the Set procedure:

```
'Property members

Property AcctNum As String
    Get
        Return acctNumber
    End Get
    Set(ByVal value As String)
        Const PASSWORD As String = "money"
        Dim passwordEntered As String = _
        InputBox("Enter password:")
        If passwordEntered = PASSWORD Then
            acctNumber = value
        End If
    End Set
End Property
```

Note that the account number can be changed only if the user knows the password.

b. Below the AcctNum property, add the LastName and FirstName properties:

```
Property LastName() As String
Property FirstName() As String
```

c. Below the FirstName property, add the read-only Balance property:

```
ReadOnly Property Balance() As Decimal
    Get
        Return acctBalance
    End Get
End Property
```

d. Save the project.

③ PRINT THE ACCOUNT CLASS CODE

④ USE THE ACCOUNT CLASS IN THE FORM1 MODULE

a. Display the Form1 Code window.

b. Create a global variable declaration that instantiates an `Account` object:

```
Dim acct1 As New Account()
```

c. Create a btnBalanceInquiry_Click event procedure and then type `acct1.` and note the IntelliSense list with the class constants and properties that have been added to the `Account` class:

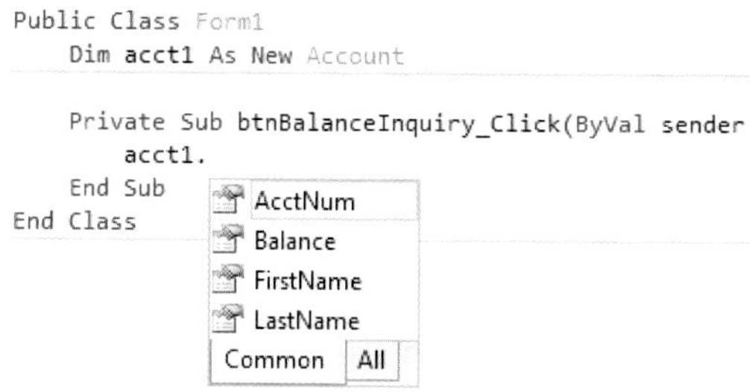

d. Delete the statement added to the event procedure and then save the project.

Methods

A method is a procedure in a class. Methods are used to perform actions on an object. For example, the `Account` class is designed to include MakeDeposit() and MakeWithdrawal() methods for making transactions. Methods often have parameters. For example, MakeDeposit() has a parameter for the deposit amount, as shown in the statements:

```
Dim acct1 As New Account()
acct1.Deposit(100)     'deposit $100
```

In the Class module, a method declaration takes the form:

```
Public Sub MethodName(parameters)
  statements
End Sub
```

`Public` declares a method that can be called by objects of the class. `MethodName` is the name describing the task performed. `parameters` are parameter declarations. `statements` is one or more statements that perform the task. `Sub` declares the method and `End Sub` ends the method. Note that a method is a procedure and can therefore also be a function procedure.

A class also typically contains methods that perform "background" work for objects of the class. These methods should not be directly accessible to objects and are declared with the keyword `Protected`. A protected method can be used by other class members only. For example, the MakeDeposit() and MakeWithdrawal() methods in the `Account` class call a protected method, AddTransaction(), for recording a transaction in the `activity` array, similar to a real bank that records all account transactions. The transaction is recorded "behind the scenes" by the protected method, without any interaction from the programmer or application user.

In the Class module, a protected method declaration requires the `Protected` keyword and takes the form:

```
Protected Sub MethodName(parameters)
      statements
End Sub
```

Review: AccountDemo – part 3 of 5

① ADD FIELD MEMBERS TO THE ACCOUNT CLASS

Just below the `Public Class Account` statement (and above the private data members), add a comment and two field members:

```
Public Class Account

    'Public field members

    Public Const MIN_REQUIRED_BALANCE As Decimal = 100  '$100
    Public Const LOW_BALANCE_FEE As Decimal = 1         '$1
```

② ADD METHOD MEMBERS

a. Below the Balance property declarations and before the `End Class` statement, add a comment and a protected method:

```
'Protected methods

Protected Sub AddTransaction(ByVal transaction As String,
ByVal code As Boolean, ByVal currentBalance As Decimal)
    'Use Length to size array because the value is one greater than the
    'current highest index value
    ReDim Preserve activity(activity.Length)
    Dim newTransaction As Integer = activity.Length - 1

    activity(newTransaction).transType = transaction
    activity(newTransaction).transCode = code
    activity(newTransaction).endingBalance = currentBalance
End Sub
```

b. Below the AddTransaction() protected method and before the `End Class` statement, add a comment and three public methods:

```
'Public methods

Public Sub ShowTransactions(ByRef displayBox As ListBox)
    Dim currentTransaction As Transaction

    displayBox.Items.Add("Error" & vbTab & "Transaction" & vbTab & "Balance")
    For transNum As Integer = 0 To activity.Length - 1
        currentTransaction = activity(transNum)
        displayBox.Items.Add(currentTransaction.transCode & vbTab &
        currentTransaction.transType & vbTab & vbTab &
```

```
            currentTransaction.endingBalance)
        Next transNum
    End Sub

    Public Sub MakeDeposit(ByVal depositAmt As Decimal, ByRef errorCode As Boolean)
        If depositAmt > 0 Then          'valid deposit
            acctBalance += depositAmt
            errorCode = False
        Else                            'deposit not valid
            errorCode = True
        End If
        AddTransaction("Deposit", errorCode, acctBalance)
    End Sub

    Public Sub MakeWithdrawal(ByVal withdrawalAmt As Decimal,
    ByRef errorCode As Boolean)
        If withdrawalAmt <= acctBalance Then               'make withdrawal
            acctBalance -= withdrawalAmt
            errorCode = False
            AddTransaction("Withdrawal", errorCode, acctBalance)
            'Determine if balance has fallen below required amount
            If acctBalance < MIN_REQUIRED_BALANCE Then  'service charge
                acctBalance -= LOW_BALANCE_FEE
                errorCode = False
                AddTransaction("Low Bal Fee", errorCode, acctBalance)
            End If
        Else                                              'withdrawal not permitted
            errorCode = True
            AddTransaction("Withdrawal", errorCode, acctBalance)
        End If
    End Sub
```

c. Save the modified project.

③ MODIFY THE ACCOUNT DEMO APPLICATION

a. Display the Form1 Code window.

b. In the btnBalanceInquiry_Click event procedure, add the statement:

```
MessageBox.Show("Account " & acct1.AcctNum & " has " &
Format(acct1.Balance, "Currency"))
```

c. Create a btnDeposit_Click event procedure and add the statements:

```
Dim textEntered As String
textEntered = InputBox("Enter amount of deposit:", Me.Text)

'Test data entered
Dim transCode As Boolean
If textEntered = Nothing Then       'Cancel or empty text box
    acct1.MakeDeposit(0, transCode)
Else                                'characters entered
    acct1.MakeDeposit(Val(textEntered), transCode)
End If

If transCode Then
    MessageBox.Show("Problem with transaction.")
End If
```

d. Create a btnWithdrawal_Click event procedure and add the statements:

```
Dim textEntered As String
textEntered = InputBox("Enter amount to withdraw.", Me.Text)

'Test data entered
Dim transCode As Boolean
If textEntered = Nothing Then        'Cancel or empty text box
    acct1.MakeWithdrawal(0, transCode)
Else                                 'characters entered
    acct1.MakeWithdrawal(Val(textEntered), transCode)
End If

If transCode Then
    MessageBox.Show("Problem with transaction.")
End If
```

e. Create a btnTransactions_Click event procedure and add the statements:

```
Me.lstTransactions.Items.Clear()          'clear previous items
acct1.ShowTransactions(Me.lstTransactions)
```

f. Create a btnModifyAccount_Click event procedure and add the statements:

```
Dim textEntered As String

'Change first name
textEntered = InputBox("First name is:  " & acct1.FirstName &
vbCrLf & "Enter new first name (Cancel to keep the same):", Me.Text)
'Test data entered
If textEntered <> Nothing Then      'new first name
    acct1.FirstName = textEntered
End If

'Change last name
textEntered = InputBox("Last name is:  " & acct1.LastName &
vbCrLf & "Enter new last name (Cancel to keep the same):", Me.Text)
'Test data entered
If textEntered <> Nothing Then      'new last name
    acct1.LastName = textEntered
End If

'Change account number
textEntered = InputBox("Account number is:  " & acct1.AcctNum &
vbCrLf & "Enter new account number (Cancel to keep the same):", Me.Text)
'Test data entered
If textEntered <> Nothing Then      'new account number
    acct1.AcctNum = textEntered
End If
```

g. Run the application. Click **Balance Inquiry**. A message box is displayed indicating the account has $0.00. Note that there is no account number listed. Select **OK** to remove the dialog box.

h. Click **Modify Account**. Input boxes are displayed for entering account holder name and an account number. The password `money` will need to be used to modify the account.

i. Use the other buttons to make deposits, withdrawals, and account modifications. View the transactions by clicking **Transactions**.

④ PRINT THE ACCOUNT CODE

Constructors

A *constructor* is a method that is automatically called by the `New` keyword when an object is instantiated. Statements for initializing object values can be placed in the constructor. In the Class module, a constructor method takes the form:

```
Sub New()
   statements
End Sub
```

`New` is the name that must be used for a constructor. `statements` is one or more statements that initialize values and perform tasks. A constructor is called only once when an object is created.

A constructor usually initializes private data members, as in the `Account` class constructor:

```
Sub New()
   Me.accountNumber = "0000"
   Me.acctBalance = 0
   Me.AddTransaction("New Account", False, acctBalance)
End Sub
```

The keyword `Me` is used where possible in a constructor as good programming style.

Review: AccountDemo – part 4 of 5

① ADD A FIELD MEMBER TO THE ACCOUNT CLASS

Below the `Public` field members in the `Account` class, add a comment and a field member that stores a `Private` default account number:

```
'Private field member

Public Const DEFAULT_ACCT_NUM As String = "0000"
```

② ADD A CONSTRUCTOR

a. Below the `Private` data members and structures, add a comment and the constructor method:

```
'Constructor

Sub New()
    Me.acctNumber = DEFAULT_ACCT_NUM
    Me.acctBalance = 0
    Me.AddTransaction("New Account", False, acctBalance)
End Sub
```

b. Save the modified project.

Check – The class code should look similar to:

```
Public Class Account

    'Public field members

    Public Const MIN_REQUIRED_BALANCE As Decimal = 100  '$100
    Public Const LOW_BALANCE_FEE As Decimal = 1        '$1
```

```
'Private field member

Private Const DEFAULT_ACCT_NUM As String = "0000"

'Private data members

Private acctNumber As String
Private acctBalance As Decimal
Private activity(-1) As Transaction
Private customer As PersonalInfo

Private Structure Transaction
    Dim transType As String
    Dim transCode As Boolean        'false if no errors
    Dim endingBalance As Decimal
End Structure

Private Structure PersonalInfo
    Dim firstName As String
    Dim lastName As String
End Structure

'Constructor

Sub New()
    Me.acctNumber = DEFAULT_ACCT_NUM
    Me.acctBalance = 0
    Me.AddTransaction("New Account", False, acctBalance)
End Sub
...
```

③ RUN THE APPLICATION

a. Run the application. Click **Balance Inquiry**. Note the default account number.

b. Click **Transactions**. Note the new account transaction.

④ PRINT THE ACCOUNT CODE

Overloading Methods

A method that performs a different action depending on the number or type of arguments it receives is said to be *overloaded*. Constructors are commonly overloaded to give more flexibility when creating objects. For example, each of the statements below creates an `Account` class object assuming four appropriate constructors are defined in the class:

```
Dim newAcct1 As New Account()          'use default values
Dim newAcct2 As New Account("1073")    'account number 1073
Dim newAcct3 As New Account(200)       'beginning balance $200
'Account number 2743, first name Grace, last name Wilson
Dim newAcct4 As New Account("2743", "Grace", "Wilson")
```

Note that `newAcct2` and `newAcct3` are instantiated with one argument, but different constructors will be called because the arguments are different types.

The four `Account` class constructors are shown on the next page. Note how the first constructor uses `Me.New` with arguments to call the constructor with an `acctNum` parameter:

```
'Constructors

Sub New()
  'Call constructor that accepts an acct number parameter
  Me.New(DEFAULT_ACCT_NUM)
End Sub

'Object instantiated with an acct number parameter
Sub New(ByVal num As String)
  Me.acctNumber = num
  Me.acctBalance = 0
  Me.AddTransaction("New Account", False, acctBalance)
End Sub

'Object instantiated with a deposit amount
Sub New(ByVal initialDeposit As Decimal)
  Me.acctNumber = DEFAULT_ACCT_NUM
  Me.acctBalance = initialDeposit
  Me.AddTransaction("New Account", False, acctBalance)
End Sub

'Object instantiated with acct number and acct holder name
Sub New(ByVal num As String, ByVal fName As String,
ByVal lName As String)
  Me.acctNumber = mum
  Me.acctBalance = 0
  Me.FirstName = fName
  Me.LastName = lName
  Me.AddTransaction("New Account", False, acctBalance)
End Sub
```

In general, methods are overloaded by writing a set of methods that each have the same name, but different parameters. Each of the `Account` constructors have the method name `New` and different parameters. The parameter list for a method can vary by changing the number of parameters or by changing the data types of parameters.

Review: AccountDemo – part 5 of 5

① ADD THREE OVERLOADED CONSTRUCTORS TO THE ACCOUNT CLASS

Below the existing default constructor, add three new constructor methods:

```
Sub New(ByVal num As String)
    Me.acctNumber = num
    Me.acctBalance = 0
    Me.AddTransaction("New Account", False, acctBalance)
End Sub

Sub New(ByVal initialDeposit As Decimal)
    Me.acctNumber = DEFAULT_ACCT_NUM
    Me.acctBalance = initialDeposit
    Me.AddTransaction("New Account", False, acctBalance)
End Sub

Sub New(ByVal num As String, ByVal fName As String, ByVal lName As String)
    Me.acctNumber = num
    Me.acctBalance = 0
    Me.FirstName = fName
    Me.LastName = lName
    Me.AddTransaction("New Account", False, acctBalance)
End Sub
```

② MODIFY THE EXISTING CONSTRUCTOR

Modify the default constructor to include just one statement:

```
Sub New()
    Me.New(DEFAULT_ACCT_NUM)
End Sub
```

③ MODIFY AND THEN RUN THE APPLICATION

a. Display the Form1 Code window.
b. Modify the global variable declaration that instantiates an `Account` object:

```
Dim acct1 As New Account("1234")
```

c. Save and run the application. Click **Balance Inquiry**. Note the account number.
d. Click **Transactions**. Note the new account transaction.

④ PRINT THE CODE AND THEN CLOSE THE PROJECT

Extending a Class

Often times an existing class can provide a basis for a new class. For example, the specification for a `CommercialAccount` class closely resembles the `Account` class. However, the `CommercialAccount` class should also include a CompanyName property and the minimum required balance should be $500 with a low balance fee of $10. Rather than create a whole new class, `CommercialAccount` could extend the `Account` class.

inheritance

Making one class an extension of another involves inheritance. *Inheritance* allows a class to define a specialized type of an already existing class. A class that inherits another class by using the `Inherits` statement in the new class:

```
Public Class CommercialAccount

  Inherits Account

  'Property member

  Property CompanyName() As String

End Class
```

derived class
base class

The `Inherits` statement gives the new class all the features of an existing class. The new class is called the *derived class* and the inherited class is called the *base class*. New properties and methods in the derived class extend the base class.

Polymorphism

Polymorphism is an object-oriented programming (OOP) feature that allows methods in a base class to be redefined in derived classes. This can make a single method appear polymorphic, changing its task to meet the needs of the object calling it. For example, a commercial account may have different withdrawal fees. Therefore, a MakeWithdrawal() method should be included in the `CommercialAccount` class to override the method in `Account`.

A base class should be written with derived classes in mind. Methods that are general purpose are declared with the keyword `Overridable`. A derived class can then redefine the method with a new method by the same name with the keyword `Overrides`. Members that are general purpose should be declared `Protected` so that they are accessible to the derived class.

The `MyBase` keyword is used to refer to the base class. It is used in a statement similar to `MyBase.New()` to call the base class constructor. The base class constructor should be called to initialize data members in the base class.

To override field members, a derived class can include data by the same name with the keyword `Shadows`. For example, a commercial account has a higher minimum balance. Therefore, a `MIN_REQUIRED_BALANCE` field with a different value is needed for the derived `CommercialAccount` class.

The `CommercialAccount` class is shown below. Note how simple it appears because it inherits a base class:

```
Public Class CommercialAccount

  Inherits Account

  'Public field members

  Shadows Const MIN_REQUIRED_BALANCE As Decimal = 500 '$500
  Shadows Const LOW_BALANCE_FEE As Decimal = 10       '$10

  'Constructor

  Sub New(ByVal num As String, ByVal acctName As String)
      MyBase.New(num)     'call base class
      Me.CommercialAcctName = acctName
  End Sub

  'Property members

  Property CompanyName() As String

  'Public method

  Public Overrides Sub MakeWithdrawal _
  (ByVal withdrawalAmt As Decimal,
  ByRef errorCode As Boolean)
      If withdrawalAmt <= acctBalance Then   'make withdrawal
          acctBalance -= withdrawalAmt
          errorCode = False
          AddTransaction("Withdrawal", errorCode,
          acctBalance)
          'determine if balance has fallen below
          'required amount
          If acctBalance < MIN_REQUIRED_BALANCE Then
              acctBalance -= LOW_BALANCE_FEE
              errorCode = False
              AddTransaction("Low Bal Fee", errorCode,
              acctBalance)
          End If
      Else                        'withdrawal not permitted
          errorCode = True
          AddTransaction("Withdrawal", errorCode,
          acctBalance)
      End If
  End Sub

End Class
```

Reusing Code

An important aspect of object-oriented programming is code reuse. Well-developed and tested classes can be used over and over again in applications or as base classes by many different classes. To add an existing class to a project, select Project → Add Existing Item. The Add Existing Item dialog box is displayed:

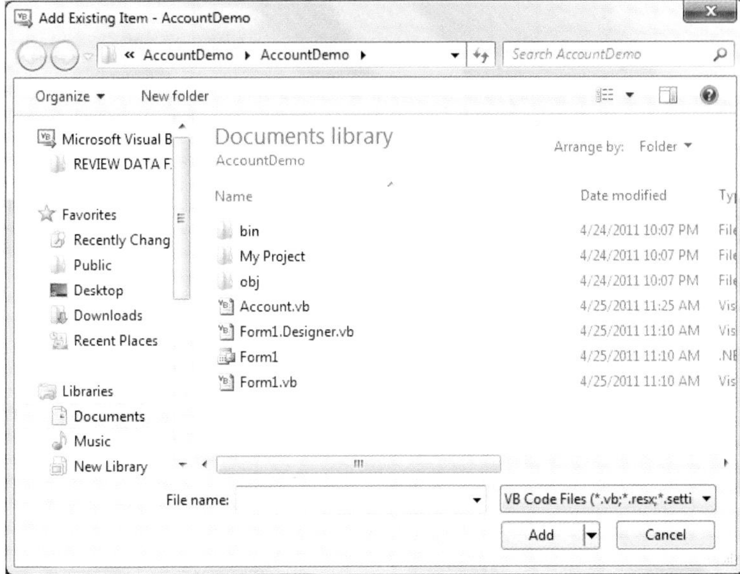

Navigate to display the project folder containing the class to add to the project. Click the class name and then select Add to add the class to the project. The class name will appear in the Solutions Explorer window where it can be opened by double-clicking it.

Another way to reuse code is to use the interface from an existing application for a new application. This is useful when an application should have an interface similar to an existing application. Just as the Add Existing Item command was used for adding a class, this command can be used to add an existing form. In the Add Existing Item dialog box, display the project folder with the form to be copied. The form file name will be `Form1.vb`. Clicking the form name and then selecting Add copies the form to the current project. Warning dialog boxes may be displayed. Yes should be selected in each. Note that the form code is copied as well as the interface overwriting any existing Form1 code.

Review: CommercialAcctDemo

① CREATE A NEW PROJECT

Create a Windows application named `CommercialAcctDemo`.

② ADD THE INTERFACE

The interface for this project will be copied from the AccountDemo project.

a. Select Project → Add Existing Item. A dialog box is displayed.

1. Navigate to display the contents of the AccountDemo project.
2. Click Form1.vb.

3. Select **Add**. Several warning dialog boxes may be displayed. Select **Yes** in each. The form from the AccountDemo project is displayed.

b. Modify the Form Text property to `Commercial Account Demo`.

c. Update comments as appropriate.

③ ADD THE ACCOUNT CLASS

The `Account` class will be copied from the AccountDemo project.

Select **Project → Add Existing Item**. A dialog box is displayed.

1. Navigate to display the contents of the AccountDemo project.
2. Click `Account.vb`.
3. Select **Add**. The Account.vb file is added to the CommercialAcctDemo project, as shown in the Solution Explorer window.

④ MODIFY THE ACCOUNT CLASS

a. In the Solution Explorer window, double-click the Account.vb file name. The `Account` class is displayed.

b. Change the `acctNumber` and `acctBalance` declarations from `Private` to `Protected` because they need to be accessed in the derived class. Move the declarations above the private data members and add a comment so that your code looks similar to:

```
...
'Protected data members

Protected acctNumber As String
Protected acctBalance As Decimal

'Private data members

Private activity(-1) As Transaction
Private customer As PersonalInfo
...
```

c. Change the MakeWithdrawal() declaration to `Overridable` because it needs to be redeclared in the derived class:

```
Public Overridable Sub MakeWithdrawal(ByVal withdrawalAmt As Decimal,
ByRef errorCode As Boolean)
```

⑤ ADD A NEW CLASS MODULE

a. Select **Project → Add Class**. A dialog box is displayed.

1. In the **Templates** list, click Class, if it is not already selected.
2. In the **Name** box, type `CommercialAccount.vb`.
3. Select **Add**. The CommercialAccount.vb Code window is displayed.

b. Save the project.

⑥ WRITE THE COMMERCIALACCOUNT CLASS

a. Below the `Public Class CommercialAccount` statement, add an `Inherits` statement:

```
Public Class CommercialAccount

    Inherits Account
```

b. Below the `Inherits` statement, add comments, two field members, and a data member.

```
'Public field members

Shadows Const MIN_REQUIRED_BALANCE As Decimal = 500 '$500
Shadows Const LOW_BALANCE_FEE As Decimal = 10       '$10

'Private data member

Private commercialAcctName As String
```

c. Below the field and data members, add a comment and a constructor:

```
'Constructor

Sub New(ByVal num As String, ByVal acctName As String)
    MyBase.New(num)     'call base class
    Me.CommercialAcctName = acctName
End Sub
```

d. Below the constructor, add a comment and a property:

```
'Property member

Property CompanyName() As String
```

e. Below the property, add a comment and a method that overrides the `Account` MakeWithdrawal() method:

```
'Public method

Public Overrides Sub Withdrawal(ByVal withdrawalAmt As Decimal,
ByRef errorCode As Boolean)
    If withdrawalAmt <= acctBalance Then        'make withdrawal
        acctBalance -= withdrawalAmt
        errorCode = False
        AddTransaction("Withdrawal", errorCode, acctBalance)
        'Determine if balance has fallen below required amount
        If acctBalance < MIN_REQUIRED_BALANCE Then      'service charge
            acctBalance -= LOW_BALANCE_FEE
            errorCode = False
            AddTransaction("Low Bal Fee", errorCode, acctBalance)
        End If
    Else                                        'withdrawal not permitted
        errorCode = True
        AddTransaction("Withdrawal", errorCode, acctBalance)
    End If
End Sub
```

⑦ MODIFY THE FORM CODE

a. In the Form1 Code window, modify the global variable declaration to instantiate a `CommercialAccount` object:

```
Dim comAcct1 As New CommercialAccount("3985", "My Company")
```

b. Select **Edit → Quick Replace** and then replace all occurrences of `acct1` with `comAcct1`.

c. Add statements to the end of the btnModifyAccount_Click event procedure to allow the company name to be modified:

```
'Change company name
textEntered = InputBox("Company name is: " & comAcct1.CompanyName &
vbCrLf & "Enter new company name (Cancel to keep the same):", Me.Text)
'Test data entered
If textEntered <> Nothing Then     'new company name
    comAcct1.CompanyName = textEntered
End If
```

⑧ RUN THE APPLICATION

a. Run the application. Click Balance Inquiry. Note the account number.

b. Use the buttons to make deposits, withdrawals, and account modifications. View the transactions by clicking Transactions. Note how the low balance fee is different for a commercial account.

c. Close CommercialAcctDemo.

⑨ PRINT THE CODE AND THEN CLOSE THE PROJECT

Case Study

In this case study a triangle calculator application will be created. This application will include a `Triangle` class.

TriangleCalculator Specification

The TriangleCalculator displays information about a triangle based on the length of its sides. The user is prompted for the length of sides a, b, and c. The user can then display the triangle area, perimeter, and type.

TriangleCalculator Design

The interface for TriangleCalculator is a form that prompts the user for the length of the triangle sides. Buttons are included to allow the user to display the area, perimeter, and triangle type:

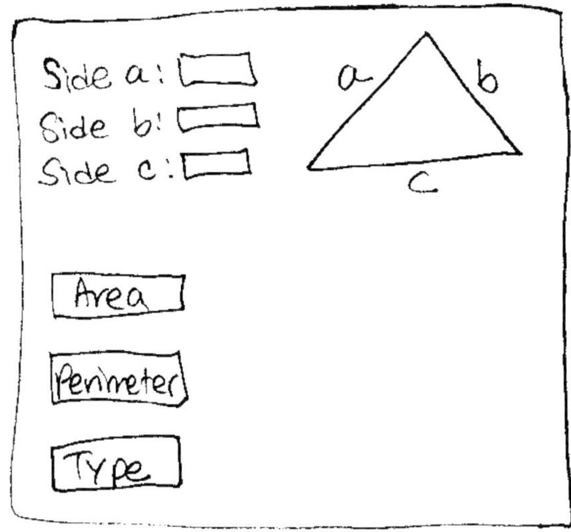

The algorithm for this Case Study is straightforward. However, since the application is about triangles, which have a clear set of related calculations and properties, a `Triangle` class should be implemented. The `Triangle` class starts with a specification:

- Triangles have three sides, commonly referred to as side a, side b, and side c. Sides a and b are the shorter sides and their sum must be greater than side c.
- The area of a triangle is computed using the semiperimeter and the length of sides a, b, and c: $\sqrt{s(s-a)(s-b)(s-c)}$
- The triangle type can be determined with the following formulas:

  right triangle: $c^2 = a^2 + b^2$

  acute triangle: $c^2 < a^2 + b^2$

  obtuse triangle: $c^2 > a^2 + b^2$

From the class specification, a list of members can be determined:

- A constructor that accepts three numeric values corresponding to side a, side b, and side c, respectively, and calculates the semiperimeter of the triangle.
- Side_a, Side_b, and Side_c properties for getting and setting side lengths.
- An s property for getting the semiperimeter.
- A private IsValidTriangle() method that indicates if sides a, b, and c form a triangle.
- A GetArea() method that returns a value corresponding to the area of the triangle and –1 if the sides do not form a valid triangle.
- The GetName() method that returns a string corresponding to the triangle type (right, acute, obtuse).

Based on the `Triangle` class design, the class pseudocode appears like:

```
Public Class Triangle
    Private SideA As Double
    Private SideB As Double
    Private SideC As Double
    Private Semiperimeter As Double

    Property a() As Double

    Property b() As Double

    Property c()

    ReadOnly Property s() As Double
        Get
            Return Semiperimeter
        End Get
    End Property
```

```
'Constructor
Sub New(ByVal a As Double, ByVal b As Single, _
ByVal c As Single)
    Me.sideA = a
    Me.sideB = b
    Me.sideC = c
    Me.Semiperimeter = 0.5 * (sideA + sideB + sideC)
End Sub

'Private method
Private Function IsValidTriangle() As Boolean
    If sideA + sideB > sideC Then        'valid triangle
        Return True
    Else                                 'invalid triangle
        Return False
    End If
End Function

'Public function
Public Function GetArea() As Double
    if IsValidTriangle() Then
        'Heron's formula
        Return Math.Sqrt(semiperimeter * _
        (semiperimeter – sideA) * (semiperimeter – sideB) * _
        (semiperimeter – sideC))
    Else
        Return -1
End Function

Public Function GetName() As String
    if IsValidTriangle() Then
        Select Case sideC ^ 2
            Case sideA ^ 2 + sideB ^ 2
                Return "Right triangle."
            Case Is < SideA ^ 2 + SideB ^ 2
                Return "Acute triangle."
            Case Else
                Return "Obtuse triangle."
        End Select
    Else
        Return "Not Valid"
End Function

End Class
```

The TriangleCalculator pseudocode is:

```
Private Sub Calculate(ByVal sender As Object, _
ByVal e As System.EventArgs) Handles btnArea.Click, _
btnPerimeter.Click, btnType.Click
    Dim sideA As Double = value from txtSideA text box
    Dim sideB As Double = value from txtSideB text box
    Dim sideC As Double = value from txtSideC text box
    Dim UserTriangle As New Triangle(sideA, sideB, sideC)
```

```
    Dim btnButtonClicked As Button = sender

    Select Case btnButtonClicked.Tag
        Case "Area"
            If userTriangle.GetArea = -1 Then
                Me.lblArea.Text = "Invalid Measurements"
            Else
                Me.lblArea.Text = userTriangle.GetArea
            End If
        Case "Perimeter"
            Me.lblPerimeter.Text = userTriangle.s * 2
        Case "Type"
            Me.lblType.Text = userTriangle.GetName
End Sub

Private Sub SideChanged(ByVal sender As Object, _
ByVal e As System.EventArgs) Handles txtSideA.TextChanged, _
txtSideB.TextChanged, txtSideC.TextChanged
    Clear labels
End Sub
```

TriangleCalculator Coding

The interface for TriangleCalculator is:

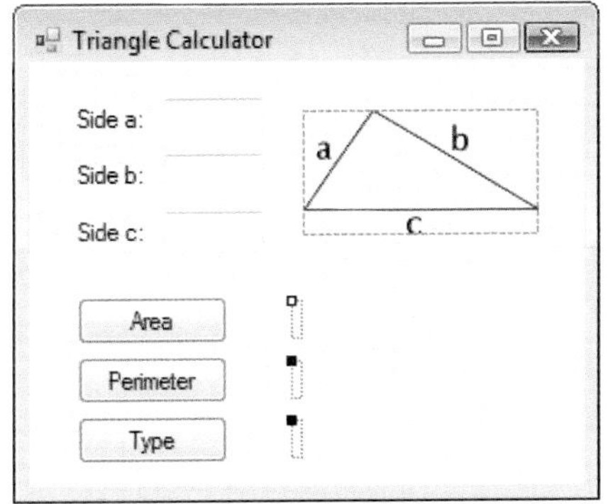

Object	**(Name)**	**Text**	**Tag**
Form1		Triangle Calculator	
Label1	lblSideAPrompt	Side a:	
TextBox1	txtSideA	*empty*	
Label2	lblSideBPrompt	Side b:	
TextBox2	txtSideB	*empty*	
Label3	lblSideCPrompt	Side c:	
TextBox3	txtSideC	*empty*	
PictureBox1	picTriangle		
Button1	btnArea	Area	Area
Button2	btnPerimeter	Perimeter	Perimeter
Button3	btnType	Type	Type
Label4	lblArea	*empty*	
Label5	lblPerimeter	*empty*	
Label6	lblType	*empty*	

The PictureBox object should display the `triangle` image.

The final coding for TriangleCalculator is:

```
Public Class Triangle

    'Private data members

    Private sideA As Double
    Private sideB As Double
    Private sideC As Double
    Private semiperimeter As Double

    'Constructor

    Sub New(ByVal a As Double, ByVal b As Double, ByVal c As Double)
        Me.sideA = a
        Me.sideB = b
        Me.sideC = c
        Me.semiperimeter = 0.5 * (sideA + sideB + sideC)
    End Sub

    'Property members

    Property Side_a() As Double

    Property Side_b() As Double

    Property Side_c() As Double

    ReadOnly Property s() As Double
        Get
            Return semiperimeter
        End Get
    End Property

    'Private method

    'Returns True if sides a, b, and c are valid for a triangle.
    '
    'pre: side a < side b < side c
    'post: True has been returned if the sum of sides a and b
    'are greater than side c. False has been returned otherwise.
    '
    Private Function IsValidTriangle() As Boolean
        If sideA + sideB > sideC Then
            Return True
        Else
            Return False
        End If
    End Function

    'Public methods

    'Returns the area of a valid triangle, -1 returned otherwise.
    '
    'post: The area of this triangle has been returned if sides
    'a, b, and c make up a valid triangle. -1 has been returned
    'otherwise.
    '
    Public Function GetArea() As Double
        If IsValidTriangle() Then
            'Heron's formula
            Return Math.Sqrt(semiperimeter * (semiperimeter - sideA) * _
            (semiperimeter - sideB) * (semiperimeter - sideC))
        Else
            Return -1
```

```
        End If
    End Function

    'Returns the type (right, acute, or obtuse) of a valid
    'triangle, Not Valid returned otherwise.
    '
    'post: The type of the triangle has been returned if sides
    'a, b, and c make up a valid triangle. Not Valid has been
    'returned otherwise.
    '
    Public Function GetName() As String
        If IsValidTriangle() Then
            Select Case sideC ^ 2
                Case sideA ^ 2 + sideB ^ 2
                    Return "Right Triangle"
                Case Is < sideA ^ 2 + sideB ^ 2
                    Return "Acute Triangle"
                Case Else
                    Return "Obtuse Triangle"
            End Select
        Else
            Return "Not Valid"
        End If
    End Function

End Class
```

```
Public Class Form1

    Private Sub Calculate(ByVal sender As Object,
    ByVal e As System.EventArgs) Handles btnArea.Click,
    btnPerimeter.Click, btnType.Click
        Dim sideA As Double = Val(Me.txtSideA.Text)
        Dim sideB As Double = Val(Me.txtSideB.Text)
        Dim sideC As Double = Val(Me.txtSideC.Text)
        Dim userTriangle As New Triangle(sideA, sideB, sideC)
        Dim btnButtonClicked As Button = sender

        Select Case btnButtonClicked.Tag
            Case "Area"
                If userTriangle.GetArea = -1 Then
                    Me.lblArea.Text = "Invalid Measurements"
                Else
                    Me.lblArea.Text = userTriangle.GetArea
                End If
            Case "Perimeter"
                Me.lblPerimeter.Text = userTriangle.s * 2
            Case "Type"
                Me.lblType.Text = userTriangle.GetName
        End Select
    End Sub

    Private Sub SideChanged(ByVal sender As Object, ByVal e As System.EventArgs) _
    Handles txtSideA.TextChanged, txtSideB.TextChanged, txtSideC.TextChanged
        Me.lblArea.Text = Nothing
        Me.lblPerimeter.Text = Nothing
        Me.lblType.Text = Nothing
    End Sub
End Class
```

TriangleCalculator Testing and Debugging

Running TriangleCalculator, entering values for sides, and clicking Area, Perimeter, and Type displays an interface similar to:

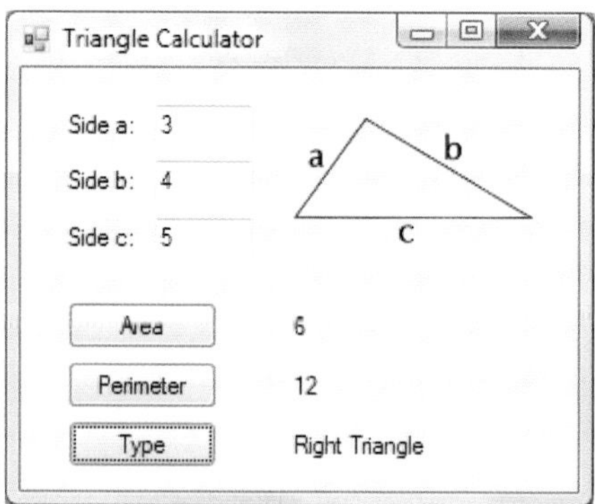

The TriangleCalculator application should be tested by typing invalid values as well as values that correspond to the three triangle types.

Review: TriangleCalculator

Modify the TriangleCalculator application to include a Height button. Clicking this button should display the height of the triangle with sides as typed by the user. The height of a triangle can be calculated with the formula height=2*area/c. Implement GetHeight() as a method of the Triangle class.

Chapter Summary

A class is an abstract data type that groups related data and procedures and is the basis of object-oriented programming. A class is used to create objects. A statement declaring a new object uses the class as the data type and is said to instantiate the object. Classes have members that can include data, properties, and methods. These members are available to objects of the class. Objects are instantiated in a `Dim` statement that includes the `New` keyword.

A class should be created when an application requires a related set of data and actions. Before coding a class, a design that includes a list of members should be created. From the design, an algorithm and pseudocode should be generated.

A class is coded in a Class module, which is added to a project by selecting Project → Add Class. A new class module contains a class declaration. There can be numerous fields, data members, properties, and methods in a class. In general, a class and its members takes the form:

```
Public Class ClassName

  Public Const field member declaration

  Private Const field member declaration

  Private data member declaration
```

```
    Property PropertyName() As DataType

    Sub New()
        statements for initializing the object
    End Sub

    Public Sub MethodName(parameters)
        statements to perform a task
    End Sub

    Protected Sub MethodName(parameters)
        statements to perform a task
    End Sub

End Class
```

The methods of a class are the only way an object can change its data values. Limiting access to data is called data hiding and is the basis for encapsulation, an important aspect of object-oriented programming.

Encapsulation is accomplished by using access modifiers. The `Private` access modifier is used to declare a field or data member as accessible to only the methods of the class. `Protected` is used to declare a member that can be used from within the class only. `Public` is used to explicitly declare a member available to an object of the class. In a Form1 module, public methods, properties, and fields appear in an IntelliSense list after typing an object name followed by a dot.

A field is used to store a constant in a class. Fields declared as `Private Const` can be used in methods of the class only. A `Public Const` field can be used by an object of the class as well as methods of the class and is called a class constant. Data members are variables used by the methods and properties in a class.

A constructor is a method that is automatically called when an object is instantiated. Statements for initializing data members can be placed in the constructor. Constructors are commonly overloaded. A set of methods that each have the same name but a different set of parameters are said to be overloaded.

A new class can extend an existing class. The `Inherits` statement is used in the class declaration to give the new class all the features of an existing class. The new class is called the derived class and the inherited class is called the base class.

Polymorphism is an object-oriented programming (OOP) feature that allows methods to be redefined in derived classes. Methods must be overridable in the base class in order to be redefined in the derived class. The `Shadows` keyword can be used to override a field member in the base class with a member of the same name in the derived class.

An important aspect of object-oriented code is code reuse. An existing class can be added to a project with the Add Existing Item command. Another way to reuse code is to use the Add Existing Item command to add an existing form.

Code conventions introduced in this chapter are:

- Class names should be a noun and begin with an uppercase letter.

Vocabulary

Access modifier Keywords that control access to members.

Base class A class that is inherited by another class.

Class An abstract data type that groups related data and procedures.

Class constant A constant in a class that is accessible to objects and methods of a class, as well as from the class itself.

Class module A separate file used to code a new class. Appears as a separate code window containing a class declaration in the IDE.

Constructor A method that is automatically called when an object is instantiated.

Data hiding Limiting access to data in a class.

Data member A variable member in a class.

Derived class A class based on another class.

Encapsulation Data hiding in a class. Implemented with access modifier keywords.

Field member A constant member in a class.

Inheritance The OOP property in which a class can define a specialized type of an already existing class.

Instantiation Creating an object of a class by using a `Dim` statement with a class name as the data type.

Method member A member of a class that is a type of procedure.

Object An instance of a class.

Overloaded A method that performs an action depending on the number and type of arguments it receives.

Polymorphic A method that can appear to change its task to meet the needs of the object calling it.

Property member A member of a class that can get (display) and set (assign) a value that is a data member of an object's class.

Add Class command Adds a new module with a Class declaration to an open project. Found in the Project menu.

Add Existing Item command Adds an existing form or class to a project. Found in the Project menu.

Get() Procedure used for returning a data member value to a calling object.

`Inherits` Statement used in a Class declaration to give a new class all the features of an existing class.

`MyBase` Keyword used to refer to a base class.

`New` Keyword used in a statement to instantiate a new object.

`Overridable` Keyword used in a base class method declaration to allow a general purpose method to be redefined in a derived class.

`Overrides` Keyword used in a derived class method declaration to redefine a method from the base class.

`Private` Access modifier keyword that declares a member of a class as accessible to the class only.

`Private Const` Declaration used in a statement to declare a field as accessible to the class only.

`Property` Statement used to declare a property for a class.

`Protected` Access modifier keyword that declares a member of a class as accessible to the class and derived classes.

`Public` Access modifier keyword that declares a member of a class as accessible to class objects.

`Public Class` Statement used to declare a new class.

`Public Const` Declaration used in a statement to declare a field as accessible to the class and class objects.

`ReadOnly` Keyword used in a property declaration to allow a class object to get the property value, but not set the value.

Set() Procedure used to give a data member a new value from the calling object.

`Shadows` Keyword used in a derived class field declaration to redefine a field.

Critical Thinking

1. Programmers using an OOP language often analyze a task to distinguish between the nouns in the problem and the verbs in the problem. This helps them decide between the needed methods and classes. Fill in either method or property:
   a) Nouns (person, place, thing) help decide the __________ needed.
   b) Verbs (action) help decide the __________ needed.

2. Imagine a band festival where many bands are playing—the TwoToos, the EggRolls, and Goop. Each band can TuneUp, PlayMusic, and TakeABow. A SetList can be read or created. If this was simulated in an object-oriented program, what would appropriate names be for:
   a) the class
   b) the objects
   c) a property
   d) the methods

3. Assume a class for a sports team named Team.
   a) List three possible object names.
   b) List three possible methods.
   c) List three possible properties.

4. What is the difference between a class and an object?

5. a) Explain the similarities and differences between field members, data members, and property members. Be sure to discuss their accessibility within the class and with objects of the class.
   b) What keyword is required to prevent a property's value from being changed?

6. State the keyword needed for each:
   a) the method in a base class that will be redefined in a derived class
   b) a field member in a base class that will be redefined in a derived class
   c) a method that is redefined in a derived class
   d) a data member that is accessible to methods of the class only
   e) a method of a class that cannot be directly called by an object of the class
   f) a method of a class that can be called by an object of the class
   g) base class field members and data members that are expected to be redefined in a derived class

7. How does Visual Basic know which overloaded method to use?

8. a) What is data hiding, and how is it related to encapsulation?
   b) How is data hiding accomplished?

9. What are two ways to reuse code?

10. Explain the similarities and differences between inheritance and polymorphism.

11. Assume a base class named `FamilyMembers` and derived classes `Parent` and `Child`.
    a) List three possible methods or properties that would be in both derived classes.
    b) List three possible methods or properties that would be specific to the `Parent` class.
    c) List three possible methods or properties that would be specific to the `Child` class.

12. Write a statement to instantiate an object named `invoice1` of type `Invoice`.

13. Use the following class code to answer the questions below:

```
Public Class Foo
    Inherits Moo

    Shadows Const ZOO As Single = 20
    Private Const VOO As String = "You"
    Private Goo As String
    Property Coo() As String
    ...
    End Property
    Public Overrides Sub Too()
    ...
    End Sub
    Protected Sub Woo()
    ...
    End Sub
End Class
```

    a) What is the derived class?
    b) What is the base class?
    c) Which method has been redefined?
    d) Which data member is new to the derived class?
    e) Which field member has been redefined?

f) Which field member is new to the derived class?
g) Which method can be called from the derived class only?
h) Which is a new property for the derived class?
i) Assume `Loo` is a string data member in the base class. How should its declaration appear in the base class if `Loo` should be accessible to members of the derived class?

14. a) Write the statement needed to instantiate a Car object of the `Vehicle` class.
    b) What does the following code in the `Vehicle` class do?

```
Private Const DEFAULT_FASTONE As _
String = "Concord"

Sub New()
    Me.Fastest = DEFAULT_FASTONE
End Sub
```

    c) Write a statement for the Form1 code module which displays the fastest car for an object in a message in a message box, similar to: The fastest car is ______.

True/False

15. Determine if each of the following is true or false. If false, explain why.
    a) Instantiation is the process of creating a new class.
    b) A class is coded in the Form1 code module.
    c) A class uses encapsulation to limit accessibility of certain members.
    d) An IntelliSense list displays all the methods of the class for an object.
    e) Constants used in a class are called fields.
    f) A protected field member can be used by the class only.
    g) A `ReadOnly` property has a Set() procedure.
    h) Overloaded methods allow different actions with the same number of parameters.
    i) Only constructor methods can be overloaded.
    j) The code for an inherited class needs to be in the same project as the derived class.
    k) All methods from a base class can be redefined in a derived class.
    l) A derived class can have methods and properties not found in the base class.
    m) Methods must always be Sub procedures.

Exercises

Exercise 1 — LocalBank

Create a LocalBank application that is based on the AccountDemo reviews created in this chapter. LocalBank should use the Account class with some modifications. LocalBank should require that an account first be retrieved before any actions can be taken. Adding an account should also be allowed when the application starts. The first image below shows the application at start up. The second image below shows the application after adding at least one account, retrieving a valid account, and making transactions.

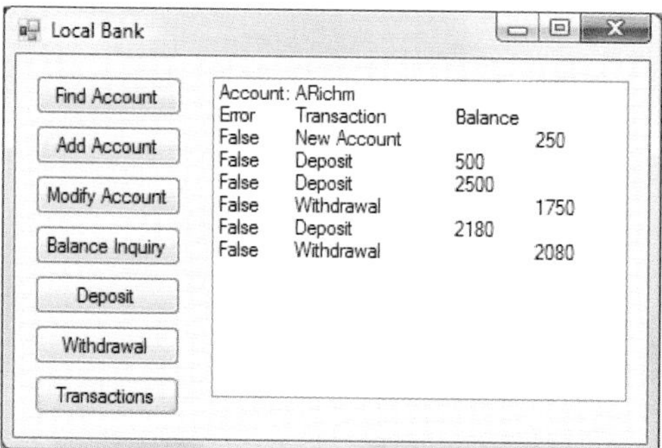

The Account class should:

- include the `Account` class, as mentioned above. However, there should not be a `DEFAULT_ACCT_NUM` member because every account number must be unique. The `Account` class should be modified to include just one constructor which accepts a first name, a last name, and an initial deposit. The constructor should set the account number to the first letter of the first name and the first 5 letters of the last name. The AcctNum property will need to be modified to be a read-only property.

The LocalBank Form1 code should:

- include two global declarations:

```
Dim activeAcct As Account        'current account to receive transactions
Dim accounts(-1) As Account      'array of accounts
```

- have the btnModifyAccount_Click event procedure coded to change only the first and last names of the account holder.
- use the active account (`activeAcct`) when any of the other buttons on the interface are clicked.
- include a GetAcctNum() function that returns the index location in the array of the account with the indicated account number or –1 otherwise.

- include the following code for the btnFindAccount_Click and btnAddAccount_Click event procedures:

```
Private Sub btnFindAccount _ Click(ByVal sender As Object,
ByVal e As System.EventArgs) Handles btnFindAccount.Click
    Dim acctNum As String
    Dim acctIndex As Integer

    acctNum = InputBox("Enter the number of the account to retrieve:",
    "Find Account")
    acctIndex = GetAcctNum(acctNum)
    If acctIndex <> -1 Then
        'Set active account
        activeAcct = accounts(acctIndex)
        'Enable actions on active account
        Me.btnBalanceInquiry.Enabled = True
        Me.btnDeposit.Enabled = True
        Me.btnModifyAccount.Enabled = True
        Me.btnTransactions.Enabled = True
        Me.btnWithdrawal.Enabled = True
    Else
        MessageBox.Show("Invalid account.")
    End If
End Sub

Private Sub btnAddAccount _ Click(ByVal sender As Object,
ByVal e As System.EventArgs) Handles btnAddAccount.Click
    Dim firstName, lastName As String
    Dim initDeposit As Double
    Dim newAcct As Account

    firstName = InputBox("Enter the account holder's first name:", "First Name")
    lastName = InputBox("Enter the account holder's last name:", "Last Name")
    initDeposit = InputBox("Enter the account holder's initial deposit:",
    "Initial Deposit")

    'Create new account and add to array of accounts
    newAcct = New Account(firstName, lastName, initDeposit)
    ReDim Preserve accounts(accounts.Length)  'increase array by 1
    accounts(accounts.Length - 1) = newAcct
End Sub
```

Exercise 2 — Employees

Create an Employees application that allows the user to enter data for as many employees as wanted and then displays information for a specific employee. The application interface should look similar to the following after adding several new employees and updating and displaying employee information:

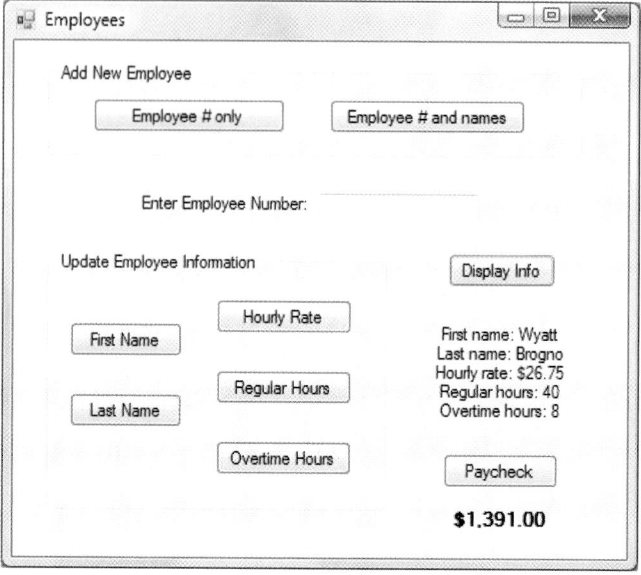

Your program code should:

- include an Employee class, as described below.
- use a dynamic array of Employee objects to maintain a set of employees.
- display input boxes for user input.
- include a FindItemIndex() function that returns the index location in the array of the employee with the indicated employee number or –1 otherwise.
- display messages indicating "Not valid." if the employee number does not exist.
- display formatted output.

The Employee class should include the following members:

- an Employee data member that is type Double. PersonalInfo is a structure that contains employeeNum, firstName, and lastName string members.
- a Payroll data member that is type Double. PayrollInfo is a structure that contains hourlyRate, regularHours, and overtimeHours single members.
- properties that allow for getting and setting of each piece of Employee and Payroll data.
- a constructor that has a string parameter for the employee number to initialize EmployeeNum. The constructor should also include statements that initialize HourlyRate to 5 and RegularHours to 40.
- a constructor that accepts an employee number, first name, and last name string parameters to initialize EmployeeNum, FirstName, and LastName respectively. The constructor should also include statements that initialize HourlyRate to 5 and RegularHours to 40.
- Paycheck() public function that returns the paycheck amount. The paycheck amount is calculated by multiplying regular hours worked by hourly rate and adding the overtime hours multiplied by time and a half (hourly rate x 1.5).

Exercise 3 — Students

Create a Students application that allows the user to enter data for as many students as wanted and then display information for a specific student. The application interface should look similar to the following after entering a first and last name, clicking Display Full Name, clicking Enter Score several times to enter scores, and clicking each button to display information:

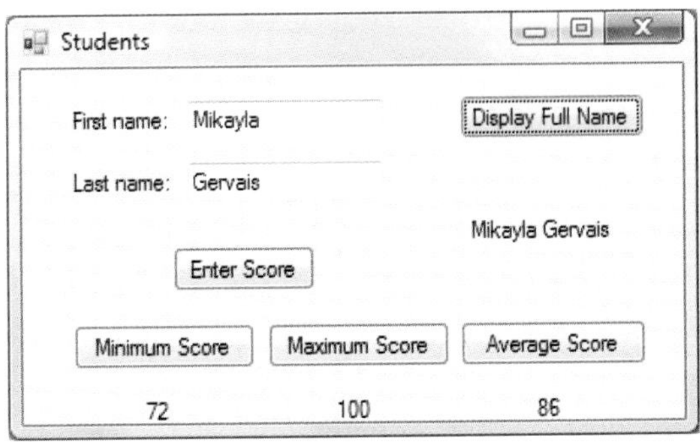

The Students application should contain a class named `Student` with the following members:

- FirstName and LastName properties.
- FullName read-only property for displaying a student's full name. Hint: Concatenate the first name and last name.
- Avg, Max, and Min read-only properties for getting the average, maximum, and minimum scores entered for the student.
- A NewScore() public method for adding a new score to the student's total score. The average, minimum, and maximum should be updated when a new score is added.

Exercise 4 — TestDynamicArray

Create a TestDynamicArray application that is similar to the DynamicArrayDemo application presented in Chapter 8. The application interface should look similar to the following after adding several values, removing values, and clicking Sum:

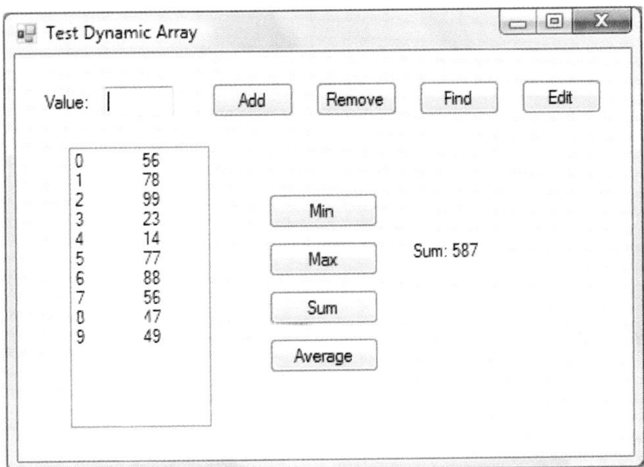

The TestDynamicArray application should contain a class named `DynamicArray` with the following members:

- a dynamic array data member with zero integer elements.
- Sum, Avg, Max, and Min read-only properties for getting the sum, average, max, and min of the numbers in the array.
- AddItem() and DeleteItem() public methods that add an item to or remove an item from the array, respectively.
- FindItemIndex() public function that returns the index of the item being searched for or –1 otherwise.
- Edit() public function that replaces an old element value with a new element value and returns 0 if successful and –1 if the index is invalid.
- GetStats() protected method that calculates the sum, average, maximum, and minimum values of the array contents and is called by AddItem, DeleteItem, and Edit every time a change is made to the array.
- DisplayContents() public method that displays the array contents in a list box.

The TestDynamicArray should contain the event procedure below:

```
Private Sub AButton_Click(ByVal sender As System.Object,
ByVal e As System.EventArgs) Handles btnAdd.Click, btnRemove.Click, btnFind.Click,
btnEdit.Click, btnMax.Click, btnMin.Click, btnSum.Click, btnAverage.Click
    Static Numbers As New DynamicArray()
    Dim num As Integer
    Dim ButtonClicked As Button = sender
    If Me.txtValue.Text = Nothing And (ButtonClicked.Tag = "Add" Or
    ButtonClicked.Tag = "Remove" Or ButtonClicked.Tag = "Find" Or
    ButtonClicked.Tag = "Edit") Then
        MessageBox.Show("Type a value before selecting a button.")
    Else
        num = Val(Me.txtValue.Text)

        Select Case ButtonClicked.Tag
            Case "Add"
                Numbers.AddItem(num)
            Case "Remove"
                Numbers.DeleteItem(num)
            Case "Find"
                Dim result As Integer = Numbers.FindItemIndex(num)
                If result = -1 Then
                    Me.lblDisplay.Text = num & " not found."
                Else
                    Me.lblDisplay.Text = num & " found at index: " & result
                End If
            Case "Edit"
                Dim newValue As Integer = Val(InputBox("Enter new value "))
                Dim result As Integer = Numbers.Edit(num, newValue)
                If result = -1 Then
                    Me.lblDisplay.Text = "The value " & num & " not found."
                Else
                    Me.lblDisplay.Text = "Value changed."
                End If
            Case "Min"
                Me.lblDisplay.Text = "Min: " & Numbers.ShowMin
            Case "Max"
                Me.lblDisplay.Text = "Max: " & Numbers.ShowMax
            Case "Sum"
                Me.lblDisplay.Text = "Sum: " & Numbers.ShowSum
```

```
            Case "Average"
                Me.lblDisplay.Text = "Average:  " & Numbers.ShowAverage
        End Select
        Numbers.DisplayContents(Me.lstOutput)
    End If
    Me.txtValue.Text = Nothing
    Me.txtValue.Select()
End Sub
```

Exercise 5 ——— MyPizzaShop

Create a MyPizzaShop application, similar to the PizzaOrder case study from Chapter 4. Use a `Pizza` class to instantiate new pizza objects. The `Pizza` class should have the following members:

- REGULAR_PRICE and LARGE_PRICE fields that store 6 and 10 respectively (for $6 and $10). Additional fields to store topping prices. Other data members will be needed for storing the base pizza price, the number of toppings, the toppings price, and the pizza size.
- A read-only PizzaPrice property for getting the price of the pizza and a Size property for getting and setting the size of the pizza.
- A constructor that takes no parameters and initializes the size to regular, the pizza price to the regular base price, the number of toppings to 0, and the toppings price to 0.
- A Public AddTopping() that increments the number of toppings and modifies the toppings price.

Exercise 6 ——— NameOptions

Create a NameOptions application that prompts the user for first, middle, and last names and provides several options for displaying the names in different ways. The project should include a `Name` class with the following members:

- a constructor with three parameters that initialize First, Middle, and Last data members.
- A FullName() read-only property that returns a single string containing First, Middle, and Last names separated by spaces.
- A LastCommaFirst() read-only property that returns a single string containing the Last name followed by a comma and a space and then the First name.
- A Signature() read-only property that returns a single string containing the First name followed by a space, the first initial of Middle name followed by a space, and then Last name.
- An Initials() read-only property that returns a single string containing the first initial of First name, first initial of Middle name, and then the first initial of Last name.
- A Monogram() read-only property that returns a single string containing the first initial of First name, the uppercase first initial of Last name, and then the first initial of Middle name.

Exercise 7 — MetricSystem

Create a MetricSystem application with options that demonstrates all the features of a `Metric` class, which should include:

- INCH_CENT_FACTOR, FEET_CENT_FACTOR, YARD_METER_FACTOR, and MILE_KILO_FACTOR field members that store the conversion factors 2.54, 30, .91, and 1.6, respectively.
- InchToCent() and CentToInch() public functions that return the unit of measurement from inches to centimeters or from centimeters to inches. Inches are converted to centimeters by multiplying the value in inches by the InchCentFactor conversion factor (2.54). Centimeters are converted to inches by dividing the value in centimeters by InchCentFactor.
- FeetToCents() and CentsToFeet() public functions that return the unit of measurement from feet to centimeters or from centimeters to feet. Feet is converted to centimeters by multiplying the value in feet by the FeetCentFactor conversion factor (30). Centimeters are converted to feet by dividing the value in centimeters by FeetCentFactor.
- YardsToMeters() and MetersToYards() public functions that return the unit of measurement from yards to meters or from meters to yards. Yards are converted to meters by multiplying the value in yards by the YardMeterFactor conversion factor (.91). Meters are converted to yards by dividing the value in meters by YardMeterFactor.
- MilesToKilos() and KilosToMiles() public functions that return the unit of measurement from miles to kilometers or from kilometers to miles. Miles are converted to kilometers by multiplying the value in miles by the MileKiloFactor conversion factor (1.6). Kilometers are converted to miles by dividing the value in kilometers by MileKiloFactor.

Chapter 11
Using Files

Key Concepts

Using files for data input
Creating, copying, and deleting files at run time
Understanding file streams
Using a text box to display file contents
Writing Keypress event procedures
Including Open and Save As dialog boxes
Reusing existing code

Case Study

Word Guess II

Review Data Files

motto.txt

Exercise Data Files

sentences.txt
verbs.txt
nouns.txt

What is a File?

Up to this point, the applications created in this text have stored data in the computer's memory in the form of variables and arrays. However, storage in memory is available only when the computer is on and an application is running. Data can also be saved in a file stored on a hard disk, CD, or memory key for later retrieval and modification. A *file* is a collection of related data stored on a persistent medium. *Persistent* simply means lasting.

persistent

Files often store data used by an application. A file is separate from the application using it and can be read from and written to by more than one application. Most applications require access to one or more files on disk.

> **Creating a Text File**
>
> A word processor such as Notepad or TextPad can be used to create a text file. When saving the document, be sure to use the **Save As** command to save the information as a TXT file with the `.txt` file name extension.

The FileInfo Class

The Visual Basic `FileInfo` class is used to create an object for a specific file. The `FileInfo` class constructor requires a file name when an object is instantiated, as in the declaration:

```
Dim schoolSuppliesList As New FileInfo("mylist.txt")
```

Property and method members of the `FileInfo` class include:

- **Exists** returns a `Boolean` value. `True` indicates the file exists and `False` indicates the file does not exist.
- **Length** returns a value that is the file size in bytes.
- **FullName** returns a string that is the full path and file name of the file associated with the `FileInfo` object.

- **Create()** creates a new, empty file using the name in the object declaration.
- **CopyTo(*newFilename*)** copies the existing file associated with the `FileInfo` object to `newFilename`, which cannot already exist.
- **Delete()** permanently deletes the file associated with the `FileInfo` object.

Using the `FileInfo` class requires an `Imports System.IO` statement at the top of the code module.

> ***Creating a File at Runtime***
>
> If a path is not specified, a file is created in the bin\Debug folder of the project folder. If the project has not yet been saved when the application is run, the file is saved in a temp folder.

The following code demonstrates the `FileInfo` properties and methods:

```
'Create object for specific file
Dim schoolSuppliesList As New FileInfo("mylist.txt")
If Not schoolSuppliesList.Exists Then     'file does not exist
  schoolSuppliesList.Create()             'create empty file
  MessageBox.Show("New file created.")
Else                   'Display full path, name, and file size
  MessageBox.Show(schoolSuppliesList.FullName &
  " exists. File size: " & SchoolSuppliesList.Length)
End If

'Copy school supplies list to a new file
schoolSuppliesList.CopyTo("newlist.txt")

'Delete file with school supplies list
schoolSuppliesList.Delete()
```

Review: MyFile

① CREATE A NEW PROJECT

Create a Windows application named `MyFile`.

② CREATE THE INTERFACE

Use the table below for setting object properties.

Object	(Name)	Text
Form1		`My File`
Button1	`btnCreateFile`	`Create File`
Button2	`btnDeleteFile`	`Delete File`

③ WRITE THE APPLICATION CODE

a. Display the Code window.

b. Add comments that include your name, application, and today's date.

c. At the very top of the code module, add an `Imports System.IO` statement. The Code window should look similar to:

```
Imports System.IO

Public Class Form1

End Class
```

d. Add a global variable declaration:

```
Const FILE _ NAME As String = "myfile.txt"
```

e. Create a btnCreateFile_Click event procedure and then add the statements:

```
Dim testFile As New FileInfo(FILE _ NAME)
If Not testFile.Exists Then                'file does not exist
    testFile.Create()                      'create an empty file
    MessageBox.Show("New file created.")
Else                                       'display full path, name, and file size
    MessageBox.Show(testFile.FullName & " exists. File size: "
    & testFile.Length)
End If
```

f. Create a btnDeleteFile_Click event procedure and then add the statements:

```
Dim testFile As New FileInfo(FILE _ NAME)
testFile.Delete()
MessageBox.Show(testFile.FullName & " deleted.")
```

④ RUN THE APPLICATION

a. Save the modified MyFile project.
b. Run the application. Click **Create File**. A message box informs that a new file has been created. Click **Create File** again. A message box informs that the file exists.
c. Close the MyFile application.
d. Run the application again. Select **Delete File**. The file is deleted.
e. Close the MyFile application.

⑤ PRINT THE CODE AND THEN CLOSE THE PROJECT

The File Stream

In Visual Basic, a file must be associated with a stream in order to perform operations on its contents, such as reading the contents, writing over the existing contents, and adding to the existing contents. The *file stream* keeps track of the *file position*, which is the point where reading or writing last occurred. File streams usually perform *sequential file access*, with all reading and writing done one character after another or one line after another. The stream can also be closed to prevent further file access.

file position

sequential access file

> **Data Streams**
>
> A stream applies to data input/output in general. For example, memory, information sent to a printer, and data sent and received from an Internet site can all be streamed.

A *stream* can be thought of as a sequence of characters. For example, a file containing a list of school supplies may look like the following when viewed in a word processor:

6 pens
binder

However, when thinking about file operations, the file should be visualized as a stream:

A file can be thought of as a stream of characters

line terminator, end of file

The carriage return character (Cr) followed by a line feed character (Lf) is called a *line terminator*. A –1 indicates *end of file*.

The FileStream and StreamReader Classes

The Visual Basic `FileStream` class is used to create a stream object for a specific file. The `FileStream` constructor requires a file name, mode, and type of access to instantiate an object, as in the declaration:

```
Dim fs As New FileStream("motto.txt", FileMode.Open,
FileAccess.Read)
```

The file mode indicates how the file should be opened or created. When reading from a file, the mode should be `FileMode.Open`, which is a constant that indicates an existing file should be opened. `FileAccess.Read` is a constant that indicates that the file should be opened for reading only.

Property and method members of the `FileStream` class include:

- **Length** returns a value that is the file size in bytes.
- **Position** can be set at run time to 0, which positions the file stream at the beginning of the file.
- **Close()** closes the file. Once a file stream is closed, a new one must be declared to access a file.

After a stream has been established, a stream reader can be used to read characters and lines of text from a file. The Visual Basic `StreamReader` class contains methods for reading data from a stream. The `StreamReader` constructor requires an existing stream to instantiate an object, as in the declaration:

```
Dim textFile As New StreamReader(fs)
```

Method members of the `StreamReader` class include:

- **Peek** returns the value of the next character without actually taking it from the stream.
- **Read** returns the next character in the stream as a integer value. ChrW() must be used to convert the integer to a character. If the character represents a number, Val() then be used to convert the character to a number.
- **ReadLine** returns the next set of characters up to the line terminator in the stream as a string.
- **Close()** closes the stream reader.

peeking

The end of file can be determined by looking ahead, or *peeking*, to the next character in the stream. A value of –1 indicates the end of the file has been reached. The code below demonstrates this as well as some methods for the `FileStream` and `StreamReader` classes:

```
Dim fs As New FileStream("motto.txt", FileMode.Open,
FileAccess.Read)
Dim textFile As New StreamReader(fs)

Dim lineOfText As String       'stores a line read from a file
Do While textFile.Peek > -1    'check for the end of file
   lineOfText = textFile.ReadLine()
   MessageBox.Show(lineOfText) 'display a line of text
Loop

textFile.Close()
fs.Close()
```

Statements are included to close the stream reader and stream when no longer needed as a matter of good programming style.

It is easiest to think of a file as a stream of characters. However, it is also important to remember that each character corresponds to a Unicode value that is numeric. For example, the character "a" corresponds to 97 and the character "5" corresponds to 53. When using the Read() method, the ChrW() function is used to convert the Unicode value to a character, as in the code:

Unicode

A space corresponds to 32, a tab to 9, carriage return to 13, and line feed to 10. Refer to Chapter 5 for more information about Unicode.

```
Dim charFromFile As Char  'stores a character read from a file
Do While textFile.Peek > -1    'check for the end of file
   charFromFile = ChrW(textFile.Read)  'convert Unicode
   MessageBox.Show(charFromFile)       'display character
Loop

textFile.Close()
fs.Close()
```

If a stream contains data that should be treated as numeric rather than as characters, then Val() should also be used. For example, the statement below converts a Unicode value to a character and then the character's numeric equivalent:

```
numFromFile = Val(ChrW(TextFile.Read)) 'number expected
```

Using the `FileStream` and `StreamReader` classes requires the `Imports System.IO` statement at the top of the code module. When procedures are written to manipulate a file stream, only the stream reader `ByRef` parameter is needed.

Advanced TextBox Features

A text box is the best choice for displaying several lines of text at a time, which may be necessary to display the entire contents of a file. For example, the application interface below contains two text boxes. The bottom text box can display many lines of text. The text box is docked, so that it changes size along with the form if the user sizes the interface at run time. Also note the scroll bars for displaying additional lines of text:

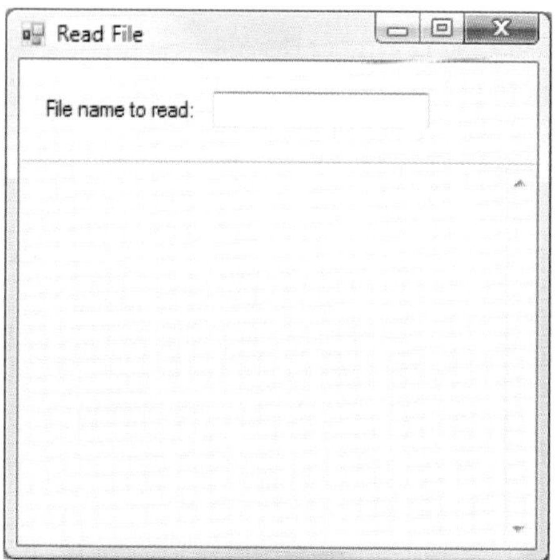

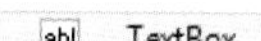

The TextBox control has the properties:

- **(Name)** identifies an object for the programmer. TextBox object names should begin with `txt`.
- **Dock** is the location of docking for the text box. Setting Dock to Bottom sizes the text box so that the bottom, right, and left borders are anchored to the form. Fill sizes the text box to the size of the form. Dock can also be set to Top, Left, or Right.
- **ReadOnly** is set to True when the text box should be used for output only. When ReadOnly is True, text can be displayed in the text box, but the user will not be able to type in the text box.
- **Multiline** is set to True to allow the text box to display multiple lines of text. The box can then be sized vertically.
- **WordWrap** is set to True to wrap lines of text at the right border of the text box. WordWrap can be set to False, but it is not recommended because only one line of text will be displayed and it may extend beyond the right border of the text box.
- **ScrollBars** is set to Vertical to add a vertical scroll bar to the text box. A vertical scroll bar appears only when the WordWrap and Mutliline properties are also set to True. ScrollBars can also be set to None, Horizontal, or Both.

The interface shown above also includes a text box for getting the file name. A TextBox object can respond to a Keypress event, which occurs when the user types in a text box. For example, the following KeyPress event procedure performs an action when the Enter key is pressed:

```
Private Sub txtFileName _ KeyPress(ByVal sender As Object,
ByVal e As System.Windows.Forms.KeyPressEventArgs)
Handles txtFileName.KeyPress
   'User pressed the Enter key
   If e.KeyChar = ChrW(Keys.Enter) Then
      Dim fileNameTyped As New FileInfo(Me.txtFileName.Text)
      If fileNameTyped.Exists Then
         Call ShowFileContents(Me.txtFileName.Text)
      Else
         MessageBox.Show("File does not exist.")
      End If
   End If
End Sub
```

In the procedure heading, the `e` parameter contains properties specific to the key pressed. These properties include KeyChar, used in the `If...Then` condition, which stores a `Char` corresponding to the key pressed. Also used in the `If...Then` condition is the Visual Basic `Keys` enumerated type with members that correspond to key names. Typing `Keys.` in the Code window displays an IntelliSense list with member names. The ChrW() function is used to convert the `Enum` member to a character.

Review: ReadFile – part 1 of 2

① CREATE A NEW PROJECT

Create a Windows application named `ReadFile`.

② CREATE THE INTERFACE

Use the table and instructions below for setting object properties.

Object	(Name)	Text
Form1		`Read File`
Label1	`lblPrompt`	`File name to read:`
TextBox1	`txtFileName`	*empty*
TextBox2	`txtFileContents`	*empty*

Set the txtFileContents ReadOnly and Multiline properties to True. Set the ScrollBars property to Vertical. Click the Dock property arrow and then click the bottom box to set Dock to Bottom, as shown on the next page:

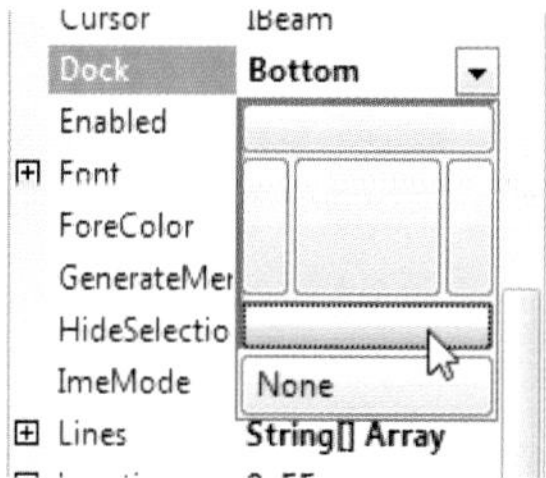

After setting properties, size the text box to extend just below the file name prompt.

③ WRITE THE APPLICATION CODE

a. Display the Code window.

b. Add comments that include your name, application, and today's date.

c. At the very top of the code module, add an `Imports System.IO` statement.

d. Create a txtFileName_KeyPress event procedure and then add the statements:

```
'User pressed the Enter key
If e.KeyChar = ChrW(Keys.Enter) Then
    Dim fileNameTyped As New FileInfo(Me.txtFileName.Text)
    If fileNameTyped.Exists Then
        Call ShowFileContents(Me.txtFileName.Text)
    Else
        MessageBox.Show("File does not exist.")
    End If
End If
```

e. Create a ShowFileContents Sub procedure:

```
Sub ShowFileContents(ByVal fileName As String)
    Dim fs As New FileStream(fileName, FileMode.Open, FileAccess.Read)
    Dim textFile As New StreamReader(fs)
    Dim lineOfText As String

    'Clear text box of previous contents
    Me.txtFileContents.Text = Nothing

    Do While textFile.Peek > -1            'check for the end of file
        lineOfText = textFile.ReadLine()
        'Display line of text
        Me.txtFileContents.Text &= lineOfText & vbCrLf
    Loop

    textFile.Close()
    fs.Close()
End Sub
```

④ RUN THE APPLICATION

You will need the `motto.txt` file that is a data file for this text. Copy `motto.txt` to the bin\Debug folder in the ReadFile project folder.

a. Save the modified ReadFile project and then run the application. Type `motto.txt` in the first text box. Press Enter. The file contents are displayed in the multiline text box. Try to type in the multiline text box. Input is not accepted because the text box is read only.

b. Close the ReadFile application.

⑤ PRINT THE CODE

The OpenFileDialog Control

Rather than expecting the user to remember the full path and file name of a file, the Open dialog box can be used. The OpenFileDialog component can be added to an application to display a predefined dialog box that allows the user to select a file by browsing:

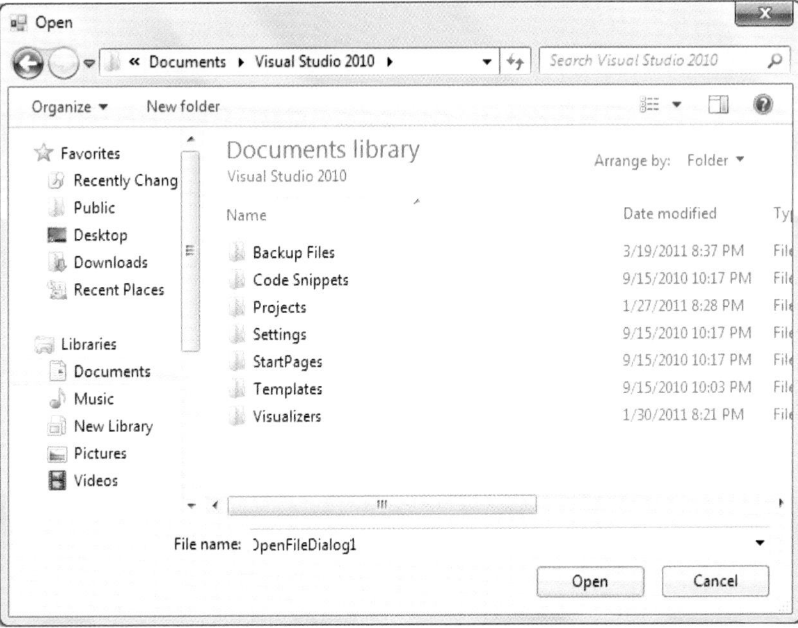

When this dialog box is displayed, the file selected by the user can be assigned to a string variable for opening a file stream.

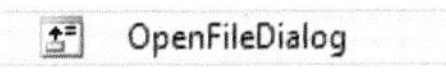

To add an Open dialog box to an application, click the OpenFileDialog control in the Toolbox, and then click the form. A component is displayed in the component tray at the bottom of the Design window. The OpenFileDialog control is a component that has no graphical element.

The OpenFileDialog control has the property:

- **FileName** is the file, including its path, selected in the dialog box.

The Open dialog box is displayed with a statement similar to:

```
Me.OpenFileDialog1.ShowDialog()
```

`OpenFileDialog1` is the name of the component added to the interface. ShowDialog() is the method of the `OpenFileDialog` class that displays the dialog box.

The FileName property of an OpenFileDialog component contains the file name selected by the user. For example, the first statement below displays the Open dialog box. The application waits until the user selects Open or Cancel in the dialog box before continuing to the next statement. The second statement assigns the selected file name to a string, and the third statement creates a file stream for the selected file:

```
Me.OpenFileDialog1.ShowDialog()        'show dialog box
Dim fileName As String = Me.OpenFileDialog1.FileName
If fileName <> Nothing Then
  Dim fs As New FileStream(strFileName, FileMode.Open,
  FileAccess.Read)
End If
```

If the user selects Cancel in the dialog box, `Nothing` is returned.

Review: ReadFile – part 2 of 2

① MODIFY THE INTERFACE

a. Delete the lblPrompt and txtFileName objects from the interface.

b. Add a MenuStrip object to the interface.

c. Type `File` for the first MenuItem.

d. For the second menu item, type `Open`.

e. For the third menu item, type `Exit`.

f. Check the names of the three menu items. Change their (Name) properties as appropriate to `FileToolStripMenuItem`, `OpenToolStripMenuItem`, and `ExitToolStripMenuItem`, if necessary.

g. Select the text box and change the Dock property to Fill (the large middle option).

h. Add an OpenFileDialog component to the interface.

Check – The menu and interface should look similar to:

i. Clear the FileName property of the OpenFileDialog1 object.

② MODIFY THE APPLICATION CODE

a. Display the Code window.

b. Delete the txtFileName_KeyPress event procedure.

c. Create an OpenToolStripMenuItem_Click event procedure and add the statements to open an existing file and display its contents:

```
Me.OpenFileDialog1.ShowDialog()      'open dialog box

'Assign selected file name
Dim fileName As String = Me.OpenFileDialog1.FileName

'Display file contents
If fileName <> Nothing Then
    Call ShowFileContents(fileName)
End If
```

d. Create a ExitToolStripMenuItem_Click event procedure and then add a statement to end the application:

```
Application.Exit()
```

③ RUN THE APPLICATION

a. Save the modified ReadFile project.

b. Run the application. Select File → Open. The Open dialog box is displayed. Navigate to the bin\Debug folder of the project folder and then select `motto` (or `motto.txt`). Select Open. The file contents are displayed.

c. Select File → Exit. The ReadFile application is closed.

④ PRINT THE CODE AND THEN CLOSE THE PROJECT

The StreamWriter Class

Writing to a file also requires setting up a stream. The following statement instantiates a `FileStream` object for a new file named `temp.txt` that can be written to:

```
Dim fs As New FileStream("temp.txt", FileMode.Create,
FileAccess.Write)
```

The `FileMode.Create` constant creates a new file and then opens it. If the file already exists, it is overwritten. Other file modes used when opening a file for writing include:

- `CreateNew` creates a new file only if a file by the same name does not exist and then opens the file.
- `OpenOrCreate` opens a file if it exists or creates a new file and then opens it.
- `Append` opens an existing file. Data written to the file is added to the end of existing data.

A stream writer is used to write characters and lines of text to a file stream. The Visual Basic `StreamWriter` class contains methods for writing data to a stream. The `StreamWriter` constructor requires an existing stream to instantiate an object, as in the declaration:

```
Dim textFile As New StreamWriter(fs)
```

Method members of the `StreamWriter` class include:

- **Write(*char*)** writes `char` character to the stream.
- **WriteLine(*string*)** writes `string` `String` followed by a line terminator to the stream. If a `string` argument is not included, then a blank line is written to the stream.
- **Close()** closes the stream writer.

The code below demonstrates writing to a file:

```
Dim fs As New FileStream("temp.txt", FileMode.Create,
FileAccess.Write)
Dim textFile As New StreamWriter(fs)
Dim lineOfText As String      'line of text to write to file

lineOfText = "This is a text file."
textFile.WriteLine(lineOfText)
textFile.WriteLine()
lineOfText = "a"
textFile.Write(lineOfText)
lineOfText = "b"
textFile.Write(lineOfText)

textFile.Close()
fs.Close()
```

The stream writer and stream must be closed for the file to be properly written to.

Reading the `temp.txt` file after the code executes displays:

```
This is a text file.

ab
```

Using the `FileStream` and `StreamWriter` classes requires the `Imports System.IO` statement at the top of the code module. When procedures are written to manipulate a file stream, only the stream writer `ByRef` parameter is needed.

The SaveFileDialog Control

Rather than expecting the user to type the full path and file name of a file, the Save As dialog box can used. A SaveFileDialog component can be added to an application to display a predefined dialog box that allows the user to select a location by browsing:

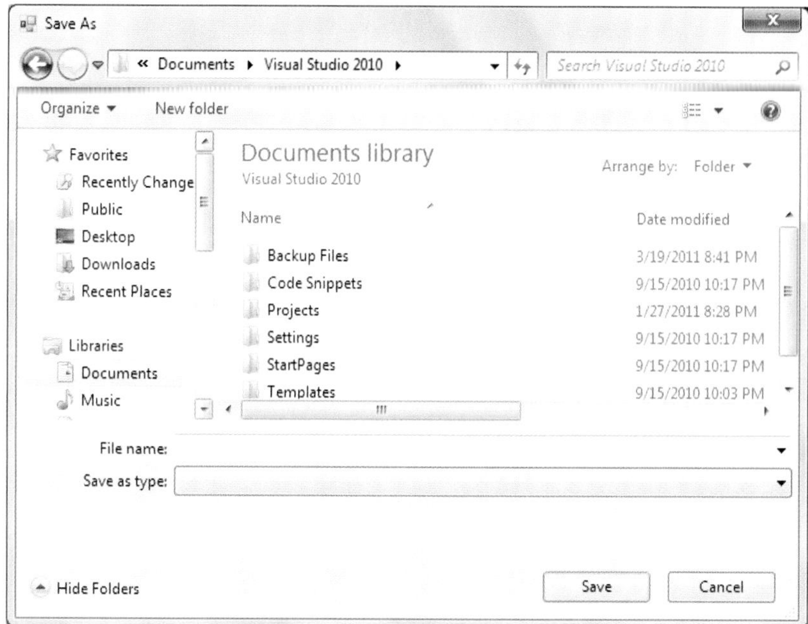

When this dialog box is displayed, the user can navigate to the folder where the file should be saved, and then type a descriptive name in the File name box. Selecting Save saves the file using the typed name.

To add a Save As dialog box to an application, click the SaveFileDialog control in the Toolbox, and then click the form. A component is displayed in the component tray at the bottom of the Design window. The SaveFileDialog control is a component that has no graphical element.

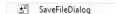

SaveFileDialog

The SaveFileDialog control has the properties:

- **FileName** can be set to a name that will be the default text displayed in the File name box of the dialog box. This text will be returned if the user selects Save without changing the name. This text is also returned if the user selects Cancel.

An application that contains this component displays the dialog box with a statement similar to:

```
SaveFileDialog1.ShowDialog()
```

`SaveFileDialog1` is the name of the component added to the interface. ShowDialog() is the method of the `SaveFileDialog` class that displays the dialog box.

The FileName property of a SaveFileDialog component contains the file name typed by the user. For example, the first statement below displays the Save As dialog box. The application waits until the user selects Save or Cancel in the dialog box before continuing to the next statement. The remaining statements create a file stream and stream writer and write the contents of a text box to the file:

```
Me.SaveFileDialog1.ShowDialog()    'display Save As dialog box
Dim fileName As String = Me.SaveFileDialog1.FileName
Dim fs As New FileStream(fileName, FileMode.Create,
FileAccess.Write)
Dim textFile As New StreamWriter(fs)
'Write text box contents to file
textFile.Write(Me.txtFileContents.Text)
```

Note that the file stream FileMode is `Create`, which overwrites an existing file or creates a new file if one does not exist. This FileMode should be used because the SaveFileDialog automatically warns the user when an existing file name is selected, allowing the user to choose whether or not to overwrite an existing file.

If the user selects **Cancel** in the dialog box, the default file name specified in the FileName property is returned.

Review: WriteFile – part 1 of 2

① CREATE A NEW PROJECT

Create a Windows application named WriteFile.

② CREATE THE INTERFACE

Use the table and instructions below for setting object properties.

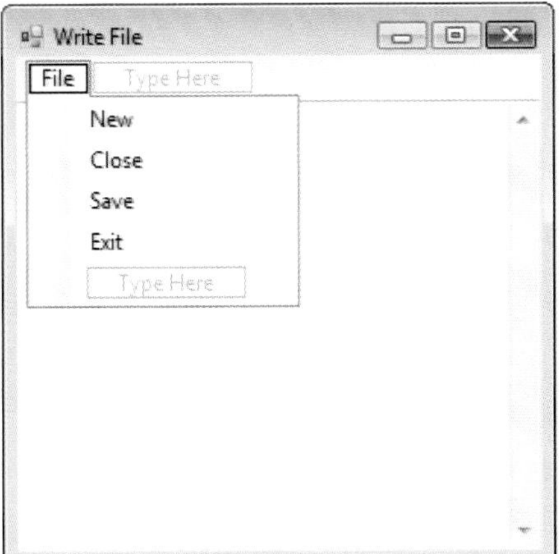

Object	(Name)	Text
Form1		`Write File`
MenuItem1		`File`
MenuItem2		`New`
MenuItem3		`Close`
MenuItem4		`Save`
MenuItem5		`Exit`
SaveFileDialog1		
TextBox1	`txtFileContents`	*empty*

a. Check the names of the menu items. Change their (Name) properties as appropriate to `FileToolStripMenuItem`, `NewToolStripMenuItem`, `CloseToolStripMenuItem`, `SaveToolStripMenuItem`, and `ExitToolStripMenuItem`.

b. Set the txtFileContents Dock property to Fill. Set the Multiline property to True. Set the ScrollBars property to Vertical.

c. Indicate a default file name in the FileName property of the SaveFileDialog1 object.

③ WRITE THE APPLICATION CODE

a. Display the Code window.
b. Add comments that include your name, application, and today's date.
c. At the very top of the code module, add an `Imports System.IO` statement.
d. Create a NewToolStripMenuItem_Click event procedure and then add a statement to clear the file contents box:

```
Me.txtFileContents.Text = Nothing
```

e. Create a CloseToolStripMenuItem_Click event procedure and then add a statement to remove any text from the file contents box:

```
Me.txtFileContents.Text = Nothing
```

f. Create a SaveToolStripMenuItem_Click event procedure and then add statements to save the contents of the text box to a file:

```
Me.SaveFileDialog1.ShowDialog()                         'display Save As dialog box
Dim fileName As String = Me.SaveFileDialog1.FileName   'get file name
Dim fs As New FileStream(fileName, FileMode.Create, FileAccess.Write)
Dim textFile As New StreamWriter(fs)

textFile.Write(Me.txtFileContents.Text)              'write text box contents to file

textFile.Close()
fs.Close()
```

g. Create a ExitToolStripMenuItem_Click event procedure and then add a statement to end the application:

```
Application.Exit()
```

④ RUN THE APPLICATION

a. Save the modified WriteFile project.
b. Run the application. Type some text in the text box. Select File → Save. The Save As dialog box is displayed. Navigate to the bin\Debug folder of the project folder and then type a descriptive file name with the `.txt` extension. Select Save. The file is saved.
c. Test the other commands.
d. Close the WriteFile application.

⑤ PRINT THE CODE

Review: WriteFile – part 2 of 2

Modify the WriteFile application created in the previous review to include an Open command. Selecting this command should display the Open dialog box, allowing the user to select a file. Use the ShowFileContents() procedure from Review: ReadFile – part 1 of 2 to display the file contents of the file selected by the user.

Reading and Writing Data

Applications often use files for data input. For example, a teacher might use an application that computes an average for a set of grades. If this application read the grades from a file, there would be no need to modify the application itself, only the file containing the data needs to be updated when a different student's grades are to be computed.

The StreamWriter class WriteLine() method converts data to a string before writing it to a file. For example, the statements:

```
Dim x As Integer = 25
Dim b As Boolean = True
Dim d As Date = #12/22/2012#
textFile.WriteLine(x)
textFile.WriteLine(b)
textFile.WriteLine(d)
```

produce the file:

```
25
True
12/22/2012 12:00:00 AM
```

Note that a default time is also written for a date.

To read numeric data from a file, the `StreamReader` class is used to read strings and then the strings must be converted to the proper data type, as in the statements:

```
Dim x As Integer = Val(textFile.ReadLine())
Dim b As Boolean = textFile.ReadLine()
Dim d As Date = textFile.ReadLine()
Me.lblFileContents.Text = x & " " & b & " " & d
```

display in the label:

```
25 True 12/22/2012
```

Note that only a date is displayed.

The Write() method can be used similarly to write data without a line terminator. The Read() method must then be used to read the file character by character.

Review: GradeCalculator

The GradeCalculator application allows a teacher to create student records and display average grades. The specification for this application is:

> The teacher must be able to enter a record for a student that includes the student's name and five grades. Selecting the **Add Student** command adds the student record to the end of a file named `stugrades.txt`. The **Clear Grades** command deletes the `stugrades.txt` file. The **Show Grades** command reads each student's name and corresponding set of grades and then displays each name and average grade rounded to 1 decimal place in separate message boxes.

① CREATE A NEW PROJECT

Create a Windows application named `GradeCalculator`.

② CREATE THE INTERFACE

Use the table below for setting object properties. There are two screens below to better show all the objects:

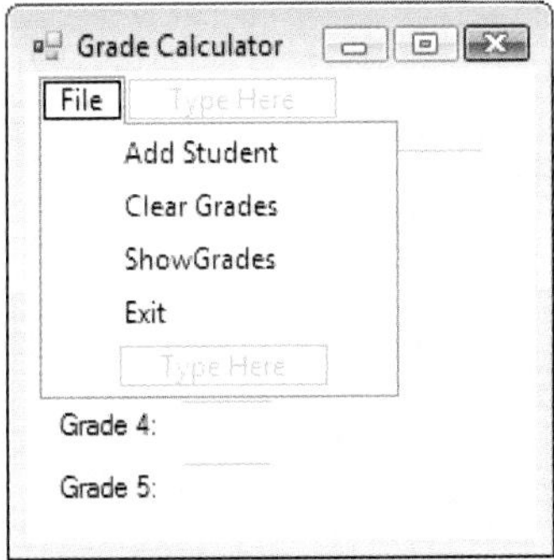

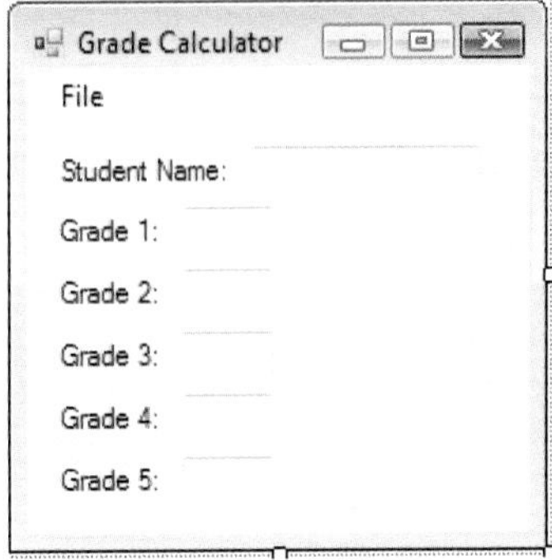

Object	**(Name)**	**Text**
Form1		Grade Calculator
MenuItem1		File
MenuItem2		Add Student
MenuItem3		Clear Grades
MenuItem4		Show Grades
MenuItem5		Exit
Label1	lblStuNamePrompt	Student Name:
TextBox1	txtStudentName	*empty*
Label2	lblGrade1Prompt	Grade 1:
TextBox2	txtGrade1	*empty*
Label3	lblGrade2Prompt	Grade 2:
TextBox3	txtGrade2	*empty*
Label4	lblGrade3Prompt	Grade 3:
TextBox4	txtGrade3	*empty*
Label5	lblGrade4Prompt	Grade 4:
TextBox5	txtGrade4	*empty*
Label6	lblGrade5Prompt	Grade 5:
TextBox6	txtGrade5	*empty*

Check the names of the menu items. Change their names as appropriate to `FileToolStripMenuItem`, `AddStudentToolStripMenuItem`, `ClearGradesToolStripMenuItem`, `ShowGradesToolStripMenuItem`, and `ExitToolStripMenuItem`, if necessary.

③ WRITE THE APPLICATION CODE

a. Display the Code window.

b. Add comments that include your name, application, and today's date.

c. At the very top of the code module, add an `Imports System.IO` statement.

d. Add two global constants and comments for each:

```
'File containing student data
Const FILE_NAME As String = "stugrades.txt"

'Number of grades entered for each student
Const NUM_GRADES As Integer = 5
```

e. Create an AddStudentToolStripMenuItem_Click event procedure with documentation and statements that add a student record to the data file and then clear the text boxes for the next student record:

```
'Adds a student name and five (5) grades to a data file. Clears
'text boxes for new record.
'
'post: A data file has been created, if necessary, and opened for adding data
'(append) to the end of existing data. Student name and five (5)
'grades (numeric scores) have been added to the end of the file.
'
Private Sub AddStudentToolStripMenuItem_Click(ByVal sender As Object,
ByVal e As System.EventArgs) Handles AddStudentToolStripMenuItem.Click
    'create new file if necessary and open file for appending data
    Dim fs As New FileStream(FILE_NAME, FileMode.Append, FileAccess.Write)
    Dim textFile As New StreamWriter(fs)

    'Write student name and data to file
    textFile.WriteLine(Me.txtStudentName.Text)
    textFile.WriteLine(Me.txtGrade1.Text)
    textFile.WriteLine(Me.txtGrade2.Text)
    textFile.WriteLine(Me.txtGrade3.Text)
    textFile.WriteLine(Me.txtGrade4.Text)
    textFile.WriteLine(Me.txtGrade5.Text)

    'Close stream writer and file stream
    textFile.Close()
    fs.Close()

    'Clear text boxes for new data
    Me.txtStudentName.Text = Nothing
    Me.txtGrade1.Text = Nothing
    Me.txtGrade2.Text = Nothing
    Me.txtGrade3.Text = Nothing
    Me.txtGrade4.Text = Nothing
    Me.txtGrade5.Text = Nothing
End Sub
```

f. Create a ShowGradesToolStripMenuItem_Click event procedure with documentation and statements that read student information from the data file, compute an average grade, and display this information in a message box:

```
'Reads student names and NUM_GRADES grades and then displays
'each student name with an average score in a message box.
'
'post: Data has been read from data file and an average score
'has been computed and displayed for each student.
'
Private Sub ShowGradesToolStripMenuItem_Click(ByVal sender As Object,
ByVal e As System.EventArgs) Handles ShowGradesToolStripMenuItem.Click
    Dim fs As New FileStream(FILE_NAME, FileMode.Open, FileAccess.Read)
    Dim textFile As New StreamReader(fs)
    Dim student As String
    Dim totalScore, averageScore As Double

    Do While textFile.Peek > -1
        student = textFile.ReadLine              'read student name
        totalScore = 0                           'initialize score for each student
        For studentNum As Integer = 1 To NUM_GRADES       'sum grades
            totalScore += Val(textFile.ReadLine)
        Next studentNum
        averageScore = Math.Round((totalScore / NUM_GRADES), 1)
        MessageBox.Show(student & " " & averageScore)
    Loop
```

```
        textFile.Close()
        fs.Close()
    End Sub
```

g. Create a ClearGradesToolStripMenuItem_Click event procedure with documentation and statements that delete the existing data file:

```
    'Deletes the existing data file.
    '
    'post: FILE _ NAME file has been deleted.
    '
    Private Sub ClearGradesToolStripMenuItem _ Click(ByVal sender As Object,
    ByVal e As System.EventArgs) Handles ClearGradesToolStripMenuItem.Click
        Dim dataFile As New FileInfo(FILE _ NAME)
        dataFile.Delete()
    End Sub
```

h. Create a ExitToolStripMenuItem_Click event procedure with a statement to end the application:

```
    Application.Exit()
```

④ RUN THE APPLICATION

a. Save the modified GradeCalculator project.
b. Run the application. Test the application by adding two students and their grades and then show the grade averages.
c. Close the GradeCalculator application.

⑤ PRINT THE CODE AND THEN CLOSE THE PROJECT

Case Study

In this case study the WordGuess application created in Chapter 5 will be modified to play a game with a randomly selected word from a file.

WordGuessII Specification

The WordGuessII application allows the user to guess the letters in a secret word. The secret word is randomly selected from a file containing 25 words that each have from 3 to 8 characters. The secret word is represented as a row of dashes on the form, with one dash for each letter. The user is prompted for a letter automatically and can enter a lowercase letter or an uppercase letter as a guess. If the letter is in the secret word, the appropriate dash(es) on the form is replaced by the letter guessed. The user may try to guess the word at any time. If the secret word is guessed, the word is displayed on the form along with the number of guesses made. If the wrong word is guessed, the user loses.

WordGuessII Design

The interface design does not need to change from the original WordGuess application.

The code design should start with an algorithm and also pseudocode. The algorithm, although similar to the WordGuess application, must take into account selecting a random word:

1. Generate a random number between 1 and 25.
2. Read *random number* number of lines in the secretwords.txt file. The word at line random number is the secret word.
3. Display the same number of dashes as in the secret word.
4. Prompt the user for a letter, but also allow the user to enter a flag if ready to guess the entire word.
5. Increment a guess counter.
6. If a letter was entered determine if the letter is in the secret word and then display the letter entered in the proper position on the form.
7. If the flag was entered, prompt the user for the entire word.
8. Repeat step 1 until the word has been guessed or the user gives up by clicking Cancel in the input box or leaves the input box empty.

The Chapter 5 case study is easily extended to read a word from a file because the original code accommodates a word of an unspecified length. The program is extended by simply adding a function that gets a secret word from a file. To match the specification, the secret word is all uppercase because the player's guesses are converted to uppercase.

The algorithm is implemented with the following pseudocode:

```
Sub btnPlayGame_Click()
    Const FLAG As Char = "!"
    Static numGuesses As Integer = 0
    Dim letterGuess As Char
    Dim wordGuess As String
    Dim letterPos As Integer
    Dim tempWord As String
    Dim endGame As Boolean
    Dim secretWord = RandomSecretWord()

    Dim wordGuessedSoFar = ""
    Dim length = SECRET_WORD.Length
    wordGuessedSoFar = wordGuessedSoFar.PadLeft(Length, "-")
    Show wordGuessedSoFar in a label

    Get letterGuess from user, ending game if Cancel is clicked
    Do While letterGuess <> FLAG And _
    wordGuessedSoFar <> SECRET_WORD And Not endGame
        Increment number of guesses
        Compare each letter of secretWord to letterGuess
        If letterGuess matches a letter in secretWord Then
            Replace dash in wordGuessedSoFar with letterGuess
        If wordGuessedSoFar <> secretWord Then
            Get letterGuess from user, ending game if Cancel clicked
    Loop
```

```
    If wordGuessedSoFar = secretWord Then
        Display message with number of guesses
    Else If letterGuess = FLAG Then
        Show input box prompting for wordGuess
        If wordGuess = secretWord Then
            Display message with number of guesses
        Else
            Display "you lose" message
    Else
        Display "game over" message
End Sub

Function RandomSecretWord() As String
    Dim wordNum As Integer = random number between 1 and 25
    Dim secretWord As String
    For textLine As Integer = 1 To wordNum–1
        textFile.ReadLine(secretwords.txt)
    Next textLine
    Return textFile.ReadLine(secretwords.txt)
End Function
```

WordGuessII Coding

The interface for WordGuessII, has new text for the form and the label and the form is wider to accommodate longer words:

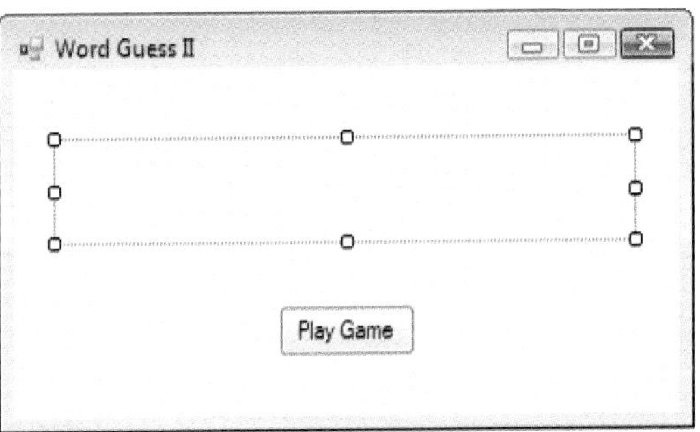

Object	(Name)	Text	TextAlign	Font
Form1		Word Guess II		
Label1	lblSecretWord	*empty*	MiddleCenter	Size 36
Button1	btnPlayGame	Play Game		

```
Imports System.IO

Public Class Form1

    Private Sub btnPlayGame_Click(ByVal sender As Object,
    ByVal e As System.EventArgs) Handles btnPlayGame.Click
        Const FLAG As Char = "!"
        Const GUESS_PROMPT As String = "Enter a letter or " & FLAG & " to guess word:"
        Dim numGuesses As Integer = 0
        Dim letterGuess As Char
        Dim wordGuess As String
        Dim tempWord As String
        Dim endGame As Boolean
```

```
    'Get secret word
    Dim secretWord As String = RandomSecretWord()
    secretWord = secretWord.ToUpper

    'Set number of dashes as letters in SECRETWORD
    Dim wordGuessedSoFar As String = ""
    Dim length As Integer = secretWord.Length
    wordGuessedSoFar = wordGuessedSoFar.PadLeft(length, "-")
    Me.lblSecretWord.Text = wordGuessedSoFar          'initialize game

    'Get first guess
    Dim tempLetterGuess = InputBox(GUESS_PROMPT, Me.Text)
    'Test data entered
    If tempLetterGuess = Nothing Then
        endGame = True
    Else
        letterGuess = tempLetterGuess
    End If

    Do While letterGuess <> FLAG And wordGuessedSoFar <> secretWord And Not endGame
        numGuesses += 1
        For letterPos As Integer = 0 To secretWord.Length - 1
            If secretWord.Chars(letterPos) = Char.ToUpper(letterGuess) Then
                'Remove dash at position of letter guessed
                tempWord = wordGuessedSoFar.Remove(letterPos, 1)
                'Insert guessed letter
                wordGuessedSoFar = tempWord.Insert(letterPos,
                Char.ToUpper(letterGuess))
                'Update interface
                Me.lblSecretWord.Text = wordGuessedSoFar
            End If
        Next letterPos

        'Get next letter if word hasn't been guessed
        If wordGuessedSoFar <> secretWord Then
            'Get user guess
            tempLetterGuess = InputBox(GUESS_PROMPT, Me.Text)
            'Test data entered
            If tempLetterGuess = Nothing Then
                endGame = True
            Else
                letterGuess = tempLetterGuess
            End If
        End If
    Loop

    If wordGuessedSoFar = secretWord Then
        MessageBox.Show("You guessed it in " & numGuesses & " guesses!")
    ElseIf letterGuess = FLAG Then
        wordGuess = InputBox("Enter a word: ", Me.Text)
        If wordGuess.ToUpper = secretWord Then
            MessageBox.Show("You guessed it in " & numGuesses & " guesses!")
            Me.lblSecretWord.Text = secretWord
        Else
            MessageBox.Show("Sorry you lose.")
        End If
    Else
        MessageBox.Show("Game over.")
    End If
End Sub
```

```
    'Reads a random word from a file with 25 words stored one word per line.
    '
    'pre: the file contains one word per line
    'post: a word has been randomly selected from a file and returned.
    '
    Function RandomSecretWord() As String
        Dim fs As New FileStream("secretwords.txt", FileMode.Open, FileAccess.Read)
        Dim textFile As New StreamReader(fs)

        Randomize()

        'Read word from file
        Dim wordNum As Integer = Int(25 * Rnd())
        For lineNum As Integer = 1 To wordNum - 1
            textFile.ReadLine()
        Next lineNum
        Return textFile.ReadLine    'return word at position wordNum

        textFile.Close()
        fs.Close()
    End Function
End Class
```

Running WordGuessII and guessing two correct letters displays:

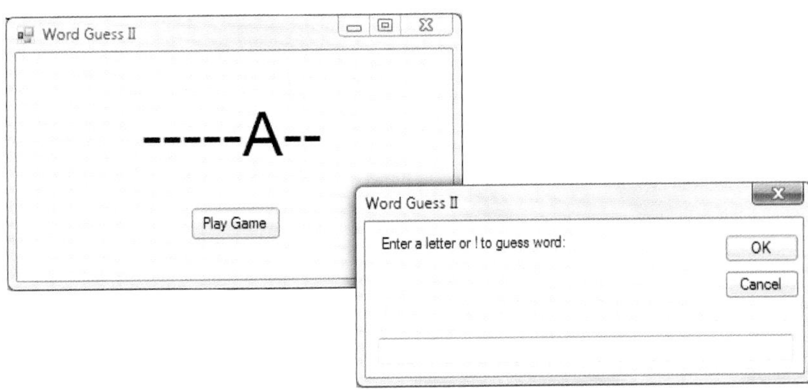

WordGuessII should be tested by entering correct and incorrect characters and correct and incorrect word guesses.

Review: WordGuessII

Modify WordGuessII to include a File menu with Add Word and New commands. The Add Word command prompts the user with an input box for a new word to add to the `secretwords.txt` file. The New command prompts the user with an input box for the number of new words and then displays that many more input boxes for getting the words. The new words are used to create a new `secretwords.txt` file, overwriting the existing words.

Chapter Summary

A file is a collection of related data stored on a persistent medium such as a hard disk. Files are often used to store data needed by applications. Text files store data as characters. However, an application can be written to convert data read to the expected data type. For example, a file containing numeral characters can be read by an application that includes the Val() function to convert strings to numbers.

The Visual Basic `FileInfo` class includes properties and methods for creating, copying, and deleting files. The `Imports System.IO` statement must be included at the top of a program using file classes.

A stream can be thought of as a sequence of characters. A file stream is used for manipulating a file. The file stream keeps track of the file position, which is the point where reading or writing last occurred, and can write to, read from, and close a file to prevent further file access.

The Visual Basic `FileStream` is used to create a file stream object for a specific file. The stream can access an existing file for reading, for appending data, or can create a new file.

The `StreamReader` class is used to create an object that can read characters from a specific stream. A stream reader object can peek ahead to determine if the end of file has been reached, and can read one character or one line of characters at a time from the stream.

The `StreamWriter` class is used to create an object that can write characters to a specific stream. A stream writer object can write one character or an entire line of characters at a time to the stream.

A TextBox object has properties that can be set to display many lines of text. A text box can be docked in the form window, include scroll bars, and automatically wrap text. A text box that is set to read-only can display text, but will not allow the user to type in the text box.

A KeyPress event procedure can be coded for a text box. A KeyPress event occurs when the user presses a key while the text box has focus. The event procedure can be coded to check for the Enter key so that actions can be taken based on the text box entry. The Visual Basic `Keys` enumerated type can be used to determine which key was pressed.

An OpenFileDialog control is an component that displays the Open dialog box at run time, but has no graphical element. The ShowDialog() method is used to display the dialog box at run time and the FileName property is used to determine which file the user has selected.

Similar to the OpenFileDialog control is the SaveFileDialog control. The SaveFileDialog control is an component that displays the Save As dialog box at run time, but has no graphical element. The ShowDialog() method is used to display the dialog box at run time and the FileName property is used to determine which file the user has selected or typed.

Vocabulary

End of file A value of –1 read from the file stream.

File A collection of related data stored on a persistent medium.

File position The point in a file stream where reading or writing last occurred.

File stream A file as a sequence of characters.

Line terminator The carriage return and line feed characters at the end of each line in a file.

Peeking Looking ahead in a file to see if the end of file has been reached.

Persistent Lasting.

Sequential Access File Reading or writing one character after another or one line after another in a file stream.

Stream A sequence of characters.

Visual Basic

`FileInfo` **class** Used for creating an object associated with a specific file. Properties include Exists, Length, and FullName. Methods include Create(), CopyTo(), and Delete().

`FileMode` Visual Basic enumerated type with members that include Open, Create, OpenOrCreate, and Append.

`FileStream` **class** Used for creating a stream object for a specific file. File modes include `Open`, `CreateNew`, `OpenOrCreate`, and `Append`. Properties include Length and Position. Methods include Close().

`Imports` Statement used to include a namespace in an application.

`Keys` Visual Basic enumerated type with members that correspond to key names.

OpenFileDialog — OpenFileDialog **control** Used to add an application component that displays the Open dialog box. Properties include FileName. Methods include ShowDialog().

SaveFileDialog — SaveFileDialog **control** Used to add an application component that displays the Save As dialog box. Properties include FileName. Methods include ShowDialog().

`StreamReader` **class** Used for creating a stream object for reading characters and lines of text from a file. Methods include Peek(), Read(), ReadLine(), and Close().

`StreamWriter` **class** Used for creating a stream object for writing characters and lines of text to a file. Methods include Write(), WriteLine(), and Close().

TextBox — TextBox **control** Used to create a control class object that can display multiple lines of text. Properties include Dock, ReadOnly, Multiline, WordWrap, and ScrollBars. Events include KeyPress.

Critical Thinking

1. List one advantage of having prices of inventory items read from a file as opposed to hard-coding them as constant values in a program.

2. Why should word wrap be allowed in a multi-line text box?

3. Labels and text boxes both can display multiple lines of data. What is the advantage(s) of using a text box?

4. Why might a programmer choose to use an OpenFileDialog component or a SaveFileDialog component instead of:
   a) prompting the user for a file name with a text box or input box?
   b) hard-coding the path and file name into the program?

5. A file named `sales_tax.txt` stores the current sales tax rate.
   a) Write statements to read the value from the file and store it in `salesTaxRate`.
   b) The sales tax value needs to be changed. To do this during run-time, which file mode should be used and why?

6. Correct the error(s) in the following code:

```
'Take info from textbox and save to a file
'of the users choice with a SaveFileDialog
'object
Me.SaveFileDialog1.ShowDialog()
If strFileName <> Nothing Then
    Dim fs As New FileStream(strFileName,
    FileMode.Create, FileAccess.Write)
    Dim textFile As New StreamWriter
    textFile.WriteLine = Me.txtFile.Text
    fs.Close()
End If
```

7. a) Write statements to read data from `namefile.txt` and then write each line, except for the line containing the string equal to "DeleteThis", to a file named `tempfile.txt`.
   b) What does the following code accomplish?

```
Dim tf As New FileInfo("namefile.txt")
tf.Delete()
Dim ttf As New FileInfo("temp.txt")
ttf.CopyTo("namefile.txt")
ttf.Delete()
```

8. CSV (comma separated values) is a common data file format, and files of this format have the file name extension `.csv`. A CSV file contains lines with data separated by commas. Each piece of data is referred to as a field.
   a) What does the following code accomplish if file file.csv contains lines with fields student name and score?

```
Dim fs As New FileStream("file.csv",
FileMode.Open, FileAccess.Read)
Dim textFile As New StreamReader(fs)
Dim p As Integer
Dim l, s As String
Dim input As String
input = InputBox("Type in value")
If input <> Nothing Then
  Do While textFile.Peek > -1
    l = textFile.ReadLine()
    p = l.IndexOf(",")
    s = l.Substring(p + 1,
    l.Length " p " 1)
    If Val(s) >= Val(input) Then
      Me.txtFile.Text = Me.txtFile.Text &
      l.Substring(0, p) &
      vbTab & e & vbCrLf
    End If
  Loop
End If
textFile.Close()
fs.Close()
```

   b) Write the statements needed to perform a linear search on the file `StudentGrades.csv`. Each line of the CSV file has three fields. The first field is a student's last name, the second is a student's first name, and the third is the student's average. Search for a last name that matches `last` and a first name that matches `first` and then display the message "________ has an average of ________", otherwise display the message "Student not found." Assume the appropriate `FileStream` has been created, `StudentFile` is the name of the `StreamReader`, and that the file contains only unique names.

True/False

9. Determine if each of the following is true or false. If false, explain why.
   a) `file1.CopyTo(file2)` will overwrite the current data in `file2`.
   b) A path must be specified when creating a new file at run time.
   c) A value of –1 in the file stream indicates the end of the file.
   d) Read gets the next piece of data up to the next space.
   e) A multiline text box can only display data from a file.
   f) An application can contain a text box which the user cannot type in.
   g) Scroll bars can always be displayed in a multiline text box.
   h) The exact keystrokes of a user typing in a text box can be determined in a KeyPress event procedure.
   i) If the full path is not provided for a file, an application expects the file to be in the Project folder.
   j) Files used in a Visual Basic program must have been created with Visual Basic.
   k) When writing data to a file, the file will not actually be written to if the file stream writer is not closed.
   l) Read and ReadLine both return data as string values.
   m) The `Append` file mode adds data to the beginning of an existing file.

Exercises

Exercise 1 — FileStatistics

a. Create a FileStatistics application that prompts the user for a file name. When Enter is pressed, the number of lines and the total number of characters in the typed text file or a message that the file does not exist is displayed. Several text files should be stored in the bin\Debug folder for testing purposes. The application interface should look similar to:

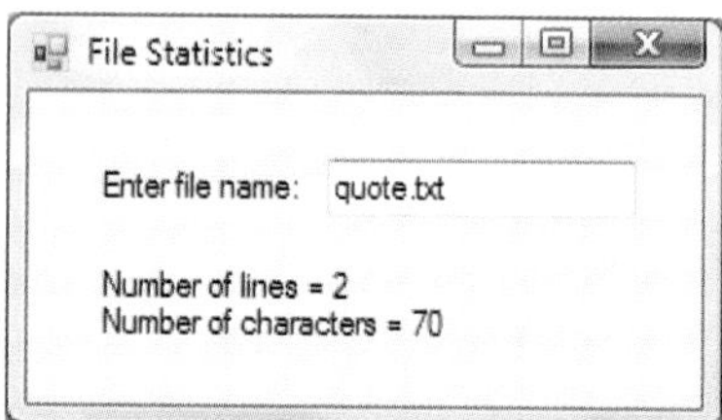

b. *Advanced* Modify the FileStatistics application to use the Read() method to report the visible number of characters in the file, ignoring all white space (tabs, carriage returns, line feeds, and spaces):

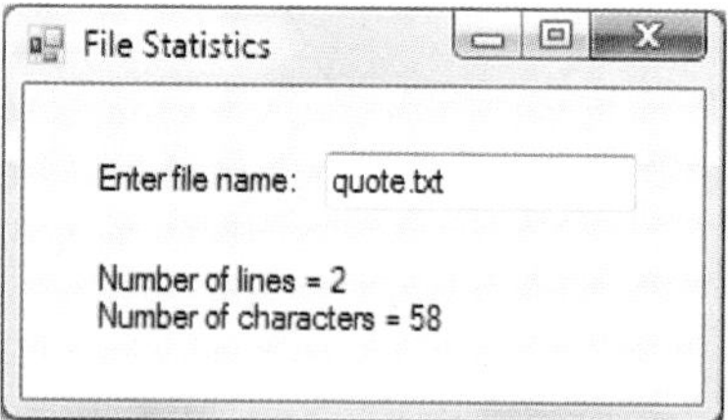

Exercise 2 — NumberStatistics

Create a NumberStatistics application that includes a File menu with Open and Exit commands. Open should display the Open dialog box to allow the user to select a file containing numeric data. The selected file's contents are then displayed in a text box, and the total and average of the numbers stored in the file can be displayed by clicking buttons, also on the interface. A file of numeric data with one number per line should be created for testing purposes. The application interface should look similar to the following after opening a file and clicking Total and Average:

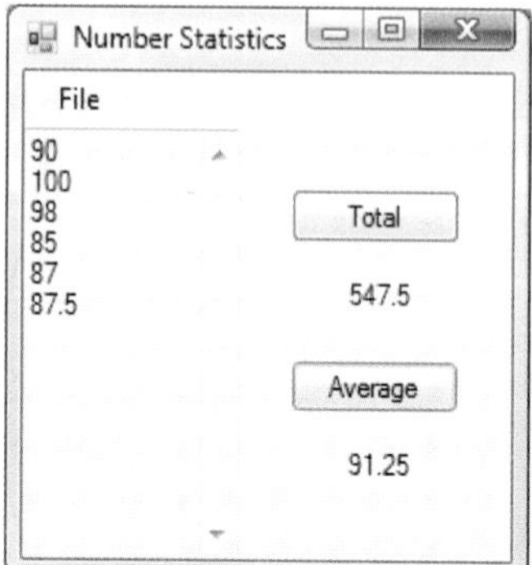

Exercise 3 — Mad-Lib

A Mad-Lib story is a story where nouns and verbs in a sentence are randomly replaced with other nouns and verbs, usually with humorous results. Create a Mad-Lib application that reads sentences, nouns, and verbs from separate text files to create a single mad-lib sentence. The following text files are data files for this text and should be copied to the bin\Debug folder of the project folder:

- `sentences.txt` contains one sentence per line, each with % signs as verb placeholders and # signs as noun placeholders. For example:

  Gloria Martin's job is to % all of the #.

- `verbs.txt` contains verbs, one per line. For example:

  run
  display
  eat

- `nouns.txt` contains nouns, one per line. For example:

  bananas
  sopranos
  elephants
  vegetables

Hint: Use the StrConv() function, mentioned in the side bar on page 139 in the text, to change lower-case nouns to proper case for sentences that begin with nouns. The application interface should look similar to:

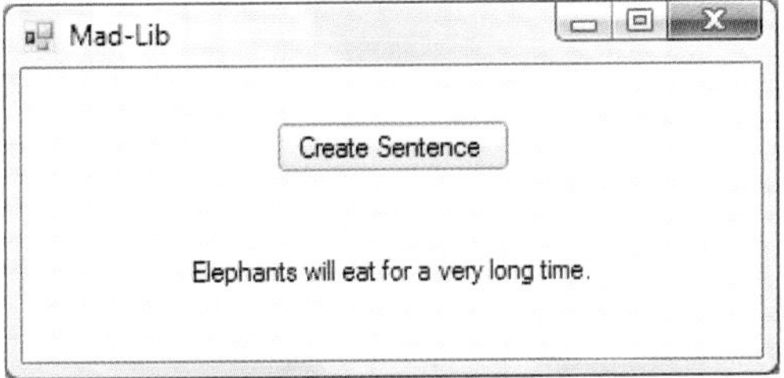

Exercise 4 — EncodeFile

Create an EncodeFile application that encodes text by replacing each letter with a coded version, leaving nonletters unchanged. Use the CodeChar() function to encode each letter:

```
Function CodeChar(ByVal plain As Char) As Char
    Select Case plain
        Case "A" To "Y", "a" To "y"
            Return ChrW(AscW(plain) + 1)
        Case "Z"
            Return "A"
        Case "z"
            Return "a"
        Case Else
            Return plain
    End Select
End Function
```

Include a File menu with New, Open, Encode, Save, Close, and Exit commands. Selecting the Encode command should encode any text in the text box and write the coded text to a file named `encoded.txt`. The application interface should look similar to the following after opening a text file, selecting Encode, closing the original file, and then opening `encoded.txt`:

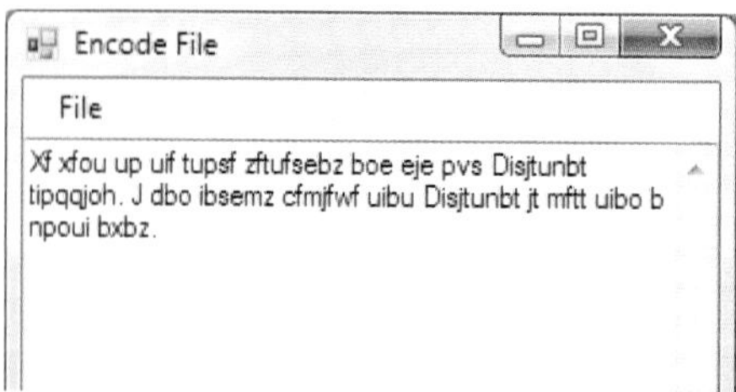

Exercise 5 — AppendFiles

Create an AppendFiles application that prompts the user for the names of two existing files. When the user clicks Append, an input box should be displayed prompting the user for the name of a third file to create from the contents of the two existing files. The third file's contents are then displayed in a text box. Display an appropriate message if either of the first two files do not exist. The application interface should look similar to the following after entering names of files stored in the bin\Debug folder of the project folder, clicking Append, and entering a new file name in the input box:

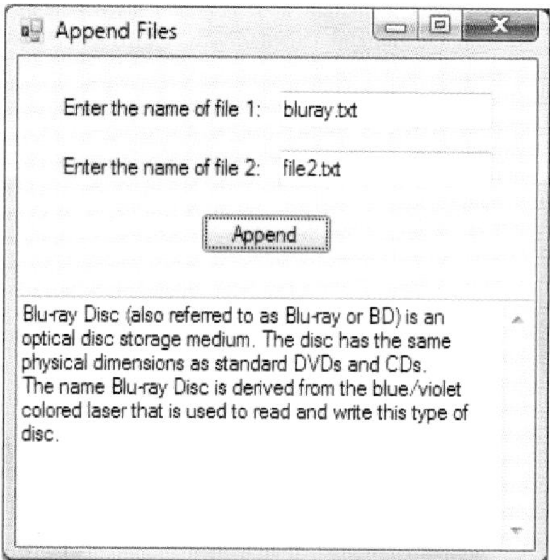

Exercise 6 — QuizResults

Create a QuizResults application that scores student quizzes. The application should append records containing student quiz responses to a file named `stuquizzes.txt`. If the file does not exist, one should be created. The records should be written with the student name on one line followed by a single T or F response on the next five lines. A separate file named `quizanswers.txt` stores the five correct answers to the quiz questions. Make up five responses and then create this file using a text editor. The QuizResults application should include a File menu with Add Student, Clear Records, Show Results, and Exit command, which allow records to be added, the `stuquizzes.txt` file to be deleted, and quiz scores to be displayed for each student in message boxes. The application interface should look similar to the following after entering data for several students and selecting Show Results:

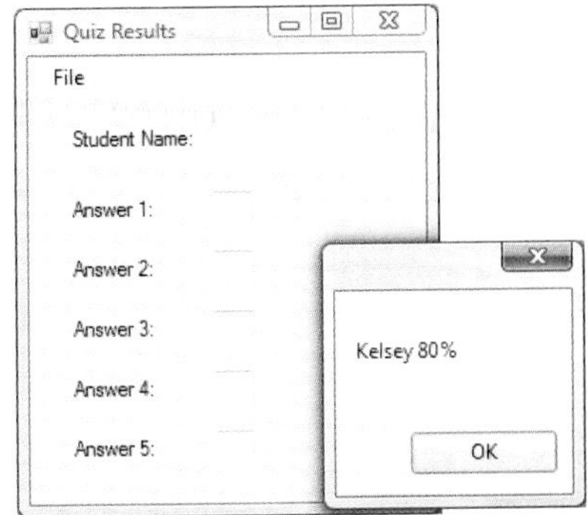

Exercise 7 — ReplaceText

Create a ReplaceText application that replaces all occurrences of a word or phrase in a file with a specified word or phrase. A text file should be stored in the bin\Debug folder of the project folder for testing purposes. The application interface should look similar to:

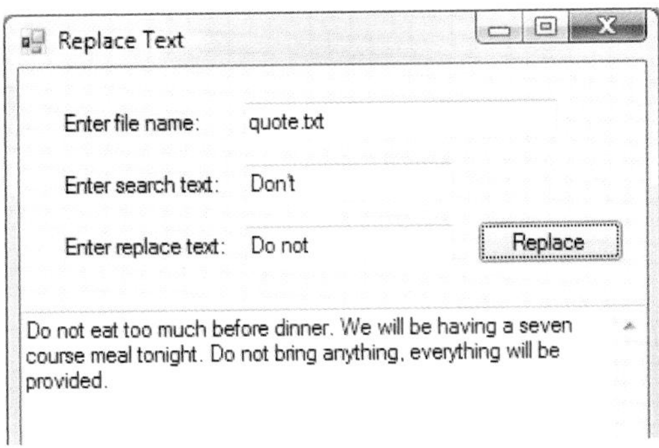

Exercise 8 — RemoveText

Create a RemoveText application that removes all occurrences of a word or phrase in a file. A text file should be stored in the bin\Debug folder of the project folder for testing purposes. The application interface should look similar to:

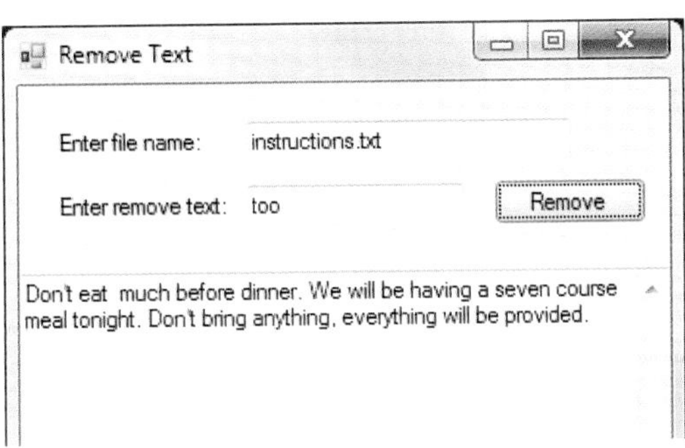

Exercise 9 — LocalBank

Modify the LocalBank application created in Chapter 10 Exercise 1 to read and write account information to a file (excluding the list of transactions). The application should include a File menu with Open Accounts and Close Accounts commands. The Open Accounts command should read all the account information from a file into an `Account` array. The Close Accounts command should write all the account information from the `Account` array to a file, overwriting existing account information.

Exercise 10 (advanced) — MergeFiles

Create a MergeFiles application that merges two files of sorted numbers into a third file of sorted numbers. For example, if the two files of sorted numbers are similar to the following and stored in the bin\Debug folder of the project folder:

file1.dat	file2.dat
12	4
23	5
34	10
45	20

then the application interface should look similar to:

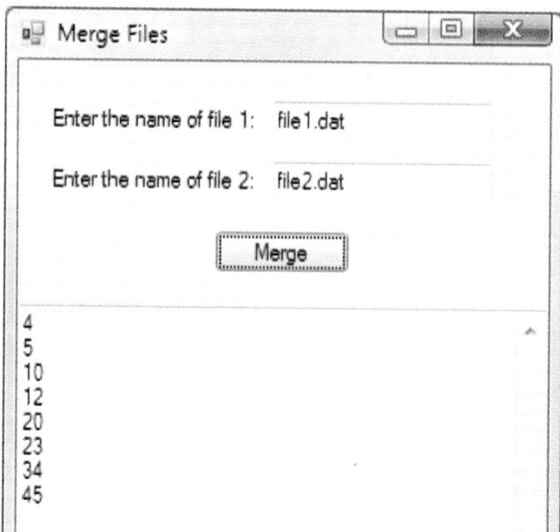

The application should not use an array to temporarily store numbers, but should merge the two files by taking one element at a time from each and writing it to the new file.

Chapter 12
Sorting and Searching

Key Concepts

Understanding the process of sorting
Implementing the bubble sort algorithm
Measuring the efficiency of a sorting algorithm
Implementing the selection sort algorithm
Implementing the insertion sort algorithm
Implementing the binary search algorithm

Bubble Sort

sorting

Sorting is the process of putting items in a designated order, either from low to high or high to low. *Bubble sort* is a basic sorting algorithm that starts at the first element of a list of items and proceeds sequentially to the last, comparing each element with the next. If the first item is greater than the second, they are swapped. Then the second item is swapped with the third, if necessary, and so on until the end of the list is reached. This process is performed on each item in the list to "bubble" up items to their proper position.

For an array of integers, the BubbleSort procedure pseudocode is:

```
Sub BubbleSort(ByRef intArray() As Integer)
    For bubbleItem = 0 To intArray.Length – 1
        For testItem = 0 To intArray.Length – 2
            If intArray(testItem) > intArray(testItem+1) Then
                Swap intArray(testItem) with intArray(testItem+1)
            End If
        Next testItem
    Next bubbleItem
End Sub
```

The BubbleSort application, shown on the next page, includes a BubbleSort() procedure to sort a list of randomly generated numbers:

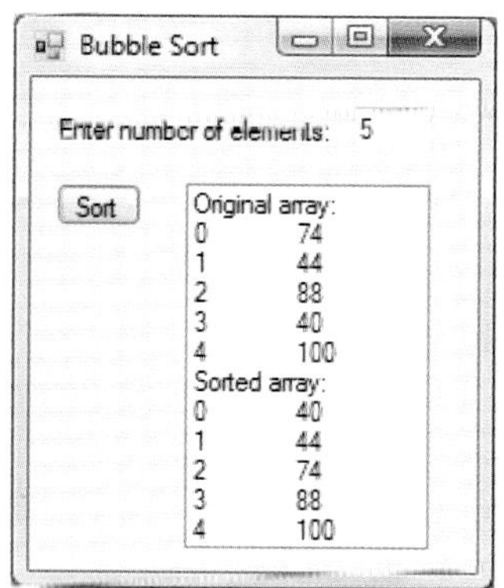


```
Private Sub btnSort_Click(ByVal sender As Object,
ByVal e As System.EventArgs) Handles btnSort.Click
    Dim itemArray(-1) As Integer
    Dim numItems As Integer

    'User chooses the number of elements for array
    numItems = Val(Me.txtNumElements.Text)
    If numItems > 0 Then
        'Create array of integers
        Call GenerateArray(numItems, itemArray)

        'Display generated array
        Me.lstArrayElements.Items.Clear()    'clear any existing data
        Call DisplayData(itemArray, Me.lstArrayElements, "Original array:")

        'Sort array
        Call BubbleSort(itemArray)

        'Display sorted array
        Call DisplayData(itemArray, Me.lstArrayElements, "Sorted array:")
    Else
        MessageBox.Show("Number of elements must be greater than 0.")
        Me.txtNumElements.Text = Nothing     'clear text box
    End If
End Sub

'Resizes the dynamic intArray to numElements elements and then assigns to
'each element a random integer between 1 and MAX_NUMBER.
'
'pre: numElements > 0
'post: intArray has been assigned numElements elements of random integers
'between 0 and MAX_NUMBER
'
Sub GenerateArray(ByVal numElements As Integer,
ByRef intArray() As Integer)
    Const MAX_NUMBER As Integer = 100
    ReDim intArray(numElements - 1)

    'Assign each array element a random value
    Randomize()
    For index As Integer = 0 To intArray.Length - 1
        intArray(index) = Int(MAX_NUMBER * Rnd() + 1)
    Next index
End Sub
```

```
'Displays the contents of intArray in a list box
'
'post: intArray items have been displayed in a list box.
'
Sub DisplayData(ByRef intArray() As Integer, ByRef lstListBox As ListBox,
ByVal title As String)
    lstListBox.Items.Add(title)
    For index As Integer = 0 To intArray.Length - 1
        lstListBox.Items.Add(index & vbTab & intArray(index))
    Next index
End Sub

'Sorts intArray from low to high
'
'post: intArray elements have been sorted low to high
'
Sub BubbleSort(ByRef intArray() As Integer)
    Dim temp As Integer

    'Bubble each element as necessary
    For bubbleItem As Integer = 0 To intArray.Length - 1
        For testItem As Integer = 0 To intArray.Length - 2
            If intArray(testItem) > intArray(testItem + 1) Then
                'Swap Elements
                temp = intArray(testItem)
                intArray(testItem) = intArray(testItem + 1)
                intArray(testItem + 1) = temp
            End If
        Next testItem
    Next bubbleItem
End Sub
```

The DateTime Structure

One measure of the efficiency of a sorting algorithm is the speed at which it can complete a sort. The Visual Basic `DateTime` structure includes members that can be used for timing:

- **Millisecond** property stores the number of milliseconds of a `DateTime` variable.
- **Now()** is a shared method that must be used with the `DateTime` structure. **Now()** returns the current time on the computer.

To time a sort, the start time can be compared to the end time, as in the statements below that time a bubble sort:

```
Dim startTime As New DateTime()
Dim endTime As New DateTime()

startTime = DateTime.Now       'start timing
Call BubbleSort(intArray)
endTime = DateTime.Now         'end timing

MessageBox.Show(endTime.Millisecond - startTime.Millisecond)
```

Review: BubbleSort – part 1 of 2

Modify the BubbleSort application to display a message box with the time required for the sort. Test the application with 1000, 3000, and 5000 elements.

A More Efficient Bubble Sort

The BubbleSort() procedure could be made more efficient by using a `Do...Loop` instead of a `For...Next` loop to process items. The `For...Next` processes every element in the array, even when no more swaps are needed to sort the list. By using a flag and a `Do...Loop`, processing need only be done until the list is sorted:

```
'Sorts intArray from low to high.
'
'post: intArray elements have been sorted low to high.
'
Sub BubbleSort(ByRef intArray() As Integer)
  Dim temp As Integer
  Dim swapRequired As Boolean = True          'flag

  Do While swapRequired
      swapRequired = False
      For testItem As Integer = 0 To intArray.Length - 2
          If intArray(testItem) > intArray(testItem + 1) Then
              'Swap elements
              temp = intArray(testItem)
              intArray(testItem) = intArray(testItem + 1)
              intArray(testItem + 1) = temp
              swapRequired = True
          End If
      Next testItem
  Loop
End Sub
```

Note that the swapRequired flag is True upon entering the loop and then immediately made False. If values are swapped, swapRequired is made True to indicate that the list was still not sorted. When one pass can be made through the list without any swaps, the loop is exited.

Review: BubbleSort – part 2 of 2

Modify the BubbleSort application to include the more efficient BubbleSort() procedure from the section above. Test and time the application with 1000, 3000, and 5000 elements.

Selection Sort

The *selection sort* is an algorithm that starts by finding the lowest item in a list and swapping it with the first. Next, the lowest item among items 2 through the last is found and swapped with item 2, and then the lowest item among items 3 through the last is swapped with item 3. This process is continued until the last item is reached, at which point all the items will be sorted.

For an array of integers, the SelectionSort() procedure pseudocode is:

```
Sub SelectionSort(ByRef intArray() As Integer)
    For itemIndex = 0 To intArray.Length – 1
        For lowItemIndex = itemIndex to intArray.Length – 1
            if intArray(lowItemIndex) < intArray(itemIndex) Then
              swap intArray(lowItemIndex) with intArray(itemIndex)
        Next lowItemIndex
    Next itemIndex
End Sub
```

The SelectionSort application below includes the SelectionSort() procedure:

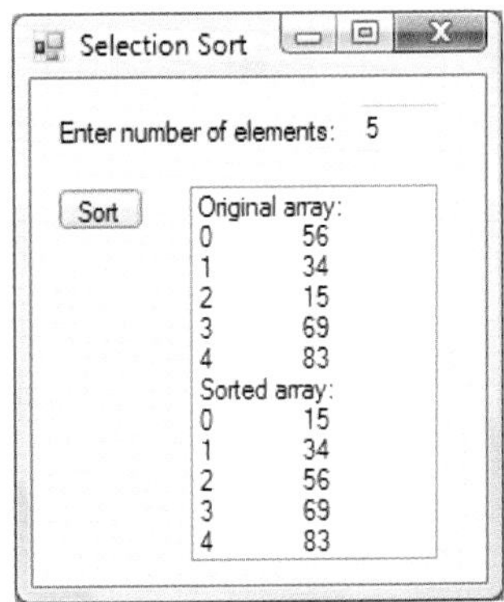


```
Private Sub btnSort _ Click(ByVal sender As Object,
ByVal e As System.EventArgs) Handles btnSort.Click
    Dim itemArray(-1) As Integer
    Dim numItems As Integer

    'User chooses the number of elements for array
    numItems = Val(Me.txtNumElements.Text)
    If numItems > 0 Then
        'Create array of integers
        Call GenerateArray(numItems, itemArray)

        'Display generated array
        Me.lstArrayElements.Items.Clear()     'clear any existing data
        Call DisplayData(itemArray, Me.lstArrayElements, "Original array:")

        'Sort array
        Call SelectionSort(itemArray)

        'Display sorted array
        Call DisplayData(itemArray, Me.lstArrayElements, "Sorted array:")
    Else
        MessageBox.Show("Number of elements must be greater than 0.")
        Me.txtNumElements.Text = Nothing      'clear text box
    End If
End Sub
```

```
'Resizes the dynamic intArray to numElements elements and then assigns to
'each element a random integer between 1 and MAX _ NUMBER.
'
'pre: numElements > 0
'post: intArray has been assigned numElements elements of random integers
'between 0 and MAX _ NUMBER
'
Sub GenerateArray(ByVal numElements As Integer,
ByRef intArray() As Integer)
    Const MAX _ NUMBER As Integer = 100
    ReDim intArray(numElements - 1)

    'Assign each array element a random value
    Randomize()
    For index As Integer = 0 To intArray.Length - 1
        intArray(index) = Int(MAX _ NUMBER * Rnd() + 1)
    Next index
End Sub

'Displays the contents of intArray in a list box
'
'post: intArray items have been displayed in a list box.
'
Sub DisplayData(ByRef intArray() As Integer, ByRef lstListBox As ListBox,
ByVal title As String)
    lstListBox.Items.Add(title)
    For index As Integer = 0 To intArray.Length - 1
        lstListBox.Items.Add(index & vbTab & intArray(index))
    Next index
End Sub

'Sorts intArray from low to high
'
'post: intArray elements have been sorted low to high
'
Sub SelectionSort(ByRef intArray() As Integer)
    Dim temp As Integer

    For itemIndex As Integer = 0 To intArray.Length - 1
        For lowItemIndex As Integer = itemIndex To intArray.Length - 1
            If intArray(lowItemIndex) < intArray(itemIndex) Then
                'Swap Elements
                temp = intArray(itemIndex)
                intArray(itemIndex) = intArray(lowItemIndex)
                intArray(lowItemIndex) = temp
            End If
        Next lowItemIndex
    Next itemIndex
End Sub
```

Note that several of the procedures are similar to those used in the DynamicArrayDemo application in Chapter 8.

Review: SelectionSort

Modify the SelectionSort application to display a message box with the time required for the sort. Test the application with 1000, 3000, and 5000 elements.

Insertion Sort

More efficient than the bubble or selection sort algorithms is the insertion sort algorithm. An *insertion sort* starts by sorting the first two items in a list. This sort is performed by shifting the first item into the second spot if the second item belongs in the first spot. Next, the third item is properly inserted within the first three items by again shifting items into their appropriate position to make room for the moved item. This process is repeated for the remaining elements.

The insertion sort is illustrated below with an array containing four elements. Step 1 shows the original list, which contains items 40, 10, 30, and 20. Step 2 shows that 40 is shifted to make room for the second item, 10. Next, 30 compared to the value in the previous position (40), 40 is shifted into position 3, 30 is then compared to the value in the previous position (10), and then 30 is placed at position 2. This process repeats for the remaining items.

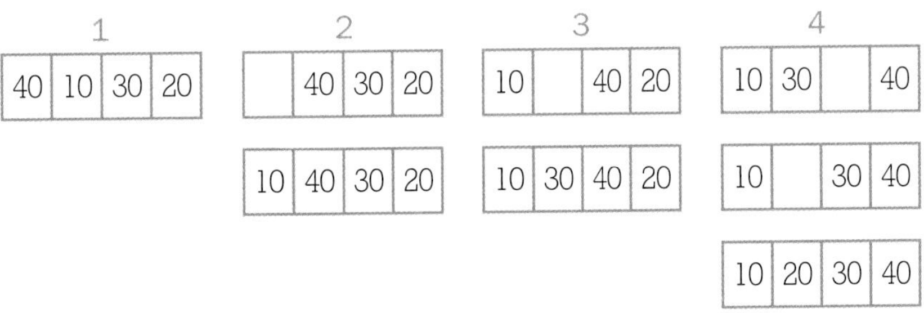

For an array of integers, the InsertionSort procedure pseudocode is:

```
Sub InsertionSort(ByRef intArray() As Integer)
    For itemIndex = 1 To intArray.Length – 1
        temp = intArray(itemIndex)
        previousItemIndex = itemIndex – 1
        Do While intArray(previousItemIndex) > temp _
        And previousItemIndex > 0
            Shift intArray(previousItemIndex) up one element
            previousItemIndex –= 1
        Loop
        If intArray(previousItemIndex) > temp Then
            Swap the two elements
        Else
            Insert element at appropriate location
        End If
    Next itemIndex
End Sub
```

The InsertionSort application on the next page includes the InsertionSort() procedure:

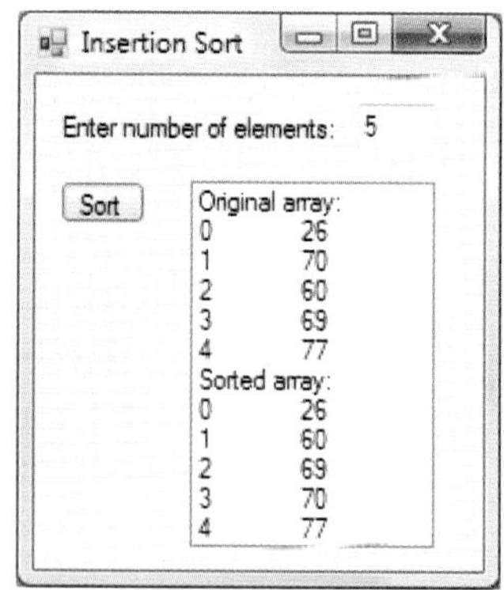


```
Private Sub btnSort_Click(ByVal sender As Object, ByVal e As System.EventArgs)
Handles btnSort.Click
    Dim itemArray(-1) As Integer
    Dim numItems As Integer

    'User chooses the number of elements for array
    numItems = Val(Me.txtNumElements.Text)
    If numItems > 0 Then
        'Create array of integers
        Call GenerateArray(numItems, itemArray)

        'Display generated array
        Me.lstArrayElements.Items.Clear()     'clear any existing data
        Call DisplayData(itemArray, Me.lstArrayElements, "Original array:")

        'Sort array
        Call InsertionSort(itemArray)

        'Display sorted array
        Call DisplayData(itemArray, Me.lstArrayElements, "Sorted array:")
    Else
        MessageBox.Show("Number of elements must be greater than 0.")
        Me.txtNumElements.Text = Nothing      'clear text box
    End If
End Sub

'Resizes the dynamic intArray to numElements elements and then assigns to
'each element a random integer between 1 and MAX_NUMBER.
'
'pre: numElements > 0
'post: intArray has been assigned numElements elements of random integers
'between 0 and MAX_NUMBER
'
Sub GenerateArray(ByVal numElements As Integer, ByRef intArray() As Integer)
    Const MAX_NUMBER As Integer = 100
    ReDim intArray(numElements - 1)

    'Assign each array element a random value
    Randomize()
    For index As Integer = 0 To intArray.Length - 1
        intArray(index) = Int(MAX_NUMBER * Rnd() + 1)
    Next index
End Sub
```

```
'Displays the contents of intArray in a list box
'
'post: intArray items have been displayed in a list box.
'
Sub DisplayData(ByRef intArray() As Integer, ByRef lstListBox As ListBox,
ByVal title As String)
    lstListBox.Items.Add(title)
    For index As Integer = 0 To intArray.Length - 1
        lstListBox.Items.Add(index & vbTab & intArray(index))
    Next index
End Sub

'Sorts intArray from low to high
'
'post: intArray elements have been sorted low to high
'
Sub InsertionSort(ByRef intArray() As Integer)
    Dim previousItemIndex As Integer
    Dim temp As Integer

    For itemIndex As Integer = 1 To intArray.Length - 1
        temp = intArray(itemIndex)
        previousItemIndex = itemIndex - 1
        Do While intArray(previousItemIndex) > temp And previousItemIndex > 0
            'Shift item up into next element position
            intArray(previousItemIndex + 1) = intArray(previousItemIndex)
            'Decrease index to compare current item to next previous item
            previousItemIndex -= 1
        Loop

        'Element at index 0 is greater than current item
        If intArray(previousItemIndex) > temp Then
            'Shift item in first element up into next element position
            intArray(previousItemIndex + 1) = intArray(previousItemIndex)
            'Place current item at index 0 (first element)
            intArray(previousItemIndex) = temp
        Else    'element at previous index is less than current item
            'Place current item at index ahead of previous item
            intArray(previousItemIndex + 1) = temp
        End If
    Next itemIndex
End Sub
```

In the InsertionSort() procedure, the `Do...Loop` moves up, if necessary, all but the element in the first position. An `If...Then` statement is then used to move the first position element up if necessary.

Review: InsertionSort

Modify the InsertionSort application to display a label with the time required for a sort. Test the application with 1000, 3000, and 5000 elements.

Binary Search

> **TIP** The linear search algorithm was introduced in Chapter 8. A linear search, also called a sequential search, is much less efficient than a binary search. However, a linear search does not require a sorted list.

Lists are sorted in order to perform a more efficient search. A *binary search* is used with a sorted list of items to quickly find the location of a value. The binary search algorithm can be thought of as a "divide-and-conquer" approach to searching. It works by examining the middle item of an array sorted from low to high, and determining if this is the item sought, or if the item sought is above or below this middle item. If the item sought is below the middle item, then a binary search is applied to the lower half of the array; if above the middle item, a binary search is applied to the upper half of the array, and so on.

For example, a binary search for the value 5 in a list of items 1, 2, 3, 4, 5, 6, and 7 could be visualized as:

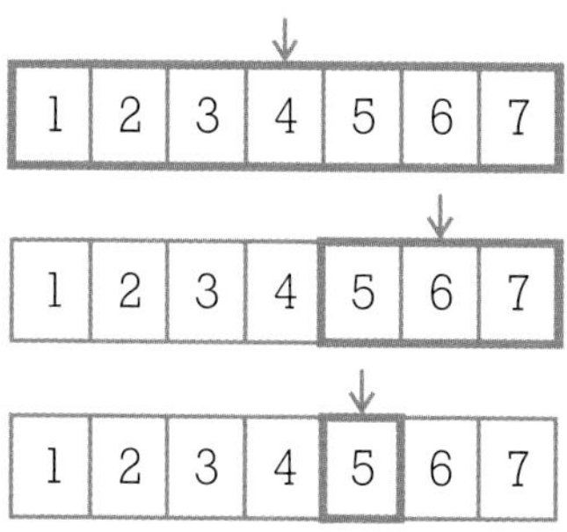

The binary search algorithm is very efficient. For example, an array of 100 elements checks no more than 8 elements in a search, and in an array of one million items no more than 20 items are checked. If a list of the entire world's population were to be searched using this algorithm, less than 40 checks are made to find any one person.

For an array of integers, the BinarySearch() function pseudocode is:

```
Function BinarySearch(ByRef intArray() As Integer, _
ByVal numToFind As Integer) As Integer
    Dim highIndex As Integer = intArray.Length – 1
    Dim midIndex As Integer
    Dim lowIndex = 0
    Dim found As Boolean = False

    Do While (Not found) And (lowIndex <= highIndex)
        midIndex = (highIndex + lowIndex) \ 2
        If intArray(midIndex) = numToFind Then
            found = True
        ElseIf intArray(midIndex) > numToFind Then
            highIndex = midIndex – 1
        Else
            lowIndex = midIndex + 1
        End If
    Loop
    If found Then
        Return midIndex
    Else
        Return –1
    End If
End Function
```

The BinarySearch application, shown below, generates an array of random numbers and then sorts the numbers using an insertion sort. The user can then enter a number to search for in the text box and click **Search** to display the index of the number, if found:

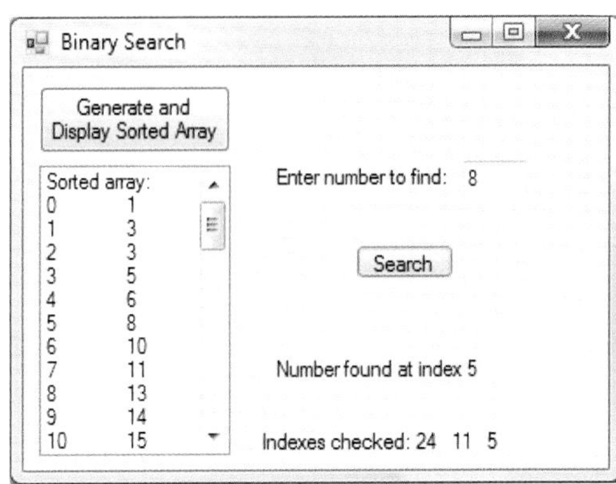


```
Private Sub btnButtonClicked_Click(ByVal sender As Object,
ByVal e As System.EventArgs) Handles btnGenerate.Click, btnSearch.Click
    Static itemArray(-1) As Integer
    Dim btnButtonClicked As Button = sender
    Dim numToFind, numFoundIndex As Integer

    Select Case btnButtonClicked.Tag
        Case "Generate"
            'Create array of integers
            Call GenerateSortedArray(itemArray)
            'Display generated array
            Me.lstArrayElements.Items.Clear()     'clear any existing data
            Call DisplayData(itemArray, Me.lstArrayElements, "Sorted array:")
        Case "Search"
            'Get search number from user
            numToFind = Val(Me.txtNumber.Text)
            'Find number
            numFoundIndex = BinarySearch(itemArray, numToFind)
            If numFoundIndex = -1 Then
                Me.lblResults.Text = "Number not found."
            Else
                Me.lblResults.Text = "Number found at index " & numFoundIndex
            End If
    End Select
End Sub

'Resizes the dynamic intArray to NUM_ELEMENTS elements, assigns a random
'integer between 1 and MAX_NUMBER to each element, and then sorts the array.
'
'post: intArray has been assigned NUM_ELEMENTS elements of random integers
'between 0 and MAX_NUMBER and then sorted from low to high.
'
Sub GenerateSortedArray(ByRef intArray() As Integer)
    Const NUM_ELEMENTS As Integer = 50
    Const MAX_NUMBER As Integer = 100
    ReDim intArray(NUM_ELEMENTS - 1)

    'Assign each array element a random value
    Randomize()
    For index As Integer = 0 To intArray.Length - 1
        intArray(index) = Int(MAX_NUMBER * Rnd() + 1)
    Next index

    'Sort array
    InsertionSort(intArray)
End Sub
```

```
'Returns the index of numToFind or -1 if numToFind is not in array.
'
'post: A -1 or the index of numToFind has been returned.
'
Function BinarySearch(ByRef intArray() As Integer,
ByVal numToFind As Integer) As Integer
    Dim highIndex As Integer = intArray.Length - 1
    Dim midIndex As Integer
    Dim lowIndex = 0
    Dim found As Boolean = False

    Do While (Not found) And (lowIndex <= highIndex)
        midIndex = (highIndex + lowIndex) \ 2
        If intArray(midIndex) = numToFind Then
            found = True
        ElseIf intArray(midIndex) > numToFind Then
            highIndex = midIndex - 1
        Else
            lowIndex = midIndex + 1
        End If
    Loop
    If found Then
        Return midIndex
    Else
        Return -1
    End If
End Function

'Displays the contents of intArray in a list box
'
'post: intArray items have been displayed in a list box.
'
Sub DisplayData(ByRef intArray() As Integer,
ByRef lstListBox As ListBox, ByVal title As String)
    lstListBox.Items.Add(title)
    For index As Integer = 0 To intArray.Length - 1
        lstListBox.Items.Add(index & vbTab & intArray(index))
    Next index
End Sub

'Sorts intArray from low to high
'
'post: intArray elements have been sorted low to high
'
Sub InsertionSort(ByRef intArray() As Integer)
    Dim previousItemIndex As Integer
    Dim temp As Integer

    For itemIndex As Integer = 1 To intArray.Length - 1
        temp = intArray(itemIndex)
        previousItemIndex = itemIndex - 1
        Do While intArray(previousItemIndex) > temp And previousItemIndex > 0
            'Shift item up into next element position
            intArray(previousItemIndex + 1) = intArray(previousItemIndex)
            'Decrease index to compare current item to next previous item
            previousItemIndex -= 1
        Loop
```

```
            'Element at index 0 is greater than current item
            If intArray(previousItemIndex) > temp Then
                'Shift item in first element up into next element position
                intArray(previousItemIndex + 1) = intArray(previousItemIndex)
                'Place current item at index 0 (first element)
                intArray(previousItemIndex) = temp
            Else    'element at previous index is less than current item
                'Place current item at index ahead of previous item
                intArray(previousItemIndex + 1) = temp
            End If
        Next itemIndex
    End Sub

    Private Sub NewFind(ByVal sender As Object, ByVal e As System.EventArgs)
    Handles txtNumber.TextChanged
        Me.lblResults.Text = Nothing
    End Sub
    End Class
```

Review: BinarySearch

Modify the BinarySearch application to display a label with the indexes of items checked in a search. Be sure to clear the label if a new array is generated or a new number is searched for.

Chapter Summary

Sorting is the process of putting items in a designated order, either from low to high or high to low. The bubble sort starts at the first item of a list and proceeds sequentially to the last, comparing each item with the next and swapping items as necessary. The selection sort repeatedly finds the lowest item from a portion of a list and swaps it with the item at index, which is incremented until index is equal to that of the last element. The insertion sort sequentially removes items from a list and adds them back to the list in the appropriate position relative to the previous items in the list.

One measure of efficiency with sorting algorithms is the time it takes the implemented algorithm to sort a list of items. The `DateTime` structure includes the Millisecond property and the Now() method for determining elapsed milliseconds.

A binary search is a very efficient way to search a sorted list of elements. The binary search takes a "divide and conquer" approach to searching a list of items.

Vocabulary

Binary search An algorithm that searches for an item in a sorted list by repeatedly comparing the middle item in a portion of a list to the search item.

Bubble sort A sorting algorithm that starts at the first item of a list and proceeds sequentially to the last, comparing each item with the next and swapping items as necessary.

Insertion sort A sorting algorithm that sequentially removes an item from a list and adds it back to the list in the appropriate position relative to the previous items in the list.

Selection sort A sorting algorithm that repeatedly finds the lowest item from a portion of a list and swaps it with the item at index, which is incremented until index is equal to that of the last element.

Sorting The process of putting items in a designated order, either low to high or high to low.

Visual Basic

`DateTime` **structure** Used for timing. Methods include Now().

Critical Thinking

1. Let 4, 6, 2, 10, 9 be a set of numbers to be sorted in ascending order. For each algorithm below, show how the numbers are ordered after each loop iteration of the algorithm.
   a) Bubble
   b) Selection
   c) Insertion

2. Compare and contrast the time that will be required for the bubble, selection, and insertion sorts. Estimate the relative times by calculating statement executions. The algorithm with the most statement executions will have the longest running time.

3. What must be done to a list of items in order to use the binary search to find a specific item?

4. List the numbers checked by a binary search when finding 10 in the list 2, 3, 7, 10, 12, 17, 25, 30, 42.

5. The `DateTime` structure also contains a Second property. A very large set of data may require seconds, rather than milliseconds, to order. Write a set of statements that checks the Second property of a `DateTime` variable. If the seconds are 0, then the Millisecond property should be checked.

6. `CDs` is a sorted array. The following procedure uses a binary search algorithm to determine where `newCD` belongs and inserts it in the correct position. Correct the errors.

```
Private Sub Insert(ByRef CDs() As String,
ByVal newCD As String)
    Dim high As Integer = CDs.Length()
    Dim low As Integer = 0
    Dim mid, spot, move As Integer

    If newCD < CDs(0) Then
        spot = 1
    ElseIf newCD > CDs(CDs.Length - 1) Then
        spot = CDs.Length
    Else
        Do While (low < high)
            mid = (high - low) \ 2
            If CDs(mid) > newCD Then
                    high = mid - 1
            Else
                    low = mid + 1
            End If
        Loop
        spot = low
    End If

        'Move existing items to insert new item
        For move = CDs.Length - 2 To spot
            CDs(move) = CDs(move + 1)
        Next move
        CDs(spot) = newCD
    End Sub
```

True/False

7. Determine if each of the following are true or false. If false, explain why.
   a) To arrange data in a specified order is called sorting.
   b) Of the bubble sort, insertion sort, and selection sort, the bubble sort is the most efficient.
   c) Sorting an array by the bubble sort can be done with one pass through the data.
   d) Selection sort can be used to order data from largest to smallest.
   e) If n items need to be sorted, the selection sort will require n passes through the data.
   f) The binary search can be done on any list of data.
   g) A binary search will usually be faster than the linear search, discussed in Chapter 8.
   h) `now = DateTime` returns the current date and time.

Exercises

Exercise 1 — AlphabetizeNames

Create an AlphabetizeNames application that allows the user to enter any number of names in input boxes and then displays them sorted alphabetically. The application interface should look similar to:

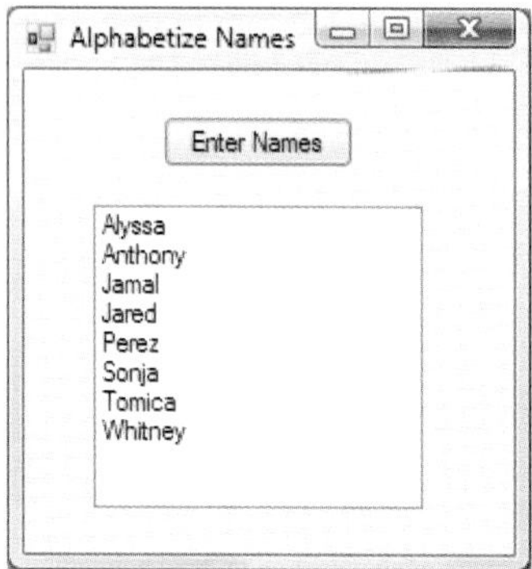

Exercise 2 — SortByField

Create a SortByField application that allows the user to enter first name, last name, and age information for any number of people and then displays the data in a list box sorted by the field selected by the user. Hint: use a structure for storing the data. The application interface should look similar to:

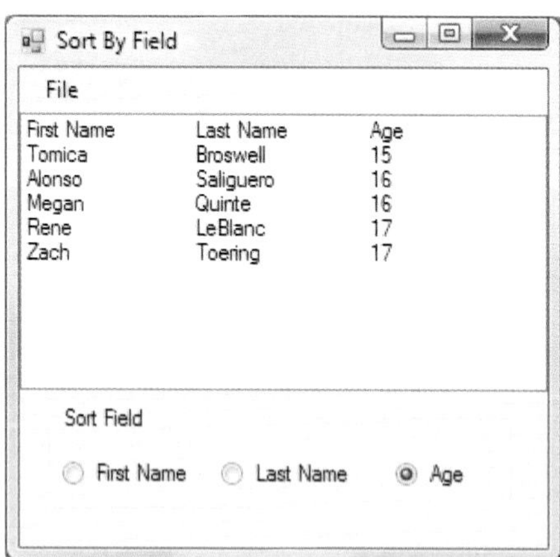

Exercise 3 —— InterpolationSearch

One variation of binary search is called the *interpolation search*. The idea is to look in a likely spot, not necessarily the middle of the array. For example, if the value sought is 967 in an array that holds items ranging from 3 to 1022, it would be intelligent to look near the end of the sorted array. Mathematically, the position to start searching at is a position 95% of the way down the array, because 967 is about 95% of the way from 3 to 1022. For example, if the array holds 500 elements, the first position to examine is 475 (95% of the way from 1 to 500). The search then proceeds to a portion of the array (either 1 to 474 or 476 to 500) depending upon whether 967 is greater or less than the 475th element.

Create an InterpolationSearch application based on the BinarySearch application presented in the text.

Exercise 4 —— TernarySearch

Create a TernarySearch application, similar to the BinarySearch application, that divides the array into three pieces rather than two. TernarySearch finds the points that divide the array into three roughly equal pieces, and then uses these points to determine where the element should be searched for. Add code to time the ternary search to compare it to the binary search.

Exercise 5 (advanced) —— SlangDictionary

a) Create a SlangDictionary application that allows the user to click Add to add a word and its definition to a file. Clicking Search reads each word and corresponding definition from the file into an array of structures. The first line of the file should contain a number indicating how many definitions are stored in the file. The array of words should then be sorted and searched for the word entered by the user. If the word is found, the word and its definition are displayed, otherwise a message box is displayed indicating the word was not found. The application interface should look similar to:

b) The SlangDictionary application sorts the file every time Search is clicked. Modify the application to be more efficient by storing the sorted status in the second line of the file. For example, when Add is clicked the second line should store Unsorted and the new word and definition appended to the file. When Search is clicked, the sort status should be Checked. If unsorted, then the words should be sorted, the second line changed, and then the file searched. If sorted, only searching need be done.

Chapter 13
MDI Applications

Key Concepts

Creating MDI applications
Understanding the parent form - child form relationship
Adding standard Windows application menus
Adding standard Windows application toolbars
Creating dialog boxes
Creating an application that enables a user to cut, copy, and paste between document windows

Case Study

Bingo

Exercise Data Files

sponges.jpg

MDI Applications

parent form

Many applications require multiple forms. An *MDI application* is a multiple-document interface application. This type of Windows application has a parent form and one or more child forms. The *parent form* is a container for the child forms. For example, the MyTextEditor MDI application below displays a parent form with two child forms:

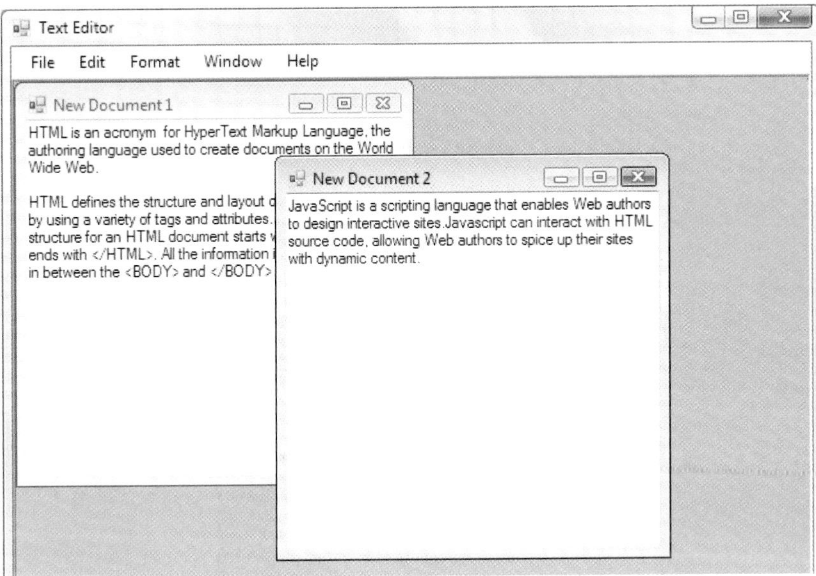

child form

TIP Child forms are moved within the parent form by dragging a title bar.

A *child form* functions completely within the parent form and cannot be moved outside the parent form. The child windows can be tiled, cascaded, and dragged to arrange them within the parent form.

Creating an MDI Application

An application can be an MDI application by first setting the appropriate Form1 properties to create a parent form. These Form control properties are:

- **IsMdiContainer** is set to True for a parent form.
- **WindowState** can be Normal, Minimized, or Maximized. A parent form is typically set to Maximized to fill the entire screen.

A parent form should also include menus and commands for controlling the child forms. These features are discussed later in the chapter.

Next, a form is added to the project. Adding a new form to a project adds a form class, which means that objects of that class to be instantiated in the Form1 module. In other words, statements can be added to the Form1 module (the parent form) to create and display child forms using the new form class. To add a form to a project, select Project → Add Windows Form. The Add New Item dialog box is displayed with the Windows Form icon selected:

TIP A form is a class, which can be used to instantiate objects (forms).

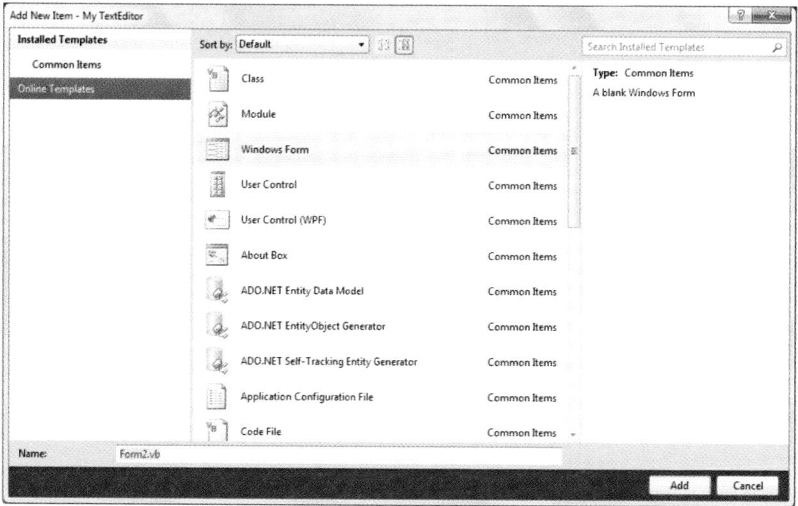

Type a descriptive form name in the Name box (be sure to keep the `.vb` extension) and then select Add. For the MyTextEditor application `NewDocument` is the child form name because it will contain a document. A Design window for the new form is then displayed in the IDE:

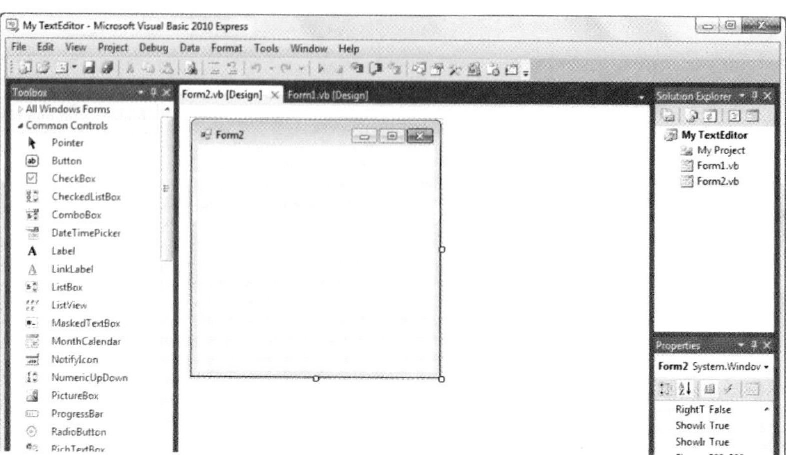

TIP An MDI application typically uses several different child forms.

The child form can be modified just as any form in the Design window. Code specific to the child form is added to the application by switching to the child's Code window.

Using Child Forms

Program code for a parent form includes statements that declare a child form, display the child form, and close the child form. For example, the following Form1 (the parent form) statements instantiate a new form, make the new form a child by assigning it to the parent, and then display the child form:

```
Dim childForm As New NewDocument()  'instantiate a new form
childForm.MdiParent = Me            'assign a parent
childForm.Show()                 'display the child form
```

The first statement above declares a variable named `childForm` using `NewDocument` as the type. The `NewDocument` form added to the project is a class, which can be used to instantiate a new form. Next, the Form control has the property MdiParent, which can be set at run time only. The property is set to `Me` to assign the child form to the current form, Form1, which has been designated as the parent form. In the last statement, the Show() method is used to display the child form.

When no longer needed, a child window should be removed from the MDI application interface. The Form control includes the following method:

- **Close()** closes a form. The form cannot be reopened after closing. A new one must be instantiated and then displayed.

The Close() method can be called from the child code or from the parent code by first determining the active child. To close the active child, the ActiveMdiChild property for the parent form is used. For example, the following statement closes the active child window:

```
Me.ActiveMdiChild.Close()  'parent form closes active child
```

Review: TextEditor – part 1 of 6

① CREATE A NEW PROJECT

Create a Windows application named `TextEditor`.

② CREATE THE PARENT FORM

a. Select the form and set the Text property to `Text Editor`, the IsMdiContainer to True, and WindowState to Maximized.

b. Add a File menu and commands. Use the table below for setting MenuItem properties.

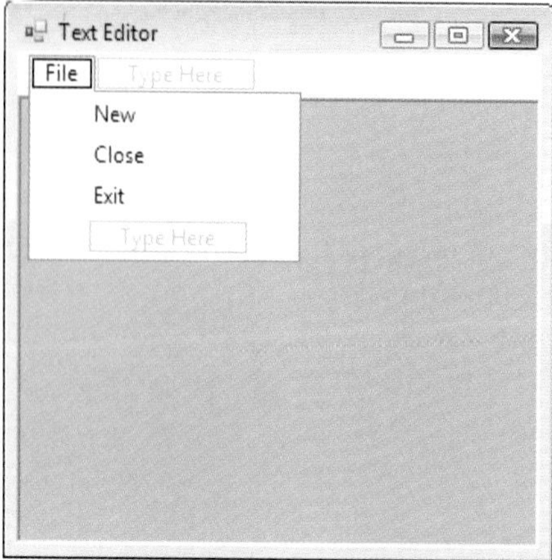

Object	Text
MenuItem1	`File`
MenuItem2	`New`
MenuItem3	`Close`
MenuItem4	`Exit`

c. Check the names of the four menu items. Change their (Name) properties as appropriate to `FileToolStripMenuItem`, `NewToolStripMenuItem`, `CloseToolStripMenuItem`, and `ExitToolStripMenuItem`, if necessary.

③ ADD A CHILD FORM

a. Select Project → Add Windows Form. A dialog box is displayed.
   1. In the Templates list, click Windows Form, if it is not already selected.
   2. In the Name box, type `NewDocument.vb`.
   3. Select Add. A form named NewDocument.vb is displayed in a Design window. Note the file added to the project as shown in the Solution Explorer window.

b. Set the Text property of the NewDocument form to `New Document`.

④ WRITE THE APPLICATION CODE

a. Display the Form1 Design window and then display the Form1 Code window.

b. Add comments that include your name and today's date.

c. Create a NewToolStripMenuItem_Click event procedure and then add statements to display a new document window with an appropriate title bar:

```
Static docNum As Integer = 0          'document number
Dim doc As New NewDocument()          'create new document window

'Assign document parent
doc.MdiParent = Me
'Create title bar that includes document number
docNum += 1
doc.Text = "New Document " & docNum
'Show window
doc.Show()
```

d. Create a CloseToolStripMenuItem_Click event procedure and then add a statement to close the active window:

```
Me.ActiveMdiChild.Close()
```

e. Create a ExitToolStripMenuItem_Click event procedure and then add a statement to end the application:

```
Application.Exit()
```

⑤ RUN THE APPLICATION

a. Save the modified TextEditor project and then run the application.

b. Select File → New. A New Document 1 window is displayed. Drag the window in the TextEditor window to move it.

c. Select File → New. A New Document 2 window is displayed.

d. Click the New Document 1 window to make it the active window. Select File → Close. The window is closed.

e. Close the New Document 2 window.

f. Select File → Exit to quit the TextEditor application.

Creating a Window Menu

An MDI application should include a Window menu with commands for arranging windows and switching between open windows. Commands for arranging open windows include Tile Horizontal, Tile Vertical, and Cascade. To switch between active windows, the name of an open window name is clicked from the list displayed at the bottom of the Window menu, as in the menu:

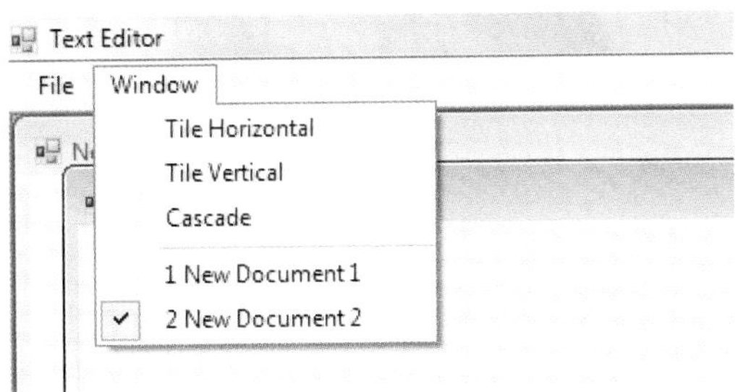

The Form control includes a method for automatically arranging windows in a parent form:

- **LayoutMdi(*LayoutOption*)** arranges open windows in a parent form. `LayoutOption` includes `MdiLayout.Cascade`, `MdiLayout.TileHorizontal`, and `MdiLayout.TileVertical`.

For example, the following MenuItem event procedure uses the Form control LayoutModi() method to tile open windows horizontally:

```
Private Sub TileHorizontalToolStripMenuItem _ Click(ByVal _
sender As Object, ByVal e As System.EventArgs) _
Handles TileHorizontalToolStripMenuItem.Click
  Me.LayoutMdi(MdiLayout.TileHorizontal)
End Sub
```

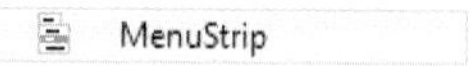

The MenuStrip control includes a property for designating which MenuItem will display the list of open child form names:

- **MdiWindowListItem** can be set to an existing MenuItem. The selected MenuItem will automatically list child form names as they are opened.

Review: TextEditor – part 2 of 6

① ADD A WINDOW MENU TO FORM1

a. Display the Form1 Design window.

b. Modify the parent form to include a Window menu. Use the table on the next page for setting object properties.

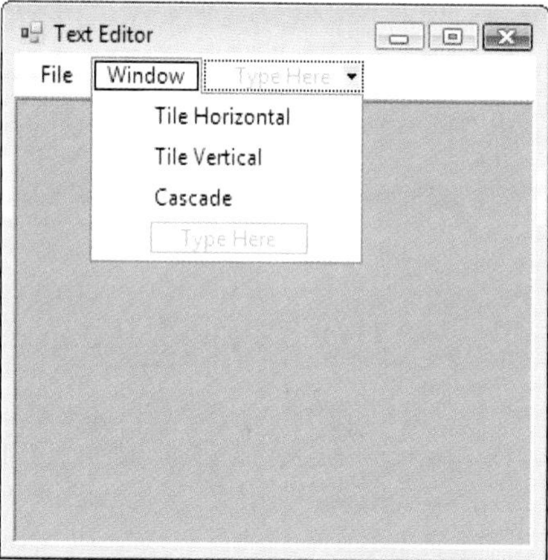

Object	Text
MenuItem1	`Window`
MenuItem2	`Tile Horizontal`
MenuItem3	`Tile Vertical`
MenuItem4	`Cascade`

c. Check the names of the four new menu items. Change their (Name) properties as appropriate to `WindowToolStripMenuItem`, `TileHorizontalToolStripMenuItem`, `TileVerticalToolStripMenuItem`, and `CascadeToolStripMenuItem`, if necessary.

d. In the Design window Component tray, click the MenuStrip1 to select it.

e. In the Properties window, change the MdiWindowListItem property to WindowToolStripMenuItem.

② WRITE THE APPLICATION CODE

a. Display the Form1 Code window.

b. Create a TileHorizontalToolStripMenuItem_Click event procedure and then add a statement to tile opened windows horizontally:

```
Me.LayoutMdi(MdiLayout.TileHorizontal)
```

c. Create a TileVerticalToolStripMenuItem_Click event procedure and then add a statement to tile opened windows vertically:

```
Me.LayoutMdi(MdiLayout.TileVertical)
```

d. Create a CascadeToolStripMenuItem_Click event procedure and then add a statement to cascade opened windows:

```
Me.LayoutMdi(MdiLayout.Cascade)
```

③ RUN THE APPLICATION

a. Save the modified TextEditor project and then run the application.

b. Select File → New three times to display three new document windows.

c. Display the Window menu. Note the document names listed at the bottom of the menu with the active window displaying a check mark.

d. Test each of the Window menu commands.

e. Quit the TextEditor application.

Advanced TextBox Methods

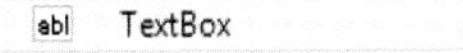

The TextBox control has methods that can be used for editing text in a text box. These methods are:

- **Copy()** copies selected text in the text box to the Windows Clipboard.
- **Cut()** removes selected text from the text box and places it on the Windows Clipboard.
- **Paste()** replaces selected text with text from the Windows Clipboard. If no text is selected, text from the Clipboard is placed at the insertion point.

The user selects text by dragging the pointer over any amount of text. Double-clicking text selects a single word. Selected text is shown as highlighted in the text box.

Commands for editing text are typically found in the Edit menu of an application. The Copy(), Cut(), and Paste() methods are typically used in the Click event procedures of these commands. For example, the CutToolStripMenuItem_Click event procedure below removes selected text from the active child form. Note that the active child must first be determined:

```
Private Sub CutToolStripMenuItem_Click(ByVal sender _
As Object, ByVal e As System.EventArgs) _
Handles CutToolStripMenuItem.Click
  Dim activeDoc As NewDocument = Me.ActiveMdiChild
  activeDoc.txtDocument.Cut()
End Sub
```

Review: TextEditor – part 3 of 6

① MODIFY THE NEWDOCUMENT FORM

a. Display the NewDocument Design window.

b. Refer to the form below to add a TextBox object. Set the (Name) property to `txtDocument`, Multiline to True, Dock to Fill (the large middle option), and Text to *empty*.

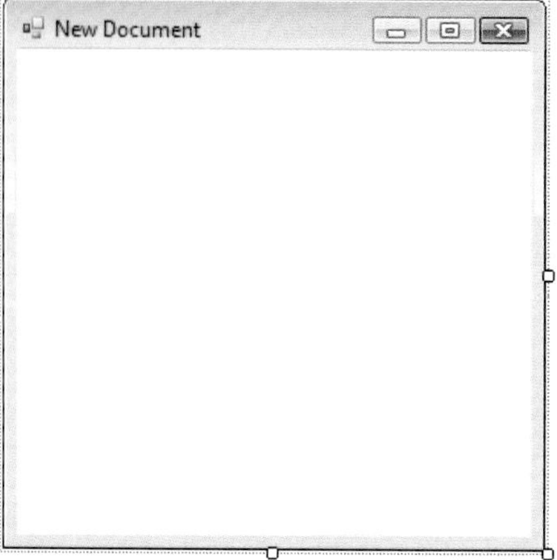

② ADD AN EDIT MENU TO FORM1

a. Display the Form1 Design window.

b. Modify the parent form to include an Edit menu. Use the table below for setting object properties.

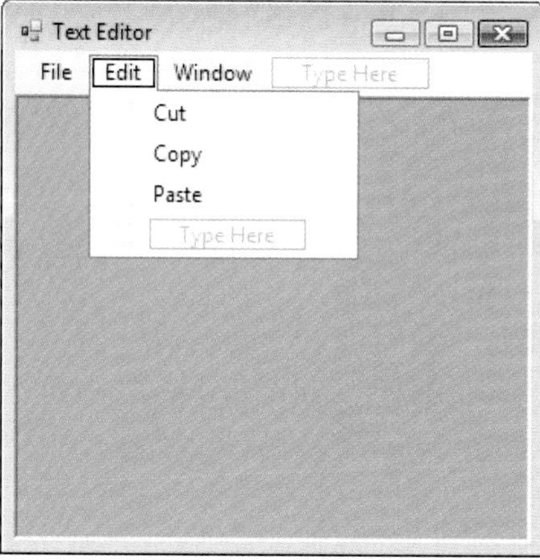

Note: To add the Edit menu between the File and Window menus, right-click the Window menu name and select Insert → MenuItem from the displayed menu.

Object	**Text**
MenuItem1	`Edit`
MenuItem2	`Cut`
MenuItem3	`Copy`
MenuItem4	`Paste`

c. Check the names of the four new menu items. Change their (Name) properties as appropriate to `EditToolStripMenuItem`, `CutToolStripMenuItem`, `CopyToolStripMenuItem`, and `PasteToolStripMenuItem`, if necessary.

③ MODIFY THE APPLICATION CODE

a. Display the Form1 Code window.

b. Create a CutToolStripMenuItem_Click event procedure and then add statements to move selected text in the active window to the Clipboard:

```
Dim activeDoc As NewDocument = Me.ActiveMdiChild
activeDoc.txtDocument.Cut()
```

c. Create a CopyToolStripMenuItem_Click event procedure and then add statements to copy selected text to the Clipboard:

```
Dim activeDoc As NewDocument = Me.ActiveMdiChild
activeDoc.txtDocument.Copy()
```

d. Create a PasteToolStripMenuItem_Click event procedure and then add statements to paste Clipboard text at the insertion point:

```
Dim activeDoc As NewDocument = Me.ActiveMdiChild
activeDoc.txtDocument.Paste()
```

④ RUN THE APPLICATION

a. Save the modified TextEditor project and then run the application.
b. Display two new document windows and then type some text into the New Document 1 window.
c. Select some of the typed text and then select Edit → Cut. The selected text is removed.
d. Click in the New Document 2 window to place the insertion point. Select Edit → Paste. The text from the Clipboard is inserted.
e. Test the Copy command.
f. Close the document windows and quit the TextEditor application.

Creating Dialog Boxes

Applications typically include menus with commands that perform actions. However, many commands require information from the user before executing. For example, an Alignment command must be told the type of paragraph alignment before it can execute. An application uses *dialog boxes* to get the information needed to execute a command.

Dialog boxes have certain features. They cannot be sized, minimized, or maximized. They include at least an OK button and a Cancel button, and they require the user to select one of these buttons before control is given back to the calling form.

A dialog box is created for an application by first adding a new form to the project. The Form control has properties for designating the form a dialog box:

- **ControlBox** is set to False because a dialog box should not offer access to the System menu.
- **MaximizeBox** is set to False because a dialog box should not be sized.
- **MinimizeBox** is set to False because a dialog box should not be sized.
- **FormBorderStyle** is set to FixedDialog to prevent the dialog box from being sized.

Commands with an Ellipsis

A command name with an ellipsis (...) after it indicates that a dialog box will be displayed when the command is selected.

The Dialog Form

Visual Basic includes the dialog form, which can be added to a project. This form includes OK and Cancel buttons. However, properties still need to be set.

TIP A dialog box can also be added by selecting Project → Add New Item and selecting Dialog.

After setting properties, the dialog box can then be customized with objects that get the needed user input. For example, an Alignment dialog box might look similar to:

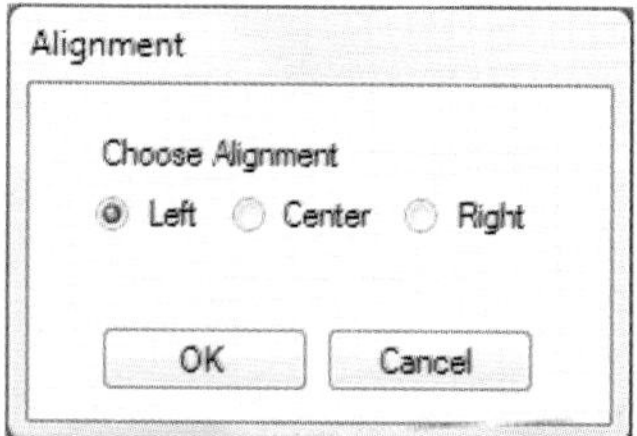

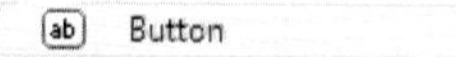

The Button control has a property that must be set for the OK and Cancel buttons in a dialog box:

- **DialogResult** can be set to None, OK, Cancel, Abort, Retry, Ignore, Yes, or No. None is the default. The option should be set to correspond to the Text property of a dialog box button. For example, a Yes button has Text set to `Yes` and DialogResult set to Yes.

The Form control has a method for displaying a dialog box as a modal form:

- **ShowDialog()** displays a form modally.

modal form

A *modal form* does not allow other forms to receive input until it has been removed from the screen. For example, a dialog box displayed as a modal form requires the user to select the OK or Cancel button, which removes the dialog box from the screen, before other forms can receive input.

The code below instantiates a dialog box object and then displays the object as a modal form. No other statements are executed until the user selects either the OK or Cancel buttons in the dialog box. If the user selected OK, the `If...Then` statement is executed to change the alignment of the text box in the active form:

```
Dim alignmentDB As New AlignmentDialogBox()
Dim activeDoc As NewDocument = Me.ActiveMdiChild

'Show dialog box
alignmentDB.ShowDialog()

'Change alignment of text in active document
If alignmentDB.DialogResult = Windows.Forms.DialogResult.OK Then
  If alignmentDB.radLeft.Checked Then
    activeDoc.txtDocument.TextAlign = HorizontalAlignment.Left
  ElseIf alignmentDB.radCenter.Checked Then
    activeDoc.txtDocument.TextAlign = HorizontalAlignment.Center
  ElseIf alignmentDB.radRight.Checked Then
    activeDoc.txtDocument.TextAlign = HorizontalAlignment.Right
  End If
End If
```

TIP The DialogResult options appear in an IntelliSense list after = is typed in a condition that involves the DialogResult property.

① ADD A DIALOG BOX TO THE PROJECT

a. Select Project → Add Windows Form. A dialog box is displayed.

   1. In the Templates list, click Windows Form, if it is not already selected.
   2. In the Name box, type `AlignmentDialogBox.vb`.
   3. Select Add. A form named AlignmentDialogBox.vb is displayed in a Design window.

b. Set the Text property of the AlignmentDialogBox form to `Alignment`.

c. Set the ControlBox, MaximizeBox, and MinimizeBox properties to False.

d. Set the FormBorderStyle to FixedDialog.

e. Use the table below for setting object properties.

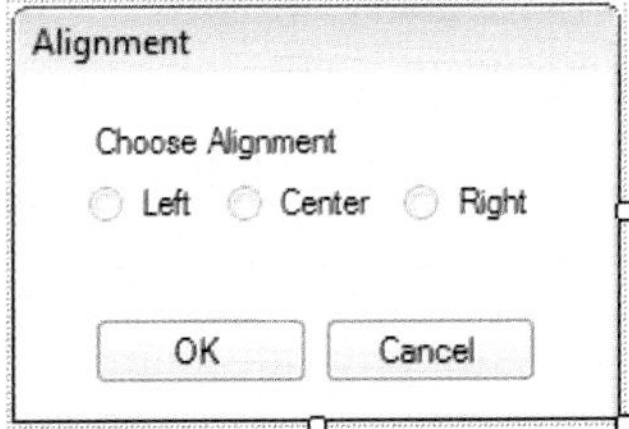

Object	(Name)	Text	DialogResult
GroupBox1	`grpAlignmentOptions`	`Choose Alignment`	
RadioButton1	`radLeft`	`Left`	
RadioButton2	`radCenter`	`Center`	
RadioButton3	`radRight`	`Right`	
Button1	`btnOK`	`OK`	OK
Button2	`btnCancel`	`Cancel`	Cancel

② ADD A FORMAT MENU TO FORM1

a. Display the Form1 Design window.

b. Modify the parent form to include a Format menu. Use the table on the next page for setting object properties.

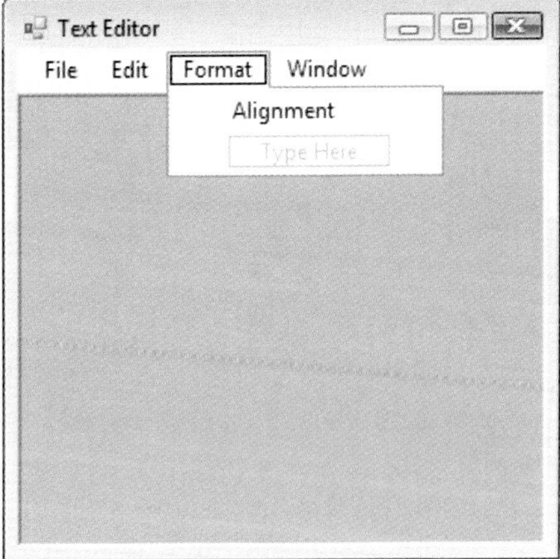

Note: To add the Format menu between the Edit and Window menus, right-click the Window menu name and select Insert → MenuItem from the displayed menu.

Object	Text
MenuItem1	Format
MenuItem2	Alignment...

c. Check the names of the two new menu items. Change their (Name) properties as appropriate to `FormatToolStripMenuItem` and `AlignmentToolStripMenuItem`, if necessary.

③ **MODIFY THE APPLICATION CODE**

a. Display the Form1 Code window.

b. Create an AlignmentToolStripMenuItem_Click event procedure and then add statements to display a dialog box and apply selected alignment:

```
Dim alignmentDB As New AlignmentDialogBox()
Dim activeDoc As NewDocument = Me.ActiveMdiChild

'Show dialog box
alignmentDB.ShowDialog()

'Change alignment of text in active document
If alignmentDB.DialogResult = Windows.Forms.DialogResult.OK Then
    If alignmentDB.radLeft.Checked Then
        activeDoc.txtDocument.TextAlign = HorizontalAlignment.Left
    ElseIf alignmentDB.radCenter.Checked Then
        activeDoc.txtDocument.TextAlign = HorizontalAlignment.Center
    Else
        activeDoc.txtDocument.TextAlign = HorizontalAlignment.Right
    End If
End If
```

④ **RUN THE APPLICATION**

a. Save the modified TextEditor project and then run the application.

b. Display a new document window and then type several paragraphs of text into the New Document 1 window.

c. Select Format → Alignment. A dialog box is displayed.

   1. Click Center.
   2. Click OK. The text is center aligned.

d. Test the other alignment options.

e. Close the document window and quit the TextEditor application.

Creating a Help Menu

A Windows application should contain a Help menu with commands for displaying information about how to use an application. The last command in the Help menu should display a dialog box with copyright, authorship, and version information. This command is referred to as the About command. For example, the About Text Editor... command displays an About dialog box similar to:

TIP An About dialog box can also be added by selecting Project → Add New Item and selecting About Box.

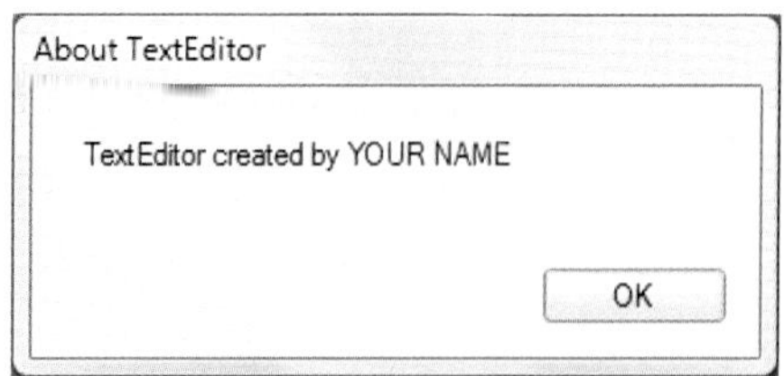

The About dialog box is created by adding a form to the project and then setting appropriate form options, adding labels, and an OK button with the appropriate DialogResult property set.

Review: TextEditor – part 5 of 6

① ADD A DIALOG BOX TO THE PROJECT

a. Select Project → Add Windows Form. A dialog box is displayed.
   1. In the Templates list, click Windows Form, if it is not already selected.
   2. In the Name box, type AboutDialogBox.vb.
   3. Select Add. A form named AboutDialogBox.vb is displayed in a Design window.

b. Set the Text property of the AboutDialogBox form to `About TextEditor`.

c. Set the ControlBox, MaximizeBox, and MinimizeBox properties to False.

d. Set the FormBorderStyle to FixedDialog.

e. Use the table below for setting object properties.

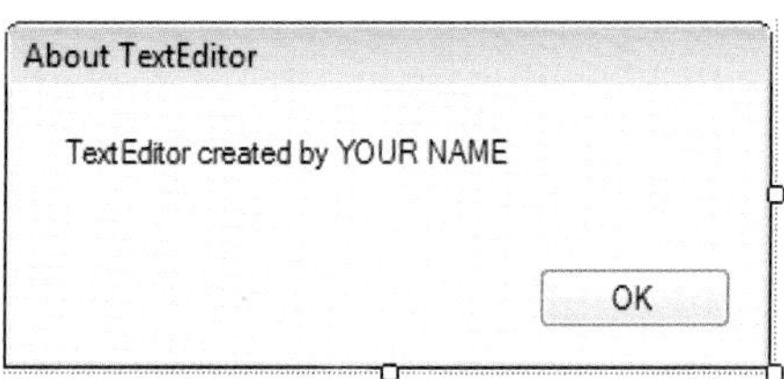

Object	(Name)	Text	DialogResult
Label1	`lblInfo`	*see form*	
Button1	`btnOK`	`OK`	OK

② ADD A HELP MENU TO FORM1

a. Display the Form1 Design window.

b. Modify the parent form to include a Help menu. Use the table below for setting object properties.

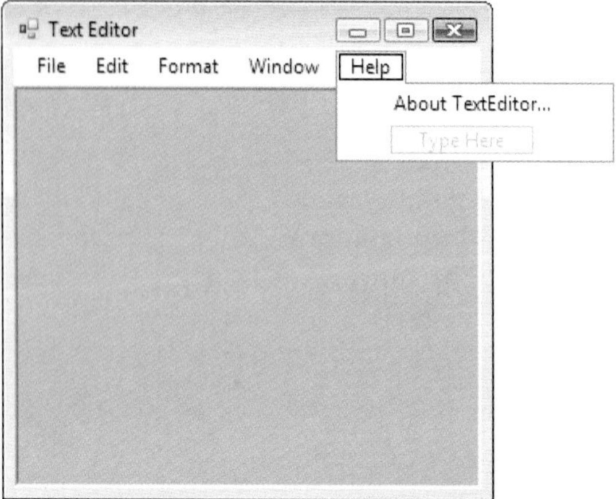

Object	Text
MenuItem1	`Help`
MenuItem2	`About TextEditor...`

c. Check the names of the two new menu items. Change their (Name) properties as appropriate to `HelpToolStripMenuItem` and `AboutToolStripMenuItem`, if necessary.

③ MODIFY THE APPLICATION CODE

a. Display the Form1 Code window.

b. Create a AboutTextEditorToolStripMenuItem_Click event procedure and then add statements to display the About dialog box:

```
Dim aboutDB As New AboutDialogBox()

'Show dialog box
aboutDB.ShowDialog()
```

④ RUN THE APPLICATION

a. Save the modified TextEditor project and then run the application.

b. Select Help → About TextEditor. A dialog box is displayed.

1. Note the application information and then click OK. The dialog box is removed.

Adding a Toolbar

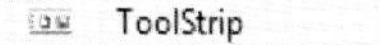

A Windows application typically includes a toolbar. To add a toolbar to an interface, click the ToolStrip control in the Toolbox and then click the form. A toolbar object is added to the form and the ToolStrip component is shown in the component tray at the bottom of the Design window. Click the shortcut arrow in the toolbar object to display ToolStrip Tasks:

TIP The shortcut arrow in the toolbar control is referred to as a 'smart tag'.

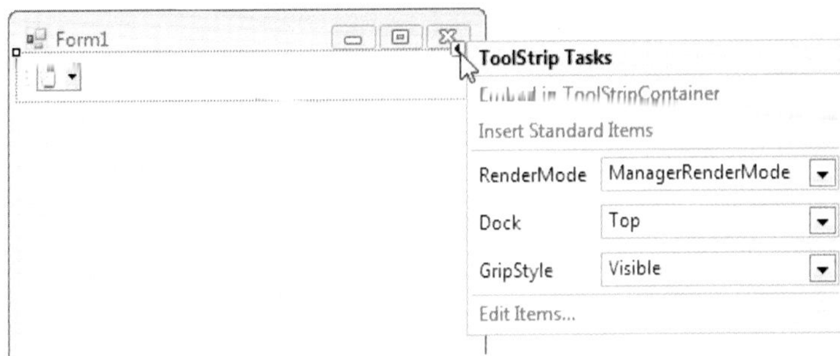

Click Insert Standard Items to automatically add a collection of standard toolbar buttons (New, Open, Save, Print, Cut, Copy, Paste, and Help):

The buttons are then made functional by writing event procedures. For example, to display an Open dialog box when the Open button is clicked, add the statement `Me.OpenFileDialog1.ShowDialog()` to the OpenToolStripButton click event procedure.

Alternatively, individual buttons are added to the toolbar by clicking the Add ToolStripButton arrow and selecting Button from the displayed menu. The default button contains a picture of a mountain, which can be modified by setting properties in the Properties window.

Toolbar buttons can be rearranged by dragging a button to a new location on the toolbar. To delete a button, right-click the button and select Delete.

Review: TextEditor – part 6 of 6

Modify the TextEditor application to include a toolbar with a New, Open, Save, Cut, Copy, Paste, and Help buttons. Write an event procedure for each toolbar button.

Case Study

In this case study a Bingo application will be created.

Bingo Specification

The Bingo application plays a game with one or two players. Each player can display any number of cards, with each card being unique. The cards are traditional Bingo cards with columns B, I, N, G, and O, and numbers that range from 1 through 75 with column B containing five numbers ranging from 1 to 15, column I with five numbers from 16 to 30, column N with four numbers from 31 to 45 and a Free Space in the middle of column N, column G with five numbers from 46 to 60, and column O with five numbers from 61 to 75. After a random number is "called," players "mark" their cards. The first player to mark five consecutive numbers has "Bingo!"

Bingo Design

A MDI application is the best design approach because this game can have more than one player and each player can have more than one card. As with any MDI application, Bingo will have File, Window, and Help menus. A button docked at the bottom of the parent form generates number calls and a label docked on the right of the parent form lists numbers already called:

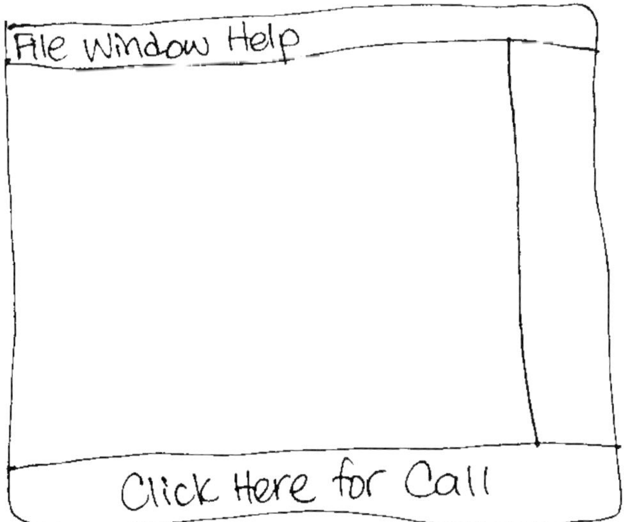

The Bingo cards in the application interface can be generated from a single child form designed with rows and columns of numbers. The player must be able to "mark" the "card," so buttons are the best choice for displaying the numbers. Before an instance of the Bingo form is displayed, a set of randomly generated numbers can be assigned to the Text property of each of the 25 buttons:

B	I	N	G	O
6	16	33	46	64
8	19	36	50	68
11	22	FREE SPACE	52	70
13	25	41	59	72
15	27	44	60	73

The player should not be able to size the card. This can be prevented by setting the FormBorderStyle property to FixedSingle. The Maximize button will not be needed on this form either.

This MDI application requires two other forms, a Help dialog box with game instructions and an About dialog box. These could look similar to:

Rules
OK
Bingo was created using Visual Basic
OK

The code design should start with an algorithm and also pseudocode. The Bingo algorithm can be based on one player with one Bingo card:

1. A Bingo card object is instantiated from the BingoCard child form by selecting File → New Card. Random numbers are generated and assigned to the buttons of the new Bingo card before displaying the card.
2. The player clicks the call button at the bottom of the screen to start the calls. Clicking this button generates a unique random number from 1 through 75 and then displays the number along with the proper row letter. The number called is also added to the label shown on the right side of the interface.
3. If a called number is also on the Bingo card, the user clicks the card so that the number is marked with Xs on both sides (for example, X14X).
4. The player continues to click the call button until five consecutive buttons on the card are marked. At this point the player has Bingo. It is up to the player to determine when the fifth consecutive number is marked on the card. The player can double-check the marked numbers by checking the call list.
5. The player quits the application by selecting File → Exit.

Based on the game algorithm, the menus and their commands for the application can be further refined:

- A File → New Card command contains a submenu with Player 1 and Player 2 commands to instantiate BingoCard objects. The title bar of the new card should state the player and card number. For example, "Player 1 Card 1."
- A File → Exit command ends the application.
- The Window menu contains commands for tiling the cards. There is no need for a Cascade command because players won't be able to see all the numbers on cascaded cards.
- The Help menu contains commands for displaying a Help dialog box with basic game instructions and an About dialog box with application information.

The algorithm for creating a Bingo card also needs further refinement. A Bingo card can be thought of as five columns of five unique random numbers with each column having numbers from a different range. In this case, column B ranges from 1 to 15, column I from 16 to 30, column N from 31 to 45, column G from 46 to 60, and column O from 61 to 75. With this approach, the task of creating a Bingo card can be divided into procedures GenerateBingoCard(), GenerateColumn(), and UniqueNumberArray():

- GenerateBingoCard() declares five arrays of Button objects, one for each row of the card. The array of Button objects is passed by reference to GenerateColumn().
- GenerateColumn() assigns each Button element a value from an array of unique random numbers. The random numbers are generated with UniqueNumberArray().
- UniqueNumbersArray() creates an array of unique numbers from 0 to a specified maximum value. The array and maximum value are passed in the procedure call. A `Boolean` array with meaningful indexes is used to keep track of which numbers have been generated by storing True in the element with the same index as the generated random number. If the value at the index is already True another number is generated. This process is continued until there are enough unique random numbers to fill the array.

The algorithm is implemented with the following pseudocode:

```
Private Sub Player1ToolStripMenuItem_Click(sender, e) _
Handles Player1ToolStripMenuItem.Click
    Create a new card using the BingoCard form
    Assign card to parent form
    Give card a title that includes the card number
    Call GenerateBingoCard(bingoCard) to give each button on
        the card a unique number in the appropriate range.
    Show the card
End Sub

Private Sub Player2ToolStripMenuItem_Click(sender, e) _
Handles Player2ToolStripMenuItem.Click
    Create a new card using the BingoCard form
    Assign card to parent form
    Give card a title that includes the card number
    Call GenerateBingoCard(bingoCard) to give each button on
        the card a unique number in the appropriate range
    Show the card
End Sub

Private Sub ExitToolStripMenuItem_Click(sender, e) _
Handles ExitToolStripMenuItem.Click
    Exit the application
End Sub

Private Sub TileHorizontalToolStripMenuItem_Click(sender, e) _
Handles TileHorizontalToolStripMenuItem.Click
    Me.LayoutMdi(MdiLayout.TileHorizontal)
End Sub
```

```
Private Sub TileVerticalToolStripMenuItem_Click(sender, e) _
Handles TileVerticalToolStripMenuItem.Click
    Me.LayoutMdi(MdiLayout.TileVertical)
End Sub

Private Sub AboutToolStripMenuItem_Click(sender, e) _
Handles AboutToolStripMenuItem.Click
    Create new About dialog box from AboutDialogBox form
    Show the dialog box
End Sub

Private Sub HowToPlayToolStripMenuItem_Click(sender, e) _
Handles HowToPlayToolStripMenuItem.Click
    Create new How To Play dialog box from HelpDialogBox form
    Show the dialog box
End Sub

Sub GenerateBingoCard(ByRef newCard As BingoCard)
    Create an array of buttons for each column on the Bingo card
    Call GenerateColumn() for each array of buttons to assign a
        unique number in the appropriate range to the text of each
        button.
End Sub

Sub GenerateColumn(ByRef btnArray() As Button,
ByVal offset As Integer)
    Generate a set of btnArray.Length numbers in the range 0 to 14
    Add the offset to each number and then assign to the Text
        properties of the buttons
End Sub

Sub UniqueNumbersArray(ByVal maxValue As Integer,
ByRef numArray() As Integer)
    Dim numChecker(maxValue - 1) As Boolean
    For num = 0 to numArray.Length – 1
        Do
            Generate a random number
        While index numChecker(randomNum) is True
        Set numChecker(randomNum) to True
    Next num

    For num = 0 to numChecker.Length – 1
        if numChecker(num) Then
            numArray(index) = num
            increment index number
        End If
    Next num
End Sub
```

```
Private Sub btnNumber_Click(sender, e) Handles btnNumber.Click
    Generate a unique random number between 1 and 75
    'Display call out
    Select Case indexToCheck
        Case 0 To 14
            Me.btnNumber.Text = "B " & callNumber + 1
        Case 15 To 29
            Me.btnNumber.Text = "I " & callNumber + 1
        Case 30 To 44
            Me.btnNumber.Text = "N " & callNumber + 1
        Case 45 To 59
            Me.btnNumber.Text = "G " & callNumber + 1
        Case 60 To 74
            Me.btnNumber.Text = "O " & callNumber + 1
    End Select
    Add call to label displaying the numbers called
End Sub
```

Pseudocode for the child form, which must mark numbers, appears like:

```
Private Sub Button_Click(ByVal sender As Object, _
ByVal e As System.EventArgs) Handles ALL BUTTONS
    Dim btnButtonClicked As Button = sender
    btnButtonClicked.Text = "X" & btnButtonClicked.Text & "X"
End Sub
```

Bingo Coding

The interface for Bingo, additional forms, and code follow. The parent form interface and BingoCard interface are:

Object	**Text**	**WindowState**
Form1	`Bingo`	Maximized
MenuStrip1		
MenuItem1	`File`	
MenuItem2	`New Card`	
MenuItem3	`Player 1`	
MenuItem4	`Player 2`	
MenuItem5	`Exit`	

MenuItem6 `Window`
MenuItem7 `Tile Horizontal`
MenuItem8 `Tile Vertical`
MenuItem9 `Help`
MenuItem10 `How To Play...`
MenuItem11 `About Bingo...`

Object	**(Name)**	**Text**	**Dock**	**Font Style**	**Font Size**
Button1	`btnNumber`	`Click Here for Call`	Bottom	Bold	18
Label1	`lblCalled`	*empty*	Right		

Object	**(Name)**	**Text**	**FormBorderStyle**	**MaximizeBox**
Form1	`BingoCard`	`Bingo Card`	FixedSingle	False

Object	**(Name)**	**Text**	**TextAlign**	**Font Style**	**Font Size**
Label1	`lblB`	`B`	MiddleCenter	Bold	14
Label2	`lblI`	`I`	MiddleCenter	Bold	14
Label3	`lblN`	`N`	MiddleCenter	Bold	14
Label4	`lblG`	`G`	MiddleCenter	Bold	14
Label5	`lblO`	`O`	MiddleCenter	Bold	14
Button1	`btnBSlot1`	*empty*			
Button2	`btnBSlot2`	*empty*			
...					
Button13	`btnNSlot3`	*empty*			
...					
Button24	`btnOSlot4`	*empty*			
Button25	`btnOSlot5`	*empty*			

The Bingo application also contains two dialog boxes, which have FormBorderStyle set to FixedDialog, and MaximizeBox, MinimizeBox, and ControlBox set to False. The dialog box form interfaces and additional properties set are:

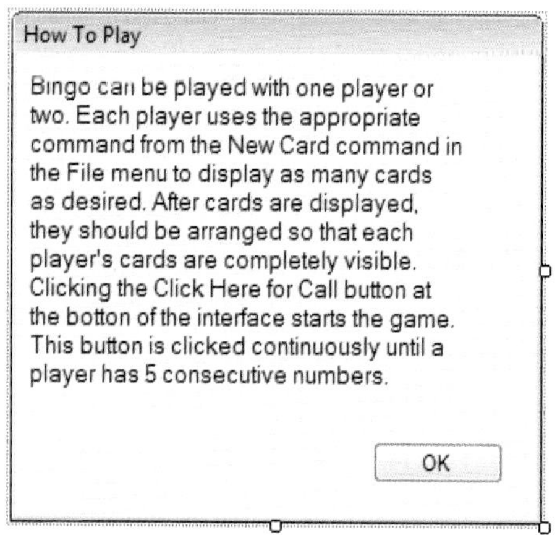
How To Play
Bingo can be played with one player or two. Each player uses the appropriate command from the New Card command in the File menu to display as many cards as desired. After cards are displayed, they should be arranged so that each player's cards are completely visible. Clicking the Click Here for Call button at the botton of the interface starts the game. This button is clicked continuously until a player has 5 consecutive numbers.
OK

Object	(Name)	Text	Font Size	DialogResult
Form1	HelpDialogBox	How To Play		
Label1	lblInfo	*see form*	10	
Button1	btnOK	OK		OK

About Bingo
Bingo was created using Visual Basic.
OK

Object	(Name)	Text	Font Size	DialogResult
Form1	AboutDialogBox	About Bingo		
Label1	lblInfo	*see form*	10	
Button1	btnOK	OK		OK

The final coding for Bingo is:

```
Public Class Form1

    'File menu commands

    Private Sub Player1ToolStripMenuItem_Click(ByVal sender As Object,
    ByVal e As System.EventArgs) Handles Player1ToolStripMenuItem.Click
        Static cardNum As Integer = 0
        Dim card As New BingoCard

        card.MdiParent = Me
        cardNum += 1
        card.Text = "Player 1 Card " & cardNum
        Call GenerateBingoCard(card)

        card.Show()
    End Sub

    Private Sub Player2ToolStripMenuItem_Click(ByVal sender As Object,
    ByVal e As System.EventArgs) Handles Player2ToolStripMenuItem.Click
        Static cardNum As Integer = 0
        Dim card As New BingoCard

        card.MdiParent = Me
        cardNum += 1
```

```
    card.Text = "Player 2 Card " & cardNum
    Call GenerateBingoCard(card)

    card.Show()
End Sub

Private Sub ExitToolStripMenuItem _ Click(ByVal sender As Object,
ByVal e As System.EventArgs) Handles ExitToolStripMenuItem.Click
    Application.Exit()
End Sub

'Windows menu commands

Private Sub TileHorizontalToolStripMenuItem _ Click(ByVal sender As Object,
ByVal e As System.EventArgs) Handles TileHorizontalToolStripMenuItem.Click
    Me.LayoutMdi(MdiLayout.TileHorizontal)
End Sub

Private Sub TileVerticalToolStripMenuItem _ Click(ByVal sender As Object,
ByVal e As System.EventArgs) Handles TileVerticalToolStripMenuItem.Click
    Me.LayoutMdi(MdiLayout.TileVertical)
End Sub

'Help menu commands

Private Sub AboutBingoToolStripMenuItem _ Click(ByVal sender As Object,
ByVal e As System.EventArgs) Handles AboutBingoToolStripMenuItem.Click
    Dim aboutDB As New AboutDialogBox
    aboutDB.ShowDialog()
End Sub

Private Sub HowToPlayToolStripMenuItem _ Click(ByVal sender As Object,
ByVal e As System.EventArgs) Handles HowToPlayToolStripMenuItem.Click
    Dim helpDB As New HelpDialogBox
    helpDB.ShowDialog()
End Sub

'Other procedures

'Generates a bingo card of random, unique numbers
'
'pre: newCard has 5 columns of 5 buttons each.
'post: Each newCard button has been assigned a unique random number
'in the appropriate range for columns B, I, N, G, and O
'
Sub GenerateBingoCard(ByRef newCard As BingoCard)
    Dim bColumn() As Button = {newCard.btnBSlot1, newCard.btnBSlot2,
    newCard.btnBSlot3, newCard.btnBSlot4, newCard.btnBSlot5}
    Call GenerateColumn(bColumn, 1)

    Dim iColumn() As Button = {newCard.btnISlot1, newCard.btnISlot2,
    newCard.btnISlot3, newCard.btnISlot4, newCard.btnISlot5}
    Call GenerateColumn(iColumn, 16)

    Dim nColumn() As Button = {newCard.btnNSlot1, newCard.btnNSlot2,
    newCard.btnNSlot3, newCard.btnNSlot4, newCard.btnNSlot5}
    Call GenerateColumn(nColumn, 31)
    newCard.btnNSlot3.Text = "Free Space"

    Dim gColumn() As Button = {newCard.btnGSlot1, newCard.btnGSlot2,
    newCard.btnGSlot3, newCard.btnGSlot4, newCard.btnGSlot5}
    Call GenerateColumn(gColumn, 46)
```

```
    Dim oColumn() As Button = {newCard.btnOSlot1, newCard.btnOSlot2,
    newCard.btnOSlot3, newCard.btnOSlot4, newCard.btnOSlot5}
    Call GenerateColumn(oColumn, 61)
End Sub

'Sets the text for each button of btnArray to a unique random number
'ranging from 0 to 14, offset by offset
'
'pre: btnArray contains 5 button objects
'post: Each button in btnArray has been assigned a unique random
'number in the appropriate range
'
Sub GenerateColumn(ByRef btnArray() As Button, ByRef offset As Integer)
    Dim numbers(4) As Integer

    'Get a unique set of numbers
    Call UniqueNumbersArray(15, numbers)
    'Assign numbers to buttons
    For buttonNum As Integer = 0 To btnArray.Length - 1
        btnArray(buttonNum).Text = numbers(buttonNum) + offset
    Next buttonNum
End Sub

'Fills numArray with unique numbers ranging from 0 to maxValue.
'
'post: numArray contains unique integers ranging in value from
'0 to maxValue.
'
Sub UniqueNumbersArray(ByVal maxValue As Integer, ByRef numArray() As Integer)
    Dim numChecker(maxValue - 1) As Boolean     'defaults to False values
    Dim indexToCheck As Integer
    Dim index As Integer

    Randomize()
    'Generate numArray.Length - 1 unique numbers
    For num As Integer = 0 To numArray.Length - 1
        'Generate a random number until one that has not
        'already been generated comes up
        Do
            indexToCheck = Int(Rnd() * maxValue)
        Loop While numChecker(indexToCheck)
        numChecker(indexToCheck) = True
    Next num

    'Store selected index values in array
    For trueNum As Integer = 0 To numChecker.Length - 1
        If numChecker(trueNum) Then
            numArray(index) = trueNum
            'increment numArray index to store next number
            index += 1
        End If
    Next trueNum
End Sub

Private Sub btnNumber_Click(ByVal sender As Object,
ByVal e As System.EventArgs) Handles btnNumber.Click
    Const RANGE As Integer = 75
    Static possibleCalls(RANGE - 1) As Boolean 'defaults to False values
    Dim callNumber As Integer

    'Generate Bingo call
    Randomize()
    Do
        'Generate random values until one that
        'has not been called is generated
```

```
            callNumber = Int(Rnd() * RANGE)
        Loop While possibleCalls(callNumber)
        possibleCalls(callNumber) = True

        'Make call
        Select Case callNumber
            Case 0 To 14
                Me.btnNumber.Text = "B" & callNumber + 1
            Case 15 To 29
                Me.btnNumber.Text = "I" & callNumber + 1
            Case 30 To 44
                Me.btnNumber.Text = "N" & callNumber + 1
            Case 45 To 59
                Me.btnNumber.Text = "G" & callNumber + 1
            Case 60 To 74
                Me.btnNumber.Text = "O" & callNumber + 1
        End Select

        'Add call to numbers called list
        Me.lblCalled.Text &= Me.btnNumber.Text & vbCrLf
    End Sub
End Class
```

The BingoCard form code:

```
Public Class BingoCard

    Private Sub Button_Click(ByVal sender As Object, ByVal e As System.EventArgs) _
    Handles btnBSlot1.Click, btnBSlot2.Click, btnBSlot3.Click, btnBSlot4.Click, btnBSlot5.Click,
    btnGSlot1.Click, btnGSlot2.Click, btnGSlot3.Click, btnGSlot4.Click, btnBSlot5.Click,
    btnISlot1.Click, btnISlot2.Click, btnISlot3.Click, btnISlot4.Click, btnISlot5.Click,
    btnNSlot1.Click, btnNSlot2.Click, btnNSlot3.Click, btnNSlot4.Click, btnNSlot5.Click,
    btnOSlot1.Click, btnOSlot2.Click, btnOSlot3.Click, btnNSlot4.Click, btnOSlot5.Click
        Dim btnButtonClicked As Button = sender
        btnButtonClicked.Text = "X" & btnButtonClicked.Text & "X"
    End Sub
End Class
```

Bingo Testing and Debugging

Running Bingo, displaying four cards, and calling a few numbers displays an interface similar to:

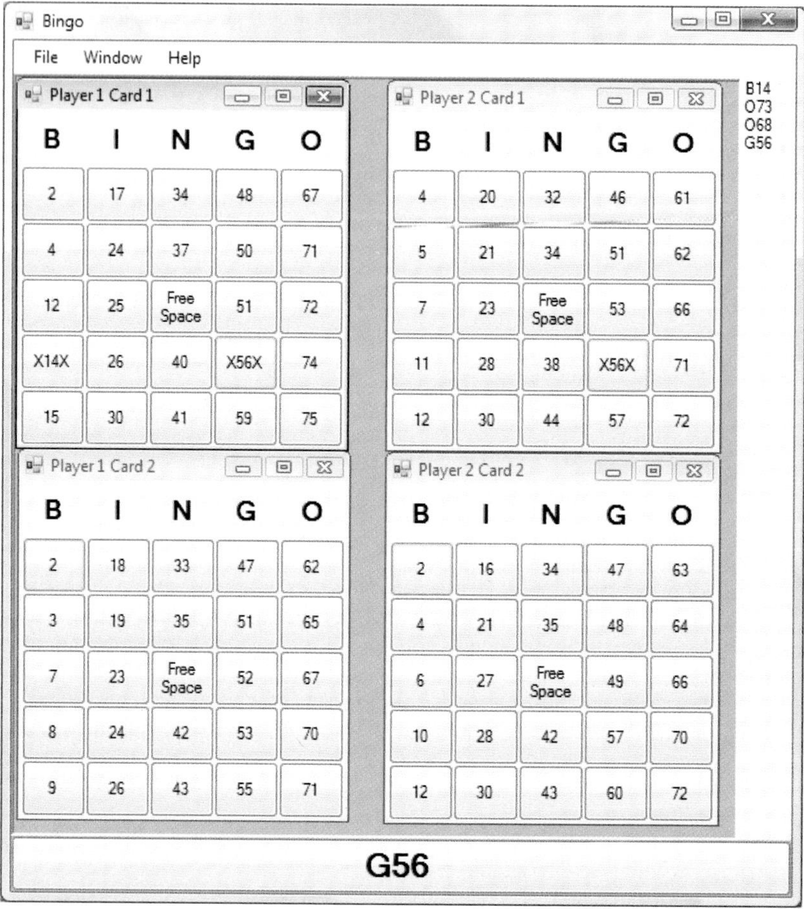

Bingo should be tested by creating multiple cards and checking for number randomness, clicking each of the slots on a card and verifying that the number "marks" as expected, verifying the call list is updated when the call button is clicked. The Help and About dialog boxes should also be tested.

Review: Bingo

Modify the Bingo case study application so that the backcolor of the buttons clicked by a player changes to a green, rather than having Xs displayed around the number.

Chapter Summary

An MDI application is an application with a parent form and one or more child forms. The parent form is a container for the child forms. The parent typically contains menus and a toolbar with commands for controlling the child forms. Windows applications contain at least File, Window, and Help menus. The File menu includes commands for opening, closing, and creating documents, which are the child forms. The Window menu includes commands for arranging windows and a list of currently open windows, and the Help menu includes a command for displaying information about the application.

The Form control is a class. As with any class, objects are instantiated in a `Dim` statement that includes the `New` keyword. The Form control has IsMdiContainer and WindowState properties for making it a parent form. A child form is added to a project by selecting Project → Add Windows Form. The Form control has an MdiParent property for making a form a child form, and a Show() method for displaying a form. The Form control Close() method is used to close a form. To close the active child form, the ActiveMdiChild property must be used as well.

The Form control includes the LayoutMdi() method for arranging open windows either tiled horizontally, tiled vertically, or cascaded. The MenuStrip control includes the MdiWindowListItem property that can be set to True so that window names are automatically added to a menu.

The TextBox control includes Copy(), Cut(), and Paste() methods for editing text in a text box. These methods are especially useful in a MDI application for editing text between open documents.

Applications use dialog boxes to get the information needed to execute some commands. A dialog box is also used to display information about an application, such as the creator's name. This dialog box is called the About dialog box.

A form is designated a dialog box by setting the properties ControlBox, MinimizeBox, MaximizeBox, and FormBorderStyle, and displaying the form as a modal form. A modal form does not allow other forms to receive input until it has been removed from the screen. The Form control ShowDialog() method is used to display a form as a modal form. A dialog box must contain at least OK and Cancel buttons. The Button control includes the DialogResult property that must be set according to the button response.

Vocabulary

Child form A form that functions completely within a parent form and cannot be moved outside the parent form.

Dialog box A form presented to the user to get the information needed to execute a command. A dialog box must contain at least an OK and a Cancel button.

MDI Application A multiple-document interface application.

Modal form A form that does not allow other forms to receive input until it has been removed from the screen.

Parent form A container for child forms.

Visual Basic

Add Windows Form **command** Adds a new form to a project. Found in the Project menu.

Button **Button control** Used to create a Button control class object. Properties include DialogResult.

Form class Used to create a control class object that can be a parent form for the application interface, a child form for application windows, or a dialog box for getting information from the user. Properties include IsMdiContainer, WindowState, MdiParent, ActiveMdiChild, ControlBox, MaximizeBox, MinimizeBox, and FormBorderStyle. Methods include Show(), ShowDialog(), LayoutMdi(), and Close().

MenuStrip **MenuStrip control** Used to add an application component that contains menu items. Properties include MdiWindowListItem.

TextBox **TextBox control** Used to add a TextBox control class object to a form. Methods include Copy(), Cut(), and Paste().

Critical Thinking

1. Why is an MDI Parent form referred to as a container form?

2. Why is it important to have menus on a parent form?

3. a) To designate a form a parent form, which property(ies) must be changed? To what?
   b) After adding a new form with the purpose of becoming a child form which property(ies) must be changed? To what? Where is this done?

4. When a command requires information from the user, should a child form or a dialog box be used?

5. a) List the Visual Basic predefined dialog boxes discussed throughout the text.
   b) What is the difference in implementing a predefined dialog box and a dialog box created for a specific application?
   c) List the similarities and differences between dialog boxes and interface forms.

6. What is a modal form? Explain.

7. a) What form properties must be changed to designate the form a dialog box? What should these properties be set to?
   b) When buttons are added to a dialog box, which button property must be set for the button response to properly work? What should this property be set to?

8. What does each procedure accomplish?
   a)
```
Private Sub AddChildrenToolStripMenuItem
_Click(ByVal sender As System.Object,
ByVal e As System.EventArgs) _
Handles AddChildToolStripMenuItem.Click
    Dim newOne As New Baby()
    Dim otherOne As New Baby()
    newOne.MdiParent = Me
    otherOne.MdiParent = Me

    newOne.Text = "Baby: NewOne"
    otherOne.Text = "Baby: OtherOne"
    newOne.Show()
    otherOne.Show()
End Sub
```
   b)
```
Private Sub btnShow_Click _
(ByVal sender As System.Object,
ByVal e As System.EventArgs) _
Handles btnShow.Click
    Dim x As Baby = Me.ActiveMdiChild
    Me.txtParent.Text = x.Text
End Sub
```
   c)
```
Private Sub DisplayToolStripMenuItem _
Click(ByVal sender As System.Object,
ByVal e As System.EventArgs) _
Handles DisplayToolStripMenuItem.Click
    Me.txtParent.Text = _
    Me.ActiveMdiChild.Text
    Dim x As Baby = Me.ActiveMdiChild
    x.txtStuff.Paste()
End Sub
```

9. a) Write code to instantiate and display a new dialog box. The form is named DataForm.vb and the specific dialog box should be named `getDataDB`.
   b) The DataForm dialog box has objects: txtName, txtAge, btnOK, and btnCancel. Write statements for the parent form that perform the following when btnOK is clicked: Assign the name from the text box to `name` and then if the age entered is less than 18 display the message "Student discount applies." and assign the value 5 to a variable named `studentDiscount`.

10. A dialog box has **OK** (`btnOK`) and **Cancel** (`btnCancel`) buttons as well as three check boxes: **Back Stage Prices** (`chkBkStage`), **VIP Refreshments** (`chkRefresh`), and **VIP Parking** (`chkPark`). Correct the errors in the following code that should determine the number of selected check boxes and assign `extraCost` appropriately:

```
Const ONE_PRIV As Double
Const TWO_PRIV As Double
Const THREE_PRIV As Double
Dim numChks As Integer
Dim extraCost As Double

SpecPrivDB.ShowDialog()
If SpecPrivDB.DialogResult =
Windows.Forms.DialogResult.OK Then
    If Me.chkBkStage.Checked Then
        numChks += 1
    End If
    If Me.chkRefresh.Checked Then
        numChks += 1
    End If
```

```
        If Me.chkPark.Checked Then
            numChks += 1
        End If

        Select numChks
            Case 1: extraCost = ONE_PRIV
            Case 2: extraCost = TWO_PRIV
            Case 3: extraCost = THREE_PRIV
        End Select
    End If
```

True/False

11. Determine if each of the following is true or false. If false, explain why.
    a) A parent form can have only one child form.
    b) There can be only one parent form in a MDI application.
    c) It is possible to close the parent form and leave children forms open.
    d) When a child form is minimized, its icon appears in the parent form, not on the taskbar.
    e) A parent form can hold different child forms.
    f) MdiList is a Form property that automatically adds the names of open child forms to a menu.
    g) If multiple open child forms are to be entirely visible, then they should be tiled.
    h) A user must respond to a dialog box before work can continue in the parent form.
    i) The DialogResult property is automatically set based on the name of the button.
    j) It is possible to ignore a displayed dialog box and continue to work in a child window.

Exercises

Exercise 1 — TheVacationStop

Create a TheVacationStop application that is used to promote the weekly special for a travel agency. The weekly special is displayed in a dialog box that can be shown in English or French. The application interface should look similar to:

The File menu contains a Quit command. The Specials menu contains a Select Language... command, which displays a dialog box prompting the user to select English or French. Clicking English displays a dialog box with the weekly special "Las Vegas, 3 days, $199." Clicking French displays a dialog box with "Las Vegas, 3 jours, 199$." The Help menu should contain an About VacationStop... command. The `sponges.jpg` image file is a data file for this text.

Exercise 2  — Mad-LibII

Create a Mad-LibII MDI application that includes standard Windows application commands and dialog boxes. Refer to Chapter 11 Exercise 3 for information about Mad-Libs. Mad-LibII should include commands that display:

- a window for adding verbs to a file.
- a window for adding nouns to a file.
- a window for adding sentences to a file. The sentences should contain placeholders for verbs and nouns.
- a window that displays random Mad-Libs using the previously created files.

Be creative with your Mad-LibII application. Add color to windows, graphics to the Mad-Lib windows, and animations where appropriate.

Exercise 3 — MathBingo

Use the Bingo case study as a guide for creating MathBingo. In math Bingo, a math problem is displayed for each call and the result of this math problem is the number to be marked. For this Bingo application, the case study should be modified so that:

- the application uses a file named mathprob.dat that stores one math problem per line. This file can be created in a text editor, such as the one discussed in Chapter 11. In this file, the first math problem should evaluate to 1, the second math problem should evaluate to 2, and so on, up to 75.
- the btnNumber_Click() procedure sets the button text to the math problem that corresponds to the selected random number. For example, if 10 is the selected random number, then the tenth math problem in the mathprob.dat file is displayed.

Exercise 4  — MyBusinessAccessories

Create a MyBusinessAccessories MDI application that includes the standard Windows application commands and dialog boxes. MyBusinessAccessories should also include commands that display:

- a window for calculating a mortgage using the Pmt() function (similar to the LoanPayment application created in the Chapter 7 reviews)
- a window for calculating the cost of financing (similar to the CreditCardLoan application created in the Chapter 7 reviews)
- a window for calculating the value of an investment after a specified period (similar to the WatchYourMoneyGrow application in the Chapter 7 reviews)

Exercise 5  — MyAccessories

Create a MyAccessories MDI application that includes the standard Windows application commands and dialog boxes. MyAccessories should also include commands that display:

- a working calculator (the Chapter 6 case study)
- a triangle calculator (the Chapter 10 case study)
- a text editor (the WriteFile application from the Chapter 11 reviews)
- the ClickIt! game (the Chapter 9 case study).

Exercise 6

Use the Visual Basic help features to research printing topics, such as printing text from a text box object. Share your research with a classmate.

Chapter 14
Databases and Web Programming

Key Concepts

Database terminology
Accessing a data source
Creating a dataset
Binding a dataset to controls on a form
Downloading Microsoft Visual Web Developer
Creating a website
Using server controls
Applying validation controls

Practice Data Files

JEWELRY.accdb
TOYS.accdb

Exercise Data Files

EVENTS.accdb

Working with Databases

A *database* is an organized collection of related data. A corporation's employee data and a store's inventory are examples of data stored in a database. Access, Microsoft SQL Server, and Oracle are examples of applications used to create databases. Visual Basic is not typically used to create new databases, but it is often used to display, analyze, and manipulate the information in an existing database:

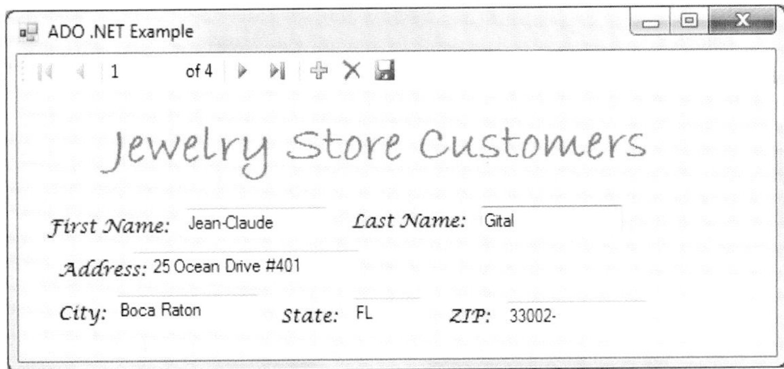

ADO.NET — *ADO.NET* is the standard data model used for database programming in Visual Basic 2010.

Working with databases requires some understanding of database terminology:

field

- A *field* is a category of information stored in a database, such as customers' last names, phone numbers, or comments.

record

- A *record* is a set of data, such as all the information about a specific customer.

table *data redundancy*

- A *table* is a database object that stores data. Data is divided into tables to eliminate unnecessary data duplication, or *data redundancy*.

relational database

- A *relational database* means that each table is related to at least one other table. For example, the Orders and Products tables are related by the Product ID fields:

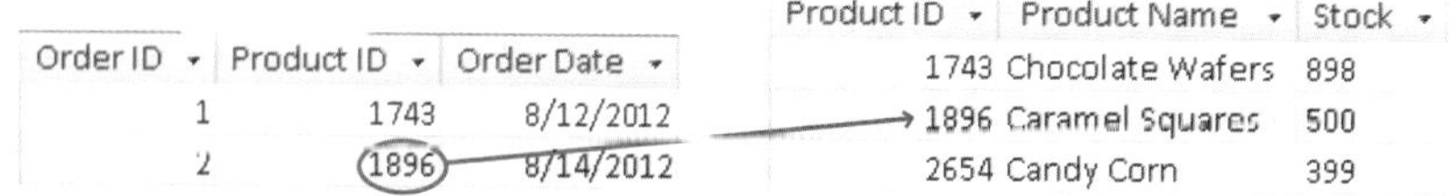

Order ID	Product ID	Order Date
1	1743	8/12/2012
2	1896	8/14/2012

Product ID	Product Name	Stock
1743	Chocolate Wafers	898
1896	Caramel Squares	500
2654	Candy Corn	399

Accessing a Data Source

To connect a Visual Basic application to a Microsoft Access database file, select Data → Add New Data Source. A dialog box is displayed. Select Database and then click Next, which displays another dialog box:

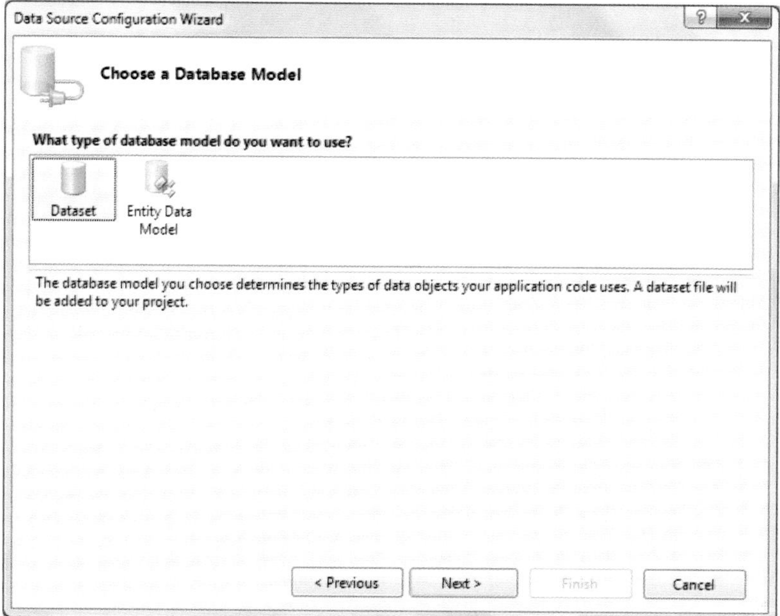

Select Dataset and then click Next. Click New Connection, which will display either the Add Connection dialog box or the Change Data Source dialog box. If the Add Connection dialog box is displayed, click Change and then select Microsoft Access Database File:

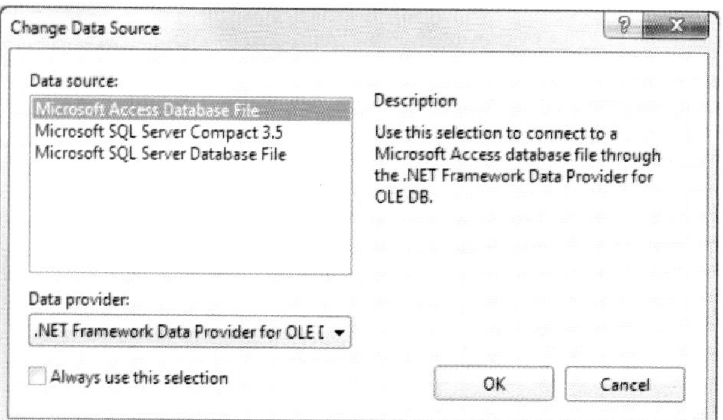

Select OK, which displays the Add Connection dialog box:

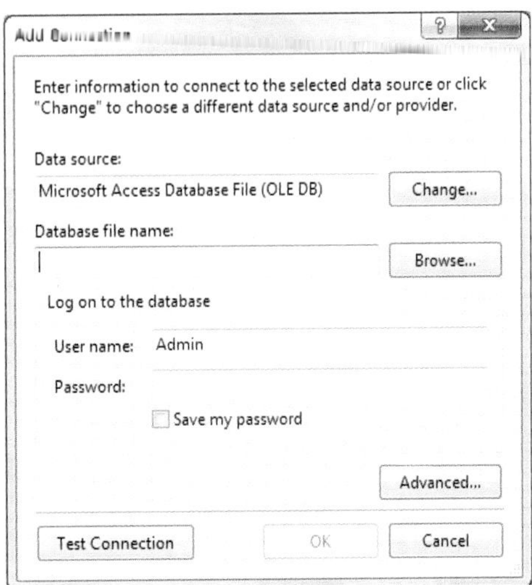

Select Browse, navigate to an Access database file, and then select Test Connection. Visual Basic will test the connection to ensure that the database is a recognized format and then display a message:

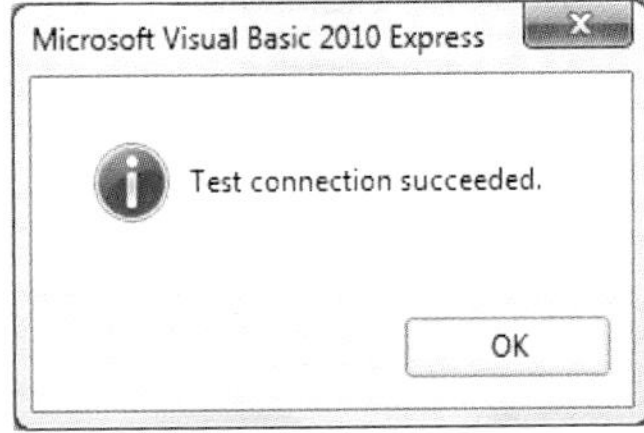

connection string

Select OK to remove the message dialog box and then select OK again. The Data Source Configuration Wizard dialog box is redisplayed. Click ⊞ to display the *connection string*, which shows the path to the database. Click Next and then click Yes to copy the database file to the project folder. Click Next again to save the connection string, which displays another dialog box:

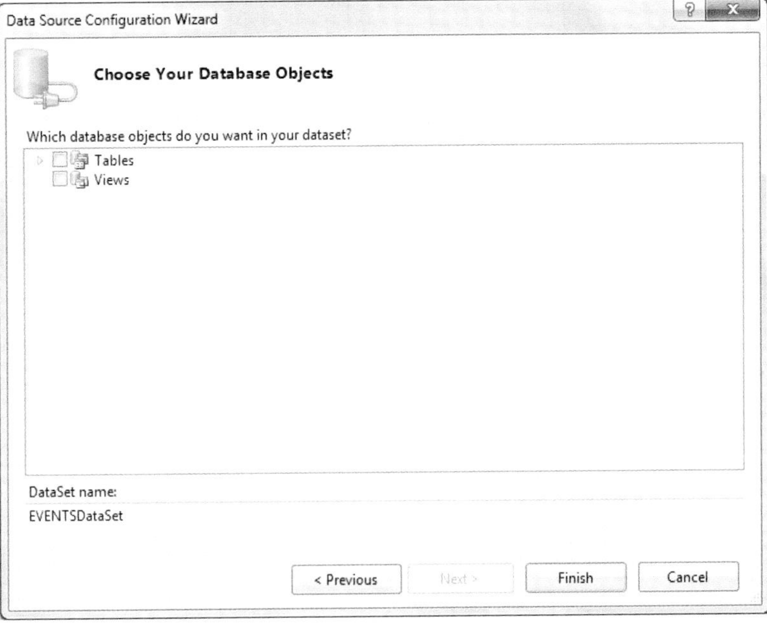

dataset A *dataset* is a representation of one or more database tables that will be accessed in the Visual Basic application. Create a dataset by clicking ⊞ and selecting the appropriate data. For example:

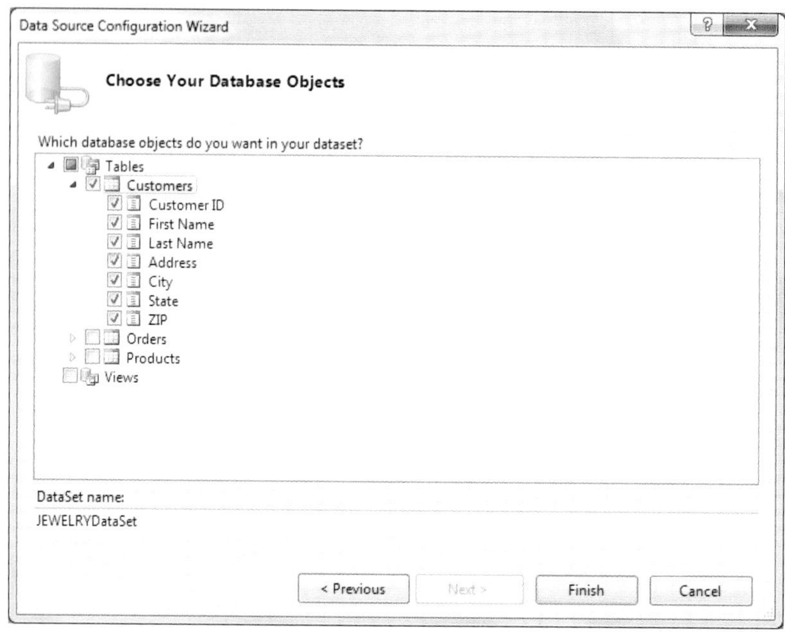

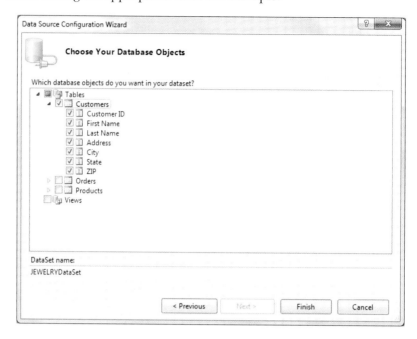

All fields in the Customers table are selected for the dataset

Click Finish. The Access database file and the dataset are displayed in the Solution Explorer window:

TIP The dataset file has a .xsd extension. This is an XML schema that describes the tables, fields, and other elements in the dataset.

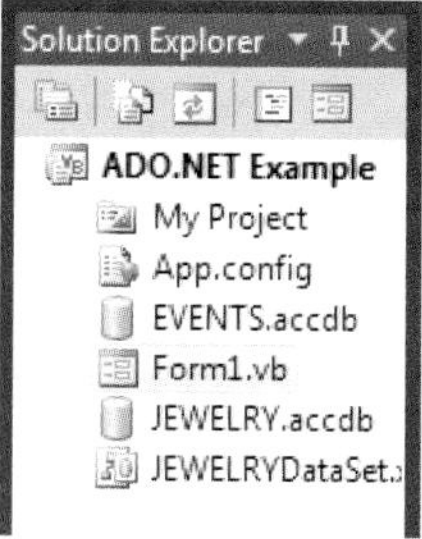

Selecting the dataset file and then clicking the View Designer button displays a visual representation of the dataset:

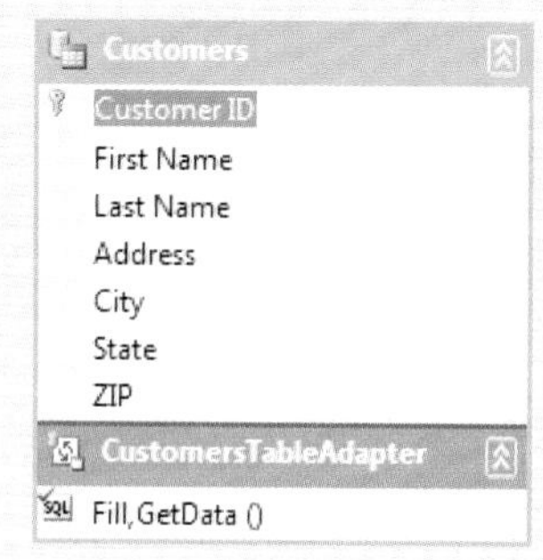

Click a field to display the field's properties, such as MaxLength, in the Properties window.

Review: Jewelry – part 1 of 2

Create a Jewelry application. Use the steps outlined in the first two sections of the chapter to establish a connection to JEWELRY.accdb, which is an Access data file for this text. Create a dataset using all of the fields in the Customers table.

Binding a Dataset to Controls on a Form

The Data Sources window is used to bind a dataset to controls on a form. Display the Data Sources window by first displaying the application form and then selecting Data → Show Data Sources:

TIP Click ⊞ to expand the data displayed.

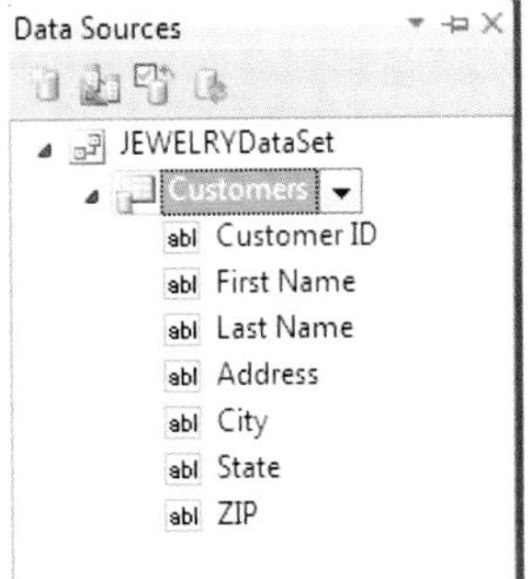

Clicking the arrow next to a field, such as First Name displays a list of options for displaying the data on a form:

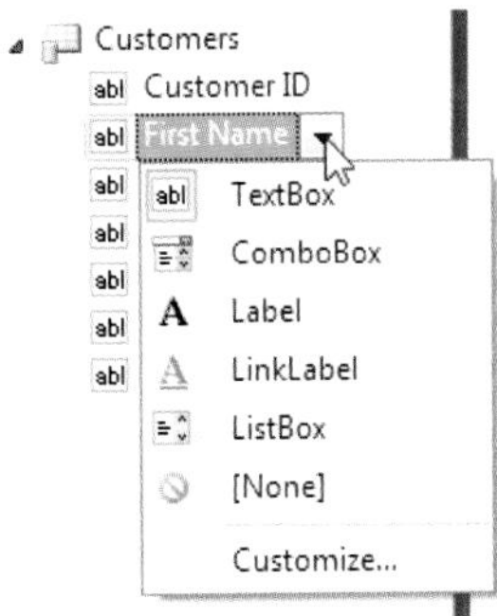

Selecting an option, such as TextBox, and then dragging the First Name field to the form displays:

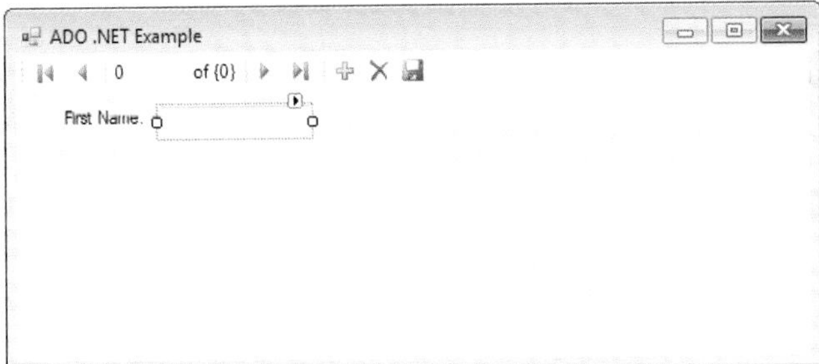

Running the application links the data in the Access database to the Visual Basic application:

TIP The dataset can be modified while the program is running but this will not affect the original database.

The Move Next and Move Previous buttons can be used to scroll through the records in the database.

Review: Jewelry – part 2 of 2

Use the steps outlined in the previous section to design a form that contains all of the fields in the Customers table. Run the application and scroll through the records in the JEWELRY database.

The DataGridView Control

The *DataGridView control* displays an entire table of information in a grid of rows and columns, similar to a spreadsheet:

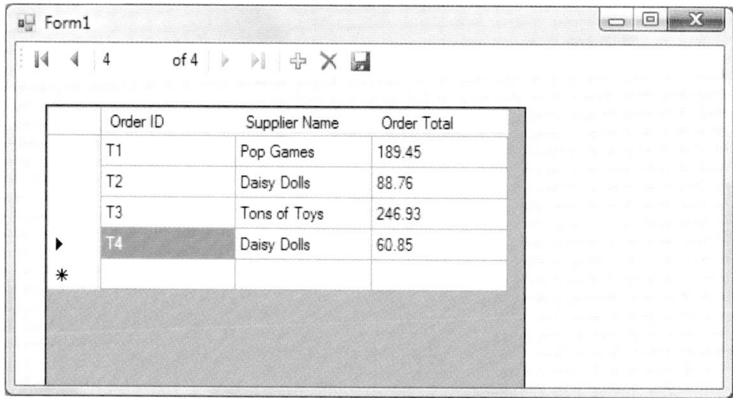

To display data from a database file using the DataGridView control, select Data → Add New Data Source and establish a connection string to the database as explained earlier in the chapter. Next, select the database table to be displayed. For example:

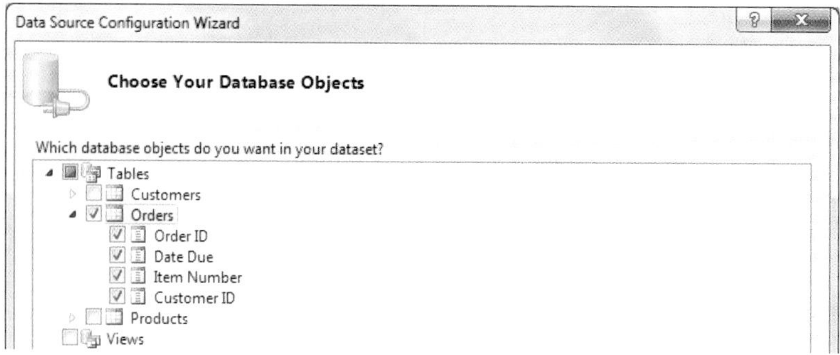

The Orders table is selected

In the Data Sources window, click the table name drop-down arrow Orders ▾ and select DataGridView. The Orders table can then be dragged to the form:

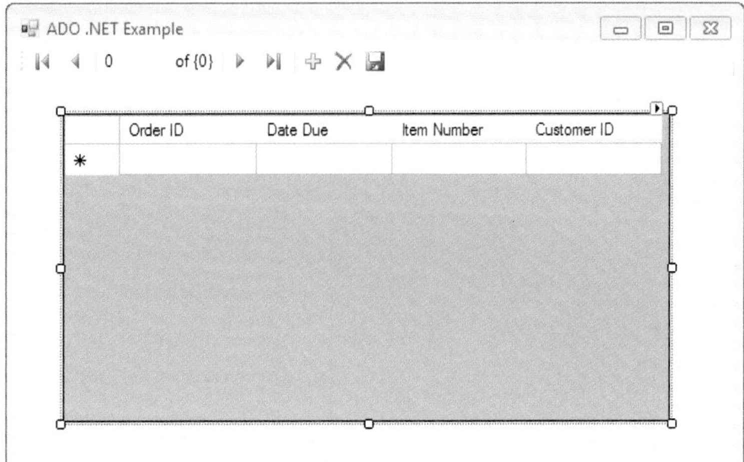

The object may need to be moved and resized so that all columns and rows of data are visible on the form. DataGridView properties can be set in the Properties window.

Selecting the table object and then clicking the shortcut arrow displays the DataGridView Tasks menu:

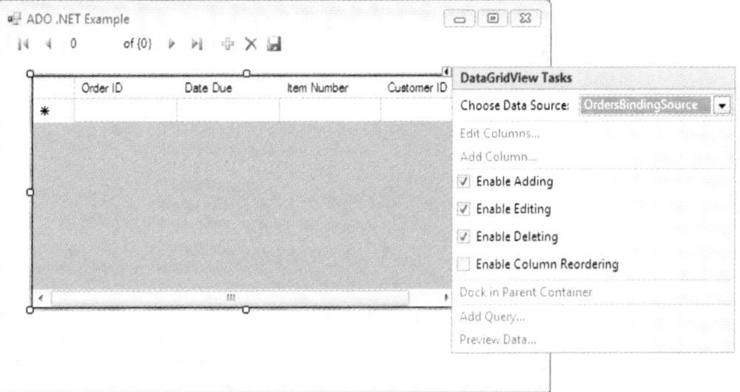

Allowing the user to edit the data can be enabled or disabled in this menu. Data can also be previewed or edited from this menu.

Review: Toys

Create a Toys application. Use the steps outlined in the first two sections of the chapter to establish a connection to TOYS.accdb, which is an Access data file for this text. Use the DataGridView control to display the Orders table on the form. Experiment with formatting the table object by setting properties in the Properties window, such as AlternatingRowsDefaultCellStyle.

Creating a Website

ASP.NET, Visual Web Developer

Once you are familiar with Visual Basic 2010, this knowledge can be applied to building websites. A *website* consists of one or more related web pages. *ASP .NET* is a Microsoft Web development framework and *Visual Web Developer* is the tool used to create ASP .NET websites. Websites are viewed in a web browser, such as Internet Explorer, and are typically stored on a web server.

In order to create a website, Visual Web Developer 2010 Express Edition must be downloaded from Microsoft's website: (www.microsoft.com/express/Downloads/#2010-Visual-Web-Developer). This is a free download.

To create a website, start Visual Web Developer 2010 Express Edition and click the New Web Site link:

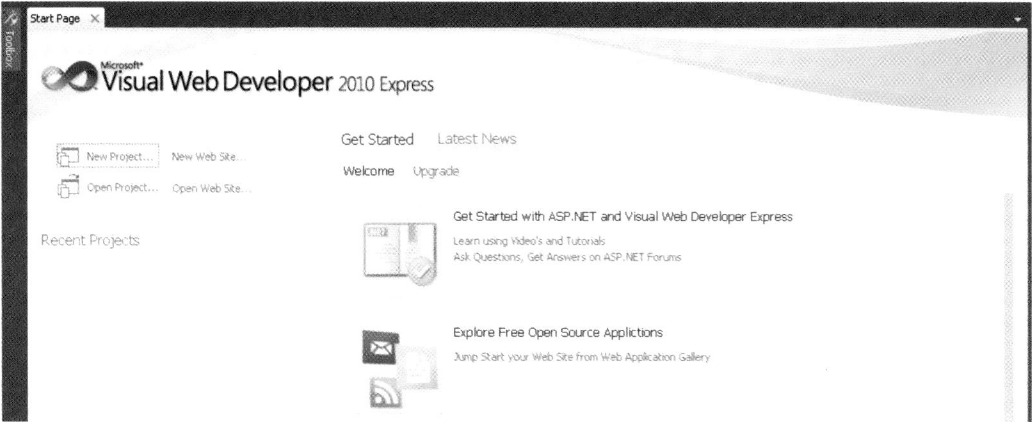

The New Web Site dialog box is displayed:

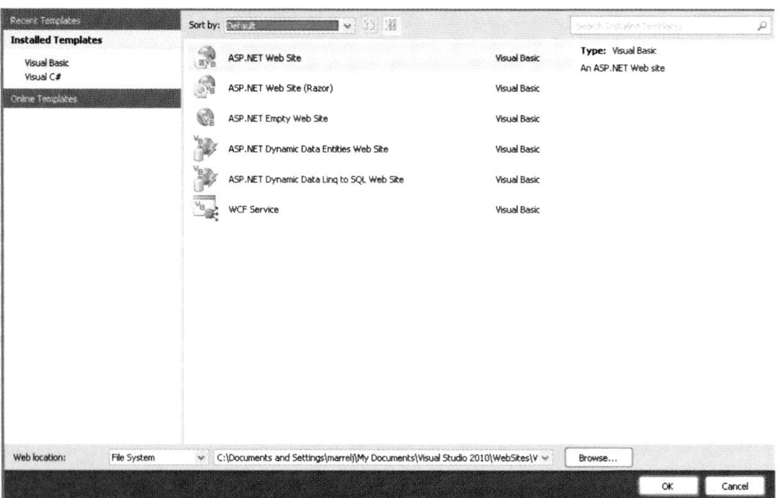

Select Visual Basic in the Installed Templates list and ASP .NET Web Site, and then select OK. The Web Application Design window opens and the Default.aspx page is displayed:

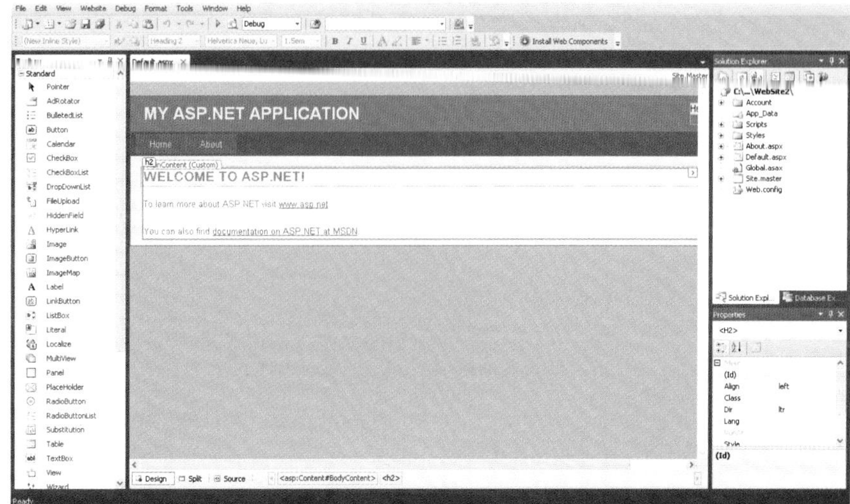

TIP Many web page controls are server controls, which run on a web server. There are many similarities between server controls and Windows forms controls including control names and properties.

Visual Basic 2010 provides a starter template to assist you in designing a Web page. The web page is initially displayed in Design view, which displays the web page as it will be viewed in a browser. The web page can also be displayed in Split view and Source view. Source view displays the HTML code created in the background and Split view is a combination of Design and Source view.

TIP A master page does not display in a Web browser.

The website template contains two web pages titled Home (Default. aspx)and About (About.aspx). The template also contains a Site.master file. This file is a *master* page which is used to create a consistent layout for the pages in the website. Changes made on the master page are automatically applied to all pages in the website.

Review: Website Design - part 1 of 2

① DOWNLOAD VISUAL WEB DEVELOPER 2010 EXPRESS

Go to www.microsoft.com/express/Downloads/#2010-Visual-Web-Developer and download Visual Web Developer 2010 Express.

② START VISUAL WEB DEVELOPER 2010 EXPRESS EDITION

③ CREATE A NEW WEBSITE

a. Click the New Web Site link.

b. Select Visual Basic in the Installed Templates list.

c. Select ASP .NET Web Site.

d. Select OK. The Web Application Design window opens and the Default.aspx page is displayed. (Click Design if the window is not displayed in Design view.)

④ EDIT THE MASTER PAGE

a. In the Solution Explorer window, double-click Site.master. The Site.master page is displayed. (Click Design if the file is not displayed in Design view.)

b. Replace the text MY ASP .NET APPLICATION with the text THE AUTO SHOP.

c. Select View → Toobars → Formatting. The Formatting toolbar is displayed.

d. Click the Foreground Color button. The More Colors dialog box is displayed.

1. Click the orange color.
2. Click OK.

⑤ EDIT THE NAVIGATION BUTTONS

a. Point to the navigation buttons. A Smart Tag is displayed:

b. Click the Smart Tag [>].

c. Select Edit Menu Items. The Menu Items Editor is displayed.

   1. Click About in the Items list.
   2. In the Properties pane, change the Text property from About to Contact.
   3. Click OK. The About navigation button is changed to Contact:

d. On the toolbar, click the Save button.

⑥ DISPLAY THE DEFAULT PAGE

Click the Default.aspx tab. The Home page is displayed. Notice the changes to the master page have been applied to this page.

Adding Objects

Objects, such as Labels and Buttons, can be added to a web page in a similar way they are added to a Windows form. First display the Standard controls in the Toolbox:

Next, place the insertion point on the form and then double-click the server control. Properties are set in the Properties window and the Formatting toolbar can be used to format objects. For example:

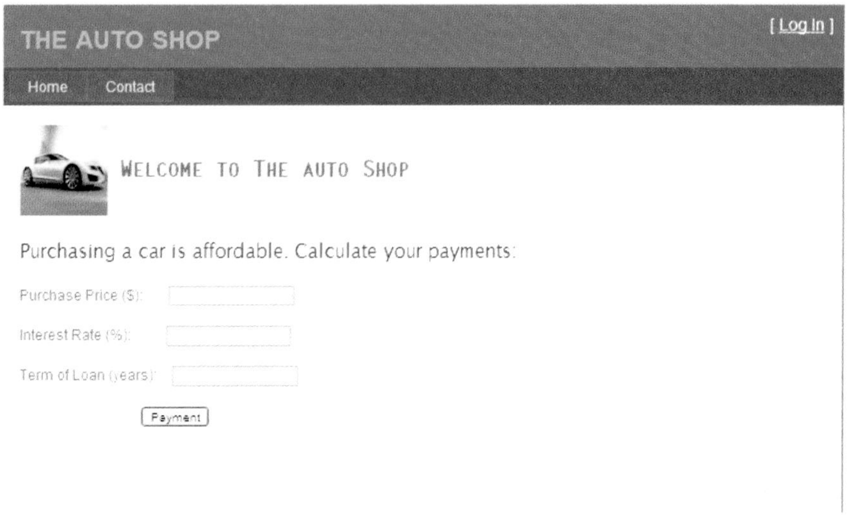

Event procedures can then be written for server controls similar to the way they are written for Windows forms. Click the Start Debugging button ▶ to run the application. If a warning dialog box is displayed, click OK to continue.

Validation Controls

Validation controls can be added to check the data entered by the user. For example, a RequiredFieldValidator object checks to see if data has been typed into a designated text box. A RequiredFieldValidator object is added by clicking the RequiredFieldValidator control in the Toolbox and dragging it to the right of the corresponding text box. In the Properties window, set the ControlToValidate property to the appropriate text box and set the ErrorMessage property to an appropriate error message.

Additional pages and Web Forms can be added to the website. For example, to add a Web Form, select Website → Add New Item → Web Form.

Review: Website Design - part 2 of 2

Use the steps outlined in the previous sections to build a home page similar to The Auto Shop example that calculates the purchase price of a car by prompting the user for the purchase price, interest rate, and term of the loan. Add appropriate validation controls. Refer to Chapter 7 in the text for the appropriate business function.

Chapter Summary

A database is an organized collection of related data. Access, Microsoft SQL Server, and Oracle are examples of applications used to create databases. Visual Basic is not typically used to create new databases, but it is often used to display, analyze, and manipulate the information in an existing database. ADO .NET is the standard data model used for database programming in Visual Basic 2010.

Database programming requires connecting to a data source and creating a dataset. The Data Sources window is used to bind a dataset to controls on a form. The DataGridView control displays information in a grid of rows and columns, similar to a spreadsheet.

Once you are familiar with Visual Basic 2010, this knowledge can be applied to building websites. ASP .NET is a Microsoft Web development framework and Visual Web Developer is the tool used to create ASP .NET websites. In order to create a website, Microsoft Visual Web Developer 2010 Express Edition must be downloaded from Microsoft's website.

Vocabulary

ADO.NET The standard data model used for database programming in Visual Basic 2010.

ASP .NET Microsoft's Web development framework.

Connection string The path to the source database.

Data redundancy A technique where data is divided into tables to eliminate unnecessary data duplication.

Database An organized collection of related data.

DataGridView control Displays information in a grid of rows and columns, similar to a spreadsheet.

Dataset A representation of one or more database tables that will be accessed in the Visual Basic application.

Field A category of information stored in a database, such as customers' last names, phone numbers, or comments.

Microsoft Visual Web Developer The tool used to create ASP .NET websites.

Record A set of data, such as all the information about a specific customer.

Relational database Each table in a database is related to at least one other table.

Table A database object that stores data.

Website One or more related web pages.

Visual Basic

Add New Data Source **command** Displays the Data Source Configuration Wizard dialog box. Found in the Data menu.

New Web Site **command** Displays the New Web Site dialog box. Found in the File menu.

Show Data Sources **command** Displays the Data Sources window. Found in the Data menu.

Critical Thinking

1. Describe two Visual Basic application examples that could be designed to display and analyze information in a database.

2. Define:
   a) Field
   b) Record
   c) Table

3. Why would it be important to eliminate data duplication in a database?

4. When establishing a connection to a database, why would you add a password?

5. List three options for displaying a field on a form.

6. Describe how the DataGridView control displays information on a form.

7. Explain how your knowledge of Visual Basic will help support the development of a website.

True/False

8. Determine if each of the following are true or false. If false, explain why.
   a) A database is an organized collection of related data.
   b) Employee Number could be an example of a field.
   c) In a relational database, each table is related to at least one other table.
   d) Access is an example of a spreadsheet application.
   e) A connection string shows the established path to a database.
   f) A dataset always consists of all of the data in the database.
   g) The length of a field cannot be modified in a DataGridView object.
   h) A website consists of one or more related web pages or web forms.
   i) Validation controls check the data entered by a user.

Exercises

Exercise 1 — Events

Create an Events application that establishes a connection to EVENTS.accdb, which is an Access data file for this text. Create a dataset using all of the fields in the Events table and design the form to display all of the fields. Add appropriate formatting.

Exercise 2 — WebAccess

Web applications often require users to register at their site. Create a WebAccess application that prompts the user for data and determines if the data is valid:

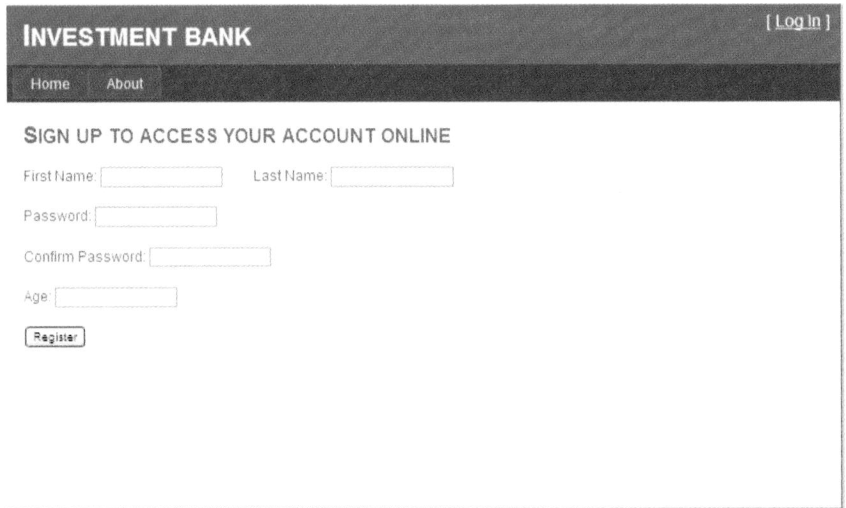

If the data is valid, a UserID is generated for the user that consists of the first 5 characters of the user's last name and their first initial. The application should include:

- RequiredFieldValidator objects for the First Name and Last Name text boxes
- CompareValidator object for the Password and Retype Password text boxes
- RangeValidator object for the Age text boxes. The user has to be 18 years or older.

The TextMode property for the Password and Retype Password text boxes should be set to Password.

Exercise 3 — BMI

Body Mass Index (BMI) is an assessment used to determine if an individual is underweight, overweight, or within a healthy weight range. Create a BMI application that calculates a user's BMI. The application interface should contain a hyperlink to the calculator and look similar to:

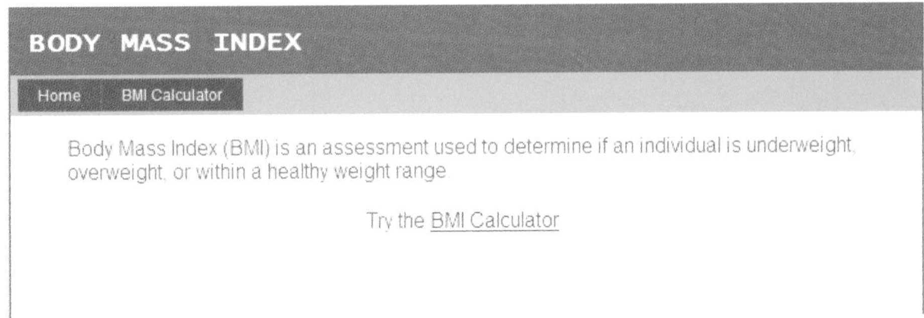

Clicking BMI Calculator displays:

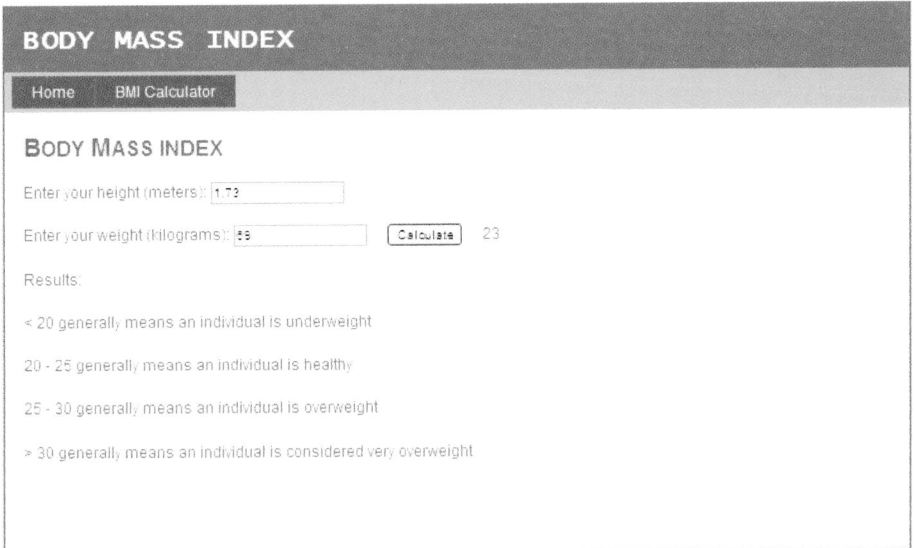

The program code should use the formula BMI = weight (kg) / [height (m)]^2 to calculate the Body Mass Index. An additional Measurement Conversion Web Form could be added to convert pounds to kilograms and feet and inches to meters.

Exercise 4 — MagicAnswer

Create a MagicAnswer application that prompts the user to ask a yes/no question and then responds by randomly displaying one of eight possible answers. The application interface should look similar to:

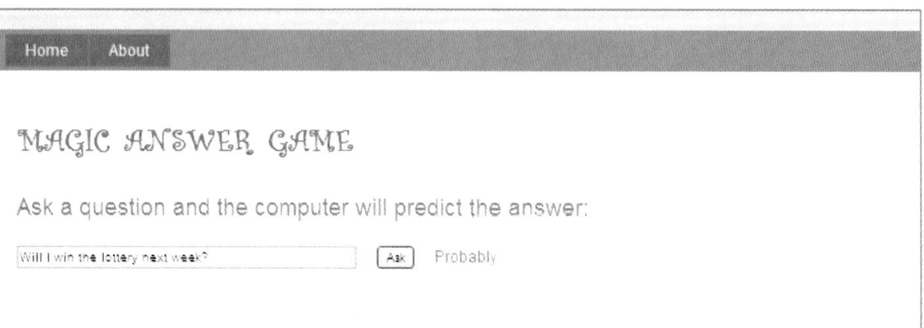

The application interface should include a RequiredFieldValidator object for the Question text box and the code should randomly display one of the following answers when a question is asked:

- Yes
- No
- Probably
- Probably not
- Maybe
- Definitely
- You are dreaming
- What?

Appendix A
Visual Basic for Applications (VBA)

Key Concepts

What is VBA?
The Developer tab
Macro Security
VBA Terminology
Viewing and Editing Excel Macro Code
Accessing VBA Help
VBA Programming

What is VBA?

Now that you have learned to program using Visual Basic 2010, you can use that knowledge to quickly master the *Visual Basic for Applications* (VBA) programming language. Visual Basic and VBA are fundamentally similar as both stem from the same programming language, Basic. The way you address objects, the way you respond to events, call methods and set properties is the same across both languages. The languages are different in that VBA can normally only run code within a host application, such as Microsoft Excel 2010 rather than as a standalone application.

Microsoft Excel 2010 is a spreadsheet application that includes a rich set of features that are used to perform tasks. However, you might want to find an easier way to perform repetitive tasks or to perform some task that the Excel application does not seem to address. VBA gives you the ability to extend those applications. VBA works by running *macros*, which are step-by-step procedures written in Visual Basic.

The Developer Tab

TIP You can download a trial version of Office 2010 from the Microsoft website.

All Office 2010 applications, including Excel use the Ribbon interface. In Excel, the Developer tab on the Ribbon is used to access the Visual Basic Editor and other developer tools:

Office 2010 does not display the Developer tab by default, you must enable it in the Excel Options dialog box. If the Developer tab is not enabled on your computer, complete the Practice below.

Practice: The Developer Tab

① START EXCEL

② DISPLAY THE DEVELOPER TAB

a. Select File → Options. The Excel Options dialog box is displayed.

1. Select Customize Ribbon.
2. Select Popular Commands in the Choose commands from list, if it is not already selected.
3. Select Main Tabs in the Customize the Ribbon list, if it is not already selected.
4. Click the Developer check box.
5. Select OK.

Macro Security

If an Excel workbook contains a macro, it is saved with a .xlsm extension instead of the default .xlsx extension. When the workbook is opened in Excel, a security warning may be displayed because macro code does have the potential to damage your computer:

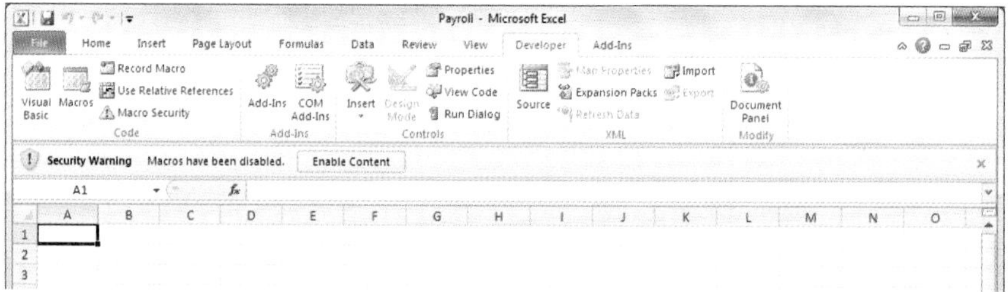

Click the Enable Content button to enable the macro.

TIP If you enable macros in a workbook stored on a local hard drive, the next time you open the workbook, macros will be automatically enabled.

The Macro Security button on the Developer tab is used to specify which macros can run and under what conditions:

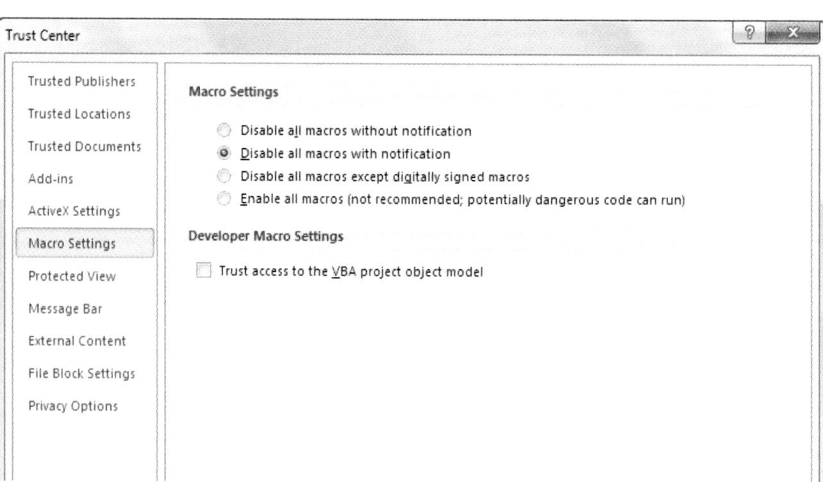

By default, the Disable all macros with notification option is selected. This option will display the security warning shown on the previous page when a macro enabled workbook is opened.

Any workbook stored in a folder that is a trusted location will automatically have its macros enabled. To specify a trusted location, select Trusted Location in the left navigation pane of the Trust Center dialog box:

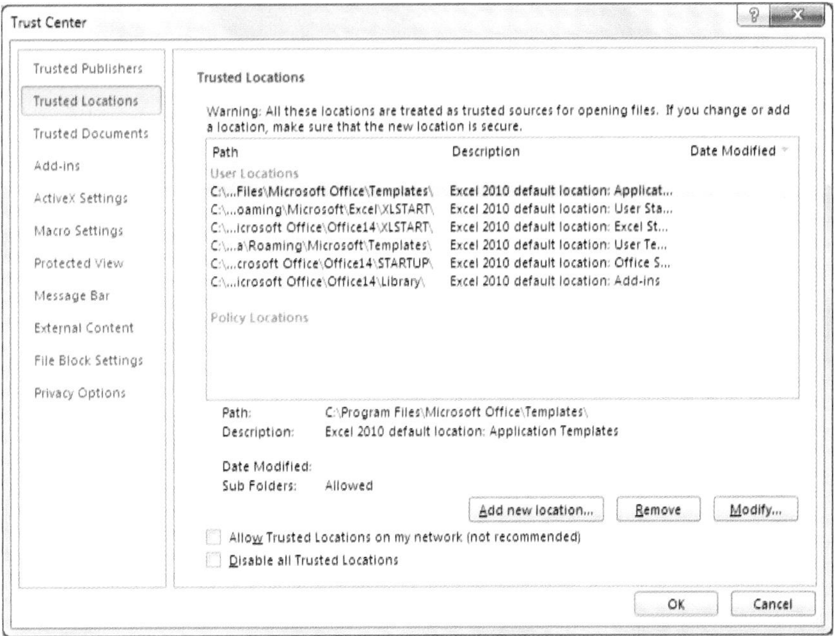

- Click Allow Trusted Locations on My Network to trust a location on a network drive.
- To add a new trusted location, click the Add new location button to display the Microsoft Office Trusted Locations dialog box:

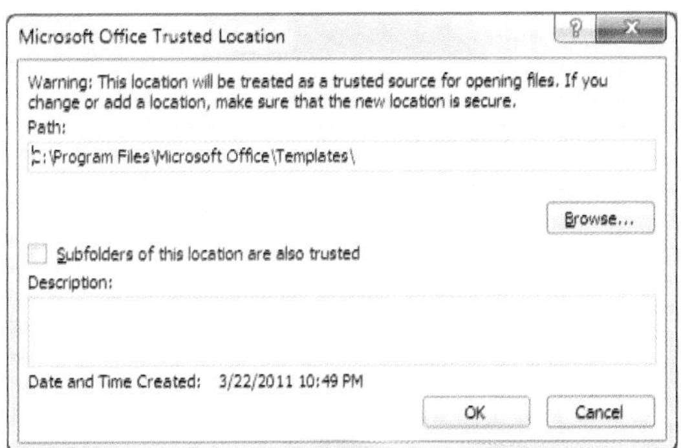

Click the Browse button and then browse to the folder you want to be a trusted location. Click OK to add the folder to the Trusted Locations list.

Macro Overview

In Excel, you record a macro by clicking the Record Macro button on the Developer tab. The Record Macro dialog box is displayed:

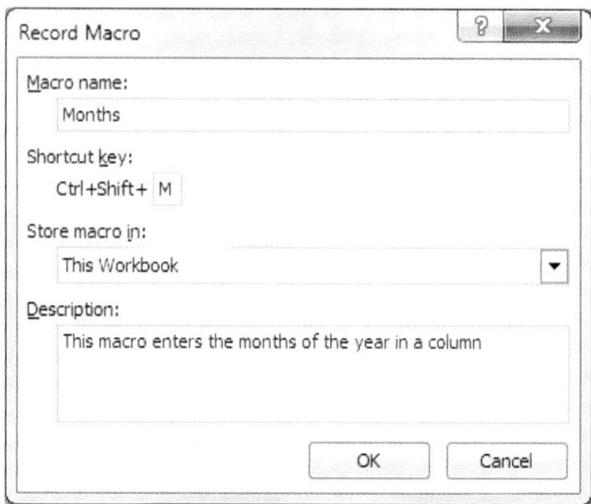

- In the Macro name box, type a name for the macro. Macro names should be descriptive of the macro task and should not contain spaces.
- A macro is assigned a shortcut key. This shortcut key is used to execute the macro. In Excel, most of the lowercase shortcuts already have a function. For example, Ctrl+ c is used to copy. If you assign a macro a shortcut key of Ctrl+c, Excel will run the macro instead of performing the copy function. To avoid this problem, hold down the Shift key when typing a shortcut key. This will assign the macro to Ctrl+Shift+C.
- In the Store macros in list, choose where the macro is saved. It is recommended that you select This Workbook if the macro is specifically related to the active workbook. If the macro performs a general Excel task, it can be saved in the Personal Macro Workbook. This workbook opens automatically when you start Excel and enables the macro.
- The Description box is used to describe the function of the macro.

Select OK to start recording the macro. Record the macro by performing all of the steps required to perform the macro's task. Click the Stop Recording Stop Recording button on the Developer tab when you are finished.

A macro is run by pressing the assigned shortcut key. Alternatively, you can create a Macro button on the Ribbon or on the Quick Access toolbar.

TIP A Macro button on the Ribbon is appropriate only if the macros saved in the Personal Macro Workbook.

Practice: Recording, Storing, and Running a Macro

① RECORD THE MACRO

a. Click the **Record Macro** button on the Developer tab. The Record Macro dialog box is displayed.

1. Fill in the Macro dialog box using the options below:

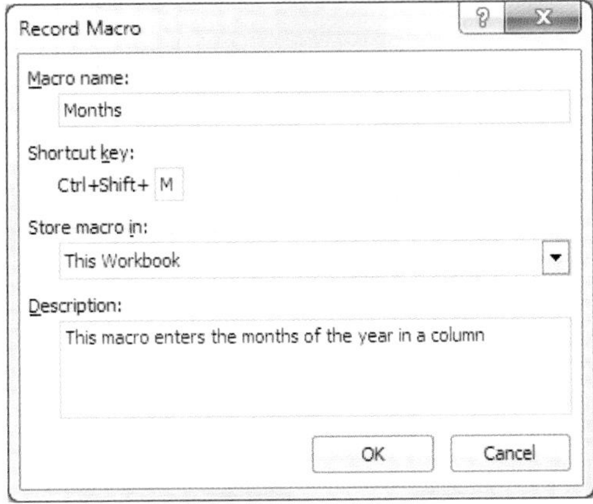

2. Click **OK**.

b. In cell A2, type January and press the Enter ✓ button on the Formula bar.

c. Drag the fill handle from cell A2 through to cell A13. The months of the year are entered in cells A2:A13.

d. Widen column A so that all of the month names fit within the column.

e. Click the **Stop Recording** button on the Developer tab.

② RUN THE MACRO

a. Click the **Sheet2** tab. Sheet2 is displayed.

b. Press Ctrl+Shift+M. The macro is run and the months of the year are entered in cells A2:A13.

③ ADD A MACRO BUTTON TO THE QUICK ACCESS TOOLBAR

a. Select **File → Options**.

b. Select **Quick Access Toolbar**. Options for customizing the Quick Access toolbar are displayed.

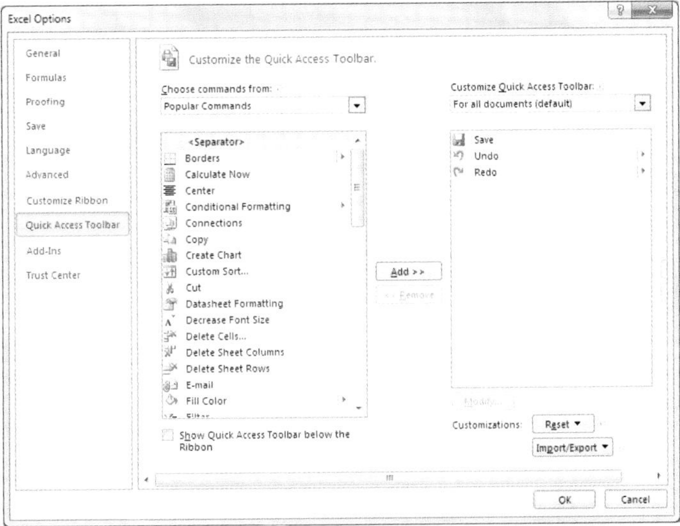

1. In the Customize Quick Access Toolbar drop-down list, change For all documents to For <FileName>. Note that the macro button will only be displayed on the Quick Access toolbar when the current workbook is open.
2. In the Choose commands from drop-down list, select Macros. A list of available macros is displayed:

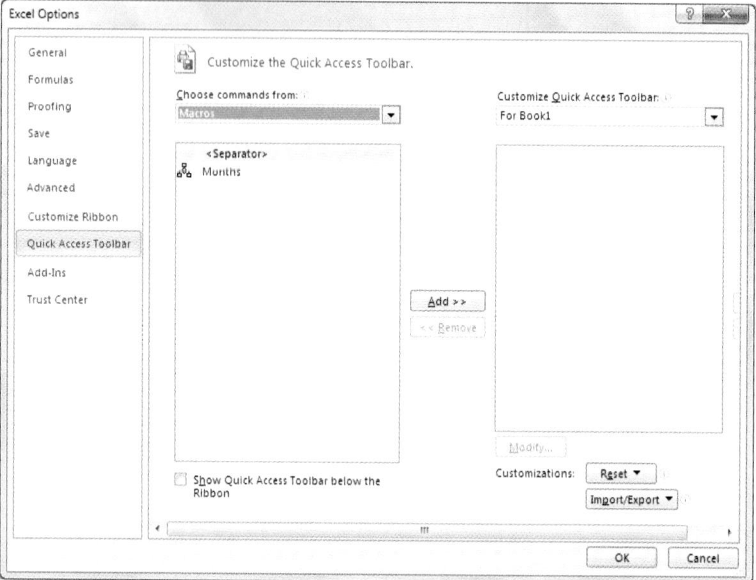

3. Click Months.
4. Click the Add button. Excel moves the macro name to the right list box.
5. Click the Modify button. Excel uses a generic VBA icon for all macros. The Modify Button dialog box displays additional icon options.
6. Click the Cancel button. The Modify Button dialog box is closed without changing the icon.
7. Click OK. The Excel Options dialog box is closed. The Months Macro button is added to the Quick Access toolbar:

④ RUN THE MACRO

a. Click the Sheet3 tab. Sheet3 is displayed.

b. Click the Months Macro button on the Quick Access toolbar. Note that the months of the year are entered in cells A2:A13.

⑤ SAVE THE WORKBOOK

a. Click File → Save. The Save As dialog box is displayed.

b. Navigate to the appropriate folder to save the workbook.

c. In the File name box, change the existing file name to Sales.

d. Select Excel Macro-Enabled Workbook in the Save as type list:

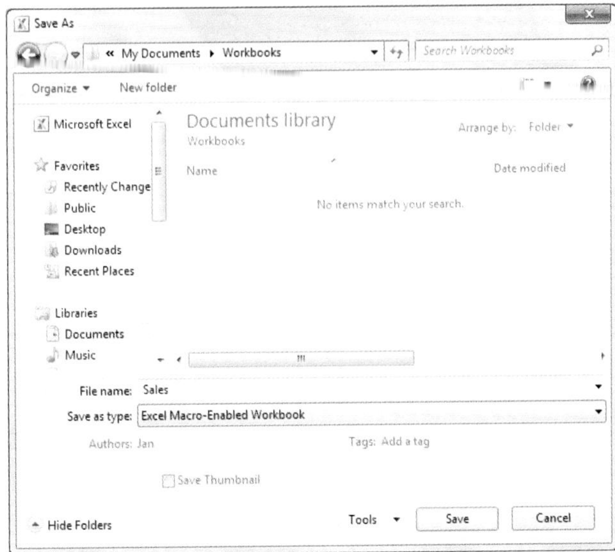

e. Click Save.

⑥ CLOSE AND THEN OPEN THE WORKBOOK

a. Select File → Close.

b. Open the Sales workbook, enabling the content.

Recorded Macro Code

TIP The VBA project resides within the corresponding Office document.

In the previous section, you learned to record and run a macro. In this section, you will view the code you recorded for the Months macro in the Microsoft Visual Basic for Applications editor. The Microsoft VBA editor is an Integrated Development Environment (IDE) that is used to write and edit VBA applications:

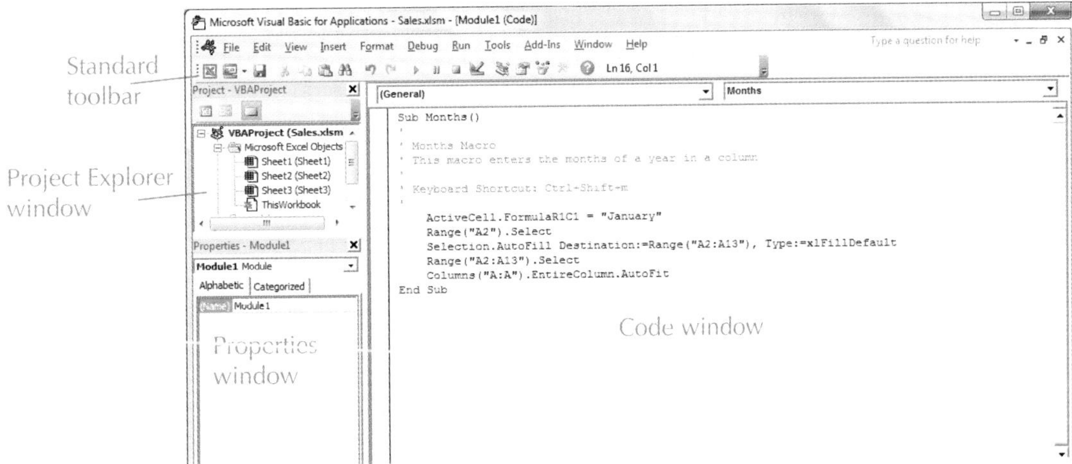

- The Project Explorer window displays the objects in the current project. The example above lists the worksheets that make up the Sales workbook. The Project Explorer window also lists modules. When you record a macro, Excel automatically creates a module in which to place the code.

- The Properties window lists the properties associated with a selected VBA object.
- The Code window is used to write and edit the application code.
- The Standard toolbar contains buttons that can be used to perform common tasks, such as Save and Run. The View Microsoft Excel button is used to switch back to Excel.

Alternative Open the editor - Developer → Macros → Edit.

To open the editor from Excel, click the Visual Basic button on the Developer tab or press Alt+F11:

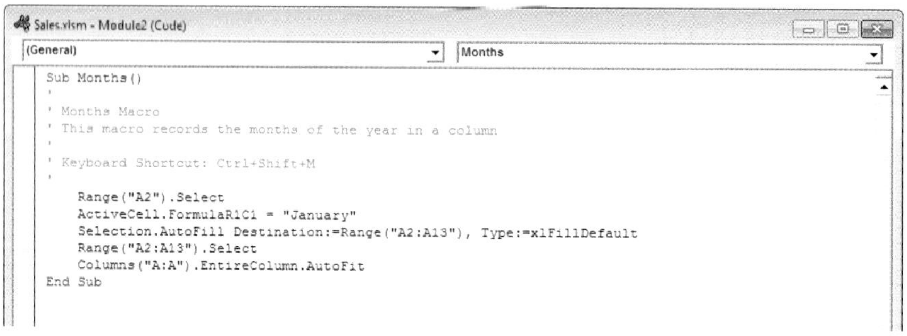

Sales.xlsm - Module2 (Code)

(General) | Months

```
Sub Months()
'
' Months Macro
' This macro records the months of the year in a column
'
' Keyboard Shortcut: Ctrl+Shift+M
'
    Range("A2").Select
    ActiveCell.FormulaR1C1 = "January"
    Selection.AutoFill Destination:=Range("A2:A13"), Type:=xlFillDefault
    Range("A2:A13").Select
    Columns("A:A").EntireColumn.AutoFit
End Sub
```

- The macro code appears between `Sub Months()` and `End Sub`. `Sub` is a short form for subroutine.
- The green lines of code that start with an apostrophe (') are comments. *Comments* provide information about the macro but are not executed. You should notice that the macro name, description, and keyboard shortcut information you entered in the Record Macro dialog box appear as comments.

VBA: An Object-Oriented Language

Like Visual Basic 2010, VBA is an object-oriented language. The basic structure of a VBA statement is:

```
Object.Method
```

You can think of an object as a noun and the method as a verb. For example, in the statement:

```
Range("A2").Select
```

`Range("A2")` is the object (*noun*) and `Select` (*verb*) is the method. Methods perform an action with an object.

Most methods have parameters that tell the method how to do the action. Parameters act as adverbs and are assigned using a colon-equal sign combination (:=). For example, in the statement below the parameter is used to indicate the autofill destination cell range:

```
Selection.AutoFill Destination:=Range("A2:A13")
```

For most objects in VBA, there is a collection of that object. For example, you can refer to more than one column:

```
Columns("A:A").EntireColumn.AutoFit
```

A collection adds an *s* to the name of the object - the object *Column* becomes *Columns*. In the example above, notice that you have to tell the programming language which column (A) or columns in the collection you are referring to.

Objects can also have properties. You can think of a property as describing the object or as an adjective that is typically set to equal something. In the example macro on the previous page, `.AutoFit` is a property assigned to the entire column A.

Practice: Editing Macro Code

① VIEW THE MACRO CODE

a. Open the Sales workbook, if it is not already.

b. Press Alt+F11. The Microsoft Visual Basic for Applications editor opens and the code for the Months macro is displayed:

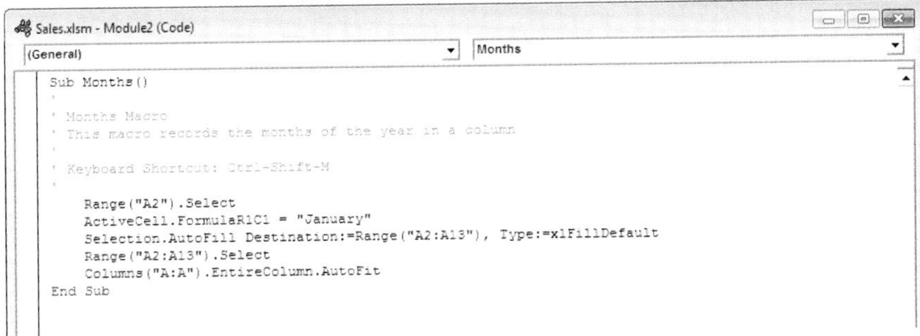

c. Locate the comment code.

② EDIT THE MACRO CODE

a. Edit the macro code so that the names of the month are entered in column D starting in cell D2:

```
Range("D2").Select

ActiveCell.FormulaR1C1 = "January"

Selection.AutoFill Destination:=Range("D2:D13"), Type:=xlFillDefault

Range("D2:D13").Select

Columns("D:D").EntireColumn.AutoFit
```

b. Click the Save button on the toolbar.

③ RUN THE MACRO

a. Click the **Sheet1** tab. Sheet1 is displayed.

b. Click cell B1.

c. Click the Months Macro button on the Quick Access toolbar. The months of the year are entered in cells D2:D13.

④ SAVE AND CLOSE THE SALES WORKBOOK

Accessing VBA Help

TIP Having an Internet connection will provide access to online help.

The F1 key is used to access VBA help. However, the VBA help library is not installed with a typical install of Office 2010. If you receive the message "Help is not available on this topic", you may have install the VBA help files from the original Office 2010 CDs.

Another source of help is the Object Browser window. This reference is used to browse the Excel object library. This is an easy way to find out all of the methods and properties associated with a particular object. Press the F2 key to access the Object Browser.

Practice: Using Help

① CREATE A NEW BLANK WORKBOOK

② OPEN THE MICROSOFT VISUAL BASIC FOR APPLICATIONS EDITOR

Press Alt+F11.

③ CREATE A MACRO

a. Select Insert → Module.

b. *You are probably familiar with message boxes. In VBA, a message box is displayed using the MsgBox function. A message box displays information and waits for a response from the user.*

Type the following code, using the Tab key to indent the second line of code:

```
Sub Msg()
    MsgBox "Hello world!"
End Sub
```

c. Click the Save button on the toolbar. The Save As dialog box is displayed.

1. In the File name box, type Message.
2. Change the Save as type to Excel Macro-Enabled Workbook.
3. Click Save. The workbook is saved and the editor is the active window.

④ RUN THE MACRO FROM THE EDITOR

a. Click the Run button. The Message dialog box is displayed.

b. Click OK. The Message box is removed. The editor is the active window.

⑤ ACCESSING HELP

a. Click within the word MsgBox.

b. Press the F1 key. Help on the MsgBox Function is displayed.

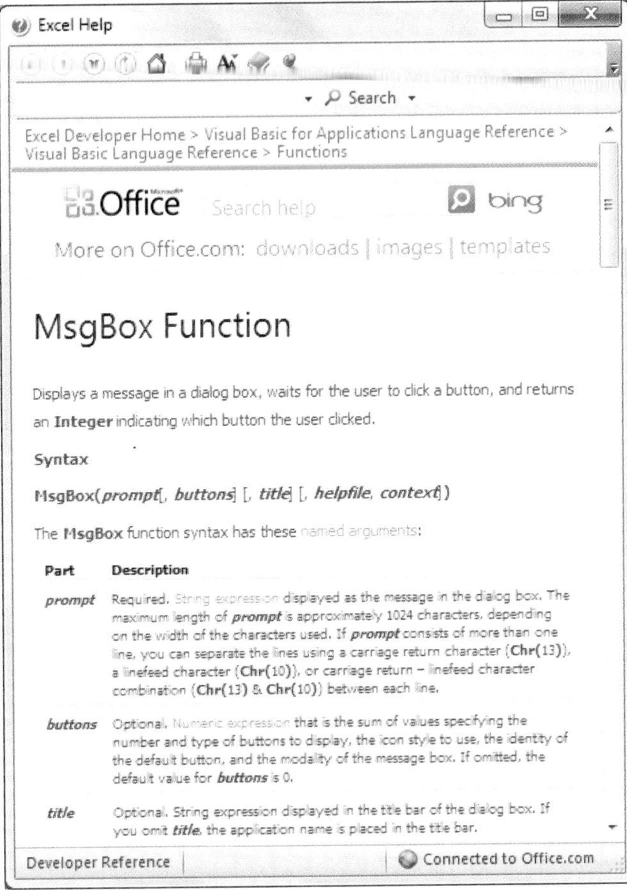

c. Scroll through the help. Note the information on the syntax and arguments.
d. Close the Help window.

⑥ USING HELP INFORMATION TO ENHANCE THE MESSAGE BOX

a. Edit the macro code by specifying button arguments, specifically a button style and Message box title. Start by positioning the insertion point after "Hello World!".
b. Type a comma. Available button styles are displayed in a drop-down list.
c. Double-click vbDefaultButton3:

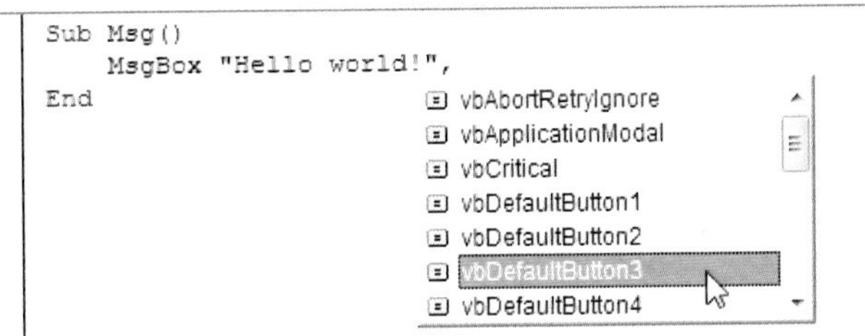

d. Type a comma, press the spacebar and then type "Message". Your code should look similar to:

```
Sub Msg()
    MsgBox "Hello World!", vbDefaultButton3, "Message"
End Sub
```

e. Save and run the modified macro from the editor.
f. Click OK to close the Message box.

⑦ EXPLORE THE OBJECT BROWSER

a. Press the F2 key. The Object Browser is displayed.

b. In the Project/Library drop down list, change <All Libraries> to **Excel**, if it is not already.

c. Select **Chart** in the Classes (left) list.

d. Explore the properties and methods that apply to the Chart object. Note that Methods appear as green books and Properties appear as index cards with a hand pointing to them.

e. Click **ChartTitle**:

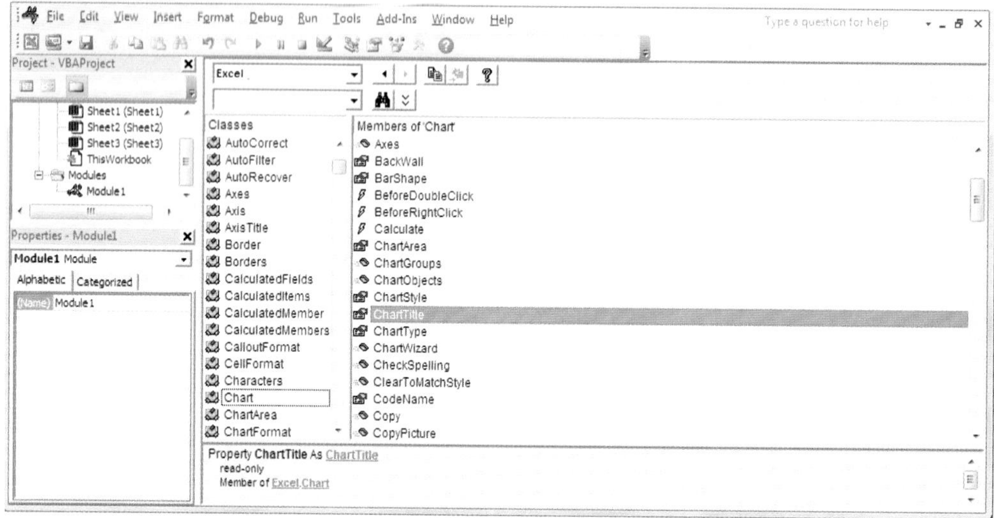

Notice the bottom of the Object Browser tells you that **ChartTitle** is a property.

⑧ CLOSE THE OBJECT BROWSER AND THE MESSAGE WORKBOOK

Loops

Loops are a fundamental component of all programming languages. Common loop constructs include: `For...Next`, `For Each...Next`, `Do...While`, `Do...Until`, and `While...Loop`. In this section, you will learn to use the `For Each...Next` loop construct to rename all of the worksheets in a workbook.

Examine the following code:

```
Sub NameWorksheets()
  Dim year as Integer
  year = 2010
  For Each Sheet In Worksheets
      Sheet.Name = year
      year = year + 1
  Next
End Sub
```

- The statement, `Dim year As Integer` declares a variable to store values of type Integer. Integer is a data type that stores positive or negative whole numbers.

TIP Declaring variables is not required in VBA, but is recommended.

- The statement, `year = 2010` assigns the value 2010 to variable *year*.
- The statement, `For Each Sheet In Worksheets` is indicating the variable *Sheet* will be used to represent each worksheet in the *Worksheets* collection.
- The statement, `Sheet.Name = year` changes the current *Name* property of the sheet to the value stored in the variable *year*.
- The statement, `year = year + 1` increases the value stored in the variable *year* by 1.
- The `For Each...Next` structure will continue to run until each worksheet in the current workbook is renamed.

Practice: Rename Sheets in a Workbook

Create a new blank workbook. Save the workbook as macro-enabled workbook, naming it Yearly Sales. Then, use the VBA editor to create a macro to rename the worksheets in the workbook 2011, 2012, and 2013. Run the macro.

Reflect on how much easier it was to rename the worksheets using a loop as opposed to the steps you would have to go through to using the Macro Recorder.

Ranges

In Excel, a range can be a single cell or a grouping of cells on a worksheet. The **Range** object is a property of the **Worksheet** object. This means that the Range object will refer to the active sheet. If you want to refer to another sheet, it must be referenced. Both statements below refer to cell A1 in Sheet1:

```
Range("A1")
Worksheets("Sheet1").Range("A1")
```

To refer to a range of adjacent cells, use the syntax:

```
Range("A1:B5").Select
```

You can also refer to the active cell in a range:

```
Range("A1", ActiveCell).Select
```

Shortcut A Range can also be referred to as [A1] or [A1:B5] or [MyRange].

To refer to a named range:

```
Worksheets("Sheet1").Range("MyRange")
```

The Range object could be used to access information on a worksheet and then use that information to rename all of the worksheets in a workbook. For example:

```
Sub NameWorksheets()
    For Each Sheet In Worksheets
        Sheet.Name = Sheet.Range("A1").Value
    Next
End Sub
```

Practice: Referring to a Range - part 1 of 3

① CREATE A NEW BLANK WORKBOOK.

② ADD DATA

a. In Sheet1, cell A1, enter the label Marketing.

b. In Sheet2, cell A1, enter the label Accounting.

c. In Sheet3, cell A1, enter the label Sales.

③ SAVE THE WORKBOOK

Save the workbook As Macro-Enabled Workbook, naming it Departments.

④ CREATE A MACRO

Use the VBA editor to write a macro that references the value in cell A1 and uses that value to rename the corresponding worksheet in the Departments workbook.

⑤ RUN THE MACRO

View the sheet names in the workbook.

Controlling the Flow

You may only want certain lines of code executed depending on a certain condition, such as if a value is not equal to 0 or if a cell is empty. You can do this using an `If..Then` statement.

Using an `If` statement to determine if a cell is empty can help avoid an error when you run a macro. For example, in the previous practice you renamed sheets based on the value stored in cell A1. However, if cell A1 on one of the sheets was empty, an error message would be generated:

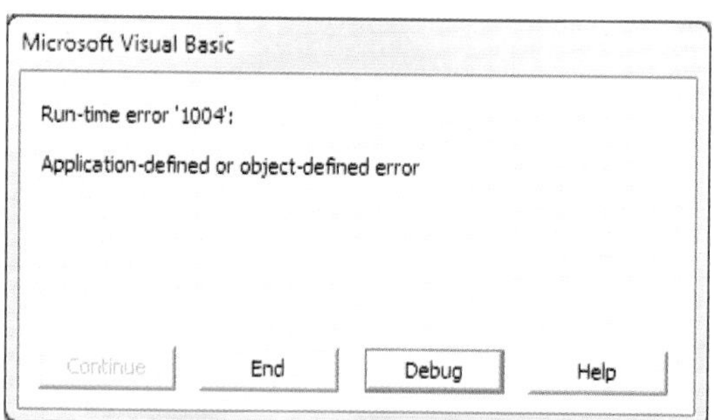

TIP If a workbook contains more than one macro, the Macro dialog box may be displayed when the **Run** button is clicked. Select the appropriate macro in the dialog box and then click the **Run** button.

Click the **Debug** button to display the macro code. The statement that is generating the error is highlighted in yellow:

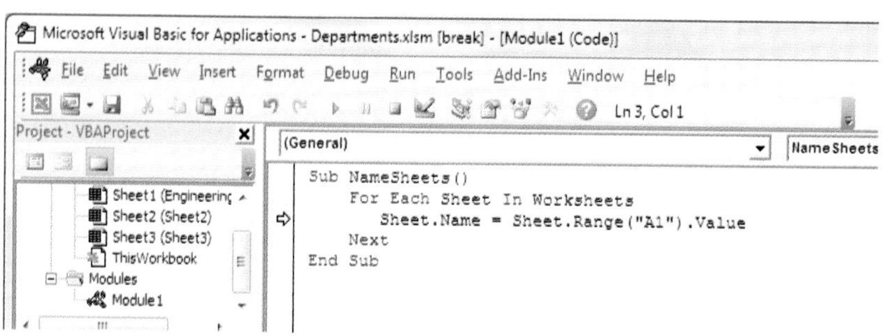

In this example, you would correct the error by adding data to cell A1. However, the problem could be avoided by checking to see if the cell was empty within the macro code:

```
Sub NameWorksheets()
  For Each Sheet in Worksheets
      If Sheet.Range("A1").Value<>"" Then
          Sheet.Name = Sheet.Range("A1").Value
      End If
  Next
End Sub
```

Practice: Referring to a Range - part 2 of 3

Modify the macro you created in the previous practice for the Departments workbook by adding an `If..Then` condition to check to see if the value in cell A1 is empty. Test the macro by changing the data in cell A1 in all three sheets, leaving at least one of the A1 cells empty.

Variable Declarations and IntelliSense

In a previous section in the chapter, you declared the variable `year` as type `Integer`. Unlike most programming languages, variable declarations are not required in VBA. However, it is recommended you declare variables especially as your macros become more complex. Using the example above, you could declare `Sheet` as type `Worksheet`. Variables are declared using a `Dim` (Dimension) statement:

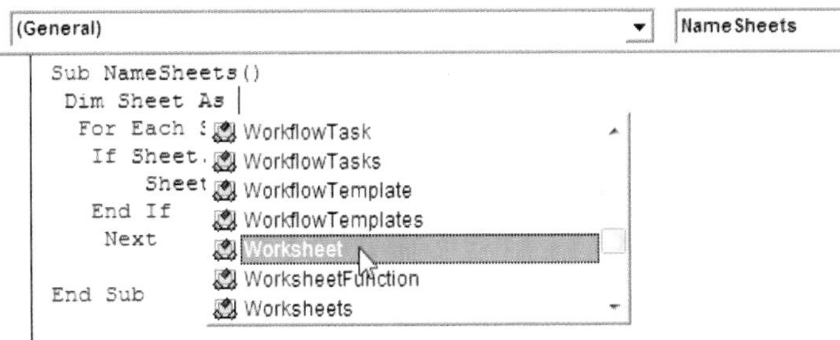

When the word `As` is typed, a list of variable types is automatically displayed. This VBA IDE IntelliSense feature makes coding easier and less error-prone. Double-click a variable type in the drop-down list to place it in the code. Once a variable is declared, IntelliSense will display a list of properties and methods associated with the object variable if it is referenced later in the macro. For example:

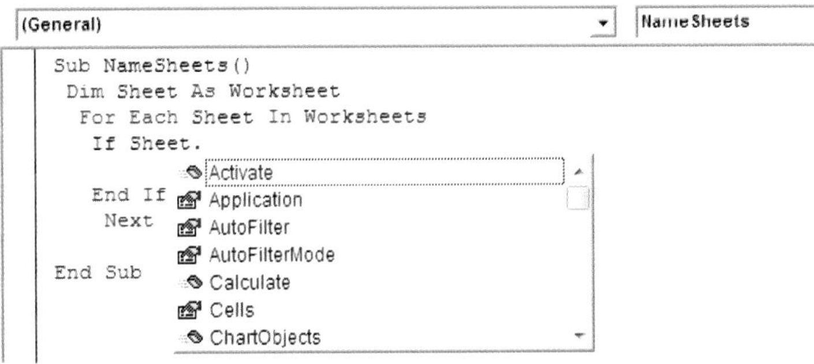

Comments

Comments provide information about the macro but are not executed. As macros become complex, it is a good idea to add comments to clarify the code. Remember that you may not be the only person working a workbook. Comments are added by typing an apostrophe (') at the start of the line:

```
(General)                                  NameSheets
Sub NameSheets()
 Dim Sheet As Worksheet
    For Each Sheet In Worksheets
        'check to see if cell A1 contains a value
        If Sheet.Range("A1").Value <> "" Then
            'use the value in cell A1 to rename the sheet
            Sheet.Name = Sheet.Range("A1").Value
        End If
    Next
End Sub
```

Within the code, comments are easily recognizable as they are automatically formatted in green text.

Practice: Referring to a Range - part 3 of 3

Modify the macro you created in the previous practice by declaring the variable used to represent the worksheets and adding at least two appropriate comments.

Charts

In Excel, you are able to create charts to visually represent numeric data. Representing numeric data in this format can make the data easier to understand and analyze as data patterns are clearly visible. If you need to create similar charts over and over again, it can become a repetitive task. An alternative, is to create a macro using VBA.

Given the following worksheet data:

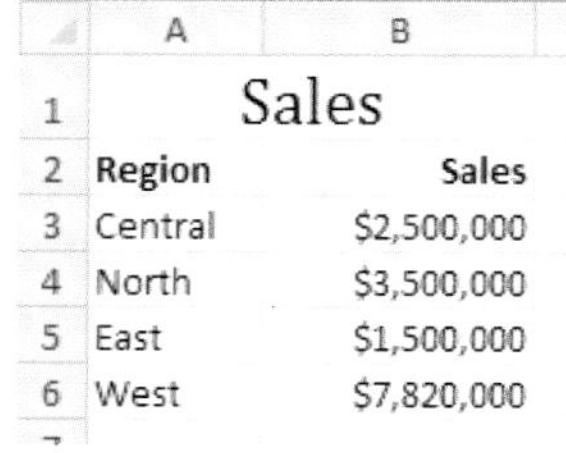

	A	B
1	Sales	
2	**Region**	**Sales**
3	Central	$2,500,000
4	North	$3,500,000
5	East	$1,500,000
6	West	$7,820,000

Examine the following code:

```
(General)                                  ChartExample
Sub ChartExample()
Dim newChart As ChartObject
Set newChart = ActiveSheet.ChartObjects.Add(150, 30, 300, 300)
    With newChart
        .Chart.SetSourceData Source:=Worksheets("Sheet1").Range("A2:B6")
    End With
End Sub
```

- In Excel, a chart can be displayed on a separate sheet or it can be embedded in a worksheet. When a chart is on its own standalone chart sheet, you work with a **Chart** object and when the chart is embedded in a worksheet, you work with a **ChartObject** object.
- The `Set newChart = ActiveSheet.ChartObjects.Add(150, 30, 300, 300)` statement creates the chart object and defines where it will be positioned on the worksheet. The first two numbers in parentheses represent the top left corner coordinates of the chart, the third number represents the width of the chart and the last number represents the height of the chart.
- The `With...End` construct is used in VBA to perform multiple actions on the same object. Within the `With...End` block, everything that starts with a period is assumed to refer to the object in the `With` statement. Cells A2 through B6 contain the source data for the chart.

Practice: Creating a Chart - part 1 of 2

① CREATE A NEW BLANK WORKBOOK

② ENTER DATA

a. Enter the following data and format as shown:

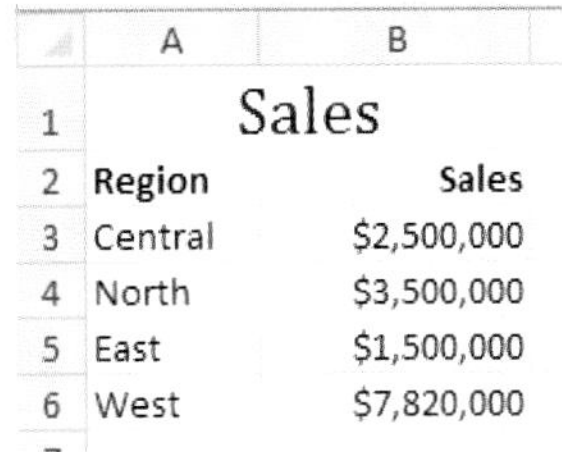

	A	B
1	Sales	
2	**Region**	**Sales**
3	Central	$2,500,000
4	North	$3,500,000
5	East	$1,500,000
6	West	$7,820,000

b. Save the workbook as a Macro-Embedded workbook, naming it Sales by Region.

③ CREATE A MACRO

a. Select **Insert → Module**.

b. Type the following code:

```
(General)                                    ChartExample

Sub ChartExample()
Dim newChart As ChartObject
Set newChart = ActiveSheet.ChartObjects.Add(150, 30, 300, 300)
    With newChart
        .Chart.SetSourceData Source:=Worksheets("Sheet1").Range("A2:B6")
    End With
End Sub
```

c. Click the Save button on the toolbar.

④ RUN THE MACRO

a. Click the Run button.

b. View the embedded chart on the worksheet:

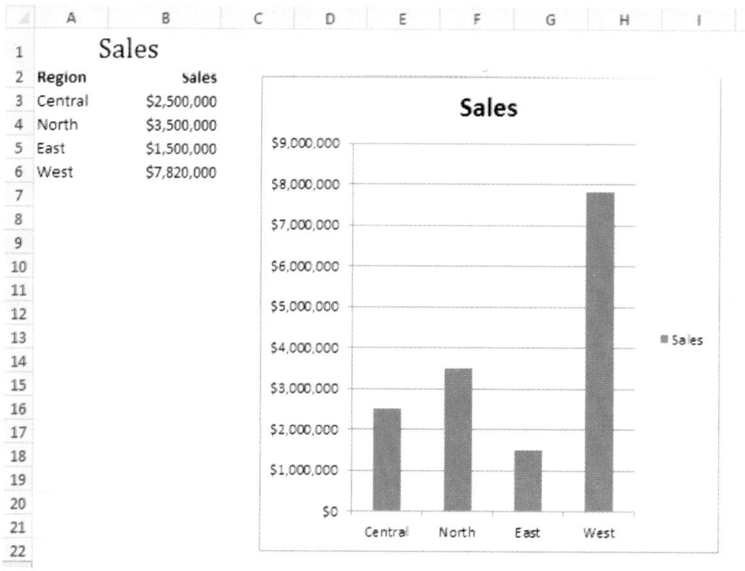

Enhancing a Chart

In Excel, the **Chart Tools Design**, **Layout**, and **Format** tabs contain commands and options used to enhance a chart. The features found on these tabs are represented as properties in VBA. For example:

- The `ChartType` property is used to change the chart type. Excel has 73 built-in chart types. In VBA built-in constants, such as `xl3DLine` and `xlArea` represent chart types.
- The `ChartStyle` property is used to apply a chart style to the active chart. The styles gallery has 48 different styles, which are represented by the numbers 1 through 48. Styles 41 through 48 appear on a dark background.
- The `Legend` property is used to change the position of the legend or to remove it from the chart.

Practice: Creating a Chart - part 2 of 2

① DELETE THE CHART

a. Display the Sales by Region workbook, if it is not already displayed.

b. Delete the chart.

c. Press Alt+F11 to switch to the VBA editor and display the ChartExample() macro from the previous practice.

② ENHANCE THE CHART

a. Modify the existing code as shown:

```
(General)                                        ChartExample

Sub ChartExample()
Dim newChart As ChartObject
Set newChart = ActiveSheet.ChartObjects.Add(150, 30, 300, 200)
    With newChart
        .Chart.SetSourceData Source:=Worksheets("Sheet1").Range("A2:B6")
        .Chart.ChartType = xlPie
        .Chart.ChartStyle = 42
        .Chart.ApplyDataLabels
    End With
End Sub
```

b. Click the Save button on the toolbar.

c. Click the Run button.

d. View the embedded chart on the worksheet:

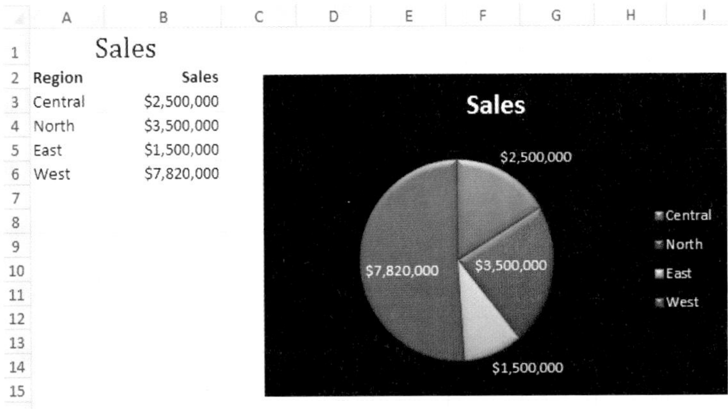

③ SAVE AND CLOSE THE REGIONAL SALES WORKBOOK

Creating a UserForm

UserForms are used to display information and obtain input from the user. A Message box, introduced earlier in the chapter, is a simple way to do this. If you need a more complex form, you can use the UserForm controls in the VBA editor.

To Insert a UserForm, select Insert → UserForm in the editor:

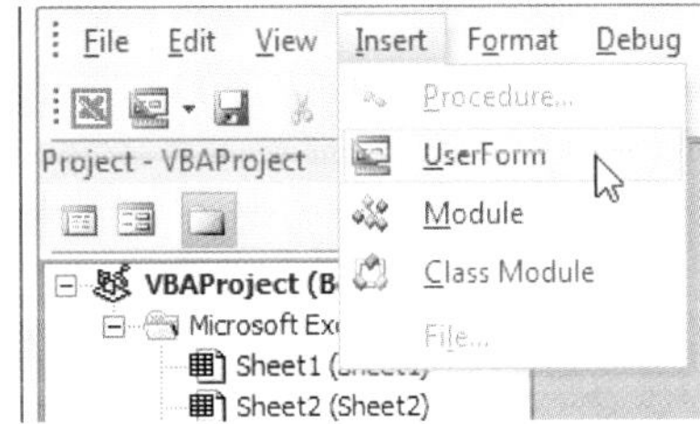

A blank form is displayed along with the Controls toolbox:

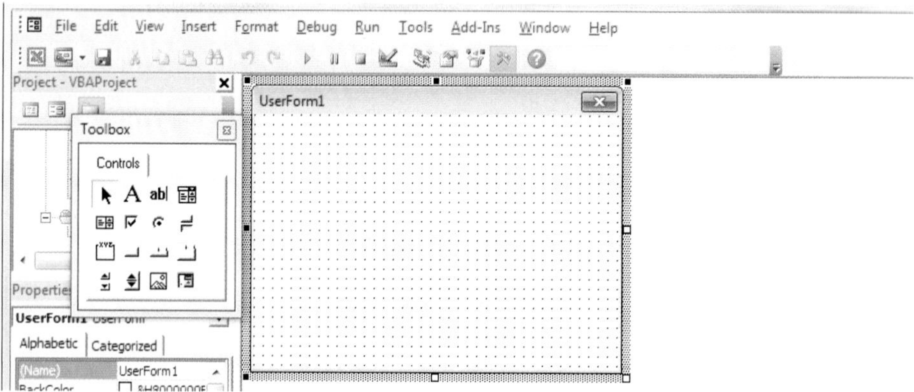

- Use the handles to size the form.
- Add controls to the form by clicking the control in the toolbox and then drawing it on the form.
- Use the Properties Window to change the properties, such as BackColor or ForeColor of the control. By default, a UserForm is named UserForm1. Use the Name property to assign the form a meaningful name. UserForm names cannot contain spaces.

TIP Many VBA programmers use a prefix when naming control objects, such as btn for a command button, frm for a form, and lbl for a label control.

Once a UserForm is designed, it can be called from any module using the statement:

```
FormName.Show
```

To hide a UserForm, use the statement:

```
FormName.Hide
```

Practice: Creating a UserForm, part 1 of 2

① CREATE A NEW BLANK WORKBOOK

a. Enter the following data and format as shown:

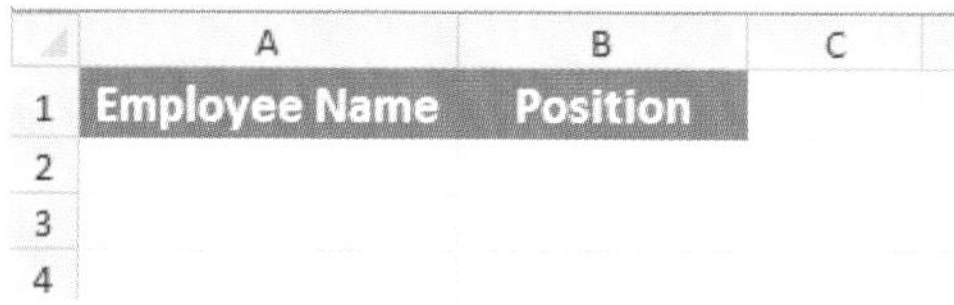

	A	B	C
1	Employee Name	Position	
2			
3			
4			

b. Save the workbook as a Macro-Enabled Workbook, naming it Employees.

② DISPLAY THE VBA EDITOR

a. Press Alt+F11

b. Select Insert → UserForm.

③ DESIGN A USERFORM

a. In the Properties Window, click the Name property and then type Employees and press the Enter key.

b. In the Properties Window, click the Caption property and then type Employees and press the Enter key. The UserForm title bar text is changed to Employees:

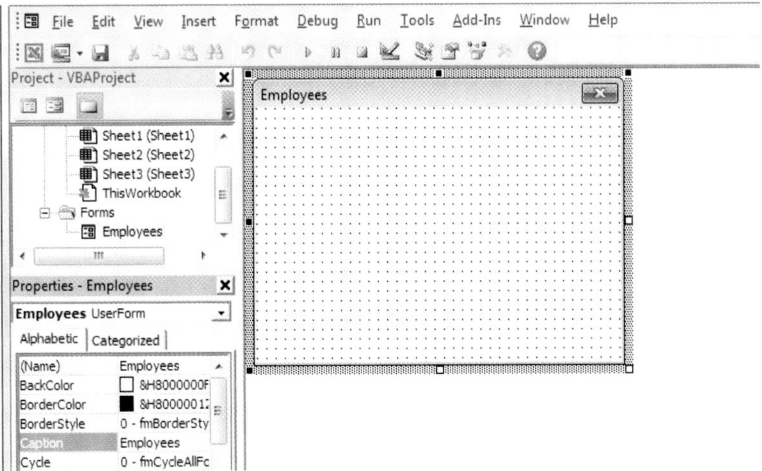

c. Click the UserForm to display the toolbox.

d. In the toolbox, click the Label control:

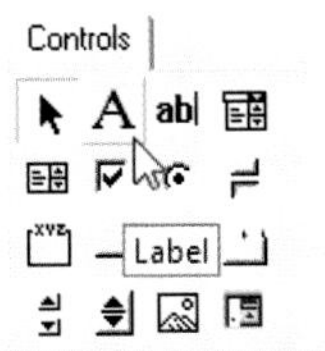

e. Click in the upper-left corner of the UserForm to place the Label control.

f. With the Label control selected, click the Caption property and type Employee Name: and then press the Enter key:

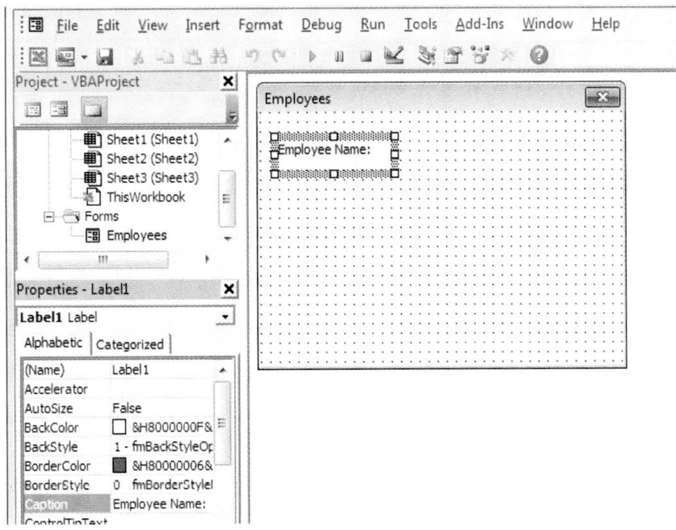

g. Click the UserForm to display the toolbox.

h. In the toolbox, click the Textbox control:

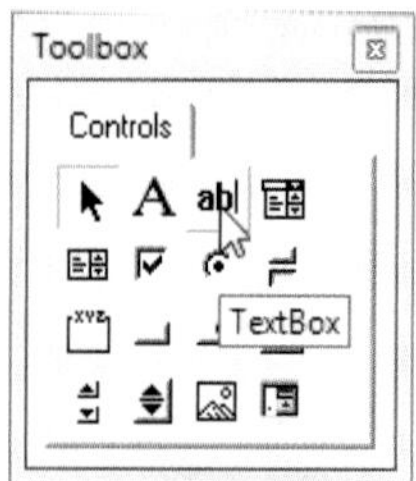

i. Draw a Textbox to the right of the Label control:

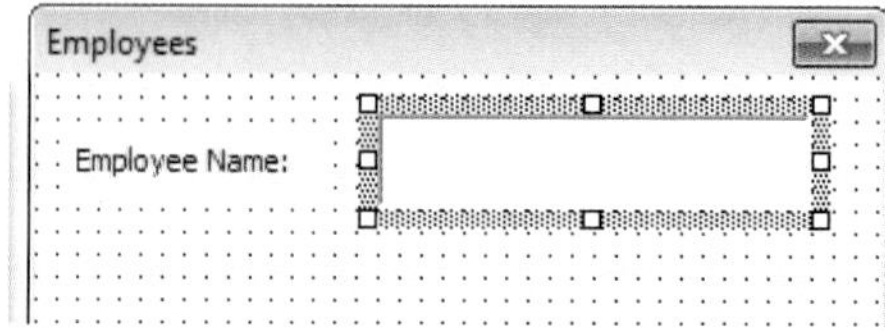

j. With the Textbox control selected, click the **Name** property and type EmpName and then press the Enter key.

k. In the toolbox, Click the Command button control:

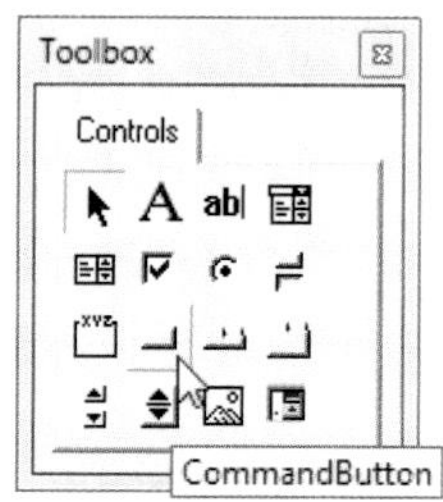

l. Add a command button to the UserForm and change the **Name** property to btnAdd and the **Caption** property to **Add**:

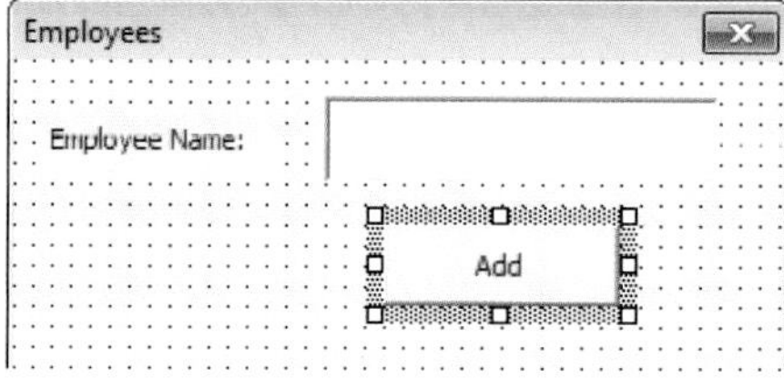

m. Click the Save button.

Programming a UserForm

The code for a control is entered in the Forms module. To do this, double-click a control on the UserForm. The form opens up in Design view:

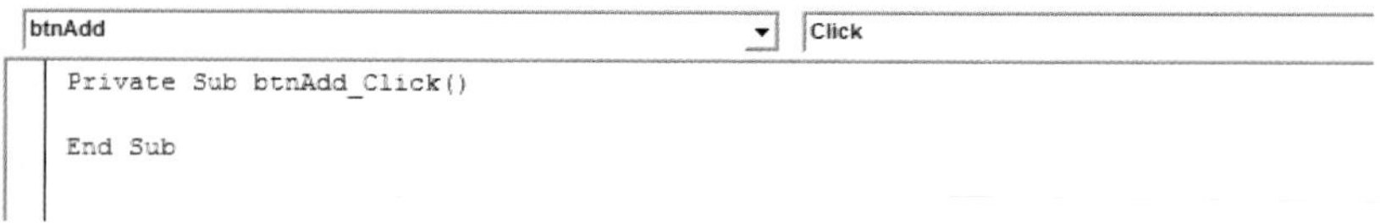

You can now write the code for the actions that are performed when the button is clicked. The example code below adds the text from a UserForm textbox to a cell on the active worksheet:

```
btnAdd                                  Click
Private Sub btnAdd_Click()
Dim LastRow As Long
LastRow = Worksheets(1).Cells(Worksheets(1).Rows.Count, 1).End(xlUp).Row + 1
Cells(LastRow, 1).Value = EmpName.Value
End Sub
```

- The Long data type is similar to the Integer data type in that it stores negative and positive whole numbers. However, the range is much larger with the Long data type. The Long data type can store values from -2,147,483,648 to 2,147,483,647.
- The `Cells` property refers to a single cell by using row and column index numbers. This returns a Range object that represents a single cell. For example `Cells(6,1)` returns cell A6 on Sheet1.
- The third line of code finds the last row in a sheet in which column A has a value and adds one to that row to move the active cell. This value is stored in the LastRow variable.
- The fourth line of code obtains the text from the `EmpName` textbox and enters it in a worksheet cell.

Practice: Creating a UserForm, part 2 of 2

① DISPLAY THE USERFORM

Display the UserForm from the last practice, if it is not already.

② PROGRAM THE USERFORM

a. Double-click the Add button.

b. Add the following code:

```
btnAdd                                  Click
Private Sub btnAdd_Click()
Dim LastRow As Long
LastRow = Worksheets(1).Cells(Worksheets(1).Rows.Count, 1).End(xlUp).Row + 1
Cells(LastRow, 1).Value = EmpName.Value
End Sub
```

c. Click the Save button on the toolbar.

③ TEST THE CODE

a. Click the Run button. The UserForm is displayed:

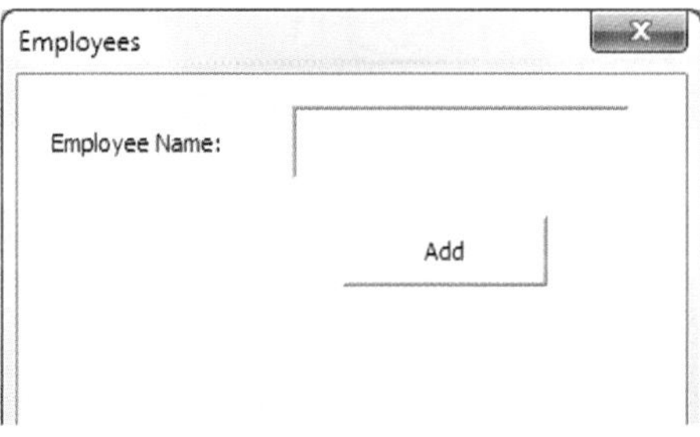

b. Type Ava Williams and then click the Add button. The text is automatically entered in cell A2:

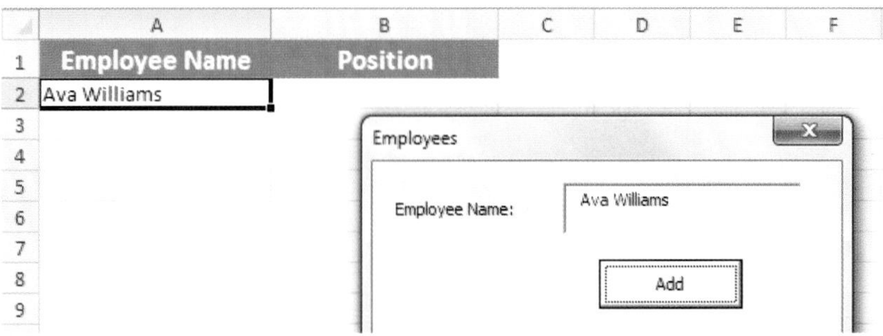

c. Close the UserForm by clicking the Close button. The VBA editor window is displayed.

④ CALL THE USERFORM

a. Click Insert → Module.

b. Add the following code to call the Employees UserForm:

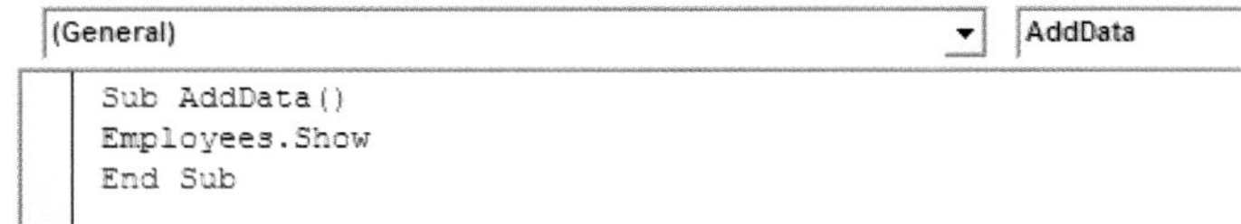

```
Sub AddData()
Employees.Show
End Sub
```

c. Click the Run button.

d. If the Macro dialog box is displayed, click the Run button. The Employees UserForm is displayed.

e. Type your name and click the Add button.

f. Close the UserForm.

⑤ ADD A MACRO BUTTON TO THE QUICK ACCESS TOOLBAR

⑥ SAVE AND CLOSE THE MODIFIED EMPLOYEES WORKBOOK

⑦ QUIT EXCEL

Index